Last Stand in the Carolinas

The Battle of Bentonville

Mark L. Bradley

Savas Publishing Company
1475 S. Bascom Avenue, Suite 204, Campbell, CA 95008

Manufactured in the United States of America

Last Stand in the Carolinas: The Battle of Bentonville
by Mark L. Bradley

Includes bibliographic references and index

Printing Number
10 9 8 7 6 5 4 3

ISBN 1-882810-02-3

Savas Publishing Company
1475 S. Bascom Avenue, Suite 204,
Campbell, California 95008
(408) 879-9073

This book is printed on 50-lb. natural acid-free paper. It meets or exceeds the guidelines for permanence and durability of the Committee on Production Guidelines for Book Longevity of the Council on Library Resources

To my Grandfather,

James Jackson Hagan,

a wonderful teacher and historian

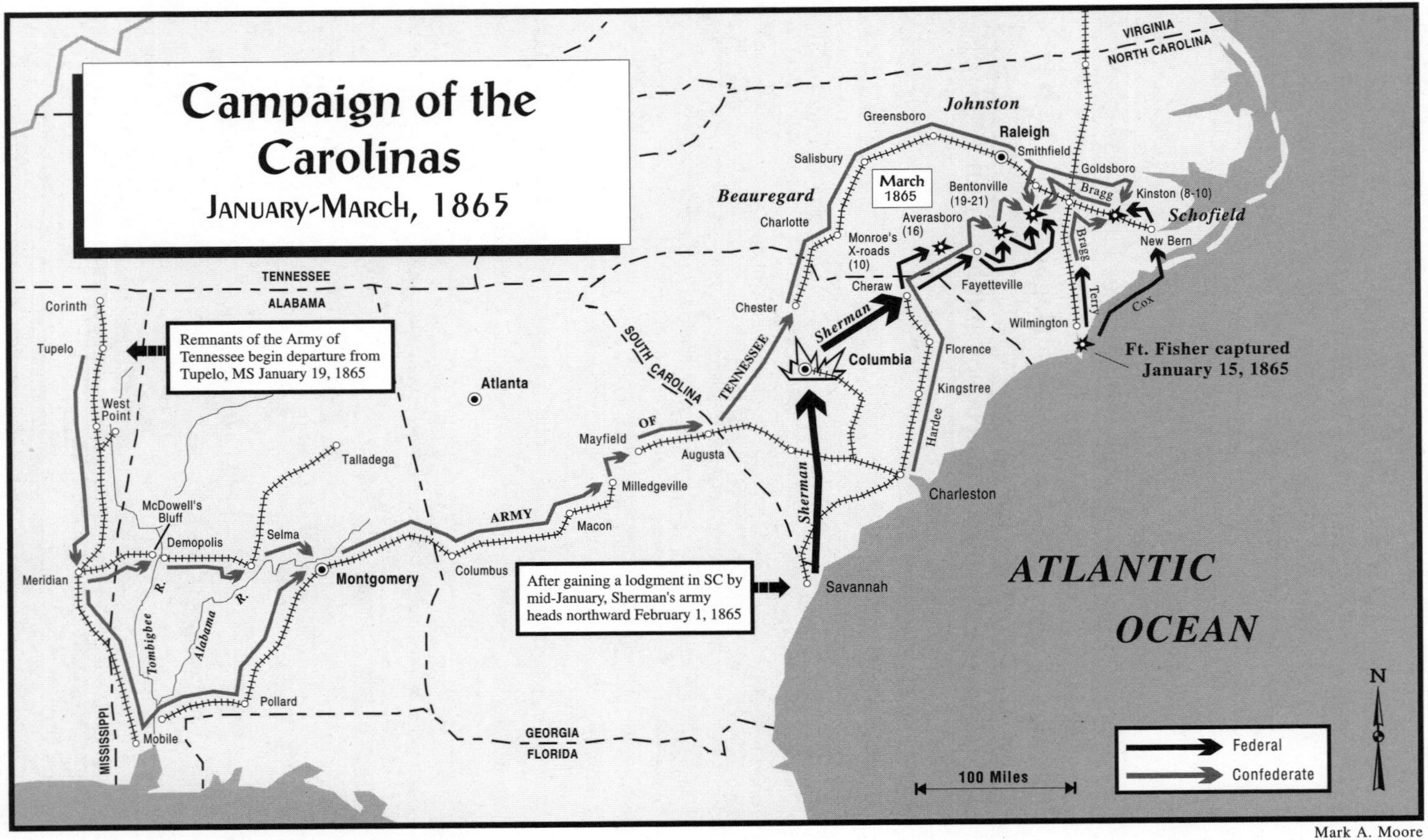
Campaign of the Carolinas
January-March, 1865
Remnants of the Army of Tennessee begin departure from Tupelo, MS January 19, 1865
After gaining a lodgment in SC by mid-January, Sherman's army heads northward February 1, 1865
Ft. Fisher captured January 15, 1865
March 1865
VIRGINIA
NORTH CAROLINA
TENNESSEE
ALABAMA
SOUTH CAROLINA
GEORGIA
FLORIDA
MISSISSIPPI
ARMY OF TENNESSEE
Johnston
Beauregard
Schofield
Sherman
Hardee
Bragg
Terry
Cox
Greensboro
Raleigh
Smithfield
Goldsboro
Kinston (8-10)
New Bern
Salisbury
Bentonville (19-21)
Averasboro (16)
Monroe's X-roads (10)
Charlotte
Cheraw
Fayetteville
Wilmington
Chester
Columbia
Florence
Kingstree
Charleston
Savannah
Atlanta
Augusta
Mayfield
Milledgeville
Macon
Columbus
Montgomery
Talladega
Selma
Demopolis
McDowell's Bluff
Corinth
Tupelo
West Point
Meridian
Mobile
Pollard
Tombigbee R.
Alabama R.
ATLANTIC OCEAN
100 Miles
N
Federal
Confederate
Mark A. Moore

Contents

Maps

THE BATTLE OF BENTONVILLE:

MAPS CONTINUED

Maps continued

Illustrations

~ Introduction to the Maps ~

In the summer of 1986 I read my first primary source on the Battle of Bentonville. It fueled my burgeoning interest in "this hotly contested fight between giants," as one veteran remembered it. For me, the reality of a big Civil War battle in North Carolina held a special allure, yet it seemed historians had largely ignored the famed "giants" after 1864. The few secondary sources available on the subject suffered at the tactical level, and there were no good maps of the action. I soon realized the level of understanding I sought on Bentonville would have to come from my own research.

With a view to eventually writing a history of the battle, I chose cartography as a more immediate means of tracking confusing troop movements and defining research goals. I wanted graphics that represented a step-by-step, regimental-level account of the fighting. As Mark Bradley and I began combining resources for a collaboration I found we shared a common vision, not just for Bentonville but for the entire campaign in North Carolina. The result is a detailed narrative with a lengthy cartographic series illustrating successive portions of the text, and covering all of the major battlefield maneuvers.

The small unit detail I was looking for did not come equally for both armies. Thankfully, the Federal material was often specific regarding placement of regiments in line of battle. Commanders and common soldiers alike wrote of battlefield alignment, many times referencing their positions by mention of neighboring units. Conversely, the Confederate sources generally kept to brigade-level description. This was evidence of the late-war condition of the Army of Tennessee, with its strings of demi-brigades and token regiments. With the exception of the North Carolina Junior Reserves, the larger Confederate units from other departments offered little better in the way of regimental detail.

I mapped the Army of Tennessee brigades on a scale proportionate to regiments in the Federal army. I drew other brigades in various larger sizes, and slightly enlarged the overall troop scale relevant to the battlefield. On the Federal side, I labeled troops above the regimental level with the names of their current commanders. In keeping with the practice of the time, I gave Confederate units their official brigade names. For example, Colquitt's Brigade is labeled as such even though Brig. Gen. A. H. Colquitt himself was not present at Bentonville. I made an exception on the Confederate side regarding Conner's Brigade, of McLaws' Division. After the Battle of Averasboro the unit appears as Kennedy's, as that commander is mentioned most often in connection with the brigade. For added clarity I chose to label Confederate corps with the names of their actual commanders, rather than official corps names.

Mark A. Moore
July 1995

Acknowledgments

My thanks go to the staffs of all the libraries and archives listed in my bibliography. Without exception I was treated with courtesy and kindness. Unfortunately, the list of those people who assisted me is so long that I have room to mention only those whose efforts were particularly helpful. I wish to thank Richard J. Sommers and David A. Keough of the United States Army Military History Institute, Carlisle Barracks, Pennsylvania; Susan Ravdin of The Library, Bowdoin College, Brunswick, Maine; Margaret Lee of the Johnston County Public Library, Smithfield, North Carolina; Mark E. Thomas of the Cincinnati Historical Society, Cincinnati, Ohio; Joanne Hohler of the State Historical Society of Wisconsin, Madison, Wisconsin; Hampton Smith and Alissa Rosenberg of the Minnesota Historical Society, St. Paul, Minnesota; DeAnne Blanton of the National Archives, Washington, D. C.; and William B. Tubbs of the Illinois State Historical Library, Springfield, Illinois.

Special thanks to Edwin C. Bearss for reading my entire manuscript. Ed's editorial assistance and commentary were invaluable, and his words of encouragement helped me to press on with what sometimes seemed an overwhelming task. I wish to thank Jay Luvaas of the United States Army War College for reading the rough draft of the Bentonville portion of my manuscript. His comments helped me to improve the final version. I also profited from several discussions with Jay on Generals Sherman and Johnston and the Battle of Bentonville.

Many thanks to John Goode, manager of the Bentonville Battleground State Historic Site. From the beginning of this project, John has provided me with assistance and encouragement. John gave me unlimited access to the site's library and research material, walked over the battlefield with me countless times, and gave me the benefit of his extensive knowledge of Civil War history. He also read the rough draft of the Bentonville chapters and made many helpful suggestions. I feel extremely fortunate to have John as a friend and colleague.

I am grateful to Morris Bass of Clinton, North Carolina, for giving me my first tour of the battlefield and the John Harper house. "Mo" and I subsequently explored much of the battleground over the span of a year. This experience taught me that in the study of military history, the battlefield is the best classroom.

I want to thank Bryce Suderow of Washington, D. C., for his helpful suggestions regarding material in the *National Tribune* and the National Archives; Raymond Gillmore of Jacksonville, Illinois, for his assistance; and the residents of the Bentonville community, who generously provided me with access to the battlefield, most of which lies on their property.

I also want to thank my good friend, Stan Campbell, for his assistance on several research trips. Thanks to all of Stan's family in Wisconsin for making me feel right at home during my stay there.

A special thanks to my editors and publishers, Theodore P. Savas and David A. Woodbury. I am grateful to Ted and Dave for all their support and guidance.

I can't thank my good friend and partner, Mark A. Moore, enough for his contribution. The series of maps that graces this volume attests to Mark's extraordinary skill and scholarship. Mark began his study of the Battle of Bentonville several years before I did, and had already drafted a set of maps depicting the March 19 battle when we first met. These maps were a revelation. Since then, we have collaborated—Mark drafting the maps while I wrote the text. Moreover, Mark's specialized knowledge of the battle enabled him to suggest many improvements to the manuscript. His contribution has resulted in a far better book than I could have written on my own.

I reserve my greatest thanks for my wife, Nancy. In addition to being my editor and research assistant, Nancy has been an unfailing source of wisdom, humor and inspiration throughout the many years of this project. When Nancy first "enlisted," she had no idea that the campaign would be so long and difficult, but she has traversed the libraries, swamps and briar thickets with grace and good cheer. For this I will always be grateful.

~ Foreword ~

Until four years ago, in the fourth week of March, when I led a tour of Civil War sites in the Carolinas, I had neither driven the roads nor walked the fields and woods associated with the battles of Averasboro and Bentonville. My knowledge of the marches that in twelve weeks took Maj. Gen. William T. Sherman's "army group" from Savannah to Raleigh and then "Uncle Billy" to James Bennett's farm house was limited to what I read in the principal sources. I was familiar with the biographies and memoirs of Sherman, Gen. Joseph E. Johnston, Lt. Gens. William J. Hardee and Wade Hampton, major players in the drama. John G. Barrett's *Sherman's March Through the Carolinas* (1956) and *The Civil War in North Carolina* (1963), and Jacob D. Cox's *The March to the Sea—Franklin, and Nashville* (1913), are excellent overviews of the campaign, but lack the detail needed for battlefield interpretation that must be site-oriented, and spiced with human interest stories. Stanley Horn's *The Army of Tennessee* (1941) and Thomas Lawrence Connelly's *Autumn of Glory: The Army of Tennessee 1862-1865* (1971) provided familiarity with the Confederate army, its leaders, and their generalship.

Maps found in the *Official Records Atlas,* coordinated with data obtained from the United States Geological Survey's 7.5-minute series for North Carolina, give an appreciation of the terrain, ground cover, and an understanding of the road network as it existed in

1865 contrasted to that found today. Two publications—*Guide to North Carolina Highway Historical Markers* (1990) and *The Battle of Bentonville* by Weymouth T. Jordan, Jr., (1990)—are indispensable to the battlefield stomper. The former, published by the North Carolina Division of Archives and History, contains the texts of the historical markers that locate and relate sites to battle actions. The latter duplicates the marker texts, graphically relating the markers to the roads, and provides an overview of the campaign and battle. Reprints of Jay Luvaas' monograph "Johnston's Last Stand—Bentonville," featured in the July 1956 issue of the *North Carolina Historical Review,* until now, has been the best available narrative history of the battle and its context.

Armed with information secured from these sources, I, in March 1991 and again in 1992, led 8-day tours of Civil War and Revolutionary War battlefield sites in North and South Carolina and Georgia. On July 9, 1993, as a member of the Congressionally-mandated Civil War Sites Advisory Commission, I returned to Averasboro and Bentonville. This was a fact-finding trip and the carpet was rolled out by state officials, Site Manager John C. Goode and the energetic and capable staff of the Bentonville Battleground State Historic Site, and historians and locals familiar with Sherman's North Carolina Campaign. Guided by John Goode and members of his staff, and Mark Bradley and Mark Moore, we toured the battlefield, which is extensive, embracing more than 6,000 acres.

My previous visits to the site had been limited to the 131 acres embraced in the state historic site and roadside pulloffs. It was different this time. Site Manager Goode had secured permission from landowners to take the Commissioners onto lands not included within the boundary of the state historic site. What we saw was impressive and exciting. We saw trenches with headlogs, after 128 years, still in place; the double-faced earthworks employed by Brig. Gen. James D. Morgan's Yanks to first repulse Maj. Gen. Robert F. Hoke's hard-charging soldiers and then scramble to the other side of the works to hurl back D. H. Hill's Confederates constituting the blade of Hardee's scythe that up to this point had swept all before them; the ground across which "Fighting Joe" Mower's Union division surged on March 21 and where 16-year-old Willie Hardee received his mortal wound; and well preserved Confederate and Union earthworks north of the "Devil's Race Track" road, where we encountered not *minié* balls but angry bees in large numbers.

Casualties were suffered in the entourage, and among those stung was our Pulitzer Prize-winning historian James McPherson.

The Commissioners returned to Wilmington that night with keen and lasting impressions of the day. Foremost was our appreciation of Bentonville, with its miles of extant earthworks in place, its mid-19th-century road network, and its pastoral setting featuring woods, swamps, and fields as an outstanding cultural resource. Of equal importance were the human resources that went so far to make a long day productive and enjoyable.

I returned to Averasboro and Bentonville with Jerry Russell's Civil War Congress on Friday, October 8, 1993. Among our war's *aficionados* aboard the two 47-passenger buses were two William T. Sherman biographers—John F. Marszalek and Eddie Vetter—and Craig L. Symonds, author of *Joseph E. Johnston: A Civil War Biography* (1992). Also present was Nathaniel C. Hughes, Jr., whose credits then included *William J. Hardee, "Old Reliable"* (1965) and *The Battle of Belmont* (1991). The afternoon spent at Bentonville highlighted the three-and-a-half-day Congress. We met John Goode and his staff, toured the visitor center and the Harper House, and chatted with living history volunteers. Then, like the Commissioners, we got out into the woods and fields and walked in the steps of history where gallant men and boys of 1865 camped, maneuvered, fought, and died.

Our hours at Bentonville that day had unforeseen and far-reaching repercussions for the Civil War community and those who enjoy good military history. Three months before when the Commissioners were onsite, John Goode had introduced Mark Bradley and Mark Moore. In doing so, he spoke of Bradley's deep interest in Sherman's and Johnston's North Carolina Campaign that climaxed at Bentonville, his extensive research on the subject, and that Bradley hoped to share this encyclopedic knowledge with the public through publication of the manuscript on which he was working. The Commissioners, while touring the site, were given copies of several handsome troop movement maps prepared and researched by Moore. We were impressed by what was said and what we saw, and urged that when completed the Bradley manuscript and Moore maps be published to call to the public's attention the Battle of Bentonville, a site which the Commission in its July 1993 report to Congress listed as one of the Nation's eleven "Priority 1

Battlefields with critical need for coordinated nationwide action by the year 2000."

A happy fallout from the Civil War Congress' Bentonville trip was the presence of Theodore "Ted" P. Savas, a California attorney, preservationist, and Civil War student. Ted Savas and David A. Woodbury—another Bay Area resident with a similar interest and a Civil War Congress veteran—had dared to implement a dream. In 1990, they established a nonprofit charitable corporation, *Regimental Studies, Inc*. The corporation, with Savas and Woodbury as owner-editors, undertook publication of a quarterly—*Civil War Regiments: A Journal of the American Civil War*. Profits from their innovative and daring venture would be donated to Civil War-related preservation organizations.

Happily for the Civil War community, the Savas-Woodbury venture is a success. The quarterly of pleasing layout became a magnet for monographs by well known and popular Civil War historians, as well as those striving for recognition. From the first the issues are theme-related, with emphasis on units, campaigns, and battles. Articles, in keeping with high standards established by the editors, are well written, relevant, footnoted, and illustrated. The editors' own maps enrich the text. Without adequate maps, campaign and battle accounts lose much of their value and disappoint the reader. Like Bob and Mary Younger's *The Gettysburg Magazine* with John Heiser's maps, the Savas and Woodbury maps give a much appreciated dimension to their publications.

At the time of Jerry Russell's 1992 Congress, Savas and Woodbury were thinking big. On the drawing board was a proposal for additional full-length titles to complement their "first book of a multi-volume study on the decisive campaign for Atlanta and the March to the Sea."

The time and place was right for bringing together key players—author Bradley and mapmaker Moore, known to their friends and colleagues at Bentonville Battleground State Historic Site as M-squared—and Savas and Woodbury, editors and publishers. As follow-up to their *The Campaign for Atlanta and Sherman's March to the Sea,* the first in Savas and Woodbury's Campaign Chronicles series, they agreed to publish the manuscript into which Mark Bradley had put, and has continued to put, so much of himself, to be supplemented by partner Mark Moore's troop position maps.

Knowing of my interest in Averasboro and Bentonville, and that I was familiar with the quality of their work and their subject expertise, the editors asked me to review and comment on the manuscript and maps. The first chapters reached me in the first week of December 1994 and were read while in Paris, France, and during the 14-hours in the air while en route from and to Washington, DC, for the fifth meeting of the *CSS Alabama* Scientific Committee. Other chapters, along with Mark Moore's maps, were read as completed.

As I read and waited for the next installment, I recalled my youth and the Saturday movie matinees, when the most anxiously awaited event was not the feature but the serial which had ended the previous Saturday with the hero or heroine confronting impossible and life threatening odds. Like the serials of the mid-1930s, Bradley's manuscript whet my intellect as I anxiously awaited the next mail.

In calling attention to Civil War books, magazines, etc., that with the advent of desktop publishing are flooding the market, the increasingly knowledgeable public is becoming wary of the promotional excerpts appearing on dust jackets with such phrases as "provide play-by-play commentary of battlefield action"; "It is doubtful that any scrap of evidence has eluded him in his relentless (perhaps obsessive) quest. . ."; or, "It is seldom that this reviewer has the pleasure of reading a 'no-fault' saga of this work's magnitude. . ."; etc.

Having called attention to these words used to promote books which when read were a disappointment and a waste of time, I insist on reading the author's manuscripts or galleys before consenting to write a foreword or prepare blurbs to appear on dust jackets. With this caveat in mind, and having walked the battlefield with John Goode, Sherman and Johnston biographers, Civil War historians Jim McPherson and Nat Hughes, and members of the Civil War Sites Advisory Commission, and read the Bradley manuscript, I welcomed the Savas-Woodbury request to prepare the foreword to *Last Stand in the Carolinas: The Battle of Bentonville*.

Mark Bradley's book is a "barnburner." He draws on a multitude of sources—primary and secondary, manuscript and printed, newspapers and periodicals—and blends these with a keen appreciation of the area to prepare a masterful story of the campaign and battle in an action-packed style. Back in the mid-1950s, when I was a graduate student at Indiana University, John Bigelow, Jr.'s, *Campaign of Chancellorsville: A Strategical and Tactical Study* (1910), with its 39 maps, three sketches, and six plans, was deemed the classic Civil War campaign study. In the last decade, I have read and applauded Edwin Coddington's *The Gettysburg Campaign: A Study in Command* (1968); Richard Sommers' *Richmond Redeemed: The Siege of Petersburg* (1981); Robert Krick's *Stonewall Jackson at Cedar Mountain* (1990); Peter Cozzens' *No Better Place to Die: The Battle of Stones River* (1990) and *The Shipwreck of their Hopes: The Battle for Chattanooga* (1994); William L. Shea's and Earl J. Hess' *Pea Ridge: Civil War Campaign in the West* (1992); Harry Pfanz's *Gettysburg: The Second Day* (1987) and *Gettysburg: Culp's Hill and Cemetery Hill* (1993); and Gordon Rhea's *The Battle of the Wilderness: May 5-6, 1864* (1994). These campaign studies measure up to Bigelow's *Chancellorsville* in scope and depth, but exceed it in style and as good narrative history. Few would read Bigelow for entertainment.

Mark Bradley's *Last Stand in the Carolinas* joins the select group of outstanding campaign and battle studies that in the years since 1968 have enlightened the reader, underscoring that good history is more entertaining and thought-provoking than a novel.

Edwin C. Bearss
Assistant to the Director, Military Sites,
National Park Service

~ Preface ~

"The true story of the battle of Bentonville remains yet to be told." This statement was written 100 years ago by Charles D. Kerr, a Union veteran of the battle, and was the most telling reminder I received along the way that this story *had to be told*. I began serious research many years ago, a few months after my first visit to the battlefield. I remember that visit well, if only because I found it all so confusing. First, there was the sheer size of the battlefield—a sprawling expanse of land that seemed to betray one historian's contention that this was "not a large battle, even by Civil War standards." Subsequent visits to the battlefield to locate and trace the miles of Union and Confederate earthworks crisscrossing the landscape reinforced my conviction that in all this there must be a story worth telling.

After a few visits to the battlefield, my curiosity was piqued. I went to the North Carolina State Library to find as many books and articles as I could on the battle, but was disappointed at the lack of secondary source material. At this point I decided to make a study of the Battle of Bentonville. Thanks to Joseph T. Glatthaar's excellent book on Maj. Gen. William T. Sherman's army, *The March to the Sea and Beyond*, I knew that I would have no trouble finding primary source material, yet I believed that the battle warranted no more than a chapter or two in a book devoted to Sherman's campaigns in North Carolina.

I was sorely mistaken. In time, I realized that the Battle of Bentonville demanded book-length treatment. As a result, I decided to devote a second—and thankfully, shorter—volume to the surrender negotiations at Bennett Place. If there is a lesson that I learned from my initial foray into Civil War historiography, it is that there appears to be no lack of material for *any* campaign study.

Because Bentonville was a major Civil War battle, I found that a book-length study was necessary to examine the battle from the perspective of both the high command and the common soldier. This approach enabled me to discuss the strategy and tactics involved, while following the men as they marched in the ranks, fought on the battlefield, and in many cases, suffered and died in the hospitals. In the course of my narrative, I used the words of the participants whenever possible, for it is only through their eyes that we can hope to glimpse "the real war" that Walt Whitman feared would never get into the books.

With the exception of a few instances I limited myself to the military aspect of Sherman's march through North Carolina. John Barrett's fine study, *Sherman's March Through the Carolinas*, is unsurpassable for its coverage of the impact of the march on the civilian population. My intention was to complement Barrett's work by writing a book that focuses on Sherman's and Johnston's military operations in North Carolina. I leave it to the (gentle, I hope) reader to determine whether I have succeeded in my purpose.

Last Stand in the Carolinas:

The Battle of Bentonville

Savannah, Georgia, December 22, 1864

To His Excellency President Lincoln,
Washington, D. C.:

I beg to present to you as a Christmas-gift the city of Savannah, with one hundred and fifty heavy guns and plenty of ammunition, also about twenty-five thousand bales of cotton.

W. T. Sherman, *Major-General* [1]

Executive Mansion,
Washington, December 26, 1864

My dear General Sherman

Many, many thanks for your Christmas gift—the capture of Savannah. When you were about leaving Atlanta for the Atlantic coast, I was *anxious*, if not fearful; but feeling that you were the better judge, and remembering that "nothing risked, nothing gained," I did not interfere. Now, the undertaking being a success, the honor is all yours; for I believe none of us went further than to acquiesce. And, taking the work of Gen. Thomas into the count, as it should be taken, it is indeed a great success. Not only does it afford the obvious and immediate military advantages; but, in showing to the world that your army could be divided, putting the stronger part to an important new service, and yet leaving enough to vanquish the old opposing force of the whole—Hood's army—it brings those who sat in darkness to see a great light. But what next? I suppose it will be safe if I leave Gen. Grant and yourself to decide. Please make my grateful acknowledgments to your whole army—officers and men.

Yours very truly, A. Lincoln[2]

~ *one* ~

"This is a Great Game That is Being Played. . ."

—Maj. Thomas Osborn, Chief of Artillery, Army of the Tennessee

The year 1864 closed brilliantly for the Western armies of the Union. First came Maj. Gen. George H. Thomas' crushing victory over the Confederate Army of Tennessee at Nashville, Tennessee, on December 15-16. Five days later Maj. Gen. William Tecumseh Sherman completed his March to the Sea by occupying Savannah, Georgia, one of the Confederacy's last viable seaports. The Federal war effort suffered a minor setback on Christmas Day when Maj. Gen. Benjamin F. Butler canceled the assault on Fort Fisher, a massive earthen fort guarding Wilmington, North Carolina, the last open port in the Confederacy. But this postponement was barely noticed by the Northern people, who saw the successes of Thomas and Sherman as proof that victory was finally at hand.

In Virginia, the armies of Lt. Gen. Ulysses S. Grant and Gen. Robert E. Lee remained deadlocked about Richmond and Petersburg, though clearly Grant's strategy of waging relentless war against the principal Confederate armies was paying dividends. While Grant kept Lee pinned down in his trenches, Sherman marched through the heartland of the South virtually unopposed, and Thomas all but destroyed the Confederacy's second-largest army.

For all its significance in the public's eye, Sherman regarded the March to the Sea as a mere change of base. He now had in mind another and far more decisive thrust into the Confederacy's vitals—one that would lead him northward through the Carolinas.

In comparing the two marches, Sherman would later write: "Were I to express my measure of the relative importance of the march to the sea, and of that from Savannah northward, I would place the former at one, and the latter at ten, or the maximum."[1]

Believing "that the most important operation toward closing out the rebellion will be to close out Lee and his army," Grant at first wanted Sherman to board his troops on transports and ship them "with all dispatch" to Virginia. Sherman was disappointed with Grant's plan of operations:

> With Savannah in our possession, at some future time if not now, we can punish South Carolina as she deserves, and as thousands of the people in Georgia hoped we would do. I do sincerely believe that the whole United States, North and South, would rejoice to have this army turned loose on South Carolina, to devastate that State in the manner we have done in Georgia, and it would have a direct and immediate bearing on the campaign in Virginia.[2]

In other words, Sherman realized that by marching his army through the Carolinas he would inevitably cut Lee's supply lines to the Deep South and induce hundreds—if not thousands—of Lee's troops from that region to desert.

Grant reconsidered Sherman's proposed plan, and decided that perhaps his lieutenant was right, particularly since he had just learned that it would take about two months to ship Sherman's entire army "with all the other calls there are for ocean transportation." He asked Sherman to submit his plans for moving his armies northward.

Sherman replied that he was pleased with the change in orders, "for I feared that the transportation by sea would very much disturb the unity and *morale* of my army, now so perfect." Then he told Grant: "I feel no doubt whatever as to our future plans. I have thought them over so long and well that they appear as clear as daylight."[3]

Sherman envisioned marching through the Carolinas after feinting northwest, toward Augusta, Georgia, while another column feinted northeast toward Charleston, South Carolina, thus compelling the enemy to divide its forces in an effort to protect

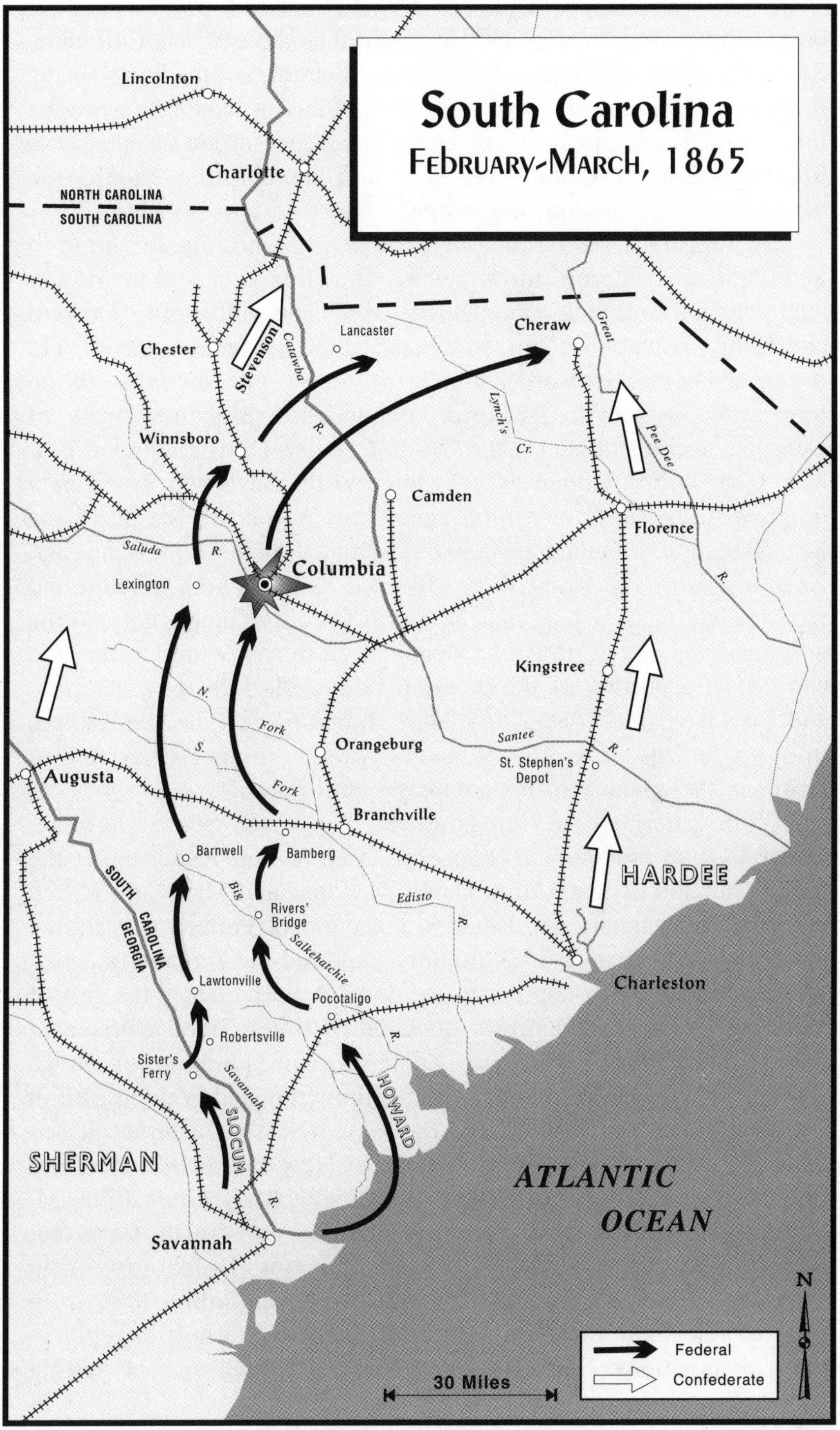

South Carolina
February-March, 1865
Lincolnton
Charlotte
NORTH CAROLINA
SOUTH CAROLINA
Chester
Stevenson
Catawba
R.
Lancaster
Cheraw
Great
Pee Dee
R.
Lynch's
Cr.
Winnsboro
Camden
Florence
Saluda
R.
Lexington
Columbia
Kingstree
N.
Fork
S.
Fork
Orangeburg
Santee
R.
St. Stephen's
Depot
Augusta
Branchville
Barnwell
Bamberg
HARDEE
SOUTH CAROLINA
GEORGIA
Big
Rivers'
Bridge
Salkehatchie
Edisto
R.
Lawtonville
Pocotaligo
R.
Charleston
Robertsville
Sister's
Ferry
Savannah
R.
SLOCUM
HOWARD
SHERMAN
ATLANTIC
OCEAN
Savannah
N
Federal
Confederate
30 Miles

Mark A. Moore

both of those important cities. He would then advance via Columbia, South Carolina, to "either Raleigh or Weldon, by the time spring fairly opens." From either of those two points, it would be a week's march for Sherman's army to Grant's trenches around Petersburg. Sherman assured Grant that he could handle Lee should the necessity of fighting him in the open arise.[4]

On January 2, 1865, Sherman received Grant's authorization to undertake his march through the Carolinas. He immediately instructed his two wing commanders, Maj. Gens. Oliver Otis Howard and Henry Warner Slocum, to advance their respective armies into South Carolina. Howard's Army of the Tennessee was to be transported by sea to Beaufort Island, while Slocum's Army of Georgia, accompanied by the Third Cavalry Division under Bvt. Maj. Gen. Judson Kilpatrick, was to cross the Savannah River via a pontoon bridge and the Union causeway. As on the March to the Sea, Slocum's command remained designated as the Left Wing, and Howard's army the Right Wing. By mid-January, both Slocum and Howard had made a lodgment in South Carolina, preparatory to the grand movement northward. Meanwhile, steady winter rains had carried off a portion of the pontoon bridge, flooded the causeway, and inundated the coastal lowlands, transforming the roads there into quagmires. The flood waters would compel Sherman to postpone the opening of his campaign until February 1.[5]

While Sherman was crossing his army into South Carolina, General Grant ordered a second expedition to Fort Fisher under the joint command of Rear Adm. David D. Porter and Maj. Gen. Alfred H. Terry. On January 15, 1865, with the aid of Porter's devastating naval bombardment, Terry's infantry captured the fort and most of the Confederate garrison. With the loss of Fort Fisher, the fall of Wilmington became merely a question of time. Grant appreciated the importance of Goldsboro as the inland junction of North Carolina's two coastal railroads—the Wilmington and Weldon, still in Confederate hands, and the Atlantic & North Carolina, under Federal control from Morehead City to New Berne. He therefore directed Thomas in Nashville to transfer Maj. Gen. John M. Schofield's XXIII Corps from Tennessee to North Carolina. Schofield's objective was to advance on Goldsboro from Wilmington (once it fell to General Terry), or failing that, from Federal-held New Berne to join with Sherman's army. In reply to these dispositions, Sherman wrote Grant: "I feel sure of getting

Wilmington, and may be Charleston, and being at Goldsboro, with its railroads finished back to Morehead City and Wilmington, I can easily take Raleigh, when it seems that Lee must come out." Thus Goldsboro, about 425 marching miles north of Savannah, became Sherman's ultimate destination.[6]

By February 1, the Right Wing was grouped about Pocotaligo, South Carolina, its inland jumping-off point, waiting for the Left Wing and the cavalry to complete their crossing of the Savannah River at Sister's Ferry. The Right Wing, or Army of the Tennessee, consisted of the XV Corps—identified by insignia featuring a cartridge box emblazoned with the legend "40 ROUNDS"— and the XVII Corps, with its arrow insignia. With the exception of one regiment, all of the men were Westerners, and on their regimental flags were stitched the names of nearly every important Western campaign or battle from Wilson's Creek and Belmont, to Forts Henry and Donelson, Pea Ridge, Shiloh, Corinth, Iuka, Vicksburg, Chattanooga, Meridian, and the various engagements that comprised the Atlanta Campaign. The Army of the Tennessee boasted a string of successes unmatched by any other Union army.

Sherman's Lieutenants

Both corps commanders in the Army of the Tennessee, Maj. Gens. John Alexander Logan and Francis Preston Blair, Jr., were politician-soldiers with no formal military training. Logan had been a Democratic congressman from Illinois when the Civil War broke out, an outspoken supporter of the Union despite the pro-secessionist feeling of his southern Illinois constituency. Indeed, it was largely through Logan's efforts that this section of the state eventually came out for the Union.[7]

Three-and-one-half years earlier, on July 21, 1861, Logan had ridden out in a carriage with a party of congressmen to watch the Battle of Bull Run, and though dressed in his Sunday best, he at one point picked up a rifle-musket and fired off a few rounds at the Southerners. Following Bull Run, Logan resigned his seat in Congress, returned to his home state, and raised the 31st Illinois—which he dubbed "the Dirty-first." Colonel Logan received his baptism of fire at Belmont, Missouri, in November 1861, during Grant's first foray against organized Confederate troops.

The politician-soldier proved his worth as a leader of men in the chaos that marked that early war engagement. By the conclusion of the Vicksburg Campaign 20 months later, Logan was a major general commanding a division in the XVII Corps. During the campaign Logan earned the respect of Grant, who deemed him qualified to command an independent army. Logan's chance to confirm Grant's judgment came on July 22, 1864, during the Battle of Atlanta, where Logan commanded the XV Corps. With the death of Maj. Gen. James B. McPherson, Logan assumed temporary command of the Army of the Tennessee, and with his customary dash, rallied a portion of the crumbling Federal line. He was the obvious choice to succeed McPherson as permanent commander of the Army of the Tennessee—insofar as Logan and his men were concerned.[8]

Instead, Sherman chose a West Pointer, General Howard, to fill the post. Sherman did not consider Logan equal to the command of an army, believing him to be a politician first and a soldier second. Logan and the men of the Army of the Tennessee were outraged, but Logan consoled himself with the belief that his opportunity to lead an army would come in due time. Logan was right, but the fighting would be over before that opportunity would arise.[9]

By mid-1864 Logan had shifted his allegiance to the Republican party, even missing the March to the Sea in order to canvass his home state on behalf of Abraham Lincoln prior to the fall elections. In December 1864, Logan traveled to City Point to confer with Grant about his military future, uncertain as to whether Sherman would restore him to his old command. Soon after Logan's arrival, Grant ordered him to proceed at once to Nashville and assume command of the Federal forces there if General Thomas still had not attacked John Bell Hood's Confederate army. Logan got as far as Louisville, Kentucky, before receiving news of Thomas' great victory. In January 1865, Logan returned to the Army of the Tennessee bearing Lincoln's reply to Sherman's Christmas greeting, and despite the latter's misgivings, Logan was restored to command of the XV Corps.[10]

John Logan cut a dashing figure on his black charger, yet he was not above climbing down from his horse to help a work party haul a wagon out of a mudhole. Because of his coal-black eyes and hair and dark complexion, Logan's men had nicknamed him "Black Jack."[11]

The commander of the XVII Corps was Maj. Gen. Francis P. Blair, Jr.—otherwise known to his friends as "Frank." His father, Francis, Sr., was a retired Washington newspaper editor and had been an advisor to Presidents Andrew Jackson, Martin Van Buren and Abraham Lincoln. Blair's brother, Montgomery, had served as postmaster general in Lincoln's Cabinet. Blair was a graduate of Princeton, but prior to that had spent a year at the University of North Carolina, where he was remembered chiefly as a prankster. A congressman from Missouri when war broke out, Blair was instrumental in keeping his state in the Union.[12]

Because of the unstable political situation in Missouri, Blair waited until mid-1862 to enter the U. S. Volunteers. A tireless recruiter, he raised seven regiments of infantry for the Union and was rewarded with a promotion to brigadier general—though he had no formal military training and almost no experience as a leader of men. In late 1862, Blair was assigned to Grant's army. Fearing that Blair would simply be one more intractable political general with whom to contend, Grant later admitted, "I dreaded his coming." But Grant was soon pleasantly disappointed. "There was no braver man than he," Grant wrote of Blair, "nor was there any who obeyed all orders of his superior in rank with more unquestioning alacrity."

Frank Blair, promoted to major general in November of 1862, first saw action in the Vicksburg Campaign leading a brigade on Sherman's Yazoo expedition, which culminated in the disastrous assault at Chickasaw Bayou. In an inauspicious combat debut, Blair lost more than a third of his command.[13] Later in the campaign, Blair commanded a division in the XV Corps, and by the time of the Atlanta Campaign, he was leading the XVII Corps. "When he came down to take command of the XVII Corps," recalled staff officer William Hemstreet, "he rode around to the various regimental headquarters and said, when the whiskey was brought out, 'Yes, let's get drunk together, boys, and learn each other's points.'" Blair was a convivial fellow, as willing to share a drink and a joke with a mud-bespattered lieutenant as with one of his division commanders. Though a political general, Blair was Sherman's best friend among his immediate subordinates—the only one, in fact, who was permitted to address his chief simply as "Sherman."[14]

Blair had a wry sense of humor. During the March to the Sea, he was accosted by the matron of a large plantation, who indignantly informed him that his soldiers were digging up all of her "ground peas." Blair regarded her for a moment while thoughtfully stroking his beard, then "drawled out with judicial and medical gravity": "Waal, Madam, I don't believe the peanuts will hurt the soldiers." According to one eyewitness, "The lady enjoyed the joke, for she flounced back with a facial mixture of humor and disdain that would be hard. . .to paint."[15]

Unlike his two corps commanders, the head of the Army of the Tennessee was a professional soldier—34-year-old Maj. Gen. Oliver Otis Howard, a native of Maine and an 1850 graduate of Bowdoin College. He continued his education at West Point, where he was graduated in 1854, counting future Confederates J. E. B. Stuart, Custis Lee and Stephen D. Lee among his friends there. After a brief stint in the Ordnance Department, Howard returned to the Point as a mathematics instructor. In his off-duty hours he studied theology with a local Episcopal priest and taught his own Bible class, also managing to find time to marry and raise a family.[16]

With the outbreak of the Civil War, Howard resigned his lieutenancy in the Regular Army and accepted command of the 3rd Maine Volunteers. He and his regiment arrived in Washington in time to participate in the battle at Bull Run, in which he commanded a brigade. By the spring of 1862, Howard was a brigadier general in command of a II Corps brigade. He subsequently lost an arm to a minie ball during the Battle of Fair Oaks, and following a brief recuperation back home in Maine, returned to the front to command another II Corps brigade at Antietam. There he assumed command of the division when its commander, John Sedgwick, fell wounded. Howard was promoted to major general on November 29, 1862, and led a division at Fredericksburg.

On April 2, 1863, Howard was named to lead the XI Corps, which had recently lost its popular—albeit inept—commander, Franz Sigel. Sigel's popularity stemmed mainly from the fact that he, like nearly half of his former command, was a German immigrant. The Germans resented Howard, whom they considered an outsider, wanting instead to be led by one of their own (preferably German) generals. The situation must have been awkward for Howard, an inexperienced 32-year-old corps commander.

Exactly one month after Howard's promotion, "Stonewall" Jackson launched a surprise attack on the Union right flank at

Chancellorsville on the evening of May 2, 1863. The exposed flank was held by Howard's XI Corps. The Confederates routed Howard's command, the first in a string of tactical successes that resulted in Gen. Robert E. Lee's most brilliant victory of the war. Both Howard and his corps had to bear the blame from the press and the Northern people for this crushing blow to the Union cause. As if that weren't enough, almost two months after its rout at Chancellorsville, the XI Corps once again found itself outflanked and falling back, this time through the streets of Gettysburg on July 1, 1863. They managed to retreat in reasonably good order and rallied on Cemetery Hill and Cemetery Ridge, thus securing the high ground for the Army of the Potomac. For this, Howard received the thanks of Congress. Nevertheless, Howard and the XI Corps emerged from the Battle of Gettysburg with an even more tarnished public image than they had had before, if such were possible.[17]

In late September 1863, following the Federal rout at Chickamauga, the XI and XII Corps were shipped by rail from Virginia to Bridgeport and Stevenson, Alabama, as reinforcements for the beleaguered Army of the Cumberland in Chattanooga, Tennessee. This transfer proved to be a boon for Howard and his much-maligned command, and the XI Corps went on to serve capably in the Chattanooga Campaign. In April 1864, it was merged with the XII Corps to form the XX Corps under the command of Maj. Gen. Joseph Hooker, giving a good account of itself throughout the Atlanta Campaign. Howard also found a place in the Western army. When the formation of the XX Corps left him without a command, he was assigned to lead the IV Corps, Army of the Cumberland.

On July 27, 1864, following the death of McPherson, Sherman named Howard to head the Army of the Tennessee, much to the chagrin of General Logan and his troops. Once again thrust into the role of unwelcome outsider, Howard faced a situation no less difficult than the one that had confronted him on assuming command of the XI Corps. He proved himself equal to the task, displaying a tactfulness in his handling of General Logan and his new command that made the transition easier for all concerned. In January, just prior to the opening of the Carolinas Campaign, Sherman designated Howard as his second-in-command. Sherman's decision was all the more surprising because his other wing commander, General Slocum, outranked Howard.[18]

According to the Army of the Tennessee's chief of artillery, Maj. Thomas Osborn, General Howard was not the "profound thinker and learned man" that Sherman was, and he lacked Sherman's "large natural ability." Nor did Howard, continued Osborn, "call out from his troops the enthusiastic applause that Generals Logan and Hooker" did. "[Y]et every officer and man has an unbounded confidence in him, and never question that an order from him is from the highest known authority. . . .I have never been in an Army where such implicit confidence was displayed in its leader." Major Osborn attributed Howard's success as an army commander to his "kindness and consideration for his troops. . .his persistent fighting when engaged, and determination to win; the reckless disregard for his own person; his implicit obedience to all authorized orders."[19]

Howard was a man of deep religious convictions, and he possessed a strong evangelical bent. Although most of his men respected him for his bravery, opinion on his religious zeal was sharply divided. He was known within the army as both "the Christian Soldier" and "Old Prayer Book." Lieutenant Colonel Andrew Hickenlooper, one of General Blair's staff officers, relates "an amusing incident which so completely illustrates General Howard's religious convictions, and the soldiers' indifference to such considerations":

> As we were riding together busily engaged amidst the general confusion incident to the falling back of our forces, we came across the driver of an ammunition wagon whose lead-mules had become tangled up in their harness. He was addressing them in terms more forceable [sic] than polite, when, notwithstanding other much more important matters demanding his attention, General Howard rode [up] to the irate teamster, and yelled out, "Hold on, hold on there my man." This caused the poor fellow while holding his lead lines to turn and look up into the General's face. Having thus attracted the driver's attention, he continued, "Suppose just as some of those vile oaths are issuing from your lips one of these passing cannon balls should take your head off?" To this the teamster unhesitatingly replied, "Well General it would just be my God d—d luck. . ." and

> proceeded to apply the lash without paying any further attention to the presence of the commanding general, who remarked to me sadly that he was afraid that man was beyond redemption.[20]

One does not have to look deep in Sherman's army to find General Howard's antithesis—Bvt. Maj. Gen. Jefferson Columbus Davis, commander of the XIV Corps in Slocum's Army of Georgia. A chaplain in Davis' command described the general as "a military tyrant, without one spark of humanity in his make-up." An Indiana soldier in the XIV Corps would never forget the tongue-lashing that Davis gave his lieutenant because a wagon in his column had broken down and was impeding the column's progress:

> Davis came along. . .and he cursed and swore around and gave our Lieutenant a terrible cursing and showed himself in his usual style. I do think our Government is hard up when such men are allowed a command. I should not [have] blamed [Lieutenant] Starbuck if he had shot him dead off his horse. I don't believe I should have taken it.

At least one of Davis' division commanders, Brig. Gen. William P. Carlin, feared and despised Davis. "There are many excellent officers in the 14th Corps, and the men are as good as any," wrote one veteran campaigner. "But the Corps is mismanaged, and a spirit of jealousy has possessed the command." Yet for all his faults, Davis retained his position because Sherman valued him as a proven battlefield commander.[21]

The 36-year-old Davis was a veteran of the Mexican War, having served as a sergeant in the 3rd Indiana at Buena Vista, where he stood just a few yards down that now-famous V-shaped battle line from Col. Jefferson Davis, the commander of the 1st Mississippi Rifles and the future president of the Confederacy. Davis later served as an officer in the 1st Artillery of the Regular Army. He was present at the bombardment of Fort Sumter and was said to have sighted the gun that fired the first Union reply. He went on to command a brigade at Wilson's Creek in southern Missouri and a division at Pea Ridge and Corinth. In May 1862, he was promoted to brigadier general of volunteers. [22]

Ill health forced Davis to take a leave of absence in the summer of 1862. In September, he volunteered to help train the civilian reserves at Louisville, Kentucky, who had been called up to oppose Braxton Bragg's advance on that city. Davis soon clashed with the commander of the Federal forces in Louisville at the time, Maj. Gen. William "Bull" Nelson, a former naval officer who proved to be as tactless and overbearing as Davis himself. Nelson had concluded their penultimate meeting by ordering Davis across the Ohio River to Cincinnati, threatening to forcibly eject him if he refused to go. Davis complied. Several days later, the commanding general in Cincinnati ordered Davis to report for duty to Maj. Gen. Don Carlos Buell, who had just assumed command in Louisville.

On September 29, accompanied by Indiana governor Oliver P. Morton, Davis paid "Bull" Nelson a visit at the Galt House, the hotel in Louisville where General Nelson was headquartered. When Davis confronted Nelson and demanded satisfaction for the earlier insult, the latter replied, "What are you doing here? Get out of my way, you contemptible puppy!" and slapped Davis across the face with the back of his hand. Then Nelson turned on Governor Morton, an old antagonist of his, and snapped, "And you came here to witness this insult, did you?" Nelson thereupon stormed out of the hotel office, slamming the glass door behind him. Davis promptly borrowed an "English bulldog" pistol from a "Captain Gibson of Louisville." When Davis saw Nelson coming back toward the office with his left hand tucked inside the right breast of his coat, he assumed that Nelson had gone to arm himself. Davis stepped into the hallway and commanded, "Stop, General Nelson, and defend yourself!" Instead, Nelson continued to walk toward Davis, his hand still concealed beneath his coat. Davis fired once, the bullet piercing Nelson's chest. Nelson died of his wound less than one hour later.[23]

As it transpired, Davis had murdered "Bull" Nelson in cold blood. Nelson was in fact unarmed when Davis shot him—it was merely his habit to walk with his left hand inside his coat. Davis was immediately placed under house arrest, but thanks to the considerable influence of Governor Morton, was soon released and ordered to report for duty. The general was indicted for manslaughter in October 1862, but was freed on $5,000 bail. On May 24, 1864, Davis' case "was stricken from the docket with leave to reinstate." Meanwhile, Davis served capably in the Army of the Cumberland both as a division and a corps commander, but never rose above the rank of major general by brevet. Nor does he seem to have profited by the lesson of the Nelson incident, for he continued to treat his own subordinates much as "Bull" Nelson had treated him.[24]

Controversy continued to plague Davis, another notable instance being the death of numerous blacks at Ebenezer Creek during the March to the Sea. Sherman, in his *Memoirs,* described the incident in Davis' favor:

> It so happened that General Davis' route into Savannah followed what was known as the "River-road," and he had to make constant use of his pontoon-train—the head of his column reaching some deep, impassable creek before the rear was fairly over another. . . .On the occasion referred to, the bridge was taken up from Ebenezer Creek while some of the [Negro] camp-followers remained asleep on the farther side, and these were picked up by Wheeler's cavalry. Some of them, in their fright, were drowned in trying to swim over, and others may have been cruelly killed by Wheeler's men, but this was a mere supposition. At all events, the same thing might have resulted to General Howard, or to any other of many of the most humane commanders who filled the army.[25]

Many of General Davis' officers and men were not as charitable as Sherman on this matter. One officer called Davis' action "a burning shame and a disgrace, and inhuman to leave them to struggle in thirty feet of water for their lives; for they prefer sinking in the water to returning to slavery." Private Timothy Pendergast of the 2nd Minnesota asked, "Where can you find in all the annals of plantation cruelty anything more completely inhuman and fiendish than this? Lagree [sic] was an angel of mercy in comparison with the author of this infamous order. . .this barbarous act has created a deep feeling against Davis in this division." Major James Connolly was outraged. "The idea of five or six hundred black women, children and old men being returned to slavery by such an infernal Copperhead as Jeff. C. Davis was entirely too much. . . .I told his staff officers what I thought of such an inhuman barbarous proceeding." Connolly believed that his statements would probably result in "a reprimand from his serene Highness" [Davis], but, Connolly warned, "if he undertakes to vent his spleen on me for it, I have the *same rights that he himself exercised in his affair with*

Nelson." Such was the character of the man who commanded the XIV Corps, as seen by some of the men who served under him.[26]

The commander of the XX Corps was Bvt. Maj. Gen. Alpheus Starkey Williams. Like Davis, Williams was a major general by brevet only, but for a different reason: he never resorted to flagrant self-promotion with the press, nor did he solicit the patronage of a powerful national politician. As a result, Williams became, according to historian Milo Quaife, "the forgotten man in the Union army." Appointed brigadier general of volunteers in August 1861, Williams did not receive his promotion by brevet until January 1865. Although he commanded a corps in one of Sherman's armies, he was outranked by several division commanders in that army, two of whom were full major generals. Moreover, for three years Williams had seen dozens of less deserving junior officers promoted above him: "[T]here is something, especially in military life," Williams wrote in October 1864, "where the gradations of command are violated and the shirking junior is foisted over the heads of long-serving and faithful officers, that falls with especial weight upon one's pride and self-respect. It can't be denied nor [sic] concealed, and he who does not feel it is not fit to hold a commission!"[27]

Williams was born in Connecticut on September 20, 1810. He was graduated from Yale in 1831 and for several years thereafter lived as a young man of means, briefly studying law in New York before embarking on a series of travels across America and Europe. Williams settled in Detroit in 1836 and established his law practice there. Among other pursuits, he worked as a probate judge, a bank president, a newspaper publisher and as postmaster of the city. He also served as an officer in two local militia companies and as lieutenant colonel in the 1st Michigan Regiment during the Mexican War.[28]

Alpheus Williams began the Civil War as commander of Michigan's school of military instruction at Fort Wayne. He first saw active duty in the Shenandoah Valley, where he commanded a brigade, and eventually a division, under Maj. Gen. Nathaniel P. Banks during the campaigns of late 1861 and early 1862. Williams assumed command of a division in the XII Corps when it was formed in September 1862, and temporarily led the corps at Antietam and Gettysburg. When the XII Corps was transferred to the Western theater, he remained with it as a division commander and continued in that capacity when the XI and XII Corps were consolidated to form the XX Corps. When Sherman formed the Army of Georgia prior to the March to the Sea, he named General Slocum to command it, and appointed Williams to succeed Slocum as commander of the XX Corps. Even so, before the war was over, Williams would again find himself demoted to division-level command.[29]

By far the oldest of Sherman's half-dozen army and corps commanders, the 54-year-old Williams was known as "Old Pap" to his men, many of whom had served under him for more than three years. In addition to being a good field commander, Williams was a diligent administrator who found that preparing for a campaign could be just as exhausting as the campaign itself:

> Reflect, how much my mind is constantly engrossed with the care of nearly 20,000 men. No sooner do I reach camp after a most arduous campaign than my labors begin in making preparation for the next. . . .Everything from wagon grease to the armament of artillery has to be attended to. With all the agents and assistance I have, I am still responsible that it is all done and done right. It must all be supervised. If it fails, or is neglected, I am the responsible man. In consequence, my mind is never at rest. My anxieties never cease. I dream of the work at night and I ponder and inquire and sometimes fret all day.

Small wonder that the veterans of the XX Corps trusted and respected "Old Pap."[30]

The commander of the Army of Georgia was Maj. Gen. Henry Warner Slocum. The 38-year-old was a native of Onondaga County, New York, and a graduate of West Point, class of 1852. Following his graduation, he served as a lieutenant of artillery in Florida and at Fort Moultrie, South Carolina. Slocum married his childhood sweetheart in 1854, and though he was promoted to first lieutenant in 1855, he regarded his pay as insufficient for raising a family. Thus, during his stint at Fort Moultrie, Slocum took advantage of his off duty hours by studying law with a prominent Charleston attorney. He resigned from the U. S. Army in 1856 and returned to Onondaga County, New York, where he established his law practice before moving to Syracuse in 1858. While there, he served as a legislator in the New York General Assembly and as colonel and instructor of artillery in the state militia.[31]

Slocum became colonel of the 27th New York on April 21, 1861, and led his regiment at Bull Run, where he was severely wounded. Later that summer he was promoted to brigadier general, and after returning to duty in the fall was given command of a brigade in Brig. Gen. William B. Franklin's division. Unlike in the peacetime army, promotion came rapidly to Slocum. In May 1862, during Maj. Gen. George B. McClellan's Peninsula Campaign, Franklin was promoted to corps commander and Slocum in turn assumed command of the division. A few months later he was promoted to major general, and following the Battle of Antietam, was given command of the XII Corps. Slocum went on to lead the XII Corps at Chancellorsville and Gettysburg, and was also nominally in command of the V Corps during the latter battle.[32]

By the time of the Gettysburg Campaign, Slocum ranked second only to Maj. Gen. Joseph Hooker in the Army of the Potomac. When Hooker was relieved of command on June 28, 1863, Maj. Gen. George G. Meade was promoted over Slocum's head, probably because Meade possessed more practical experience than his senior in rank. Nevertheless, Slocum's rise had been a meteoric one, but his contempt for Joe Hooker was such that he submitted his resignation to President Lincoln in the fall of 1863, after learning that he was to serve under Hooker in the Western theater. Slocum had been the most outspoken advocate of Hooker's removal from command following the Federal defeat at Chancellorsville and refused to serve under him again. Lincoln rejected Slocum's resignation, deeming him too valuable a man to lose. Instead, he was eventually reassigned to the District of Vicksburg, which he commanded from April 20 to August 14, 1864, during which time he missed most of the Atlanta Campaign. In one of the war's interesting ironies, Slocum succeeded Hooker as commander of the XX Corps when the latter resigned in a huff after being passed over for the command of the Army of the Tennessee. Prior to the March to the Sea, Sherman appointed Slocum to head the newly-formed Army of Georgia, which consisted of the XIV and XX corps.[33]

"General Slocum enjoys the reputation of a thoroughly accomplished soldier," wrote Sherman aide Maj. George W. Nichols. Nichols described Slocum as "brave, cool, experienced," and referred to his "complete mastery of all the details of his profession, his keen sense of order and discipline, and his energetic and magnetic manner." But Slocum was also prickly at times, and Major Osborn's characterization of him as an "unpleasant man" seems to have been an apt one.[34]

Slocum's Army of Georgia brought a diverse wealth of combat experience to Sherman's army. The XIV Corps was a predominately veteran Western aggregation that had formerly belonged to the Army of the Cumberland. A few of the regiments had seen action in Missouri as early as 1861, and most had fought in the bloody engagements at Shiloh, Corinth, Perryville and Stones River. At Chickamauga, the valiant stand by units of the XIV Corps on Snodgrass Hill and Horseshoe Ridge had saved the Army of the Cumberland from annihilation, and its subsequent charge—purely on the initiative of the enlisted men—up the slopes of Missionary Ridge sent the Confederates reeling back into Georgia, thus raising the siege of Chattanooga. The XIV Corps, with its distinctive acorn badge, had fought well throughout the Atlanta Campaign, particularly at Jonesboro, where its rout of Patrick Cleburne's stellar division cut the Confederates' last railroad line into Atlanta and led to the fall of that important industrial city.

The XX Corps, as stated earlier, was composed principally of regiments from the old XI and XII Corps of the Army of the Potomac. Many of these troops had fought in the Shenandoah Valley Campaign, Cedar Mountain, Antietam, Fredericksburg, Chancellorsville and Gettysburg. The men of the XX Corps were products of the incessant drill and strict discipline of the Eastern army. As a result, they presented a stark contrast to their Western comrades in the other three corps, whose free and easy ways struck the Easterners as unsoldierly. But the spit and polish soldiers of the XX Corps—who wore the star emblem formerly used by the now-defunct XII Corps—would undergo a startling transformation on the march through the Carolinas, and by the end of the campaign would emerge as ragged and rough-looking as the Westerners. Though the Easterners never quite blended in with the rest of Sherman's men, they came to respect the fighting ability of their Western comrades and took pride in being members of "Uncle Billy" Sherman's army.

Sherman's cavalry was commanded by 29-year-old Maj. Gen. Judson Kilpatrick, whose audacity was exceeded only by his ambition. Just before Sherman set out on his March to the Sea, he described Kilpatrick's virtues as a commander in rather odd terms.

"I know Kilpatrick is a hell of a damned fool," Sherman reportedly told Maj. Gen. James H. Wilson, "but I want just that sort of man to command my cavalry on this expedition."[35]

Kilpatrick was born near Deckertown, New Jersey, on January 14, 1836. He had little formal schooling, but was admitted to West Point in 1856 and was graduated there in 1861. On the day of his graduation Kilpatrick married Alice Nailer and carried a silken banner bearing her name with him when he went off to war. Eager for fame and rapid promotion, Kilpatrick saw that the best means of attaining both was to join the U.S. Volunteers. He enlisted in the 5th New York Infantry—the renowned Duryée's Zouaves—and was commissioned captain. He was wounded at Big Bethel on June 10, 1861, the first Regular Army officer struck down by enemy fire in the Civil War.[36]

When Kilpatrick returned to active duty later that year, it was as lieutenant colonel of the 2nd New York Cavalry. During the campaigns of 1862, "Little Kil" led numerous raids behind enemy lines, and by December was promoted to colonel of the regiment. Two months later he received a brigade command and took part in Maj. Gen. George Stoneman's unsuccessful raid on Richmond, during which Kilpatrick's command approached to within two miles of the Confederate capital's defenses before being driven back. Kilpatrick's fame reached its zenith in June 1863 following Brandy Station, the largest mounted engagement of the Civil War and the first important action of the Gettysburg Campaign. In that battle Kilpatrick and his brigade fought gamely, giving notice to "Jeb" Stuart's Confederate horsemen that they could no longer expect to dominate Federal cavalry in an equal fight. Four days after the battle, he received his brigadier general's star, and later that month was given command of a division that included the brigades of Brig. Gens. George A. Custer and Elon J. Farnsworth. Kilpatrick's ambitions were being realized.[37]

His foolhardy streak was in evidence at Gettysburg on July 3, when he ordered Farnsworth to lead his brigade in an attack on the Confederate right flank following the repulse of Pickett's charge. Farnsworth's charge was as doomed to failure as Pickett's had been. When he protested on the grounds that his troopers "were too good men to kill," Kilpatrick shot back, "Do you refuse to obey my orders? If you are afraid to lead this charge, I will lead it." Farnsworth rose up in his stirrups and demanded, "Take that back!" Kilpatrick retracted his statement, but the order stood. Farnsworth agreed to lead the charge, but served notice to his commanding officer, "you must bear the responsibility." The mounted assault, over boulder-strewn ground and against infantry waiting behind rocks and trees, was a disaster. Farnsworth was mortally wounded, struck in five places, and his brigade was cut to pieces. On this day Kilpatrick truly earned his other nickname: "Kill cavalry."[38]

As if that weren't a dark enough stain on Kilpatrick's career, on October 19, 1863, Jeb Stuart routed Kilpatrick in a lopsided affair known as the "Buckland Races." Soon afterward, Kilpatrick's wife died. Beset by personal tragedy and professional disaster, Kilpatrick found solace in his newly-formed ambition to become president of the United States. This chain of circumstances combined to make "Little Kil" even more reckless than he had been before. Seeking a way to retrieve his sinking fortunes, Kilpatrick hatched the scheme which became known as the Kilpatrick-Dahlgren raid. President Lincoln, catching wind of the scheme, invited Kilpatrick to the White House to explain it to him. The cavalry officer told the president that the objective of his plan was to enter Richmond, free the Federal prisoners incarcerated there, and capture any Confederate high officials he happened to find in his path. Then Kilpatrick played his trump card by assuring Lincoln that his raid would be the perfect means of distributing the president's amnesty proclamation for Rebels who were ready to return to the Union. In a rare lapse of judgment, Lincoln gave his approval.[39]

The raid began promisingly enough on the night of February 28, 1864, but Kilpatrick's 3,500-man column was beaten back just as it reached the outskirts of Richmond. Kilpatrick's other column, a 500-man detachment under the command of Col. Ulric Dahlgren, was ambushed and Dahlgren was killed. Papers were allegedly found on Dahlgren's body declaring Kilpatrick's intention to burn Richmond and assassinate the Confederate president and his cabinet. Following this disaster, Kilpatrick was transferred to the Western theater and ordered to report to General Sherman. His reassignment was regarded within the army as a demotion, and Kilpatrick himself must have believed that all his grand ambitions were crushed.[40]

Bad luck continued to follow the diminutive cavalryman. At Resaca in May 1864, only a few weeks into the Atlanta Campaign,

Kilpatrick was severely wounded and knocked out of action for several months. Eager to return to the army and participate in the capture of Atlanta, Kilpatrick ignored his doctor's advice and was back at the front by late July. Unable at first to ride on horseback because of the lingering effects of his wound, Kilpatrick conducted operations from a carriage. Sherman was pleased with the work of Kilpatrick and his cavalry on the March to the Sea, crediting them with preventing the enemy's horsemen from wreaking havoc on his infantry columns and wagon trains. "Little Kil" had found his niche at last.[41]

Though he spurned strong drink and gambling, Kilpatrick had a fondness for the fairer sex, which he seems to have indulged quite freely following his wife's death. "Little Kil" compensated for his short, slight build by wearing expensive tailored uniforms, great boots and a black felt hat which he kept tilted at a rakish angle. He drove his men and their mounts hard, but he was a popular commander, always seeing to it that his troopers were well-provisioned. He also had a tendency to look the other way as they plundered and pillaged their way across Georgia.[42]

Kilpatrick's command was officially known as the Third Cavalry Division, and like their infantry counterparts, the troopers boasted a sum total of experience that included nearly every important campaign and engagement in the Western theater. Most of Kilpatrick's troopers were old hands at fighting dismounted alongside infantry, a tactic generally believed to have been the exclusive province of the Confederate cavalry under Maj. Gens. Joseph Wheeler and Nathan Bedford Forrest.

* * *

On February 1, 1865, Sherman's combined armies numbered 60,079 officers and men. The core of this army consisted of veteran volunteers who had first enlisted in 1861 and 1862, then re-enlisted in 1864 after their two- and three-year terms had expired. These veterans were the survivors of what one soldier called "a rigorous weeding-out process" effected by Rebel bullets, hardship and disease. Moreover, prior to both the Savannah and Carolinas campaigns, Sherman ordered the Medical Department to examine all soldiers with health problems and ship out all those deemed unfit for active campaigning. As a result, the army that Sherman led into

South Carolina was an elite force unmatched by any other comparably-sized body of men in the Federal army.[43]

Before the March to the Sea, Sherman had also reduced the number of wagons, baggage and artillery pieces in his army. The trains consisted of 2,500 wagons, with six mules to each wagon, and 600 ambulances pulled by two horses each. Sherman reported that his army carried with it "an ample supply of ammunition for a great battle," but just seven days' forage and 20 days' hard bread, coffee, sugar and salt, plus some beef on the hoof. The army had to rely on foraging to supply it with food gathered from the countryside through which it passed. As for baggage, Sherman allowed just one wagon per regiment. Even the commanding general slept under a tent fly, reserving his headquarters wall tent for clerical work. The number of field pieces was reduced to 68, or roughly one cannon per 900 men. Each gun and caisson (with its limber) was pulled by eight horses, two more than the regulations called for.[44]

Even on good roads the marching column of each wing often stretched out for 10 miles. As a result, whenever possible each of the four corps marched on a separate road. Under ordinary circumstances this arrangement would have rendered the trains vulnerable to the far-ranging Confederate cavalry, but Kilpatrick's horsemen and the numerous mounted foraging details did a superb job of shielding the main columns.[45]

As Sherman swept into the interior of South Carolina, his armies occupied a front more than 40 miles wide. His tactic of feinting on both Charleston to the east and Augusta to the west made it nearly impossible for the Confederates to determine in which direction the Federals were headed. Sherman simply moved between the forces of his divided and outnumbered opposition.

Opposing the Union advance through South Carolina was a miscellaneous array of Confederate forces commanded by Gen. Pierre Gustave Toutant Beauregard, the head of the Military Division of the West. Beauregard called a council of war which met on February 2 at Green's Cut Station, near Augusta. Among the Southern luminaries present were Lt. Gen. William Joseph Hardee, commander of the Department of South Carolina, Georgia and Florida; Maj. Gen. Daniel Harvey Hill, commander of the District of Georgia from his headquarters at Augusta; and Maj. Gen. Gustavus

W. Smith, who led the Georgia state militia. Beauregard estimated that his combined forces amounted to 33,450 troops. But Beauregard was basing his estimate on reinforcements he expected to receive, as well as troops on hand. The actual number of troops present—including Hardee's command, Maj. Gen. Joseph Wheeler's Cavalry Corps and a contingent of Lee's Corps from the Army of Tennessee—amounted to about half of Beauregard's optimistic estimate.[46]

Prior to the council of war, Wheeler had notified D. H. Hill that Sherman's army appeared to be headed for Branchville, a rail junction lying roughly midway between Augusta and Charleston. Branchville was important to the Confederacy because it provided the sole remaining rail link between Virginia and Georgia. The generals considered the option of concentrating at Branchville "and there offer battle to Sherman," but Beauregard dismissed the idea with a rhetorical flourish, deeming it "in violation of all maxims of the military art" to attempt a concentration at a point Sherman's larger army might reach first. As it later materialized, the Federal Right Wing struck the railroad at Midway, 15 miles west of Branchville. Believing that "the pending negotiations for peace" impelled him to hold Charleston and Augusta for "as long as it was humanly possible," Beauregard divided his forces to defend those two cities, but still hoped to oppose Sherman's advance into South Carolina. Although Beauregard allowed for the contingency of uniting these disparate forces at Columbia, Sherman succeeded in interposing his army between Hardee's command to the east and the Army of Tennessee contingent to the west. Thus the Confederacy was unable to mount an effective defense of South Carolina.[47]

The "pending negotiations" in which Beauregard placed so much faith came to be called the Hampton Roads Conference, held on the morning of February 3. The conference came about largely through the efforts of Francis Preston Blair, Sr., a long-time presidential advisor and the father of Maj. Gen. Frank Blair, Sherman's XVII Corps commander. Acting as intermediary between Presidents Abraham Lincoln and Jefferson Davis, Blair arranged a meeting "with a view to secure peace to the two countries," as Davis phrased it, or in Lincoln's words, "with the view of securing peace to the people of our one common country." Though both presidents wanted to appear eager to exploit every opportunity for peace, neither was willing to compromise his objectives to attain it.

Given the irreconcilable differences between the two presidents' viewpoints, the Hampton Roads Conference was doomed to failure.[48]

The conference took place in the saloon of Lincoln's steamer, the *River Queen,* near Fort Monroe, Virginia, off the tip of the Virginia peninsula. The Confederate commissioners were Senator Robert M. T. Hunter, Assistant Secretary of War John A. Campbell, and Vice President Alexander H. Stephens, all well-known peace advocates. President Davis was conspicuously absent. Representing the Union were Lincoln and Secretary of State William H. Seward. The Federal and Confederate representatives soon reached an impasse: Lincoln would settle for nothing less than restoration of the Union, and the Confederates were empowered to negotiate solely on the basis of an independent Confederacy. The four-hour meeting was both amicable and inconclusive—the war would have to grind on inexorably until a victor and a vanquished emerged from the gunpowder smoke.[49]

On the same day of the Hampton Roads Conference, Lt. James Royal Ladd, an officer in Sherman's army, no doubt expressed the belief of most of his comrades when he wrote:

> A great many rumors are rife at the present time in regard to peace, or at least a cessation of hostilities. Blair's visit to Richmond many think is based upon such a mission but my opinion is that Sherman's visit [to the Carolinas] will have a greater tendency to bring a peace about than all the Blairs on earth.[50]

Beauregard's decision to defend Augusta and Charleston instead of concentrating his scattered forces played directly into Sherman's hands, and the Federal advance through South Carolina was virtually unopposed. When Sherman reached the outskirts of Columbia on the afternoon of February 16, the city was defended by a small Confederate force consisting of portions of Wheeler's cavalry and a contingent of Stephen D. Lee's Corps from the Army of Tennessee, as well as by Maj. Gen. Matthew C. Butler's cavalry division, newly arrived from the Army of Northern Virginia. Beauregard and Lt. Gen. Wade Hampton were present in Columbia to direct operations there. Also on hand was Gen. Joseph E. Johnston, who was acting in an unofficial capacity, and still in disfavor with the Davis administration—dating back to his removal from command of the Army of Tennessee seven months before. Johnston and his wife Lydia had since moved to Columbia to be near their friends and relatives, but were already feeling pressed to relocate. “The expenses of living here are much above our means,” Johnston had written a former staff officer in late January. “We can't remain here three months longer, even with Sherman's consent.”[51]

Columbia fell to Sherman's army on February 17, and by the next morning much of it had burned to the ground, the result of high winds, burning cotton—initially set afire by Hampton’s cavalry—and drunken Federal soldiers. With the fall of Columbia, the port city of Charleston became untenable. While the fires raged through Columbia, General Hardee's command evacuated Charleston under prior orders from Beauregard.[52]

On February 19 Sherman's army resumed its march, heading northward toward Winnsboro. Once again Beauregard was mistaken as to Sherman's intentions. “He [Sherman] will probably be at Charlotte about the 24th, before my forces can concentrate there,” wrote Beauregard. “He will doubtless move then on Greensborough, Danville, and Petersburg, or if short of supplies, on Raleigh and Weldon, where he will form a junction with Schofield.” In truth, Sherman's next destination was Fayetteville, or failing that, Wilmington. On the 18th Beauregard had directed Hardee's Corps to move northward by rail to Cheraw, but he countermanded that order a day later and ordered Hardee to take the trains to Greensboro, North Carolina, via Wilmington, somehow overlooking the fact that Wilmington was about to fall to General Schofield's Federal command. On the 21st, Department of North Carolina commander Gen. Braxton Bragg wired Hardee that the Federals had cut the Wilmington & Manchester Railroad, thus necessitating a march to Cheraw. Wilmington fell to Schofield on the following day, February 22.[53]

By now it was clear to the Confederacy's newly-appointed general-in-chief, Robert E. Lee, that Beauregard was not up to the task of stopping Sherman. In a letter to President Davis, Lee wrote: “Genl Beauregard makes no mention of what he proposes or what he can do, or where his troops are. He does not appear from his despatches to be able to do much.”[54]

Beauregard's subsequent dispatches did nothing to dispel his superiors' doubts about his fitness for battlefield command. At noon on February 21, President Davis received a message from the Creole general reminiscent of his grand—and preposterous—schemes of the past:

> Should enemy advance into North Carolina toward Charlotte and Salisbury, as is now almost certain, I earnestly urge a concentration in time of at least 35,000 infantry and artillery at latter point, if possible, to give him battle there, and crush him, then to concentrate all forces against Grant, and then to march on Washington to dictate a peace. Hardee and myself can collect about 15,000, exclusive of Cheatham and Stewart [of the Army of Tennessee], not likely to reach in time. If Lee and Bragg could furnish 20,000 more the fate of the Confederacy would be secure.[55]

Davis forwarded Beauregard's "startling" telegram to Lee. Although Lee tactfully replied, "The idea is good, but the means are lacking," he must have shared Davis' belief that Beauregard's proposal betrayed a commander who was unable to come to grips with military reality. In a February 19 dispatch to the new Confederate secretary of war, John C. Breckinridge, Lee had already broached the idea of replacing Beauregard with General Johnston, citing Beauregard's rumored failing health as the reason:

> Should his strength give way, there is no one on duty in the department who could replace him, nor have I any one to send there. Genl J. E. Johnston is the only officer whom I know who has the confidence of the army & people, & if he was ordered to report to me I would place him there on duty.[56]

Two days later Lee again raised the subject with Breckinridge, requesting that Johnston be ordered to report to him for duty. Lee thereby secured Breckinridge's consent (and by implication Davis' own grudging permission), and on February 22 sent the following message to Johnston:

> Assume command of the Army of Tennessee and all troops in Department of South Carolina, Georgia, and Florida.

> Assign General Beauregard to duty under you, as you may select. Concentrate all available forces and drive back Sherman.[57]

~ *two* ~

". . .And Great Men Are Playing It"

—Maj. Thomas Osborn, Chief of Artillery, Army of the Tennessee

Like many other refugees from Columbia, General Johnston was staying in Lincolnton, North Carolina, during the latter part of February in the hope that Sherman would bypass this backwater of the Confederacy. But Lee's directive suddenly thrust Johnston back into the maelstrom. "It is too late to expect me to concentrate troops capable of driving back Sherman," Johnston wired Lee. "The remnant of the Army of Tennessee is much divided. So are other troops." Johnston regarded his new assignment with a jaundiced eye, telling fellow refugee Mary Chesnut that he "was only put back to be the one to surrender."[1]

Despite his misgivings, Johnston traveled to Charlotte on February 23 to assume command and begin the concentration of his scattered forces. But first he conferred with Beauregard. Ever mindful of a fellow general's prerogatives, Johnston secured Beauregard's assurance that the new arrangement "was agreeable to him" before assuming command. With that item of business settled, Johnston directed Beauregard to remain as his second in command and to order the immediate concentration of all available forces. On February 24, Johnston reviewed a remnant of Lee's Corps of the Army of Tennessee. In the words of an Alabamian from Manigault's Brigade:

> Today Johnston received our Corps and as he passed each Brigade, three cheers were given in a very joyful tone and manner expressive of great satisfaction. The old General

> looks as usual, hearty and soldier like. He is the most soldierly looking general I have ever seen. He is as well loved in this army among the men, as an officer can be. They have every confidence in him, and that alone will benefit the army and the service.[2]

Though gratified at the reception accorded him by the Army of Tennessee veterans, the review merely confirmed what Johnston had suspected about the condition of the army. On February 25, Johnston wrote Robert E. Lee that his small army comprised a force "too weak to cope with Sherman." His force consisted of, first:, Hardee's troops, numbering some 12,000 effectives; second, the Army of Tennessee veterans, comprising Lee's Corps (3,500), Stewart's Corps (1,200), and Cheatham's Corps (1,900); and third, the cavalry under Wade Hampton, about 6,000 troopers in all. This motley array totaled fewer than 25,000 men, and in the words of Hampton, "It would scarcely have been possible to disperse a force more effectually."[3]

That this disparate assemblage came together at all is remarkable. Following its rout at Nashville, the remnant of the Army of Tennessee had fallen back into northeastern Mississippi and had established winter camp at Tupelo. "If not in the strict sense of the word, a disorganized mob, it was no longer an army," recollected Col. Alfred Roman of Beauregard's staff. Moreover, in early January Gen. John Bell Hood had instituted a system of furloughs that, though well-intentioned, only accelerated the disintegration of the once-grand army. Following Hood's resignation on January 13, President Davis completed the dispersal of the Army of Tennessee by directing Beauregard to send a portion of it eastward to oppose Sherman's expected march into South Carolina. This operation proved to be the Confederacy's last major railroad troop transfer of the war.[4]

The first soldiers to undertake the journey were the men of Maj. Gen. Carter L. Stevenson's Division of Lee's Corps. The long and circuitous trip began at dawn on January 19, 1865, when the first trainload of troops headed southward on the Mobile & Ohio for Meridian, Mississippi, where they switched to the eastbound Alabama & Mississippi Rivers line. When the train reached McDowell's Bluff, Alabama, the men boarded ferries and crossed the Tombigbee River to Demopolis, where they boarded cars to

Selma. From Selma the troops took a steamboat ride up the Alabama River to Montgomery, Alabama,. The next stage of their eastbound journey carried them over a patchwork rail system consisting of the Montgomery & West Point, the Muscogee, the Southwestern, and the Central of Georgia, to Milledgeville, Georgia. From there the men marched northeast 35 miles to Mayfield, where they again boarded cars, this time on the incomplete Augusta & Milledgeville line, which carried them to Warrenton. At Warrenton they switched to the Georgia Railroad for the 30-mile ride to Augusta. The first trainload of Stevenson's troops arrived at Augusta on the evening of January 27. The 500-mile journey from Tupelo had taken nine days.[5]

The remnant of Lee's Corps (under the temporary command of General Stevenson) was the only portion of the Army of Tennessee to arrive in time to dispute Sherman's progress through South Carolina, first near Branchville along the Edisto Rivers line, then at Orangeburg, and finally at Columbia. On February 17, Stevenson's command withdrew northward toward Winnsboro and Chester, the latter point having been the terminus of the Charlotte & South Carolina Railroad since the fall of Columbia. They reached Chester on the 20th, but for some reason marched for Charlotte instead of traveling there by rail. On the 21st, the men of Lee's Corps tramped 20 miles to the Catawba River, which they waded at Landsford Ford, then marched another six miles before camping at the North Carolina state line. They reached Charlotte on February 23, where a part of Stevenson's command passed in review before General Johnston that afternoon, followed by the remainder on the next day. To the veterans of Lee's Corps, who had fought under Johnston for the bulk of the Atlanta Campaign and subsequently under Hood in Tennessee, Johnston's return to command made for a happy reunion.[6]

For the men of Stewart's and Cheatham's corps, the long journey from Tupelo, Mississippi to Augusta, Georgia, was lengthier and more tedious than it had been for the men of Lee's Corps. Because of a lack of rolling stock, the troops were forced to march the 50 miles from Tupelo to West Point in order to board the cars there. Moreover, a massive backlog had developed along the Demopolis-to-Selma leg, which resulting in the use of a detour to Mobile, adding another 100 miles to their journey. Even so, by February 25 the balance of Stewart's and Cheatham's troops were within 80 miles of Charlotte, marching northward from Newberry and Pomaria to Chester.[7]

Discipline during the numerous rail stopovers and along the route of march was uncertain at best. A Texan in Cheatham's Corps branded his comrades "a set of thieves": "Our Brig behaved shamefully all the way around from Tupelo, Miss." But, he explained, "The boys had not been paid off for ten months," nor had they received their accustomed whiskey and tobacco rations. As a result, the men resorted to plundering to supply the deficiency. Beauregard's quartermaster, Capt. John M. Goodman, wrote that the Army of Tennessee "is now a complete mob. I never have witnessed so much demoralization in my life. . . . I have feared [for] my life in contending with our own troops and in the attempt to keep them in some kind of discipline." But Goodman expressed the hope that General Johnston would be able to restore the army's discipline and morale.[8]

While the Army of Tennessee concentrated at Charlotte, Lt. Gen. William J. Hardee's Corps was hurrying northward from Charleston to beat Sherman's army to Cheraw, South Carolina, which now appeared to be the Federals' next destination. Most of the men in Hardee's command were former coastal artillerymen or garrison troops unaccustomed to hard marching. At first they welcomed the march as a change from the monotony of picket duty, but "[o]ur feet soon became blistered and sore," recalled Cpl. A. P. Ford, a South Carolinian in Hardee's Corps. "[M]any of us had no shoes, but trudged along in the cold and mud barefooted as best we could." Hardee's soldiers quickly learned a valuable lesson: travel light. "Our men had started on this march with as much baggage as they. . .could carry," Corporal Ford continued,

> but soon began to throw aside the impedimenta and settle down to. . .one blanket per man and the suit of clothes each actually wore. For some miles both sides of the road were strewn with knapsacks, articles of clothing, etc., . . .and the highway appeared as if fleeing troops in panic had passed along.[9]

Some of Hardee's troops were fortunate enough to ride the trains out of Charleston, but most of them had to march the 40 miles to St. Stephen's Depot, where they were to board the cars for

Cheraw. The footsore soldiers began arriving at St. Stephen's on February 20.[10]

According to Hardee's adjutant, Lt. Col. Thomas B. Roy, there occurred a "Great many desertions from the command on the march from Charleston. Some art[illery] companies almost disbanded by desertions." Corporal Ford supported Roy's observation:

> All along the line of march large numbers of men were constantly deserting. Nightly, under cover of darkness, many would sneak from their bivouacs and go off, not to the enemy, but to their homes. . . .The most influential cause of desertions was the news that reached the men of the great suffering of their wives and children at home, caused by the devastations of Sherman's army.[11]

Attrition whittled away at Hardee's command from both bottom and top, and not solely because of desertion. First there was Hardee himself, so sick at the time of the evacuation of Charleston that he had to relinquish command to his senior division commander, Maj. Gen. Lafayette McLaws. Moreover, South Carolina governor Andrew Magrath recalled several of the state militia units serving in Hardee's Corps, and in the coming weeks would press Hardee and Johnston to return additional state troops to him. On February 22 Hardee consolidated his rapidly dwindling command from three divisions to two, eliminating the division commanded by Maj. Gen. Ambrose R. "Rans" Wright. In the ensuing shake-up Wright was granted a leave of absence to attend a session of the Georgia legislature, and one of Wright's former brigade commanders, Brig. Gen. Hugh Mercer, was transferred to Macon, Georgia. Wright's troops were reassigned to Hardee's two remaining divisions, McLaws' and Brig. Gen. William B. Taliaferro's. Lieutenant Colonel Roy stated that the two divisions numbered 5,000 effectives each—2,000 less than Johnston's February 25 estimate of Hardee's troop strength. That number would dwindle even further in the coming weeks.[12]

JOHNSTON'S LIEUTENANTS

Aside from Conner's Brigade from the Army of Northern Virginia, commanded by Brig. Gen. John D. Kennedy, and a few other veteran regiments, McLaws' makeshift division was a command consisting mostly of untested infantry and some Georgia and South Carolina "reservists," a euphemism for those men deemed earlier in the war as either too old or too young to fight. Their commander, Lafayette McLaws, was a veteran division commander in the Army of Northern Virginia under Lt. Gen. James Longstreet, a former West Point classmate. Early in the war McLaws had proved himself a capable division commander, but his reputation had lost much of its luster by the time of Gettysburg. Following the Battle of Chickamauga, McLaws angered Longstreet by refusing to support his effort to oust Gen. Braxton Bragg from command of the Army of Tennessee. This had disastrous consequences for McLaws—or so he believed. During the Knoxville Campaign a few months later, Longstreet accused McLaws of bungling the assault on Fort Sanders and relieved him from duty. Although later exonerated by President Davis and restored to his old command, McLaws was quietly shuffled off to Savannah in May 1864, when Longstreet threatened to resign in protest.[13]

Controversy continued to haunt McLaws. In January 1865, he was accused of being drunk the night his division evacuated its position at Pocotaligo, South Carolina. Several troopers of the 3rd South Carolina Cavalry stated that during the retreat they had seen McLaws "so intoxicated that he was vomiting freely." When Hardee ordered an investigation into the matter, more than a dozen eyewitnesses stepped forward and attested to McLaws' sobriety on the night in question. Although sustained by Hardee and his brigade commanders, the incident left McLaws angry and bitter.[14]

Brigadier General William B. Taliaferro commanded the other division in Hardee's Corps. A wealthy Virginia planter before the war, Taliaferro was a graduate of William & Mary College, had studied law at Harvard, and had served in the Mexican War as a major in the 9th U. S. Infantry. Taliaferro had commanded a brigade under "Stonewall" Jackson during the Shenandoah Valley Campaign, and briefly led Jackson's old division before being wounded at Groveton on August 28, 1862, during the Second Manassas Campaign. Although Taliaferro returned to active duty in time to lead a division at Fredericksburg, his status as division commander was only temporary. When he was passed over for promotion in January 1863, the humiliated general requested a transfer. Having little confidence in the abilities of his disgruntled subordinate, General Jackson was happy to oblige him. Taliaferro was duly shipped off to Savannah one month later. By mid-1863 he was commanding garrison troops in the Charleston Harbor defenses, where he remained until the evacuation two years later.[15] As things later unfolded, Hardee was less than pleased with his two division commanders, judging by his determination to replace them at the first opportunity.

The brigade commanders under McLaws and Taliaferro were not as tested in the field as their superiors. Taliaferro's Division consisted of three brigades: Col. Alfred Rhett's, Col. A. D. Goodwyn's, and Brig. Gen. Stephen Elliott, Jr's. The balance of Rhett's Brigade had garrisoned Fort Sumter for most of the war. Their commander was a fire-eating secessionist, and though his troops had seen no field combat service, they had defended Fort Sumter bravely and could at least be counted on to fight. While Rhett had no pitched combat experience, his counterpart, Stephen Elliott, had seen plenty of action during his brief tenure as a brigade commander in the Army of Northern Virginia. Elliott's old brigade had manned the works blown up by the Federal mine explosion that opened the Battle of the Crater in July of 1864. Elliott had been severely wounded during the fight, and was still suffering from those wounds in February 1865. There was even some doubt as to whether Elliott would be able to withstand the rigors of the coming campaign. His present command was no less an uncertainty, being composed of coastal artillerymen, militia troops and a battalion of Citadel cadets. Much like Elliott's command, Goodwyn's Brigade consisted of South Carolina militia troops of limited usefulness, particularly since Governor Magrath had ordered them not to leave the state.[16]

Who better to command a corps so riddled with uncertainties than the general known as "Old Reliable?" In February 1865, Lt. Gen. William J. Hardee was 49 years old and for the past 27 years had been a professional soldier. An 1838 graduate of West Point, Hardee was a veteran of the Seminole Wars and the Mexican War, and had spent much of his antebellum career on frontier duty with the 2nd U. S. Dragoons.[17]

In 1853 Secretary of War Jefferson Davis assigned Hardee the task of compiling an infantry tactics manual for the U.S. Army. The result was Hardee's *Rifle and Light Infantry Tactics,* a two-volume treatise detailing the evolutions of the infantry battalion. Hardee's *Tactics* subsequently became the standard text on small unit maneuver for both the Union and Confederate armies. Yet even at the time of its publication, Hardee's *Tactics* was obsolete. The advent of the rifle-musket had seen to that. A vast improvement over the old smoothbore musket in both range and accuracy, the rifle-musket rendered the sort of close order formations called for in the *Tactics* suicidal. It would take the better part of the Civil War for most of the generals to learn that tragic lesson—and some would never learn it. Even so, the *Tactics* brought Hardee great prestige in the pre-war army. In 1855 Hardee was promoted to major and assigned to the 2nd U. S. Cavalry, a prestigious posting that included such future Civil War luminaries as Col. Albert Sidney Johnston, Lt. Col. Robert E. Lee, Maj. George H. Thomas, Capts. Earl Van Dorn, Edmund Kirby Smith and George Stoneman, and Lt. John Bell Hood. One year later, Davis appointed Hardee to the post of commandant of cadets at West Point, where he remained until 1860.[18]

Hardee resigned from the U. S. Army on January 29, 1861, ten days after his home state of Georgia seceded from the Union. By July he was a brigadier general organizing and training a brigade of Arkansas troops in that state. In the fall of 1861, Hardee was commanding a division in Kentucky under Gen. Albert Sidney Johnston. He was promoted to major general on October 21, 1861, and by the spring of 1862 was commanding a corps in the Army of the Mississippi—the forerunner of the Army of Tennessee. At Shiloh, Hardee and his corps established a pattern (later repeated at Perryville and Stones River) of making assaults that enjoyed initial success, only to come to grief because of Confederate tactical blunders or the Federal army's numerical superiority. Nevertheless, during this time Hardee earned his nickname, "Old Reliable," and a reputation as the Confederate army's finest corps commander in the West. On October 11, 1862, he was promoted to lieutenant general. In July 1863, Hardee was reassigned to duty under Gen. Joseph E. Johnston in Mississippi and Alabama, where his duties included reorganizing and re-equipping the paroled men of the Vicksburg garrison. As a result, Hardee missed leading his old corps in the Battle of Chickamauga, the Army of Tennessee's only major tactical victory. In transferring Hardee, the War Department had unwittingly removed Army of Tennessee commander Braxton Bragg's most subtle and influential enemy. Had Bragg known of Hardee's clandestine efforts to remove him from command, it is unlikely he would have consented to his return. In any case, Hardee was ordered to rejoin his old corps near Chattanooga in late October. Upon his return, Hardee found the army demoralized and rife with dissension. Nevertheless, at Missionary Ridge Hardee's troops repulsed the repeated assaults of the Federal XV Corps, personally commanded by Maj. Gen. William T. Sherman. When the Army of Tennessee's line collapsed, Hardee's elite division, led by Maj. Gen. Patrick R. Cleburne, held off Sherman's force, enabling most of the routed Confederates to escape capture. Following the disaster at Missionary Ridge, Bragg resigned his command of the Army of Tennessee. Hardee assumed command of the army on December 2—but only temporarily. "I fully appreciate the compliment paid to me by the President," Hardee wrote the War Department, "but feeling my inability to serve the country successfully in this new sphere of duty, I respectfully decline the command if designed to be permanent." Hardee no doubt dreaded the increased responsibility, and may also have feared a renewal of the intrigues and conspiracies that had racked the army throughout Bragg's tenure. Whatever the reason, Hardee refused the top post. It would not be offered to him again.[19]

The Atlanta Campaign saw the waning of close order, open-field warfare as Hardee practiced it, and the emergence of trench warfare, a concept foreign to both Hardee's training and temperament. Aside from a few isolated defensive victories at Pickett's Mill and Kennesaw Mountain, neither Hardee nor his corps enjoyed even the limited success of their pre-1864 days. When Lt. Gen. John Bell Hood replaced Johnston as commander of the Army of Tennessee, he immediately launched a series of desperate assaults against the Federals encircling Atlanta. Hardee's Corps spearheaded two of those assaults, the Battle of Peachtree Creek and the Battle of Atlanta. Both attacks failed, in part because of Hardee's poor tactical judgment. At the Battle of Jonesboro six weeks later, Hardee turned in perhaps the worst performance of his Civil War career, mismanaging the attacks of both his own and Lee's corps.[20]

Soon after the fall of Atlanta, Hardee requested a transfer, which General Hood eagerly endorsed. Hood blamed Hardee for the fall of Atlanta, and Hardee deemed Hood unqualified to lead the Army of Tennessee. President Davis reluctantly granted Hardee's request and ordered him to assume command of the Department of South Carolina, Georgia and Florida. When Sherman opened his siege of Savannah in December 1864, Hardee skillfully evacuated his garrison across the Savannah River, thus saving his troops to fight another day. Though Hardee regarded the withdrawal from Savannah as his finest achievement of the war, the Confederacy could ill-afford any more such triumphs.[21]

During the evacuation of Charleston on February 17, Hardee was so sick that he had to be sent ahead to Kingstree, about 70 miles north of Charleston on the Northeastern Railroad, and about halfway to Cheraw. But by February 20 Hardee was back on duty. In compliance with Beauregard's orders, he asked Bragg whether it was still possible to send his troops into Wilmington ahead of General Schofield's Federals. On the 21st he received word from Bragg that Schofield had cut the rail line into Wilmington. Hardee consequently had no choice but to send his troops on to Cheraw. When he attempted to notify Beauregard of the change in plans, he discovered that the telegraph lines had been cut. Hardee now assumed that he had no time to lose if he wanted to beat the Federals to Cheraw.[22]

The first trainload of Hardee's troops, consisting of Col. John C. Fiser's Brigade of McLaws' Division, arrived at Kingstree on the afternoon of February 21. On the 22nd they rode the cars as far as Florence, and arrived at Cheraw the following day. The trains carrying McLaws' troops were crowded to overflowing, and some of the men from Conner's Brigade spent a miserable night riding on top of the cars in a driving rain. By the 27th most of McLaws' Division had arrived at Cheraw, but Hardee grew concerned that neither his artillery nor the bulk of Taliaferro's Division would reach him before the Federals cut the rail line to Cheraw. "This road, like all others in the Confederacy, is wretchedly managed," an exasperated Hardee wired General Johnston on February 28. "With proper management I ought to have had everything here by this time. . . .A rapid march of the enemy will bring him here to-morrow." But Hardee's luck soon changed, as Taliaferro's troops began to arrive in force that afternoon, and the incessant rains had finally succeeded in stalling Sherman's army—something the Confederates had been unable to do.[23]

Most of the Federal XIV Corps had been stranded on the south bank of the Catawba River since February 23. When Kilpatrick's cavalry and the XX Corps made the crossing on the 22nd, the Catawba was placid, but torrential rains transformed the once-peaceful stream into a raging torrent which carried off most of the Left Wing's 660-foot pontoon bridge. For the next several days Sherman's army was at a standstill while the 58th Indiana Pontoniers frantically recovered their bridging material and sought another site for their bridge. The Federals could not afford to remain in this sparsely settled region for more than a few days, because they had already exhausted the few provisions the foragers had managed to gather. Sherman lost all patience and ordered General Davis to spike his guns, burn his wagons, swim his horses and mules, and ferry his men across before he wasted any more time in bridge-building. But Davis' pontoniers came through quite literally at the eleventh hour, and by midnight on the 28th, the soldiers of Baird's Division began to cross the 680-foot bridge at Kingsbury Ferry.[24]

Samuel Beight of the 105th Ohio found the experience unforgettable:

> The river overflowed its banks, and at the ford designated for our crossing the water surged and roared like the falls of a great cataract. . . .The heavens were weeping, and the rain poured down upon us in torrents. As we approached the bridge four abreast, all jesting and laughter so common with the boys at once ceased. A serious crisis confronted us, and we realized that there was no fun in it. At the south end of the bridge stood [an officer], with drawn sword, directing each file to break step as we came upon the bridge and to keep a distance of five paces between the lines. It is doubtful if ever an order was more scrupulously obeyed. Our hearts palpitated wildly. . . .In every alternate pontoon on the left sat a brave soldier boy holding aloft a flaming, resiniferous pine torch to light the way across. The black soot from the torches filled our ears, eyes and nostrils. . . .When we stepped off the last plank at the north end of the bridge we breathed regularly once more.[25]

While the XIV Corps crossed the treacherous Catawba River, about 40 miles to the east the XV Corps was stalled on the west bank of Lynch's Creek. Brevet Major General John M. Corse's division had the advance and reached the creek on the morning of February 26. Corse's foragers and scouts found the bridge intact, but the approaches were flooded by several feet of water which extended for about a half-mile beyond the creek. Corse ordered his lead brigade, commanded by Brig. Gen. Elliott Rice, to wade the freshet and make a lodgment on the opposite side. General Rice sent forward the 2nd Iowa as skirmishers.[26]

John Blume of the 66th Indiana recalled that his regiment followed close behind the Iowans. "The water was about knee-deep on the west side," Blume wrote:

> but on the east side, for about a quarter of a mile, the road was through a dense jungle of briers, grapevines and underbrush, and the depth of the water varied from one to four and a half feet. And cold! Holy Moses, that was the coldest water I ever waded through. Most of our boys had taken off their clothes and had them tied in bundles, which they carried on their heads.[27]

This proved to be quite a balancing act, for the men often found themselves wading in water up to their armpits and having to hold their rifles and cartridge boxes over their heads.

Before Rice's men could reach dry land, several hundred troopers of Maj. Gen. Matthew C. Butler's Confederate cavalry appeared, pursuing a squad of XV Corps foragers. The 2nd Iowa received the order to charge: "[A] great splashing of water followed," Blume noted, "and the 2nd Iowa boys reached the land, piled their clothes in a heap and took off after the Johnnies." Aided by the 7th Illinois Mounted Infantry, the Iowans drove off Butler's troopers, then returned to where they had left their clothing.[28]

The XV Corps spent the next three days building two trestle bridges across the flooded lowlands and corduroying the approaches. On the 26th the XVII Corps reached Lynch's Creek a few miles to the east and found the 270-foot-long bridge at their crossing untouched. "Here, however, we found the road [and] bottom lands adjoining overflowed for a considerable distance on either side," General Blair reported, "the water being from two to six feet in depth for a distance of about 200 yards on west and 1,500 yards on east side." Blair sent one of his regiments over to secure the crossing, then ordered his battalion of the 1st Michigan Engineers and Mechanics to build a footbridge across the swamp. After working all night, the 1st Michigan Engineers and Blair's pioneer corps completed a bridge that stretched for more than a mile.[29]

Blair ordered the indefatigable 1st Michigan to tackle a far more ambitious undertaking on the following day: the construction of a wagon bridge and road. About 2,500 men worked on the project, and according to Blair's estimate, by 5:00 p.m. they had "completed 850 feet of bridging and 7,000 feet of corduroyed road on stringers." While the XV Corps continued to work on their bridges, Blair's command crossed Lynch's Creek on the 28th and marched to within 13 miles of Cheraw before receiving orders from General Howard to halt and fortify their position. Blair could hear Hardee's troop trains "running in and out of Cheraw all day, and the whistle blowing continually." He pressed Howard for permission to move on Cheraw the next morning, but Howard told him not to advance beyond his present position until the XV Corps had crossed Lynch's Creek.[30]

From a group of Confederate deserters Blair received the startling news that Joe Johnston had been restored to command. Blair immediately notified Howard, and on March 1, Howard passed the news on to Sherman, who at that time was accompanying Slocum's wing. Outwardly Sherman remained as confident and unconcerned as before. In answer to the rumor that Johnston was in Cheraw personally directing operations there, Sherman wrote Blair: "Big generals may be there but not a large force." Yet Sherman later admitted: "I knew that my special antagonist, General Jos. Johnston, was back with part of his old army; that he would not be misled by feints and false reports, and would somehow compel me to exercise more caution than I had hitherto done."[31]

Sherman was right. Johnston would not be as easily misled as Beauregard had been. On March 1 Johnston wrote Lee, discounting Beauregard's and Wade Hampton's reports that Sherman appeared to be heading toward Charlotte:

> The route by Charlotte, Greensboro, and Danville is very difficult now, as you remark. It would also leave your army

> exactly between those of General Grant and General Sherman. It seems to me, therefore, that. . .General Sherman ought not to take it. His junction with General Schofield is also an object important enough. . .to induce him to keep more to the east. Such a course would render his junction with General Grant easier.[32]

Johnston told Lee that he was anxious to combine Hardee's troops with those from the Army of Tennessee. "These forces united may impede the march of the Federal army, and even find opportunities to strike heavy blows, or at least prevent it from gathering food." If this show of confidence gave Lee a flicker of hope, the following sentence must have extinguished it: "Would it be possible to hold Richmond itself with half your army, while the other half joined us near Roanoke to crush Sherman? We might then turn upon Grant." Lee must have found Johnston's proposal sadly reminiscent of Beauregard.[33]

It was only fitting that Robert E. Lee and Joseph E. Johnston should find themselves fighting virtually back-to-back at the war's close. The Lee-Johnston destinies had been joined since the American Revolution, when Johnston's father, Peter, had fought in the cavalry legion commanded by Lee's father, Henry—better known as "Light Horse Harry" Lee. Moreover, the two men were native Virginians, they were the same age (Lee was just two weeks older) and both had graduated in the class of 1829 at West Point, where they became close friends. In 1865 Johnston confided to Confederate senator Louis T. Wigfall of Texas: "In youth & early manhood I loved & admired him more than any man in the world." Following graduation, Lee's and Johnston's paths diverged, although for the next 20 years duty would occasionally throw them together.[34]

From West Point Johnston went on to routine service for several years with the U.S. Artillery. During the mid-1830s he participated in the Indian wars in Illinois and Florida while on special duty, serving as a staff officer under the nation's foremost military hero, Maj. Gen. Winfield Scott. Only after Johnston resigned from the army in 1837 did he take part in his first skirmish. As a civilian engineer working for the U.S. Topographical Bureau, Johnston accompanied a joint army-navy expedition to Florida in order to survey a stretch of the Florida coastline. The United States was at war with the Seminoles, and Johnston soon found himself caught in the middle.

The commander of the expedition was a rash man, and when his squad encountered a force of the Seminoles, he ordered an attack. The balance of his small command consisted of navy recruits who not only refused to fight, but retreated. Since most of the officers were killed or wounded at the outset, Johnston assumed command of the rear guard—a squad of two dozen Regular Army troops. Under Johnston's guidance, the soldiers held the Seminoles at bay throughout the retreat to their ship. Some of Johnston's detractors would later contend that he had not stopped retreating since his experience in Florida. Nevertheless, this incident seems to have convinced Johnston that he truly belonged in the military. He rejoined the army in 1838, entering the Corps of Topographical Engineers.

The Mexican War was the great proving ground for many future Civil War generals, and Johnston was no exception. Once again Johnston served as an aide on Winfield Scott's staff, where he resumed his old friendship with fellow staff officer Robert E. Lee. Though wounded at Cerro Gordo, Johnston returned in time to play a prominent role in the war, leading a battalion of light infantry in the successful charges at Contreras and Chapultepec.

Johnston emerged from the Mexican War as one of the most promising of a cluster of younger officers, and in 1855 became lieutenant colonel of the First Cavalry, equivalent to Robert E. Lee's position with the Second Cavalry at about that time. On June 28, 1860, Johnston was promoted to Quartermaster General of the Army, a position which carried with it the rank of brigadier general and was considered one of the choicest assignments in the army. But when Virginia voted to secede from the Union on April 19, 1861, Johnston knew that he had to go with his state, and sadly resigned his commission three days later.

Johnston's first major battle as an army commander was at Manassas on July 21, 1861, and it also proved to be his only outright victory (although he shared the laurels with P. G. T. Beauregard). Yet Johnston immediately came under criticism from President Davis and others for failing to pursue the routed Federal army, when in truth the victorious Confederates—owing to exhaustion and inexperience at all levels of command—were scarcely less disorganized than their beaten enemy. Despite this minor flap, Davis and Johnston continued on friendly terms—that is, until Johnston first read Davis' list of full generals. Johnston exploded when he saw himself ranked fourth on the list, behind Gens. Samuel Cooper, Albert Sidney Johnston and Robert E. Lee. Johnston was well aware of a law passed by the Confederate Congress that stipulated that all officers of the same rank would retain the relative seniority of their old Regular Army rank. Thus, according to Confederate law, and Johnston's interpretation of that law, his former U. S. Army rank of brigadier general should have made him the ranking general in the Confederate service. Not so, said Davis, who explained that he ranked his full generals according to their *line* rank in the Regular Army. And since Johnston had been a brigadier general by *staff* rank only, Davis placed him according to his old line rank of lieutenant colonel, thus leaving him behind Cooper, Sidney Johnston and Lee. Angry and hurt because he believed that he had been done a grave injustice, Johnston sent Davis a tactless letter of protest. Davis' reply was terse and cold—the first of many such letters to pass between the two men. Thus began what may have been the most disastrous command misalliance of the Civil War.[35]

The spring of 1862 found Johnston on the Virginia Peninsula confronting his one-time friend and protégé, Maj. Gen. George B. McClellan, whose 100,000-man Federal army outnumbered his own by 30,000. McClellan began his deliberate advance up the peninsula in April, his objective Richmond, the capital of the Confederacy. Both Davis and his chief military advisor, Robert E. Lee, believed that Johnston's best defense was to contest every foot of ground on the peninsula, where McClellan would be unable to deploy his superior force to full advantage. Johnston disagreed, arguing that his smaller but more mobile army stood its best chance of defeating the Federals in the open ground near Richmond. Johnston consequently retreated up the peninsula before McClellan, who by mid-May had advanced to within seven miles of the city. Finally, Johnston launched an assault against an isolated Federal corps at Seven Pines on May 31. Although it looked good on paper, Johnston's plan was overly complicated and the subsequent attack was badly mismanaged. Johnston, moreover, having ridden to the front near the close of the first day's fight, fell severely wounded and had to relinquish command of his army. Though his second-in--command, Gustavus Smith, assumed the reins of power, President

Davis immediately recognized that Smith was not up to the task. The army was turned over to Johnston's old friend, Robert E. Lee.

While recuperating from his wounds in Richmond, Johnston formed a friendship and political alliance with Texas senator Louis T. Wigfall, one of President Davis' most influential and outspoken enemies. By now the break between Davis and Johnston was complete. Yet in November Davis entrusted Johnston with command of the newly formed Department of the West, consisting in part of Bragg's Army of Tennessee at Murfreesboro and Lt. Gen. John C. Pemberton's Army of Mississippi at Vicksburg and Port Hudson. Even with the aid of the telegraph and the railroad, this proved to be a far-flung command assignment. Johnston believed that the two armies would function more efficiently as independent entities, and that the distance separating them made the shuttling of reinforcements from one to the other a self-defeating proposition. Moreover, he resented what he saw as Davis' constant meddling in his department's affairs.

In May 1863, Johnston was ordered to travel to Mississippi and assume personal command of the Confederate forces there. At the head of his 32,000-man Army of Relief, he advanced to the Big Black River 10 miles east of Vicksburg only to find General Sherman's 30,000-man Army of Observation guarding the river crossings. As Johnston looked on, Vicksburg fell on July 4, and Pemberton's command surrendered with the fallen city. Both Pemberton and Davis blamed Johnston's failure to come to Pemberton's relief for the loss of Vicksburg and its garrison, while Johnston saw the fall of Vicksburg as inevitable, and accused Pemberton and Davis of allowing the garrison to fall with it.

Although it galled him to do so, Davis bowed to popular opinion and appointed Johnston commander of the Army of Tennessee in December 1863, after that army's disastrous defeat on the hills overlooking Chattanooga. Johnston immediately put his experience as quartermaster general to work and dramatically improved the flow of supplies to the army. He also implemented a system of furloughs for the men, many of whom hadn't been home since the outbreak of the war. The improved rations (including a regular supply of whiskey and tobacco), the issuance of new shoes, tents and uniforms, together with the furloughs, transformed the morale of the Army of Tennessee. Johnston also reunited the Tennessee brigades of Maj. Gen. Benjamin F. Cheatham's Division, which the soldiers believed Bragg had separated as punishment for their outspoken hatred of him. Upon learning the good news, Cheatham's Tennesseans immediately marched to Johnston's headquarters. When Johnston stepped out of the house to acknowledge their cheers, Frank Cheatham put his arm around him, patted his bald pate a few times, and said, "Boys, this is old Joe!" Though patrician to the core, "Old Joe" suffered this indignity in silence, and as a result won the undying love of Cheatham's men.[36]

In addition to restoring the morale of the Army of Tennessee, Johnston also pressed the War Department for reinforcements. By the second week of the Atlanta Campaign in mid-May 1864, Johnston's army numbered about 70,000 men, an increase of nearly 30,000 from its January troop strength. Nevertheless, Sherman's force numbered 110,000 men and was able to maneuver Johnston out of one defensive position after another. Davis repeatedly urged Johnston to bring Sherman to battle, but Johnston, for a variety of reasons, was unable or unwilling to do so. By mid-July Sherman had advanced to the outskirts of Atlanta. Convinced that Johnston intended to surrender Atlanta without a fight, Davis relieved him from command on July 17.[37]

Johnston's conduct of the Atlanta Campaign was embroiled in controversy, and remains so today. Yet whatever ability Johnston may have possessed as an army commander was undermined by the mutual animosity and distrust that existed between him and President Davis. For his part, Johnston displayed a tactless indifference to Davis' role as commander-in-chief. He refused to take Davis into his confidence, something that Robert E. Lee never failed to do. Worse yet, whenever Davis pressed him to attack, Johnston inevitably replied that he would do so as soon as there was an opportunity—exactly the sort of noncommittal response that infuriated Davis.[38]

Following his dismissal Johnston had ample time to nurse his anger and resentment, for he was in virtual retirement with slim prospects for another command assignment. But as the tide of the war turned decisively against the Confederate cause in late 1864, the anti-Davis faction (Johnston's friend and ally Senator Wigfall foremost among them) began to call for Johnston's restoration to command. On the face of it, Davis' enemies were merely acceding to the popular outcry, when in fact they perceived Johnston's resurgence as a means of eroding the president's power and influence. In January 1865, both Houses of the Confederate Congress drafted resolutions calling for Johnston's reinstatement. Though their opinion may have mattered little in Richmond at this time, Johnston's former soldiers also longed to see "Old Joe" back in command. They remembered his solicitude for their welfare, and in contrast with Hood's disastrous Tennessee Campaign, Johnston's cautious retreat through northern Georgia must have seemed a pleasant memory.[39]

On February 4, 1865, Confederate vice president Alexander H. Stephens and 17 senators (including Wigfall) signed a petition addressed to General-in-Chief Robert E. Lee recommending that Johnston be reappointed as commander of the Army of Tennessee. "I entertain a high opinion of Genl Johnston's capacity," Lee replied, "but think a continual change of commanders is very injurious to any troops & tends greatly to their disorganization." As to the senators' contention that he possessed the authority to reinstate Johnston, Lee wrote:

> I do not consider that my app[ointmen]t as Genl in Chief of the Armies of the C[onfederate] States confers the right which you assume belongs to it, nor is it proper that it should. I can only employ such troops & officers as may be placed at my disposal by the War Dept. Those withheld or relieved from service are not at my disposal.

Despite his refusal to act on the senators' recommendation, Lee certainly favored it, but doubtless hesitated to act given Davis' antipathy for Johnston.[40]

On February 18 Davis drafted a scathing indictment of Joseph E. Johnston's Civil War career. In the course of his closely-reasoned, 5,000-word paper, Davis stated that he had entrusted Johnston with three important command assignments, and that he had utterly failed in each. Davis characterized Johnston as:

> deficient in enterprise, tardy in movement, defective in preparation, and singularly neglectful of the duty of preserving the means of supply and transportation. . . .It should be added, that [it had not] been possible for me to obtain from General Johnston any communications of his plans or purposes beyond vague statements of an intention

> to counteract the enemy as their plans might be developed.[41]

In conclusion, Davis wrote: "My opinion of General Johnston's unfitness to command has ripened slowly and against my inclinations into a conviction so settled that it would be impossible for me again to feel confidence in him as the commander of an army in the field." Davis intended to submit his paper to the Confederate Congress in answer to the several resolutions recommending Johnston's restoration to command, but on further reflection he thought better of it. Within a few days of writing his paper, Davis assented to General Lee's request (as well as to overwhelming public opinion) and approved Johnston's reinstatement, expressing the hope that "General Johnston's soldierly qualities may be made serviceable to his country when acting under General Lee's orders." In truth, Davis had long since ceased to believe in Johnston, and doubtless assumed that he would retreat all the way to Richmond without bringing Sherman to battle.[42]

Prospects for the new Lee-Johnston command partnership were less than favorable. In a letter to Senator Wigfall, Johnston confided that he had long supposed that Lee had forgotten their earlier friendship. This statement reveals far more about Johnston's attitude toward Lee than the reverse. Johnston envied the success Lee had enjoyed with his old army. Regarding Lee's crushing defensive victory at Fredericksburg, Johnston had told Wigfall, "What luck some people have. Nobody will ever come to attack me in such a place." On the day that Johnston left Lincolnton to assume command of the army, he took a walk with Mary Chesnut. "He explained. . .all of Lee and Stonewall Jackson's mistakes," she recorded in her diary. "He was radiant and joyful." Underlying Johnston's envy and resentment was his suspicion that Lee had become one of Davis' inner circle.[43]

* * *

General Joseph Eggelston Johnston was 58 years old in March 1865; his Federal counterpart, Maj. Gen. William Tecumseh

Sherman, was thirteen years his junior. Johnston was reserved in demeanor; Sherman was garrulous and animated. The former dressed impeccably, his double-breasted general's coat always looking crisp and freshly brushed; the latter dressed carelessly, and when on the march wore a rumpled field officer's coat without insignia of rank. No two men could have been more dissimilar, and yet, although Sherman and Johnston had never met, during the Atlanta Campaign they had forged a bond of mutual respect that would remain unbroken for the rest of their lives.

By March 1865, both generals knew that the war was grinding to a close. Johnston had assumed command believing that the most the Confederacy could hope to gain by continuing the war was "fair terms of peace; for the Southern cause must have appeared hopeless then, to all intelligent and dispassionate Southern men." Sherman stated the matter with characteristic bluntness: "From the moment my army passed Columbia S. C. the war was ended. All after that was the necessary consequences of foregone conclusions, the manner of the conclusion only being left for Johnston." A foregone conclusion, perhaps, but one of Howard's staff officers, Maj. Thomas Osborn, found the unfolding of the campaign no less absorbing: "This is a great game that is being played," he wrote, "and great men are playing it."[44]

Sherman was one of those great men. Born in Lancaster, Ohio, on February 8, 1820, he was the sixth of 11 children. His debt-ridden father died in 1829, leaving his mother destitute and unable to care for the younger children. The nine-year-old "Cump" was taken in by Thomas Ewing, one of the wealthiest and most influential men in Ohio. In 1836 Ewing procured an appointment to West Point for young Sherman, who proved to be an excellent student. Unfortunately, Sherman's prankishness and unkempt appearance earned him so many demerits that he graduated sixth instead of fourth in the class of 1840, and thereby missed out on the opportunity of joining the elite Corps of Engineers.[45]

Like Johnston, Sherman was assigned to the artillery and served on garrison duty in Florida and South Carolina. He made many friends in the Deep South, and enjoyed living in that region. Although he couldn't have known it at the time, his travels through the wilds of Georgia and South Carolina enabled him to plot the advance of his army through those regions during the Civil War. In 1846 the army transferred Sherman to California, far from the battlefields of the Mexican War, where careers were being made by ambitious young officers. The California Gold Rush followed on the heels of war, and once again, Sherman could only look on while others took advantage of an extraordinary opportunity.

In California Sherman became increasingly dissatisfied with his low pay and dim prospects of advancement, so following his marriage to his foster sister Ellen Ewing in 1850, he left the army to seek his fortune in the civilian world. But Sherman might never have resigned had his new wife and father-in-law not urged him to do so. Though Ellen wanted Sherman to work for her father, by now a prominent national politician, "Cump" was too proud to give in. Instead, he spent the next several years working as a banker in San Francisco and New York, and briefly as a lawyer in Leavenworth, Kansas. Sherman's civilian career was marked by a few minor successes and several notable failures. Yet through it all, he had remained hard-working, conscientious and resourceful, and though he once pronounced himself "the Jonah of banking," his failure as a banker had more to do with the volatility of the national economy than with financial ineptitude.

Thanks in part to the influence of two Southern army friends, Braxton Bragg and P. G. T. Beauregard, in 1859 Sherman was elected superintendent of the newly-founded Louisiana Military Seminary, the forerunner of Louisiana State University. Despite the absence of his wife and children (who, characteristically enough, remained behind at the Ewing family home in Ohio) Sherman's brief term at the military school was a happy and productive one. But with Louisiana's secession from the Union and the seizure of the Federal arsenal at Baton Rouge, Sherman sadly and reluctantly tendered his resignation. Convinced that civil war was imminent, Sherman despaired at the North's lack of preparation, and accepted the presidency of a St. Louis streetcar company rather than throw in his lot with the Union's half-hearted war effort.

West Point-trained officers were in short supply, however, and in due course Sherman was offered a commission as brigadier general of volunteers. He refused, but accepted the colonelcy of a Regular Army regiment, regarding volunteer soldiers as altogether too untrustworthy. Sherman received his baptism of fire at First Bull Run, where—against his better judgment—he commanded a brigade of volunteers. While most of the other volunteer soldiers broke ranks and fled in panic, Sherman's men at first fell back slowly and in good order, until they reached Cub Run, where they, too, panicked and fled the field. The rout at Bull Run taught Sherman an invaluable lesson: his volunteers had the makings of good soldiers, but lacked the necessary training and discipline.

In the fall of 1861, Sherman assumed command of the Union forces in Kentucky, though he didn't want the responsibility and had previously extracted a promise from Lincoln that it would not be thrust upon him. Sherman's alarmist telegrams to the War Department prompted a visit to his headquarters by Secretary of War Simon Cameron and his coterie, which included—unbeknownst to Sherman—a group of reporters. While the newspapermen looked on and listened, Sherman nervously paced up and down the room as he briefed the secretary on the military situation in Kentucky. The situation as Sherman painted it was bleak: the Confederates were poised to capture Louisville, and Sherman needed at least 60,000 troops to defend it. To go on the offensive would require nothing less than 200,000 men. (At the time, Sherman's Confederate counterpart, Albert Sidney Johnston, had fewer troops than Sherman, and was convinced that Sherman was about to attack *him*.) If Secretary of War Cameron was astounded by Sherman's calculations, the reporters were overjoyed, for here was a story too good to pass up: the military commander in Kentucky had allowed his own fears to unhinge him. The *New York Tribune* published Sherman's assessment verbatim; Sherman perceived this as a betrayal of Cameron's assurance that he could speak his mind "freely and without restraint." Thus began the bitter feud between Sherman and newspapermen in general, and *Tribune* publisher Horace Greeley in particular. In addition to the unflattering newspaper accounts, many of the civilian and military men who saw Sherman at this time began to whisper that he was insane.[46]

Although Sherman's true condition was a far cry from insanity, he *was* in a state of nervous exhaustion, prompted in part by the public furor over his remarks to Cameron. Of this dark period in his life, Sherman later confided to his brother John that he saw himself as disgraced and probably would have committed suicide had it not been for his children.

Sherman was relieved from duty in Kentucky and transferred to St. Louis, where a pre-war army friend, Maj. Gen. Henry W. Halleck, was preparing the Department of the Missouri for war. After a few weeks of routine duty there, Sherman applied for a leave and returned home to Ohio, accompanied by his wife Ellen. The rest seems to have benefited Sherman, for he was soon back on duty in St. Louis. In February 1862, he was in Paducah, Kentucky, supervising the shipment of men and supplies to Brig. Gen. Ulysses S. Grant, who was providing the North with its first major victory of the war at Fort Donelson, Tennessee. Though his superior in rank, Sherman cooperated wholeheartedly with Grant. "I should like to hear from you," Sherman wrote Grant, "and will do everything in my power to hurry forward to you reinforcements and supplies, and if I could be of service myself would gladly come, without making any question of rank with you."[47]

Sherman's attitude impressed Grant, for unlike many of his own subordinates, Sherman appeared to place Union victory above personal ambition. Conversely, Sherman saw in Grant the positive force that he had formerly believed was lacking in the Union war effort. "Until you had won Donelson," Sherman later wrote Grant, "I was almost cowed by the terrible array of anarchical elements that presented themselves at every point; but that victory admitted the ray of light I have followed ever since." And so began the most productive command partnership of the Civil War.[48]

That partnership received its first severe test at Shiloh in early April 1862. After narrowly averting disaster on the first day of the battle, Grant, with a reinforced army, emerged victorious on the second day, but at a terrible loss in killed, wounded and captured. Grant's victory at Shiloh cost him both his command and his popularity with the Northern people. Finding himself superseded by General Halleck, Grant considered leaving the army, but Sherman persuaded him to stay. Soon afterward, the popular outcry against Grant died down, and in due course he was restored to his old command.

For Sherman the Battle of Shiloh was the great turning point of his life. He emerged from that horrific struggle with a new self-confidence. Though his division was at first driven back in disorder, Sherman remained cool and unflappable, and by his own example was able to rally his raw troops. This was in sharp contrast with the timid fellow who preferred the presidency of a streetcar company to the colonelcy of a regiment, and while commanding in Kentucky saw Rebels lurking behind every corner.

After the Battle of Shiloh, Sherman was transferred to Memphis, where he acted as military governor. While there, Sherman saw firsthand that he was battling not just the Southern armies but the Southern people as well. Prior to this time Sherman had been conventional in his thinking on the acceptable limits of warfare, believing that civilian property was inviolable. But his experience at Memphis quickly disabused him of that notion. When Sherman learned that local guerrillas were firing on Federal ships plying the Mississippi River, he retaliated by burning the town from which the shots were fired. Sherman also exercised a more positive form of coercion, however, by encouraging Memphis businesses, theaters and churches to reopen, and by exercising leniency in his dealings with the city's law-abiding citizens.

In late 1862 Sherman rejoined Grant at the opening of the Vicksburg Campaign. At stake was control of the Mississippi River, or "the grand artery of America," as Sherman called it. Sherman's first operation of the campaign, the assault on Chickasaw Bayou, ended in a bloody repulse of his command. But this time Sherman neither brooded nor sulked over his reverse; instead, he resolved to wage war from then on with unrelenting ferocity, in the belief that the harsher the North made the war for the South, the sooner it would end.[49]

The Vicksburg Campaign of 1863 saw Sherman's first systematic use of foraging as a means of subsisting his command. Even so, Sherman remained tied to the belief that an army could range neither far nor long from its supply line. So when Grant proposed doing just that, Sherman argued that it was an unnecessary risk. Undaunted, Grant went ahead with his plan. His transports ran the batteries guarding Vicksburg, and his men were then ferried from the west bank of the Mississippi to the east bank below the town. There, Grant's army was able to sustain itself on the bounty of the countryside, far from its Grand Gulf supply depot. This lesson in tactics made a profound impression on Sherman.[50]

After attempting two unsuccessful frontal assaults on the fortifications ringing Vicksburg, Grant decided to starve the Confederate garrison into submission. With the fall of Vicksburg on Independence Day, Grant's perseverance was vindicated. Despite numerous setbacks, he had repeatedly displayed what Sherman once referred to as his "simple faith in success. . .which I can liken to nothing else than the faith a Christian has in his Savior." Recalling his Fort Donelson analogy, Sherman declared the fall of Vicksburg "the first gleam of daylight in this war."[51]

In the autumn of 1863 Grant assumed command of the sprawling Military Division of the Mississippi. His first task was to raise the Confederate siege of Chattanooga. Grant turned over command of the Army of the Tennessee to Sherman, and sent it east to reinforce the Army of the Cumberland, bottled up inside Chattanooga since its defeat at Chickamauga. In the Battle of Missionary Ridge, Sherman personally led his old command, the XV Corps, which had the misfortune of colliding with Pat Cleburne's crack division. While the rest of the Confederates fled in disorder before the Federal assaults, Cleburne's troops held Sherman's men in check—despite the fact that Sherman's divisions were designated as the primary assault troops. Nevertheless, the battle was a decisive Union victory and secured Chattanooga as a base from which the Federals could conduct future campaigns into the Deep South.

Sherman's next important operation was the Meridian expedition, the precursor of his marches through Georgia and the Carolinas. In February 1864, Sherman and his 20,000-man raiding force set out from Vicksburg. His objective was to weaken Confederate morale and resistance east of the Mississippi River by destroying the enemy's railroads and supply depots in and about Meridian. Sherman's Meridian expedition bore all the features of his later, bigger raids: miles of twisted railroad track, columns of smoke denoting his route of march, and an outraged and terrified Southern citizenry left in his wake. While on the march Sherman announced that his eventual destination was Mobile, Alabama—a ruse intended to prevent the Confederates from concentrating in his front, and one that he would later utilize to good advantage in Georgia and the Carolinas.

On March 18, newly promoted Lt. Gen. Ulysses S. Grant headed east from Nashville to assume command of all the armies of the United States and to make his headquarters with the Army of the Potomac. Accompanying him on the long train ride as far as Cincinnati was Sherman, Grant's successor to the command of the Federal armies of the West. Sherman recalled that, "Amidst countless interruptions of a business and social nature," the two generals plotted a joint strategy. In the spring Grant would assume the offensive against Lee's army in Virginia, while Sherman would move against Johnston's army in Georgia. Grant's intention was to maintain the initiative against the two main Rebel armies and thus prevent one from reinforcing the other. Though Grant gave Sherman complete discretion in sorting out the details of his own campaign, the Union would prosecute the war with a unity of action that until that time had been conspicuously lacking.[52]

In a parting letter to Grant, Sherman professed his faith in his friend and chief: "I knew wherever I was that you thought of me, and if I got in a tight place you would come—if alive." Though separated by hundreds of miles, Grant and Sherman would maintain a frequent correspondence by telegraph and letter.[53]

Sherman's preparation for the Atlanta Campaign was a masterful utilization of logistics and military technology. It was Sherman's ability to organize and exploit the resources at his disposal that ensured the successful outcome of his campaign. He was able to keep his army well-supplied because he understood the logistical requirements for waging modern war. "I reiterate," Sherman wrote ten years after the war, "that the Atlanta campaign was an impossibility without these railroads; and only then because we had the men and the means to defend and maintain them." Sherman's far-reaching grasp of technology and logistics entitles him to consideration as the Civil War's most modern general as much as his notoriety as the so-called inventor of total war.[54]

In keeping with the Union's grand strategy, Sherman maintained the offensive against Johnston from the opening of the campaign in May until mid-July, when Johnston was replaced by Gen. John Bell Hood. Hood briefly seized the initiative with his three sorties outside Atlanta, but was repulsed with heavy losses each time. Sherman displayed a resourcefulness rivaling Grant's in outmaneuvering Hood at Jonesboro and cutting the Confederates' last open rail line, thereby compelling Hood to evacuate the city on the night of September 1.

Sherman chased Hood out of Georgia and into Alabama, but soon tired of the pursuit. He detached a portion of his army under Maj. Gen. George H. Thomas to deal with Hood, then shifted his focus to the southeast, toward Savannah and the Atlantic coast. Sherman found that selling Grant on the March to the Sea was a difficult proposition, but he astutely emphasized the march's strategic virtues. "Instead of being on the defensive," Sherman explained, "I would be on the offensive; instead of guessing at what [Hood] means to do, he would have to guess at my plans. . . .I can make the march, and make Georgia howl." Grant relented, and

Sherman kept his word. Earlier in the war, Grant's victories at Fort Donelson and Vicksburg had provided Sherman with a guiding "ray of light"; now it was the success of Sherman's March to the Sea that, in Lincoln's words, brought others "who sat in darkness to see a great light."[55]

No one saw this "great light" more clearly than Sherman's own troops. By the opening of the Carolinas Campaign, their faith in "Uncle Billy" was absolute. "[T]here never was such a man as Sherman or as they call him (Crazy Bill)," wrote one XV Corps soldier, "and he has got his men to believe they cant be whip[p]ed." Staff officer William Hemstreet agreed with the assessment, calling Sherman:

> the most blazing figure of the continent. He was not only commander-in-chief but the smartest man in an army that idolized him. He knew everything from mending a mule's harness to grand tactics and civil diplomacy.

Hemstreet then described Sherman's appearance:

> He was tall and gaunt, and although only forty-[five], his face was deeply furrowed. . .[H]is voice was a positive, quick, and rough basso. . . .His customary appearance was to walk along the roadside with his hands in his trousers' pockets. . .and talk good earnest common-sense with the person nearest him, regardless of rank.[56]

Sherman slept fitfully and could often be found poring over his maps by the light of the campfire, a familiar sight to sentinel and courier alike. He held his ever-present cigar between compressed lips at an angle that his brother-in-law Lt. Col. Charles Ewing described as "a line of communication between mouth and ear." Sherman's aides worried whenever they found the sheet on his cot covered with ashes, for it meant that their chief had passed another sleepless night. At times the cares and anxieties of command told on Sherman. Of one such episode, Major Osborn wrote:

> I understand that no one can approach Sherman without being snubbed. His high nervous temperament and sarcasm are now at their highest pitch. . . .It makes but very little difference whether one be a major general or a private

> soldier, they do not tamper with Sherman during these spells of deep anxiety and care.[57]

But such episodes were rare. Far more typical was the Sherman who eagerly questioned the passing forager or runaway slave as to the roads or the lay of the land along the line of march. Sherman could be brusque, often supplying the answers as well as the questions. Lieutenant Colonel Ewing dubbed these rapid-fire question-and-answer sessions "Sherman's catechism." "Had catechism yet?" was a familiar refrain around Sherman's headquarters.[58]

Sherman's young clerk, Vett Noble, wrote that his chief "has so much on his mind that his orderly has to tell him when to put on clean shirts. . . .he is a queer old coon, but cant he just settle the Rebels?"[59]

* * *

Corps Commander Francis Blair spent the afternoon of March 1 waiting impatiently at his headquarters for the go-ahead from Howard. Instead, he received disturbing news from his Third Division commander, Brig. Gen. Manning F. Force, that one of his foragers had been murdered. "I have the honor to state," Force's dispatch began,

> that the body of Private R. M. Woodruff, "H" Co. 30th Ill. a regularly detailed forager was found to day, about 12 miles from camp in the roadside near Blackneys [Blakeny's] Bridge. There was no bullet wound his skull was broken in with something blunt perhaps a club, possibly the butt of a musket. . . .This appears to be such a case as Genl. Sherman refers to in his letter of instructions. I have no prisoners and respectfully request that the Corps Provost Marshal turn over a prisoner for retaliation.[60]

On February 22 Sherman had received a dispatch from General Kilpatrick informing him that more than two dozen of his men had been murdered after surrendering to the Rebels. Some of them were found with their throats cut and a paper pinned to their breasts saying, "Death to all foragers." The murders infuriated Sherman, who ordered Kilpatrick to retaliate by executing an equal number of Confederate prisoners and leaving them by the roadside with labels attached to their bodies "stating that man for man shall be killed for every one of our men they kill." Sherman also instructed Howard, "If any of your foragers are murdered, take life for life, leaving a record of each case."[61]

Kilpatrick's threat to retaliate led to an exchange of prisoners and a reunion under flag of truce with his old West Point chum, Gen. Joe Wheeler. Unfortunately, the result of Sherman's order to Howard was far more tragic.[62]

In response to Force's dispatch, General Blair ordered the retaliatory execution to take place on the morning of March 2. On that fateful morning, the XVII Corps' 100 Confederate prisoners were drawn up in single file and ordered to draw a slip of paper from a hat as they marched past it. The letter "G" was written on all of the slips of paper except one, which was blank. Finally, after most of the prisoners had filed by and drawn their lots, a South Carolinian named James Miller drew the fatal blank slip. Miller was immediately halted and informed that he had "half an hour to prepare for death," then was led away.[63]

The prisoner was "an old man, on the shady side of 50 years," wrote Pvt. George Lawson, an Illinoisan in Force's division. "I spoke to the poor man and he was quite resigned to his fate, [but] when speaking of his wife and seven children, the tears streamed down his furrowed cheeks."[64]

As the guard detail led Miller to the place of execution, hundreds of Federal soldiers gathered about him in order to witness the fatal volley. The detail halted in a ravine and formed a hollow square around Miller, who was placed against a tree and left untied at his request. The chaplain of the 31st Illinois prayed with Miller, who told him, "I was forced into the army, never was in a battle, never wished the Yankees any harm."[65]

The firing squad consisted of 12 men from the slain Woodruff's regiment, the 30th Illinois. The 30th's historian noted that Woodruff "was not well thought of and many regrets were heard that a good man" would have to die for him. It was said that when the colonel of the 30th, William C. Rhoades, was ordered to command the firing squad, he at first refused. Only the threat of an immediate court-martial induced Rhoades to obey.[66]

Miller was blindfolded and given a handkerchief to drop as a signal to the firing squad. "When all was ready, there were a few seconds of death-like stillness and suspense," wrote one eyewitness, "every eye being riveted on the handkerchief in the old man's fingers." The handkerchief fluttered to the ground.

"Fire!" Rhoades cried. "The fatal volley was fired," Lawson recorded, and six bullets struck his body, the other six rounds being blanks. Another onlooker noted that Miller died "like a man a soldier and a christian. It was a sad and imposing scene." Lawson "saw many an eye moistened, and many a soldier who would never say 'Surrender' wiping his eyes after this scene." General Force noted that "this one death produced more perceptible feeling than the gore of a battle field."[67]

Soon after Miller's comrades "heard the volley that put an end to his existence," a guard detail marched into the prison pen and led one of the prisoners to General Blair's headquarters. The prisoner had been Miller's neighbor for most of his life. Blair asked him several questions regarding the dead man's character. The neighbor replied that Miller had been a good man, and had left a wife and children behind. Blair then remarked that if he had known these facts before the execution, he would have spared Miller's life. "But then," he added, "if I had spared him, his fate would have fallen on one of the rest of you." Following Miller's execution, there were no more reports of murdered Union foragers in South Carolina.[68]

Later that afternoon, Blair received welcome news from Howard's headquarters: "The general directs that in accordance with General Sherman's instructions you move forward on Cheraw at as early an hour as possible to-morrow morning."[69]

~ *three* ~

"You could have played cards on der coat-tails"

—Anonymous South Carolina Slave

On the evening of March 2, General Hardee summoned Maj. Gen. Matthew C. Butler to his headquarters in Cheraw. Butler arrived about 9:00 p.m., and found the commanding general holding a council of war with his two division commanders, McLaws and Taliaferro, and some lower-ranking officers. Hardee turned to Butler and asked, "General, after your experience in today's operations, what do you advise in regard to the evacuation of Cheraw?" Butler had just taken part in the skirmishing with the XX Corps at Chesterfield about 10 miles to the west, and had received reports from his pickets that the XVII Corps had finally resumed its advance on Cheraw from the southwest. At both points the enemy was less than a day's march away. Butler advised Hardee to get his army "across the Pee Dee [River] at the earliest possible moment." Butler later recalled that General McLaws and several other officers argued "that there was no occasion for haste." Butler remained adamant. "Well, gentlemen," he said, "you have asked my opinion and I have given it frankly, and have heard nothing to induce me to change it."[1]

Hardee heeded Butler's warning and began dictating an order to his adjutant for the withdrawal of his corps. As Butler later remembered it:

> The first paragraph directed the chiefs of the quartermaster, ordnance and subsistence departments to begin the moving of their trains next morning at daylight. When the paragraph was finished I suggested that the order be changed to take

> effect at once that night, and the change was accordingly made. The last paragraph of the order directed that my division should bring up the rear, destroy what public stores might be left and burn the covered bridge over the Pee Dee.

Hardee also ordered Butler to deploy his troopers along Thompson's Creek to delay the enemy's advance for as long as possible.[2]

That night Hardee began the evacuation of Cheraw. Because both the railroad and the navigable portion of the Pee Dee terminated at Cheraw, Hardee had only his wagons to carry off supplies. As a result, he was forced to abandon most of his munitions stockpile, and gave orders to issue extra rations to the men from the storehouses in town. By dawn Hardee's wagon train, artillery and most of his infantry were across the Pee Dee. Only Col. John C. Fiser's Brigade of McLaws' Division remained behind in Cheraw to serve as Hardee's rear guard.[3]

At 7:00 a.m. on March 3, the Federal XVII Corps began its march on Cheraw, with Maj. Gen. Joseph A. Mower's division in the advance. Mower's lead brigade, commanded by Brig. Gen. John W. Fuller, marched seven miles before encountering Butler's cavalry at Thompson's Creek, about five miles southwest of Cheraw. The Southerners had dug a line of entrenchments on a hill overlooking the creek. The veteran troopers had also torn some planks off the bridge and were setting fire to it when Fuller's skirmishers came into view. General Mower directed Fuller's brigade to deploy in front, then sent Col. John Tillson's brigade to the left in order to flank the Confederate troopers. "We raised a yell," recorded Lt. John H. Ferguson, one of Tillson's skirmishers:

> and came crashing through the woods like a herricane. the rebs thought the yankee nation had broken loos. the[y] did not wait to fire another shot, but flead every man for himself, a great many of them throwing away their arms, knapsacks, haversacks &c in order to make the best time the[y] could.[4]

Meanwhile, Fuller's skirmish line drove off the Confederates in their front and halted a few minutes to put out the fire on the bridge and replace the missing planks. Then, in the words of the 27th

Ohio's Capt. Charles H. Smith, the Federals resumed the pursuit, "advancing across the fields, climbing over or tearing down the fences, passing through woods, thick underbrush and other obstructions" until they reached the outskirts of Cheraw, having covered the last two miles at the double-quick.[5]

Howard's chief of artillery, Maj. Thomas Osborn, marveled at the speed of the pursuit: "I have never seen troops moved with such energy as Mower moved his division." One of Mower's staff officers called his commander "the Murat of the army. . . .He should have been a cavalry leader, because infantry was too geometrical and slow for his impetuous blood and quick military instincts." Fittingly enough, Howard had recently told Sherman that should he ever organize a cavalry corps, the ideal commander would be Joe Mower.[6]

Mower's champion was none other than Sherman himself, who regarded his protégé as "the boldest young soldier we have." Mower first came to Sherman's attention during the Vicksburg Campaign, when "Fighting Joe" commanded a brigade in Sherman's XV Corps. At that time Sherman marked him for greatness. During most of 1864, Mower served outside Sherman's immediate command, but he was far from forgotten. In a letter to Mower's superior, Sherman asked whether the rumor was true that "Fighting Joe" had killed the dreaded Southern cavalryman, Nathan Bedford Forrest. "If so," Sherman jested, "tell General Mower I am pledged to him for his promotion, and if Old Abe don't make good my promise then General Mower may have my place." If ever any man filled the void in Sherman's life left by McPherson's death, that man was Joe Mower.[7]

Joseph Anthony Mower was 37 years old in March 1865. General Howard described him as being "[a]bout six feet in height, well-proportioned and of great physical strength." In his youth Mower had been a journeyman ship's carpenter. He began his military career in 1846, enlisting as a private in the U. S. Engineers Battalion before serving in the Mexican War. Although he was discharged in 1848, civilian life did not suit him and he rejoined the army in 1855 as a lieutenant of infantry. At the outbreak of the Civil War, Mower was stationed in San Antonio, Texas. There he disobeyed the orders of his commander, the future Confederate major general David E. Twiggs, by refusing to surrender with the rest of the garrison. Mower's Civil War career was as varied as it was successful. As colonel of the 11th Missouri Infantry, Mower took part in the battles of Iuka and Corinth. He was severely wounded during the latter fight and briefly fell into the hands of the enemy. He soon recovered from his wounds and went on to command his XV Corps brigade at Vicksburg. Later, Mower's brigade was transferred to the XVI Corps, where his daredevil command was dubbed, "Mower's Guerrillas."[8]

In the spring of 1864, he was elevated to the command of the First Division, XVI Corps, which he led on the ill-fated Red River Campaign. Mower's capture of Fort De Russy and his raid on Henderson Hill numbered among the few Federal successes of that expedition. In July Mower and his division took part in Maj. Gen. A. J. Smith's expedition against Nathan Bedford Forrest in Mississippi. Mower also participated in the pursuit of Sterling Price in Missouri, and joined Sherman's grand army in time to lead the First Division of the XVII Corps on the March to the Sea.[9]

The opening days of the Carolinas Campaign found Mower's division slogging through the icy swamps of South Carolina. After a night spent wading the freezing waters of the Salkehatchie River with his troops, Mower was seen the next morning breaking icicles off his coat. In honor of the occasion Mower's men nicknamed him the "Swamp Lizard." While they respected the courage and boldness of their commander, they also believed that he was too reckless with their lives. One private in Fuller's brigade described Mower as both "imprudent" and "desperately brave." There was a saying rife in Sherman's army that, "If you become assigned to Mower's staff go and make your will."[10]

Following the fight in the Salk—during which Mower had taken his usual place on the skirmish line—he greeted one of his regimental commanders by saying, "I want to take a drink with a man who can ride as far into hell as I can." Mower's adjutant, Col. William Hemstreet, marked that winter day as the beginning of the end for his chief, who thenceforth "suffered pulmonary trouble until the day of his death" five years later.[11]

Several days after the Salk engagement, Mower's skirmishers ran up against a section of artillery at their Edisto River crossing, forcing Mower to bridge the swamp beyond range of the Southerners' guns. The Confederates across the way whooped and hollered and dared the Yankees to attack them. "[I]n plain sight of [the] roystering, defiant enemy," Mower rose up in his stirrups, and shaking his fist, turned to Hemstreet and said: "God, man, wouldn't you like to wade in there with a sabre?"[12]

There was no time for fist-shaking on the advance to Cheraw—Mower was too busy urging his troops forward. He ordered up the six guns of Lt. William W. Hyser's battery (Battery C, 1st Michigan) to join in the pursuit. The road leading into Cheraw was so narrow that for most of the way Lieutenant Hyser had to advance his guns in column. But the battery kept pace with Mower's skirmishers, and even took the lead once or twice.[13]

Meanwhile, the 1st Georgia Regulars of Fiser's Confederate brigade deployed on the edge of town to give Butler's hard pressed cavalrymen some much-needed support. The troopers soon came galloping into view, then thundered past the Georgia infantrymen "without so much as by your permission," recalled Sgt. William H. Andrews of the Regulars. Led by the 27th Ohio in skirmish formation, the men of Fuller's brigade trotted across an open field in the Regulars' front. Sergeant Andrews and his comrades looked beyond their left flank and saw the Federals "about 150 yards off, like a drove of blackbirds making for our rear." Colonel Richard A. Wayne ordered his Regulars to fall back into town.[14]

The Georgians readily complied, and the Ohioans followed in hot pursuit. The skirmishing was from house-to-house and street-to-street. "It was a running fight," Andrews recollected. "We would load on the run, wheel and fire while the women and children were screaming and waving everything they could get hold of that was white." The improvised white banners infuriated the Regulars' color sergeant, Sam Bennett, who violently waved the regimental flag over his head while shouting, "You may wave your handkerchiefs and newspapers, but I will be d—d if this is not the battle flag."[15]

The Federals "went through the town like a dose of salts," wrote Pvt. Joseph M. Strickling of the 39th Ohio, in a race to cut off the fleeing Confederates and save the Pee Dee Bridge. As Pvt. Benjamin F. Sweet of the 39th dashed past an open window, he grabbed a handful of hot biscuits that had been left on the sill to cool. When the Federals came to within a few hundred yards of the bridge, General Mower ordered Lieutenant Hyser to unlimber a section of his battery and open fire on the Rebels defending it, who happened to be a detachment of Butler's cavalry and the 1st Georgia Regulars. The canister tore through the ranks of the Regulars,

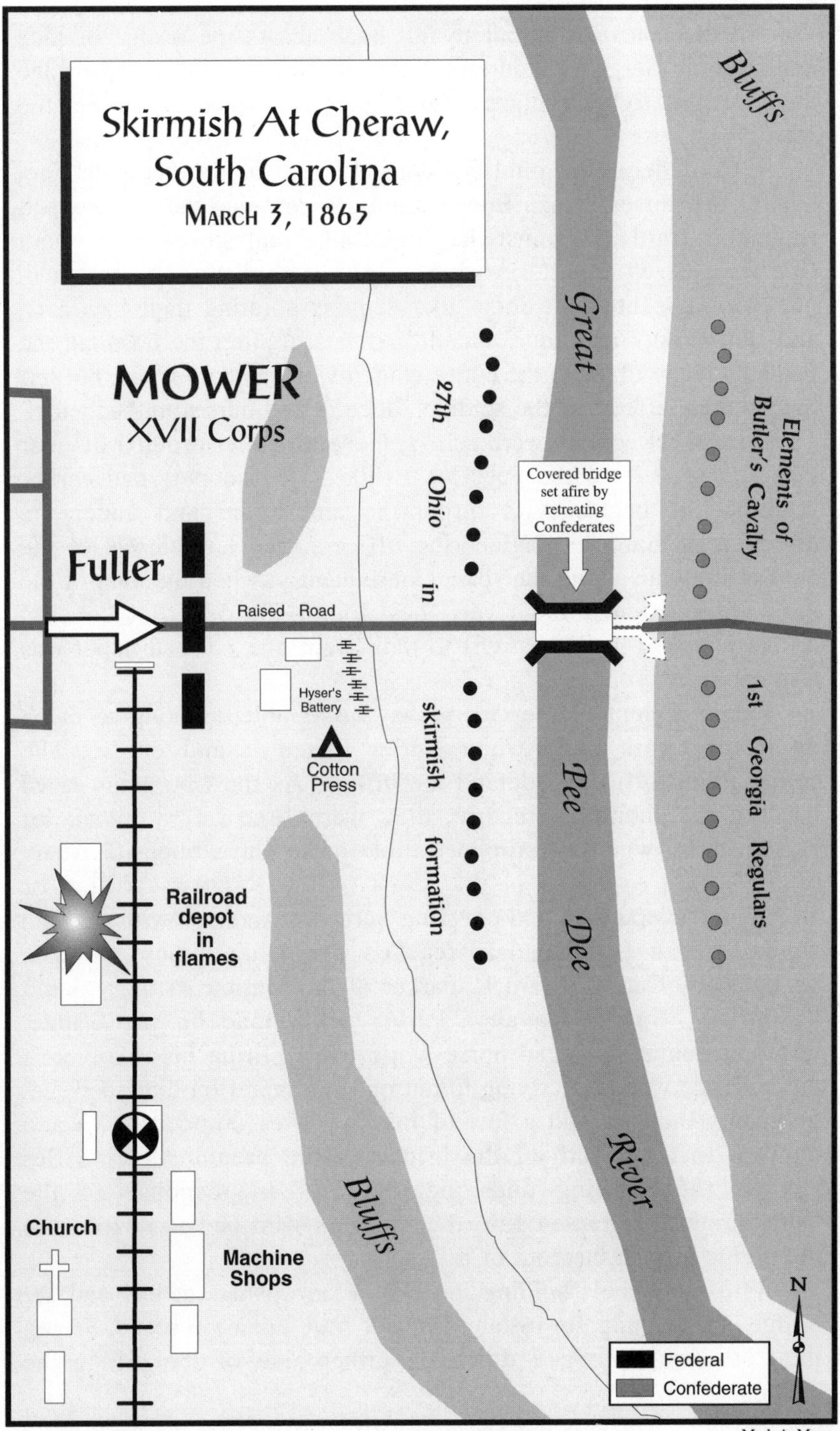

Skirmish At Cheraw, South Carolina
March 3, 1865
MOWER
XVII Corps
Fuller
Raised Road
Hyser's Battery
Cotton Press
27th Ohio in skirmish formation
Great Pee Dee River
Covered bridge set afire by retreating Confederates
Elements of Butler's Cavalry
1st Georgia Regulars
Bluffs
Bluffs
Railroad depot in flames
Church
Machine Shops
Federal
Confederate
N

Mark A. Moore

leaving them no choice but to fall back across the bridge or face annihilation. Sergeant Andrews called the brief stand at the bridge "one of the tightest places the [R]egulars were in during the war."[16]

A Confederate hospital stood in the path of the Federals' fire. One of the nurses, Susan Bowen Lining, wrote that the "bullets and fragments [rattled] against the House like hail stones—but thank God we escaped unhurt." A squad of Union soldiers, she continued, burst through the front door "like demons pointing their bayonets, and calling out *Surrender!* Stand!" After searching the hospital, the Federals made off with the entire contents of the store room, but left the personal effects of the soldiers, doctors and nurses untouched.[17]

Once the Regulars were across, General Butler ordered his rear guard to set fire to the Pee Dee Bridge. The troopers had earlier smeared the bridge with turpentine and rosin, and under the direction of Hardee's engineering officers, had left barrels of the stuff at intervals along the span. Consequently, when the men of the 27th Ohio reached the river, they found the 500-foot covered bridge wrapped in flames. Off to their right, the railroad depot was also on fire.[18]

A detachment of the Georgians was double-quicking to catch up to the main body when Butler halted it and ordered the commanding officer to defend the bridge. As the Georgians raced back to the flaming structure, they were fired on by all six of Hyser's guns, which had dropped trail on the bluffs opposite. Many of the shells exploded in the midst of the Regulars, killing or wounding several men and covering Sergeant Andrews with dirt and smoke. When the Regulars reached the bridge, they found it defended by Capt. Edward L. Parker of the Marion Artillery and a handful of Butler's cavalry. Parker was alone on the bridge, kneeling behind his dead horse while coolly firing his revolver at the Federals who were trying to put out the flames on the other end. Sergeant Andrews and a few of his comrades dropped down and crawled to the mouth of the bridge before propping their rifles against the flooring and opening fire. In response to the Confederates' increased fire, the Federals who had ventured onto the bridge now dashed out of it.[19]

With the Rebels holding the Union skirmishers at bay and the bridge still burning, an irritated Mower rode upon the scene. Seeing the 27th Ohio plopped down on either side of the bridge, he immediately ordered them to get on their feet and charge across the structure. By this time the bridge was covered in flames from end to end. The men glanced at Mower, then the burning bridge. They didn't budge.[20]

Mower was enraged. He cursed the 27th Ohio and called the men cowards. Then, in the words of one Ohioan, he "relieved his mind as usual by a conversation with God." Mower sent for the 18th Missouri and ordered *them* to charge across the bridge. Fortunately, the 18th's commander, Col. Charles Sheldon, persuaded Mower to cancel the assault by suggesting that the men cross the river in pontoon boats instead. Soon afterward, the burning bridge crashed into the waters of the Pee Dee amid the cheers of the Confederates across the way. That evening, Mower visited the camp of the 27th Ohio and apologized to the men for his tirade, telling them that on further reflection he realized that it would have been impossible for them to capture the burning bridge.[21]

* * *

Though Cheraw suffered less than most other South Carolina towns lying in the path of Sherman's march, it suffered all the same. No sooner had the XVII Corps occupied the town than the plundering and pillaging began. Although the residential district was left standing, the business district was ransacked and then burned. "Cheraw has been quite a business place," observed one Federal soldier, "but now all the stores[,] shops &c are in ashes while the houses on another street still remain." In the words of a local citizen:

> every house, large and small, of whatever class of tenant, black or white, free or slave, was pillaged and stripped of all valuables that could be carried away. . . .[General Blair] made his headquarters in the residence of one of our wealthiest citizens [a blockade runner by trade] . . . .When appealed to by the lady of the house to interfere with the plundering of the common soldiers, who, in the basement were breaking [open] and robbing trunks, &c, he repaired to

> the scene, but only to share in the spoil. This is, as I understand, the late member of the Federal Congress.[22]

In the basement of the blockade runner's house Blair discovered a treasure trove of vintage wines and Brussels carpets that had been sent north from Charleston for safekeeping. After seeing to it that his own headquarters wagon was well-stocked, Blair distributed the remainder "to the army generally, in fair proportions." Among those benefiting from Blair's munificence was General Sherman, who received "a dozen bottles of the finest madeira I ever tasted," and enough carpets to outfit his staff and escort with tent rugs and saddle blankets. As Blair's men soon discovered, the entire town was a storehouse for precious goods transported from Charleston.[23]

General Blair reported that his corps had also captured 25 pieces of field artillery, 16 limber chests and caissons, 5,000 rounds of artillery ammunition, 20,000 rounds of small arms ammunition, 2,000 stand of small arms, and 1,000 sabers. The XVII Corps also captured one railroad locomotive with a dozen cars and burned several thousand bales of cotton. But the most dangerous prize of all proved to be 44,000 pounds of powder left behind by Hardee. A sizable mule train hauled the barrels of powder and the boxes of ammunition to the river bank, where work crews from the 1st Michigan Engineers dumped the contents into a stream that ran through a large ravine. The Michigan Engineers also destroyed a stockpile of captured rifles by bending the barrels between the spokes of a locomotive wheel before throwing them onto a pile of boards and setting fire to the whole.[24]

The most notable of the captured cannon was a 20-pounder Blakely rifle adorned with a brass plate that bore the inscription, "Presented to the Sovereign State of South Carolina by one of her citizens residing abroad, in commemoration of the 20th of December, 1860." The men of Hyser's battery took this Blakely gun and two other captured field pieces with them as trophies. The rest were dumped into the Pee Dee River or were loaded with massive charges and burst in honor of Lincoln's second inauguration on March 4.[25]

* * *

On the morning of the inauguration, Sherman left Slocum's wing at Chesterfield and headed for Cheraw. He soon reached a road that branched off to the right, which corresponded to the Cheraw Road on his map. "Seeing a negro standing by the roadside," Sherman recalled, "I inquired of him what road that was." When told that it led to Cheraw, Sherman asked, "Is it a good road, and how far?"

"A very good road," the black man replied, "and eight or ten miles."

Sherman inquired of the man if he had seen any Rebels. "Oh! no," he laughed, "dey is gone two days ago; you could have played cards on der coat-tails, dey was in sich a hurry!"[26]

The general took the man at his word, and rode ahead of the main body accompanied only by his staff. When Sherman reached Cheraw, Howard's pontoon bridge was well underway, Mower having made a lodgment on the north bank early that morning. The rest of the XVII Corps began crossing in the afternoon, followed by the XV Corps on the 5th.[27]

The crossing of the XVII Corps was punctuated by numerous explosions. First there was the cannon fire celebrating Lincoln's inauguration. Then later that evening, the retreating Confederates ignited a stockpile of abandoned ammunition. The resulting fireworks cast an eerie glow in the northern sky, and the din led many of the Federal soldiers to believe that a distant battle was taking place. In Mower's camp, bugles sounded the assembly and drums beat the long roll, but the skirmishers soon came in reporting that there was no cause for alarm—the enemy was long gone. But these explosions were nothing in comparison to the blast that was to follow.[28]

On the morning of March 6, soldiers of Bvt. Maj. Gen. Charles R. Woods' division of the XV Corps were lounging on the bluffs overlooking the Pee Dee River while awaiting their turn to cross. Some of the men were bored and wandered over to the ravine where the powder and the ammunition had been dumped. The ravine was from 10 to 12 feet deep and filled with powder—at least 36,000 pounds of it. There was so much powder, in fact, that the little stream that was being used to douse it had long since vanished beneath it. The men scooped up handfuls of the powder and carried it to their cooking fires a few hundred yards away, where they exploded it amid much shouting and laughter. With each new handful they grew more careless, and left numerous crisscrossing trails of powder running back to the ravine.[29]

Sergeant Theodore Upson of the 100th Indiana had just started his coffee boiling when he saw "a little flash of powder [running] along the ground." A moment later he noticed that the powder flashes had multiplied and were running in all directions. Someone yelled, "Look out for the magazine!" Upson and his comrades "made some pretty quick moves" in putting as much space between themselves and the ravine as the burning powder trails would allow.[30]

"Then there was a tremendous explosion," Upson recorded. "The dirt and stones flew in evry [sic] direction." The flash was so bright that "the whole sky seemed to burst into flame," thought one Iowa soldier. The ground shook for miles as if in the grip of an earthquake. The force of the blast razed several houses and shattered nearly every window in town. A storm of shell and shrapnel rained down for a half-mile in every direction.[31]

Susan Bowen Lining was cooking breakfast for herself and her son when she heard the explosion. The force of the blast knocked a frying pan out of her hand and sent objects hurtling about the kitchen. "My poor child clung to me screaming," Lining wrote. "I expected every moment to see him in a convulsion." She later discovered that the blast had knocked some plaster off the walls and had torn the shutters off their hinges.[32]

The XV Corps wagon train was crossing the Pee Dee when the blast occurred. Dozens of wagons and teams were crowded along the road and atop the bluffs, waiting to cross. As assistant quartermaster of the XV Corps, Lt. James E. Graham was supervising their crossing when he heard a "terrific noise," followed by:

> an immense cloud of smoke filled with sand, stones, roots, timbers &c. . .which alarmed the horses and mules & put that densely crowded mass in motion. Drivers were away from their teams & the mules dashed forward or to either side & carried everything before [them]. Mounted men were borne along by their frightened animals which tried to avoid being crushed by the wagons. All was confusion & as we approached the high bluff destruction seemed inevitable. . . . [M]en were trying to stop the mules and were yelling at the

> top of their voices, women and children (refugees) shrieked screamed & prayed, but the trains went dashing on to their own destruction, until at last the foremost [animals] having arrived at the bluff. . .planted their feet in the sand & stopped the moving multitude & all was over except the confused murmur of voices in conversation over the affair & inquiries after the killed & wounded.[33]

One officer and three enlisted men were killed as a result of the blast, and more than a dozen were wounded. Rumor had it that Sherman at first believed the explosion was an act of sabotage, and was on the verge of issuing orders to burn the rest of the town and execute the mayor in retaliation. He relented, however, when he learned that it was the carelessness of his own men that had caused the devastation.[34]

* * *

The Right Wing of Sherman's army was across the Pee Dee by the afternoon of March 6. Some 10 miles to the northwest, the Left Wing had crossed the state line and was laying its pontoon bridge near Sneedsboro, North Carolina. Unfortunately, the Pee Dee proved to be more than 900 feet wide at the crossing point, leaving the 58th Indiana Pontoniers several hundred feet short of bridging material. While Gen. Jefferson C. Davis raged and fumed over the lack of enterprise in the 58th's officers, the pontoniers worked through the night, completing the bridge by stretching canvas sheets over some wagons and using them as pontoon boats. Kilpatrick's cavalry began crossing at sundown on the 6th. Sherman ordered his cavalry chief to swing northeastward to Rockingham, keeping his command on the extreme left of the army in order to shield the XIV Corps from Wheeler's probing cavalry. Although the improvised wagon-boats eventually sank, the pontoniers made the necessary repairs, and the XIV Corps was across by 10:00 p.m. on the 7th. To save time Slocum sent the XX Corps to Cheraw on the morning of the 6th, where it crossed on the Right Wing's bridge. "Let General Davis lead into Fayetteville," Sherman told Slocum, "holding the Twentieth [Corps] in support with the cavalry on his

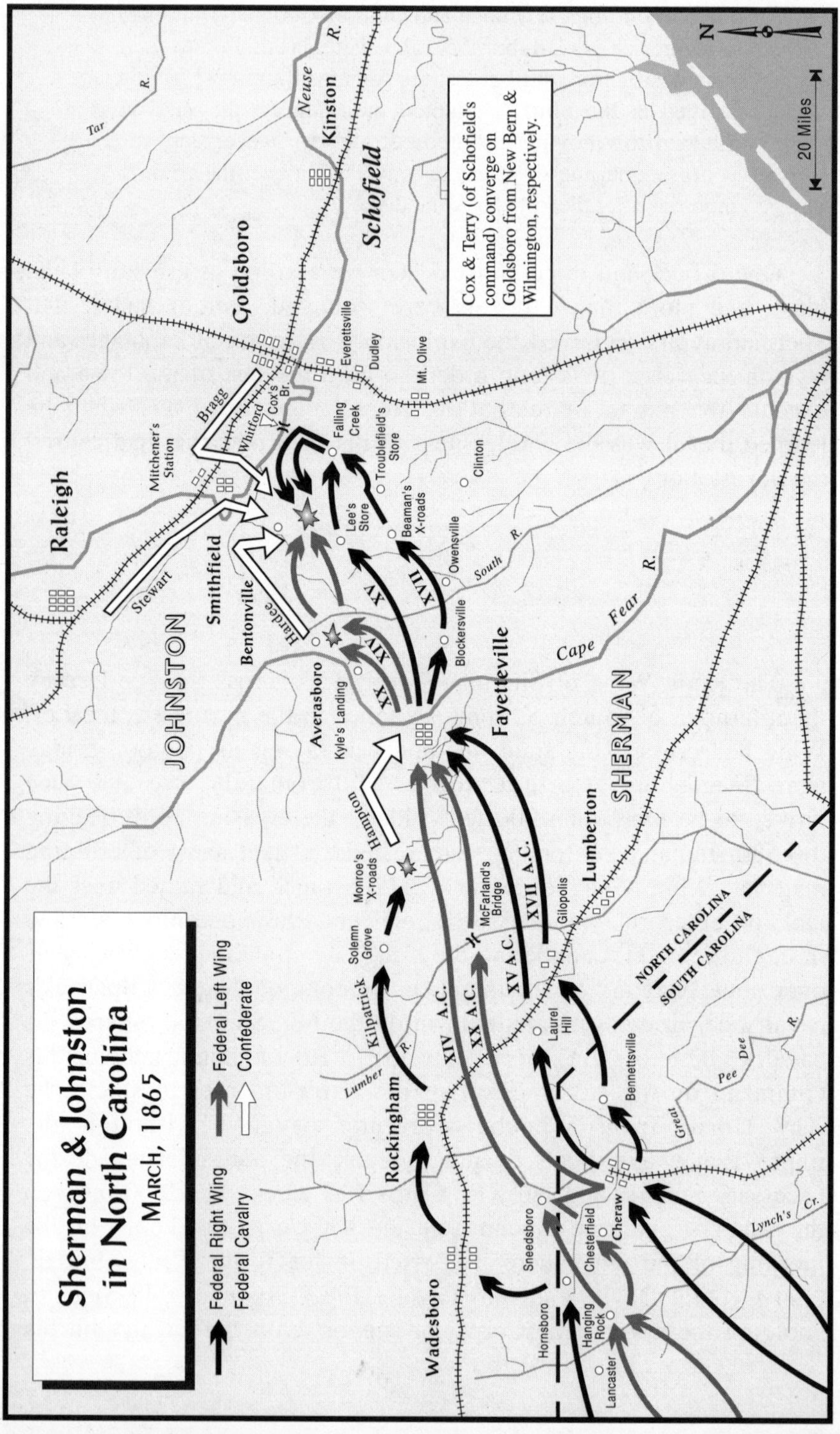
Sherman & Johnston in North Carolina
March, 1865
Federal Right Wing
Federal Left Wing
Federal Cavalry
Confederate
Cox & Terry (of Schofield's command) converge on Goldsboro from New Bern & Wilmington, respectively.
20 Miles
N
Raleigh
Goldsboro
Kinston
Schofield
Smithfield
Bentonville
JOHNSTON
Stewart
Hardee
Bragg
Mitchener's Station
Whitford
Cox's Br.
Everettsville
Dudley
Mt. Olive
Falling Creek
Troublefield's Store
Lee's Store
Beaman's X-roads
Clinton
Owensville
Averasboro
Kyle's Landing
Blockersville
Fayetteville
SHERMAN
Lumberton
Gilopolis
Hampton
Monroe's X-roads
Solemn Grove
Kilpatrick
McFarland's Bridge
XIV A.C.
XX A.C.
XV A.C.
XVII A.C.
XIV
XX
XV
XVII
Laurel Hill
Bennettsville
NORTH CAROLINA
SOUTH CAROLINA
Rockingham
Wadesboro
Sneedsboro
Chesterfield
Cheraw
Hornsboro
Hanging Rock
Lancaster
Tar R.
Neuse R.
South R.
Cape Fear R.
Lumber R.
Great Pee Dee R.
Lynch's Cr.

Mark A. Moore

left rear. I will hold General Howard back, but close enough to come up if Joe Johnston wants to fight. I will now fight him if he dares."[35]

During his stay in Cheraw, Sherman visited the house that Hardee had occupied as his headquarters. When the owner asked him where he expected to go next, Sherman replied, "I have about 60,000 men out there and I intend to go pretty much where I please." In one of the rooms, Sherman chanced upon a recent copy of the New York *Tribune*—the first Northern newspaper that he had seen in almost a month. The *Tribune* confirmed the rumors he had heard regarding the fall of Charleston and Wilmington. Of far greater interest to Sherman—and presumably Hardee—was a brief paragraph in which "the editor had the satisfaction to inform his readers that General Sherman would next be heard from about Goldsboro, because his supply-vessels from Savannah were known to be rendezvousing at Morehead City." Sherman later blamed this "extremely mischievous" news item for enabling Johnston and Hardee to anticipate his line of march, and he held his old nemesis, *Tribune* editor Horace Greeley, personally responsible. "Up to that moment," Sherman wrote, with the benefit of hindsight, "I had endeavored so to feign to our left that we had completely misled our antagonists; but this was no longer possible, and I concluded that we must be ready for the concentration in our front of all the force subject to General Jos. Johnston's orders."[36]

* * *

Hardee may well have read the *Tribune* news item concerning Sherman's intended destination, but whether he credited it or not was another matter. At any rate, Hardee's most recent dispatch from General Beauregard directed him to march from Cheraw to Greensboro, a full 130 miles northwest of Goldsboro. In obedience to those orders, on March 3 Hardee led his corps toward Rockingham, about 25 miles north of Cheraw. He marched only a few miles on the 3rd and halted at Harrington's Station to dole out extra rations to his men, secure in the knowledge that the Federals had not yet attempted a crossing of the Pee Dee. On the 4th Hardee resumed the march to Rockingham, arriving there late that afternoon.[37]

At Rockingham Hardee informed Johnston that he was setting out for Greensboro in the morning, and that he had intended to march northward via Fayetteville until Bragg had warned him of Schofield's advance in that direction. Hardee added that he believed Sherman's army was marching to Fayetteville in order "to form a junction with Schofield and to obtain supplies." So much for Sherman's theory concerning Hardee's utilization of the "extremely mischievous" *Tribune* report.[38]

While Hardee was writing to Johnston, Johnston was wiring Hardee from a railroad depot near Greensboro that he was on his way to join him at Fayetteville. When Johnston received Hardee's dispatch a few hours later, he was shocked to learn that Hardee was marching toward Greensboro instead of Fayetteville, in accordance with erroneous and outdated information received from Generals Bragg and Beauregard. Johnston immediately sent Hardee orders to march for Fayetteville, then wired the other two generals for explanations. Bragg replied that the false report concerning Schofield's advance on Fayetteville had come from another source, and that the moment he had learned of it he sent Hardee a correct report of the situation. Beauregard shot back that Hardee was following his February 24 instructions instead of those sent him on the 26th; then he sent Hardee orders to march at once for Fayetteville.[39]

A confused state of affairs continued within the Confederate hierarchy. Hardee received Johnston's orders on the night of March 5, and accordingly set out for Fayetteville on the 6th. Johnston, meanwhile, began to doubt that Hardee could reach Fayetteville ahead of Sherman and sent him an order to march toward Raleigh instead. But then "Old Joe" thought better of it and instructed "Old Reliable" to march to Fayetteville after all. By the time Hardee received Beauregard's order and Johnston's two contradictory orders, his command was already well on its way to Fayetteville. "I had already informed you, in repeated dispatches, of my change of route toward Fayetteville and the progress of my march," a perturbed Hardee wrote Johnston on March 7. Hardee added that he expected to reach Fayetteville by March 9 or 10.[40]

The muddled marching orders did nothing to increase the morale of the men in the ranks, and Hardee continued to lose troops from desertion. Some of the men talked openly of mutiny, and one soldier even tried to make good his threat. On the 7th Rhett's Brigade held a drumhead court-martial for a Sergeant O'Keefe of Company B, 1st South Carolina Artillery. O'Keefe had been charged with mutinous conduct for inciting the men in his company to desert, and for attempting to shoot an officer who was reprimanding him for his misconduct. The sergeant was found guilty and condemned to be shot on the spot. As O'Keefe was led away, the 1st's chaplain offered to pray with him. "Preacher," O'Keefe said, "I never listened to you in Fort Sumter, and I won't listen to you now." He was shot in view of the brigade, then buried without ceremony. Few of the men mourned O'Keefe, as most of them were too footsore and hungry to feel much pity for the dead sergeant.[41]

While Hardee's Corps trudged northward toward Fayetteville, General Johnston arrived there on March 6. An Irishman named Thomas Conolly met Johnston and his staff on the Raleigh Road. Conolly described the general as "a lithe shaped little man, with good address & very quiet manner." Johnston was "followed by an ambulance drawn by 4 mules containing his camp equipage & his own camp wagon with a splendid pair of bays & 2 led horses."[42]

The Confederate commander had traveled from Charlotte to Fayetteville in order "to obtain quick intelligence of the enemy's movements, and to direct those of the Confederate troops." Encouraged by the Federals' difficult and time-consuming crossings at the Catawba River, the Pee Dee River and Lynch's Creek, he hoped to unite the Army of Tennessee troops with those of Hardee's Corps in time to attack one of Sherman's wings as it was crossing the Cape Fear River. Johnston had left Beauregard behind at Charlotte to forward the Western army troops by rail to Smithfield, 40 miles northeast of Fayetteville. Smithfield also happened to be just 50 miles northwest of Kinston on the railroad, which would put the Western army troops within easy supporting distance of Bragg's command. And it looked as if Bragg would need all the help he could get, for the Federal XXIII Corps of General Schofield's command was advancing westward from New Berne. Its objective was Goldsboro and a junction with Sherman's army.[43]

At Johnston's request, on March 4, Gen. Robert E. Lee placed Bragg's Department of North Carolina troops under his command.

When Bragg received the news, he fired off a letter to President Davis:

> I beg that you will relieve me from [this] embarrassing position. I seek no command or position, and only desire to be ordered to await assignment to duty at some point in Georgia or Alabama. The circumstances constraining me to make this request are painful in the extreme, but I cannot blindly disregard them.

Bragg had good reason to be alarmed. Just eight months before, as Davis' chief of staff, he had strongly recommended Johnston's removal from command. To make matters worse, Johnston had been Bragg's superior in 1863, and had sustained Bragg when Davis and nearly everyone else were pressing for his dismissal. Bragg therefore must have found his new subordinate relation to Johnston embarrassing, to say the least.[44]

Braxton Bragg was a tragically flawed general. He had commanded the Army of Tennessee longer than any other man, and had proved himself capable in many respects. If nothing else, he was a fighter, something that his successor, Joseph E. Johnston, was not. But Bragg lacked the one essential quality that Johnston possessed above all others—charisma. In fact, most of Bragg's officers and men found him repulsive. "Bragg is our evil genius," was how one veteran characterized the general's effect on the army.[45]

However much sympathy Davis may have felt for Bragg's plight, the authority to transfer him was no longer his. And so Bragg remained where he was. To his credit, Bragg refused to sulk about the awkward situation and instead prepared to hurl back the Federal force advancing on Kinston. On March 6 he asked Johnston to send him the Army of Tennessee troops massing at Smithfield. "A few hours would suffice to unite [those] forces with mine and insure a victory," noted Bragg. Abandoning his plan of opposing Sherman at Fayetteville, Johnston granted Bragg's request, but told him to return the Western troops to Smithfield immediately after the battle, where they would be closer to Sherman's line of march.[46]

The troop transfer led to an uneasy alliance between Bragg and Maj. Gen. Daniel Harvey Hill. The two men had been bitter enemies since the latter's dismissal at Bragg's hands 17 months before.

Given the circumstances, it is remarkable that they managed to set aside their differences long enough to concentrate on the task at hand. Hill commanded the 2,000-man Army of Tennessee contingent and reported directly to Bragg. Bragg's command also included Maj. Gen. Robert F. Hoke's Division and the North Carolina Junior Reserves Brigade, numbering about 6,000 effectives in all. Bragg and Hoke had worked well together in recapturing Plymouth, North Carolina, the previous year. For his efforts, Hoke had received a congratulatory telegram from President Davis, the thanks of Congress, and a major general's commission. Bragg had received nothing. Since Plymouth, however, their command partnership had suffered one setback after another. Perhaps the impending battle with the Federals would revive their waning fortunes.[47]

The Federal XXIII Corps was commanded by Maj. Gen. Jacob D. Cox, a capable battlefield commander whom General Schofield relied upon implicitly. On March 8 Cox's Federals collided with Bragg's men at a crossroads four miles east of Kinston known as Wise's Forks. Bragg's command routed a portion of the Federals forces, capturing one cannon and more than 800 men. Cox's troops dug in during the night of the 8th and after desultory skirmishing the next day, the Southerners resumed the offensive on the 10th. The well-entrenched Federals repulsed the Confederates' assaults easily. Upon learning that Cox was being reinforced, Bragg withdrew on the night of the 10th toward Kinston. Once again, Bragg had seen an apparent victory end in retreat.[48]

Regardless of the outcome, Johnston was correct in diverting the Army of Tennessee troops to Kinston for two reasons. First, it was doubtful that they could have reached Fayetteville in time to assist Hardee in opposing Sherman. Second, Schofield's force was weaker and more vulnerable than Sherman's. In the end, Johnston had no alternative, since the rapid shuttling of troops along the railroad was his only means of offsetting the Federals' overwhelming numerical superiority.[49]

Now that Bragg was retreating on Goldsboro, Johnston resumed his efforts to concentrate his scattered forces in front of Sherman. In this he had the considerable advantage of the North Carolina Railroad, which extended in a 220-mile-long arc from Charlotte to Goldsboro. At first the shipment of Army of Tennessee troops to

Smithfield proceeded smoothly under Beauregard's capable supervision, and by March 10 most of Lee's and Stewart's Corps had reached Smithfield. But Johnston invited disaster when he gave Bragg a free hand in transporting those troops from Smithfield to Kinston. Bragg monopolized the rolling stock, since his only concern was to speed D. H. Hill's troops to the front. As overall commander, Johnston should have exercised tighter control over Bragg's operations. His failure to do so resulted in a crisis situation on Beauregard's end of the line.[50]

On March 11, Beauregard informed Johnston that there was a 120-car backlog of troops, artillery and wagons awaiting transportation at Salisbury, with 65 additional carloads waiting at Chester. The bottleneck occurred at Salisbury because the width of the track narrowed there—which required a change of cars—and because most of the narrow gauge rolling stock sent to Smithfield had not yet returned. For some reason, the rolling stock that had been used to ship Bragg's troops to the front was later sent back to Raleigh, where it stood idle for six days, aiding neither Beauregard nor Bragg in their respective troop movements. Though aware of the problem, Johnston once again failed to issue orders directing the rolling stock to be sent where it was needed. As a result, Bragg's command had to march the 22 miles from Goldsboro to Smithfield, and the backlog at Salisbury rapidly worsened.[51]

Most of the troops awaiting transportation at Salisbury belonged to Maj. Gen. Frank Cheatham's Corps. General Cheatham was a fiery sort, and after several days of waiting for the trains to arrive, his patience had worn thin. When the cars finally did pull in, they couldn't be loaded and moved out fast enough to suit him, so he decided to take matters into his own hands.

"Where is the conductor of this train?" Cheatham demanded.

According to one onlooker, a man "all dressed up in a dudish uniform" stepped forward and said, "I am the conductor."

"Why don't you move out with your train," Cheatham prodded, "what are you waiting on?"

The conductor puffed himself up and replied, "*I* am running that part of the business, sir." The conductor had hardly finished speaking when the general struck him with "the full weight of his fist, and landed him full length out in the mud" beyond the railway platform.

"It is needless to say," the eyewitness recorded, "the conductor was up and had his train moving before he took time to shake off the mud."[52]

Like Cheatham, Johnston blamed the North Carolina Railroad officials for bungling the later troop shipments. "This railroad, with its enormous amount of rolling-stock, has brought us only about 500 men a day," he complained. Yet Johnston had only himself to blame, for he exercised ultimate authority. At stake was his ability to strike Sherman with his entire army when the opportunity offered, and in this he failed. A substantial number of his troops would still be waiting to board the cars at Salisbury when that crucial moment arrived.[53]

To add to Johnston's woes, General Lee and Secretary of War Breckinridge informed him that the subsistence stores collected in the depots along the North Carolina Railroad were for the exclusive use of the Army of Northern Virginia. (Johnston was later chagrined to learn that there were enough rations on hand to feed an army of 60,000 men for four months.) Lee told Johnston that he would have to supply his army by foraging on the countryside. Lacking the wagons and teams to undertake the effort, Johnston turned to North Carolina governor Zebulon Vance and Maj. Archibald H. Cole of the Quartermaster General's office in Richmond for assistance. Acting under Johnston's authority, Vance's and Cole's agents impressed wagons and draft animals along the expected route of Sherman's march. By means of this impressed field transportation, Johnston's army was able to collect enough provisions to feed itself until its own wagons came up.[54]

Johnston was further frustrated by the Richmond bureaucracy. When he sought to obtain pay for his men (many of whom had not been paid in more than a year), Secretary of War Breckinridge informed him that the Confederate Treasury was broke, and suggested that he should "make the best of the circumstances." When Johnston asked that a large store of supplies in Charlotte belonging to the navy (which had virtually ceased to exist by this time) be transferred to the army, Secretary of the Navy Stephen R. Mallory refused to part with it. Worse yet, Johnston was unable to procure rifle-muskets for almost 1,300 of his men. They remained unarmed to the end of the war.[55]

With the Federals advancing in superior force on two fronts, the concentration of his own army hampered by tie-ups along the railroad, and that army dependent on a sparsely settled region for subsistence, prospects appeared bleak for Johnston. On March 11 he informed Lee: "I will not give battle with Sherman's united army. . .but will if I can find it divided." And so Johnston gathered his own divided army, in the hope that he could defeat either Sherman or Schofield before one could combine with the other.[56]

* * *

On March 8 the columns of the Federal Right Wing marched into North Carolina on a carpet of pine needles, surrounded by a forest of loblolly pines whose limbs formed a green canopy 70 feet above the soldiers' heads. Many of these turpentine-producing trees were ablaze, creating a thick smoke which, in the words of one soldier, "hung like a pall over our heads, while the fire below lighted up the trunks of the trees that seemed to be supporting a roof, creating a feeling of awe as though we were within the precincts of a grand old cathedral." The troops added to the solemnity of the scene by singing "John Brown's Body."[57]

That night General Sherman made camp at Laurel Hill Church, on the extreme right of the army. He sent off his scout, Cpl. James Pike, with a message addressed to "Commanding Officer, Wilmington, N. C.:"

> We are marching on Fayetteville; will be there Saturday, [March 11,] Sunday, and Monday, and then will march for Goldsborough. If possible send a boat up Cape Fear River, and have word conveyed to General Schofield that I expect to meet him about Goldsborough. We are all well and doing finely. The rain makes our roads difficult, and may delay me about Fayetteville, in which case I would like some bread, sugar, and coffee. We have an abundance of all else. I expect to reach Goldsborough by the 20th instant.

This was Sherman's first attempt to communicate with the outside world in more than a month.[58]

On March 9th Sherman accompanied the XV Corps on its march, crossing the Lumber River with Maj. Gen. William B.

Hazen's division. Hazen's boys were said to be Sherman's pets, for he had led many of them since Shiloh. As he rode between the columns of soldiers waiting to cross, the men gave a cheer that was taken up by regiments a mile back. The veterans at the rear of the column recognized the exceptional quality of this cheer, for they invariably remarked, "Listen to them cheering Billy Sherman."[59]

Sherman camped at Bethel Church, 26 miles southwest of Fayetteville. An aide had fashioned a crude bed out of carpet for the general. "No," Sherman said with a wave of his hand, "keep that for some of you young fellows who are not well." Then he stretched out on a wooden pew for the night.[60]

While Sherman slept (fitfully, no doubt) on his hard bed, several regiments from Bvt. Maj. Gen. John E. Smith's division of the XV Corps were hard at work pulling wagons out of the mud in the midst of a blinding rainstorm. One of the laborers, Pvt. George Lambert of the 4th Minnesota, remarked that he hoped never again to see such a deluge. The division train was soon stuck, many of the wagons having sunk to the axle in quicksand. Lambert and his comrades now realized that they were in for "an all night's work in the rain and mud:"

> Louder and deeper cursed the teamsters, as down would go mules and wagons into some bottomless hole. . . .After tugging away, the steaming mules would be unloosed from the wagons and the men would take their places—some in the rear, some at the wheels and more at the tongue and trace chains, and with a tug and a yell would land the cumbrous wagons upon a few feet of solid ground. . . .The gloomy forest was resounding with the swinging of axes, the crash of falling trees and the mingling curses of a multitude of mule drivers, while it thundered, rained, and the wind blew beyond description. To add to the wildness of the scene, every few hundred feet would be seen a pitch pine in full blaze of light, its smoky flames tossing away up in the air.[61]

Each supply wagon was pulled along by means of a pair of two-hundred-foot ropes, with a hundred men at each rope. Among those tugging at the ropes was XV Corps commander John Logan, who was covered with mud from head to foot. The men kept at it until 2:00 a.m., when Logan finally called a halt to give them a few hours' rest. At first light the men were roused and the work was resumed. By 9:00 a.m. on the 10th, nearly 24 hours since breaking camp the day before, the men had hauled the last wagon onto dry land and were marching off to rejoin their brigade. "[T]his was undoubtedly the hardest day of my soldier life," one exhausted fellow scrawled in his diary. "I wonder how much it takes to kill a fellow anyhow."[62]

Sherman was up at daybreak to check the condition of the XV Corps' road. To his disappointment, the rains had transformed it into a canal. He decided to let the XV Corps troops rest for a day and give the road a chance to dry. Then he returned to the church and sat down to write dispatches to his two wing commanders. Now that his grand army was converging on Fayetteville, Sherman told Howard that he wanted to "let Slocum break into town" first (to salve his disappointment at not taking part in the capture of Columbia), but to come to his support if Johnston offered battle. Then Sherman urged Slocum "to do all that is possible to secure the bridge across Cape Fear River."[63]

Meanwhile, at a remote crossroads 15 miles to the north, Kilpatrick and his command were fighting to regain their camp, having been surprised and driven out by an overwhelming force of Confederate cavalry.

~ *four* ~

"An Infernal Surprise"

—Gen. Judson Kilpatrick

The ablest subordinate in Johnston's patchwork army was a cavalryman, Lt. Gen. Wade Hampton of South Carolina. Before the war Hampton had been a planter and reputedly the wealthiest man in the South. The slave-holding aristocrat had opposed secession because he believed it was more apt to topple the old order than perpetuate it. Yet when the time came, he threw all his support behind South Carolina's decision to leave the Union. With the approach of war, Hampton formed his eponymously-named legion, which he armed and outfitted with his own funds. A novice at war, the 43-year-old Hampton proved to be a born combat leader. At Manassas he was no less green than the troops under his command. Yet, even though his unit sustained 20% casualties—including Hampton himself—he led them as coolly and confidently as a seasoned veteran. His pragmatic approach no doubt sprang from the belief that war was a grim business, devoid of romance and chivalry. This was ironic, for in 1865 Sherman's troops would contemptuously refer to Hampton and his South Carolina cavalry as "the chivalry."[1]

Hampton and Joe Johnston were old comrades. He had served under Johnston during the Peninsula Campaign in 1862, at the head of a brigade of infantry. Like Johnston, Hampton was wounded at Seven Pines on May 31, early in the campaign. During his service on the peninsula, Hampton formed a high opinion of Johnston's abilities, and later referred to his removal from command during the Atlanta Campaign as a "national calamity."[2]

In July 1862, Hampton was transferred to the cavalry and given command of one of "Jeb" Stuart's brigades. One year later, he was severely wounded at Gettysburg, receiving two deep saber cuts across his scalp and a shrapnel wound in his body. By the time of General Stuart's death on May 12, 1864, Hampton was a major general and the cavalry corps' senior division commander. Yet General Lee hesitated to designate Hampton as Stuart's successor to the command of the Army of Northern Virginia's cavalry. Lee's reluctance stemmed from Hampton's lack of formal military training as well as from his desire to see whether the South Carolinian would prove himself equal to the increased command responsibility. Hampton again demonstrated his mettle at Trevilian Station, where he defeated Maj. Gen. Philip H. Sheridan's Federal cavalry in a fierce two-day battle. Other successes followed, and on August 11, Hampton received the long-deferred appointment. In the final autumn of the war, when more than a third of his command was without horses, the ever-resourceful Hampton still managed to hold his own against the enemy. But the days of improbable success were numbered.[3]

In January 1865, Hampton applied for a transfer to South Carolina. He requested that Maj. General Matthew C. Butler's Division accompany him in order to remount itself, for half the men were without horses. General Lee reluctantly granted Hampton's request. "I think Hampton will be of service," Lee wrote President Davis, "in mounting his men and arousing the spirit and strength of the State." Pledging to "fight as long as I can wield my sabre," Hampton arrived in his hometown of Columbia in early February.[4]

Despite still being able to "wield his sabre," there was little Hampton could do except retreat once Sherman's army reached Columbia. The two Hampton family mansions, Sand Hill and Millwood, were burned on the night of February 17. "I have given far more than all my property to this cause," Hampton wrote a friend, "& I am ready to give *all*." This was no idle boast: Hampton had lost a brother and a son to the war, and had been wounded in battle numerous times.[5]

On February 16, President Davis had notified Hampton that the Senate had confirmed his nomination promoting him to lieutenant general. For Hampton in 1865, this was a rare piece of good news, because it meant that he would not have to serve under Maj. Gen. Joseph Wheeler. On the contrary, it meant that Wheeler would have to serve under him, a prospect that the independent-minded Wheeler did not relish. Wheeler had been the Army of Tennessee's cavalry chief since October 13, 1862, and until Hampton's promotion had been the ranking general in the Confederate cavalry. In March 1865, he was only 28 years old, a full 18 years Hampton's junior.[6]

Like Johnston and Sherman, Hampton and Wheeler present a study in contrasts. Hampton was a broad man, nearly six feet tall and possessing great physical strength; Wheeler was five-feet-five inches tall and slight of build. He was known variously as "Little Joe," "Fighting Joe" and the "War Child," nicknames that attest to his small stature, his combative spirit and his relative youth. A West Point graduate (class of 1859), Wheeler possessed the formal military education that Hampton lacked. But he was an indifferent student, and ironically his poorest grades were in cavalry tactics.[7]

While Hampton managed his vast estates in the months prior to the war, Wheeler served in New Mexico with the Regiment of Mounted Rifles, an outfit that had been formed as an experiment in the use of mounted infantry. Wheeler liked the idea of a cavalry force equally adept at fighting on foot and on horseback, and would later utilize it with great success in the broken and wooded terrain of the South.

When his home state of Georgia seceded, Wheeler resigned his second lieutenant's commission and headed east. He enlisted as a lieutenant in the Georgia state forces, and first served in the coastal artillery at Pensacola, Florida, under Braxton Bragg. At Shiloh Wheeler commanded the 19th Alabama Infantry, again under Bragg. Transferred to the cavalry service in July 1862, Wheeler commanded Bragg's cavalry during the Kentucky invasion. He did such a good job of covering the Confederate army's retreat that Bragg appointed him to be his cavalry chief in the newly-organized Army of Tennessee, and on October 30, 1862 was promoted to brigadier general. Though Wheeler lacked Stuart's dash and Bedford Forrest's savage brilliance, Bragg appreciated "Fighting Joe's" tenacity and grit, and above all, his strict adherence to orders.

Wheeler reinforced Bragg's confidence in him by proving to be an excellent raider and intelligence gatherer. During the Stones River (Murfreesboro) Campaign, he rode around the Federal army and smashed up its wagon train in a manner reminiscent of Stuart's rides around McClellan's army. "Fighting Joe" even found time to write a cavalry tactics manual, in which he set forth his method of utilizing cavalry as mounted infantry. Soon afterward, Wheeler received confirmation of his promotion to major general, and at the age of 26 ranked second only to "Jeb" Stuart in the Confederate cavalry service.

Although Wheeler went on to serve capably in the Chickamauga Campaign, during the Knoxville expedition his weaknesses as a commander became apparent. Straggling and depredations threatened to disintegrate his command, yet he seemed incapable of restoring discipline. Fortunately, Bragg's resignation and Johnston's assumption of command helped to restore the morale of Wheeler's men. During the Atlanta Campaign, Wheeler's cavalry once more displayed its old fighting spirit, and its leader proved himself superior to the Federal cavalry commanders in Sherman's army. Wheeler's most conspicuous triumph of 1864 was his repulse of the McCook-Stoneman Raid on Macon and Andersonville, in which his troopers killed, routed or captured more than half of Sherman's cavalry force.

In the fall of 1864 Gen. John B. Hood, Johnston's successor in command of the Army of Tennessee, assigned Wheeler the futile task of contesting Sherman's March to the Sea. Since Wheeler had only 4,500 troopers under his command, offering serious opposition to Sherman's army was out of the question. The Georgian had to content himself with battling General Kilpatrick's cavalry and the Federals' numberless foraging details. Meanwhile, Wheeler's cavalrymen gained a reputation for plundering and wanton destruction that made them almost as feared among the citizens of Georgia as the infamous bummers of Sherman's army. Once more, Wheeler came under fire for failing to control his command.

General Beauregard thought the accusations serious enough to send his inspector general, Col. Alfred Roman, to Wheeler's camp in December 1864, for a thorough inspection of his cavalry corps. In his report to Beauregard, Roman noted that the citizens in Georgia and South Carolina regarded Wheeler's cavalry "more as a band of highway robbers than as an organized military Body." Though Roman pointed out that this reputation was largely undeserved, he nevertheless perceived a critical lack of discipline in Wheeler's Cavalry Corps at all levels of command. Roman placed the blame squarely on Wheeler's shoulders, calling him "too gentle, too lenient." Though Roman recommended replacing Wheeler immediately, he conceded that finding a replacement would be difficult, for "the Forrests, the Hamptons, are not easily found." As if in answer to Roman's recommendation, Hampton arrived in South Carolina in late January, and by virtue of his promotion, assumed command of Wheeler's cavalry on February 16.[8]

By all accounts Wheeler obeyed Hampton's orders without question, and in Wheeler's own words, Hampton "exercised his authority with all possible deference." Yet beneath this veneer of courtesy there existed a spirit of rivalry between the two commanders as well as their respective commands. This competitiveness later erupted into a post-war battle of the books. For the time being, however, Hampton and Wheeler focused their energies on battling the Federals.[9]

Following the withdrawal from Columbia, Hampton accompanied Wheeler's command, which was shadowing the Federal cavalry and Left Wing. General Butler's division was on the enemy's right flank. When the Federal Right Wing suddenly shifted its line of march to the east toward Cheraw, Butler found himself cut off from Wheeler, and for the next two weeks was "operating on my own hook," as he phrased it, striking "an occasional blow at detachments foraging and plundering the helpless inhabitants." Butler's Division also served as the rear guard for Hardee's Corps at Cheraw.

Meanwhile, Wheeler's horsemen clashed several times with Kilpatrick's troopers, most notably near Hornsboro, North Carolina, on March 3-4, and again near Rockingham on March 7. That same day, Butler's Division had its first scrape with Kilpatrick's cavalry in the streets of Rockingham. On the 8th, Butler's and Wheeler's cavalry forces reunited ten miles north of the town. In a dispatch to General Hardee, Hampton wrote, "As soon as my command can be concentrated I shall move round the left flank of the enemy to his front." Hampton now found himself at a disadvantage, for Kilpatrick was nearer to both Fayetteville and Hardee's column than he was. Only hard riding could close the gap.[10]

* * *

General Kilpatrick's cavalry left Rockingham at 7:00 a.m. on March 8, riding for most of the day in a cold rain, "over the worst roads it has been my fortune to travel," wrote Lt. Col. Robert H. King of the 3rd Kentucky Cavalry. King did not exaggerate, for the Federals' artillery and wagon train bogged down while crossing Drowning Creek and had to be dragged out by men working in water up to their armpits. The Confederate cavalry made frequent dashes on the rear and left flank of the Union column, yet caused little damage. Nevertheless, the rear of Kilpatrick's straggling column did not reach camp until 4:00 a.m. on March 9.[11]

The Federal cavalry broke camp a few hours later and was back on the march at 8:00 a.m., heading eastward on the Morganton Road for Fayetteville. He reached Solemn Grove at 2:00 p.m. and halted for three hours to enable the column to close up. Colonel George E. Spencer's brigade had the advance, followed by Lt. Col. William B. Way's brigade of dismounted troopers. Brigadier General Smith D. Atkins' brigade came next, with Col. Thomas J. Jordan's brigade bringing up the rear. Kilpatrick learned from Confederate prisoners that Hardee's Corps had passed Solemn Grove the day before. More importantly, "Little Kil" also learned that Hampton's cavalry was proceeding eastward on the Yadkin Road several miles to the north, and on the Morganton Road behind the Union column.[12]

This was wonderful news to Kilpatrick, for it meant that he had only to block those roads to prevent Hampton from reaching Hardee. He planned to do just that, disregarding Sherman's most recent instructions to him to "Keep your horses in the best order for the day when we must have a big fight—not, however, on this turn." Nevertheless, an excited Kilpatrick sent Sherman a message that Hampton was behind him and that he would attempt to cut him off. Thus far in the campaign, Kilpatrick had done a superb job of shielding the Left Wing from the enemy's cavalry. Moreover, his feints on Augusta and Charlotte had prevented the Confederates from concentrating in the army's front. In short, Kilpatrick had been on his best behavior so far, but the opportunity as he saw it was too good to pass up.[13]

There was just one problem: Kilpatrick did not have enough men to stop Hampton's entire force. As of March 1, Kilpatrick had 4,317 officers and men in his command, compared to roughly 4,000 troopers under Hampton. Once again, Kilpatrick was

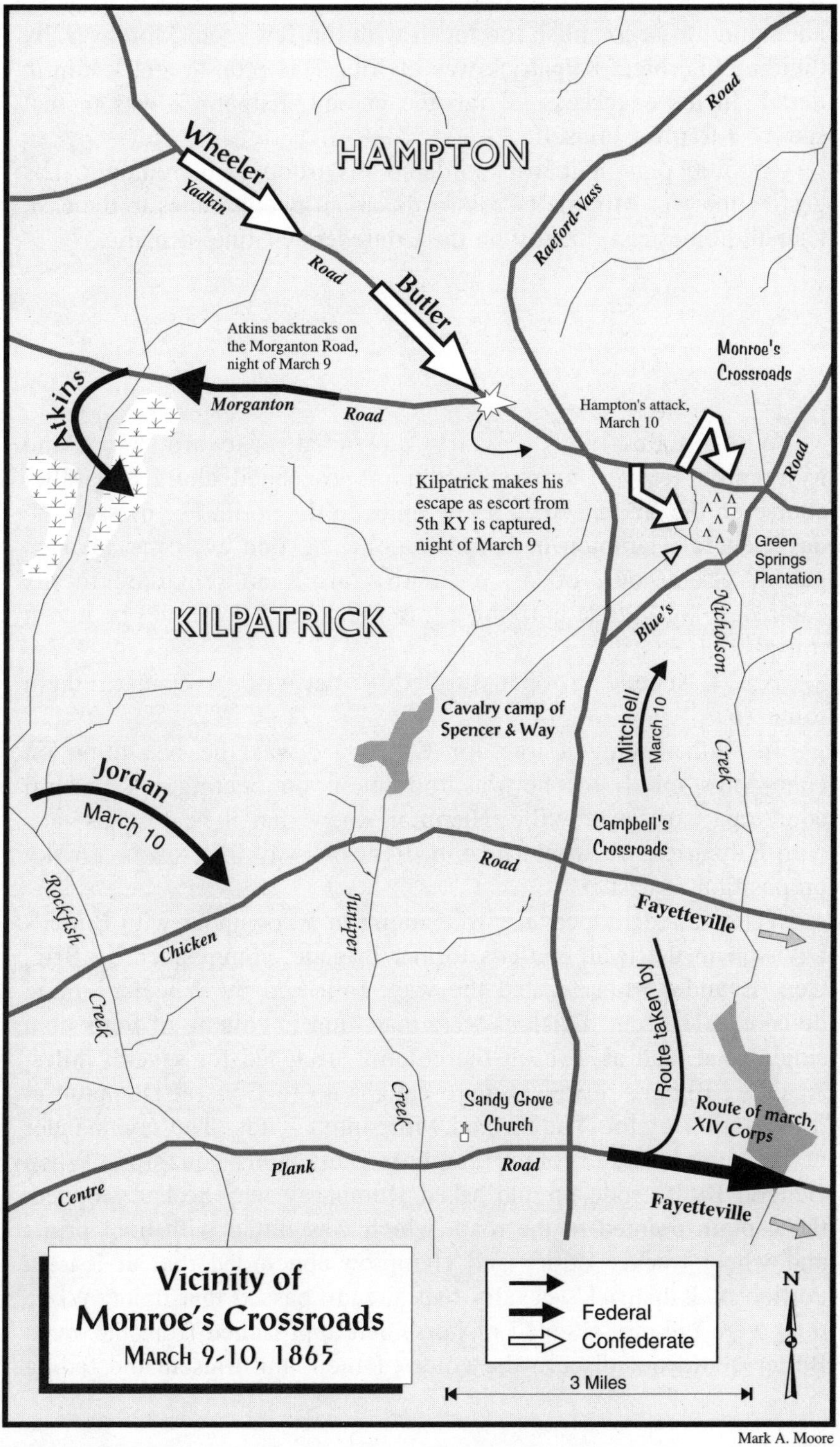
HAMPTON
Wheeler
Yadkin
Road
Butler
Raeford-Vass
Road
Atkins backtracks on the Morganton Road, night of March 9
Atkins
Morganton
Road
Monroe's Crossroads
Hampton's attack, March 10
Road
Kilpatrick makes his escape as escort from 5th KY is captured, night of March 9
Green Springs Plantation
KILPATRICK
Blue's
Nicholson
Creek
Mitchell
March 10
Cavalry camp of Spencer & Way
Jordan
March 10
Campbell's Crossroads
Road
Rockfish
Creek
Chicken
Juniper
Creek
Fayetteville
Route taken by
Route of march, XIV Corps
Sandy Grove Church
Centre
Plank
Road
Fayetteville
Vicinity of Monroe's Crossroads
March 9-10, 1865
Federal
Confederate
3 Miles
N

Mark A. Moore

attempting to accomplish too much with too few men. Moreover, by dividing his force, Kilpatrick was inviting Hampton to attack him in detail. In his eagerness to trap the enemy, Kilpatrick was in fact setting a trap for himself.[14]

At 5:00 p.m. Kilpatrick ordered his troopers to remount. His destination was Monroe's Crossroads, about twelve miles to the east, a small homestead directly on the Confederates' line of march.

* * *

While Kilpatrick's cavalry advanced eastward down the Morganton Road, Hampton's column proceeded along a parallel course on the Yadkin Road a few miles to the north. For most of the day General Hampton had ridden alone, beyond even the advance guard. "Look out, boys," a South Carolinian remarked to his comrades, "old Wade is fixing a trap for them[.] [W]e will be into it tonight."

No, a second trooper replied. "We will give it to them tomorrow."[15]

In truth, laying a trap for Kilpatrick was the last thing on Hampton's mind, for he was too intent on beating his Federal counterpart to Fayetteville. Hampton knew that if he lost his race with Kilpatrick, he would have to fight his way into town—a risky proposition at best.

The Confederate cavalry rode along in a downpour with Butler's Division in the lead. Butler's former brigade, commanded by Brig. Gen. Evander M. Law, led the way, followed by Wheeler's three divisions. The four divisions were marching in column of fours on a single road, and as a result the column stretched for several miles. At dusk, Butler's advance guard caught up to General Hampton at the junction of the Yadkin and Morganton roads. The commander of the guard, Capt. John Humphrey, halted his squadron. When General Butler rode up and asked Humphrey why he had stopped, the captain pointed to the road, which was rutted with hoof prints and wheel tracks. Butler and Hampton concluded that at least a portion of Kilpatrick's cavalry had already passed that point. While they were talking, a squad of horsemen approached from the west. Butler could not discern the color of their uniforms in the fading light, so he asked Humphrey if any of his men were on the Morganton Road. When Humphrey answered in the negative, Butler rode forward and challenged the squad:

"Who comes there?"

"Fifth Kentucky," came the reply.[16]

Butler knew this to be one of Kilpatrick's regiments, and concluded that this squad was the rear guard of the column that had just passed. He said, "Ride up, sir; I want to speak with you."

Two men rode forward—the officer commanding the guard and his orderly. Butler led them back a few steps to where Humphrey's squadron was halted, then turned upon them with drawn pistol and demanded their surrender. In Butler's words, "Nothing else was left for them to do." A veteran of Humphrey's squadron called Butler's capture of the two Federals "the coolest thing I ever witnessed."[17]

Butler now ordered Captain Humphrey to surround and capture the squad of the 5th Kentucky, which Humphrey accomplished without firing a shot. The capture netted Humphrey 16 Federals and the 5th Kentucky's regimental colors. Without knowing it, Butler had bagged Kilpatrick's escort and had come within a whisker of capturing the general himself. But the alert Kilpatrick had led his staff into the woods when the Kentuckians halted and had made his escape. Even so, the excitement had only begun for Kilpatrick.[18]

Matthew Calbraith Butler was the same age as General Kilpatrick, having turned 29 the day before (March 8). "It used to be said his skin glanced bullets," one veteran wrote of Butler, "and that it required a twelve-pounder to carry away" his right foot at Brandy Station. Butler's men told numerous stories about his coolness under fire. According to one anecdote, when a courier galloped up with a message from one of his colonels that he was being flanked by the enemy, Butler's nonchalant reply was, "Tell him to flank them back."[19]

Butler was Hampton's favorite subordinate. The two South Carolinians had been friends since before the war, but there was no cronyism involved in the younger man's rise in rank and command responsibility. Butler had amply demonstrated his capability, first as a captain in the Hampton Legion's cavalry, then as colonel of the 2nd South Carolina Cavalry, and finally, as both a brigade and a division commander.

Butler and Hampton discussed the situation that now confronted them. They concluded that the squad just captured was a picket detail for the Union cavalry force that had passed the fork in the road. The two generals further concluded that this portion of the Federal cavalry was now isolated from the main body. This was the glimmer of daylight Hampton had been looking for. He thereupon decided to attack the isolated Union cavalry force, and ordered the assault for dawn the next morning. Butler accordingly ordered his column to fall in and begin its pursuit of the Federal cavalry.[20]

* * *

Spencer's cavalry brigade and Way's dismounted brigade reached Monroe's Crossroads at 9:00 p.m., just 17 miles west of Fayetteville. The men knew that with luck, they would reach the outskirts of town by the following night.[21]

General Kilpatrick rejoined Spencer's brigade following his narrow escape. When Kilpatrick had stumbled into Butler's advance, he had been riding ahead of Atkins' brigade, having given Atkins instructions to bivouac at the fork now occupied by Butler's Confederate Division. This fork was three miles west of Spencer's camp at Monroe's Crossroads. Kilpatrick had also instructed Colonel Jordan to post his brigade at a junction on the Chicken Road about three miles south of Spencer's camp, thereby hoping to block Hampton's advance while keeping his three brigades within supporting distance of one another. Given his close call at the fork, Kilpatrick must have suspected that his plan was unraveling, but as events later demonstrated, he displayed no apparent concern.[22]

Kilpatrick and Spencer made their headquarters at the Charles Monroe house, which stood near the southwest corner of the crossroads that bore the owner's name. Monroe's Crossroads was formed by the intersection of the Morganton and Blue's roads. Monroe had wisely fled the premises, perhaps on the advice of Confederate general Lafayette McLaws, who had camped near his house the night before. The Federals' wagons were parked along either side of Blue's Road just east of the house. Kilpatrick's own two horses were grazing in the yard near an expensive carriage that carried the general's two female companions, refugees from South Carolina who were traveling with the general in order to flee to the North. Their presence in the general's entourage was the talk of

"Kil's" men, "making much scandal," in the words of one Ohio trooper.[23]

Way's dismounted brigade made its camp in a small field just north of the Monroe house and along the Morganton Road. The so-called "bull pen" containing about 150 Confederate prisoners stood in Way's camp. The two 3-inch ordnance rifles of Lt. Ebenezer W. Stetson's section of the 10th Wisconsin Battery were parked on a knoll about 500 feet south of the Monroe house and just west of Blue's Road. Of Colonel Spencer's three regiments, the 5th Ohio Cavalry was camped along a ridge just north of the two guns, the 5th Kentucky Cavalry just south of them, and the 1st Alabama Cavalry between Stetson's guns to the east and Nicholson Creek to the west. Spencer's camp was situated in an open wood, protected on its southern and western sides by a swamp. Most of his troopers probably slept in the open wrapped in their shelter tents. Since the men of the 5th Ohio and Way's brigade were camped near the Monroe house, many were able to drape their tents over fence rails. Some of them doubtless found shelter in the barn and the other farm buildings that stood near the house.[24]

Unbeknownst to the Confederates, Kilpatrick's scouts had bivouacked across Blue's Road several hundred yards southeast of Colonel Spencer's camp. The scouts had arrived at Monroe's Crossroads at noon, about nine hours ahead of the main body. Although the commander of the scouts, Capt. Theo F. Northrop, found the Monroe house "a very comfortable place. . .to spend the night," he considered it "too exposed." Instead, Northrop chose a more remote site across Blue's Road. As events later developed, Northrop would have no cause to regret his decision.[25]

Despite a drizzling rain, the men fed their horses, then cooked and ate their own suppers before turning in. Spencer later reported that he posted pickets along his end of the camp; Way presumably did the same. By 11:00 p.m. the camp was still and almost everyone was asleep.[26]

While Kilpatrick and his men slept, Atkins' brigade was struggling through a swamp about five miles to the west in an attempt to march around Hampton's flank. Earlier, Atkins had reached his assigned campsite only to discover that Hampton had camped there ahead of him. So Atkins countermarched several miles, then turned left and headed south in an effort to strike the Chicken Road. Instead, he struck a swamp. Atkins now concluded that the earliest he could reach Kilpatrick was mid-morning. Jordan's brigade had also failed to reach its assigned position and was bivouacked at Rockfish Church, a few miles west of Atkins' position. At 1:00 a.m. Jordan's scouts informed Colonel Jordan that the enemy held the Morganton Road in force, thus cutting him off from both Atkins' and Spencer's brigades. And so the three Federal cavalry brigades were now isolated from each other and from their nearest infantry support.[27]

As Kilpatrick slept, the trap slowly closed around him.

* * *

Generals Hampton, Wheeler and Butler reached Kilpatrick's camp shortly before midnight. Hampton and Wheeler rode forward with Wheeler's chief of scouts, Capt. A. M. Shannon, to reconnoiter the area. After dismounting some distance away, they approached on foot and located the house that they assumed was Kilpatrick's headquarters. They also located the position of the Federal pickets and artillery. It is unclear whether they took note of the swamp that bordered the western side of the Federal camp along Nicholson Creek. In any event, the Southerners failed to take the swamp into account when planning their attack, an oversight that would prove costly.[28]

Wheeler directed Captain Shannon to capture the Federals' pickets stationed along the western side of the camp, and to do so without firing a gun. Meanwhile, Butler's scouts were to capture the Federal pickets guarding the Morganton Road and the northern end of camp. Shannon's scouts carried out their orders to the letter. Shannon even sent two of his men into the camp to locate the prison pen. They soon returned, leading two captured horses each. When Wheeler joined Shannon's scouts on the picket line, he asked, "Where are the enemy?"

One of the scouts pointed to the dim outline of the camp and replied, "There they are, General."

"What, that near and all asleep?" Wheeler said, dumbfounded. "Won't we have a picnic tonight."[29]

While Hampton and Wheeler reconnoitered the enemy's camp, Butler halted his division about one mile to the west, throwing out dismounted skirmishers in his front and videttes beyond the skirmishers. Butler ordered his men to keep their horses saddled and to make no fires. The men filed off on either side of the Morganton Road and ate such rations as they had, then lay down on the cold, damp ground and went to sleep.[30]

Butler also dozed off, but was soon awakened and informed that his skirmishers had captured a Federal lieutenant who had ridden into their lines. The lieutenant told Butler that he was Kilpatrick's acting quartermaster, and that the general had sent him back to find a broken-down wagon. He also said that Kilpatrick had established his headquarters in a house on the north end of camp. When Hampton and Wheeler returned from their reconnaissance, Butler passed this information on to them. Hampton instructed his two subordinates to lay a trap for "Little Kil." Wheeler assigned Captain Shannon the task of bagging Kilpatrick. Not to be outdone, Butler instructed Col. Gilbert J. Wright, the commander of Young's Brigade, to choose "a prudent but bold" man for the job. "Gib" Wright chose Captain Bostick of Cobb's Legion to command the detail charged with capturing Kilpatrick. When Bostick reported to Butler for instructions, the general described the location of the Monroe house, then instructed the captain "to rush straight for the house, surround it. . .and if he could live there, hold the position until we could get up, as I wished to make Kilpatrick a prisoner."[31]

Soon after Butler issued his orders to Bostick, he had his men mount up. He led his two brigades at a walk to the edge of Monroe's field just north of the Morganton Road, where they halted. Butler's Division now faced south, and was arrayed in column of regiments. Young's Brigade had the advance, and Captain Bostick's squadron of Cobb's Legion had the honor of leading the charge. Butler's old brigade under General Law was drawn up in reserve. Butler instructed Colonel Wright to follow Bostick closely with the rest of his brigade, but to throw only one regiment at a time into the charge. Butler assured Wright that as soon as all of his regiments had gone in, he would send in Law's Brigade as support.[32]

As Butler's Rebels deployed for the assault, Wheeler's command, on Butler's right, filed into position on a ridge overlooking the western boundary of the Monroe farm. Wheeler's men had suffered a grueling, all-night march to reach this point, and as dawn approached they were still arriving. Wheeler's line faced east and at a 90-degree angle, to Butler's. "Fighting Joe" deployed four of his brigades in column of regiments as his striking force. From left to right they were: Hagan's and Anderson's of Allen's Division, and Ashby's and Harrison's of Humes' Division. He held his two remaining brigades, Dibrell's and Breckinridge's of Dibrell's Division, in reserve.[33]

The rain, which had been falling steadily that night, stopped just before dawn on March 10, only to be replaced by a thick blanket of fog. The Federal camp was perfectly still. Fortunately for the Confederates, the wet leaves and pine needles muffled the tramping of their horses' hooves.[34]

General Wheeler placed Shannon's scouts on the left and in front of Hagan's Brigade to enable them to reach Kilpatrick's headquarters first. Wheeler would ride in with Shannon, eager no doubt to catch his old West Point chum napping. When General Hampton rode up to issue some last-minute instructions, Wheeler saluted him and said, "General Hampton, with your permission I will give the order to dismount, so as to make the capture of this entire camp sure."

"General Wheeler," Hampton replied, "as a cavalryman I prefer making this capture on horseback."

General Wheeler again saluted and said, "General Hampton, all is ready for action; have your headquarters bugler blow the charge."[35]

Hampton returned Wheeler's salute and rode back to Butler's column, where he took his place at the head of Cobb's Legion. He instructed Butler to "bring off the artillery as soon as it was captured." As dawn broke, Hampton ordered his bugler to sound the charge.[36]

At the same instant Butler shouted, "Troops from Virginia follow me! Forward! Charge!" Led by Bostick's squadron, Cobb's Legion burst out of the woods shrieking the Rebel yell and brandishing their sabers and revolvers. They struck Lieutenant Colonel Way's camp at the gallop, stampeding the prison guard and overrunning the awakening Federals, many of whom promptly surrendered. One of the Northerners, Pvt. J. W. Swan, crawled out of the hen house where he had been sleeping and joined his dazed comrades in a foot race for the woods southeast of their camp. As General Butler rode into the Federal camp behind Young's Brigade, he saw dozens of dim figures running toward him through the mist. At first the general thought that his attack had been repulsed and

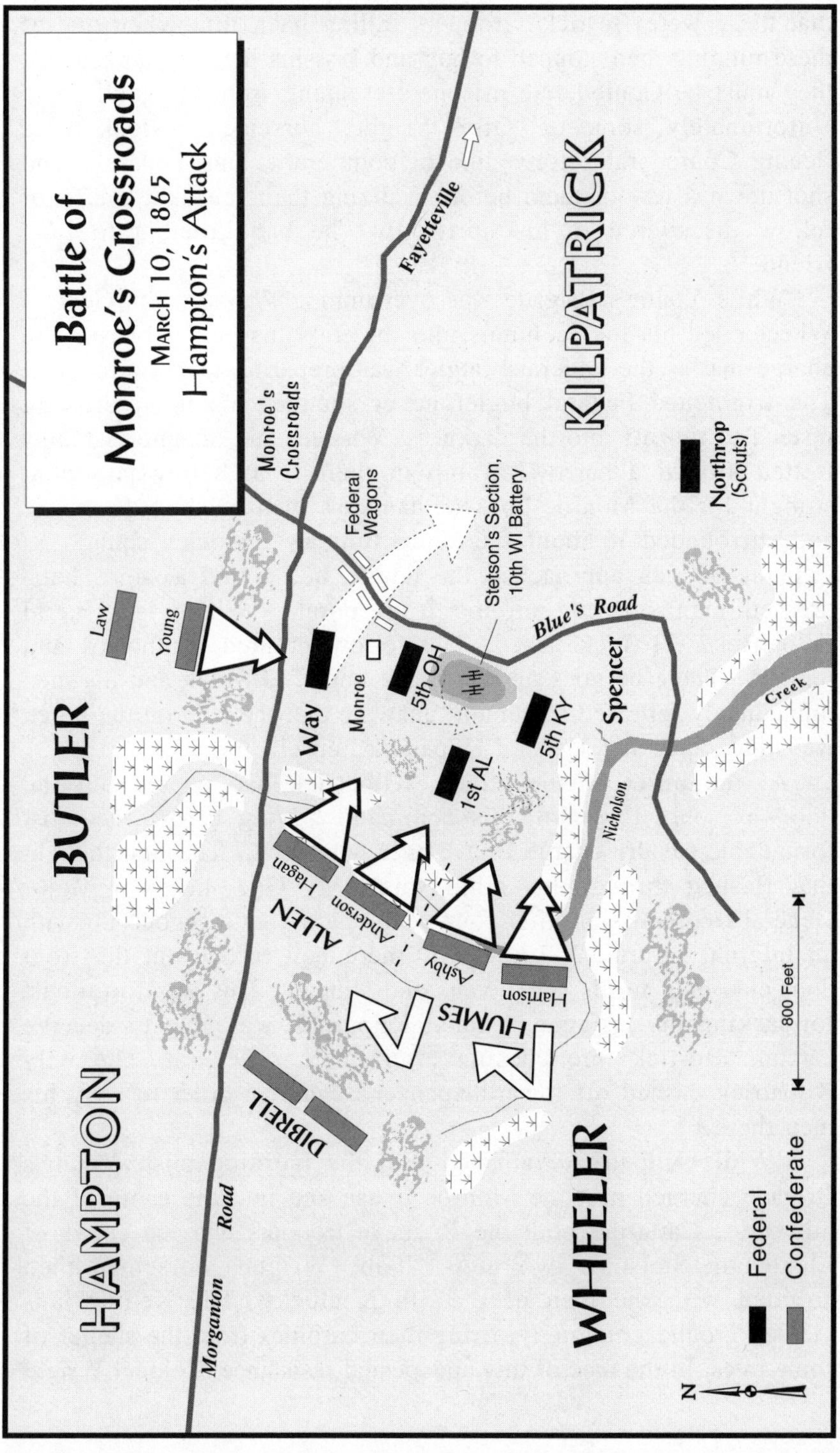
Battle of
Monroe's Crossroads
March 10, 1865
Hampton's Attack
BUTLER
HAMPTON
WHEELER
KILPATRICK
Law
Young
Way
Monroe
5th OH
5th KY
1st AL
Federal Wagons
Stetson's Section,
10th WI Battery
Northrop
(Scouts)
Monroe's
Crossroads
Fayetteville
Blue's Road
Spencer
Nicholson
Creek
Hagan
Anderson
ALLEN
Ashby
Harrison
HUMES
DIBRELL
Morganton
Road
800 Feet
Federal
Confederate
N

Mark A. Moore

that these were Bostick's troopers falling back. But when one of these running men stopped to hug and kiss his leg, he realized that they must be Confederate prisoners escaping from the "bull pen." Unfortunately, some of "Gib" Wright's horsemen mistook these fleeing Confederates for a line of counterattacking Federals, and shot down a few of them before realizing their mistake. One poor fellow discovered to his horror that he had killed a lifelong friend.[37]

While Young's Brigade was overrunning Way's camp, General Wheeler led his four columns into the fray, his bugler blaring the charge just as the Federals' bugler was preparing to blow reveille. The frightened Federal bugler never sounded a note, preferring instead to run off into the darkness. Wheeler and Shannon's scouts trotted around a narrow swamp in their front before galloping straight for the Monroe house. Shannon's men reached the house and surrounded it about the same time as Bostick's squad. As Captain Bostick approached the house, he spotted a short, half-dressed man standing on the front porch. "Where is General Kilpatrick?" Bostick asked. The fellow pointed southward and replied, "There he goes on that black horse!" Bostick and his men immediately followed in pursuit, unaware that the man on the porch was none other than General Kilpatrick himself.[38]

At the onset of the attack, Kilpatrick had peered out the doorway, only to behold his command "flying before the most formidable cavalry charge I have ever witnessed." The first thought that flashed through his mind was: "My God, here's a Major General's commission after four years' hard fighting gone up with an infernal surprise." "Little Kil" thereupon rushed out the front door clad only in his shirt, pants and slippers. This was fortuitous, for lacking his insignia of rank, Kilpatrick was able to deceive Captain Bostick into chasing after another Federal. The wily Kilpatrick dashed off toward Spencer's camp in order to rally his men there.[39]

While Kilpatrick vanished into the morning mist, Young's Brigade charged past the Monroe house and into the camp of the 5th Ohio, scattering both the Buckeye troopers and the crews of Lieutenant Stetson's two guns. "Gib" Wright's horsemen then collided with the men of the 5th Kentucky. The Kentuckians yielded ground grudgingly, firing their carbines from the shelter of some trees. In the face of this unexpected resistance, Colonel Wright halted his brigade to reform his line. This was a wise decision, for Wright's command was somewhat disorganized, the men having disobeyed Butler's orders and charged in one rush, rather than in the prescribed column of regiments. Elements of Wheeler's two left brigades, led by Col. James Hagan and Brig. Gen. Robert H. Anderson, finally reached the Monroe house area after floundering through a swamp, but their presence only added to the confusion. Worse yet, some of the Southerners succumbed to temptation and began to plunder the wagons parked along Blue's Road. Despite the problems inherent in a dawn attack, the Confederates were still better organized than the Federals, and now controlled most of their camp, including their wagons and artillery.[40]

The hiss of passing bullets terrified the two women inside the Monroe house. One of the ladies ran out to the carriage, only to discover that there were no horses hitched to it. Her rescuer, a South Carolinian named Edward Wells, dismounted and led her to a nearby ravine to get her out of harm's way. Wells observed that despite the whizzing bullets, the woman occasionally peered over the ravine, "thus showing. . .that female curiosity is stronger even than love of life." The other woman called out from the doorway to Capt. Samuel Pegues of the 3rd Alabama Cavalry, and begged him to rescue her. Pegues was understandably moved by her pleas, for he described her as "a beautiful young Irish woman, in scanty night-dress." The captain reassured the frightened woman and urged her to "retire to the security of her chamber."[41]

The fighting around the Monroe house was a jumble of small battles at close quarters. According to one South Carolina trooper, even a missed shot was bound to hit *someone*. At one point, General Butler witnessed what he later called, "the gamest fight I ever saw," between a Federal horseman and one of his own men whose back was turned to him. Both men fired several times at close range before the Federal tumbled from his saddle. The general later learned that the unknown Confederate was his brother, Capt. James Butler. Nearby, Pvt. Bill Martin was fighting dismounted, his horse having been shot from under him. In the midst of the hand-to-hand combat, Martin saw that a Federal was biting his friend J. H. Moses' finger, so he "lifted the Yankee off" Moses with a blast from his revolver. During the melee an Alabamian named Scales made off with "Spot," one of Kilpatrick's two prized horses. Brigadier

General William W. Allen, one of Wheeler's division commanders, mounted the other, a black stallion, after his own horse was killed in the yard of the house.[42]

While the left half of Wheeler's command was fighting around the Monroe house, the right half, consisting of Brig. Gen. Thomas Harrison's Brigade and Col. Henry M. Ashby's Brigade, was still struggling across a swamp in its front. Several hundred yards to the east, the 1st Alabama Cavalry (U. S.) laid down a heavy fire into the swamp, forcing Harrison's and Ashby's troopers to dismount and seek cover.[43]

The men of the 1st Alabama Cavalry were fiercely independent Unionists from the hilly northern region of the state who refused to truckle to the secessionist cotton planters of the flatlands farther south. In 1862 they formed their own regiment and joined the Union army. For most of the war, these bluecoat Alabamians had served as scouts, raiders, and railroad guards. At the moment, however, they were doing just what they had enlisted to do—fight Rebels.[44]

Stymied by the swamp and the Unionist Alabamians' galling fire, Harrison's and Ashby's troopers withdrew to the west bank and rode northward to find an easier—and safer—route into the Federal camp. As the Confederate fire slackened along the swamp to the west, the men of the 1st Alabama shifted their attention to the fighting north of their bivouac. Assisted by the 5th Kentucky on their right, the Alabama Federals began to press back the Confederates on the ridge to the north. They were joined by some troopers from the 5th Ohio who had grabbed their seven-shot Spencer carbines before bolting for the rear. The combined firepower of the Federals succeeded in pressing back Wheeler's and Butler's men to the vicinity of the Monroe house and enabled the Northerners to recapture their artillery. The veteran Federal troopers were rallying swiftly: the turning point of the battle had arrived.[45]

Realizing that the Yankees had recovered from their initial shock and that Colonel Wright's command had become disorganized, General Butler sent a courier back to order General Law to charge with his brigade. Wheeler rode up and asked Butler where his command was. "Scattered like Hell," the South Carolinian replied. "Where is yours?" Wheeler said that most of his command had encountered a bog and was struggling to get across.[46]

Meanwhile, Lieutenant Stetson and a few artillerymen of the 10th Wisconsin Battery crept up to one of their two guns, rammed a canister round down the barrel, and opened fire. The blast tore a gaping hole in the crowd of Confederate horsemen rallying near the Monroe house. Butler wanted the Federal gun silenced at once, but Young's Brigade was too disorganized to mount a charge. A few of Law's men rode up about this time, but there was no sign of General Law or the rest of the brigade. According to Butler's courier, Hampton had ordered Law to attack at some other point.[47]

Butler scraped together an assault force consisting of detachments from both Law's and Wright's brigades, and placed them under the command of Lt. Col. Barrington S. King of Cobb's Legion. While Butler was massing his force, a handful of dismounted troopers fired on the Federal gun crew, killing or wounding all save Lieutenant Stetson, who in the words of one South Carolinian, "seemed to bear a charmed life." The dismounted Confederates rushed the lone Federal lieutenant, but he steadfastly stood by his piece and yanked the lanyard, mowing them down with a round of canister. Stetson loaded another round just as Lieutenant Colonel King's force came thundering toward him. The brave officer patiently watched the Rebel horsemen bear down upon him. At the last moment, he pulled the lanyard and sent a hailstorm of shrapnel into the charging gray line. One fragment tore through King's thigh, severing an artery and splattering the man next to him with his blood. King was helped to the rear, where he died soon afterward. Moments after King's wounding, Stetson was struck by a pistol shot while loading his cannon. Though the Confederate charge had succeeded in silencing the Federal gun, the 5th Ohio cavalrymen were pouring a murderous fire into the Southerners with their Spencer repeaters. General Butler later wrote that his command sustained 62 casualties during the five-minute battle for the two Union cannon.[48]

The bloodied Confederates fell back and reformed for another charge as Wheeler's and Butler's commands combined for a final onslaught on Kilpatrick's camp. But they failed to drive back the Federals, who refused to yield the ground they had won back. From the swamp, Captain Northrop and his scout company galloped up Blue's Road past Lieutenant Colonel Way's fugitives, and headed straight for the Confederate left flank. Believing that these horsemen were reinforcements from Colonel Jordan's command,

Way's men shouted, "Here comes the 1st Brigade!" The fugitives of the dismounted brigade took heart, and advanced behind Northrop's scouts. The Confederates saw Northrop and his men bearing down on their flank, followed by a line of battle bristling with Springfield rifles and shiny bayonets, and concluded that Kilpatrick's infantry support had arrived.[49]

General Hampton knew that his cavalry had shot its bolt. Moreover, both Butler and Wheeler had already lost too many irreplaceable veterans. Among the severely wounded in Wheeler's command were division commander Brig. Gen. W. Y. C. Humes, and brigade commanders Hagan and Harrison. To add further weight to the already top-heavy casualty list, every field officer in Hagan's Brigade had been killed or wounded. With the apparent arrival of Federal infantry support, there was nothing left for Hampton to do but retreat. The Southerners fell back northward a quarter-mile on Blue's Road, then veered eastward into the woods, with Col. George G. Dibrell's Division serving as rear guard. The Federals pursued Dibrell for about a half-mile before breaking off the chase.[50]

At 8:00 a.m., roughly 30 minutes after the last shot had been fired, Brig. Gen. John G. Mitchell's infantry brigade came double-quicking up Blue's Road from the south. Mitchell's brigade belonged to Morgan's division of the XIV Corps, and had been ordered to Kilpatrick's relief when a breathless cavalryman stumbled into the infantry's camp with news of "Little Kil's" disaster. Guided by the sounds of battle, Mitchell's troops trotted overland through woods and fields for nearly five miles before reaching Kilpatrick's camp. One infantryman recalled that Kilpatrick "looked a little worse for wear, as we saw him without hat, coat or shoes." General Mitchell immediately threw out a skirmish line to cover the northern and eastern sides of the camp. When Mitchell and his command marched back to their camp later that day, they were accompanied by the two ladies, who evidently found life with the cavalry a bit too exciting for their taste. The women traveled with the XIV Corps column to Fayetteville.[51]

Kilpatrick's cavalrymen remained at Monroe's Crossroads until 3:00 p.m., tending their wounded and burying both their own and the Confederate dead. Although General Kilpatrick reported his total loss at 19 killed, 68 wounded and 103 missing, Colonel Spencer reported an almost identical loss for his brigade alone.

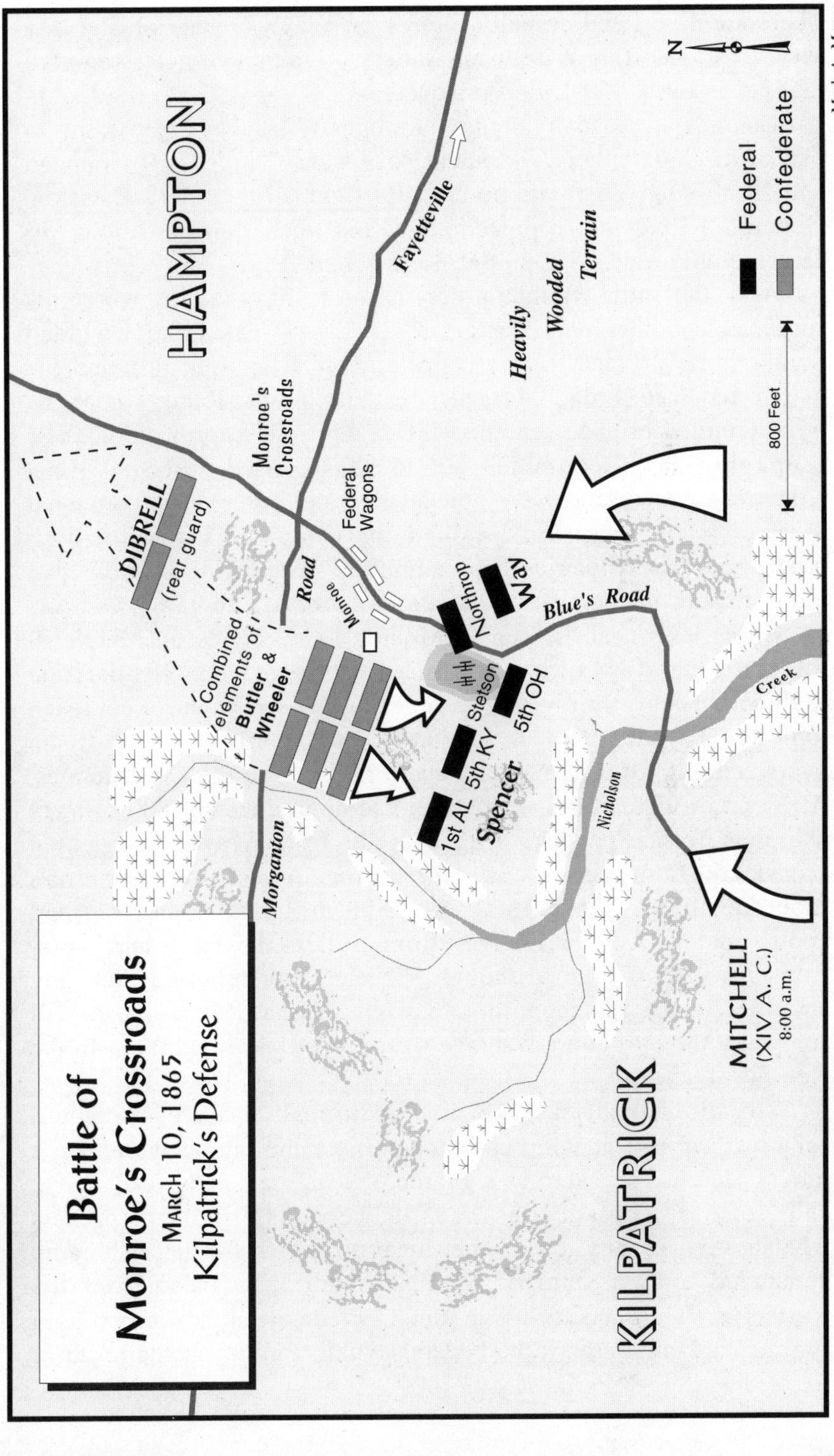
Battle of
Monroe's Crossroads
March 10, 1865
Kilpatrick's Defense
HAMPTON
KILPATRICK
Monroe's Crossroads
Federal Wagons
DIBRELL
(rear guard)
Combined elements of
Butler &
Wheeler
Monroe
Road
Morganton
Fayetteville
Blue's Road
Northrop
Way
Stetson
5th OH
5th KY
1st AL
Spencer
Heavily
Wooded
Terrain
Nicholson
Creek
MITCHELL
(XIV A. C.)
8:00 a.m.
800 Feet
Federal
Confederate
N

Mark A. Moore

There are no official casualty figures for Way's brigade or Stetson's section of the 10th Wisconsin Battery. General Wheeler reported that he captured 350 Union prisoners.[52]

Confederate casualty figures are equally sketchy. According to one of his biographers, Wheeler's loss was 12 killed, 60 wounded and 10 missing. There are no casualty figures for Butler's Division. General Kilpatrick reported that his men buried about 80 Confederate dead and captured 30 prisoners.[53]

After the battle, Hampton pressed on to Fayetteville, where his surgeons and the local doctors and nurses treated the wounded Southern cavalrymen. Later that afternoon, Kilpatrick resumed the march and met Jordan's brigade on the Chicken Road, where his three reunited brigades camped just a few miles north of the XIV Corps' bivouac. Determined not to be surprised a second time, Kilpatrick threw out a heavy picket line and ordered his command to erect a log breastwork around the camp. This was the first prudent act that Kilpatrick had committed since laying his defective trap for the Confederates on the afternoon of March 9.[54]

Kilpatrick's near-disaster at Monroe's Crossroads on March 10 was the result of his own recklessness and imprudence. His decision to divide his cavalry division in order to block Hampton's approach routes to Fayetteville was foolhardy, particularly in view of the overwhelming local numerical superiority it gave the Confederates. At Monroe's Crossroads, Kilpatrick had approximately 800 officers and men from Spencer's brigade, 600 from Way's dismounted brigade, 50 from Stetson's artillery section, and 50 from Northrop's scout company, for a total of 1,500 troopers. Hampton had approximately 1,000 effectives from Butler's Division and 3,000 from Wheeler's Corps. Although Wheeler later reported that only about 1,200 of his men took part in the battle, Hampton still enjoyed a three-to-two advantage over Kilpatrick, in addition to the element of surprise.

Nor did Kilpatrick take any additional measures to guard against a surprise attack, even though his camp lay on the enemy's line of march. The camp was guarded by only a small picket force, and several Confederates recalled encountering no pickets whatsoever. In any case, the location of the Federals' camp demanded a high state of readiness, but it is clear from the Northerners' initial shock that the Confederate attack came as a surprise to them. Perhaps the Federals' vulnerability was the result of fatigue—yet fatigue did not prevent the Confederates from staging a dawn attack. In short, Kilpatrick's lack of concern in the face of such potential danger is inexplicable. Sherman's alleged description of Kilpatrick as "a hell of a damned fool" is particularly apt in the case of Monroe's Crossroads.

Given the Confederates' advantage of surprise and overwhelming numerical superiority, why did their attack fail? The first and foremost reason is that the Confederate cavalrymen were facing veterans like themselves. Although the initial Southern assault succeeded in driving most of the Federals from their camp, these veteran Union troopers had the presence of mind to grab their carbines or rifles as they fled. One Confederate cavalryman, Col. J. F. Waring of the Jeff Davis Legion, credited the Federals with "rallying promptly after the first surprise." Moreover, the Northerners were able to mount an effective resistance even before their officers could gain control of the situation. From the Union standpoint, the Battle of Monroe's Crossroads was a classic soldier's fight.[55]

Another reason for the Confederate repulse was the breakdown in Confederate tactical organization that occurred the moment the attack commenced, when the troopers of Young's Brigade disobeyed orders and rushed the Federal camp in a confused mass rather than in the prescribed column of regiments. Even success contributed to the Southerners' problems, for a substantial number of Confederate troopers broke ranks to plunder the captured wagons. General Butler contended that his assault lost momentum because both his reserve and Wheeler's command failed to support his initial success. General Wheeler echoed Butler's complaint regarding his own reserve. Both generals blamed Hampton for failing to bring up their reserves, but Hampton denied their accusations, claiming that Butler's failure to carry off the enemy's artillery and Wheeler's inability to keep his men in the ranks and out of the captured wagons led to the collapse of the assault. Such finger-pointing among the Confederate cavalry's three senior officers points to the fact that they had lost tactical control of the situation.[56]

Third, the swamp along Nicholson Creek prevented half of Wheeler's striking force from reaching Kilpatrick's camp. The swamp proved to be such an impediment to the Confederates of Humes' Division that they never seriously threatened the 1st

Alabama Unionists. By the time the Georgians and Alabamians of Allen's Division got across the swamp on Wheeler's left, the Federals had recovered from their initial shock and repulsed the attacks. It is difficult to believe that such experienced horsemen as Hampton and Wheeler would have misjudged the nature of this swamp. Perhaps in their haste to reconnoiter Kilpatrick's camp they simply overlooked it. In any case, the swamp nullified the effectiveness of Wheeler's cavalry.

For all their blunders, both sides claimed the Battle of Monroe's Crossroads as a moral and a tactical victory. In his report, Kilpatrick stated that his men "regained their camp, animals, artillery, and transportation, and drove the enemy from the ground he had taken by surprise and force of numbers alone." On the other hand, the Confederates declared themselves the victors because they had captured hundreds of Federals, had freed all of their own men held prisoner by Kilpatrick, and had succeeded in opening the road to Fayetteville.[57]

In any case, Kilpatrick was grateful for Hampton's abrupt departure, and Hampton equally so for Kilpatrick's half-hearted pursuit. For the next few days, the Federal cavalry could rest and lick its wounds, whereas for some of the Confederate horsemen the excitement was far from over.

~ *five* ~

"Remember Us Very Kindly to Mr. Sherman"

—Fayetteville *Daily Telegraph*

Hardee reached Fayetteville on the afternoon of March 9, and met General Johnston at his headquarters in the Fayetteville Hotel. Johnston told Hardee that he was leaving for Raleigh that evening to direct the concentration of the Army of Tennessee troops; then he explained Hardee's new orders to him. There would be no battle at Fayetteville. Instead, Hardee was to withdraw northward on the Raleigh Plank Road east of the Cape Fear River. He was to keep between the Federals and Raleigh, and to govern his movements according to their line of march. Johnston instructed Hardee to burn the bridge across the Cape Fear and to delay the enemy's advance as much as possible without jeopardizing his own command. Hardee assigned General Hampton the task of burning the bridge. Shortly after midnight on the 10th, Hardee received a dispatch from Johnston suggesting that the enemy might be moving on Goldsboro instead of Raleigh, and if so, that he should fall back toward Smithfield in order to combine with the Army of Tennessee troops arriving there.[1]

On the morning of the 10th, Hardee deployed his two divisions in a semi-circle to guard the southern and western approaches to Fayetteville. He also sent his wagon train and reserve artillery across the Cape Fear River with orders to camp on the Raleigh Road two miles north of town. He began the evacuation of the main body at 8:00 p.m. Marching at the head of the column was Hardee's Foreign Battalion—so called because it consisted of Union prisoners who preferred serving as pioneers in the Confederate army to wasting away in a Southern prison. These "galvanized Yankees" were armed only with axes, picks and shovels. They were followed by the ammunition wagons and artillery.[2]

Hardee's infantry marched into town next. "Footsore, weary, dirty and hungry they came," recalled Sarah Tillinghast. "No time for them to cook rations. . . .So on that memorable 10th we all went to work as cooks for Hardee's army." The women of Fayetteville opened their houses to soldiers and kept their tables filled with food. "A good many of them came to get little jobs of sewing or mending done," remembered Fayetteville resident Josephine Bryan Worth:

> One of them stopped at our gate and asked for a hat, and about fifty, more or less, stopped to see what kind of hat he would receive. Now, the only masculine headgear about the house was a wheat-straw hat, whole but rather the worse for the wettings it had received. I ran and got that; it was received with shouts of "New spring hat from Nassau," "Ain't it pretty now," "Give it to me," &c. As the soldier received it he waved it around with three cheers, in which he was joined by all the rest. It is needless to say that I retired in confusion.

In addition to the countless private soldiers, the Bryan home was also visited by a group of grim-faced officers who spoke in hushed tones while studying a large map spread out before them.[3]

The procession continued all night. By dawn the foot soldiers had filed past, only to be replaced by row upon row of horsemen. Twelve-year-old Robert K. Bryan (a cousin of Josephine Bryan) was standing in the doorway of his family's house when "a small man dressed in the uniform of a Confederate general" dismounted before the front gate. Leaving his horse with an orderly, the general walked to the door and asked young Robert to bring him a bowl of water and a towel, which the boy promptly did. The general remarked that he had not washed his face in three days, then added, "Bud, your mother would lick you if you didn't do better than that, wouldn't she?" As the general turned to leave, a staff officer told Robert, "That man you were talking to was General Wheeler."[4]

Seven-year-old Sally Hawthorne and her sister were sent out early by their mother to hand out sandwiches to the soldiers, blissfully unaware of the fact that Sherman's army was also in the vicinity. The two girls entered a wide avenue filled with Confederate horsemen "riding pell mell up the street, on the sidewalk, anywhere, so as to be going uptown" toward the bridge, Sally recalled. She and her sister held up their baskets so that the troopers could grab a sandwich as they rode by. The girls were startled by the sound of gunfire, which caused some of the horses near them to rear and plunge. A "dapper young officer" rode up and told the girls to run home as fast as they could, because "The Yankees are all over town." Then he spurred his horse and galloped up the street. Hand in hand, the two sisters dashed off for home.[5]

General Hampton was eating breakfast at the Fayetteville Hotel with two of his aides when he heard a commotion outside. He went out to investigate and found a detachment of Confederate cavalry galloping down the street toward the bridge. Learning from one of his scouts, Hugh Scott, that the Federals had cut off their approach to the bridge, Hampton called together seven of his men who happened to be nearby—Scott, his two aides, three troopers from Butler's escort company, and a member of Wheeler's command. "Scott, where are they?" Hampton asked, referring to the Federals. The scout replied that they were just beyond the market house (which straddled the main street), and were approaching from the right-hand street corner. Since the Northerners blocked his path to the stable where his horse was, Hampton mounted the nearest horse at hand and gathered his small force about him.[6]

The Federal horsemen belonged to General Howard's scout company, commanded by Capt. William H. Duncan and numbering about 50 men. At daybreak, Howard had sent Duncan ahead with both the scouts and the headquarters escort to reconnoiter the roads into Fayetteville. On reaching the outskirts, Duncan's men drove the Confederate pickets easily and soon reached the center of town. Although Southern cavalrymen appeared to be everywhere, they seemed more anxious to flee than to fight. Duncan ordered the escort company to seize the Cape Fear River Bridge to cut off the enemy's escape, while his own command scouted the town. Duncan was riding so far ahead of the main body that when Hampton's force appeared, the Federal captain found himself cut off from his command.[7]

"Charge them!" Hampton cried. Raising the rebel yell, the Confederates galloped past the market house. The Federals drew their carbines, fired a ragged volley, then wheeled their horses about and fled. In their haste to turn the right-hand corner, the Union horsemen crowded together, making excellent targets for the onrushing Southerners. Hampton shot at least two Federals with his revolver, and another South Carolinian, Edward Wells, later boasted, "I had the pleasure of cleaving one fellow's head with my sabre, besides using my pistol freely."[8]

Captain Duncan found himself trapped between Hampton's force in front and a second enemy detachment approaching from the rear. Putting the spurs to his horse, Duncan galloped into the midst of Hampton's band, alternately firing his revolver to his right and left. Duncan succeeded in dashing past the Confederates, but was overtaken at the edge of town. He was taken back to the hotel, where he was stripped of his uniform and all his personal effects. Hampton received Duncan's sword belt and holster. The wily Duncan made his escape from the Confederates a few days later.[9]

Most of Duncan's command eluded Hampton's squad and galloped back to the Right Wing's advance with news of their repulse and Captain Duncan's capture. The advance consisted of 200 mounted men from Bvt. Maj. Gen. Giles A. Smith's division of the XVII Corps. General Smith had ordered the commander of the mounted force, Lt. Col. J. J. Hibbets, "to take the city if possible, and guard it until forces from the left wing entered it." Hibbets ordered Duncan's men to follow him as he led his augmented command into Fayetteville, skirmishing with Hampton's rear guard all the while. During the fight, Lt. Col. William E. Strong of General Howard's staff rode up and ordered Hibbets to seize the Cape Fear River Bridge. Soon afterward, Fayetteville mayor Archibald McLean surrendered the town to Strong.[10]

Meanwhile, Hibbets' force drove the Confederate cavalry down the street toward the bridge. "Observing a large volume of smoke in the direction of the river," Hibbets assumed that the Southerners had set fire to the bridge, and so turned his attention to posting guards about the town. But he soon learned that the bridge was still intact and that it might yet be saved. When Hibbets and his men dashed up to within a few hundred yards of the bridge, however, Hampton's cavalrymen ignited it. The old covered bridge burned swiftly, having been doused with turpentine. The Federals and

Confederates traded shots from opposite sides of the river until noon, when General Smith arrived with his division. The Southerners prudently fell back.[11]

While the Federal Right Wing entered Fayetteville from the south, the Left Wing approached from the west. Brevet Major General Absalom Baird's division of the XIV Corps had the advance, with the 75th Indiana of Lt. Col. Thomas Doan's brigade thrown forward as skirmishers. The Hoosiers drove Hampton's troopers for five miles before reaching the outskirts of town, where they encountered a line of barricades. The Indianians halted to reform their line before storming the barricades, driving the Confederates before them. The men of the 75th found themselves racing against several other Federal regiments to reach the town first. "Halt!" barked one company commander of the 75th, whose order went unheeded. "Well then, go to hell if you won't halt," he called after them. Despite their haste, Baird's skirmishers reached the center of town just after Mayor McLean had surrendered the city to Lieutenant Colonel Strong, and just as a detail of General Smith's men was raising the Stars and Stripes over the market house. But when General Slocum rode up, General Howard turned over the town to him in obedience to Sherman's orders. "So this question of who should occupy the town first closed up in a very amusing manner," Maj. Thomas Osborn recorded, "and in a way no one could take exception to."[12]

Baird's division occupied the town and immediately cleared out all stragglers. He also posted guards at all public buildings and most private homes. Acting under Sherman's orders, Baird's men destroyed two iron foundries, four cotton mills and the offices of the town's three newspapers—the *Observer*, the *North Carolina Presbyterian* and the *Daily Telegraph*. The Federals no doubt found the *Telegraph's* parting editorial of interest:

> We do not know that we may be compelled to suspend publication of the *Telegraph* before next year. If all the accounts of excited couriers be correct there must be 500,000 Yankees within two hundred yards of Fayetteville to-day. . . .As soon as 400,000 of these dear fellows enter the city from the South, we propose to retire by the road leading North. Some of them don't like us, and rather than have a difficulty, we shall fall back. We beg that some of

> our friends will remember us very kindly to Mr. Sherman. . .and inform him that the speediest way of ending this war is to hang the last man of his command and make his way back to his family. If he don't like this proposition, he can trade his army off for a dog and hang the dog.[13]

General Sherman left Bethel Church at 6:00 a.m. on the 11th, and rode the 26 miles to Fayetteville in six hours. He made his headquarters at the old U. S. Arsenal, where he was greeted by a former Regular Army comrade named Thomas Stevens, the Arsenal's quartermaster. Sherman smiled when he first saw his old friend, but then his face abruptly darkened. The general told Stevens that "a man who had turned traitor to the flag he had served under was too vile a thing to be in his presence," but sent him away with the assurance that his house would be protected. Sherman kept his promise: by March 14, Stevens' house would be the only building left standing on the Arsenal grounds.[14]

At 6:00 a.m. on Sunday, March 12, the morning stillness was broken by the shrill whistle of the tug *Davidson*, which had arrived at Fayetteville after a hazardous night journey from Wilmington. The skipper, Capt. Andrew Ainsworth, immediately proceeded to Sherman's headquarters. On the way, a throng of cheering Union soldiers surrounded Ainsworth and bombarded him with questions. Sherman and his staff welcomed the skipper with no less enthusiasm, though they were disappointed to learn that he had brought along neither letters nor newspapers. The general instructed Ainsworth to remain at Fayetteville until 6:00 p.m., then spent the day writing dispatches and letters. This delay also provided Sherman's men with their long-awaited opportunity to write home. "An hour ago, we were all astounded by the announcement that a mail would leave headquarters at four P.M.," Lt. Col. Charles F. Morse of the 2nd Massachusetts wrote his mother. "If you had quietly stepped up to my shelter and asked me to come and take a comfortable Sunday dinner at home, I should have hardly been more astonished."[15]

General Sherman was proud of what he and his army had accomplished thus far on the march through the Carolinas, as his letters demonstrate. "I have done all I proposed," he boasted to Secretary of War Edwin M. Stanton, "and the fruits seem to me ample for the time employed." In a letter to his wife Ellen,

Sherman wrote, "We have achieved all I aimed to accomplish." And to his close friend and superior, General Grant, he stated, "The army is in splendid health, condition, and spirit, although we have had foul weather and roads that would have stopped travel to almost any other body of men I ever read of." Only to his father-in-law, Thomas Ewing, did Sherman confide his uncertainty: "Thus far I have succeeded admirably and must trust somewhat to chance. War though a science must like all other domains sometimes approach the doubtful."[16]

Sherman also dealt with the mundane—though essential—matter of logistics. "I want you to send me all the shoes, stockings, drawers, sugar, coffee, and flour you can spare," Sherman told General Terry, the commander at Wilmington. "Have the boats escorted, and let them run at night at any risk." Sherman told General Schofield to press on with the rebuilding of the railroad from New Berne to Goldsboro, and Terry was instructed to do the same on his advance from Wilmington. Sherman also expected to make a junction with Schofield at or near Goldsboro, whereupon "we can go wherever we can live."[17]

There was also the matter of the Fayetteville Arsenal, which had been the property of the U. S. government before the war. Believing that "the United States should never again confide such valuable property to a people who have betrayed a trust," Sherman ordered his chief engineer, Col. Orlando M. Poe, to destroy the Arsenal's buildings and machinery. Poe assigned the task to the 1st Michigan Engineers and Mechanics.[18]

The Michiganders began their work at 9:00 a.m. on March 12. "A number of us were given sledge hammers and told to smash all that machinery," recalled Pvt. Henry C. Hackett. "Our hammers were kept busy until all that fine machinery was scrap." Colonel Poe complained that "the clang of hammers & axes wielded by more than a thousand men, is almost enough to drive one crazy." Then the Engineers built battering rams using railroad iron, which they suspended from wooden tripods with chains. The men hammered away at each building from several sides until it collapsed, then moved on to the next one. "The work seemed to please all present," Private Hackett remembered. But the work was also dangerous, as Pvt. James Greenalch discovered. "We were undermining a large building," Greenalch wrote to his family, "and a part of it come down and kild one of our Sargeants that stood by my side and hurt two others. If I had not sprang for my life it wouldent of ben worth a peney to any one."[19]

The work of battering down the Arsenal continued until March 14, when only a heap of rubble and lumber remained, which the Michigan Engineers set ablaze. "A couple of hours sufficed to reduce to ashes everything that would burn," Colonel Poe reported, "so that only a few piles of broken bricks remained of that repossessed arsenal."[20]

On the morning of the 14th, General Sherman and his staff moved out of their quarters on the Arsenal grounds and crossed the Cape Fear River on one of the army's two pontoon bridges. Once across, Sherman set to work writing dispatches, sitting at the same desk as his aides and clerks. He kept a small staff and wrote most of the dispatches himself, utilizing his clerks chiefly as copyists. Sherman's powers of concentration were a frequent source of wonder to his staff. "There is a Band playing in front of the quarters," wrote Sherman's clerk, Vett Noble, "he sits on the opposite side of the desk from me now, and forty bands might be making the nicest music in the world and he wouldn't notice it."[21]

"I am now across Cape Fear River with nearly all my army," Sherman wrote Grant. "I shall. . .draw out ten miles and begin my maneuvers for the possession of Goldsboro." Sherman's plan included a feint on Raleigh with four light divisions from the Left Wing, while the remaining two divisions escorted all nonessential wagons in rear of the Right Wing. Slocum would advance northward up the Raleigh Plank Road until he came to the Goldsboro Road five miles south of Averasboro. From there he would head eastward toward Goldsboro via Bentonville, while Kilpatrick's cavalry and a division of infantry would continue to feint on Raleigh by striking the North Carolina Railroad near Smithfield. Meanwhile, Howard would advance northeastward on a more direct line toward Goldsboro, keeping five divisions in light marching order and ready to assist Slocum. Of Slocum's march toward Bentonville, Sherman wrote, "I do think it is Johnston's only chance to meet this army before an easy junction with Schofield can be effected."[22]

Sherman therefore wanted his army stripped down to fighting trim. All of the army's sick and wounded were loaded onto steamers and sent to Wilmington. Another hindrance that taxed the army's efficiency was the multitude of refugees that had flocked to the Federal army during the march through South Carolina. "I must rid my army of 20,000 to 30,000 useless mouths," Sherman told General Terry. Some of the refugees were sent to Wilmington by steamer, but most of them traveled on foot, accompanied by an escort of several hundred soldiers whose enlistments had expired, all under the command of Maj. John Windsor of the 116th Illinois. As the refugee column wound past Howard's headquarters, the general and his staff stood by the roadside and watched. "It was a singular spectacle," Howard wrote:

> that immense column of every color and every possible description. . . .Bundles on their heads, children in arms, men on mules, women in old wagons, all poorly clad & many with little to eat. They will do anything suffer anything for freedom. They go they know not where. I can only think & say to myself God will care for them.

Major Osborn noted that it took the column three hours to pass Howard's headquarters.[23]

The Federal army also rid itself of all its surplus horses and mules by herding them together and shooting them. The carcasses were left for the townspeople to burn, "and you may try to imagine the odor, if you can," wrote Alice Campbell of Fayetteville.[24]

Several steamers arrived at Fayetteville with supplies of hard bread, sugar, coffee, shoes and oats, but without mail or clothing. "Sending this steamer with forage shows a great lack of appreciation by the commander at Wilmington of the real necessities of the Army," Osborn observed. But in sending the forage, General Terry was merely obeying Sherman's orders to "finish off the loads with oats or corn." The mail and clothing were en route to Beaufort, in anticipation of Sherman's arrival at Goldsboro. Sherman's men would have to wait a few more days for clean clothes and news from home.[25]

Though confident of success, Sherman intended to exercise caution. "I can whip Joe Johnston," he wrote Terry, "provided he don't catch one of my corps in flank, and I will see that my army marches hence to Goldsborough in compact form."[26]

~ *six* ~

"We Heard the Bullets Whistling Their Death Song"

—Peter Funk, 150th New York

Following its withdrawal from Fayetteville on the night of March 10-11, Hardee's Corps marched on the Raleigh Plank Road to Smithville, where it halted. The halt gave many of Hardee's soldiers their first opportunity to write home in nearly a month. "I have again reached a post office from which I can write to you with some prospect of my letter reaching you," Col. George Wortham of the 50th North Carolina wrote his father. "Ever since the fall of Wilmington and Columbia I have been shut off from all communication with home." General Lafayette McLaws noted that he had his clothes washed on Sunday, March 12, and that the washerwoman "satisfied her conscience by charging double price" for working on the Sabbath.

March 14 was payday for the 1st Georgia Regulars, who received six months' back wages in nearly valueless Confederate paper money. Sergeant William H. Andrews sent $50 of his pay home to his mother, who later told him that she had used it to buy 50 pounds of lard—quite a bargain in March 1865.[1]

Smithville (not to be confused with Smithfield) lay about five miles south of Averasboro, at a point where the Cape Fear River and the Black River converged to within two miles of each other. Hardee chose this ground to oppose Sherman's advance in order to use the two rivers and the adjacent swamps to protect his flanks. Furthermore, Hardee's position blocked the junction of the Raleigh

Road and the Goldsboro Road, which meant that the Federals would have to attack him regardless of their destination.[2]

In a post-war memorandum, Hardee stated that he made his stand south of Averasboro to ascertain the strength and destination of the Union forces in his front. If so, he rashly employed his corps in a reconnaissance operation that should have been assigned to a few brigades of Wheeler's cavalry. Moreover, by blocking the roads to Raleigh and Goldsboro, Hardee in fact *prevented* the Federals from disclosing their objective. At any rate, Hardee neglected to mention the two most important reasons for disputing the Federal advance: to buy time for the concentration of Johnston's army, and to give his inexperienced and demoralized command a chance to prove itself.[3]

By mid-March, Hardee's Corps was in danger of disintegrating. On March 10, Goodwyn's Brigade and the Citadel Cadets battalion had left Hardee's command and returned to South Carolina under orders from Governor Magrath. Moreover, desertions continued to erode Hardee's troop strength. By March 15, the corps numbered only 6,455 effectives—a reduction of one-half from the 13,000 who had evacuated Charleston one month earlier. Hardee realized that if he did not fight soon, he would not have a command to fight with.[4] Flagging morale was a constant concern. At dawn on March 15, the men of Rhett's Brigade were assembled to witness the execution of another of their comrades for desertion. Thus far in the campaign, Colonel Rhett had been responsible for more deaths in his command than the Federals. But Rhett's men would soon have a chance to shoot the enemy instead of their own comrades.[5]

At 8:00 a.m. on March 15, Hampton notified Brig. Gen. William Taliaferro that the enemy was advancing up the Raleigh Road in force, driving back Wheeler's cavalry. Taliaferro ordered Colonel Rhett's Brigade into a position straddling the Raleigh Plank Road, along the upper edge of a field about 400 yards north of the John Smith house. From left to right, Rhett's Brigade consisted of the 1st South Carolina Infantry (Regulars), Lucas' Battalion and the 1st South Carolina Artillery (Regulars). While Rhett's troops threw up light earthworks, Taliaferro sent out skirmishers and ordered up a section of 12-pounder howitzers from Capt. G. LeGardeur's Battery and one 12-pounder Napoleon from Capt. Henry M. Stuart's Battery. The three field pieces unlimbered on the extreme right of Rhett's line. Taliaferro then deployed Stephen Elliott's

Brigade behind a swamp about 200 yards in rear of Rhett's position. At 11:00 a.m., Hardee instructed McLaws to deploy his division about 600 yards in rear of Elliott's line. Hardee's decision to oppose the Federals surprised McLaws: "Never thought about making a stand about Averasboro," he confided to his journal.[6]

When Hardee reached the front, he ordered Taliaferro to push Rhett's skirmishers forward until they developed the enemy. Now it was Taliaferro's turn to be surprised. He had intended to withdraw Rhett's Brigade to Elliott's line once his wagon train was out of danger; instead, Hardee chose to employ a three-line defense. "Old Reliable" was keenly aware that most of Taliaferro's troops lacked field combat experience. His intent was for them to delay the Federals before falling back to the main line, which was occupied by McLaws' more seasoned troops.[7]

As the South Carolinians advanced southward through the pine woods searching for Federals, Wheeler's rear guard fell back through their line. About 3:00 p.m. Rhett's skirmishers collided with the 9th Michigan Cavalry of Atkins' brigade a half-mile south of Rhett's main line. The Michiganders dismounted and drove back the outgunned Confederates by laying down a steady fire with their repeating Spencer carbines. Meanwhile, the rest of Atkins' brigade deployed on either side of the road and built barricades. Once Kilpatrick's other two brigades were up, the 9th Michigan withdrew to the main line, closely followed by Rhett's aggressive skirmishers. Taliaferro's three field pieces joined in by hurling shells at the Federals. Atkins' section of the 10th Wisconsin Battery replied in kind, although neither side gained any significant advantage. By nightfall the skirmish firing gave way to a downpour of rain.[8]

During the afternoon's skirmishing, Kilpatrick's chief of scouts, Capt. Theo Northrop, together with three of his men, ventured beyond the Federal lines to reconnoiter the Confederate position. The day was rainy and foggy, limiting visibility in the thick pine woods. As Northrop and his men rode up the bank of a small ravine, they glimpsed Colonel Rhett's main line lying just beyond the field in their front. The Federal scouts also spied a group of mounted Confederate officers surrounded by their staffs and couriers 100 yards to the left. One of Northrop's men raised his Spencer carbine and took aim at them, but Northrop—"remembering about the boy and the hornet's nest"—checked him before he could squeeze off a shot. Northrop concluded that he and his men had somehow slipped through the Confederates' skirmish line and were now in danger of being captured. The Federal captain wheeled his horse about, and as he led his scouts back into the ravine, spied two approaching horsemen. One of the men asked him, "Where are Gens. Hampton and Taliaferro?"[9]

Northrop could not believe his good fortune. "They are right back here a short distance on the road," he said, delighted that the two unsuspecting Confederate officers had fallen into his grasp. As the two Southerners passed by, Northrop said, "You will have to come with us."

"Do you know who you're talking to?" one of the Confederates shot back. "I am Colonel Rhett." Undeceived as to Northrop's identity, Rhett reached for his revolver, but one of the Federals pressed the muzzle of his carbine to Rhett's ear. "Well, this is cool," Rhett said, dropping his pistol.[10]

Northrop and his trio of scouts eluded the Confederate skirmishers and returned to Kilpatrick's headquarters with Colonel Rhett and his adjutant. "Hello, Northrop," Kilpatrick said. "What troops are these we are fighting?"

"Taliaferro's Division. . .from Charleston," Northrop replied. "I have one of the brigade commanders with me."

"The hell you have," Kilpatrick retorted.

"So I introduced him [to] Col. Alfred Rhett," Northrop recalled. The ensuing conversation was both brief and heated. When Rhett told Kilpatrick that he had been taken in by a "D— Yankee trick," "Little Kil" answered him with a laugh. But when Rhett boasted that there would soon be "50,000 fresh men ready and waiting" to fight him, Kilpatrick's smile vanished. "Yes," he said, "and if that is true we will have to hunt the swamps to find the d—d cowards."[11]

Kilpatrick turned his prisoners over to General Sherman, who had his headquarters in an old cooper shop. Sherman described Rhett as "a tall, slender, and handsome young man, dressed in the most approved rebel uniform, with high jackboots beautifully stitched." Rhett's reception at Sherman's headquarters was a good deal more hospitable than it had been at Kilpatrick's. In fact, it proved to be a reunion of sorts, for the South Carolinian knew Generals Sherman, Slocum and Davis from their pre-war army days in Charleston. During dinner the four men talked over old times. Davis and Rhett might even have laughed over the irony of their having lobbed shells at each other during the firing on Fort Sumter four years earlier, for Rhett had commanded an artillery battery at Fort Moultrie across the harbor from Davis.[12]

Not everyone at Sherman's headquarters was taken with Colonel Rhett. One of Sherman's aides, Maj. Henry Hitchcock, called Rhett a "devil in human shape":

> He was a complete specimen of his class: well-educated, fluent, "a gentleman," in all *exterior* qualities, of an easy assurance of manner and well-bred self-confidence admirably calculated to make an impression. . . .but. . .whose polished manners and easy assurance made only more hideous to me the utterly heartless & selfish ambition & pride of class which gave tone to his whole discourse.[13]

Hitchcock would not have been surprised to learn that the 35-year-old Alfred Moore Rhett was a graduate of Harvard (class of 1851); that the two recurrent topics of his correspondence were his rice plantation and his hunting dogs; and that he had a penchant for dueling, having fought three between 1853 and 1862. Rhett's most recent duel was waged in response to a challenge from his superior officer, Col. W. R. Calhoun, who was mortally wounded in the gentlemen's *affaire d'honneur*. Although dueling between officers was forbidden under Confederate military law, Rhett escaped punishment because the law conflicted sharply with the Southern gentleman's code of honor at that time, and because his father was the noted newspaper publisher and secessionist firebrand, Robert Barnwell Rhett. Nevertheless, it was a source of some embarrassment to the commander at Charleston, General Beauregard, that Colonel Calhoun's death resulted in Rhett's elevation to command of the Fort Sumter garrison and his promotion to colonel.[14]

Rhett had remained in command at Fort Sumter until the evacuation of Charleston. During his tenure he earned a reputation as a stern disciplinarian. As Rhett told his audience of Union generals:

> discipline's the thing: all you have to do is establish the principle. Why, I've shot twelve men myself in the last six weeks, and not long ago I took a pack of dogs and went into the swamps, and in three days I caught twenty-eight men with them.

As Rhett talked on, Sherman smiled in amusement, while Hitchcock gaped in horrified disbelief.[15]

That night, Rhett slept in Slocum's tent, but the following morning he was turned over to General Davis' provost marshal. Soon afterward, Kilpatrick applied for Rhett's transfer to his care, having heard that the South Carolinian had mistreated some Federals captured in the Monroe's Crossroads fight. As the cavalry escort led him away, Rhett boasted to one of his guards that he was the man who had ordered the firing of the first shot on Fort Sumter—hardly the sort of talk calculated to endear him to his captors. Following Captain Duncan's return to the army—minus his uniform and accouterments—Kilpatrick retaliated by authorizing his men to treat Rhett in like manner, and the Confederate colonel was compelled to exchange his fine boots for a pair of mud-caked brogans.[16]

* * *

While the opposing forces were converging in the vicinity of Averasboro, Henry Slocum's infantrymen slogged along in a sea of mud, thankful to be encumbered by no more than their ambulances and a few dozen headquarters and ordnance wagons. Slocum's four light divisions marched in the following order: William T. Ward's and Nathaniel J. Jackson's divisions of the XX Corps, followed by James D. Morgan's and William P. Carlin's divisions of the XIV Corps. Slocum had 20,000 men in all, including Kilpatrick's cavalry. The column halted at dusk, and soon the pine woods were aglow with campfires.[17]

The men of Col. William Hawley's brigade of Jackson's division encamped at Bluff Church and ate their suppers in a drenching rain. By 7:30 p.m. many of them were already dozing among the grave mounds and headstones when a courier galloped up with a message for Hawley. Moments later came the order to fall in. The cemetery was suddenly alive with hundreds of darting figures illuminated by lightning flashes. By 8:00 p.m. Hawley's brigade was packed up and on the march to reinforce Kilpatrick's cavalry at the front.[18]

"The men furnished themselves with [burning] pine-knots," wrote Capt. Daniel Oakey of the 2nd Massachusetts:

> and our weapons glistened in the torch-light, a cloud of black smoke from the torches floating back over our heads. The regimental wits were as ready as ever, and amid a flow of lively badinage we toiled on through the mud. When the column was halted. . .to give us an opportunity of drawing breath, I found Sergeant Johnson with one arm in the mud up to the elbow. He explained that he was trying to find his shoe.

Hawley's men floundered on for five miles, reaching the front at 12:30 a.m. on March 16, when they relieved Atkins' brigade at their barricades. "Those who were exhausted sank down in the mud to sleep," Captain Oakey recalled, "while others speculated on the future."[19]

At 2:00 a.m. on March 16, a courier rode up to Sherman's headquarters with dispatches from Generals Howard and Terry. Sherman was awake when the messages arrived and anxiously tore them open. The news was good: Howard's wing was crossing South River and so far had met with only token opposition from Butler's cavalry; Terry reported that Schofield had reached Kinston en route to Goldsboro. "So all is working well around us and we must not scatter," Sherman wrote Howard, "but aim to converge about Bentonville, and afterward Goldsborough." Although Hardee blocked the route to Goldsboro, Sherman calculated that his opponent had only 10,000 men and could be shoved back once Slocum was in position. "Hardee is ahead of me and shows fight," Sherman told Terry. "I will go at him in the morning with four divisions and push him as far as Averasborough before turning toward Bentonville and Cox's Bridge."[20]

During the night the rain slackened and the musicians of the 2nd Massachusetts brass band played an impromptu concert for the soldiers at the front. Just a few hundred yards to the north, Lt. Edward Middleton and his picket force from the 1st South Carolina Artillery listened to the strains of "'Cottage by the Sea' & several other airs," Middleton noted in his diary.[21]

At daybreak, the musicians packed up their instruments and reported to the division hospital for duty as stretcher bearers and hospital stewards in the coming battle near Averasboro.

* * *

Thursday, March 16, dawned gray and cloudy, promising another day of heavy rainfall. The 8th Indiana Cavalry of Jordan's brigade rode forward at 6:00 a.m., passing around the right flank of Hawley's brigade, whose skirmishers greeted them with, "Here comes the cavalry! It will be a whoop and a yell, and back they will come!" Angered by the foot soldiers' insults, the Hoosier cavalrymen plunged into the pine forest, driving the Confederate pickets and skirmishers into their works "in the wildest confusion," reported the 8th's commander, Lt. Col. Fielder A. Jones, who was laboring under the delusion that he had routed Rhett's Brigade. "Had our infantry then pushed forward it is my firm belief that we could have captured the enemy's works, artillery, and many prisoners, without the firing of a shot." Jones no doubt made this contention with the infantrymen's taunts still ringing in his ears. "Had there been solid ground I should have taken their works with cavalry," Jones added, "but the rains of the previous night had made the country one vast mire, which checked the impetus of our charge, and gave the enemy time to reform behind their works." The ground proved so spongy that Jones ordered his regiment to dismount, and had the horses led to the rear.[22]

The new commander of Rhett's Brigade, Col. William Butler, reinforced his skirmish line and sent it forward again. Although the 8th Indiana was armed with Spencer carbines, the Hoosiers soon found themselves outgunned and outflanked and were driven back. Colonel Jordan sent the 9th Pennsylvania Cavalry in on the 8th's right to bolster the advance, followed in rapid succession by the 2nd and 3rd Kentucky Cavalry regiments. Butler's South Carolinians attacked Jordan's position repeatedly, but were repulsed each time. The fighting on the right became so hot that Kilpatrick directed General Atkins to advance to Jordan's support and assume command in that sector. Atkins reached Jordan's position about 10:00 a.m., when he learned that the latter's brigade had nearly run out of ammunition. He ordered his two Spencer-toting regiments, the 9th Michigan Cavalry and the 92nd Illinois Mounted Infantry, to relieve Jordan's troopers, whose ammunition wagons were well to the rear.[23]

In contrast to the Federal right flank, the rest of the line was quiet. "We hoped that the rebels had left," wrote Peter Funk of the 150th New York, Hawley's brigade,

> but we were bitterly disappointed. . . .The skirmishers advanced, we followed close at their heels. They had not gone more than 50 yards before they were saluted by a volley from the rebel picket [sic], and we heard the bullets whistling their death song as they hummed by us.

Hawley's skirmishers soon discovered that the Confederates in their front were strongly entrenched and supported by artillery, so Hawley decided to wait for the rest of the XX Corps to arrive before launching an attack.[24]

While awaiting the order to advance, an officer in the 13th New Jersey overheard Sherman and his cavalry chief discussing the situation:

"General Kilpatrick, I want you to move your cavalry to the left and develop the enemy's line."

"How do you propose that I shall do it?" Kilpatrick inquired.

"Move your men to the left and engage the enemy," Sherman replied. "Develop their line—make a damn big time—you know how to do it, you know how to do it."

Kilpatrick accordingly ordered Spencer's brigade to deploy on Hawley's left flank.[25]

The three brigades of Bvt. Maj. Gen. William T. Ward's division reached the battlefield about 9:00 a.m. and deployed in line of battle. From left to right, Ward's line consisted of the brigades of Col. Daniel Dustin, Bvt. Brig. Gen. William Cogswell, and Col. Henry Case. Soon afterward, the two remaining brigades of Brig. Gen. Nathaniel J. Jackson's division joined Hawley's brigade at the front. Jackson's division in turn formed on Ward's right, beginning with Hawley on the left, followed by Brig. Gen. James S. Robinson's brigade in the center, and Col. James L. Selfridge's brigade on the right. Selfridge's brigade had no sooner gotten into position than Kilpatrick's cavalry came tumbling back in retreat on its right. When the pursuing South Carolinians burst into view,

Selfridge's first line opened fire on the advancing enemy. The initial Federal volley took the Confederates by surprise, and they soon fell back in disorder. Union officers quickly rallied the disordered cavalry, directing the horsemen to their place on Selfridge's right.[26]

Jackson's and Ward's divisions now advanced to within 500 yards of Rhett's main line. Dustin's brigade held the extreme left of the Federal line, relieving Spencer's brigade, and now faced the John Smith house and field. From left to right, Dustin's four regiments were: the 33rd Indiana, 22nd Wisconsin (which faced the house), 85th Indiana and 19th Michigan, whose right flank touched the left of the Raleigh Plank Road. Only the 33rd enjoyed the comparative safety of the woods; the other three regiments were drawn up in the open field. Dustin ordered his men to lie down to avoid the enemy artillery's shells, which "whizzed and burst dangerously. . .close at hand," the 22nd's William McIntosh noted.[27]

As if on cue, three XX Corps batteries rumbled into the Smith field and orchard in Dustin's front, and brazenly unlimbered their 12 guns on a rise less than 500 yards from the South Carolinians' line. From left to right, these batteries were: Lt. Jerome B. Stephens' (Battery C, 1st Ohio), Capt. Charles E. Winegar's (Battery I, 1st New York), and Lt. Edward P. Newkirk's (Battery M, 1st New York). While Dustin's men laid down a steady supporting fire, the three Union batteries blasted the right and center of the South Carolinians' line with a deadly combination of solid shot, spherical case and fused shells. The fire soon silenced the Confederate artillery. A Federal projectile disabled one of Captain LeGardeur's two howitzers, while another scored a direct hit on one of LeGardeur's limber chests. The resulting explosion killed or wounded several nearby artillerymen and draft horses.[28]

Having blocked the Federal advance for nearly five hours, Rhett's Brigade was now hard pressed along its entire line. But the South Carolinians had accomplished their task. Although numbering only 1,051 men, they had fought with the tenacity of veterans, forcing Sherman to consume most of the morning deploying Kilpatrick's cavalry and the two divisions of the XX Corps—12,000 men in all. On the afternoon of the 15th, Hardee had instructed Taliaferro to hold the line occupied by Rhett's Brigade "until it was no longer tenable, then fall back upon" Elliott's line. Clearly the time to withdraw had arrived, but the South Carolinians' position was now under such a heavy and continuous

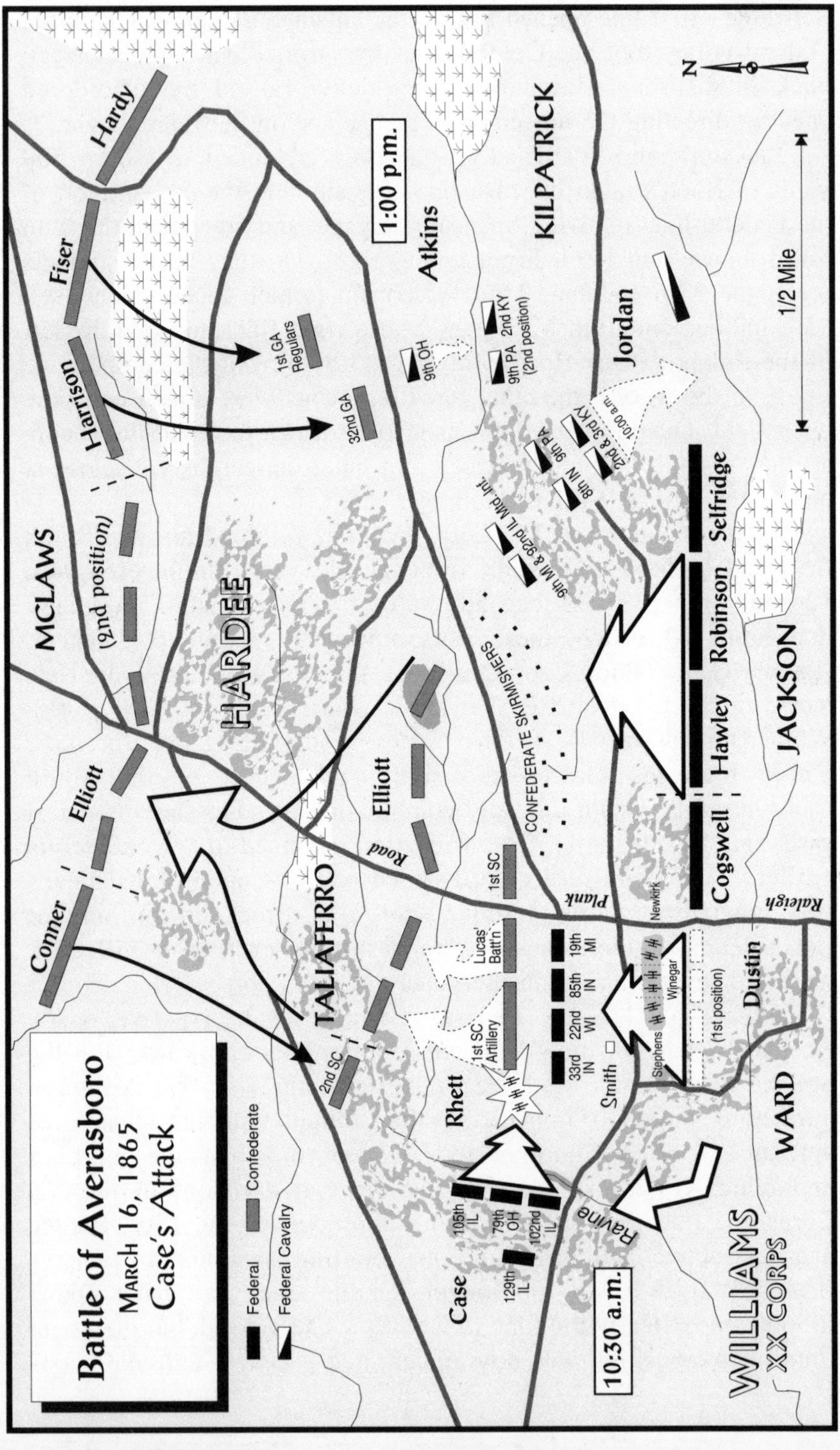
Battle of Averasboro
March 16, 1865
Case's Attack
Federal
Federal Cavalry
Confederate
MCLAWS
HARDEE
KILPATRICK
JACKSON
WARD
WILLIAMS
XX CORPS
1:00 p.m.
10:30 a.m.
Hardy
Fiser
Harrison
(2nd position)
Elliott
Conner
Taliaferro
2nd SC
1st SC
Elliott
Rhett
1st SC Artillery
Lucas' Batt'n
1st GA Regulars
32nd GA
Atkins
9th OH
2nd KY
9th PA
(2nd position)
Jordan
CONFEDERATE SKIRMISHERS
9th MI & 92nd IL Mtd. Inf.
8th IN
9th PA
2nd & 3rd KY
10:00 a.m.
Selfridge
Robinson
Hawley
Cogswell
Dustin
Newkirk
Winegar
Stephens
(1st position)
33rd IN
22nd WI
85th IN
19th MI
Smith
Plank
Road
Raleigh
Ravine
Case
105th IL
79th OH
102nd IL
129th IL
1/2 Mile
N

Mark A. Moore

fire that an orderly withdrawal would have been a difficult proposition even for seasoned veterans—to say nothing of Rhett's green troops. Even so, their situation was about to become far more desperate.[29]

About 10:30 a.m. Sherman directed Slocum to send a brigade around Rhett's right flank in order to turn it. Slocum passed the order on to Williams, who sent a staff officer to Col. Henry Case with instructions to withdraw his brigade from the main line and make the attack. Colonel Case fell back a short distance, waited for Cogswell and Hawley to close the gap in his front, and then led his column around Dustin's left flank. Case deployed his brigade as it advanced through the woods and swamps west of the John Smith farm, positioning the 79th Ohio and 102nd Illinois, left to right, in the main line of battle, and the 129th and 105th Illinois regiments in reserve, formed in column of divisions. (As used in this instance, a *division* signifies two companies of a regiment.) Case's fifth regiment, the 70th Indiana, remained in the rear as a train guard.

As Case's line moved forward through the woods, the skirmishers of the 102nd Illinois collided with a portion of Rhett's skirmish line and easily drove them off. As his advance entered a ravine, Colonel Case dismounted and crept up to the treeline. The woods and brush were so thick that he had to lie prone to see into the Smith field. About 300 yards in his front stood the open right flank of Rhett's line. Leaping to his feet, Case dashed back to his command and ordered the 105th Illinois to form on the left of the 79th Ohio. Then Case ordered a charge. "[We] broke for. . .the Johnnies. . .on the run," wrote Pvt. Thomas Finley of the 102nd Illinois, "and [with] a demoniac yell we rushed in on [their] flank pouring volley after volley from our Spencers."[30]

While Case pushed his men forward to deliver the *coup de grace* to Rhett's unsuspecting battle line, Colonel Dustin received the order to advance against Rhett's front. As Dustin's line of battle passed through the Federal batteries, the men shouted three loud huzzah's. Rhett's men wasted little time in training their weapons on Dustin's advancing columns. Fire from the Confederate line was so severe on the 19th Michigan and the 85th Indiana that Dustin ordered his brigade to execute a left oblique to exploit the cover of the woods and the Smith farm buildings. After the line halted to reform, Dustin ordered his men to fire a volley and advance at the double-quick. The Federals rushed across the field, "fully expecting to meet a charge of. . .canister," recorded Sgt. Charles H. Dickinson of the 22nd Wisconsin, "but nothing came but a volley of musketry. . .and fortunately for us. . .the bullets nearly all went over us." Seeing that the Federals were charging them from both their front and right flank, the men of Rhett's Brigade fled their position at the "treble-quick," noted Lt. Bill Colcock of the 1st South Carolina Artillery, which had been holding the right of Rhett's battered line. "[T]he Johnnies showed their heels as fast as God would let them," the 102nd Illinois' Thomas Finley wrote. One of Finley's comrades, Laforest Dunham of the 129th Illinois, admitted, "I was never so pleased in my life as I was to see the rebs get up and try to get out of the way."[31]

Raising a cheer, the Federals broke into a sprint. Case's troops reached the South Carolinians' works first, closely followed by Dustin's men. When the Federals saw the carnage behind those works, their cheering abruptly ceased. "It was the terriblest slaughter of men that I ever witnessed," Private Finley recorded. Sergeant Dickinson of the 22nd Wisconsin found a wounded Confederate artilleryman lying:

> in the mud in the bottom of the ditch; he had been hit by a cannon ball from one of our guns, which had gone through at least six feet of earth works, it had torn off the whole right side of his body, and he begged of our men to shoot him, to put him out of misery and pain; but he only lived a few minutes.

Dickinson also learned why he had not had to face artillery fire during the charge. He saw six white horses, "dead and horribly mangled, which had evidently. . .been hitched to the limber" that had exploded earlier in the fight. "[T]he gunners and drivers were laying about, what was left of them, mangled. . .past recognition; it was no wonder that gun was silenced."[32]

Of the three field pieces on Rhett's line, the Federals captured two—one howitzer and one Napoleon. The XX Corps' chief of artillery, Maj. John A. Reynolds, ordered the captured Napoleon turned and fired on the Confederates, using their own ammunition. Meanwhile, the three XX Corps batteries arrived and unlimbered on the reverse side of Rhett's former works.[33]

While Case's and Dustin's men rounded up prisoners, Federal stretcher bearers carried the wounded of both sides to the John Smith house—also known as Oak Grove—where Union hospital stewards put up tents, unloaded the wounded from ambulances, and helped the surgeons at the amputation tables.[34]

About 1:00 p.m., the two XX Corps divisions and Kilpatrick's cavalry advanced against Elliott's line 200 yards to the north—Hardee's second line of defense. Scouts from the 9th Ohio Cavalry, which held the extreme right flank of the Federal line, informed General Kilpatrick that they had found a road leading around the Confederates' left flank, and recently captured Confederate prisoners claimed that their units were falling back. Kilpatrick accordingly ordered the 9th's commander, Col. William D. Hamilton, to advance up that road and find the Confederate flank. When Colonel Hamilton replied that his regiment was almost out of ammunition, Kilpatrick told him not to fire upon the enemy—a strange order to give a commander embarking on an offensive operation.[35]

At about the same time, McLaws received a report from one of his staff officers that "the enemy's cavalry were about flanking [Elliott's] left flank." McLaws immediately ordered forward two of his veteran regiments, the 32nd Georgia of Col. George P. Harrison's Brigade and the 1st Georgia Regulars of Col. John C. Fiser's Brigade, to intercept the Federal cavalry. Sergeant W. H. Andrews commanded the right wing of the Regulars' Company M, and though his unit was on the skirmish line, he was under orders not to fire because Elliott's Brigade was somewhere in his front. McLaws later noted that the woods in his front were so thick that Elliott's line was invisible to him from his vantage point on the third line. As Andrews recalled it:

> The 32nd Georgia was about 150 yards in front, a little to my right, lying down in the bushes, and when the enemy's cavalry was within 75 yards [the 32nd] rose up and fired a volley into them. . . .The cavalry without changing their gait obliqued to the right. . .while the 32nd moved by the left flank, still firing into them. It was the first cavalry I had ever seen under fire, and they looked so grand and imposing that I almost forgot I had a gun, but I did wake up and ordered the right of Company M to give them a little lead

> while they were passing. I had three shots at them, and I saw a number of horses pass out from there without any riders, but at the same time retaining their place in line.[36]

The firing of the right wing of Company M soon brought the company's commander, Capt. James R. DuBose, "up the line to see what the trouble was," Andrews continued. "I told the captain I could not help it for the [Union] cavalry was too tempting a target to pass up. . . .He gave me Hail Columbia for disobeying orders." Their flanking maneuver blocked, the 9th Ohio Cavalry fell back several hundred yards and rallied. The 32nd Georgia pursued the Federal horsemen for a short distance, then withdrew to the main line.[37]

McLaws sent a third veteran regiment forward—the 2nd South Carolina of Conner's Brigade—to protect Elliott's right flank. Although the 2nd connected on the right of Elliott's line and drove back the Federal skirmishers in its front, the Northerners soon returned in line of battle and drove off Elliott's troops and Rhett's dazed fugitives with little trouble. The post of rear guard thus fell to the 2nd South Carolina by default. "As our force was not large enough to hold Sherman's army," W. A. Johnson, a member of the 2nd, observed, "we retired decently and in order. . .until we reached. . .our old position."[38]

As the second line of defense crumbled, General Hardee directed Taliaferro to deploy Elliott's Brigade in the center of the third line, astride the Raleigh Plank Road, with Rhett's Brigade drawn up in reserve. McLaws' Division accordingly deployed on either side of Elliott. Colonel Washington Hardy's Brigade of North Carolinians held the extreme left of Hardee's main line, extending to the swamps along Black River. Fiser's Brigade formed on Hardy's right, and Harrison's Brigade occupied the left center of the line between Fiser and Elliott. Conner's Brigade deployed on the right of Elliott. Hardee was delighted to see General Wheeler ride up at this time at the head of Humes' and Allen's divisions. The cavalrymen immediately deployed on Conner's right, extending Hardee's line to the Cape Fear River. Thanks to the addition of Wheeler's two cavalry divisions, Hardee now had about 8,000 well-entrenched soldiers to oppose Sherman's veteran force of 20,000, tolerable odds given the situation.[39]

Wheeler's troopers had arrived none too soon, for Brig. Gen. James D. Morgan's division of the Federal XIV Corps was now advancing on the left of Ward's division with the intention of turning Hardee's right flank. Brigadier General John G. Mitchell's brigade formed on the left of Ward's division, closely followed by Bvt. Brig. Gen. Benjamin D. Fearing's brigade, which deployed on Mitchell's left, extending the Federal line toward the Cape Fear River. Morgan held Brig. Gen. William Vandever's brigade in reserve. Fearing was so confident of turning the Confederates' right flank that he ordered his brigade to execute a right half-wheel without first reconnoitering his position. "Contrary to the expectation of all," Fearing wrote, "we found works in our front and extending far to our left." Fearing now deployed skirmishers to develop the Southerners' line—something he should have done *before* he had attempted his flanking maneuver. The skirmishers reported that Hardee's line extended a half-mile to the bluffs overlooking the Cape Fear River. There was no longer an exposed Rebel flank to turn.[40]

Fearing notified Morgan that the Confederates were well-entrenched in his front and on his left, but for some reason failed to mention that he had developed the enemy's line all the way to the river. Morgan therefore ordered Vandever's five regiments to form on Fearing's left in the mistaken belief that they could turn Hardee's right flank from that position. After securing Davis' permission to make the attack, Morgan ordered Vandever forward. Vandever's men encountered a ravine "some 40 feet in depth, with. . .almost perpendicular banks," wrote a private in the 10th Michigan who signed himself "W. F." "We could only descend by the help of bushes which grew on either bank, swinging down from point to point, crossing a stream at the bottom, and again drawing ourselves up by the shrubbery on the opposite side."[41]

After his men had gained the top, Vandever deployed his brigade in two lines. From left to right, the 16th Illinois, 17th New York, and 14th Michigan manned the front line, and the 60th Illinois and 10th Michigan followed in reserve. They advanced only 400 yards before encountering a second ravine. Vandever sent forward several companies of the 60th Illinois and the 17th New York as skirmishers, but the fire of Wheeler's troopers pinned them down on the opposite bank. A few hundred yards to the rear, Vandever's main line dashed for the cover of nearby trees, logs

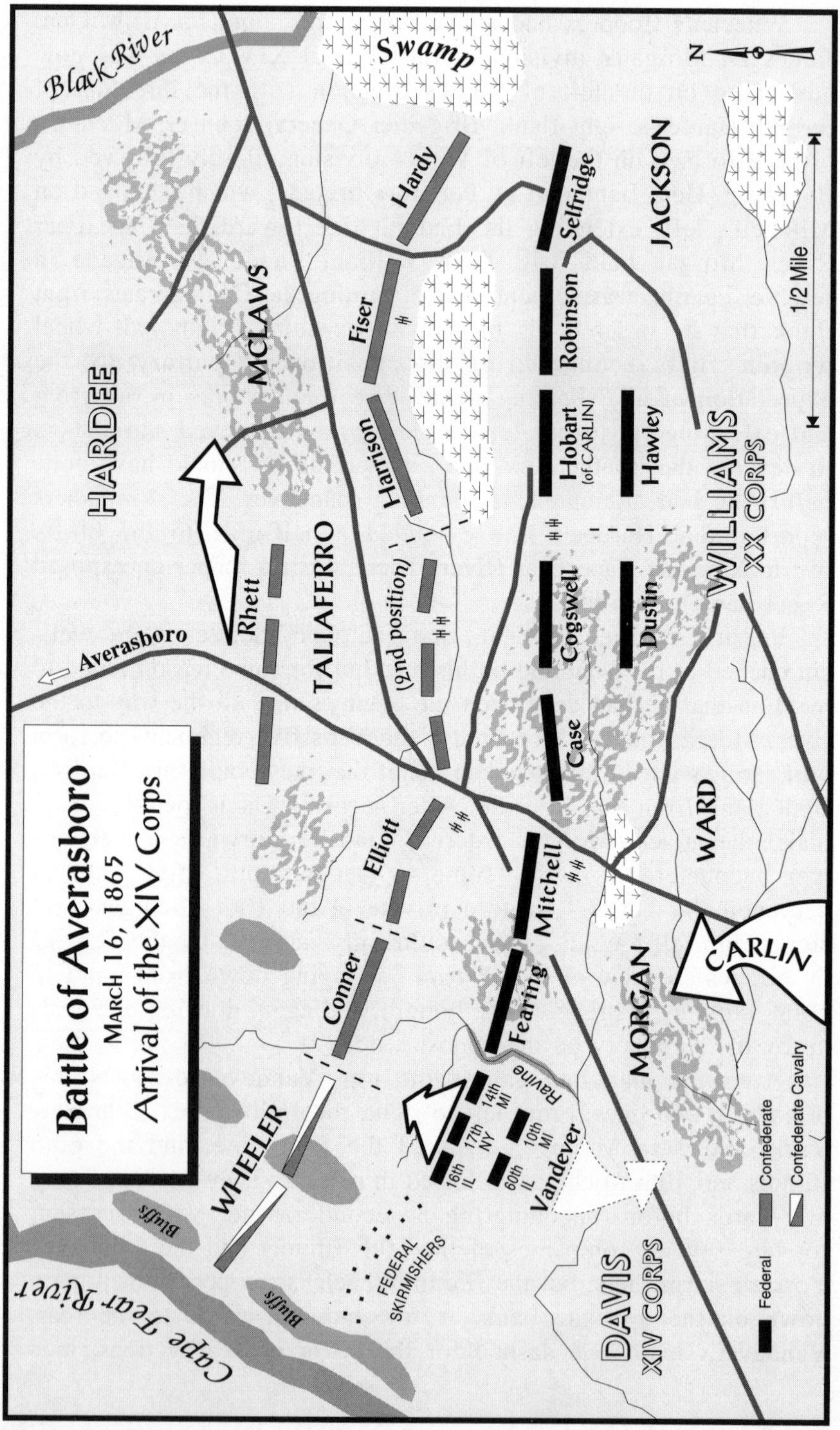
Battle of Averasboro
March 16, 1865
Arrival of the XIV Corps
Mark A. Moore
Black River
Swamp
Cape Fear River
Bluffs
Bluffs
Averasboro
HARDEE
MCLAWS
TALIAFERRO
Hardy
Fiser
Harrison
Rhett
(2nd position)
Elliott
Conner
WHEELER
FEDERAL SKIRMISHERS
16th IL
17th NY
14th MI
60th IL
10th MI
Ravine
Vandever
Fearing
Mitchell
Case
Cogswell
Dustin
Hobart (of CARLIN)
Hawley
Robinson
Selfridge
JACKSON
WARD
MORGAN
CARLIN
WILLIAMS
XX CORPS
DAVIS
XIV CORPS
1/2 Mile
N
Federal
Confederate
Confederate Cavalry

and—in the case of two companies of the 10th Michigan—a pile of corn. On the skirmish line, the 17th New York's commander, Lt. Col. James Lake, raised his sword to lead a charge, but was shot in the right forearm. Slipping the knot from his wrist, Lake grasped the sword in his left hand, then fell with a bullet wound in the groin. Consequently, the attack was never made.[42]

Seeing that the Confederates were dug in all the way to the river, a bitterly disappointed Morgan concluded that "it would have been worse than folly to have attempted a farther advance." He left a skirmish line behind to observe Wheeler's position and ordered Vandever's brigade to fall back to the rear of Fearing's brigade.[43]

As the afternoon wore on, the XX Corps line advanced beyond Elliott's abandoned works in fits and starts. The enlisted men considered this a foolish tactic. "The bugle would sound the forward and we would advance a few steps and lie down," recalled Charles Castle of the 129th Illinois. "This was repeated about every hour, the intention being merely to press the enemy." Castle knew that the bugle calls signaling "Attention" and "Forward" were also signals for the enemy to open fire, and at each advance, "the canister would rattle around lively for a while." One of Castle's comrades, Orange Daniels of the 102nd Illinois, thought a charge "would have taken the force confronting us with less casualties than by following the lying down tactics."[44]

Recent rains, and the resulting sea of mud, had a good deal to do with the stop-and-go advance. Slocum's orders to Williams were to press the enemy, but not to attack until both divisions of the XIV Corps were up. The muddy roads and rainy weather prevented all of Carlin's division from reaching the front until dusk, when Sherman decided to postpone the assault until morning. Hence the cautious advance on Hardee's third line. [45]

Lafayette McLaws noted that the Federals who attacked his line had been "checked in every instance easily and with but little loss." But he feared for his left flank, having seen the Northerners filing off in that direction for a supposed assault. Rhett's battered brigade was accordingly shifted to the left to reinforce Hardy's Brigade, but the Federals did not attack. At any rate, McLaws believed that they "probably would have turned that flank" had they tried.[46]

By dusk the downpour resumed and the fighting slackened to desultory skirmishing, but sharpshooters continued to force the men on both sides to lay low. For the soldiers of Hawley's brigade, the battle had raged from 6:00 a.m. until 4:00 p.m., when they were relieved by Bvt. Brig. Gen. Harrison C. Hobart's brigade of Carlin's division, XIV Corps. During those 10 hours, they had suffered 144 casualties—the most of any Union brigade that had fought in the battle. "It was the longest, and in some respects, the hardest engagement our regiment was ever in," wrote the 150th New York's historian, S. G. Cook. William Grunert of the 129th Illinois, Case's brigade, agreed: "Never before had we been exposed to such a fire of shells and [canister], as in that afternoon at the battle of Averysboro [sic]."[47]

Hardee ordered his outnumbered command to evacuate under cover of darkness. The Confederates began withdrawing their artillery at nightfall, and the infantry followed at 8:30 p.m. Private Robert W. Sanders of Elliott's Brigade recalled that his command built fires in rear of their works as if going into camp, then crawled away on all fours, not speaking above a whisper. As the Southerners crept off, they could hear the Federal sharpshooters' bullets thudding against the trees.[48]

Hardee's stand at Averasboro was a classic delaying action. He had succeeded in stalling Sherman's advance for one day, and had given his green troops their first taste of field combat. From prisoners Hardee learned that he had faced elements of the XIV Corps, the XX Corps and Kilpatrick's cavalry. These gains, however, came at a substantial cost. Hardee's Corps suffered 500 casualties in the day's fighting, most of them coming from Rhett's Brigade. Of the 458 troops the 1st South Carolina Artillery had brought into the battle, 215 had been killed, wounded or captured. Yet for all his losses, Hardee remained uncertain as to Sherman's destination.[49]

While Sherman had also accomplished his immediate objective of clearing the road to Goldsboro, the Battle of Averasboro had cost him 682 casualties, and of that number, 533 were wounded. Their loss was particularly burdensome since the wounded had to be transported with the column. This logistical consideration accounts for Sherman's decision to press Hardee rather than risk a general assault, for every additional wounded man would have further slowed his progress. Moreover, Sherman was confident that Hardee would withdraw of his own accord—as he indeed did.[50]

Yet the Federal commander was surprised at the stubbornness of the Confederate resistance at Averasboro. Major George W. Nichols, one of Sherman's staff officers, recorded that Rhett's Brigade had "fought well, and suffered severely both in officers and men. . . The Rebels have shown more pluck [today] than we have seen in them since Atlanta."[51]

~ *seven* ~

"Old Hampton Is Playing a Bluff Game"

—One of Hampton's Troopers

The Federal skirmishers crept forward at daybreak on March 17 and discovered that the Confederates had abandoned their breastworks. Ward's division pursued Hardee's rear guard—Humes' Division of Wheeler's cavalry—as far north as Averasboro to maintain the feint on Raleigh. Kilpatrick's cavalry advanced northward on a parallel road to the east toward Elevation to determine whether Hardee was headed for Raleigh or Smithfield. But General Sherman abandoned his plan of striking the North Carolina Railroad. "Our true tactics would be to push all our columns to Smithfield," he wrote General Howard, "but I will only follow Hardee far enough to give him impulse." Having shoved Hardee's Corps out of the way, Slocum's wing could now begin its eastward advance on the Goldsboro Road.[1]

While the Federals broke camp and buried their dead, Sherman visited the hospital at Oak Grove, where hundreds of Union and Confederate wounded were being treated. As the general approached the house, he saw amputated "arms and legs lying around loose, in the yard and on the porch." Hospital steward Charles Gottlieb Michael noted his visit: "Sherman went through every ward and tent, and talked to his brave Boys, and the poor criples seemed to lifen up when they heard and seen the Comander in Chief. the[y] all smiled at him."[2]

In one room Sherman met "a pale handsome young fellow, whose left arm had just been cut off near the shoulder." The young man was Capt. J. Ravenel Macbeth of the 1st South Carolina Artillery. Macbeth told Sherman that he remembered him from the visits Sherman had made to his father's house in Charleston. Sherman had Macbeth dictate a note to his mother, which the general promised to mail as soon as he reached his destination.[3]

The homes of John Smith's two brothers, Farquhard and William, also served as hospitals. In the William Smith house, behind Federal lines, Union surgeons used the family's piano as an operating table. The Farquhard Smith house—also known as Lebanon—stood just in rear of the Confederates' third line. At Lebanon, 17-year-old Janie Smith and her family rolled bandages and brought food to the sick and wounded soldiers. Every barn and shed on the property was filled with wounded men. Amputations were performed under the cedar trees, using tables that had been carried from the house. "The scene beggars description," Janie wrote. "[T]he blood lay in puddles in the grove, the groans of the dying and the complaints of those undergoing amputation was horrible. The painful impression has seared my very heart." [4]

Four miles north at Averasboro, the Confederates left some of their grievously wounded men to the mercy of the townspeople. "My heart grew sick as I passed through Aversboro [sic]. . .and saw the wretched condition the poor [soldi]ers were in who had been wounded the day before," wrote Col. Baxter Smith, a brigade commander in Wheeler's cavalry. "There they lay stretched upon the hard floor, many of them still weltering in their blood, and some of them with broken limbs that had not been attended to." When the men of Ward's division occupied the town, they found 32 wounded Confederates in one building alone.[5]

While Ward's troops occupied Averasboro, the rest of Slocum's wing waited for the bridge across Black River to be rebuilt. Brigadier General William P. Carlin's division had the advance. For the past two days, Carlin's division had brought up the rear, and the men looked forward to marching over roads that had not been churned up by the rest of the column. But on crossing the river, Carlin discovered that Morgan's division was again in front of him, having crossed on a bridge to the north. An angry Carlin protested that his division was entitled to the advance, but Morgan replied that his orders had come from General Davis himself. Carlin believed —orders or no orders—that Morgan had usurped his rightful place at the head of the column, and he determined to redress this insult at the first opportunity.[6]

Sherman's forces continued their inexorable advance on the 17th. Morgan's division marched to within 20 miles of Bentonville, followed by the rest of the Left Wing. Sherman's Right Wing advanced only six miles because Howard wished to remain near Averasboro pending news of the battle from Sherman. Schofield and the XXIII Corps halted at Kinston to collect supplies, while General Terry and the 10,000 men of the Provisional Corps advanced northward from Wilmington toward Goldsboro. So far the concentration of the Federal grand army was proceeding on schedule, and Sherman expected to reach the vicinity of Goldsboro by the afternoon of Sunday, March 19.[7]

* * *

Following his departure from Fayetteville, General Johnston arrived in Raleigh on the morning of March 10 and resumed the work of concentrating his army. On the 11th, Johnston decided that if Sherman advanced on Raleigh, Bragg would march to Hardee's assistance; but if Sherman headed toward Goldsboro, Hardee would join Bragg. Since Johnston was uncertain as to Sherman's destination, he gathered his forces at Smithfield, midway between Raleigh and Goldsboro. Two days later, on March 13, he ordered Bragg to transfer his troops from Goldsboro to Smithfield. Rumors, speculation, and intelligence regarding Sherman's destination continued to flood into Johnston's headquarters. Beauregard wrote Johnston on March 14 that Sherman was "moving doubtless to form junction with Schofield's forces about Goldsborough." The Creole suggested that since Johnston presently lacked the numbers to check Sherman, he should instead turn on Schofield and crush him before the junction could be made. Though Beauregard's plan had merit, it meant uncovering Raleigh—a risk Johnston would not take. General Lee had recently informed him that the loss of the Raleigh & Gaston Railroad would soon reduce the Army of Northern Virginia to starvation. Johnston clung to his plan of striking an isolated portion of Sherman's army.[8]

On the same day, Johnston received heartening news from Senator Louis Wigfall in Richmond. "You are mistaken as to the motive which induced your being ordered to the command,"

Wigfall wrote the general. "It was out of confidence & kindness & a real desire to obtain the benefit of your ability in this crisis." Then Wigfall named the man responsible for Johnston's reinstatement: "It was Lee & not Davis. . . .For God's sake communicate with Lee fully & freely & with kindness & confidence & give him the full benefit of your judgment in this hour of peril."[9]

Johnston replied:

> What you write me of Lee gratifies me beyond measure. In youth & early manhood I loved & admired him more than any man in the world. Since then we have had little intercourse & have become formal in our personal intercourse . . . .I have long thought that he had forgotten our early friendship. To be mistaken in so thinking would give me inexpressible pleasure. Be assured[,] however, that knight of old never fought under his King more loyally than I'll serve under General Lee.

Thanks to Wigfall's missive, Johnston and the Confederate War Department would be working in near harmony for the first time in nearly four years. Yet Johnston still feared that his appointment had come too late.[10]

The general traveled to Smithfield on March 15 and established his headquarters there. As "Old Joe" rode through town, he was met by a band from the Army of Tennessee that struck up "Dixie" in his honor. The townspeople and a passing column of soldiers cheered him. "The old Gen. acknowledged the complement [sic] by raising his hat every few yards," one band member observed. A staff officer who met Johnston later that day found the general "surprisingly social," and noted that he "endeavors to conceal his greatness rather than to impress you with it."[11]

At Smithfield, Johnston formed the Army of the South by combining the four distinct forces under his command—Hardee's Corps, Maj. Gen. Robert Hoke's Division, the Army of Tennessee contingent, and Wade Hampton's cavalry. On the 16th, he officially announced Beauregard's appointment as his second-in-command, and in a second order, stated that Lt. Gen. A. P. Stewart was assuming command of the remnants of the Army of Tennessee.[12]

Alexander Peter Stewart was 43 years old in March 1865. In recognition of his ramrod-straight posture and his devout Presbyterianism, his men called him "Old Straight." A native Tennessean, Stewart was a West Point graduate, class of 1842. Upon graduation, he commanded a company of the 3rd U. S. Artillery at Fort Macon, near Beaufort, North Carolina, then taught mathematics for two years at his alma mater. Stewart resigned his commission in 1845 to teach at Cumberland University in Lebanon, Tennessee. With the exception of two years spent at the University of Nashville, Professor Stewart remained at Cumberland until the outbreak of the war.[13]

Stewart opposed slavery and secession, but conceded the constitutional right of any state to leave the Union. Thus, when Tennessee voted to secede, he abided by his home state's decision. He entered the state service as an artillery instructor. By the fall of 1861, he was a major in the Confederate army, commanding a battery of heavy artillery in the Battle of Belmont. He was promoted to brigadier general on November 8, 1861, and led his infantry brigade at Shiloh, Perryville and Stones River (Murfreesboro). By mid-1863, Stewart commanded a division in Hardee's Corps of the Army of Tennessee, and was promoted to major general to rank from June 2, 1863. He led his division at Chickamauga, Missionary Ridge, and during the first two months of the Atlanta Campaign. On July 7, 1864, the Tennesseean assumed command of the corps formerly led by the recently-deceased Leonidas Polk; he was promoted to lieutenant general on the same day. Stewart led his corps in the Battle of Peachtree Creek on July 20, and eight days later in the Battle of Ezra Church, where he was struck in the head by a spent ball. He recovered from his wound and went on to command his divisions at Franklin and Nashville.[14]

Johnston rewarded Stewart's competence and perseverance by elevating him to the command of the Army of Tennessee contingent. It was now an army in name only, numbering just 4,500 men—about the size of a small division in the Army of Tennessee of the previous spring. Johnston feared that it was "too late to make it the same army." In his report for the Battle of Wise's Forks, Maj. Gen. D. H. Hill noted that the Army of Tennessee's officers had warned him that their men would not "attack earth-works, their experience in the late [Tennessee] campaign not being favorable to such an undertaking." As a result of the disastrous defeats at

Franklin and Nashville, Johnston and Stewart wondered whether the Army of Tennessee veterans could still fight with their old grit.[15]

Robert Hoke's Division reached Smithfield on March 15. The newest addition to this veteran division was the North Carolina Junior Reserves Brigade. Although all of the Reserves' field officers and some of the line officers were veterans, the ranks were filled with teenage boys who had seen minimal field service. The Junior Reserves regiments originally had been assigned the comparatively safe duty of guarding railroad bridges and depots vulnerable to Federal raiding parties, thus freeing the veteran Confederate guard details to serve at the front. As the manpower shortage worsened, the Junior Reserves were called upon to serve on the front line. President Davis once referred to this policy as "grinding up the seed corn of the Confederacy."[16]

According to D. H. Hill, the Junior Reserves' inexperience had told at Wise's Forks, where a portion of the brigade had broken under fire and the rest had refused to advance further. Lieutenant Colonel Charles W. Broadfoot, the commander of the 1st Junior Reserves Regiment, later refuted Hill's statement by explaining that only a part of his regiment had fallen back, and that it had done so in obedience to orders intended for the skirmish line. Under the circumstances, it is a credit to the Junior Reserves Brigade that it did not flee en masse, because the Battle of Wise's Forks was its first pitched engagement.[17]

Such was the composition of the Army of the South—an unpromising mixture of jaded veterans and raw youths. How it would stand in the field against Sherman's veterans remained to be seen.

On the morning of March 16, Johnston ordered General Hardee to withdraw toward Smithfield, but by the time "Old Reliable" received the dispatch, his command was fighting the Battle of Averasboro. Hardee replied that he would fall back on Smithfield at nightfall, but that doing so would uncover Raleigh. Johnston received Hardee's reply at 4:00 p.m., and directed him to remain in front of the Federals if they were advancing toward Raleigh, but to march for Smithfield if they headed east. At 10:00 p.m. Johnston received encouraging news from Hardee: "The enemy have made repeated attempts to carry my line and turn my flanks, but have been repulsed in every attempt." Hardee also reported that he would withdraw toward Smithfield that night in obedience to

Johnston's orders, not yet having received Johnston's more recent instructions to govern his actions according to the Federals' movements. Hardee finally received the dispatch at 11:00 p.m., but by then his command was already on its way to Smithfield. At 6:00 a.m. on the 17th, Johnston informed Hardee that if Sherman headed toward Raleigh, the troops at Smithfield would join Hardee at a point as far south of Raleigh as possible.[18]

During the night of March 16-17, Hardee's Corps marched to a point several miles north of Averasboro over "the worst road I ever saw," noted Lt. Col. James Welsman Brown, an officer in Taliaferro's Division, who added that "the sole of my boot was drawn off." Taliaferro's men went into camp at 2:00 a.m. and drew rations—their first opportunity to eat since the evening of the 15th. They resumed the march three hours later. On the morning of the 17th, Hardee issued an order to his officers and men thanking them "for their courage and conduct of yesterday," and congratulating them "upon giving the enemy the first serious check he has received since leaving Atlanta." But the South Carolinians of Rhett's Brigade had little use for Hardee's words of praise. According to Capt. Charles Inglesby of the 1st South Carolina Artillery, "it was constantly said by the weary, footsore officers and men. . .that they would a thousand times rather stand and fight old Billy Sherman, at any odds, than run from him as we were being forced to do."[19]

Even the dapper Hardee looked tired and demoralized. Sergeant Andrews of the 1st Georgia Regulars of McLaws' Division was tramping across a stream when Hardee and his staff rode by, splashing Andrews and his comrades with muddy water. The sergeant noticed that Hardee's uniform was badly soiled and that the general had the look of a man who "had drawn more corn meal than he could carry with him and had to leave it behind."[20]

Hardee's Corps marched to Elevation, a point midway between Averasboro and Smithfield, where the intersection of the Raleigh and Smithfield roads supposedly was. There Hardee discovered that his map was in error and the intersection was actually two miles nearer to Smithfield. (This proved to be only the first of many instances over the next few days in which the North Carolina state maps betrayed the generals of both sides.) He therefore resumed the march and, in obedience to Johnston's orders, halted at the intersection to await the Union advance. "I do not believe the enemy is moving on Raleigh," Hardee wrote Johnston. "I can't believe the enemy intends a serious advance on [the Smithfield] or the Raleigh Road. If he divides his forces you will have the opportunity to concentrate and whip him." Hardee closed with these prophetic words: "To-day will develop the purposes of the enemy."[21]

As Hardee marched toward Smithfield, Hampton's cavalry disputed the progress of the Federal columns farther south. Humes' and Allen's divisions of Wheeler's Cavalry Corps screened Hardee's rear and right flank, which were threatened by Ward's division and Kilpatrick's cavalry. Butler's Division sparred with the Federal Right Wing, which had crossed South River and was heading northeastward. While the Union Left Wing crossed Black River (actually the northern extension of South River), General Hampton and Dibrell's Division of Wheeler's Corps fell back on the Goldsboro Road to the Willis Cole plantation. Early that morning, Hampton had told Hardee that he believed the Federals were heading toward Goldsboro; since then, the Left Wing's abrupt shift to the east had further reinforced Hampton's belief, Ward's and Kilpatrick's feint notwithstanding. Moreover, Hampton received reports from Wheeler and Colonel Dibrell that recently captured Union prisoners, as well as local citizens living along the Federals' line of march, stated that Sherman's destination was Goldsboro, and not Raleigh.[22]

Hampton made his headquarters at the Cole house near the junction of the Goldsboro and Smithfield roads two miles south of Bentonville. The South Carolinian planned to use Dibrell's Division to contest Slocum's advance up the Goldsboro Road. He posted Butler's Division at Blackman Lee's store six miles to the southwest to oppose Howard's wing. In a 6:00 p.m. dispatch to Hardee, Hampton reiterated his belief that Sherman's destination was Goldsboro. "I will keep in front of the enemy, between him and Smithfield and Goldsborough, until the very last moment," Hampton assured Hardee.[23]

At 7:00 p.m. Johnston sent Hardee word that the time to act had come. "Something must be done to-morrow morning," Johnston wrote, "and yet I have no satisfactory information as to the enemy's movements. Can you give me any certain information of the force you engaged yesterday?" Hardee's reply has not come down to us, but it likely indicated that Hampton was better informed as to the Federals' movements than he was. That evening, Johnston ordered

Generals Bragg and Stewart to prepare to march at dawn the next morning, and then he sent a message to Hampton.[24]

It was almost midnight when two horsemen dashed up the lane leading to Willis Cole's house and delivered a dispatch to Hampton:

> Please send by the bearer all the information you have of the movement and position of the enemy, the number of their columns, their location and distance apart, and distance from Goldsborough, and give me your opinion whether it is practicable to reach them from Smithfield on the south side of the [Neuse] river before they reach Goldsborough.
>
> J. E. JOHNSTON,
> *General*[25]

Hampton replied that the two Federal wings were indeed advancing on Goldsboro, and that they were widely separated. He added that the wing advancing up the road from Averasboro was more than a day's march from the Cole plantation, which was 18 miles south of Smithfield. The South Carolinian suggested that the plantation was an excellent site for an attack, and assured Johnston that he would delay the Union advance so as to enable the Confederate army to concentrate there.[26]

Of the two riders who had delivered the message to Hampton, one galloped off for Smithfield bearing Hampton's reply, and the other, Lt. Wade Hampton, Jr., remained behind to visit with his father. An aide-de-camp on Johnston's staff, the younger Hampton later assured the general that he had urged upon his father "the necessity of frequent and full dispatches." History has failed to record the elder Hampton's reply to his son's urgings.[27]

Johnston received Hampton's dispatch at dawn on March 18, and immediately ordered Stewart and Bragg to march their commands to Bentonville. A glance at the state map made it clear to Johnston that the two Federal wings were 12 miles apart, thus separated by a day's march. He therefore decided to attack the nearest enemy column. At 7:40 a.m. "Old Joe" wrote Hampton: "We will go to the place at which your dispatch was written. The scheme mentioned in my note, which you pronounce practicable, will be attempted."[28]

What induced the normally timorous Johnston to order the attack? The only other full-scale assault he had launched during the war was at Seven Pines, where he had attacked because his back was to Richmond and his only other option was the unthinkable one of evacuating the Confederate capital without a fight. But Johnston's strategic situation in North Carolina in March 1865 was different. Of the two principal Confederate armies, Lee's Army of Northern Virginia was pinned down in Richmond, whereas Johnston's was still comparatively free to maneuver. Johnston could have fallen back toward Raleigh and awaited Sherman's advance on that city, as Sherman hoped (and President Davis expected) he would do. After all, whenever Johnston had the option to retreat, was that not what he invariably did?

Instead, Johnston decided to attack; he did so for three reasons. The first was based on tactical considerations. In order to have any hope of success, Johnston knew that he had to strike Sherman before the latter could combine with Schofield. The second reason sprang from Johnston's character: he saw the impending battle with Sherman as one he could not lose, since the outcome of the war was already decided. By March 1865, Johnston regarded Confederate defeat as inevitable, and believed that a stunning blow to Sherman's army might give the South greater leverage at the bargaining table. The third reason was an emotional one: due to Senator Wigfall's recent letter, Johnston's former regard for Robert E. Lee had returned. "Old Joe" was determined to do all in his power to aid his long-time friend and comrade. Johnston had assured Wigfall "that knight of old never fought under his King more loyally than I'll serve under General Lee," and he intended to keep his word.

* * *

The approach march to Bentonville was a tiring one for Bragg's and Stewart's men, but it passed without mishap. The long gray columns marched most of the way on the Smithfield-Bentonville Road—also known as the Devil's Race Path. Johnston also directed Hardee to march for Bentonville. Since the state map indicated that Elevation and Bentonville were just 12 miles apart, Johnston assumed that Hardee's column would have no trouble reaching its destination before nightfall. Unfortunately for the Confederates, the state map was wildly inaccurate and led Johnston to underestimate Hardee's distance from Bentonville while overestimating the distance separating the Federal columns. Although the Confederates had the services of Johnston County sheriff William Cullom, he failed to recognize the state map's inaccuracies. In this case, Johnston's access to local information availed him next to nothing.[29]

Hardee's march to Bentonville was fraught with difficulty from the start. Although Hardee received Johnston's dispatch at 8:50 a.m., he did not get his command underway until 11:00 a.m. Moreover, he was unaware of the road that Johnston had suggested as his shortest route to Bentonville. Hardee finally succeeded in locating the road, but as the afternoon wore on the distance to Bentonville proved to be much greater than the supposed 12 miles.[30]

While Johnston's infantry marched toward Bentonville, Dibrell's Division, with Hampton at its head, disputed the Federal Left Wing's progress on the Goldsboro Road. The Confederate horsemen had ridden out at dawn and collided with some of the enemy's mounted foragers soon afterward. The Southerners fell back to Bushy Swamp, about five miles west of the Cole plantation. Hampton ordered a section of his horse artillery to open fire on the Union foragers, who prudently awaited the arrival of the head of the infantry column.[31]

General Morgan's division of the XIV Corps once again had the advance of the Federal Left Wing. On reaching the swamp, Morgan deployed Vandever's brigade on the right of the road and Mitchell's brigade on the left. The Federal skirmishers easily drove off the Confederate horsemen about noon. Soon afterward, Sherman arrived at the front and ordered Morgan to halt so that the column could close up. The men were allowed to fall out and eat lunch. "We feel in excellent spirits," wrote Lt. John Marshall Branum of the 98th Ohio, Mitchell's brigade. "Everything promises for a smooth entry into Goldsboro."[32]

From Confederate prisoners Morgan learned that he had faced Wade Hampton and two brigades of cavalry. This came as no surprise to Morgan, for his infantry had skirmished with Confederate cavalry from the outset of the campaign. Yet General Carlin's reminiscences indicate that he believed a major battle was imminent. Carlin had spied the enemy's scouts lurking in the woods near the roadside, and he believed that the Rebel cavalry and artillery in Morgan's front were buying time for the concentration of Johnston's army.[33]

The strongest evidence of all was the behavior of the Cox family, whose farmhouse had briefly served as General Hampton's headquarters and now served as General Sherman's. Carlin remembered sitting on the veranda of the house with the Coxes while Generals Sherman, Slocum and Davis "had an earnest conversation" in the yard. Meanwhile, the Cox children were crying aloud, and Carlin noted that Mr. and Mrs. Cox "seemed to have been weeping, as their eyes were still red." Carlin assumed that the family was distraught because they feared the ravages of the Union soldiers. When he offered to provide the Coxes with a guard and a store of provisions, Mr. Cox shook his head and exclaimed, "Oh, that won't save us." Carlin inferred from Cox's reply that the Rebels had warned him that a battle would take place on or near his farm.[34]

Carlin whispered his suspicions to General Davis, who passed them on to Sherman. "Oh, no," Sherman said, "they will not fight us till we get near Smithfield or Raleigh." Given all the indications, Carlin recalled, "it seemed incredible that Gen. Sherman believed no battle was to take place." If we credit Carlin's story, we must conclude that Carlin was the unsung Federal hero of the Battle of Bentonville, for he had tried to warn Sherman of its approach. At first glance, Carlin's story appears plausible enough, but it renders his behavior on the morning of the 19th all the more inexplicable, as will be seen.[35]

Contrary to Carlin's recollection, as of 2:00 p.m. on March 18, Sherman expected the Confederates to contest his advance: "I think it probable that Joe Johnston will try to prevent our getting Goldsboro," he wrote Howard. However, several circumstances induced Sherman to change his mind a few hours later. First, Kilpatrick reported that Hardee was retreating on Smithfield and that Johnston was concentrating his army near Raleigh. Then the 10th Michigan of Vandever's brigade advanced northward one-and-a-half miles on the Smithfield-Clinton Road to Mill Creek, where they found that a detachment of Wheeler's cavalry had burned the bridge. In this instance, Sherman's map deceived him, for it indicated that the Confederates had burned the bridge over their only approach route to Bentonville (Sherman's map omitted the Devil's Race Path five miles east of the Smithfield-Clinton Road). This further indicated that Johnston was falling back on Raleigh.

Believing that Johnston had conceded Goldsboro to him, Sherman instructed Slocum to advance on the 19th to Cox's Bridge via the Goldsboro Road, where his wing would converge with Howard's, which was marching on the lower, or new, Goldsboro Road five miles to the south. From Cox's Bridge across the Neuse River, it was a 12-mile march to Goldsboro.[36]

At 4:00 p.m., Sherman instructed Slocum and Howard to halt for the night. Slocum's head of column had reached the intersection of the Smithfield-Clinton and the Averasboro-Goldsboro roads. Howard and the XV Corps were encamped about Blackman Lee's store just two miles to the south, while the XVII Corps was bivouacked in the vicinity of Troublefield's store six miles south of Howard, whose XV Corps occupied a four-mile front. Both Slocum and Howard stood within 25 miles of Goldsboro. The two Federal wings presented a 12-mile front, as compact as Sherman's grand army had ever been while on the march.[37]

* * *

Dibrell's Confederate division fell back to the Reddick Morris farm just west of the Cole plantation. Hampton deemed it "vitally important" that he hold this ground until the arrival of Johnston's infantry. He deployed Dibrell's Tennesseans and Kentuckians in the woods on either side of the Goldsboro Road, then ordered them to dismount and throw together some rail barricades along the eastern edge of Morris' cornfield. Hampton also placed his two artillery batteries in a commanding position north of the road. As the South Carolinian mounted his horse to ride off to another part of the line, he overheard one of his veterans remark, "Old Hampton is playing a bluff game, and if he don't mind Sherman will call him." "Old Hampton" conceded the trooper's ready grasp of the principles governing both war and poker: "I knew that if a serious attack was made on me the guns would be lost," the South Carolinian wrote, "but I determined to run this risk in the hope of checking the Federal advance."[38]

Hampton's two batteries were the newest addition to his command. Captain William E. Earle's Battery had served with McLaws' Division until a few weeks before. Its ordnance consisted of one 12-pounder Napoleon, one 10-pounder Parrott, and two 12-pounder howitzers. Although Capt. Edwin L. Halsey's Battery had joined Hampton's command just the day before, it had previously served under him in Virginia, where it had begun its service in the Hampton Legion. When Hampton was transferred to South Carolina in January 1865, the men of Halsey's Battery petitioned him to take them along. The general gratefully assented and obtained the necessary authorization.[39]

Prior to their transfer, the men of Halsey's Battery had drawn crisp new uniforms and boot leather. At this late date in the war, their starched white collars and well-greased boots belied their veteran status. According to Louis Sherfesee, the battery's guidon bearer, some of Wheeler's troopers mistook the artillerymen for "some militia company" and taunted them with, "Come up out of those collars!" and "You needn't hide—we see you in those boots." The cavalrymen "kindly offered to snap a cap on their rifles (to show greenhorns how it was done) if we would give them five cents," Sherfesee wrote. Halsey's men bore the troopers' taunts in silence, for they had nothing to prove. During nearly four years of service, his battery had fought in 143 battles and skirmishes, and had fired more than 30,000 rounds of artillery ammunition, wearing out in the process the four 12-pounder Blakely rifles which Hampton had bought to arm it in 1861. The battery now fielded four captured 12-pounder Napoleons, which were presently trained on the Goldsboro Road in anticipation of the enemy's advance.[40]

They did not have long to wait. A column of Federal horsemen came thundering up that road at dusk. Led by Maj. James Taylor Holmes of the 52nd Ohio, this mounted force consisted of 90 foragers from Fearing's brigade of Morgan's division. Major Holmes' detail had skirmished with Dibrell's cavalry for most of the day, and Holmes hoped that one more attack would push the Confederates out of the way. Instead, Holmes was met by a volley of musketry and artillery from the woods across the field in his front, which told the major that he had run into a force too large for him to drive. After skirmishing with the Rebel cavalry for about an hour, Holmes and his command returned to camp empty-handed. Hampton could breathe a sigh of relief, for his bluff had not been called.[41]

When Major Holmes reached camp, he reported to Generals Morgan and Fearing. Holmes stated that he had run into Hampton's cavalry behind barricades five miles to the east, and had developed both musketry and artillery. The major told Morgan and Fearing that he expected the Rebels to put up a fight the next morning, but the two generals disagreed. "We shall see," Holmes jotted in his diary.[42]

* * *

Robert Hoke's Confederate division reached Bentonville at nightfall, followed by the Army of Tennessee. The men were ordered to keep quiet and make no fires, for the enemy was close at hand. "It is supposed we are to meet & encounter part of Sherman's army," wrote Lt. William Calder, the adjutant of the Junior Reserves Brigade. "May God grant us a telling victory, and may He enable us to rid ourselves of this dread nemesis." Major Bromfield Ridley of A. P. Stewart's staff found the veterans of the Army of Tennessee "in high spirits and ready to brave the coming storm."[43]

Meanwhile, after a 14-mile march, Hardee's Corps made camp six miles north of Bentonville, the distance from Elevation proving to be 20 miles instead of the supposed 12. Hardee rode ahead one mile to Sneed's house, where he and his staff spent the night. "I shall start at 4 o'clock [a.m.], so as to reach Bentonville at an early hour in the morning," Hardee informed Johnston, "but if it be necessary I can start my command at an earlier hour."[44]

That evening, Hampton reported to Johnston at Bentonville, saying his cavalry had successfully defended the ground chosen for the assault. The South Carolinian stated that the Federals were encamped five miles west of the proposed battlefield. Johnston replied that the enemy was much closer to the site than Hardee's Corps was, and expressed the regret that he could no longer "hope for the advantage of attacking the head of a deep column."[45]

Since it was too late for Johnston to reconnoiter the ground, Hampton proposed a plan of attack that would exploit the heavily wooded terrain surrounding the Willis Cole house. Hampton described the ground as "the eastern edge of an old plantation, lying principally on the north side of the [Goldsboro] road, and surrounded, east, south, and north, by dense thickets of blackjack." He suggested that Johnston place Hoke's Division astride the

Goldsboro Road to act as a blocking force against the Union advance. Hampton recommended deploying Hardee's Corps on Hoke's right and at a 45-degree angle to Hoke's line, followed by Stewart's Army of Tennessee contingent, which would form on Hardee's right, and whose line would run parallel to the Goldsboro Road. From their position north of the road, Hardee and Stewart would strike the left flank of the Union column as it collided with Hoke's line. Only Hoke's blocking force would be visible to the advancing Federals, since Hardee and Stewart would be concealed in the woods a half-mile north of the Goldsboro Road. In order to buy time for the deployment of the infantry, Hampton suggested placing Dibrell's troopers behind the same barricades they had occupied that afternoon. The cavalry would give ground slowly to the Federals, then retire through Hoke's line once the deployment had been completed.[46]

Johnston approved Hampton's plan. "Old Joe" regretted that the Union advance was so near and that Hardee's Corps was so far away, but he knew that this would be his last opportunity to strike Sherman with any hope of success. Johnston therefore directed that the deployment commence at dawn the next morning.

While Generals Johnston and Hampton discussed their battle plan, two young veterans of Halsey's Battery exchanged angry words, leading one to challenge the other to a duel. The challenge was immediately accepted. The two duelists, or *principals*, were Pvts. Marx E. Cohen, Jr. and Thomas R. Chew. Chew was an original member of the Hampton Legion. Cohen, who at the advanced age of 23 was known to his comrades as "Doctor," was a relative newcomer to the battery, having served only for about a year. Cohen chose William J. Verdier to be his second, and Chew chose Leonidas Raysor; both Verdier and Raysor were battery mates of the principals. The seconds were charged with loading their respective principal's revolver and with arranging the time and place of the duel. Since the impending battle demanded a prompt settlement, Raysor and Verdier set the time of the duel for dawn the next morning.[47]

At midnight on the night of March 18-19, the duel—and the opening of the Battle of Bentonville—were just six hours away.

~ *eight* ~

"The Rebels Don't Drive Worth a Damn"

—Sherman's Bummers

At 3:00 a.m. on March 19, Capt. Charles E. Belknap ordered the 90 men of his foraging detail awakened. The men were Ohioans and Michiganders detailed from Buell's brigade of Carlin's division. They were well-armed, some of them carrying Springfield rifle-muskets, while the rest brandished either Colt revolving rifles or Spencer repeating carbines. Belknap's bummers broke camp after feeding their horses and drinking their coffee, and rode eastward on the Goldsboro Road. It was 4:00 a.m. According to Belknap, his troops were "tired, sore, cross, and ugly," but every man was in his place.[1]

Belknap was even more tired than his men. He had not reached camp until midnight, having first gone to division headquarters to receive the pickets' countersign for the next five days. While there, the 18-year-old captain reported his suspicions to General Carlin concerning the enemy's intentions. Like Major Holmes, Belknap had skirmished with Dibrell's horsemen for most of the preceding day, and he noted that they had yielded ground with greater stubbornness than usual. The statements of some local citizens and a mortally wounded trooper from Dibrell's command also indicated to Belknap that the Confederates were preparing a repetition of their stand south of Averasboro. Carlin passed on Belknap's report to General Sherman, who did not credit it. Neither did Carlin, for he ordered Belknap to rejoin the division at Cox's Bridge on the evening of the 19th. Carlin's final instructions to the young captain were, "If you cannot drive the enemy, flank them," a far cry from the tone of his reminiscences, in which he stated that he expected a battle to take place on that day. This is only the first of many such inconsistencies between Carlin's actions and his later statements.[2]

Major Holmes' foraging detail broke camp at the same time as Captain Belknap's. General Morgan was up early as usual, and ambled over to see the major off. Morgan told Holmes that he expected his detail to be in Goldsboro by sundown. As Holmes swung into his saddle, he replied that he did not think that would be possible. "You'll go right in, young man," the general assured him. Morgan's complacency, coupled with the dismissal of his report the night before, left Major Holmes feeling "out of humor."[3]

Holmes led his detail to the Federal picket line. One of the pickets advised the foragers "to be careful, as the Johnnies' cavalry was only a short distance in front."

"To h— with the Johnnies," one of the bummers roared. "We want something to eat, and we'll have it or bust."

"Well, I guess you'll bust," the sentry shot back, "for you won't get anything but lead to eat."

"All right," said the bummer. "We'll see." Indeed they would.[4]

At dawn, Belknap's foragers surprised one of Dibrell's picket posts and drove off the dazed Confederates without firing a shot. The Federals continued eastward down the Goldsboro Road until they came to a swampy ravine, where they were met by Dibrell's skirmish line deployed along the eastern side of the swamp. The Southerners leveled their rifles and carbines at the Yankees and opened fire, then wheeled their horses about and galloped off for the main line. Belknap's men pursued the Confederate horsemen up a gradual slope, then drew rein when they came to within a few hundred yards of Hampton's barricades. "As far as I could see to the right and left," Captain Belknap recalled, "the dirt from thousands of shovels was flying in the air." Belknap briefly surveyed the confusion his approach had inspired—"[Rebel] officers shouting to their men to fall in line and the men throwing away their shovels and securing their guns"—then he led his force back to the western side of the swampy ravine. Belknap dispatched one of his best men to inform General Carlin of his discovery, but the courier never reached his destination. "He must have been killed by a bushwhacker," Belknap wrote in 1893, "for he is still one of the missing."[5]

In obedience to Carlin's injunction to flank the Rebels if he could not drive them, Belknap left 30 of his men to picket the swamp, then led the rest on a ride around the Confederate right flank. Belknap soon found a grist mill with an ample supply of corn, but before his men had a chance to grind any meal a squadron of Confederate cavalry drove off the Federal bummers. The captain was fortunate to emerge from the scrape with his life, for as soon as he reached friendly lines, his mortally wounded horse collapsed and died. The Battle of Bentonville was already over for Captain Belknap, but for most of his comrades, it had not yet begun.[6]

Meanwhile, Major Holmes' command found the Confederates behind the same barricades they had occupied the evening before. Even with the addition of several other XIV and XX Corps foraging details, Holmes lacked the manpower to dislodge the Confederates, and he discovered that flanking them was a more difficult operation than it had been for Belknap's detail. As he had done at Bushy Swamp the morning before, Holmes ordered his men to skirmish with the Confederates until the infantry arrived. The major's hunch had proved correct: there would be no easy ride into Goldsboro that day.[7]

* * *

The Confederate camps were astir at daybreak on Sunday, March 19. While most of the soldiers were preparing breakfast, a group of men from Halsey's Battery stole away from their bivouac and found a secluded place to conduct their duel. Privates Cohen and Chew stepped off their positions, and probably stood no more than 60 feet apart, in accordance with dueling's code of honor. Given the short range and the fact that the two men were armed with revolvers, the duel was certain to have a bloody outcome. At a given signal, the two duelists opened fire on each other and emptied their revolvers. Miraculously, both men emerged from the duel unscathed. The two principals were stunned: they each had fired six rounds at point blank range, yet neither of them was hurt.[8]

"I can't understand it," Cohen said several times on the way back to camp. Then he turned to his second, Verdier, and demanded to know whether the seconds had tampered with the ammunition. Verdier just smiled in reply.

"I understand now," Cohen snapped. "I shall hold you to account for this!"

Cohen had guessed Verdier's and Raysor's secret: the two seconds had agreed to load both revolvers with blanks in order to prevent their two comrades from killing or maiming each other. The war had taken enough of their comrades already.

A bugle in the distance sounded the familiar refrain of "Boots and Saddles." Cohen, Chew and the other artillerymen raced back to camp. Once again, the veteran battery was going into battle.[9]

* * *

Reveille sounded at 4:00 a.m. in the camp of Carlin's division. The night had been mild, and rather than pitch their tents, the men had spread out their bedrolls and slept under the stars. For the first time since leaving Fayetteville, Carlin's men would march in the advance. They would not have to choke on the dust kicked up by thousands of feet or wallow in the quicksand churned up by the wagons and ambulances. They would also reach camp first that night, giving them access to the best ground and the purest water to be had. Moreover, these soldiers knew that they were just two days' march from Goldsboro, where they would receive mail from home and new clothing and shoes. All signs indicated that the Rebels had fallen back toward Raleigh. Victory must have seemed no more than an arm's length away to these weary veterans of the XIV Corps. Yet many of them would face their sternest test of the war on this March Sunday, and some of them would not survive it.[10]

In observance of the Sabbath, a brigade band intoned the solemn strains of "Old Hundred." The men had their usual breakfast of hardtack and coffee, their spartan fare enlivened here and there by chicken or ham or a sweet potato. But not all of the XIV Corps soldiers were so fortunate. According to Capt. William F. Allee of the 22nd Indiana, his men had had to subsist on roasting ears for the past few days. Such were the pitfalls of the brigade foraging system: while one part of the camp feasted, another part starved.[11]

At 6:00 a.m. Generals Sherman, Slocum and Davis sat together on their horses at the intersection of the Smithfield-Clinton and Goldsboro-Averasboro roads. Convinced that the danger of a Confederate attack had passed, Sherman prepared to rejoin the Right Wing in order to communicate with Generals Schofield and Terry more quickly. Before setting out, Sherman told Slocum and Davis that he was sure Hardee had fallen back toward Raleigh, and that the Left Wing could easily reach Cox's Bridge across the Neuse River that day. Slocum agreed, but Davis had his doubts, according to the recollection of his chief of staff, Lt. Col. Alexander C. McClurg. Davis told Sherman that he believed his advance "was likely to encounter more than the usual cavalry opposition." "No, Jeff," Sherman replied. "There is nothing there but Dibbrell's [sic] cavalry. Brush them out of the way. . . .I'll meet you to-morrow morning at Cox's Bridge." With that, Sherman led his staff and escort down the Clinton Road to rejoin Howard's wing.[12]

* * *

At 7:00 a.m. Carlin's division moved out in the advance, passing between the waiting ranks of Morgan's division. Carlin's troops marched in column of fours, arms right shoulder shift, with regimental flags flying, while a band played national airs. Carlin was wearing his newest uniform for the occasion. He indulged in this display of pomp as a dig at Morgan's division for stealing the advance from him two days before. Carlin later wrote that he wore this uniform so that the enemy could identify his rank in case he was killed or captured. Of course, his new uniform also made him an inviting target for enemy marksmen, a fact that the veteran brigadier would not have overlooked. It is doubtful that Carlin would have worn his best uniform had he suspected that a battle would take place that day. In this instance, Carlin's post-war reminiscences fail to explain his actions.[13]

As the Federal column headed east down the Goldsboro Road, the thick black smoke of countless pine knot campfires vanished to reveal a clear blue sky. Some of the Westerners noticed that the apple and peach trees were blossoming a full month before they did back home.[14]

Before long Carlin's troops could hear the incessant rattle of musketry in their front, a sure sign that the bummers had met with some stubborn opposition a mile or two up the road. As a precaution, Carlin ordered his wagons and pack mules to the rear of the column. Generals Carlin and Davis no doubt discussed the situation, albeit none too cordially. "Gen. Davis was not communicative to me," Carlin later wrote, "and I had no unnecessary communication with him." To Sherman, Carlin confided: "During the whole of the Georgia and Carolina Campaigns I have been compelled to feel that I was under the command of an enemy. . . .I was convinced that if an opportunity should occur he would ruin my reputation."[15]

A native of Carrollton, Illinois, the 35-year-old Carlin was a graduate of West Point (class of 1850), had seen action against the Sioux and Cheyenne nations, and had served in Col. Albert Sidney Johnston's Mormon expedition. A Regular Army captain when the Civil War broke out, Carlin was commissioned colonel of the 38th Illinois Volunteer Infantry on August 15, 1861. From November 1861 to March 1862, Carlin commanded the District of Southeast Missouri, and by May 1862, was leading a brigade in Brig. Gen. Jefferson C. Davis's division of the XX Corps. In the Battle of Perryville, Carlin attracted the favorable notice of the Army of the Ohio's commander, Maj. Gen. Don Carlos Buell, who reported: "Sheridan was reinforced by Carlin's Brigade, which charged the enemy with intrepidity and drove him through the town to his position beyond." Two months later, on November 29, 1862, Carlin was promoted to brigadier general of volunteers.[16]

The Illinoisan fell out with Davis in January 1863, following the Battle of Stones River. Carlin was angered by Davis' after-action report and fired off a six-page letter of protest to him. By September of that year, relations between Carlin and Davis had so deteriorated that Carlin's report for the Battle of Chickamauga was little more than a thinly disguised diatribe against his superior. Twentieth Corps chief Maj. Gen. Alexander McCook recommended that Carlin be transferred to another command. Before the ink on McCook's endorsement could dry, however, Carlin went directly to Army of the Cumberland commander Maj. Gen. William S. Rosecrans and applied for a transfer. Rosecrans granted Carlin's request, and he went on to serve with distinction in the Chattanooga and Atlanta campaigns.[17]

Carlin's and Davis' paths crossed again in August 1864. Carlin now led the First Division of the XIV Corps, and Davis was promoted to commander of that corps. "For many days," Carlin later wrote, "I seriously thought of leaving the Corps when he [General Davis] was assigned to command of it, believing such a course due myself and him both; but regretting to part with troops I had commanded and known so long[,] I decided to hold on and endeavor to avoid difficulty with him." Thus matters stood between Carlin and Davis on the morning of March 19, 1865.[18]

As Carlin's veterans marched eastward, they noticed that the musketry was increasing instead of diminishing, as it usually did. Lieutenant Allen Dougall of the 88th Indiana knew that there would be some hard fighting up ahead. "If the foragers could not clear the way, nothing less than a brigade need try it."[19]

At the moment, Major Holmes would have been only too willing to agree with Lieutenant Dougall's assessment, as it was his men whose musketry Dougall heard. Holmes and his foragers had been skirmishing with Dibrell's troopers for several hours, and during that time the Union bummers found new use for a phrase that had not been heard since the Atlanta Campaign: "the Rebels don't drive worth a damn." Major Holmes galloped back to warn Carlin.[20]

The major had no trouble finding Carlin, for the general was conspicuous in his crisp new uniform. As the two officers rode to the front, Holmes told Carlin that his foragers had "pushed down on Johnston's line. . . .and developed both musketry and artillery." According to several of Holmes' men, "Carlin pooh[-]poohed the idea of infantry being in his front, and did not propose to be delayed in his movements by cavalry." Once his advance brigade—Brig. Gen. Harrison C. Hobart's—was up, Carlin turned to Holmes and said, "Get your d—d bummers out of the way, and I will drive the rebels out with a skirmish line!"[21]

"This somewhat 'riled' the Major," recalled onlooker Cyrus Fox of the 86th Illinois, but Holmes managed to control his temper. He rode back to his command and ordered it to make way for Hobart's brigade.[22]

General Hobart deployed his brigade in two lines, or wings. The front line, or right wing, consisted of the 88th Indiana, 33rd Ohio and 94th Ohio, the whole commanded by Lt. Col. Cyrus E. Briant.

The rear line, or left wing, was comprised of the 21st Wisconsin, 42nd Indiana and 104th Illinois, and was led by Lt. Col. Michael H. Fitch. So far in the campaign, neither Briant nor Fitch had exercised independent command of his wing, but that would change before noon.[23]

Hobart ordered forward two companies from each regiment of Briant's wing to form his skirmish line. The skirmishers deployed in a field to the right, south, of the Goldsboro Road, and were supported by Briant's three regiments. The time was 10:00 a.m.[24]

As Carlin's men deployed to drive off the Rebels before them, the rest of Slocum's column continued on its eastward course as if Carlin had met with no opposition. "We were so confident of success," wrote Chaplain L. W. Earle of the 21st Michigan, "that civilians, baggage, horses, mules, and wagons, all kept along with, or close up to our advansing [sic] column," Carlin's marching orders notwithstanding. The column soon slowed to a crawl, and Chaplain Earle noted that "the scattering shots" up the road "seemed to increase" in fury. The chaplain saw Slocum gallop past toward the front, his staff and escort trailing close behind. Slocum fell in beside Capt. Arthur Prince, who commanded the 21st Michigan, the first regiment in the column behind Hobart. "Why don't you hurry up this column?" Slocum asked Prince. "From the best information that we have, there are only about eight hundred [Confederate] cavalry concealed in the underbrush."[25]

A few minutes later, two of Slocum's staff officers, Lt. Joseph B. Foraker and Maj. William G. Tracy, asked the general if they might "ride to the front and find out exactly what the situation was." Slocum gave his consent. The two young officers galloped about a mile to the front, where they entered "an open space of ground, perhaps a quarter of a mile in width," Foraker recalled, "beyond which there was [sic] the usual pine woods." This open field was the Reddick Morris farm. Foraker and Tracy rode up while Briant's wing of Hobart's brigade was forming for the assault. Foraker noted that the skirmishers had already advanced halfway across the field. By the time the two staff officers reached the supporting regiments, they, too, were advancing. The 33rd Ohio moved forward on the left, an inviting target in the open field, while the 88th Indiana advanced in the center, its right flank concealed by thick woods. The right (or southernmost) regiment, the 94th Ohio, which was completely hidden by the woods, moved in tandem with the Hoosiers and their fellow Ohioans. Briant's entire wing was now advancing against the extreme left of Wade Hampton's barricades.[26]

The skirmishers ran across the Goldsboro Road to the edge of the woods, the main line following a few hundred yards behind. According to Lieutenant Foraker, Hampton's dismounted troopers opened upon Briant's skirmish line "a fierce musketry fire." Despite the heavy fire laid down by the dismounted Southern horsemen, the Federal skirmishers plunged into the woods and encountered Hampton's "line of outposts, each post more or less protected by a light intrenchment or barricade made of logs, rails, etc.," Foraker observed. "These outposts were situated far enough back in the pine woods not to be seen until we got near them." Hampton's works extended for a short distance on either side of the Goldsboro Road.[27] With his bluff finally called, Hampton was compelled to fall back.

The Union skirmishers drove Dibrell's Tennesseans and Kentuckians "through a big Swamp," wrote Pvt. John Herr of the 94th Ohio. "We had to wade mud and water knee deep." Briant's wing now changed front in order to move eastward on a line with the Goldsboro Road.[28]

In riding forward with the main line of Briant's wing, Foraker and Tracy came within range of the enemy's bullets. The two staff officers had tagged along as "mere volunteers," Foraker noted, and were now under fire, although neither officer was carrying sidearms nor had any specific duty that required him to remain at the front. They were also mounted and each had an orderly riding alongside him. "We made a rather conspicuous mark for the enemy," remarked Foraker, who also believed that "to be killed under such circumstances would look like a waste of raw material." The trouble was that neither Foraker nor Tracy could think of a way to exit gracefully while Hobart's men were looking on. A spent ball which pierced Major Tracy's boot, giving him a slight but painful leg wound, solved the staff officers' dilemma. Nineteen-year-old Joe Foraker, spared a hero's death at Bentonville, would one day serve as the governor of Ohio.[29]

When Hobart saw that Briant's skirmishers were easily driving back the Confederates, he ordered Lieutenant Colonel Fitch, who had been following Briant's wing, to halt his line. Fitch looked on as

Briant's wing "advanced out of sight through the woods and thick undergrowth."[30]

General Davis accompanied Carlin to the front. Davis bore no trace of the anxiety he had manifested in his conversation with Sherman back at the crossroads, although he conceded that "the enemy's pickets yielded their ground with unusual stubbornness for cavalry troops." He was confident, however, that Carlin faced nothing more than a division of Confederate cavalry and a few pieces of artillery. In his report, Davis noted that the first batch of prisoners were cavalrymen, and that they "gave no information of an infantry force behind them." Davis therefore directed Carlin "to attack vigorously and push on." Carlin was already doing just that.[31]

While Hobart's brigade was driving back Dibrell's cavalry, Slocum rode up alongside Davis and Carlin to view Hobart's progress. Slocum told the two generals that he had just learned from one of Kilpatrick's staff officers—a lieutenant who had escaped from the enemy at Smithfield two days before—that Johnston's army was concentrating at or near Raleigh in expectation of Sherman's advance on that city. Slocum and Davis agreed that nothing stood between them and Goldsboro except some Rebel cavalry with a few pieces of artillery. Slocum ordered Carlin to send his Second Brigade, commanded by Bvt. Brig. Gen. George P. Buell, "some distance to the left of the [Goldsboro] road for the purpose of developing the enemy's line." Buell led his men down "a dim road" that branched off the Goldsboro Road "in a north-easterly direction, and passed about fifty yards to the right of a frame building that looked like a country schoolhouse or church," Carlin wrote. The road soon petered out, and Buell's men found themselves slogging through a briar-infested swamp.[32]

* * *

Unbeknownst to Hobart or his men, they were heading straight for Maj. Gen. Robert F. Hoke's Division, which had marched from its encampment at dawn and had since fortified its position along the Bentonville Road and astride the Goldsboro Road. Hoke's veteran command numbered 3,655 effectives, and was augmented by the 689 men of the division's artillery contingent, plus the 1,213 boys of the Junior Reserves Brigade, for a total of 5,557 officers and men.[33]

General Hoke and his division were on loan from the Army of Northern Virginia. Robert E. Lee had deemed the defense of Fort Fisher, which guarded the river approach to Wilmington, of such strategic importance that in December 1864, he had pulled Hoke's Division out of its Petersburg fortifications and shipped it by rail to the Confederacy's last open seaport. Lee knew that if Fort Fisher fell, his army was doomed. At Wilmington, Hoke resumed his service under Department of North Carolina commander Gen. Braxton Bragg.[34]

On January 15, 1865, Hoke's Division crouched behind its entrenchments and watched as Fort Fisher fell after a fierce struggle, thus sealing the fate of both Wilmington and the blockade running traffic that General Lee had deemed indispensable to the survival of his army. Bragg had refused to commit Hoke's Division to the relief of Fort Fisher because he believed that an attack upon the entrenched Union position north of the fort would have proved disastrous. From the fall of Fort Fisher to the battle of Wise's Forks on March 8-10, Hoke—and consequently Bragg—endured one setback after another. Only the capture of about 800 Union soldiers on March 8 had served to brighten an otherwise dismal campaign.[35]

Since his elevation to division-level command, Hoke had proved to be a disappointment. He had been a superb regimental and brigade commander, yet aside from the recapture of Plymouth, North Carolina, on April 20, 1864, he had demonstrated little capacity for division command. According to Douglas Southall Freeman, Hoke's fatal flaw was his unwillingness to cooperate with others. This criticism is unfair, however, particularly in light of Hoke's record as a regimental and brigade commander. If anything, Hoke's fatal flaw was his inflexibility, which often manifested itself in a tendency to put too literal a construction on his orders, even if the conditions governing those orders had changed. As a regimental or brigade commander, Hoke's rigid adherence to orders was commendable, but at the division level it spelled disaster whenever independence of action was needed. Ironically, Hoke's only success as a division commander came at Plymouth, where his superior, General Bragg, gave him a free hand in making his tactical decisions.[36]

Hoke deployed his four veteran brigades in two lines just south of the fork of the Goldsboro and Bentonville roads. On the left, he placed Brig. Gen. Johnson C. Hagood's Brigade on the front line, with Brig. Gen. William W. Kirkland's Brigade behind Hagood. On the right, Hoke deployed Colquitt's Brigade (under Col. Charles T. Zachry) in front, and Clingman's Brigade (under Col. William S. Devane) in rear of Colquitt.

Colonel John H. Nethercutt's Junior Reserves Brigade occupied a position that straddled the Goldsboro Road and extended northward along the west side of the Bentonville Road. The Reserves supported a six-gun battery from the 13th North Carolina Battalion (a.k.a. Starr's Battalion of artillery) commanded by Capt. George Atkins. Nethercutt's line was partially concealed by a narrow stand of pine trees that stood between the Willis Cole plantation and the Bentonville Road. From left to right, the 1st Reserves (70th North Carolina) held the Goldsboro Road, followed by the 2nd Reserves (71st North Carolina), Atkins' Battery, and the 3rd Reserves (72nd North Carolina). Millard's Battalion of Reserves formed in rear of the main line as a reserve.[37]

The Cole house, a whitewashed, two-story frame structure, stood on the northern edge of an open field about 200 yards west of the Junior Reserves' line. A barn and several other outbuildings also dotted the Cole field.[38]

* * *

As Hoke's veterans and Nethercutt's neophytes waited behind their works, Briant's Federal skirmishers continued driving Dibrell's dismounted cavalry with ease—that is, until the Confederate troopers halted about halfway across the Cole field and fired a parting volley into the faces of their pursuers. After unleashing the well-timed volley, the Southern cavalrymen vanished into the woods behind them.[39]

Meanwhile, Hobart ordered Lieutenant Colonel Fitch to advance his wing eastward along the right, or south, side of the Goldsboro Road. Fitch's three regiments—from left to right, the 104th Illinois, 21st Wisconsin, and 42nd Indiana—had moved forward about a mile when Carlin ordered the lieutenant colonel to form his line on

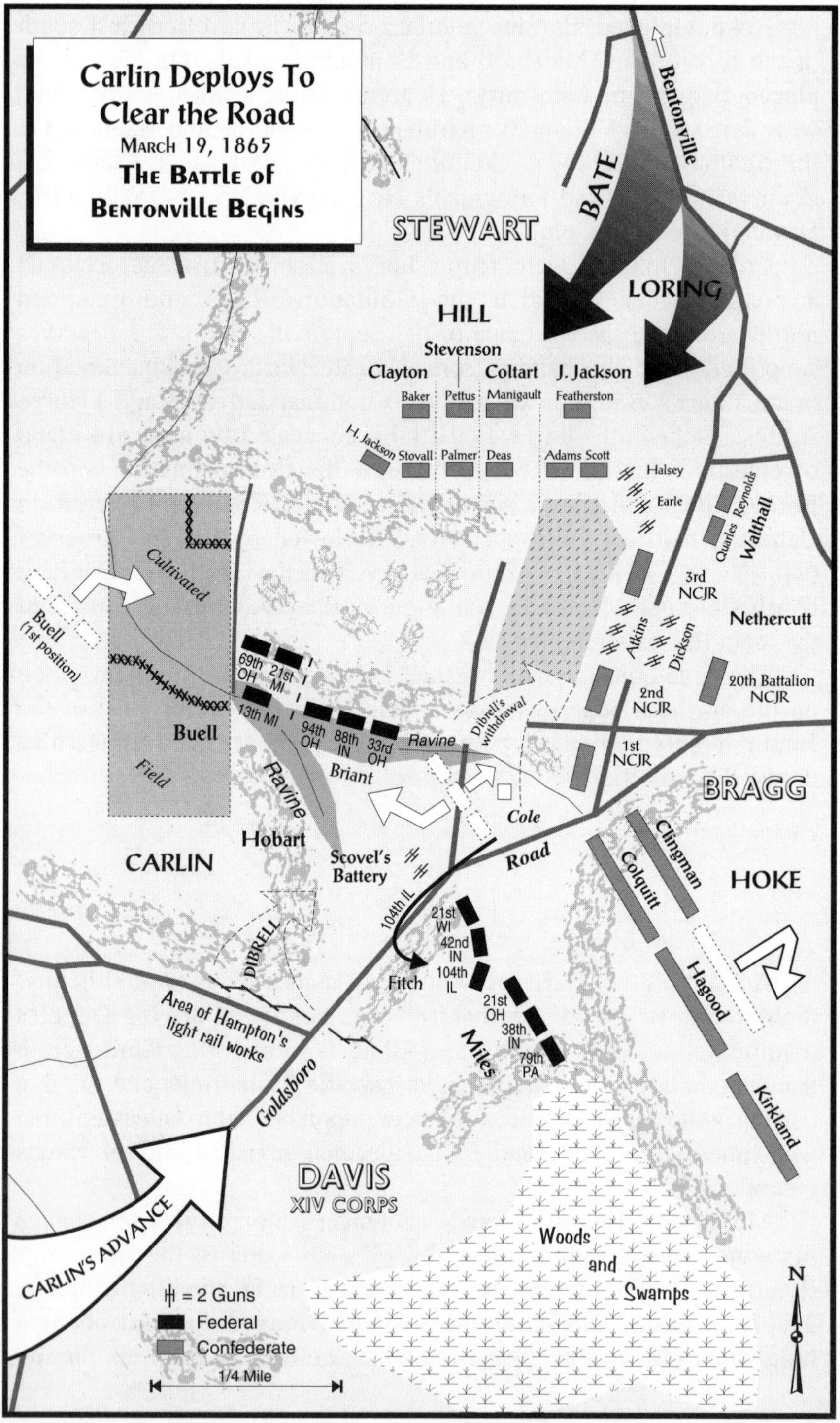

Carlin Deploys To Clear the Road
March 19, 1865
The Battle of Bentonville Begins
Bentonville
BATE
STEWART
LORING
HILL
Stevenson
Clayton
Coltart
J. Jackson
Baker
Pettus
Manigault
Featherston
H. Jackson
Stovall
Palmer
Deas
Adams
Scott
Halsey
Earle
Reynolds
Quarles
Walthall
3rd NCJR
Nethercutt
Atkins
Dickson
20th Battalion NCJR
2nd NCJR
1st NCJR
Cultivated
Field
Buell (1st position)
Buell
69th OH
21st MI
13th MI
94th OH
88th IN
33rd OH
Ravine
Dibrell's withdrawal
Briant
Ravine
Cole
BRAGG
Hobart
CARLIN
Scovel's Battery
Road
Clingman
Colquitt
HOKE
104th IL
21st WI
42nd IN
104th IL
Fitch
DIBRELL
Hagood
Area of Hampton's light rail works
21st OH
38th IN
79th PA
Miles
Goldsboro
Kirkland
DAVIS
XIV CORPS
CARLIN'S ADVANCE
Woods and Swamps
= 2 Guns
Federal
Confederate
1/4 Mile
N

Mark A. Moore

the right of Briant's wing. While Fitch maneuvered into position south of the road, his left regiment, the 104th Illinois, obliqued to the north side and formed on the right of the 94th Ohio of Briant's wing.[40]

Hobart now advanced both wings of his brigade. When Briant's wing reached the Cole house north of the Goldsboro Road, the Junior Reserves and Atkins' Battery opened fire. Some of Briant's men took shelter inside the house or the barn, while the rest hugged the earth and frantically scooped out crude entrenchments while the Rebel minie balls zipped by just above their heads.[41]

Captain Atkins directed two of his gunners to train their 12-pounder Napoleons on the Cole house and surrounding buildings. "Their shells and canon [sic] balls soon began to knock these Buildings to pieces," wrote Pvt. Joseph Hoffhines of the 33rd Ohio. A few brave Yankee souls withstood the barrage and poured a deadly fire from the second story windows of the Cole house into the ranks of the Junior Reserves. The boy soldiers cheered wildly when Atkins' Battery, "with a few well-directed shells, caused [the Yankees] to pour out [of the house] like rats out of a sinking ship," remembered one Reservist.[42]

The 33rd Ohio was thus driven from what little shelter the men had chanced to find. "We were in plain sight, in the open field, in musket range. . .we found the place a little unhealthy," recalled Capt. Joseph Hinson, the 33rd's commander. Hinson's men sprinted to a wooded ravine on their left and began to entrench on its forward slope, for they had discovered the enemy in force to the north as well. "During all this time," an uneasy Private Hoffhines noted, "the Bullets were whistling all around us and cutting the timber on every side." The 88th Indiana and 94th Ohio remained pinned down in the Cole field opposite the Junior Reserves' skirmishers, who were performing their work like veterans while kneeling behind a rail barricade at the edge of the woods.[43]

After driving the Ohioans from the Cole buildings, Atkins' Battery directed its fire on Fitch's wing south of the road. A few errant rounds tore through the pines behind Fitch's main line, narrowly missing Generals Slocum, Davis and Carlin. Lieutenant Colonel Fitch responded to this fire by shifting his command about 200 yards to the right (south) in an effort to conceal his line from Atkins' gunners. Consequently, the 104th Illinois left the Cole field and returned to the south side of the Goldsboro Road. A few misplaced Southern shells had broken the tenuous connection between Hobart's two "wings." Although his troops were now concealed from the enemy gunners' view, Fitch's view was likewise obstructed by the dense woods bordering the Goldsboro Road. Fitch assumed that Briant was still within supporting distance, but he was mistaken: the two wings would operate as separate entities for the rest of the day. Hobart would remain with Briant's wing, thus leaving Fitch in independent command of his three regiments.[44]

Fitch abruptly forgot his left flank when Carlin galloped up and warned him that his right flank was in danger of being turned. Carlin had been reconnoitering the ground just beyond Fitch's right when he spotted a line of Confederates moving in for a flank attack. He ordered Maj. John Widmer, the commander of the 104th Illinois, to double-quick his regiment over to the right of the 42nd Indiana, the far right of Fitch's line. Major Widmer sent out Company F, under Capt. William Strawn, as his skirmish line. While groping their way through a thicket, Strawn's men collided with Hoke's skirmishers. Captain Strawn recalled:

> It didn't take long for every man to seek cover behind the nearest tree or sapling and then keep a sharp look-out for a Rebel uniform. This was not always safe, for discovering a blue blouse a few paces in front, and supposing it belonged to one of my men, I tried to restrain one of my boys from firing at it. I had hardly spoken when a puff of smoke arose and a bullet from the gun of the man in the blue blouse barked the sapling where my skirmisher stood. The rebel dropped as he fired and crawled away. . . .I did not caution any one again not to fire to the front.[45]

Company F maintained such a rapid and continuous fire that the men soon ran low on ammunition. Captain Strawn sent back for more and informed Widmer that the force in his front was indeed infantry—*Rebel* infantry. There was now no doubt that Hampton's troopers were supported by foot soldiers, but how many were there?[46]

Major Widmer crept up to the skirmish line to see for himself. He was soon hit by a bullet that sent him sprawling.

One of his men called out, "Major, are you hurt?"

"N-o-o," Widmer replied, "with a look of disgust I shall never forget," wrote Captain Strawn.

The missile that had struck Widmer proved to be a spent ball which had merely torn off the heel of his boot, leaving him with a painful bruise nonetheless.[47]

While Strawn's skirmishers engaged Hoke's men, Fitch deployed his line for battle. The 21st Wisconsin faced due east, its left touching the Goldsboro Road. On the 21st's right, the line of the 42nd Indiana and 104th Illinois was swung back to defend against an expected Confederate flank attack from the southeast. Without waiting for orders, Fitch's men wisely began to entrench.[48]

Meanwhile, Lt. Palmer Scovel's battery (Battery C, 1st Illinois Light Artillery) rolled into view and unlimbered just above the Goldsboro Road and to the left of the 21st Wisconsin, 350 yards south-southwest of the Cole house. Scovel's battery consisted of four 3-inch ordnance rifles and was attached to Carlin's division. Scanning the terrain in their immediate front, battery commander Scovel and his gunners glimpsed what appeared to be a broken line of Confederate earthworks in the woods along the eastern edge of the Cole field. They could also see Atkins' Confederate battery northeast of the Cole house. The gunners accordingly sighted their ordnance rifles and began firing shot and shell at the half-concealed Rebel targets.[49]

* * *

While Hoke's Division skirmished with Hobart's brigade, Lt. Gen. A. P. Stewart's 4,500-man contingent of the Army of Tennessee began marching into position. The two divisions of Stewart's old corps led the way, commanded by Maj. Gen. William W. Loring. Loring's former division had the advance and was commanded by Col. James Jackson, while Loring's other division was led by Maj. Gen. Edward C. Walthall. Both Loring's (Jackson's) and Walthall's divisions had been shattered the previous autumn in the futile charge at Franklin and in the rout at Nashville. Going into the fight at Bentonville, Loring's Division numbered just 650 effectives and Walthall's a paltry 240, leaving Stewart's Corps with 890 officers and men—less than an early-war regiment. But what

Walthall's Division lacked in strength of numbers, it more than compensated for in toughness and tenacity. No less an authority than cavalryman Nathan Bedford Forrest esteemed Walthall's Division and its commander so highly that on the retreat from Nashville he chose Walthall's two brigades to form the core of the army's rear guard and Walthall to command the rear guard's infantry. When told that Walthall had accepted the post, Forrest said, "Now we will keep them [the enemy] back."[50]

Wade Hampton's battle plan had called for Hardee's Corps to occupy the center of the Confederate line, but since Hardee's troops had not yet reached the field, Hampton recommended placing his two horse artillery batteries, Halsey's and Earle's, in the resulting gap. General Johnston adopted Hampton's suggestion. By the time the head of Stewart's column came into view, Hampton's two batteries were already in position, occupying an open field and facing southwest at a 45-degree angle to Hoke's line. Stewart ordered Loring's Division to deploy in the woods on the right of the horse artillery. Scott's and Adams' Brigades, commanded respectively by Capt. John A. Dixon and Lt. Col. Robert J. Lawrence, manned the first line, while Featherston's Brigade, led by Maj. Martin A. Oatis, formed the second line.[51]

As Col. Jackson moved Loring's old division into position, Stewart directed Walthall to deploy his division on the left of the horse artillery. Walthall led his troops into position, accompanied by his two brigade commanders, Maj. Gen. D. H. Hill, and several other officers. Generals Johnston and Hampton rode up and viewed the procession. An anxious Johnston noted that "the deployment of the troops consumed a weary time." Although the men were under strict orders to make no unnecessary noise, the veterans of the Army of Tennessee loudly cheered "Old Joe," who tipped his hat in reply. Moments later, a few cannon balls screamed by overhead and plummeted into the woods behind the cheering soldiers.[52]

Walthall deployed his division in a blackjack oak and pine wood about 200 yards in rear of the Junior Reserves' right flank, and formed his command in a single line. Quarles' Brigade, under Brig. Gen. George D. Johnston held the left of the line, and Brig. Gen. Daniel H. Reynolds' Brigade manned the right. Walthall's line faced a little north of west, enabling it, if necessary, to swing out beyond the Reserves' flank and advance into the open field, either to support the artillery or to join in a general assault.[53]

While Walthall's troops marched into position along the northeastern edge of the field, an enemy shell came hurtling down on the generals and struck "Old Bob," General Reynolds' mount. Reynolds later recorded the incident in his diary:

> It [the shell] entered my horse's breast & came out under my left leg, cutting away my stirrup & breaking my leg just below the knee & tearing off a great part of the calf of [my] leg & then killed a horse standing next to mine. My horse reared up & taking my right foot out of the stirrup, with my hands I threw myself out of the saddle, falling on the dead horse, the blood from my Horse's side spurting over me, & fearing my horse would fall on me[,] I, by aid of a bush got out in front of him, the noble animal still standing tho' a stream of blood larger than my arm was gushing from his breast. Fearing he might fall forward on me[,] I called for help but it was already there, my litter bearers seeing me fall had come running.

General Reynolds was then carried to an ambulance, which took him to the main Confederate hospital at Bentonville.[54]

The shell that struck Reynolds may have overshot its intended target. Just a few yards away, Halsey's and Earle's Batteries stood in the middle of the open field, an inviting target for counter-battery fire. Moreover, they were under orders not to open fire and thereby call attention to themselves. The shell that wounded Reynolds and killed Old Bob bore grim testimony to the fact that these orders had outlasted their usefulness. Halsey's men scrambled for cover amid the bursting shells, some crouching beneath their guns while others sprawled behind field stumps. One of the first shell bursts killed duelist Marx Cohen. Minutes later, Cohen's dueling adversary, Thomas Chew, fell mortally wounded. Chew's second, Leonidas Raysor, lost an arm to a shell fragment. Soon Cohen's second, William Verdier, could hear the familiar voices of his battery mates cry out above the din: "Look out, Verd! Your turn next!"[55]

Fortunately for Private Verdier, Generals Johnston and Hampton rode up to investigate. Halsey requested permission to open fire, which the generals granted. The battery roared into action.[56] Aside from Cohen, Chew and Raysor, Halsey's Battery lost four more men with severe wounds. A passing Confederate counted a dozen horses lying dead or wounded in the area of Halsey's guns.

The quiet suffering of these wounded creatures made a lasting impression on him: “To this day I recall the piteous expressions of two or three of these wounded horses, as they raised their heads in their suffering and looked at us as we passed them.”[57]

The wounding of Reynolds and the ravaging of Halsey's Battery were the result of Lieutenant Scovel's fire, since his battery was the only Federal artillery on the field at that time. Although Scovel could not have seen these targets from his position near the Goldsboro Road, his fire was too accurate to have been accidental. Perhaps he had received some assistance from the 33rd Ohio in sighting his field pieces.

The Confederate batteries replied with solid shot, killing or wounding several of Scovel's and Fitch's men. The commander of the left-most company of the 21st Wisconsin, Capt. James M. Randall, observed the artillery duel from the roadside. At one point, one of Slocum's staff officers rode up to where Randall was standing, looked “wisely towards the front,” and asked, “What regiment is this?”

Capt. Randall replied, “The Twenty-first Wisconsin.”

“Why don't you move on,” the staff officer said, “there is nothing but cavalry there.”

Suddenly, an artillery projectile shrieked past: the startled staff officer wheeled his horse about and galloped for the rear and safety.[58]

* * *

Shortly after 10:00 a.m. Stephen D. Lee's three-division corps began filing into position on the right of Loring's Division of Stewart's Corps. Lee's Corps numbered 2,687 effectives, by far the largest representation of the Army of Tennessee's three corps. Lieutenant General Lee was not present to lead his corps into battle, having been wounded during the retreat from Nashville. After a slow recuperation, he was leading a column of stragglers and convalescents northward from Augusta, Georgia. Filling in for Lee at Bentonville was Maj. Gen. Daniel Harvey Hill, whose indisputable talent for field command was marred by his sharp tongue and waspish disposition.[59]

D. H. Hill was feeling sick this Sunday morning. This was not unusual, as poor health had plagued Hill throughout the war. He attributed his chronic malaise to the rigors of a soldier's life, but his critics would later assert that he suffered from hypochondria, a malady also ascribed to his late brother-in-law, Thomas J. "Stonewall" Jackson. Hill shared at least two other traits with Jackson: he was a devout Presbyterian, and he was absolutely fearless in battle.[60]

Hill was born in 1821. A graduate of West Point (class of 1842) and a veteran of the Mexican War, Hill was superintendent of the North Carolina Military Institute when the Civil War broke out. As colonel of the 1st North Carolina Volunteers, Hill had led his command in the Battle of Big Bethel, the first Southern victory of the war. He went on to serve as a major general under Joseph E. Johnston during the Peninsula Campaign. Following Johnston's wounding at Seven Pines, Hill served under Robert E. Lee. The North Carolinian was something of a gadfly to Lee, openly criticizing his conduct of the battles of Malvern Hill and South Mountain. Hill was also a notorious croaker, or prophet of doom, and it didn't help matters that his prognostications were usually correct. Despite Hill's superb performance in defending the "Bloody Lane" at Antietam, Lee found his behavior insufferable.[61]

Confederate president Jefferson Davis hoped to salvage the deteriorating situation by transferring Hill to the Western theater. On July 10, 1863, Davis notified Hill that he had promoted him to lieutenant general, pending Senatorial approval. Within a week Hill was ordered to report to Gen. Braxton Bragg at Chattanooga, Tennessee. He went on to command a corps in Bragg's Army of Tennessee, and enjoyed a role in that army's only major victory. But before the year was out, he found himself a virtual outcast in an army well-stocked with outcasts.[62]

The Battle of Chickamauga was fought on September 19-20, 1863, about five miles southeast of Chattanooga. Although the first day's fighting was inconclusive, the second day's battle resulted in a Union rout. Only Maj. Gen. George H. Thomas's valiant stand on the Federal left flank prevented Bragg from crushing the Army of the Cumberland. On the 21st, Bragg allowed the Yankees to slip unmolested into their fortifications around Chattanooga.[63]

Most of Bragg's generals, D. H. Hill included, were furious with Bragg for bungling what they believed had been the Confederacy's golden opportunity to change the course of the war in the West. All the fighting had gained them was 20,000 casualties, more than one-fourth their number. The disaffected generals drafted and signed a petition that called for the removal of Braxton Bragg from command of the Army of Tennessee. They had intended to send their petition by courier to President Davis, but when Davis arrived unannounced at their camp in mid-October, they decided to shelve the petition and appeal to the president in person. Hill filed the petition among his personal papers.[64]

After conferring with Bragg, Davis summoned the army's corps commanders to Bragg's headquarters tent. Davis asked the assembled generals to voice their opinion on whether Bragg should remain in command. In Bragg's presence each of the generals stated that Bragg was unfit to command the Army of Tennessee. The result of this singular conference was that Davis sustained Bragg, and Bragg thereupon sacked Hill.[65]

Hill was a convenient scapegoat. Since he had the petition in his files, Bragg incorrectly assumed that he was its author and the leader of the anti-Bragg faction. Moreover, at the time of his dismissal, Hill had no powerful political allies whom he could call upon for support. As far as Davis was concerned, Hill's dismissal would enable the president's old friend, Lt. Gen. Leonidas Polk, to slip off the hook, for after the battle of Chickamauga Bragg had suspended Polk and charged him with dereliction of duty. It was an endless source of consternation to Davis that two of his favorites, Polk and Bragg, were such bitter enemies.[66]

Hill waited several months for orders assigning him to a new command. None came. In December 1863, the Confederate Senate reconvened, but Hill's name was not on Davis' list of promotions. Hill's rank therefore reverted to that of major general. He responded by peppering Davis and Adjutant General Samuel Cooper with applications for a court of inquiry, without success. Hill refused several command assignments because they were not accompanied by an official expression of undiminished confidence in his capabilities. In July 1864, he returned to his old job as mathematics professor at Davidson College near Charlotte, North Carolina. Meanwhile, his father-in-law, newly elected Senator William A. Graham of North Carolina, lobbied for him in Richmond. In October, Hill asked North Carolina governor Zebulon Vance to sound out President Davis. Vance proposed that Hill be given command of the eastern portion of the Department of North Carolina. This was an unfortunate suggestion, for none other than Braxton Bragg commanded that department. Davis referred the letter to Robert E. Lee, whose reply is a masterpiece of understatement: "General Hill is brave, watchful, and patriotic. . .[but] I fear there may be a want of harmony between the two [Bragg and Hill]."[67]

Thanks to Senator Graham's adroit political maneuvering, Hill received orders in late December to report to General Beauregard in Charleston. By mid-January 1865, Hill was commanding the District of Georgia from his headquarters in Augusta, and on March 3, he assumed command of Edward Johnson's old division and with it temporary command of Lee's Corps. Hill had finally resumed his old place in the Army of Tennessee —that is, what was left of it.[68]

On March 7, Johnston ordered Hill to report with his troops to Bragg, who was preparing to oppose Jacob Cox's Federals at Wise's Forks. Johnston closed his dispatch to Hill with this plea: "I beg you to forget the past for this emergency." In deference to "Old Joe," Hill swallowed his pride and joined Bragg at the front. By March 16, however, Hill had reached the end of his rope. He wrote Johnston: "I hope that it may be possible & consistent with interests of the service to give us another commander than Genl Bragg. He has made me a scape-goat once & would do it again. I cant feel otherwise than unpleasantly situated."[69]

Hill got his wish. But as he sat upon his horse that fine Sunday morning and supervised the deployment of his troops, he knew that Bragg was somewhere nearby doing the same thing. Hill also knew that given the capricious nature of battle, the army's fate might eventually rest in Bragg's hands. The ailing Hill must have reflected on this state of affairs with a mixture of dread and despair.

While General Hill looked on, Col. John G. Coltart led Hill's old division into position on Loring's right. Deas' Brigade, under Lt. Col. Harry Toulmin, occupied the front line, while Manigault's Brigade, under Lt. Col. John C. Carter, formed in reserve.[70]

The second division of Lee's (Hill's) corps, under Maj. Gen. Carter L. Stevenson, deployed on Coltart's right. Brigadier General Joseph B. Palmer's Brigade manned the front line, while Brig. Gen. Edmund W. Pettus' Brigade deployed about 250 yards in rear of Palmer.[71]

Major General Henry D. Clayton's command, the corps' third division, equaled A. P. Stewart's entire corps in number of effectives. Clayton placed his two smaller brigades on the front line, deploying Stovall's Brigade, commanded by Col. Henry C. Kellogg, on the left, and Jackson's Brigade, led by Lt. Col. Osceola Kyle, on the right. Brigadier General Alpheus Baker's Brigade occupied the rear line. Major L. P. Thomas of the 42nd Georgia, Stovall's Brigade, recalled that while his regiment marched into position, "firing could be heard in the distance, and the movements of couriers and aides rushing here and there indicated a battle on hand."[72]

While Hill's (Coltart's) Division faced thick pine woods, the terrain in Stevenson's and Clayton's front, while wooded, was more open. A few hundred yards beyond the woods on Clayton's right flank lay a narrow, open field which extended for several hundred yards to the south.

While his command was thus deploying, Hill rode out to reconnoiter the ground in his front and on his right. Just south of the open field, Hill glimpsed a ragged line of Federals advancing toward him through a tangled thicket. He galloped back to his command and ordered Coltart to send out a skirmish line. Lieutenant S. A. Roberts of the 39th Alabama and a handful of men from Deas' Brigade answered Coltart's call for volunteers. [73]

What Hill had caught sight of was George P. Buell's skirmish line feeling for the Confederate right flank. Buell's undersized brigade consisted of the 13th Michigan, 21st Michigan and 69th Ohio. Fielding just 630 officers and men, it was the smallest brigade in Slocum's Army of Georgia. As Buell's skirmishers dashed from woodline to woodline across the southern end of the field, they traded shots with Lieutenant Roberts' squad. "Before we had developed our own strength. . .to the enemy," Buell reported, "orders reached us to return and take position on the left of General Hobart's brigade." But if Buell had managed to conceal his strength from the Confederates, he had also failed to develop *their* strength, which was the reason Slocum had sent him out in the first place. Buell—and Slocum—would later have cause to regret this missed opportunity.[74]

About 11:00 a.m. Carlin ordered Hobart to shift the 88th Indiana and the 94th Ohio of Briant's wing from their exposed position in the Cole field northwest to a ravine, where they formed on the left of the 33rd Ohio. As soon as the two regiments reached their new position, they began to entrench. Thanks to nearly a full hour's head start, the 33rd's works were already well underway.[75]

As Hobart shifted his regiments north of the Goldsboro Road, Buell's brigade fell back after its skirmish with pickets from the Army of Tennessee and deployed on Briant's left, along the northern slope of the same ravine occupied by Briant's wing. "I do not remember seeing any troops on our right," wrote one of Buell's officers, Lt. Marcus Bates of the 21st Michigan. "Briant was there, but beyond our sight in thick pine woods. It looked as if any forward movement of the enemy would surround us." Buell arranged his line in two ranks and set his men to work building rail barricades. The brigade ambulance train parked alongside a road that ran behind and parallel to Buell's line. This road continued past Buell's refused left flank and curved northward, running straight into the Confederate line 600 yards to the north. Buell deployed two companies of skirmishers under Capt. George M. Rowe along his front and his left flank stretching across the road. As a further safeguard, Buell directed a detachment of his mounted foragers to build a barricade across the road in advance of the skirmishers at a point where the road veered sharply toward the enemy lines. The skirmishers noted with some unease that they were advancing into the same field they had dashed across under enemy fire just a few minutes before.[76]

On the right of Carlin's line—south of the Goldsboro Road—Fitch's wing held steady, though it was hard pressed to do so, especially along the front and right flank of the 104th Illinois. As a precaution, Carlin ordered his Third Brigade, Lt. Col. David Miles commanding, to form in reserve behind Fitch's line and Scovel's battery. Under a galling fire of artillery and musketry, the 38th Indiana and the 21st Ohio deployed south of the Goldsboro Road and the 79th Pennsylvania deployed north of it in support of Scovel's battery. As Company C of the 79th was marching into position, an enemy shell exploded in its ranks, wounding three men. In response to the enemy's artillery barrage, Miles shifted the 79th Pennsylvania to the south side of the road, where it formed on the right of the brigade. The 38th Indiana was now the center regiment, and the 21st Ohio remained on its left. The brigade executed a right oblique and advanced until it connected with Fitch's right flank.

Miles refused the line of the 79th Pennsylvania and ordered his entire brigade "to throw up temporary works."[77]

No sooner had Miles gone into position on Fitch's right than his own right flank came under a severe fire from Hoke's Division, several hundred yards to the east. General Davis therefore ordered Brig. Gen. James D. Morgan's division to "feel forward for the right of Carlin's line and form thereon." According to Morgan, it was just after 11:00 a.m. when he received Davis' order "to hurry forward two of his three brigades to Carlin's assistance."[78]

The 54-year-old Morgan had led an adventurous life. At the age of 16 he signed on as a hand aboard the merchantman *Beverly*. What followed might have come from a Herman Melville novel. One month into Morgan's first voyage some of the crew mutinied, the ship burned at sea, and Morgan drifted in a lifeboat for two weeks before reaching the South American coast. It is hardly surprising that Morgan lost his taste for the seafaring life at an early age.[79]

A native of Boston, Morgan moved to Quincy, Illinois, in 1835, where he prospered as a businessman catering to the ever-increasing traffic along the Mississippi River. During the 1840s he led the town's militia company, the Quincy Greys, and served as a captain in the 1st Illinois Infantry during the Mexican War. These early experiences in company-level command taught Morgan the importance of drill in sharpening a unit's fighting capabilities.[80]

Morgan began his Civil War service in April 1861, as lieutenant colonel of the 10th Illinois. He rose in rank steadily, if unspectacularly, and by the opening of the March to the Sea, was leading the Second Division of the XIV Corps. One of Morgan's staff officers wrote that the general believed his first duty was "to follow exactly his orders. This was his fundamental principle as an officer. . . .There were many officers who could have planned campaigns better than he, but no one who could carry out a definite program and hold on in defense of a position he was assigned to, with a more obstinate determination and indomitable purpose than he." Morgan was a literalist cut from the same mold as his adversary Robert Hoke. Though he lacked brilliance and dash, Morgan was the sort of man who could be relied upon to hold a position to the last.[81]

Morgan was popular with his men, in part because he lived like them, sleeping under a tent fly while his staff usually slept in a nearby house. One of Morgan's veterans remembered that "Old Jimmy [was] brave, active, unostentatious, patient, and untiring. He earned his pay, and it ever seemed to be his endeavor to make the boys earn theirs." Another soldier wrote, "Morgan. . .is a man of small and wiry figure, . . .an earnest, modest, and conscientious soldier."[82]

He was also fond of a prank, even if it was played at his own expense. In his *Personal Recollections*, Chaplain George Pepper relates an anecdote about Morgan that goes far in explaining why his men liked him:

> Morgan in his dress looks more like a wagon-Master than a General. On a certain occasion a new recruit, who had just arrived in camp, lost a few articles and was inquiring for them among the veterans in hopes of finding them. An old soldier, fond of his sport, told the new recruit that the only thief in the brigade was in Jim Morgan's tent. The recruit immediately started for Jim's quarters, and poking his head in, asked: "Does Jim Morgan live here?"
>
> "Yes," was the reply. "My name is *James* Morgan."
>
> "Then I want you to hand over those books you stole from me!"
>
> "I have none of your books, my man."
>
> "It is an infernal lie!" exclaimed the recruit. "The boys say you are the only thief in camp. Turn out them books, or I'll grind your carcass into apple sass!"
>
> The general relished the joke very much, but seeing the sinewy recruit peeling off his coat, [the general] informed him of his relations to the brigade, and the recruit walked off. . .remarking, "Wall, blast me if I'd take you for a Brigadier. Excuse me, General, I don't know the ropes yet."[83]

In response to Davis' orders, Morgan's troops trotted past ammunition wagons, batteries and ambulances until they reached the front, where they left the Goldsboro Road and plunged into a wooded swamp on Lieutenant Colonel Miles' right. Morgan's Second Brigade, commanded by Brig. Gen. John G. Mitchell, led the way. Mitchell sent out the 78th Illinois to find the enemy's position. On his front line, Mitchell posted, from left to right, the 98th, 108th and 113th Ohio regiments, with the 34th Illinois and

121st Ohio anchoring the flanks of the rear line. Morgan's Third Brigade, led by Brig. Gen. Benjamin D. Fearing, formed in close column of regiments behind Mitchell and somewhat to his right. As listed in its March 19 order of march, Fearing's brigade consisted of the 52nd Ohio, 86th Illinois, 22nd Indiana and 125th Illinois. The 85th Illinois remained behind on train guard duty and would not take part in the battle.[84]

"As soon as these positions were established," wrote Sgt. Lyman Widney of the 34th Illinois, "our first line began to build intrenchments from force of habit, as we had no idea that we would find any use for them, [sic] the enemy had been so little disposed to stand long on the defensive, much less to attack intrenchments." Mitchell's second line quickly followed suit. Finding the ground "boggy and interspersed with little swamps," Mitchell's men discarded their shovels and took up their axes or hatchets. They piled up "logs, stumps, limbs. . .and anything [else] that could be got hold of for turning bullets," recalled one soldier, then cemented their "rude breast-work of timber" with shovelfuls of muddy soil. While Mitchell's brigade was entrenching, Fearing's troops formed a double line in rear of Mitchell and began building their own works. Morgan also ordered Fearing to send out the 125th Illinois to cover the division's right flank and rear.[85]

Meanwhile, the 78th Illinois and Miles' skirmishers drove Hagood's Rebel skirmishers back to their main line. The Confederate skirmishers reported that the Federals were massing on their left flank. Hagood accordingly sent a warning to Hoke that his left was in danger of being turned. In response, Hoke pulled Kirkland's Brigade out of its supporting position and hurried it forward to deploy on Hagood's left. The Confederate line once again extended beyond the Federals' right flank. Morgan therefore requested that Davis send forward his First Brigade, which had remained at the rear guarding the trains.[86]

While Davis ordered his sixth and last available brigade to the front, Slocum, "fearing that the firing would be heard by Sherman and cause the other wing of the army to delay its march," sent Maj. Eugene W. Guindon of his staff to Sherman "to tell him that I had met a strong force of cavalry, but that I should not need assistance, and felt confident [that] I should be at the Neuse [River] at the appointed time." Slocum also hurried forward the XX Corps, intending to deploy it on Morgan's right "with a view of turning the left of the enemy's position." In the meantime, he instructed Morgan and Carlin "to press the enemy closely and force him to develop his position and strength." In accordance with Slocum's order, Davis directed Carlin to attack the enemy with Buell's brigade (Davis evidently did not order either of Morgan's two brigades to attack because they were still deploying). "In order to multiply the chances of success," Carlin directed Briant's wing to support Buell's assault, and Miles' brigade to attack south of the Goldsboro Road as well. Carlin ordered the assault to commence at noon.[87]

* * *

D. H. Hill was eager to attack the Yankees. But as time passed and no advance was ordered, he saw no reason for his men to remain idle. Although A. P. Stewart did not think it advisable to entrench so long as the plan was to attack, Hill ordered his men to start digging anyway, believing that time wouldn't weigh so heavily on their hands if they were kept busy. Hill also ordered forward a strong skirmish line, which he placed under the command of Lt. Col John P. McGuire, to cover his front and right flank. McGuire deployed his skirmishers about 300 yards in front of the main line.[88]

As Lee's (Hill's) Corps began to entrench, Maj. Gen. William B. Bate arrived on the field with his command, a remnant of Cheatham's Corps numbering a scant 900 effectives. Bate's contingent consisted of his own division, now led by Col. Daniel L. Kenan, and two brigades of Cleburne's Division commanded by Brig. Gen. James A. Smith. Bate led Cleburne's Division into position, placing Govan's Brigade, commanded by Col. Peter V. Green, on the left of the front line, and Smith's Brigade, under Capt. J. R. Bonner, on the right. Bate's (Kenan's) Division manned the reserve line, and consisted of Tyler's Brigade, led by Maj. W. H. Wilkinson, which deployed behind Govan, and Finley's Brigade, under Lt. Col. Elisha Washburn, which filed into position behind Smith.[89]

As soon as the enemy's bullets began to zip by, Bate ordered the men on the front line to lie down. The sound of the passing minies terrified the veterans of Smith's Brigade, who had last heard them during the debacle at Nashville three months before. As Bate calmly sat on his horse in rear of the front line, he remarked that Pat Cleburne's boys were hugging the ground "mighty close," and chided them for having poked fun at his own men for doing the same thing.[90]

Like so many other of his fellow generals in the Army of Tennessee, the 38-year-old Bate was a lawyer and a self-educated man, and he had a nickname "Old Grits." Prior to the war he had held a variety of jobs, from clerk to newspaper editor, before finally establishing his law practice in Nashville. A Mexican War veteran, Bate began the war as colonel of the 2nd Tennessee Infantry. Beginning at Shiloh, a series of wounds had shattered the health of the once-brawny Bate, who now rode with a pair of crutches strapped to his saddle; when leading his troops into battle, he was more apt to brandish a crutch than his sword.[91]

Now that Bate's contingent was in position, the Confederates had approximately 10,000 officers and men on the field. Although Hardee's Corps had not yet deployed, the Southerners outnumbered the Federals, whose commanders still labored under the assumption that they faced only a division of cavalry. Thus, Carlin prepared to assault the Confederates with just 2,000 effectives, though his men, such as Lieutenant Bates of Buell's brigade, suspected that the Rebels in their front outnumbered them by a substantial margin. Before the day was done, many of Carlin's men would lose their lives proving their commanders wrong.

* * *

In accordance with Carlin's orders, Miles' brigade attacked Hoke's position just before noon. The Federals struggled across a briar-choked swamp while Hagood's and Kirkland's Confederates subjected them to a severe fire from the relative safety of their entrenchments. Miles' brigade obliqued to the right in feeling for the Confederate flank, and as a result, his line of battle advanced across Mitchell's front, striking both Hagood's and Kirkland's positions.[92]

The men of Miles' three regiments—the 38th Indiana, 21st Ohio and 79th Pennsylvania—dropped to the ground and crept forward to within 50 yards of Hagood's and Kirkland's entrenchments. The gunpowder smoke grew so thick that the advancing Federals became disoriented. As a result of this confusion, the commander of the 38th Indiana, Capt. James H. Low, received a report that his troops were firing on their own men. Low ordered his command to cease fire until he could determine who they were firing upon. It proved to be Captain Low's final order, for he fell mortally wounded only moments after issuing it.[93]

Not surprisingly, Miles' assault ground to a halt within 50 yards of Hoke's line. Realizing that his brigade stood "no chance of carrying the [enemy's] works in consequence of the impenetrable thicket and the depth of the swamp"—a difficulty compounded by the veteran opposition he faced—Miles called off the costly attack. As the Federals fell back, Hagood's and Kirkland's skirmishers pursued them, while Rebel details brought off the wounded and gathered the Federals' abandoned rifles and accouterments. "Our loss was trivial," Confederate general Hagood recalled, "the men having with great rapidity covered themselves with earth and log obstructions."[94]

Given the decisive repulse of Miles' brigade, the assault can only be regarded as a Union failure. Yet, Hampton believed that it may have saved the day for the Federals. Although Miles' assault had failed, his brigade had struck with enough force to induce Bragg to apply to Johnston for reinforcements. Relying on his experienced subordinate's judgment, Johnston promptly reinforced Bragg. But "Old Joe" came to regret his decisión so much that he later omitted his name from his account of the incident: "Lieutenant-General Hardee, the head of whose column was then near, was directed, most injudiciously, to send his leading division, McLaws', to the assistance of [Hoke's Division]." When Johnston notified Hampton of his decision to reinforce Bragg, Hampton urged him to reconsider. "This movement," Hampton wrote, "was in my judgment the only mistake committed on our part during the fight." Hampton believed that if McLaws' Division had assumed its assigned position in the center and the attack had commenced two hours earlier than it did, the Confederates would have routed Slocum's wing. Instead, Johnston sent McLaws to Bragg's assistance, and committed the one irretrievable tactical blunder of the day, or so Hampton thought. In any case, the assault of Miles' brigade bought valuable time for the Federals by delaying the main

Confederate attack, and led Johnston to detach one-quarter of his infantry from his striking force.[95]

* * *

On the morning of March 19, Lafayette McLaws' Division had broken camp before dawn and marched southward six miles on the Devil's Race Path, reaching Bentonville at 9:00 a.m. McLaws noted that on his arrival he "shook hands warmly with Genl. Johnston & Genl. Bragg." The Army of Northern Virginia veteran permitted his men to fall out and rest in the yard of the Bentonville Methodist Church while they waited for A. P. Stewart's column to clear the road. Since they had been denied a chance to eat breakfast before setting out on the march, McLaws' troops, Pvt. Kinchen J. Carpenter of the 50th North Carolina among them, "ate such rations as we had— generally fat bacon and hardtack."[96]

McLaws' men were able to snatch a few hours' rest before receiving the order to fall in. They marched south on the Bentonville Road, past the Army of Tennessee's position on their right, until they reached the intersection of the Goldsboro Road. Bragg, mounted on his horse by the roadside, was doubtless relieved to see the head of McLaws' column come tramping into view. A Georgian in McLaws' Division described the dour Bragg's appearance on the morning of the battle: "He was clean-shaven except [for] closely[-]trimmed side whiskers, a tall man, weighing 160 or 175 pounds."[97]

McLaws reported that he deployed his division "with great difficulty" because of the dense thickets, the knee-deep swamps, and the clouds of gunpowder smoke that obstructed its path. Nor did it help that the staff officers Bragg had sent along to guide McLaws to Hoke's left "lost their way every time." McLaws finally sent out the 3rd South Carolina of Conner's Brigade to feel for Hoke's flank, which the veteran regiment found just as Hoke was repulsing Miles' assault. Bragg ordered McLaws to remain on Hoke's left nonetheless, informing his temporary subordinate "that General Stewart would attack the enemy in flank," and that McLaws "must be ready to strike a blow if an opportunity offered." McLaws sent out some skirmishers in his front, deployed his division in two lines, and set his men to work building fortifications.[98]

As for Stewart's contemplated attack, it would have to wait. The Federals confronting the Army of Tennessee contingent were about to launch an assault of their own.

~ *nine* ~

"Old Joe Will Give Billy Sherman Hell To-day"

—Southern Teamster

General Buell received Carlin's order to undertake a flanking maneuver against the Army of Tennessee just before noon. Buell already had his men marching to the left when Carlin countermanded the order and instructed Buell to return to his position on the left of Briant's wing of Hobart's brigade. Carlin now ordered Generals Buell and Hobart to "charge the enemy and discover what force was in our front." Carlin had altered his tactics: instead of flanking the Confederate position, he would test its strength by subjecting it to a frontal assault.[1]

As commander of Company C, 21st Michigan, Lt. Marcus Bates was briefed on Buell's plan of attack. The brigade would advance in two ranks, the 69th Ohio on the left and the 21st Michigan on the right of the front rank, with the 13th Michigan following in reserve. The front rank would advance on the enemy position as far as possible; if it faltered, the 13th Michigan would charge through the front rank and carry the Confederate works—at least according to Buell's plan. Lieutenant Bates scanned the terrain before him:

> On our right was a thick woods filled with a dense undergrowth, on our front an open pine woods through which we could see the works and lines of the enemy, and on the left the open field we had crossed coming into our present position, and beyond this field thick woods.[2]

About 600 yards separated the opposing lines. Briant's wing would have to struggle through the undergrowth, whereas Buell's brigade would have an easier time of it in advancing through the open woods and the field. But their blessing might prove to be a curse if they failed to drive the enemy, for in the open they would make easy targets for the Confederates' rifle-muskets.[3]

Lieutenant Bates had no qualms about the quality of his command. "I knew every man perfectly," he wrote, "and felt entire confidence in every one." Moreover, General Carlin appeared certain of success as he walked along the line speaking words of encouragement to the officers and men. Yet Bates feared the worst: "As we waited the final order, my thoughts wandered to Michigan where my wife and boy, all unconscious of the situation, were, I knew, thinking of me, and a silent prayer ascended to the God of battles to protect and care for them should I fall in what seemed a hopeless charge."[4]

At noon "the order came ringing down the line," Bates recalled, and the Federals sprang forward. The Union line of battle left the cover of the ravine and ascended the slope in its front. As Buell's men climbed over a rail fence, they were fired on by Lieutenant Colonel McGuire's Confederate skirmishers.[5]

About 600 yards to the north, the men of Clayton's Division were gathering rails and logs for their breastworks when they were alerted by the sharp staccato of rifle fire. They barely had time to fall in before McGuire's skirmishers came running into view. Clayton's men had not had time to entrench, and lay down behind field pines or whatever loose timber they had managed to scavenge.[6]

Buell and Briant followed close upon McGuire's heels. "Here they came," wrote Maj. L. P. Thomas, commander of the 42nd Georgia, Stovall's Brigade. "It was a grand sight to see them moving on us, 'Old Glory' floating in the breeze so proudly." On the Federal right Briant's wing approached Stovall's position in line of battle, the 94th Ohio on the left, the 88th Indiana in the center, and the 33rd Ohio on the right. Captain Hinson marched at the head of the 33rd, wondering "whether the object of this movement was any[thing] more than a reconnoisance [sic]." Hinson kept the right of his regiment just inside the tree line. To his surprise, he found the woods in his front entirely free from underbrush.[7]

From his vantage point beyond Stovall's left, Maj. Gen. Carter Stevenson noted that the Union line of battle was advancing obliquely on his division's works, as if the Federals expected to strike the Confederate right flank. Hence, Briant's left flank had advanced to within a few hundred yards of Stovall's position, while his right barely came within range of Palmer's line, where Stevenson was standing. But there may have been another reason for Briant's skewed alignment: Hampton's horse artillery. Halsey's and Earle's Batteries poured a hailstorm of canister into the woods where the 33rd Ohio was advancing, causing Deas' Brigade of Hill's (Coltart's) Division to fire into the woods as well, though "without [their] seeing any object at which to fire," a disgruntled D. H. Hill reported. Their advance slowed by the heavy Confederate fire, the 33rd trailed along behind Briant's other two regiments.[8]

"Attention, Forty-Second Georgia!" Major Thomas shouted from his position on Stovall's line. "Hold your fire for my orders, and when you fire, give the rebel yell." Meanwhile, Lieutenant Colonel McGuire galloped back to his command, the 32nd Tennessee of Palmer's Brigade, in time to issue orders nearly identical to Thomas'. While McGuire had been out leading the Confederate skirmish line, his Tennesseans had used their bayonets to dig a rude breastwork 18 inches high, topping it off with pine logs they had cut to size with some old axes.[9]

"[B]ravely onward the enemy marched in grand style," Thomas recalled, "nearer and nearer they came." The Georgia major reminded his soldiers to hold their fire until he gave the order. The tension became almost unbearable for the waiting Confederates. It seemed to Sgt. Tom Corn of the 32nd Tennessee that McGuire was allowing the Yankees to "come disagreeable clos[e] to us." Corn stole a backward glance at McGuire, who appeared "verry calm and just as it seamed they would run over us he gave the order [to] fire." The Tennesseans gave the Federals "the le[a]d and they came to a stand[,] swaid [swayed] right and left[,] and weald [wheeled] on a ded run for thear brest works," Corn remembered.

Major Thomas of Stovall's Brigade waited until the Northerners had approached to within 40 yards of his line to give:

> the order so anxiously awaited. . .a sheet of fire blazed out from the hidden battle line of the Forty-second Georgia. . .

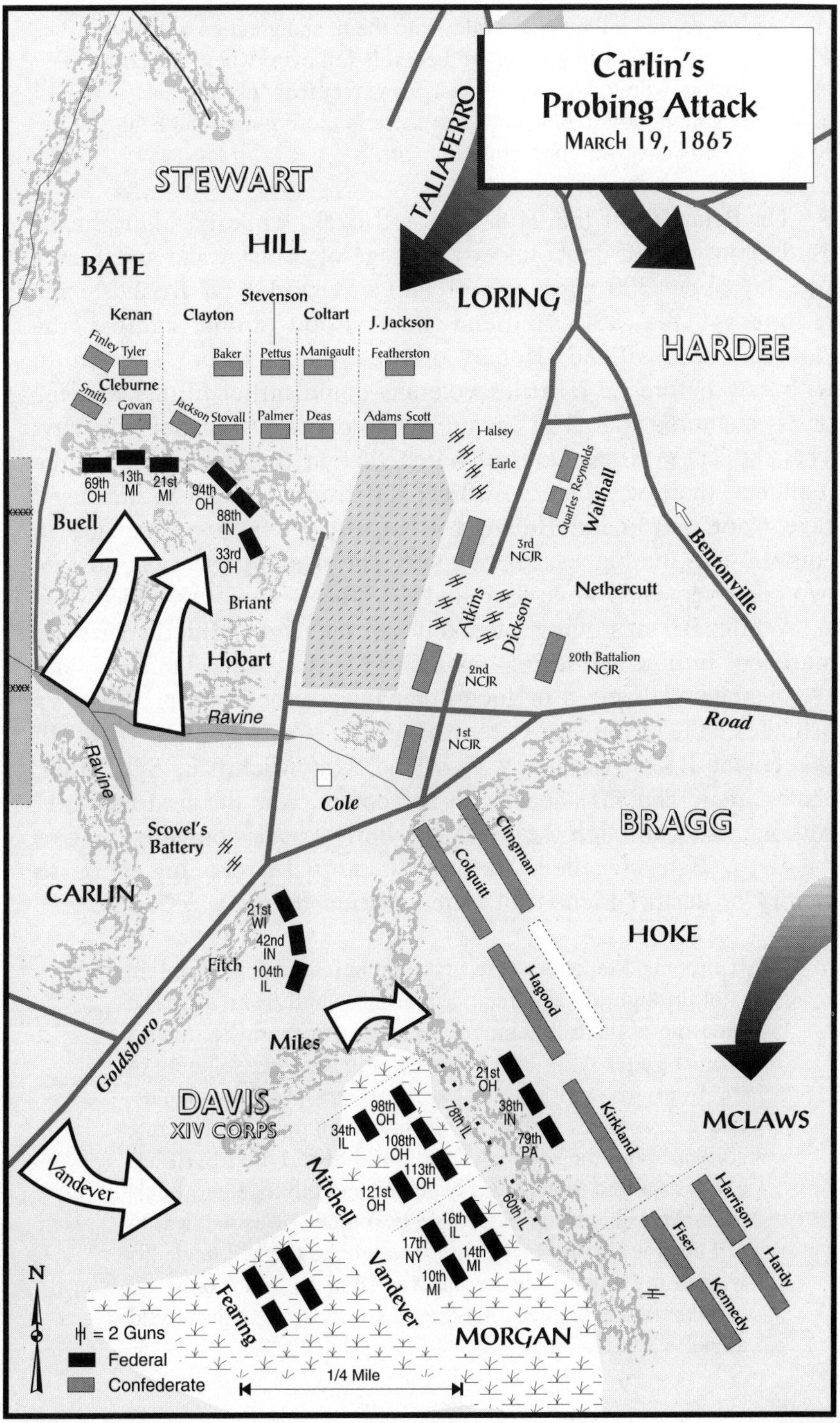

Carlin's Probing Attack
March 19, 1865
TALIAFERRO
STEWART
HILL
BATE
LORING
HARDEE
Stevenson
Kenan
Clayton
Coltart
J. Jackson
Finley
Tyler
Baker
Pettus
Manigault
Featherston
Cleburne
Smith
Govan
Jackson
Stovall
Palmer
Deas
Adams
Scott
Halsey
Earle
Quarles
Reynolds
Walthall
69th OH
13th MI
21st MI
94th OH
88th IN
33rd OH
Buell
Briant
Hobart
3rd NCJR
Atkins
Dickson
Nethercutt
20th Battalion NCJR
2nd NCJR
1st NCJR
Bentonville
Road
Ravine
Ravine
Cole
Scovel's Battery
BRAGG
Clingman
Colquitt
CARLIN
21st WI
42nd IN
104th IL
Fitch
HOKE
Hagood
Miles
Goldsboro
DAVIS
XIV CORPS
21st OH
38th IN
79th PA
78th IL
98th OH
34th IL
108th OH
113th OH
121st OH
Mitchell
Kirkland
MCLAWS
Harrison
60th IL
16th IL
17th NY
14th MI
10th MI
Vandever
Vandever
Fiser
Hardy
Kennedy
Fearing
MORGAN
N
= 2 Guns
Federal
Confederate
1/4 Mile

Mark A. Moore

> we poured volley after volley into them, and great gaps were made in their line, as brave Federals fell everywhere—their colors would rise and fall just a few feet from us, and many a gallant boy in blue is buried there in those pines who held "Old Glory" up for a brief moment.[10]

On Briant's left the 94th Ohio fell back, while on his right the 33rd Ohio, pinned down under a barrage of canister and small arms fire, lay about 300 yards shy of Palmer's works. Of Briant's three regiments, the 88th Indiana now stood alone against the Confederate fusillade. Hobart ordered the Hoosier regiment to withdraw before D. H. Hill's veterans could inflict further damage on its shattered line. The Indianians paid dearly for their tenacity. The 88th's Lt. Allen Dougall noted that in the right wing of the regiment, there was "not an officer left from the right to the flag," save Capt. Ferdinand Boltz of Company F. In one company, a corporal was the highest-ranking survivor. The regiment had lost its two color sergeants—one dead and the other severely wounded.[11]

While Briant's wing attacked on the right, Buell's brigade marched into a withering small arms fire. The Ohioans and Michiganders advanced in good order toward Jackson's and Govan's brigades, the front rank returning the Confederates' fire. In Lieutenant Bates' Company C of the 21st Michigan, Sgt. Frank Foster, marching far ahead with the colors, was the first casualty. Although shot through the wrist, the burly Foster "bravely clung to the flag," Bates recalled, "keeping it aloft[,] beckoning us on to victory or death." Lieutenant Bates continued:

> [Corporal] Mauch was the first man in [Company] C to fall, shot through the abdomen, a mortal wound from which he died the night following. We passed [Corporal] Kilmer a moment later lying on his back dying, his feet squarely to the front, his smoking musket firmly grasped in his hands, and a few paces farther along lay a young [C]onfederate soldier about the same age and build also dying[.] [I]t has always seemed to me these two fired and fell together. Louis Messaker, one of my oldest and best men[,] was the next to fall dead. . .my brother[,] shot through the thigh[,] made his way to my side to tell me he was shot[.] I could only tell him to make his way to the hospital as best he could alone.[12]

"I tell you it was a tight place," wrote another lieutenant in the 21st, Charles S. Brown. "I was awfully scart [scared], but I'll be hanged if I was going to show it." Lieutenant Brown was indeed in a tight place, but to paraphrase the English lexicographer, Samuel Johnson, he should have been thankful for anything short of hanging. The previous fall, Brown—then an ambitious private—had prepared his own application for a first lieutenant's commission, going so far as to forge his commanding officer's signature. Brown justified his action by pointing out that as the 21st Michigan's adjutant, he was performing the duties of a regimental staff officer and was therefore entitled to a first lieutenant's rank and pay. Within a few months Brown received his commission bearing Michigan governor James G. Blaine's signature. The officers of the 21st sent a petition to Governor Blaine protesting Brown's promotion, and the men ostracized the roguish young lieutenant, threatening dire consequences if he didn't resign his lieutenancy. "[A]ll the 21st can't bluff me out of it," Brown wrote, "but it is very annoying & unpleasant."[13]

Buell's brigade enjoyed a brief respite while the Confederate main line absorbed its skirmishers. The Southerners held their fire until the Federals approached to within 50 yards of their line, then "they opened fire and gave us an awful volley," Lieutenant Brown recalled. When the front rank faltered, the 13th Michigan charged through it as planned. With their commander, Maj. Willard Eaton, and their regimental color bearer leading the way, the 13th gave a yell and rushed to within 30 yards of the Confederate works. Lacking even the rudimentary fortifications constructed by Lee's Corps, the men of Govan's Brigade abandoned their position and sought refuge behind Smith's Brigade on their immediate right. The gap in the line created by the withdrawal of Govan's once-stalwart fighters was abruptly enlarged when Jackson's brigade on Govan's left also fled. The situation on the right flank of the Army of Tennessee had become precarious.

Two shots soon ruined an inviting opportunity for Buell's Federals to rout the vulnerable Confederates. Before the 13th Michigan could enter the breach, Major Eaton was killed by a bullet through the brain and the regimental color bearer was severely wounded—both men fell while at the head of the regiment. The 13th Michigan hesitated, and though the 69th Ohio and 21st

Michigan formed on either side of the 13th, neither regiment would advance further. Buell's charge had stalled at the critical moment of its advance.[14]

Perhaps it was just as well for Buell's men that their assault had faltered when it did. "We could have went in the works easy enough," noted Pvt. William Carroll of the 13th Michigan, "the rebels all nearly went to the left [but] if we had went in they would have come in on our left and taken us all prisoners[.]"[15]

As Buell's assault crested before the Army of Tennessee's line, Briant's wing fell back, exposing the 21st Michigan to an enfilade fire from Stovall's Brigade and Hampton's horse artillery. The two Confederate batteries raked the 21st with fused shells and case shot. "I did *not* love how they pitched lead & iron into us," Lieutenant Brown wrote. "by jove it looked hard to see intimate friends blown to pieces before your eyes[,] but such is life." Meanwhile, Bate's troops blasted away at the 69th Ohio and the 13th Michigan. When the soldiers of Govan's and Jackson's brigades saw the blue line wavering, they rushed back to their positions on the front line, where the added weight of their fire proved too much for Buell's brigade to bear. A few Yankees who had ventured too near to Clayton's line threw down their rifles and surrendered, while the rest fell back to the protective cover of the ravine, leaving their dead and wounded on the field. "[We] charged and were handsomely repulsed with a heavy loss on the Sixty-ninth [Ohio]," reported a bitter Capt. Jacob Rarick. The assault of Buell's brigade had ended in a bloody failure.[16]

Some of Buell's less gravely wounded men walked, hobbled or crawled back to the creek at the base of the ravine, where brigade surgeon Maj. John Avery had his hospital—that is, until the enemy's bullets began to zip past with alarming frequency. While Dr. Avery was preparing the wounded for evacuation to the rear, one of the ambulance drivers panicked, and in the words of an eyewitness, "jumped from his seat to cut the traces and fly." The good doctor coolly drew his pistol and held the driver to his work while the orderlies helped the wounded aboard. The ambulance, and Dr. Avery's hospital, made it to the rear safely.[17]

A triumphant D. H. Hill rode among his cheering Army of Tennessee troops and complimented them on their repulse of the Yankees, while 600 yards to the south, General Buell roundly criticized his men for faltering before the enemy's works. Perhaps it was this episode (and others like it) that moved Lieutenant Brown to write, "Buell our Brigadier is a regular mutton head & is cordially hated through[out] the Brig[ade]." Venturing beyond their lines, some of the Confederates gathered up the enemy's dropped weapons and ammunition and carried in the wounded of both sides. They also plundered the Union corpses for clothing, food and any other articles they happened to find. After the battle, several men of the 13th Michigan would return to this area to recover the bodies of their fallen comrades, and would find Major Eaton's corpse stripped to its underwear and lying in a mass grave.[18]

Carlin's probing attacks had cost him several hundred casualties and had succeeded only in developing a strong but undetermined force of Confederate infantry and artillery in his front. Although Slocum was now convinced that he "had to deal with something more formidable than a division of cavalry," he wasn't about to concede that the enemy force confronting him presented a serious threat to his command. Other events would soon convince Slocum to believe otherwise.[19]

While the weary men of Buell's and Briant's regiments strengthened their breastworks, an officer presented three gray-clad prisoners to Carlin. The spokesman of the trio, whom one eyewitness described as "an emaciated, sickly-appearing young man," stepped forward and insisted on being taken to the Federals' commanding general. When Carlin replied that he was the officer in command at that point, the youthful prisoner told him "that he and his two companions had been Union soldiers and had been captured, and to avoid starvation, they had enlisted in the Confederate army, with the intention of deserting it and joining the Union army as soon as the opportunity should present itself." Carlin continued:

> He informed me also that General J. E. Johnston. . . was in supreme command. . . .He stated that Johnston. . .had ridden through the several divisions of [his] army, and made speeches calculated to incite the troops to desperate efforts to overthrow the left wing of Sherman's army.

The prisoner concluded by telling Carlin that Johnston intended to crush the Left Wing, then fall upon the Right Wing and destroy it in turn.[20]

Carlin deemed this man's information to be of such importance that he mounted him on his own gray stallion, Rosy (so named in honor of Maj. Gen. William S. Rosecrans), and sent him off to Slocum under the watchful eye of his adjutant, Capt. James E. Edmonds. The young man repeated his story to Slocum, who questioned him closely. Slocum soon learned that the man was a native of Syracuse, New York, and that he had enlisted in a company there at the outbreak of the war. Slocum had also lived in Syracuse, and was able to corroborate much of the young fellow's story. "There is a very large force immediately in your front," the young Syracusan warned Slocum, "all under the command of General Joe Johnston." He also told the general "that it was understood among the Rebel soldiers that this force amounted to 40,000 men." Slocum remained skeptical. While he continued to question the "galvanized Yankee," Major Tracy and Lieutenant Foraker rode upon the scene. Tracy also happened to be a former resident of Syracuse, and instantly recognized the man in tattered gray as an old acquaintance and a former comrade in arms.[21]

Just then Lt. Col. Henry G. Litchfield, General Davis' inspector general, rode up to report on the situation at the front. Davis had earlier dispatched Litchfield to supervise Morgan's deployment on the right. When Slocum asked Litchfield what he had seen, the staff officer replied, "Well, General, I have found something more than Dibrell's cavalry—I find infantry intrenched along our whole front, and enough of them to give us all the amusement we shall want for the rest of the day."[22]

Regretting now that he had sent Major Guindon to reassure Sherman, Slocum "at once concluded to take a defensive position and communicate with the commanding general." Slocum countermanded his order sending the XX Corps to Morgan's right. Instead, he directed XX Corps commander Williams to send his wagons southward to join the XV Corps column, and to deploy his corps on Morgan's left. Slocum also ordered that all foragers be dismounted and placed in the ranks. When a nervous staff officer suggested that even a single day's delay in reaching Goldsboro might later prove embarrassing, Slocum said: "I can afford to be charged with being dilatory or overcautious, but I cannot afford the responsibility of another Ball's Bluff affair."[23]

Slocum's reply impressed Joe Foraker, who now realized "that there was really serious work before us." Slocum took out his watch: it was 1:30 p.m. He scribbled out a message, then motioned to Foraker. Handing the dispatch to his youngest staff officer, Slocum told him that it was for Sherman. Foraker was both surprised and pleased that his chief was entrusting him with so crucial a task. Slocum told Foraker in a general way where he could expect to find Sherman. He sent off the young lieutenant with these words: "Ride well to the right, so as to keep clear of the enemy's left flank, and *don't spare horseflesh*."[24]

* * *

At noon the commander of Morgan's First Brigade, Brig. Gen. William Vandever, received General Davis' order to hurry forward his command, which had been guarding Morgan's wagon train far to the rear. Leaving the wagons behind, Vandever's troops jogged the three miles to the front, arriving in time to hear the din of Buell's and Briant's fight off to the north. Vandever led his command into position on the right of Mitchell's brigade, while just a few hundred yards to the east, McLaws was deploying his Confederate division on General Hoke's left.[25]

Vandever arrayed his brigade in two lines of battle about 100 yards apart. From left to right, the 16th Illinois and 14th Michigan occupied the front line, and the 17th New York and 10th Michigan manned the rear line. The 60th Illinois deployed as skirmishers on the right of the 78th Illinois of Mitchell's brigade, thus relieving the 125th Illinois, which returned to Fearing's position. Vandever's right flank rested on a swamp which the general described as "not wholly impassable," although one of his men recalled that this "vast swamp. . .was impassable for large bodies of men." Vandever's troops on both lines immediately began building log works in extension of Mitchell's already substantial fortifications. Though Mitchell's and Vandever's men could not have known it at the time, within a few hours these log works would prove invaluable to them.[26]

* * *

On the morning of March 19th, Brig. Gen. William B. Taliaferro's Division of Hardee's Corps was marching south on the Devil's Race Path toward Bentonville. They were "a sleepy, worn out, hungry and altogether unhappy body of men," recalled Capt. Charles Inglesby of Rhett's Brigade, having been "routed up" before dawn and "marched off" before breakfast. But above all else, Taliaferro's men were sick and tired of running away from Sherman. Before long they could hear the occasional boom of a cannon. As they marched on, the booming grew louder and more frequent, which told them that they were no longer retreating from the enemy—they were now hurrying to meet him. The effect of this realization was electrifying. "The officers and men forgot they were tired and hungry," Captain Inglesby noted, "and [their] step was unconsciously quickened." As Taliaferro's troops neared the battlefield, their pace further quickened when they heard the unmistakable rattle of musketry amid the booming of the artillery.[27]

The South Carolinians of Rhett's Brigade marched past a slow-moving wagon train. An old teamster gazed at the winding gray column that appeared to stretch for miles in either direction. "Great God!" he cried. "I didn't know there were that many men in the world. Old Joe will give Billy Sherman hell to-day, sure."[28]

Taliaferro's two brigades filed off to the right when they reached the Army of Tennessee's line. They were halted in rear of Bate's position, where they fell out to enjoy a much-needed rest. Their enjoyment was short-lived though, for their resting place lay just in front of the field hospitals. Stretcher bearers hauling the wounded from Buell's assault stepped, or sometimes stumbled, over the reclining soldiers. Taliaferro's men would never forget the sight of the bloody amputated legs and arms littering the grass around the operating tables. Nor would they soon forget the cries and groans of the wounded above the insistent rasp of the surgeon's saw. As if that weren't enough, Federal cannon balls frequently screamed past just over their heads. Captain Inglesby found the whole experience "far from inspiriting." Yet just a few yards off a regimental band "played some music that gave us an uplift and inspiration for the coming fray," recalled Robert Sanders, a soldier in Elliott's Brigade.[29]

Nearby a dozen badly wounded Federals lay helpless on the ground, several of them crying out for a drink of water. A few of

Taliaferro's men took pity on the Union soldiers and offered them a drink, "even to the emptying of several canteens," noted Cpl. A. P. Ford of Elliott's Brigade. One Confederate produced a flask of whiskey, which he handed to a Yankee whose leg had been crushed by an artillery projectile. The Federal took a stiff drink and said: "Thank God, Johnny[.] [I]t may come around that I may be able to do you a kindness, and I'll never forget this drink of liquor." Oblivious to these scenes of mercy and mortality, Lt. Col. James Welsman Brown of Elliott's Brigade devoured a letter from his sister that had just been delivered to him.[30]

While Taliaferro's men rested, and the surgeons worked on, Wade Hampton was at the head of one of his cavalry regiments trying to find the left flank of the enemy. Hampton informed General Johnston that the Federals had just attacked the Army of Tennessee's position, and that Taliaferro's Division was going into position. "I think whatever we do should be done quickly," Hampton advised. "An advance of the line would break them, I think."[31]

Johnston received Hampton's dispatch at 1:45 p.m. Although the deployment of his forces had consumed most of the morning, Johnston knew that the Federals were still strung out for miles along the Goldsboro Road and therefore vulnerable to a sudden attack. But he also knew that he would have to strike soon if he hoped to exploit his numerical superiority and the four hours of daylight left to him. In order to streamline his chain of command prior to the assault, Johnston placed Hardee in command of Taliaferro's Division and the Army of Tennessee contingent, or the Confederate right wing. Although Hardee's reassignment effectively stripped A. P. Stewart of his command, Hardee later divided his wing into two halves, retaining command of Taliaferro's and Bate's forces, while placing Stewart in command of Loring's and D. H. Hill's. Against his better judgment, Johnston left Bragg in command of McLaws' and Hoke's divisions, or the Confederate left wing. Johnston ordered his two wing commanders to launch the assault at 2:15 p.m.[32]

* * *

For several hours Scovel's Federal battery had been fighting a war of attrition with the three Confederate batteries in its front. Although it had enjoyed some initial success, the momentum had shifted and now it was clearly on the losing end. Outgunned by a margin of fourteen cannon to four, Lieutenant Scovel and his crews desperately needed help. About 1:00 p.m. the XIV Corps chief of artillery, Maj. Charles Houghtaling, sent forward his reserve artillery—the 19th Indiana Battery, commanded by Lt. Samuel D. Webb—to the front. The Hoosier battery must have been a welcome sight to Scovel's men as it unlimbered nearby. Once Lieutenant Webb's four Napoleons began firing, General Carlin ordered Scovel's battery to take up a position on the left in rear of Buell's line, but south of the ravine. Minutes later, the Confederates scored a direct hit on one of Lieutenant Webb's caissons, sending a geyser of flames and shell fragments into the air. The explosion killed several draft animals and wounded a few artillerymen.[33]

Meanwhile, about a half-mile to the rear Slocum dispatched Davis' chief of staff, Lt. Col. Alexander C. McClurg, to find General Williams, the XX Corps commander, and order him "to push his troops to the front with all possible speed." McClurg found "Pap" Williams less than a mile to the rear, the general having ridden far in advance of his troops. On receiving Slocum's order, Williams galloped back to the junction of the Smithfield and Goldsboro roads, where his column had halted for lunch.[34]

Williams' First Division, Brig. Gen. Nathaniel J. Jackson commanding, had the advance. In obedience to Slocum's orders, Williams instructed Jackson to march his division to the front at once, to send his trains south toward the XV Corps' column, and to post a strong guard at the crossroads. Since 6:00 a.m. Jackson's Second and Third Brigades, commanded respectively by Col. William Hawley and Brig. Gen. James S. Robinson, had taken turns corduroying the Goldsboro Road, which the XIV Corps had transformed into a quagmire. It is therefore no surprise that as these tired soldiers fell in they grumbled and cursed about their dinner break being cut short. Hawley's brigade had the advance and reached the Morris farm sometime after 2:00 p.m. It deployed in reserve north of the Goldsboro Road, about a mile in rear of Carlin's and Morgan's line. Robinson's brigade continued to the front, where Slocum intended to use it to plug the gap in Carlin's line along the Cole field, and to support the two XIV Corps batteries there.

Jackson's First Brigade, led by Col. James L. Selfridge, brought up the rear and had not yet reached the Morris farm, though through no fault of Hawley's or Robinson's pioneers. Colonel Selfridge found the Goldsboro Road "well corduroyed, and [the] wagons moving along without any trouble."[35]

Robinson deployed his brigade between the separated halves of Carlin's division. On the front line Robinson placed the 31st Wisconsin on the right flank, in rear of Webb's battery, while the 61st and 82nd Ohio regiments occupied the left flank and center. The 82nd Illinois and 143rd New York manned the left and right of Robinson's rear line, respectively. Robinson's sixth regiment, the 101st Illinois, was left behind to guard the Smithfield-Goldsboro crossroads. Robinson's brigade faced a shallow ravine, beyond which stretched the Cole field. His line skirted the edge of a dense pine forest which extended to the rear for several hundred yards. Since they were carrying no entrenching tools, Robinson's men used their hatchets to fashion a rail and log breastwork, but before they could make much headway Williams ordered Robinson's two reserve regiments, the 82nd Illinois and 143rd New York, to report to Colonel Hawley, who was deploying his brigade back at the Morris farm. Robinson was left with just half of his command, and neither of his flanks connected with any part of Carlin's line, because Robinson simply hadn't enough men to fill the gap. "I was so d—d mad over the position in which my brigade was placed," Robinson later wrote, "that I felt like pitching into the whole fraternity of commanding Generals. In fact I told Slocum the next time 3 Regmnts [sic] of my Brigade were sent to the front and 3 to the rear, I would go with the latter."[36]

For 14 years Robinson had wielded his pen as editor and publisher of the Kenton, Ohio, *Republican*, until he relinquished that mightier weapon for the sword five days after the firing on Fort Sumter. As colonel of the 82nd Ohio, Robinson had led his regiment through some of the Army of the Potomac's darkest days. The 82nd Ohio had served in Maj. Gen. O. O. Howard's luckless XI Corps, which had been routed at Chancellorsville by "Stonewall" Jackson's surprise flank attack. Two months later the XI Corps was again driven headlong, this time through the streets of Gettysburg during the first day's fighting. On that fateful day Robinson was severely wounded, and was unable to return to duty until the following spring. By then the XI Corps had been transferred to the

Western theater, where it was consolidated with the XII Corps to form the XX Corps. Upon his return Robinson assumed his present brigade command and was promoted to brigadier general following the March to the Sea. In keeping with his high rank, Robinson's chiseled features and voluminous beard suggested nothing less than an Olympian deity or an Old Testament prophet.[37]

Thanks to the hard lessons learned at Chancellorsville and Gettysburg, Robinson—or any veteran member of his command, for that matter—knew an untenable position when he saw one. As he reconnoitered the ground on his left, he noted that Buell's left flank, instead of being refused, was thrust forward in conformity to the swampy ravine in its front. "A most dangerous and unfortunate arrangement," the Ohio general reported, "as it rendered it much more easy to be flanked than it ought to have been." Robinson also noted that Carlin had not posted a skirmish line across the Cole field as he should have. Of course Robinson did not know about Hobart's failed attempt to establish a line across that hotly contested field earlier in the day. His own skirmishers would learn soon enough the difficulty of holding the high ground near the Cole house.[38]

According to Captain Hinson of the 33rd Ohio, the situation on the right flank of Lieutenant Colonel Briant's line was equally bad:

> at no time was [sic] there any Union troops between the right of Co. A[, 33rd Ohio] and the [Goldsboro] road. . .a distance at least equal to the length of six regiments. The ground at the [Cole] house, and to the north of it, was higher than any in that immediate vicinity, and was, I think, the key to the whole position. . . .Gen. Carlin and Gen. Hobart were frequently along our line. . .and I repeatedly called attention to this gap in the line. . .[although I] assured them that we could hold our front against any force that might be brought against us.

Carlin and Hobart must have ignored Hinson's warning in the belief that neither they nor the Confederates could have held the Cole field for long. The two generals were no doubt content to let the field remain a no man's land, since they lacked the troops to defend it. Not surprisingly, this gap would later prove to be Hobart's undoing.[39]

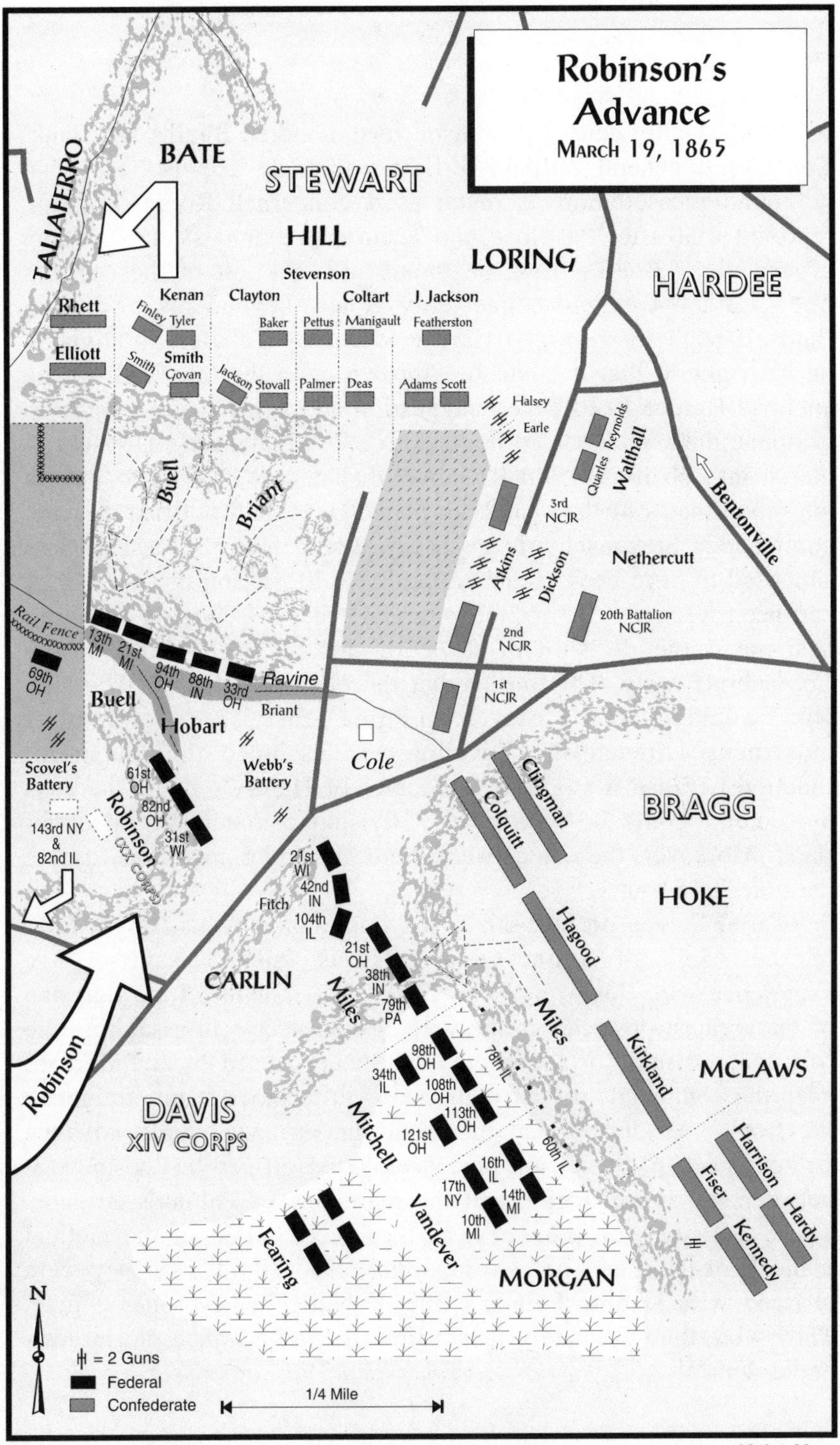
Robinson's Advance
March 19, 1865
BATE
TALIAFERRO
STEWART
HILL
LORING
HARDEE
Stevenson
Kenan
Clayton
Coltart
J. Jackson
Rhett
Finley
Tyler
Baker
Pettus
Manigault
Featherston
Elliott
Smith
Smith
Govan
Jackson
Stovall
Palmer
Deas
Adams
Scott
Halsey
Earle
Reynolds
Quarles
Walthall
Bentonville
Buell
Briant
3rd NCJR
Atkins
Dickson
Nethercutt
20th Battalion NCJR
2nd NCJR
1st NCJR
Rail Fence
13th MI
21st MI
94th OH
88th IN
33rd OH
Ravine
69th OH
Buell
Briant
Hobart
Cole
Scovel's Battery
Webb's Battery
61st OH
82nd OH
31st WI
143rd NY & 82nd IL
Robinson (XX CORPS)
Clingman
Colquitt
BRAGG
21st WI
42nd IN
104th IL
Fitch
HOKE
Hagood
21st OH
38th IN
79th PA
CARLIN
Miles
Miles
98th OH
78th IL
34th IL
108th OH
113th OH
Kirkland
MCLAWS
Robinson
DAVIS
XIV CORPS
Mitchell
121st OH
60th IL
16th IL
17th NY
14th MI
10th MI
Harrison
Fiser
Hardy
Kennedy
Fearing
Vandever
MORGAN
N
= 2 Guns
Federal
Confederate
1/4 Mile

Mark A. Moore

* * *

While Union general Robinson reconnoitered Buell's left flank, Confederate general William B. Bate was doing likewise, and what he found pleased him as much as it concerned Robinson. Bate reported that after "a close and accurate reconnaissance" of the ground along Buell's front, he found "that the left of the enemy's line. . .did not extend connectedly at all" beyond his own right flank. Bate therefore urged Hardee to deploy Taliaferro's Division on his right so that it could be "thrown upon the left flank of the enemy." Hardee liked Bate's suggestion and persuaded Johnston to postpone the assault for 30 minutes to allow Taliaferro's Division to march into position. "Old Reliable" dispatched couriers to inform his subordinates of the change in plans. D. H. Hill notified division commander Stevenson of the delay just before the assault was supposed to have been launched. Hill told Stevenson that the attack had been rescheduled for 2:45 p.m., and that his division had been designated the division of direction for the right wing of the Confederate army. This meant that the other divisions of Hardee's wing would *guide on* Stevenson's line—that is, conform to its movements. Stevenson's Division was assigned this important function because it stood in the center of Hardee's line, where its movements could be seen by the division commanders on either flank. Moreover, the center was where General Hardee would give the order to advance.[40]

Carter Stevenson recognized the importance of his task in light of the Army of Tennessee's previous failed assaults. "My experience with this army," he wrote, "has convinced me that one of the greatest obstacles in the way of our success in assaulting the fortified positions of the enemy has been caused by a failure to keep the commands properly aligned, and to move them straight to the front." To ensure that his front line brigade would advance without mishap, Stevenson placed mounted officers in the interval between his skirmish line and the main line of Palmer's Brigade. These officers—or *markers*, as they were called in the tactical manuals of the time—had an important responsibility, for they were charged with leading Palmer's line of battle in its proper course. They were thus ultimately responsible for the advance of Hardee's entire wing.[41]

While the Army of Tennessee formed ranks for the assault, the cry of "Fall in!" echoed along the woods where Taliaferro's troops were resting. The men seized their rifle-muskets and sprang to their feet. Major A. Burnet Rhett, the commander of Taliaferro's light artillery battalion, rode down the line, announcing that France had officially recognized the Confederacy and was sending warships to break the Federal blockade. The men whooped and cheered. According to Corporal Ford, Major Rhett's morale-boosting ploy worked because, "We were blinded by our patriotism. . .few of us realizing that the end was so near." Elliott's Brigade had the advance. As it marched into position on Bate's right, a private exclaimed, "Well, boys, one out of every three of us will drop to-day. I wonder who it will be?"[42]

About 600 yards to the south, Buell received a report from Captain Rowe, his skirmish line commander, that an enemy column was snaking past his left flank under cover of the timber. Buell in turn reported the Confederate flanking maneuver to Carlin, stretched Rowe's skirmish line a half-mile to his left, then posted the 69th Ohio behind a rail fence in rear of Rowe's skirmishers. The 69th numbered fewer than 100 men, and it occupied an exposed position in the middle of the open field on Buell's left, some distance behind the left rear of the 13th Michigan. But thanks to the strong back of the 69th's ordnance sergeant, John McAllister, the Buckeye regiment could at least rely on a plentiful ammunition supply. McAllister unslung his haversack and dumped the boxes of cartridges on the ground, then turned and trotted back to the brigade ordnance wagon for another thousand-round load—each load weighing in at more than 60 pounds.[43]

Sergeant McAllister was a survivor. After being wounded and captured during the Battle of Stones River, he was shipped off to Libby Prison, where he languished for three months before being exchanged. A year later, during the fighting at Resaca, Georgia, a bullet shattered McAllister's larynx. His doctors urged him to spend the remainder of the war on guard duty, but the veteran sergeant insisted on rejoining his regiment at the front. Although McAllister had since recovered from his wound, he would never again be able to speak above a hoarse whisper.[44]

Before the day was done, McAllister would need to call upon both his experience and his two strong legs to survive the impending Confederate onslaught.

About the time that Buell's report of an enemy flanking maneuver reached him, Carlin received a message from General Davis directing him to hold his position and make demonstrations as though he were about to attack again. Davis hoped that Carlin could thus occupy the enemy long enough to enable the XX Corps to come to his support. But Carlin, believing that the Confederates had assumed the offensive, disregarded Davis' order and instead continued strengthening his present position. While Carlin supervised the work of entrenching, yet another messenger appeared—Lieutenant William Ludlow, Slocum's chief engineer. Slocum had sent Ludlow to evaluate the strength of Carlin's position. Ludlow advised Carlin to fall back across the ravine in his rear and to construct a line of works, probably at a 90-degree angle to Robinson's line. Once again, Carlin decided to remain where he was. "Being confident of my ability to hold my position until the troops in rear should come up," he asserted, "I decided not to fall back, but made dispositions to fortify my left flank against movements of the enemy in that direction."[45]

Of these dispositions Davis' chief of staff, Lieutenant Colonel McClurg, later wrote:

> The first division—Carlin's—was. . . very much extended and attenuated. It had been deployed without reference to any such force as that which now confronted it; its position was weak, and its strength much impaired by the serious work it had already gone through.

In short, Carlin's division was ripe for a thrashing.[46]

* * *

General Williams was at the Morris farm overseeing the deployment of Jackson's division of the XX Corps when some scouts and foragers galloped up from the northeast and reported that a large force of the enemy's infantry was marching around Carlin's left flank and was within a mile of the Morris farm. (The enemy force referred to was Taliaferro's Division, which was marching into position on Bate's right.) This news concerned

Williams, because the Morris farm was where most of the XIV Corps' wagons were parked and where the XIV Corps' chief surgeon, Waldo Daniels, had established his hospital. Moreover, the farm was presently undefended. To meet this threat, Williams ordered Hawley's brigade into position about a quarter-mile north of the Goldsboro Road.[47]

Hawley's men advanced to a swampy, wooded ravine that ran roughly east-west along the northern edge of the Morris farm. Along the southern lip of this ravine Hawley deployed his brigade in two ranks facing a little east of north. Hawley's right flank rested on a second ravine that ran northward from the Goldsboro Road, and connected with the first ravine about 100 yards north of Hawley's line. Anchoring Hawley's right flank were the 2nd Massachusetts, which manned the front line, and the 13th New Jersey, which formed in rear of the New Englanders along the edge of a cornfield and in column of divisions (in this tactical sense, a *division* signifies two companies of a regiment). The 13th New Jersey was therefore arrayed in a column of two companies per rank because such a formation could, with equal rapidity, reinforce any portion of Hawley's line or refuse and support the right flank of the 2nd Massachusetts. The two regiments that Williams had earlier ordered from Robinson, the 82nd Illinois and 143rd New York, now reported to Hawley, who placed them in rear of his left flank, with instructions "to be ready to move at a moment's notice to any part of his line."[48]

Selfridge's brigade of Jackson's division also reached the Morris farm at this time, having double-quicked the last two miles of their march. Without breaking stride, Selfridge's veterans filed through a gap in the rail fence that bordered Reddick Morris' cornfield, each man snatching up a rail as he passed. Forming on Hawley's left, they stacked the rails in front and began to entrench, tossing the earth onto the rails, which served as the skeleton of their breastwork.[49]

* * *

For more than an hour Lieutenant Scovel, his four ordnance rifles unlimbered yet silent, had awaited orders from Carlin to open fire from his new position behind Buell's brigade. Perhaps Carlin was so preoccupied with the enemy in his front that he had forgotten about his artillery in the rear. While Scovel marked time, Lieutenant Webb moved the left section of his battery several hundred yards north to Robinson's left flank in the hope of obtaining a better field of fire from there.[50]

About 2:30 p.m. Robinson's skirmishers ventured into the Cole field. The Confederate skirmish line, consisting of several companies of Junior Reserves, fired a few rounds at the Federals, then fell back to the main line. Lieutenant George Lyman of the 31st Wisconsin led his Union skirmishers in a dash across the open field to occupy the Cole house and buildings. "By this time," Robinson noted, "the firing became very lively."[51]

So lively, in fact, that a number of stray bullets whistled over the heads of Captain Hinson and the rest of the 33rd Ohio. Turning to face the Cole field, Hinson glimpsed Lieutenant Lyman's men sweeping past his position. "I shouted to these skirmishers to be careful what they were about or we would retaliate," recalled Hinson. Just then Hinson's own skirmishers came in on the run and bounded over the 33rd's breastwork, shouting, "Here they come!"[52]

~ *ten* ~

"We Run Like the Duce"

—Lt. Charles Brown, 21st Michigan

At 2:45 p.m. General Hardee rode down the front of the long gray and butternut line of the Confederate right wing and waved his troops forward. With Joseph B. Palmer's Brigade of Stevenson's Division leading the way, the Confederates left the safety of their entrenchments and marched into the fields and pine woods in their front. Most of the men could not see the Federal line for the trees and underbrush, but they knew that it was not far distant. Although they could not have known it at the time, their impending assault would be the last grand charge of the Army of Tennessee. Palmer's troops "advanced with a yell," recalled one Tennessean, confident that "we could take the [enemy's] works or old Joe would not order it." Palmer reported that his brigade "moved steadily forward. . .in common time," that is, at a moderate walk, "preserving its alignment almost as if on parade." In order to maintain this alignment and to prevent the men from becoming winded, Palmer continued the advance at a relaxed pace for the first 400 yards. Edmund Pettus' Brigade followed at a distance of 300 yards, close enough to support Palmer's advance if necessary, yet beyond range of any missiles aimed at Palmer's line.[1]

On the left of Hardee's wing, Loring ordered Stewart's Corps forward. Loring had earlier instructed Walthall to advance his division—which was posted behind Halsey's and Earle's batteries—across the open field in his front and to join on the left of Loring's Division (under Jackson) in the woods southwest of the field. But Loring had also cautioned Walthall to march in rear of Jackson's command if the Junior Reserves Brigade of Hoke's Division advanced into his allotted place on the front line.[2]

Edward Walthall rode into the field at the head of his 240-man division, where it immediately drew fire from Robinson's and Briant's skirmishers and Webb's battery. The eight cannon of Hampton's horse artillery fell silent while Walthall's Division marched across the field "in as perfect order as [if] on dress parade, at [the] quick step, with bright guns at right shoulder shift, directly towards the gap [between Loring's and Hoke's divisions], through this iron and leaden hail," remembered Col. Henry Bunn, who was in temporary command of Reynolds' Brigade. Walthall turned around in his saddle and gazed in admiration at the "perfect line" of his veteran division. He turned to Colonel Bunn and said, "I have been in all, or nearly all[,] the battles fought by the Army of Tennessee, and have seen many brave sights, but nothing comparable to this." A. P. Stewart agreed. More than 30 years later, he wrote: "It was an inspiring sight. . .to see the firm, steady lines, their intrepid commander towering above them on his horse, advancing under a shower of bullets into the storm of battle. . . .I love to think of Gen. Walthall as he appeared on that occasion." Halcott Pride Jones, a gunner in Hoke's artillery, called the charge of Walthall's Division "the most splendid thing I ever witnessed."[3]

The Junior Reserves on Walthall's immediate left cheered and applauded their veteran comrades. Colonel Charles Broadfoot of the 1st Reserves recalled:

> It looked like a picture and at our distance was truly beautiful. Several officers led the charge on horseback across an open field in full view, with colors flying and line of battle in such perfect order as to be able to distinguish the several field officers in proper place and followed by a battery [of Hampton's horse artillery] which dashed at full gallop, wheeled, unlimbered, and opened fire. It was gallantly done, but it was painful to see how close their battle flags were together, regiments being scarcely larger than companies and [the] division not much larger than a regiment should be.[4]

Unfortunately for the Confederates, the Army of Tennessee's splendid advance was not properly supported. For reasons known only to General Bragg, Hoke's and McLaws' divisions did not join in the grand assault as ordered. As a result, the Junior Reserves remained stationary, and Walthall's Division was thus free to form on Loring's left. After Walthall's men advanced several hundred yards, they left the field and came to a steep ravine, where they encountered an immense thicket of briars. After trampling and hacking their way through, they found the men of Loring's Division huddled in the ravine on their right. Because of its steep southern bank, this ravine made a superb natural breastwork. About 400 yards to Loring's right, Briant's Federals were fighting to defend this same ravine. Walthall utilized the shelter of the ravine to dress his line, which had been thrown into confusion by the struggle through the briar patch. But when the time came to advance, the soldiers of Stewart's Corps refused to budge. The officers threatened and cajoled their men, but to no avail. For a few tense moments Loring's and Walthall's boys glowered at each other. "Right at this point," Colonel Bunn wrote, "occurred one of those little episodes, which often during. . .war, accomplish greater results than genius." Most of Loring's Division hailed from Mississippi, whose sons were known throughout the Army of Tennessee as "Mudheads." Many of Walthall's soldiers were Arkansans—they were called "Joshes." It was a "Josh" who spoke up first:

"Mudheads, ain't you goin'[?]"

"We'll go if you will, Josh."

"All right, here's at ye."[5]

The men of Walthall's and Loring's divisions burst out of the ravine raising the Rebel yell, and swept past the Cole house. They overran many of Robinson's skirmishers, capturing more than 30 of them, including their commander, Lieutenant Lyman, who was too severely wounded to make his escape. Walthall sent his prisoners to the rear without a guard because he could not spare the men to furnish one. The skirmishers of Stewart's Corps pressed their Union counterparts so closely that some of the men at Robinson's main line panicked and opened fire on friend and foe alike. Finding themselves on the receiving end of a deadly cross fire, Robinson's skirmishers "skedaddled for the works," recalled S. J. Packer, a skirmisher from the 82nd Ohio. Meanwhile, Webb's Indiana battery "would shoot holes through the rebel ranks," wrote a soldier in the 31st Wisconsin, "but they would fill up." The Confederates surged into the ravine facing the Union works and lay down to avoid the plunging fire of Robinson's troops and Webb's battery. Once they realized that their position was a comparatively safe one, the Southerners taunted the Federals by shaking their battle flags at them. For the moment, Loring was content to await the arrival of D. H. Hill's command before resuming the advance.[6]

On Loring's right, Lee's Corps (under D. H. Hill) increased its pace to the quick step, or a brisk walk, as the Federal works loomed up ahead. Once the troops of Deas' and Palmer's brigades had advanced side-by-side through the woods to within a few hundred yards of the 33rd Ohio's position, the defenders "began to give them the best we had in store," wrote the 33rd's commander, Captain Hinson. "But it made no difference. . . .On came the enemy." Following one Northern volley, Pvt. R. S. Cowles of the 45th Tennessee, Palmer's Brigade, looked down at his rifle-musket and saw that a Yankee bullet had shattered the stock: "My gun was literally shot to pieces in my hands," he wrote. Palmer's men clambered over a high rail fence, then double-quicked to within 50 yards of the 33rd Ohio's position, where they fired off a round or two before resuming their downhill advance. So far, Hinson noted, the 33rd's entrenchments had provided excellent cover for his men, whose "shoulders when standing erect in the ditch were about on a level with the ground in front."[7]

But with Palmer bearing down on his center and Deas on the verge of overlapping his right, Hinson knew that it was time to fall back. Before doing so, he wanted to notify Lieutenant Colonel Briant, whom he had just seen standing to the left of the 33rd's line. Hinson set out to find his superior, and on the way met Briant's adjutant, who warned him that an undetermined force of the enemy had gotten in rear of their position. Hinson correctly assumed that the Rebels had advanced through the Cole field on his right without his having seen them. The Rebel soldiers in rear of Briant's position were the 890-man remnant of Stewart's Corps under Loring.[8]

When Hinson at last found Briant, he told him, "I can't hold my line." Without waiting for orders, Hinson continued, "I turned about to give the command to retreat, when I saw the right of the regiment break to the rear, and I was thankful for that much time gained." The rest of Hinson's Buckeyes held on until the Confederates approached to within a few yards of their line:

"They're getting pretty close," remarked an edgy Ohio private.

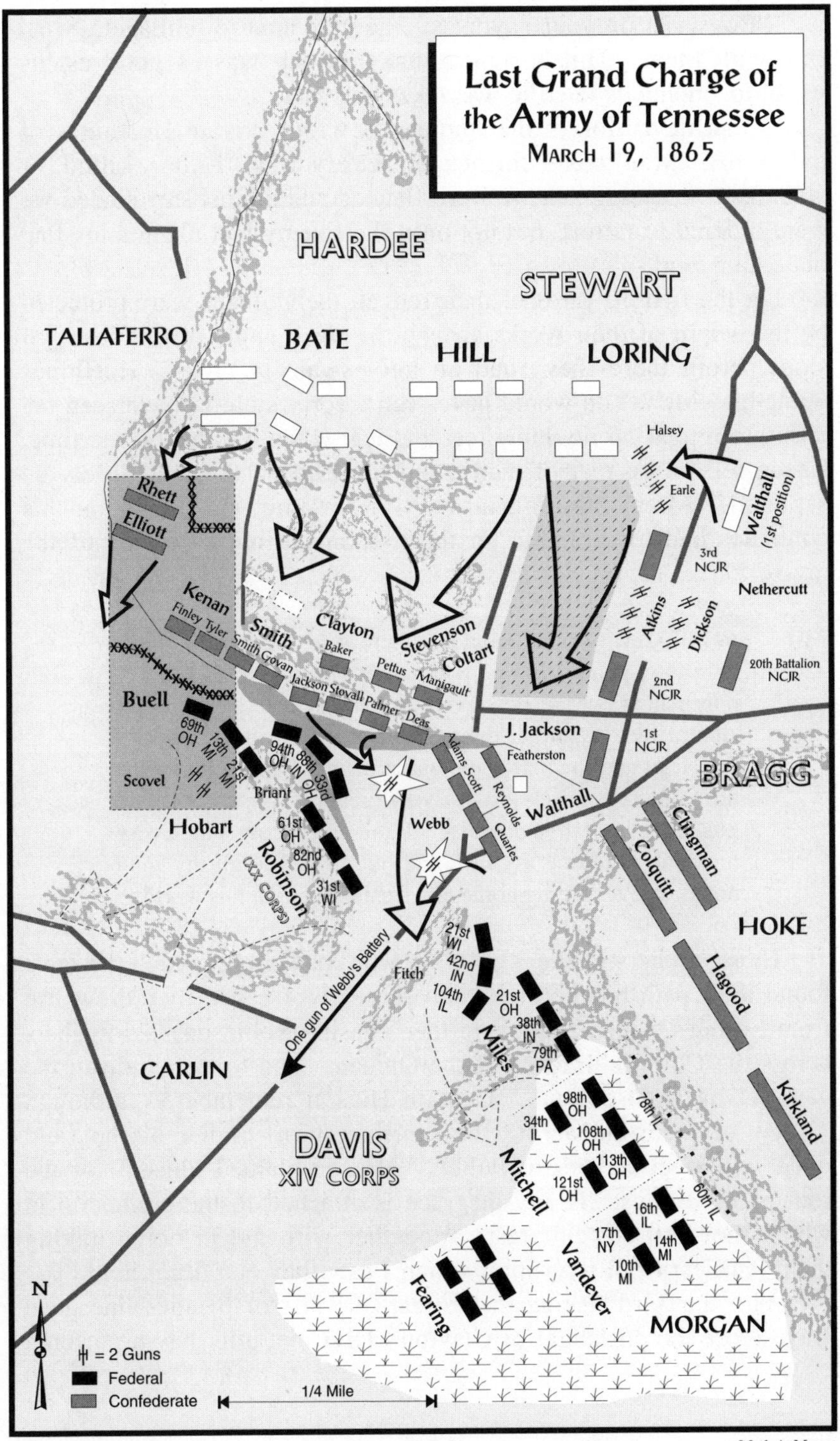
Last Grand Charge of the Army of Tennessee
March 19, 1865
HARDEE
STEWART
TALIAFERRO
BATE
HILL
LORING
Halsey
Earle
Walthall (1st position)
Rhett
Elliott
Kenan
Finley
Tyler
Smith
Govan
Jackson
Stovall
Palmer
Deas
Smith
Clayton
Baker
Pettus
Manigault
Stevenson
Coltart
Atkins
Dickson
3rd NCJR
Nethercutt
20th Battalion NCJR
2nd NCJR
1st NCJR
J. Jackson
Featherston
Adams
Scott
Reynolds
Quarles
Walthall
BRAGG
Clingman
Colquitt
HOKE
Hagood
Kirkland
Buell
69th OH
13th MI
21st MI
Scovel
Briant
94th OH
88th IN
33rd OH
Hobart
61st OH
82nd OH
31st WI
Robinson (XX CORPS)
Webb
21st WI
42nd IN
104th IL
Fitch
One gun of Webb's Battery
21st OH
38th IN
79th PA
Miles
CARLIN
98th OH
78th IL
34th IL
108th OH
113th OH
121st OH
DAVIS
XIV CORPS
Mitchell
16th IL
60th IL
17th NY
14th MI
10th MI
Vandever
Fearing
MORGAN
N
= 2 Guns
Federal
Confederate
1/4 Mile

Mark A. Moore

"Boys, put on your bayonets," the man next to him said, "we'll stay with them." Hinson noted that the man was as good as his word, for moments later he was taken prisoner.

"I can never forget that moment," wrote Private Hoffhines of the 33rd. "Men were falling on Every side Either killed or wounded. . . .seeing that we were flanked and almost surrounded we were ordered to retreat, but not until the Enemy had planted his flag on. . .our works."[9]

For the first 50 yards of their retreat, the Ohioans were protected by the height of their works and by the steep angle of the downhill slope. From there they "had an ugly swale to cross," Hoffhines wrote his wife. "You would have seen a sorry sight to have seen me trying to retreat on my lame feet and leg which was bad at the time. I soon fell in the rear of many, and thought that I would surely be captured." After splashing through the swamp, Hoffhines and his comrades had to scramble up the rise on the opposite side of the ravine:

> in full view of our Enemies. . .here was our greatest peril. here they poured in one continuous fire of destruction. . . one man was Shot down right by my side. . .on the other side of me. . .another poor fellow was shot in the back of the Head and the ball come out at his nose and had tore his nose allmost entirely off[.] Every breath he drew the Blood gushed out at his nose. . . .I did not know but Every moment would be my last, and put an end to all my fond hopes of Ever seeing home and friends again in this world.[10]

Those soldiers of the 33rd Ohio who managed to reach the crest found their path blocked by a rail fence. Worse yet, they drew fire from Loring's troops, who were then chasing Robinson's skirmishers across the Cole field. Most of the Ohioans "had to turn and run the gauntlet by right-oblique," Captain Hinson remembered, although "a few of them cut across the [northwestern] corner of the field under a perfect shower of bullets." Hinson blamed himself for the rout of his troops: "If any disgrace is attached to the confusion in which they retired. . .it rests altogether with me in not. . .taking them [earlier] from a position which I saw they could not hold."[11]

With the 33rd fleeing to the rear, the rest of Briant's line gave way before the onslaught of Clayton's Division, after having offered what General Clayton described as "only a feeble resistance." By laying down a furious fire, the 88th Indiana briefly held the center, but was soon outflanked on either side by swarms of screaming Rebels. "They came down upon us like an avalanche," recalled the 88th's Lt. Allen Dougall. "Our Situation at this time was truly awfull [sic]," wrote Hoosier captain Ferdinand Boltz.[12]

On Hardee's right, General Bate's command advanced to the assault, led by the two-brigade remnant of Cleburne's Division under Brig. Gen. James A. Smith. In advancing on the right, Smith's Brigade was tripped up by its own abatis and had to double-quick to catch up to Govan's Brigade, which continued its advance notwithstanding. Smith's Georgians suffered the misfortune of emerging into an open field, while on their left, Govan's Arkansans moved in relative safety through a pine wood. After advancing 200 yards up the gentle rise in the field, Smith's Brigade "obliqued too far to the left," Bate reported, "in order to get under cover of the timber," and got tangled up in Govan's line just as Buell's Michiganders poured a devastating volley into their ranks. General Smith's line wavered under this fire and seemed about to break.

Bate now saw his opportunity to settle an old score while lighting a fire under Smith's demoralized command. "Old Grits" motioned his second line forward, which happened to be the remnant of the division he had commanded at Nashville the previous December. At some point during that battle, Govan's Brigade had passed his division hollering: "Lie down, Mr. Bate—Mr. Govan is gwine to pop a cap." And now, when Bate's old division came up to within earshot of Govan's Brigade, Bate later said, "I made my men halloo out, 'Lie down, Mr. Govan—*Mr. Bate* is gwine to pop a cap.'" Bate reported that his second line "approached in such fine spirit and order as to reassure the first [line] and excite an emulation which caused the first line to move rapidly forward." "Old Grits" must have chuckled in his beard as he penned the above sentence.[13]

In resuming the advance Bate's men passed the bodies of the Federals who had been killed in Buell's assault and whose faces, according to one soldier, "had turned almost black. . .from exposure to the sun." It is equally plausible that their black faces were the result of standing near too many pitch pine fires and too little soap.

As Bate's men mounted the crest of the slope, the Federal works came into view. Led by their color bearer, Pvt. Frank Stone, the 1st Georgia Volunteers of Smith's Brigade pressed on. Stone was carrying the distinctive flag of Cleburne's Division—a white disc centered on a dark blue field, which in turn was framed by a narrow white border. Cleburne's Division was the only infantry division in Confederate service permitted to carry its own colors in lieu of the standard Confederate battle flag. The division had earned this signal honor, for in its heyday it had been one of the elite fighting units of the Confederacy.[14]

Bate's men reached the tree line marking the edge of the ravine. "Down the slope we charged," wrote Sgt. Walter A. Clark of the 1st Georgia, "half the distance had been covered and the enemy's line is only a hundred yards away. The 'zips' of the minies get thicker and thicker and the line partially demoralized by the heavy fire suddenly halts." In the ensuing confusion, Private Stone and Sergeant Clark jumped for the same pine tree. According to one comrade, Stone was so thin that, if he wished to protect himself, he had merely "to present a side view to the enemy, as a minie ball would never reach his anatomy in that position."[15]

But on this occasion Private Stone was not thin enough, at least not for Sergeant Clark, with whom he was sharing the inadequate cover of that little pine. Clark momentarily forgot his own plight when he heard a sharp cry, then turned and saw comrade Jim Beasley "clasp his hand to his face as the blood spurt[ed] from his cheek." Seconds later a minie ball slammed into Clark's cartridge box, which Clark had slung around the front of his body to use as a shield and to make the loading of his rifle easier. The impact of the ball drew forth a grunt from Clark. "Are you hurt?" asked Stone. Miraculously, Clark was uninjured; in passing through his cartridge box, the ball had ricocheted off the butt-end of a cartridge and exited out the right side of the box.[16]

While their supports on the right fell back before the enemy onslaught, Buell's two Michigan regiments fired coolly and deliberately, holding Bate's troops at bay. But the Michiganders were hungry, having had no coffee or hot food since sunup, and their bloody noon assault had taken a heavy toll. Those who had escaped unhurt were exhausted, as much from the strain of awaiting the Confederate assault as from the labor expended on their unfinished breastworks. According to the 21st Michigan's

Lieutenant Bates, his men ignored their hunger and fatigue, for they had more pressing business to attend to. Bates described the Confederate advance:

> As far as we could see on both our right and left they were coming in unbroken lines with that old yell we had learned to know so well. We held our position, keeping up a continuous and rapid fire, until we could plainly see their trap closing around us as they enveloped our flanks and subjected them to their fire. It was impossible to maintain our position.[17]

The Michiganders could see enough of the Confederate line to realize that it overlapped their own on either flank. No one was more aware of this fact than General Carlin, who had been pacing back and forth along Buell's line, awaiting word from one of his couriers or for the return of Captain Edmonds and Rosy. Carlin had stopped near the extreme left of Buell's line, where he observed "the enemy advancing over the open field" and in the woods "considerably beyond Buell's left flank. . .but I saw no need of retreating." Carlin walked over to Buell's right, where the situation appeared to be less threatening than it had been on the left: "The enemy," Carlin wrote, "had advanced to within 30 steps of Buell's line on the right and halted." Carlin stood so close to Lt. Charles Brown's position on the line that "I could have laid my hand upon him," Brown wrote. "[H]e was as cool a man in a fight as I ever saw."[18]

General Buell, however, did not share his superior's confidence. Buell calculated that the flanking column the Rebels had sent beyond his left was now in position to strike Captain Rowe's skirmish line, if it had not done so already. He also knew that he lacked the manpower to hold his left flank, for the Confederates were present in sufficient numbers to simply brush aside Rowe's skirmishers and the 69th Ohio. When Buell turned to examine the situation on his right flank, he was stunned to see the Confederates swarming through the woods where Briant's line had been. Buell also noted that Carlin "was just at the right of my line, but was evidently not aware of the condition of things to his right, for he was at that time looking intently to the front at the enemy as he faltered before the fire of my men."[19]

Buell waited for Carlin to act, but "seeing that too much delay would cause our certain capture, and there being no time for consultation, I ordered the retreat. Half a minute's delay, and Carlin, myself, and most of my brigade would have been captured." Lieutenant Brown believed that he and his comrades had "stood as long as man could stand & when that was no longer a possibility [we] run like the duce."[20]

While brigade bugler William Worley sounded the retreat, Carlin was firing the rifle-musket of an anxious soldier in an effort to steady the man's nerves. When Carlin returned the rifle to its owner, he noticed that Buell's entire line had vanished. Rifle firmly in hand, the nervous soldier scampered off after his regiment. "I was absolutely alone," Carlin recalled, "not an officer or man who wore the Union blue was in sight. There was a compact line of Confederates not 30 yards from me. I was dressed in a new uniform of Brigadier-General." Carlin thought of surrendering, but abruptly dismissed the notion. In order to avoid calling attention to himself, Carlin walked slowly down the slope until he reached the swale at the bottom of the ravine. Lieutenant Brown spotted Carlin as he was hunched over in the middle of the swamp, ducking beneath a hail of Rebel bullets. Pointing to the general, Brown turned to his mates and quipped: "use him as a stepping stone to cross dry shod."[21]

Carlin left the relative safety of the swamp and began climbing up the slope, where he came into view of the advancing Confederates. "It was then that a regular fusilade [sic] . . .was opened on me," he recalled, "cutting the twigs and bushes all around me, and throwing up black dirt around my feet; even the earth under my feet seemed to be cut away by the bullets." For the second time in minutes, Carlin considered surrendering to the Confederates, but a sudden lull in their fire convinced him to press on in search of his command. At that point, Carlin resolved to surrender only if he were struck down by a bullet.[22]

* * *

On the Confederate right, Brig. Gen. Stephen Elliott, Jr., who led a brigade in Taliaferro's Division, swept the pine woods to the south with his field glasses. To his left he saw what appeared to be a Union skirmish line, but when he looked straight ahead or to the right, he saw only empty woodland.[23]

Elliott was still suffering from several wounds he had sustained during the Battle of the Crater the previous July. The wounds had not healed properly and would prove fatal within a year. But at the moment Elliott was jubilant, for he saw that his line overlapped the Federal left flank. He rode back to his brigade, which formed the front rank of Taliaferro's line of battle. Rhett's Brigade (under Col. William Butler) was drawn up in support of Elliott. The officers of both brigades ordered their men to remove their blankets, knapsacks and haversacks to afford them greater freedom of movement.[24]

General Elliott gave the command: "Forward!" Lieutenant Colonel James Welsman Brown, Elliott's second-in-command, wrote in his diary: "we started in entirely ignorant of what was expected of us." Although Brown found this singular lack of intelligence lamentable, it seems to have made no difference to Elliott's rank and file. Raising the Rebel yell, they "advanced through a very thick black jack oak woods full of briars, and then double-quicked," recalled Cpl. A. P. Ford. They overran Buell's skirmish line, killing or capturing several of the Union skirmishers before scattering the rest. "One picket was in the act of eating his dinner," wrote Ford, "and as we ran upon him he dropped his tin bucket, which. . .had rice and peas boiled together. Our lieutenant grabbed it up, and carried it, with the spoon still in the porridge."[25]

* * *

With the Michigan regiments of Buell's brigade in full retreat, Bate's line, on Elliott's immediate left, once again lurched forward and passed over the abandoned Federal breastworks. Sergeant Clark paused at the works to pick up a frying pan, a hatchet and an Enfield rifle left behind by the fleeing Yankees. Tossing aside his inferior Austrian rifle, Clark raised his new Enfield and took aim at a crowd of Federals scrambling up the opposite bank of the ravine. Clark sent "one of their own balls after them" and missed because, as he explained, "the cartridge was faulty and failed to reach its mark."[26]

Some of Buell's men fell back fighting, but most of them simply "showed to the Rebs as well as our side some of the best running ever did," wrote the 21st Michigan's Lieutenant Brown. Seeing his infantry support dashing past his guns, Lieutenant Scovel ordered his Illinois battery to limber up and head for the rear. Nearby, Lt. O. C. Townsend was helping the hospital stewards load the wounded of Carlin's division into his ambulances. A staff officer galloped up and asked Townsend if he was in charge of Carlin's hospital train.

"I am," Townsend replied.

"Then get it out of there!" barked the staff officer, "and quick as God will let you. Our lines are broken and the boys are falling back."

Townsend ordered the ambulances to the rear at once, then mounted his horse and sped back to the division hospital, where he reported the rout of Carlin's troops north of the Goldsboro Road. Major Reuben Dyer, the chief surgeon of Carlin's division, ordered all hospital tents struck and the wounded evacuated to the XIV Corps hospital on the Morris farm.[27]

Sergeant Lyman Widney of the 34th Illinois, a regiment in Morgan's division, had walked a short distance to the rear in search of his regiment's commissary pack mule, when he was greeted by the sight of dozens of ambulances and ordnance wagons jolting and bumping toward the rear via the Goldsboro Road and the adjoining fields. Seeing that this wild "caravan" blocked the way back to his regiment, Sergeant Widney sat back against a tree and "watched with no small amusement the frantic efforts" of the teamsters "to infuse some of their own terror into their mules[,] which refused to be led any faster than usual." One of the Federal quartermasters, Capt. Alexander Ayers, later told his wife that the Rebels "come on to us a little *harder & closer* than I ever saw them before. I do not now see why they did not take my whole train & myself in. I never before saw myself entirely helpless & at their mercy but can say that I was not scared in the least though in the midst of a most terrible stampede."[28]

When Sergeant Widney rose to his feet he found that his path was again blocked, this time by a straggler line, whose task was to stem the Union rout. "Shoot any men who try to pass your line," ordered the commanding officer. "There will be a fight here in five minutes." Widney recalled that when the fleeing Federals burst into view, "and the bullets of the advancing enemy began to sing around our ears," the straggler line evaporated.[29]

* * *

From its position behind a rail fence straddling the field in Bate's right front, the 69th Ohio poured a steady fire into Smith's Brigade as it crossed the swampy ravine. General Bate responded to the 69th's oblique fire by swinging out his old division (the brigades of Finley and Tyler) and forming it on Smith's right. Although he had yet to make contact with Taliaferro's line, Bate's augmented right flank had no difficulty in sweeping aside the company-sized 69th Ohio. No sooner did Bate strike the Ohioans than Taliaferro threatened to cut off their escape route, and in so doing, trap them and the rest of Carlin's fugitives. Lieutenant Brown called the Federals' foot race to the rear "the best thing we ever did, for [in] falling back we met a line of Rebs marching straight for our rear & in 15 minutes more we would have been between two lines of the buggers[.]" The grand assault of the still-formidable Army of Tennessee had routed the Federal left flank. For the rest of the day, the portion of Carlin's division north of the Goldsboro Road was finished as an effective fighting force.[30]

On Bate's left, D. H. Hill's line of battle advanced across the swampy ravine, closely followed by Hardee and his mounted escort. G. B. Gardner, a member of Hardee's escort, described what he saw:

> As I passed along through the charge, I saw the poor fellows that but a few minutes ago were full of life, lying about on the ground dead and dying and hundreds of wounded, going and being carried to the rear. I was carrying the General's flag in the charge. . . .While I was passing through a pond poor Charley [Gardner's horse] bogged and fell and caught my leg under him. I held the flag out of the water,[sic] I expect it was amusing to see me lying there in the middle of the pond, with my leg fastened under a fallen horse, holding up the flag, for fear it would be soiled. But without assistance we recovered, and in less time than I have been giving an account of the scene, we were passing along in the midst of a peal of laughter from the men. It is

> astonishing that men can indulge in laughter in the midst of such sadness, but they do.[31]

Hill's troops were halted at the southern bank of the ravine, where they were given a breather, much as Loring had earlier done for his command. And much as Loring's troops had done, Hill's veterans peered over the lip of the ravine and decided they did not like what they saw. Before them stretched the Cole field, and beyond it, a tree line bristling with the cannon of Webb's battery and the rifles of Robinson's Federals, who were kneeling behind formidable-looking log works. When the officers gave the order to advance, the soldiers balked. "Franklin was fresh in their minds and they hesitated," explained Hardee's adjutant, Lt. Col. Thomas B. Roy.[32]

Hardee spurred his horse up the slope of the ravine to investigate the delay. A single glance across the field told him all he needed to know. Although he was not given to battlefield heroics—he was called "Old Reliable" for good reason—Hardee rode into the field, and in full view of the Federals, waved his men forward. The soldiers raised a cheer, then climbed to the rim of the ravine and dashed across the field.[33]

General Robinson saw that his position was hopeless. Hill's and Loring's advance threatened his center and right flank, and the rout of Buell's brigade "permitted the enemy to come directly in upon my left flank and rear," Robinson reported, "and left me no alternative but to withdraw my command or have them captured. The line was held until to have remained upon it would have been madness. I therefore reluctantly gave the command to fall back." With the general himself carrying the brigade colors, Robinson's three regiments retired in good order toward the Morris farm, their withdrawal aided by the cover of the thick woods west of the Cole field. However, knots of Buell's and Briant's fleeing troops occasionally broke through the ranks of Robinson's brigade, and threatened to sweep it along in the tide of panic-stricken men.[34]

Just as Buell's retreat had uncovered Robinson, Robinson's withdrawal uncovered Webb's battery, which was left to fend for itself. The two sections of the battery were separated by a distance of several hundred yards, and stood on either end of what had been Robinson's line. The crews of the left section managed to limber up their guns and get them underway, but Stevenson's troops cut off their escape route. General Palmer's men shot two Hoosier artillerymen off the limber chests of one fleeing Napoleon while they were tossing out shells in a desperate effort to lighten their load. Lieutenant E. C. Thornton, the adjutant for Jackson's Brigade of Clayton's Division, single-handedly captured the other field piece with the caisson and team intact.[35]

The ground occupied by the right section of Webb's battery was littered with horse and mule carcasses and the debris of the blown-up caisson. The crew of one gun had to abandon it, for want of draft animals. But the other Napoleon was limbered up and standing just a few yards north of the Goldsboro Road, General Loring's skirmishers having driven off its crew. Bearing off their mortally wounded commander, the men of Webb's battery fell in behind Robinson's retreating line.[36]

Private Peter Anderson of the 31st Wisconsin, Robinson's right regiment, was falling back with his comrades when he heard someone shout: "For God's sake, bring out that battery!" Anderson turned to a comrade and asked him to "come with me and attempt to save the battery. He refused." So Private Anderson ran back alone, and found one of the two abandoned guns limbered up, the horses hitched and ready to be moved. Turning the lead horses into the Goldsboro Road and using his ramrod as a whip, he started the team after Robinson's retiring line. Anderson recalled:

> I tried to mount one of the horses, but the stirrup was shot off just as I put my foot in it and I was obliged to follow along behind. The distance to our lines was from one-third to half a mile, and all this way I was under a hot rebel fire from both sides. At one time the rebels were on all sides of me and demanding my surrender. I had previously fired my gun and was now trying to reload. I had nearly succeeded when a shot struck the barrel and broke it in the middle. The same shot knocked off the tip of my right forefinger. I raised my musket and blazed away, sending ramrod and all into the rebels. An officer rode up close to me, pointed his revolver at my head and shouted: "Surrender, you damned Yankee!" A shot from some quarter killed him outright the next moment. I finally reached my regiment which, observing my predicament, had taken a stand waiting for me to come up.

Anderson continued on his way until he reached the Morris farm, where he was met by a grateful Major Houghtaling, the XIV Corps' chief of artillery. Within a week Anderson would receive the personal thanks of General Sherman, and three months later he would be awarded a captain's commission and the Medal of Honor. But for now Anderson simply wanted to get a new rifle and rejoin his comrades.[37]

At the front, Sergeant Widney was making his way back to the 34th Illinois when he observed Union "officers mounted and on foot,. . .brandishing their swords, running hither and thither, frantically endeavoring to rally the disorganized masses of men." Lieutenant Colonel McClurg recalled riding up to the front amid:

> masses of men slowly and doggedly falling back along the [Goldsboro] road, and through the fields and open woods on the left of the road. . . . Minie-balls were whizzing in every direction, although I was then far from the front line as I had left it only a short time before. . . .[T]he roar of musketry and artillery was now continuous.

McClurg was racing past the gunless crews of Webb's battery when its new commander, Lt. Clinton Keeler, called out, "For Heaven's sake, don't go down there! I am the last man of the command. Everything is gone in front of you."[38]

"Checking my horse," McClurg continued, "I saw the rebel regiments in front in full view, stretching through the fields to the left as far as the eye could reach, advancing rapidly, and firing as they came. . . .The onward sweep of the rebel lines was like the waves of the ocean, resistless."[39]

During the rout Chaplain Earle of the 21st Michigan remained at the front tending the wounded. Earle was bent over dressing a wound when a surgeon tapped him on the shoulder and said, "Chaplain, look out there." The chaplain looked up and saw:

> a whole column of Gray-backs coming. . .just out side [sic] of our men. And I turned around and looked in the oposite [sic] direction, and there were coming, just outside of our men, another force of these chaps. And things looked blue, yes, decidedly pitious [sic]. You ask, if we run? Yes, like

> whiteheads. And, I know that my old bob-tailed rone [sic], never made such time before.[40]

From his position just south of the Goldsboro Road, Lieutenant Colonel Fitch witnessed the Rebel advance across the Cole field: "Approaching our flank was a line of Loring's and [Walthall's] divisions," he wrote, "parallel with the road and at right angles with our line. It stretched to the rear farther than I could see through the timber. I could not help admiring for the moment, their fine soldierly bearing."[41]

Fitch had just dashed over from the right of his line at the urging of Captain Randall, who commanded the company of the 21st Wisconsin nearest the Goldsboro Road. Randall and several men of Webb's battery warned Fitch that a large force of the enemy had passed around his flank and into the woods, and were now advancing on his left rear. This news came as a shock to Fitch, who had assumed since late morning that Briant's wing held the Cole field. Because his view of the Cole field was obscured by a thicket which bordered the Goldsboro Road, Fitch had expected Hobart to inform him of any change in the line to the left of Webb's battery. Since receiving Carlin's injunction to secure his right flank, Fitch had focused his attention on that part of his line in the belief that it was unsupported.[42]

Fitch now glanced rearward down the Goldsboro Road for a sign of Union blue—he saw none. "It was evident at once," Fitch wrote, "that we could not remain an instant in [our] isolated position—three little regiments had no show whatever against the forces in sight—or we would have [met] the same fate that had overtaken the left. We would either be captured or annihilated." As he peered through the thicket at the approaching Rebel line, Fitch noticed that Webb's battery had abandoned one of its field pieces by the roadside. Fitch ordered a squad of his men to wheel the gun into position and mimic the various functions of an artillery crew. He then swung Randall's company of the 21st Wisconsin around to face the enemy and sent it forward. Fitch thus hoped to buy enough time for the rest of his wing to change front by the left flank, and so face the Confederates advancing across the Cole field. But just as the main line began to wheel about, the skirmishers came dashing in—with their return Fitch noticed that the Confederates' fire along his old front continued unabated. Suddenly, Rebel minie balls from behind began to zip past his head. Fitch abruptly halted his wheeling maneuver and cried out above the din: "About face! Left oblique! Double quick! March! March!" Fitch led his three regiments about 200 yards to the right and rear of their former position in the field. During the retreat, Fitch's men had to endure a constant harassing fire while stumbling through a swamp overgrown with briars, vines and blackjack oaks. On emerging from the morass, Fitch and his men entered an open wood: no soldier in Fitch's wing was more surprised than Fitch to see the log breastworks of General Morgan's division looming up before him. Fitch was delighted to find a veritable Union fortress where he had expected to encounter only Confederates, but he was also incensed that no one had bothered to inform him that Morgan had deployed on his right.[43]

On Fitch's right, Miles' brigade likewise withdrew in the direction of Morgan's division. Captain J. L. Keller of the 21st Ohio blamed Miles, perhaps unfairly, for placing his brigade in such a precarious position. "Bullets from our rear, bullets from our left flank, and a few from our front, were too much for even veterans," Captain Keller recalled. "Every man in the regiment knew somebody had blundered." According to Keller, neither Miles nor any other officer ordered a retreat; instead, Keller believed that the brigade "intuitively moved" before disaster struck.[44]

The fight was now over for Capt. John Eicker of Company C, 79th Pennsylvania of Miles' brigade. Minutes after witnessing the death of his good friend Fred Myers, Eicker was disabled by a bullet wound in the left thigh. Turning over his command to the company's first sergeant, Eicker limped to the rear, helped along by two of his men. Somehow they managed to thread their way through what had been the Federal rear and was now rapidly becoming the Confederate front. Soon after reaching the Morris farm—the site of the XIV Corps hospital—Eicker found a comrade of the 79th, Pvt. Vincent Lee, lying in the yard, "the Blood oozing out of his mouth and Nose." Captain Eicker continued:

> I said to him Vince are you wounded bad[?]
> he said yes I am shot right through my Bowells
> I guess I will die to night
> so he did[.] the next morning he was a corps[e].[45]

The men of Fitch's and Miles' commands passed through Mitchell's brigade's line in a "rapid and disorganized retreat," General Mitchell reported. "It was impossible to gather any definite information from them. All that was known was that the troops on their left had given way and the enemy had turned their flank." Some of these frightened men paused in their flight long enough to warn Mitchell's troops that the enemy would surround them if they remained in their present position. Most of Mitchell's veterans ignored these warnings and stayed put.[46]

To guard against this threat to his left, Mitchell ordered Fitch and Miles to deploy their commands—or what remained of them—on his left flank and at a 90-degree angle to his entrenched line, which faced eastward. As added insurance, Mitchell directed his two rear-line regiments, the 34th Illinois and the 121st Ohio, to deploy on either side of Carlin's fugitives. The 34th Illinois changed position first, deploying on the left of the 98th Ohio, and thus forming a right angle on that part of Mitchell's line. The 121st Ohio then left its works and deployed on the extreme left of the new line, which faced north toward the Cole field and the Goldsboro Road. "All this was done in a swamp covered with water and thickly overgrown with underwood and brambles as well as larger trees, and under a continual fire, which was growing hotter every minute," wrote the 121st's commander, Maj. Aaron Robinson.[47]

While Mitchell was making these dispositions, Morgan sent over his adjutant, Capt. Theo Wiseman, to order Mitchell to refuse his left flank and deploy the 34th Illinois and the 121st Ohio on this new line. But as Morgan happily observed, "This cool and gallant officer had already anticipated my order." As the firing on the left grew louder, Morgan ordered General Vandever to shift his two rear-line regiments, the 10th Michigan and the 17th New York, about 100 yards to the left so that they could advance with equal rapidity to either Mitchell's or Vandever's support. Vandever placed these two regiments under the temporary command of Col. Charles Lum of the 10th Michigan, and sent them on their way.[48]

* * *

"General, I congratulate you on your success," General Johnston said, shaking Hardee's hand, "or rather on doing what you always do." Hardee had every reason to feel satisfied, for his troops had just swept the Federals from the field, and he had led the way. Johnston and Hardee had only to scan the Cole field for evidence of the Federals' rout: rifles, cartridge boxes, knapsacks, haversacks, canteens and blankets lay scattered everywhere—there was also the wreckage of Webb's battery along the far corner of the field. It was with understandable reluctance that Hardee called a halt to the pursuit. Hardee knew that his wing had smashed the Union left flank, but he also knew that his own line was badly disordered, owing to its rapid advance across a swampy, broken and heavily wooded terrain. Hardee no doubt assumed that the Federals would rally beyond the woods west of the Cole plantation, and he wanted his line of battle in a proper condition to assault the enemy's new position.[49]

Hardee asked Johnston to return McLaws' Division to him. Johnston readily granted Hardee's request, perhaps miffed by Bragg's failure to attack as ordered. McLaws, ironically enough, was making his first tentative advance since deploying on Hoke's left, when he received Hardee's order to report to him with his division. McLaws called in his skirmishers and a section of Brooks' Battery that had somehow slogged through the swamp in its front. Once more, McLaws found himself leading his division toward the sound of the guns, only this time the sound seemed to be emanating from all directions.[50]

While McLaws was withdrawing from his position on Hoke's left, General Bragg ordered Hoke to assault Morgan's line. Bragg's order reached Hoke about 3:45 p.m., one hour after the scheduled time for the attack. Bragg clearly had disobeyed Johnston's order to attack at 2:45 p.m. Instead, Bragg had notified McLaws (and presumably Hoke) "that General Stewart would attack the enemy in flank," and that his two division commanders "must be ready to strike a blow if an opportunity offered." In other words, Bragg delayed his attack pending the outcome of the Confederate right wing's assault, making his own assault contingent upon the success of Hardee's and Stewart's attack. Bragg therefore either misunderstood Johnston's order or he deliberately disobeyed it. In a post-war letter to General Hoke, Johnston stated that he repeatedly urged Bragg to attack, implying that Bragg's disobedience was intentional. We can only guess as to Bragg's motives, since he did not write an after-action report on the battle.[51]

In preparation for his assault, Hoke swung out Colquitt's and Clingman's brigades to join on General Loring's left. In response to orders from A. P. Stewart, Loring halted Stewart's Corps just south of the road, facing Mitchell's refused left flank, and D. H. Hill stopped Lee's Corps along the road and on Loring's right. Hardee halted Bate's line, which faced south-southwest, at the tree line bordering the Morris farm. The Confederate line now extended for more than a half-mile down the Goldsboro Road. In the meantime, Taliaferro's Division struggled through the woods west of the Cole plantation and had yet to form on Bate's right.[52]

General Hill ordered his division commanders to form a line of battle parallel to, and on the north side of, the Goldsboro Road. During the advance, however, Palmer's Brigade of Stevenson's Division had strayed south of the road; it was recrossing the road in obedience to Hill's orders when Hill instructed General Palmer to halt his command. Meanwhile, Baker's Brigade of Clayton's Division blundered into the road, cutting Palmer's Brigade in two, General Clayton having ordered Baker forward to relieve Stovall and Jackson. Baker's men found the road littered with the enemy's discarded baggage, and broke ranks to sift through it, thereby worsening an already chaotic situation. Private B. F. Watson of the 40th Alabama inventoried his regiment's haul:

> Some of our men grabbed up [the] knapsacks, and one of our Co., Frank Lee, found a silk dress, while some found ladies' garments and Daguerreotypes, and Chevalier of Capt. Coleman's company hauled out a little bag of silver of about 12 dollars. . . .I grabbed up a frying pan and stuck the handle under my belt as a sort of shield.[53]

But the confusion was short-lived. The two wings of Johnston's army converged on Morgan's salient from three sides. So far, the Confederate grand assault was proceeding according to plan.

* * *

General Morgan received an order from Lieutenant Colonel Litchfield of General Davis' staff to relieve Miles' brigade with Fearing's brigade. General Fearing was getting his command underway when Davis galloped up on his white mare and informed Morgan that the Rebels had swept away Carlin's line and were heading for his left rear. Then Davis turned to his inspector general and asked,

"Where is that brigade, Litchfield?"

"Here it is, sir," the lieutenant colonel replied, pointing to Fearing's brigade. Massed in column of regiments, the brigade was faced to the front. Davis ordered it to wheel to the left, then he told Fearing to push his brigade as rapidly as possible to the Goldsboro Road, where the Rebels were forming for another assault.

"Advance upon their flank, Fearing!" Davis shouted. "Deploy as you go. Give them the best you've got, and we'll whip them yet!"

"Hurrah for old Jeff!" the men cheered. "We'll whip 'em yet!"

As the Federal brigade plunged into the swampy thicket and splashed off toward the Goldsboro Road, one of Fearing's veterans overheard Davis tell his staff that Fearing's brigade was marching straight into Hell.

"And so we did go there," recalled the old veteran.[54]

As Lt. Col. Allen L. Fahnestock marched past at the head of the 86th Illinois, Davis hollered, "Col., for God Sake get your Regiment out to the road, the Enemy are capturing our Men." Fahnestock saluted Davis and led the 86th after the rest of Fearing's brigade. An uneasy Fahnestock noted that with each step his regiment took toward the Goldsboro Road, the further away it moved from the left of Mitchell's line. Meanwhile, General Fearing was at the head of his brigade, deploying it in line of battle and wondering what lay beyond the swamp he was crossing. Fearing hadn't long to find out. About thirty paces shy of the Goldsboro Road, Fearing's line collided with General Bate's skirmishers. The Federals drove the Confederates across the road and upon the left flank of Cleburne's Division, which in turn fell back from its position near the road and on Clayton's Division's right.[55]

Fearing's troops struggled "through numerous swamps, over bushes, vines, and briers," reported the commander of the 125th Illinois, Lt. Col. James W. Langley, before halting just south of, and parallel to, the Goldsboro Road. The 22nd Indiana, commanded by Capt. William H. Snodgrass, joined on the right of the 125th Illinois, the two regiments forming the left wing of Fearing's line. Lieutenant Colonel Charles W. Clancy posted his command, the 52nd Ohio, on Snodgrass' right. "The firing from my line was well directed," Clancy reported, "at once breaking the enemy's line, and he retreated a short distance in disorder and confusion." Finding his front secure for the moment, Clancy shifted his attention to the right flank of his regiment, which he refused pending the arrival of the 86th Illinois. Meanwhile, Fearing threw out a heavy skirmish line across the Goldsboro Road, extending it 250 yards to the left in order to connect with the XX Corps' skirmishers. Fearing also tried to locate Carlin's troops on the right, but reported that he "could find or hear nothing of them."[56]

General Bate reacted to Fearing's spoiling attack by applying to General Stevenson for reinforcements. Stevenson had just ordered his reserve brigade, Pettus', to advance southward across the Goldsboro Road when he received Bate's request. Fortunately for Bate, General Pettus was at that moment leading his Alabamians in the direction of the loudest firing, which happened to be along Bate's left flank. Pettus noted that the musketry seemed to be approaching his left, and that some stragglers—probably from Bate's skirmish line—were sprinting from that direction for the rear. Pettus accordingly refused his left flank and advanced into the marshy thicket south of the road.[57]

Bate also appealed to Stevenson's superior, D. H. Hill, for help. Since half of Palmer's Brigade was already south of the Goldsboro Road, Hill ordered it to bolster Bate's battered left flank, then sent Clayton's Division to Bate's support as well. While following Baker's Brigade across the road, General Clayton noticed that the enemy was firing on it from the right and across its line of march. Clayton sent forward a few scouts, who found the right of Fearing's line posted just south of the Goldsboro Road and to the right of where Baker had just passed. Clayton instructed Col. Osceola Kyle, the commander of Jackson's Brigade, to collect whatever force he could from his own and Stovall's Brigade, and use it to check Fearing's advance, thus securing the right flank and rear of Baker's Brigade.[58]

On Fearing's right, the 86th Illinois arrived and formed on the right of the 52nd Ohio. Lieutenant Colonel Fahnestock deployed a skirmish line in his front and along his right flank. Baker's and Palmer's Confederates soon pressed back the 86th's skirmishers and attempted to steal around the Illinoisans' right flank. Fahnestock countered by swinging back his right and ordering his men to "lay down and shoot low." Private R. A. Lambert of the 42nd Alabama, Baker's Brigade, recalled that he and his comrades suddenly found themselves "in a hornets' nest of bullets. We quickly obeyed the orders to lie down, but still made use of our guns."[59]

On Fearing's left, Lieutenant Colonel Langley stepped into the Goldsboro Road and looked to his right to learn the cause of the heavy firing coming from that direction. "I observed a strong column of the enemy, four lines deep," Langley reported, "moving against the point where I supposed the right of the brigade rested." General Fearing also stood in the road and watched the procession. He later reported that "many officers" of his brigade assured him that "these were the columns of [Carlin's] Division, Fourteenth Army Corps, as many soldiers composing this force were wearing the Federal uniform."[60]

Meanwhile, Fahnestock sent word to Fearing that a double column of Confederates was turning his position. Fearing hurried over to the right to inform Fahnestock that his troops were in fact firing on their own men. "I told him they were Rebbles," Fahnestock wrote, but Fearing ordered his nonplused subordinate to cease fire anyway.[61]

The woods in Fahnestock's front were so thick with gunpowder smoke that by the time it began to lift, the Confederates had approached to within 20 yards of the 86th Illinois' right flank. Disregarding Fearing's cease-fire order, Fahnestock ordered his men to open fire. The Rebels responded with a volley of their own, which was so devastating that, according to Fahnestock, it claimed no less than 23 of his men in killed and wounded, even though his regiment was prone at the time. "The Bullets flew like hail among the Pine trees," Fahnestock noted. Fearing was among those severely wounded, losing his right thumb and forefinger to a Rebel bullet, yet he remained on the field until loss of blood forced him to relinquish his command.[62]

Fearing attempted to fend off the Confederates by ordering the 86th to refuse its right flank again, but it was too late. "The whole of my line was doubled up and thrown into confusion," he reported. The Confederates mounted a charge against the 86th Illinois and the 52nd Ohio that routed Fearing's two right regiments. Luckily for the Federals, the enemy "did not, or could not, follow up with his broken and straggling ranks the seeming

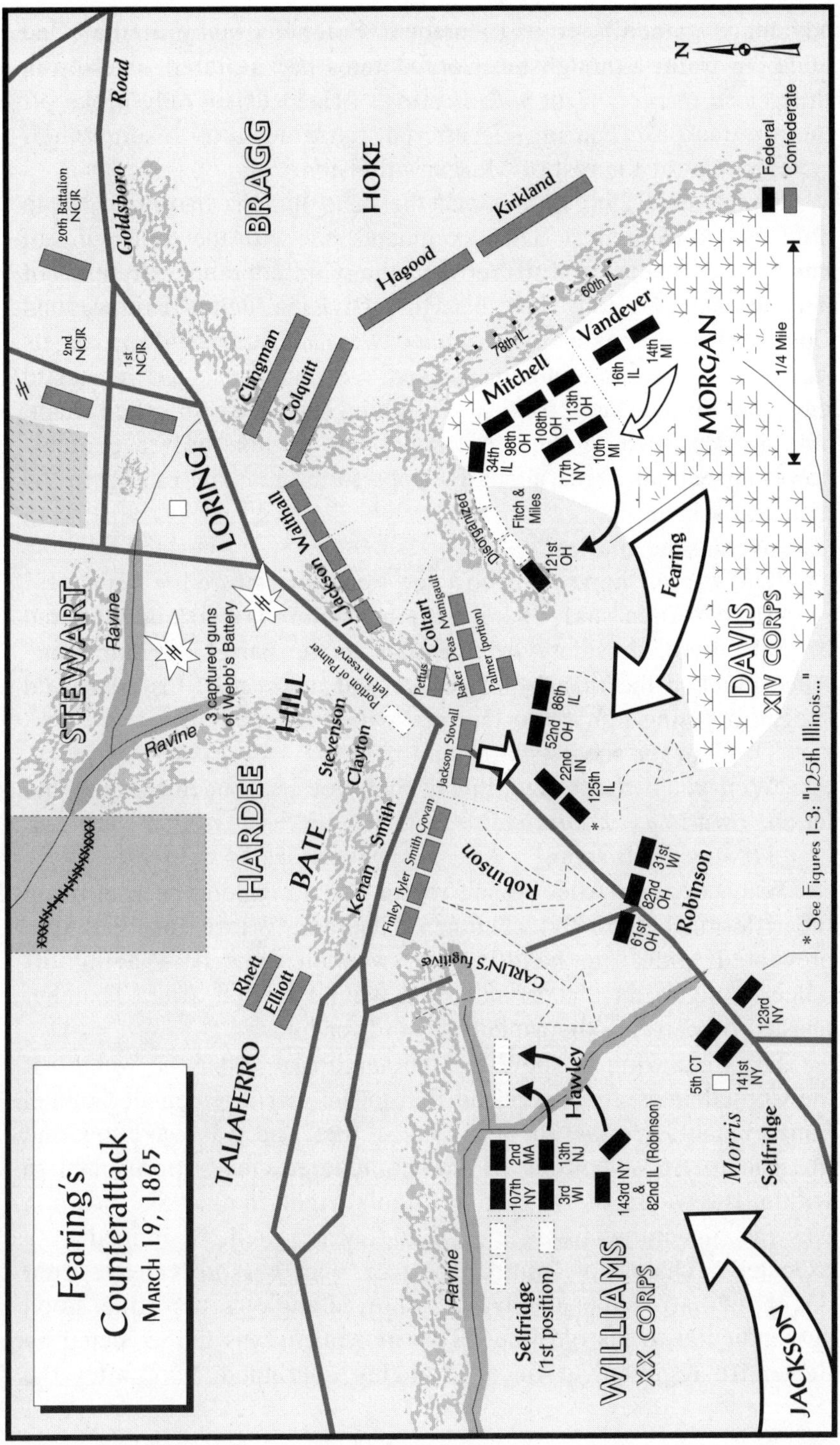
Fearing's Counterattack
March 19, 1865
Goldsboro Road
BRAGG
HOKE
Hagood
Kirkland
Clingman
Colquitt
20th Battalion NCJR
2nd NCJR
1st NCJR
LORING
STEWART
Ravine
Ravine
3 captured guns of Webb's Battery
J. Jackson
Walthall
HARDEE
HILL
Stevenson
Clayton
Portion of Palmer left in reserve
Pettus
Coltart
Baker
Deas
Manigault
Palmer (portion)
Jackson
Stovall
BATE
Kenan
Smith
Finley
Tyler
Smith
Govan
Rhett
Elliott
TALIAFERRO
CARLIN'S fugitives
Robinson
Mitchell
Vandever
78th IL
60th IL
34th IL
98th OH
108th OH
113th OH
17th NY
10th MI
16th IL
14th MI
Disorganized
Fitch & Miles
121st OH
MORGAN
Fearing
DAVIS
XIV CORPS
86th IL
52nd OH
22nd IN
125th IL
31st WI
82nd OH
61st OH
Robinson
123rd NY
5th CT
141st NY
Morris
Selfridge
Hawley
2nd MA
13th NJ
107th NY
3rd WI
143rd NY & 82nd IL (Robinson)
Selfridge (1st position)
WILLIAMS
XX CORPS
Ravine
JACKSON
1/4 Mile
N
Federal
Confederate
* See Figures 1-3: "125th Illinois..."

Mark A. Moore

advantage gained," wrote Lieutenant Colonel Clancy of the 52nd Ohio. In truth, although the Confederates had suffered severely in their close quarters fight with Fearing's brigade, they only broke off their pursuit of Fearing's scattered right wing to resume their envelopment of the rest of Morgan's division.[63]

So far, the 125th Illinois and the 22nd Indiana had managed to hold their own against Bate's command, but with the right wing of Fearing's brigade in full retreat, the Confederates' strength of numbers began to tell. Now that Hill's Division, Pettus' Brigade, and Colonel Kyle's makeshift command were all bearing down on its right flank, the 22nd Indiana needed every man it could muster to the front line—skulkers and stragglers included. So when Capt. William F. Allee of the 22nd spied one of his "coffee coolers" cowering behind a tree about 10 steps to the rear, he ran up to the man and asked,

"What's the matter?"

"Oh, I loose mine ram-rod," the skulker answered.

"Hell!" Allee said, "here are guns, ramrods and all, scattered over the field—besides, your own is in the barrel of your gun." Allee grabbed the man by the collar and the seat of his pants and "began boosting him up to the line" when he cried,

"Oh, I never scoot (shoot) any before."

"Well you'll shoot now, or I'll pitch you in front of the line and let our own boys *shoot you*."

"I'll scoot! I'll scoot!"

When Captain Allee wasn't routing up stragglers, he was firing the rifle-musket of Pvt. Thomas Thatcher, whose disabled arm prevented him from handling the weapon himself. Waving off Allee's suggestion that he have his wound looked after, Thatcher insisted on carrying the captain's sword for him.[64]

The right wing of the 22nd Indiana broke under the weight of the Confederates' firepower and fled to the rear. Lieutenant Colonel Langley could see that the left wing of the 22nd was wavering, and that the foremost column of the Confederates had approached to within 100 yards of the 125th Illinois' right flank. "My position was fast becoming untenable," Langley reported. "I immediately executed a change of front to the rear, and thus presented a front direct to that of the enemy." In short, Langley's new line stood perpendicular to his old line. "This movement was not executed by the entire regiment at once," Langley continued, "nor after the approved system of battalion drill, but by detaching two companies at a time from the right and placing them on the new alignment."[65]

Langley's men had to execute the change of front while under a severe enfilade fire—a difficult proposition at best, even for Langley's veteran command. At the time that Langley ordered the 125th Illinois to change front, it was facing the Goldsboro Road:

FIG. 1: To initiate the change of front to the rear, Langley ordered his two right companies to face about and wheel to the left.

FIG. 2: The textbooks recommend that the right, or *first*. company initiate the movement, followed by the rest of the regiment, which would form on the first company's right. Langley dispensed with the textbook method because it would have rendered his line vulnerable while it was pivoting into position on the first company. By shifting just two companies into position at a time, the 125th Illinois was able to maintain a steady fire on the enemy while extricating itself from a dangerous position. The 125th Illinois now confronted the enemy head-on.[66]

FIG. 3: The Confederates responded to the 125th's maneuver by shifting from a narrow front with a depth of four lines to a wide, two-line front. Seeing that the Rebels were turning his right flank, Langley again ordered a change of front to the rear. But this time the Confederates were on to Langley, who soon realized that his regiment was all but surrounded. "I directed my regiment to retire firing," Langley wrote. The Confederate line of battle was now within 50 yards of the 125th Illinois' position.[67]

The 125th fell back about 300 yards along the Goldsboro Road and rallied in an open field. Langley was pleased to find that his regiment remained intact, having retired in good order. The other regiments in Fearing's brigade were less fortunate. Captain Snodgrass managed to rally about 100 of his men from the left wing of the 22nd Indiana, but the right wing, together with the 52nd Ohio and the 86th Illinois, could not be found. A few minutes before 4:00 p.m., Capt. Charles Swift of General Fearing's staff informed Langley that Fearing was severely wounded and was therefore turning over command to him. (Langley enjoyed the dubious distinction of being the brigade's fifth commander in less

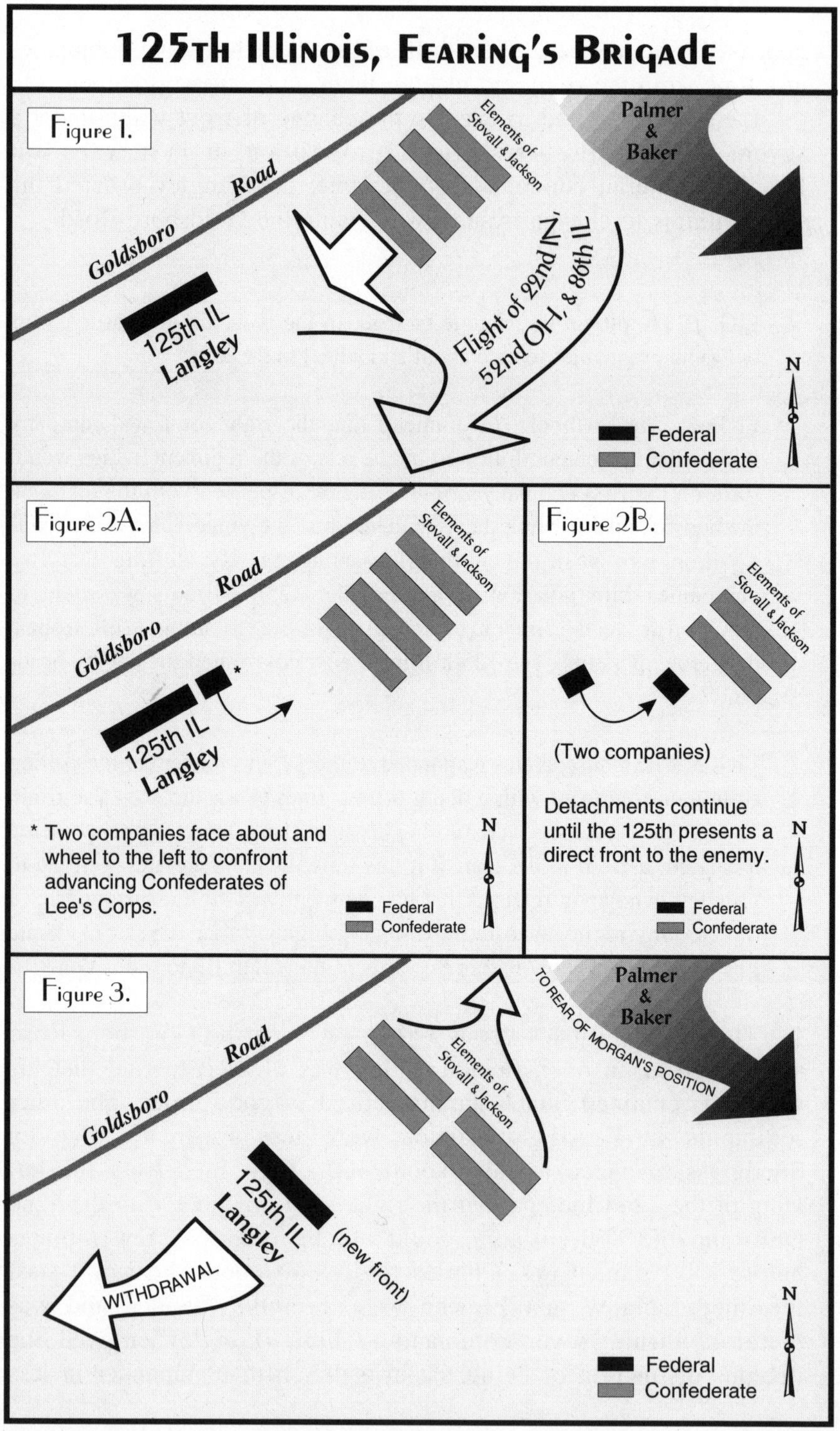
125th Illinois, Fearing's Brigade
Figure 1.
Goldsboro Road
Elements of Stovall & Jackson
Palmer & Baker
Flight of 22nd IN, 52nd OH, & 86th IL
125th IL Langley
N
Federal
Confederate
Figure 2A.
Goldsboro Road
Elements of Stovall & Jackson
125th IL Langley
* Two companies face about and wheel to the left to confront advancing Confederates of Lee's Corps.
Federal
Confederate
Figure 2B.
Elements of Stovall & Jackson
(Two companies)
Detachments continue until the 125th presents a direct front to the enemy.
Federal
Confederate
Figure 3.
Goldsboro Road
Palmer & Baker
TO REAR OF MORGAN'S POSITION
Elements of Stovall & Jackson
125th IL Langley
(new front)
WITHDRAWAL
Federal
Confederate

Mark A. Moore

than a year.) On assuming command Langley advanced his reformed line about 75 yards to the eastern edge of the field. He ordered that each of his men carry a load of rails to the new position, which lay south of, and perpendicular to, the Goldsboro Road. Langley also sent two of his staff officers after the 52nd Ohio and 86th Illinois, instructing them to guide the two regiments into position on the right of the new line.[68]

Just a few hundred yards east of Langley's position, four brigades of D. H. Hill's command poured into the gap opened by Fearing's retreat and headed straight for the rear of Morgan's position, while Hoke's Division began its assault on Morgan's front and left flank. It was 4:00 p.m. The struggle south of the Goldsboro Road was about to commence.

~ *eleven* ~

"It Seemed More Than Men Could Bear"

—Lt. Col. Alexander C. McClurg, Adjutant, Staff of Gen. Jeff C. Davis

"They are coming!" The words echoed up and down the line of the 34th Illinois of Mitchell's brigade. The men of the 34th dropped their axes and hatchets and grabbed their rifles. Pacing back and forth in rear of the angle, General Mitchell kept his pre-battle speech brief: "Every man in his place, and do your duty, boys. They have driven everything else; we must whip them or go to Andersonville." Although Mitchell had dispatched every axman in his brigade to assist in fortifying his new line, there had not been enough time. The 34th's log works were only substantial enough to lie down behind, and the works begun by Fitch's and Miles' troops and the 121st Ohio offered even less cover. Nevertheless, Bragg's one-hour delay in attacking had given Mitchell's and Vandever's men an invaluable opportunity to strengthen their position.[1]

Led by their commander, Col. Charles Zachry, Colquitt's Georgia Brigade assaulted the angle of Mitchell's works, with Clingman's North Carolina Brigade following in support. Sergeant Widney had rejoined the 34th Illinois and was standing near the point of the angle when the Georgians made a dash for the works. The 34th fired a volley into the Georgians from point-blank range: "The surging masses of our assailants recoiled from our barricades like spray from the sides of a well-built ship," Widney wrote. While Mitchell's Ohioans and Illinoisans on either side of the angle swept their front with a deadly cross-fire, Colonel Zachry's Georgians subjected Mitchell's intersecting lines to an equally devastating enfilade fire. A few of the Georgians who had dashed up to within several yards of the Yankee works became trapped in this lethal exchange and surrendered rather than risk being shot by friend and foe alike.[2]

Lieutenant John Marshall Branum of Company C, 98th Ohio, was one of the first defenders to fall at the angle. Branum's company commander and friend since boyhood, Capt. John Carson, was standing just a few feet away from the lieutenant when he received his death wound. "The ball struck him near the upper part of the chest, passing directly through him," Carson wrote Branum's father. Branum turned to Carson and said, "I'm killed, Captain." The lieutenant took one step toward Carson, then collapsed in his arms. "Take care of my things and send them to Mother," he whispered, and died. "I let him down slowly to the ground," Carson continued, "he was dead—died without a struggle or [a] moan."[3]

For a time the bullets flew so thick that the men of the 98th Ohio dared not raise their heads above the parapet. At one point a squad of Colonel Zachry's Georgians rushed up to within 20 yards of the Ohioans' works. It appeared to the their commander, Lt. Col. John S. Pearce, that the Confederates would overrun his position. Pearce rose up and ordered his men to fix bayonets, then was shot down an instant later. Private William H. Seaman and a comrade of Company G, 98th Ohio, jumped to their feet and fired a round into the faces of two onrushing Confederates. When Seaman crouched down again, he saw his comrade lying dead beside him.[4]

Prior to Hoke's assault, most of the men of the 121st Ohio felled trees to strengthen their position on the extreme left of Mitchell's refused line. A few soldiers, Pvt. C. R. Warfield among them, played cards instead. A falling tree crashed down on Private Warfield, striking him on the back of the neck. Before Warfield could give the responsible party a tongue lashing, he heard the distant report of two pistol shots, followed by a chorus of Rebel yells. Yet Warfield and his comrades could see nothing, the dense thicket in their front masking the Confederate advance.[5]

Although the minie balls began to zip past, the 121st Ohio received no order to open fire. Even when Zachry's Georgians emerged from the cover of the thicket 100 yards away, the commander of the 121st, Maj. Aaron Robinson, still hesitated to give the order, believing that the men in the "dusty, threadbare, and faded uniforms" advancing toward his line might be reinforcements from the XX Corps. The major sent out Lt. James Ball and six enlisted men of Company G to ascertain whether the unidentified troops were friend or foe. Robinson instructed his Ohioans to lay low and hold their fire in the meantime. But when the men of the 121st saw that the advancing soldiers were shooting at them, they disregarded Major Robinson's orders and opened on them. As Robinson passed down the line with his hands raised, begging his men to cease fire, a private caught him by the arm and pointed to a Confederate battle flag that was bobbing above the clouds of gray smoke. The startled Robinson ordered his men to open fire.[6]

The Ohioans of the 121st lay behind their incomplete works and fired on Zachry's Georgians, who appeared to be obliquing across their front toward the Ohioans' unsupported left flank. While the 121st was thus occupied, Lieutenant Ball returned from his reconnaissance to warn Major Robinson that the Confederates were indeed massing on his left, which dangled dangerously in the air.[7]

On the right of the 121st, Miles' brigade was withdrawing from its counterattack against the skirmishers of Stewart's Corps when Zachry's Georgians attacked Mitchell's position. Mitchell had ordered Lieutenant Colonel Miles to make the sortie to enable the rest of his makeshift command to fortify the refused line. During the withdrawal Miles was severely wounded, and command was turned over to Lt. Col. Arnold McMahan of the 21st Ohio. Soon afterward, McMahan was struck down by a bullet in the chest. Fortunately for McMahan, the bullet had flattened against a brass uniform button, leaving the him briefly stunned, but otherwise unhurt.[8]

McMahan's 21st Ohio was a regiment of unsung heroes. At Chickamauga the 21st had defended its crucial position on Horseshoe Ridge until it was surrounded, thereby sacrificing itself to save the XIV Corps from destruction. As a result, McMahan and more than 100 of his men were captured and sent to prison. After his exchange, McMahan found himself the scapegoat of Brig. Gen. John M. Brannan, who implied that McMahan's surrender on Horseshoe Ridge was the result of either cowardice or incompetence. Although it was clear even then that Brannan had unfairly slighted McMahan and his regiment, they never received official recognition for their defense of Horseshoe Ridge. Instead, they would have to wait 130 years for historian Peter Cozzens' tribute: "The six-hour stand of the Twenty-first Ohio [was] the most distinguished service rendered by any single regiment at Chickamauga."[9]

After withdrawing from its advanced position, Miles' brigade fell in between the right of the 121st Ohio and the left of the 104th Illinois of Fitch's wing. The 42nd Indiana occupied the center of Fitch's line, and the 21st Wisconsin the right, which in turn joined on the left of the 34th Illinois of Mitchell's brigade. Fitch's command had been at the front since mid-morning, and was running low on ammunition, having had no opportunity to replenish its supply. The troops fixed bayonets as they ran out of cartridges, and remained in position beside the few comrades who still had a round or two left to fire.[10]

As the firing diminished along Fitch's front, Zachry's Georgians of Colquitt's Brigade raised a yell and charged Fitch's position. Fearing that his regiment would be overrun by the screaming Rebels, Major Widmer ordered the 104th Illinois to retreat. The urge to flee proved contagious, as the balance of Fitch's wing and Miles' brigade quickly followed suit. The withdrawal soon degenerated into a rout. Captain Keller had served with the 21st Ohio since its formation, yet he could remember no time "when gloom and discouragement settled so thick and fast upon us" as it did in the swamps of Bentonville.[11]

No sooner did Major Robinson learn that the 121st Ohio's left flank was threatened than the musketry on his right erupted into "a perfect tempest," and sounded as if it were heading straight for his position. As Fitch's and Miles' fugitives streamed past him, Robinson concluded that to remain any longer in his present position "would have been madness." He ordered the 121st Ohio to retreat. The 121st fell back several hundred yards to the edge of the swamp on Vandever's right flank. Robinson soon discovered that his regiment was so badly scattered that about half his command was missing. The major counted three regimental flags flapping alongside the 121st's, which told him that Fitch's and Miles' commands were no less disorganized than his own.[12]

Having caught his breath, Robinson now set about to reform his line when a question presented itself: where were the Rebels? Why weren't they exploiting their breakthrough? Robinson assumed that the Confederates had shifted their attention to another part of the

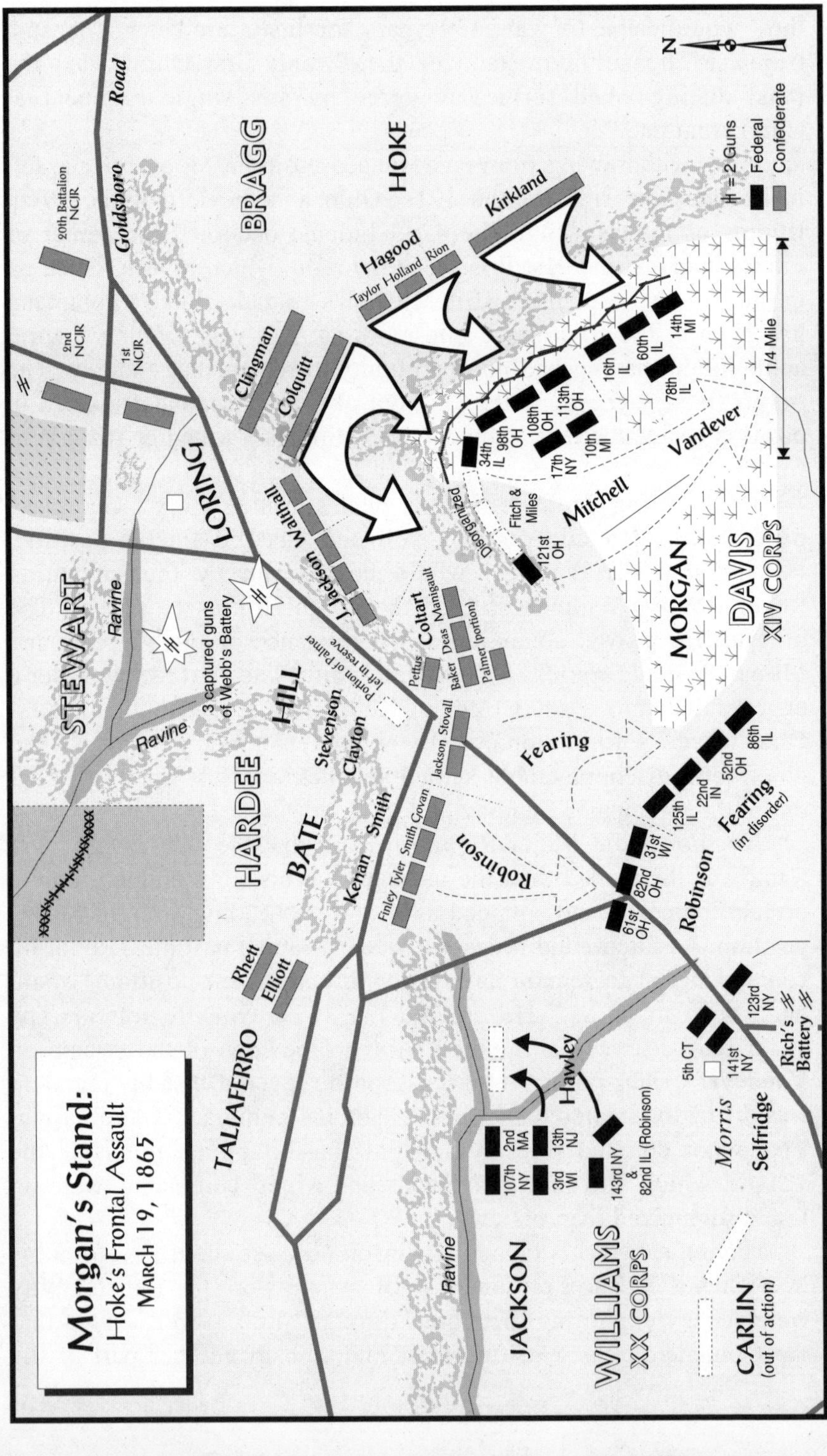

Morgan's Stand:
Hoke's Frontal Assault
March 19, 1865
Goldsboro Road
BRAGG
HOKE
Kirkland
Hagood
Taylor Holland Rion
Clingman
Colquitt
20th Battalion NCJR
2nd NCJR
1st NCJR
LORING
J. Jackson Walthall
STEWART
Ravine
3 captured guns of Webb's Battery
Portion of Palmer left in reserve
HILL
Stevenson
Clayton
Coltart
Pettus Deas Manigault
Baker Palmer (portion)
Jackson Stovall
HARDEE
BATE
Smith
Kenan
Finley Tyler Smith Govan
Rhett
Elliott
TALIAFERRO
34th IL
98th OH
108th OH
113th OH
17th NY
10th MI
16th IL
60th IL
14th MI
78th IL
Disorganized
Fitch & Miles
121st OH
Mitchell
Vandever
MORGAN
DAVIS
XIV CORPS
Fearing
125th IL
22nd IN
52nd OH
86th IL
Fearing (in disorder)
31st WI
82nd OH
61st OH
Robinson
123rd NY
Rich's Battery
5th CT
141st NY
Morris
Selfridge
Hawley
2nd MA
13th NJ
107th NY
3rd WI
143rd NY & 82nd IL (Robinson)
JACKSON
WILLIAMS
XX CORPS
CARLIN
(out of action)
= 2 Guns
Federal
Confederate
1/4 Mile
N

Mark A. Moore

field. In any case, he was grateful for the reprieve, for which he had the 10th Michigan and the 17th New York of Vandever's brigade to thank. (The role of these two Federal regiments will be covered later in this chapter.)[13]

As the northern face of Morgan's position disintegrated, the battle continued down the eastern side of his line, raging on the right of Mitchell's line, which was held by the 108th and 113th Ohio. The two Buckeye regiments faced the North Carolina contingent of Hagood's Brigade, consisting of Lt. Col. John Douglas Taylor's command and six companies of the 40th North Carolina under Maj. William A. Holland. Taylor's command occupied the right of Hagood's advancing line, flanked by Colquitt's Brigade on the right and the 40th North Carolina on the left.[14] Lieutenant Colonel Taylor led an array of coastal artillery units that had spent most of the war manning the heavy ordnance guns of Fort Caswell and Fort Campbell on the Cape Fear River below Wilmington. The strategic purpose of these and other forts along the Cape Fear was to protect the blockade running traffic, which for a time had provided the Confederacy with its only link to the outside world. Prior to 1865 these Confederates must have felt cut off from the war, having only the occasional duel with a Union blockade steamer to enliven an otherwise dull routine.[15]

During the withdrawal before General Schofield's Union forces in February 1865, Taylor collected several companies of the 36th North Carolina, the 9th North Carolina Battalion, and a few other seacoast artillery units. This makeshift command was assigned to Hagood's Brigade and became known as the "Red Infantry," in recognition of the officers' red kepis and the red trim on the artillerymen's uniforms. The 40th North Carolina also had been orphaned by the loss of the coastal forts below Wilmington, and since then had marched and fought alongside Taylor's contingent. The 40th shared the *nom de guerre* of its brother artillery command, and would soon share its fate in this, their first and—as it transpired—last pitched battle.

Across the swamp from Hagood's Brigade, the men of the 113th Ohio knelt down in two ranks behind their stout works. The woods in the Ohioans' front were so overgrown with briars and brush that the 40th North Carolina approached unseen to within point-blank range of the Federals' rifles. The Tarheels found this to be a mixed blessing. "We opened upon [the Rebels] such a fire as carried death and destruction with it," recalled Sgt. Francis McAdams of the 113th Ohio, "and before which a man might not hope to advance and live." The Ohioans maintained this rapid fire "for a long while," McAdams added, the rear rank of the 113th loading the rifles and the front rank firing them. At one point McAdams' file partner, Mike Huddleston, leaned forward and shouted into his ear: "My God, Mack, these guns of ours are getting too hot; we had better rest." McAdams merely shrugged and continued firing.[16]

Sergeant T. C. Davis of Company C, 40th North Carolina, recalled that when he and his comrades approached to within a short distance of the 113th Ohio's works, the 40th's skirmishers were nowhere to be seen. During the advance, Hoke's line of battle had obliqued to the left, and as a result the 40th's skirmishers now occupied Colquitt's front. According to Sergeant Davis, the 40th was ordered to halt before the Union works, where it "dressed to the right under a heavy fire from the enemy." Davis noted that "the command was obeyed with as much coolness. . .as if [the men were] on dress parade." But the decision to halt proved costly, for it robbed the 40th's assault of its momentum and led to most of the regiment's casualties. The sergeant considered the maneuver a needless sacrifice of brave men.[17]

On the 40th North Carolina's right, Lieutenant Colonel Taylor and his command struck hard, driving the 108th Ohio from its fortifications. The "Red Infantry" mounted the 108th's works and directed a plunging fire into the Ohioans, who sprinted for the cover of Mitchell's second line of works. The impetuousness of the "Red Infantry's" assault ultimately led them to disaster, for Taylor's troops were the only Confederates to carry the Federal works. As they stood atop the smoking earthen entrenchments, their exposed flanks were cut to pieces by a succession of enfilade volleys. Seeing its chance, the 108th Ohio surged forward and poured a murderous fire into the center of the Tarheels' rapidly-thinning line. Taylor was standing atop the Ohioans' works when he saw a Federal about 20 paces away aim his rifle at him and fire. The bullet struck Taylor in the left arm near the shoulder and knocked him off his feet. The men who carried Taylor from the field had to step carefully, for the ground was covered with the dead and wounded of his command. Of the commissioned officers in Taylor's command, only two emerged from the fight unscathed: the "Red Infantry" was now led by a lieutenant. Of the 267 officers and men in Taylor's contingent,

152 were killed, wounded or captured—a casualty rate of 57 per cent.[18]

Lieutenant Colonel Taylor was carried to the division hospital, where surgeons examined his shattered arm and told him that it would have to be amputated. Following the operation, Taylor awoke in his tent that night and discovered that he was sharing it with three of his company commanders, and that each of these officers likely would be dead before sunrise. Taylor survived both his wound and the surgery that removed his limb. Instead of enduring a painful trip to Smithfield in an ambulance, he rode the distance on horseback, less than 24 hours after his amputation.[19]

On the 40th North Carolina's left, Lt. Col. James H. Rion's contingent of South Carolinians from Hagood's Brigade struck Mitchell's skirmishers from the 78th Illinois, who soon realized that the Confederates were driving them back toward the 14th Michigan's position on Vandever's line. The 78th's commander, Lt. Col. Maris R. Vernon, sent word to the 14th Michigan's commander, Lt. Col. George W. Grummond, that his Illinoisans were low on ammunition and would have to withdraw through the 14th's line. Grummond instructed his men not to fire until he gave the command, then told Vernon to retire through the 14th's works without halting and form in reserve. Vernon ordered his men to fire a parting volley at the Rebels, and under cover of the smoke the 78th Illinois withdrew behind the main line.[20]

On Rion's left, General Kirkland's North Carolina Brigade shoved back Vandever's skirmish line—the 60th Illinois—so rapidly that the Tarheels cut off Companies C and K from the rest of the Federal regiment. Seeing that the Confederates had surrounded them, the men of the two beleaguered companies called upon Lieutenant Allen, the only commissioned officer present, to lead them in a charge through the enemy lines. "We went forward with a yell," remembered Pvt. Frank L. Ferguson of Company C, "then the fun commenced[.] [W]e had the regimental flag with us[,] and as soon as the rebels saw [it] they wanted it so they took [off] after the color bearer with fixed bayonets." In the ensuing melee, one Confederate reached out to grab the colors just as a soldier of the 60th Illinois stabbed him with his bayonet. The Illinoisans cut their way through the Confederate lines and rejoined their comrades crouching behind Vandever's main line of works. The 14th

Michigan manned the right, the 60th Illinois the center, and the 16th Illinois the left of Vandever's front line.[21]

Lieutenant Colonel Grummond noted that Kirkland's North Carolinians "advanced steadily, firing rapidly," until they came to within 30 yards of the 14th Michigan's position. "I then gave the command," Grummond continued. "The men rose steadily as one man and poured into the enemy the most terrific fire I ever listened to; nothing could withstand it." On the other end of Vandever's line, the 16th Illinois' commander, Capt. Herman Lund, reported that Rion's South Carolinians "charged furiously, advancing [to] within seventy-five yards of our works. Our fire, however, was too severe to be withstood, and their line broke and ran in confusion." From his vantage point on the reserve line, Lieutenant Colonel Vernon observed that Vandever's "whole line opened a terrible fire, under which the rebel lines melted away."[22]

The Confederates of Hoke's Division fell back and reformed for another assault. During the lull, Sergeant McAdams and two privates from the 113th Ohio were detailed to gather up the ammunition of the Confederate dead and wounded. McAdams happened upon a mortally wounded Southerner who gasped, "Is there no help for the widow's son?"

"I told him he was beyond help, and that I had no time to give to his wants," McAdams wrote. "But. . .as he had no further use for the cartridges in his box [or] for the knapsack on his back, I would relieve him of both, which I did."[23]

Another scavenger, Lt. John Schenck of the 16th Illinois, found a North Carolinian with a nasty leg wound. The Tarheel asked Schenck whether he was looking for cartridges.

"Yes," Schenck replied.

"Well, Yank," said the Tarheel, "turn me over keerfully and look in my knapsack. You'll thar find 40 rounds. Take 'em and use 'em. I hope you'll whip our army and end the wah. I am tired of it."

Lieutenant Schenck took the wounded Tarheel's "40 rounds," and with the help of a few comrades, carried the Confederate back to the 16th Illinois' works.[24]

Hoke's second assault was heralded by the shrieking of the Rebel yell. The 40th North Carolina rushed forward and again obliqued to the left, striking Vandever's line. Vandever's troops now had to contend with the 40th as well as Kirkland's and Rion's troops. According to the 16th Illinois' Captain Lund, the Confederates

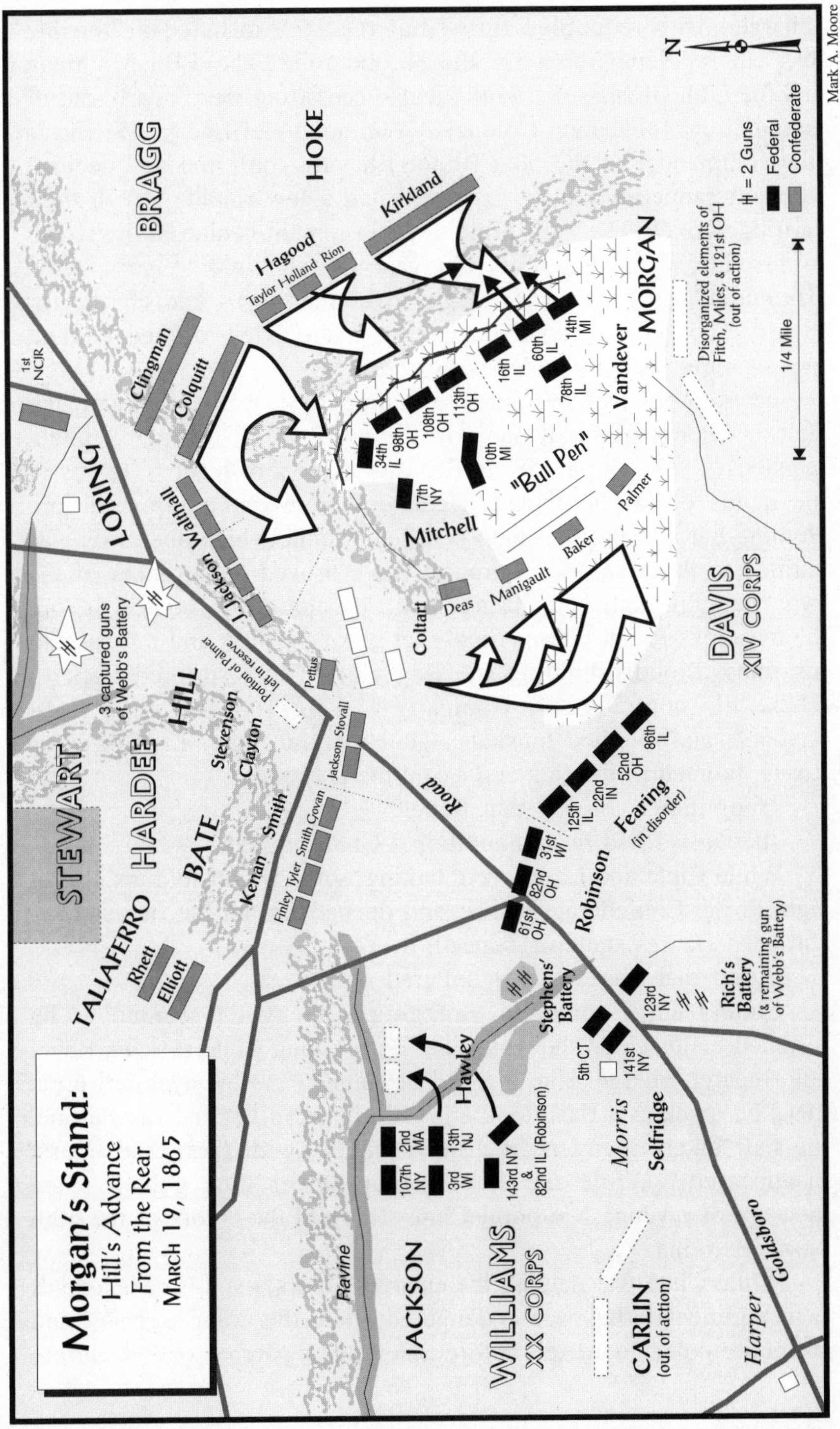
Morgan's Stand:
Hill's Advance
From the Rear
March 19, 1865
STEWART
HARDEE
BATE
HILL
LORING
BRAGG
HOKE
TALIAFERRO
Rhett
Elliott
Kenan
Smith
Stevenson
Clayton
Finley Tyler Smith Govan
Jackson Stovall
Pettus
Portion of Palmer left in reserve
3 captured guns of Webb's Battery
J. Jackson
Walthall
Colquitt
Clingman
1st NCJR
Hagood
Taylor Holland Rion
Kirkland
Coltart
Deas
Manigault
Baker
Palmer
Mitchell
"Bull Pen"
Vandever
MORGAN
34th IL
98th OH
108th OH
113th OH
16th IL
60th IL
14th MI
78th IL
10th MI
17th NY
Disorganized elements of Fitch, Miles, & 121st OH (out of action)
125th IL
22nd IN
52nd OH
86th IL
Fearing (in disorder)
61st OH
82nd OH
31st WI
Robinson
DAVIS
XIV CORPS
Road
Stephens' Battery
5th CT
141st NY
123rd NY
Rich's Battery (& remaining gun of Webb's Battery)
Hawley
107th NY
2nd MA
3rd WI
13th NJ
143rd NY & 82nd IL (Robinson)
Morris
Selfridge
Ravine
JACKSON
WILLIAMS
XX CORPS
CARLIN (out of action)
Harper
Goldsboro
= 2 Guns
Federal
Confederate
1/4 Mile
N
Mark A. Moore

"charged with redoubled fury," but the 16th inflicted a "terrible loss" in repulsing them for the second time. The 14th Michigan and the 60th Illinois met with equal success, but were nearly out of ammunition. Lieutenant Colonels Grummond and George W. Evans (the commander of the 60th Illinois) hastily conferred and decided to counterattack while the men still had a few rounds left in their cartridge boxes. The 16th Illinois would remain behind at the works to provide a rallying point in case Mitchell's line gave way. Grummond gave the order to go "over the works and charge for them." The fighting soon degenerated into hand-to-hand combat in a swampy thicket clouded with smoke.[25]

For Cpl. George W. Clute of Company I, 14th Michigan, the fight became a personal one. "In the midst of the struggle," Clute recalled, "I saw a Confederate flag and made a rush for it. It was in the hands of [a] lieutenant. He and I were out of ammunition. Nothing but a trial of strength could determine which one of us was entitled to those colors." Corporal Clute proved the stronger of the two, dragging both color bearer and flag along for 100 feet before the tenacious Rebel officer finally let go of the staff and ran back to his lines. Proudly holding the flag aloft, Clute sprinted back to where his comrades of Company I were fighting with fixed bayonets and clubbed muskets. Clute's commander, Lt. Cornelius Losey, pointed to the flag and asked the corporal:

"Why didn't you kill that Rebel?"

"Because I had no ammunition," Clute replied.

While Clute and Losey were talking, some Union soldiers caught sight of the Confederate banner and opened fire on the two smoke-shrouded figures standing beneath it.

"Drop that flag!" Losey hollered.

Clute readily complied, dragging it along the ground as he resumed his place on the front line. Before long Clute saw the Rebel color bearer emerge from a cloud of smoke: "As his eyes fell upon me[,] he quick as a flash took aim with his revolver and fired at me, the ball entering my right arm. Then he, with like suddenness, disappeared." While the Rebel color bearer thus gained some measure of revenge, Corporal Clute still held the colors of the 40th North Carolina.[26]

While Clute was seizing the enemy's colors, the 14th Michigan's own regimental flag was endangered when the color sergeant and the entire color guard fell before a devastating Rebel volley. Before the Confederates could reach the flag, little Henry E. Plant, a private in Company F, seized it from the hands of the mortally wounded color bearer, Sgt. Ezra Davis, and waved it for all to see. Plant's comrades responded with a loud "Hurrah!," and ran to his assistance. After the battle, Plant was named the 14th's color bearer and carried his regiment's flag in the Grand Review at Washington, D. C., two months later. This honor was all the more noteworthy because the post of color bearer usually fell to tall men, and the five-foot-three-inch Plant was one of the shortest men in the regiment.[27] For their heroism at Bentonville, both Corporal Clute and Private Plant would receive the Medal of Honor—more than 30 years later.[28]

The close quarters fighting along Vandever's front was sharp but brief. The Federals drove Hagood's and Kirkland's Confederates back to their works, the 14th Michigan netting in the process 38 wounded and 125 unwounded prisoners. Grummond estimated that 70 enemy dead lay in his front. General Vandever claimed that his men had bagged General Hoke himself, but that the Tarheel commander had made his escape while being escorted to the rear.[29]

Above the cheering and yelling of his men Grummond could hear the rattle of musketry coming from somewhere behind his breastworks—followed by the Rebel yell. "I concluded there was trouble there," Grummond wrote, "and I immediately gathered my men together and fell back to my works." When Grummond returned to his position, he found the 16th Illinois kneeling behind the front side of their fortifications. Grummond glanced at the front line of works built by Fearing's brigade: the enemy now swarmed behind those works, and three of their regimental flags waved above the parapet. The Rebels were cheering loudly and demanding the Yankees' surrender.[30]

Grummond no doubt shook his head in disbelief. For the first time in the war he faced the prospect of storming Union earthworks.

* * *

Now that Fearing's brigade had been driven out of the way, the officers of Baker's Brigade ordered their men to get up and resume the advance on the rear of Morgan's embattled position. Alpheus

Baker's Alabamians soon happened upon a double line of works—the same works that Fearing's troops had abandoned when ordered forward by General Davis. Beyond Fearing's works stood a third breastwork, which the Federals appeared to hold in force. This third breastwork was Vandever's second line of works. To one of Baker's Alabamians the double line of works appeared to curve outward in a semicircle, terminating at the third, or main, breastwork. The double line stretched slightly beyond either of Baker's flanks. Near the center of these works there was a narrow gap. The Alabama soldier mistook the extreme left of Mitchell's refused line for a continuation of Fearing's line. This misunderstanding explains the apparent outward curve of the Federal works and the gap, which marked where Mitchell's line ended and Fearing's line began. There also was an open space about 15 yards wide between the double line of works and the third line, which the Alabama private referred to as the "bull pen."[31]

"Here we met a condition I have never been able to understand," wrote Claude Lee Hadaway, a veteran of the 54th Alabama, Baker's Brigade. "We got [to] within possibly fifty yards of the breastworks and everything stopped, firing had ceased, and there was not a Federal in sight." Nor was there a Confederate officer above the rank of lieutenant to be seen. "There we stood, not knowing whether to advance or retreat," Hadaway recalled. Not only were there no field officers in evidence, but the regimental standards of Baker's Brigade were bunched together, making a rapid reorganization of the line impossible. Another of Baker's soldiers, Pvt. B. F. Watson of the 40th Alabama, wrote that his regiment struck Fearing's works "in disconnected groups." It is clear from the recollections of Baker's troops that Fearing's spoiling attack had thrown Baker's Brigade into confusion and had bought valuable time for the rest of Morgan's division, which had its hands full repulsing the determined assaults of Hoke's Division.[32]

Private Hadaway nevertheless "could see no reason why we should not advance to the breastworks," but since no orders to that effect had been given, the young private informed Lt. Joe Abney, the ranking officer present, that he "was going to see what was behind those breastworks." Hadaway had crept up to within 20 feet of the works, when seven Federals rose up from behind the parapet, threw down their rifles, and raised their hands in surrender. The ecstatic Hadaway turned over his prisoners to Lt. John Carpenter of

Company H of the 54th Alabama. Writing of his exploit 50 years later, Hadaway assured his readers that he did not mention it "in a spirit of braggadocio [or] egotism, for I have passed through too many dangerous and risky places to boast of them now."[33]

While Lieutenant Carpenter and his men escorted their prisoners to the rear, Brig. Gen. Joseph B. Palmer led the Tennesseans and Virginians of his brigade into position about 300 yards south of the Goldsboro Road, and beyond the extreme right of Fearing's works. "These works," Palmer reported, "were occupied by the enemy with about the usual number of men in their lines." Palmer did not specify what the "usual number" was, nor is it clear to whose command these Federals belonged. Perhaps they were fugitives from Miles' brigade or Fitch's wing of Carlin's division, or perhaps they belonged to the 121st Ohio or the 78th Illinois of Morgan's division.[34]

Whoever these Federal soldiers were, they had concentrated behind the works nearest Palmer's left flank, for Baker's men reported seeing few Union troops behind the double line of works in their front. Although the Northerners had no works in Palmer's front, the general concluded that it would be "wholly unsafe to move farther forward or pass" the works on his left without first driving off the Federal soldiers occupying them. Palmer confessed his ignorance of the purpose of his advance south of the Goldsboro Road, but supposed that carrying the enemy's three lines of works "was in part the objective point of my movement."

Palmer ordered his brigade to execute a left wheel and strike the enemy's works on the flank. His Confederates chased the Federals out of their first two lines of works and were preparing to assault the third line when some of the Union soldiers threw down their rifle-muskets. Private R. A. Lambert of the 42nd Alabama recalled that the Yankees behind the third line of works "began to wave [their] hats and handkerchiefs, so it was natural for us to suppose they were wanting to surrender, for we knew full well that we were in behind them." Lambert and his comrades called out to the Federals to raise their hands and come over—the Federals responded by telling the Alabamians to do the same. "And thus we found there was a misunderstanding," Private Lambert wrote. The men on both sides crouched behind their works, only to repeat the whole process a few minutes later. Private Lambert and his comrades no doubt wondered what the Yankees were up to.[35]

The Yankees were buying time. Following the collapse of Mitchell's refused left flank, the 17th New York and 10th Michigan had had to defend the resulting gap in Morgan's line of defense. Captain Alexander S. Marshall of the 17th New York reported that the panic-stricken Federals of Miles' brigade and Fitch's wing had fled through his ranks, "carrying a few of the faint-hearted with them." Major Michael H. Locher of the 79th Pennsylvania, Miles' brigade, tried to put the rout of his regiment in the best possible light when he reported that it was "relieved" by the 17th New York.[36]

The 17th New York Veteran Volunteer Infantry was one of two Eastern regiments in the XIV Corps, and the only one to wear the Zouave uniform. A Wisconsin soldier found the 17th New York Zouaves to be "funny looking fellows as far as their Costume was concerned." The Westerners nicknamed them the "Red-Headed Woodpeckers." One soldier in Fearing's brigade referred to them as "those fellows that wore the red turbans." In truth, the men of the 17th wore a red fez with a long blue tassel, a waist length navy blue jacket with red trim, a crimson sash, navy chausseur trousers and white canvas leggings. By this stage of the campaign, however, it is doubtful whether their uniforms were little more than rags. The regiment was composed mostly of Germans and Irishmen, whose thickly-accented, bilingual chatter must have underscored their exotic appearance. But in spite of their "funny" dress, the Wisconsinite added, "the fellows understood their business as the Johnnies found out at their cost."[37]

Captain Marshall observed a Confederate column—the Georgians of Colquitt's Brigade—stealing around his left flank. Marshall ordered the 17th New York to open a left oblique fire upon the enemy column, which replied with a sharp fire of its own as it continued to snake around the New Yorkers' exposed flank. The Confederates also seized the abandoned works on the left of Mitchell's refused line. The three left companies of the 10th Michigan swung back and added their firepower to the 17th New York's. The aggressive Georgians forced the 17th to change front twice to protect its threatened left flank. Despite the desperate conditions under which they labored, the veteran Zouaves fought tenaciously, maintaining a heavy fire on Colonel Zachry's Georgians, who finally withdrew to the safety of the swamp in their rear. Marshall ordered his men to cease fire.[38]

The New Yorkers' plight had not yet ended, however. Moments later, Marshall discovered a second column advancing from the left and rear of the 17th New York's position. Were they friend or foe? "The woods on our left were on fire," wrote Sgt. William Westervelt of Company K, "and the smoke was so thick we could see but indistinctly." Westervelt and his comrades could see the troops "moving on our left, but in the thick smoke [we] could not tell the color of their uniforms." To further confuse matters, the uniforms of both sides bore "the same muddy hues," according to one Union soldier. A private in the 10th Michigan wrote that some of his comrades believed "it was the enemy and some reported it as the 20th army corps [sic]." A volley from the rear, and the appearance amid the billowing smoke of several Rebel battle flags quickly disabused even the most optimistic Yankee. As the Federals leaped over to the front side of their fortifications, less than 100 yards away the Southerners were dashing forward to Fearing's abandoned works. These Confederates were the South Carolinians and Alabamians of Hill's (Coltart's) Division, Lee's Corps.[39]

Captain William Dunphy of the 10th Michigan decided to mollify the Rebels—at least for the moment. Dunphy had assumed temporary command of his regiment when Vandever had placed Colonel Lum in overall command of the 10th Michigan and the 17th New York. Both Lum and Dunphy knew that the 14th Michigan and the 60th Illinois had counterattacked Hoke's troops and had met with some success. According to Lum, "but few shots came from that direction." (Evidently Dunphy and Lum were confident that Mitchell could hold his own as well, but of course they could not afford to believe otherwise.) Dunphy concluded that his best course was to stall for time until Vandever's front line should return. Instead of laying down a heavy fire, he ordered his men to cease fire and wave their hats above the parapet. Once the Michiganders had gotten the Southerners' attention and all firing had ceased, Dunphy and an escort of two men climbed over their breastworks and walked about 30 paces toward the Confederate position. Colonel Lum estimated that the distance "from our colors to those of the enemy. . .was about sixteen or eighteen rods," or between 90 and 100 yards. Dunphy and his two-man escort confronted the troops of Hill's Division in the open and at point-blank range. In a loud voice Dunphy announced that he wanted to speak to the Rebels' commanding officer.[40]

Lieutenant Colonel John C. Carter stepped forward. Carter commanded Manigault's Brigade of Hill's Division and was the ranking Confederate officer on that part of the field. Dunphy told Carter that he had come forward to demand the Rebels' surrender—an astonishing proposition, given that Morgan's division was hemmed in by the Confederates on three sides and by an all but impassable swamp on the fourth. Carter refused Dunphy's ultimatum, offering instead to parole Dunphy and his troops on the spot if they surrendered to him. Dunphy declined Carter's offer and started back for his lines. But before Dunphy could reach the safety of his works, the Confederates fired a volley at him and his escort. There is no mention of whether Dunphy was carrying a flag of truce, but regardless of the circumstances, it was a mean trick of the Confederates to fire on the three defenseless Yankees. Perhaps this action betrays Lieutenant Colonel Carter's realization that he had been duped. Some measure of Carter's disappointment may be detected in a passage from D. H. Hill's after-action report. Concerning Carter's inconclusive parley with Dunphy, Hill wrote that Carter had been "in actual negotiation with a Yankee general" for the surrender of his command. Hill presumably heard this from Carter himself. Dunphy no doubt would have found Lieutenant Colonel Carter's misapprehension both amusing and flattering, for it indicated that his ruse had been a complete success.[41]

Miraculously, Dunphy and his escort reached their lines unhurt. While the soldiers on both sides once more blazed away at each other, Captains Dunphy and Marshall discussed the situation. They decided to order a bayonet charge.[42]

* * *

Meanwhile, some scattering fire from behind had prompted the soldiers of Mitchell's brigade to jump over to the front (eastern) side of their works and prepare to meet an assault from what had been their rear. Fortunately for the Federals, Hoke's troops, whom they had just repulsed, were nowhere in sight. A soldier in the 34th Illinois wrote that "it was a ludicrous sight" to see the regiment's Rebel prisoners, about 20 in number, "performing gymnastics across the works alongside of our boys." The overriding concern of the men in the 34th was that they hadn't enough ammunition to repel another Confederate assault. The 34th's commander, Capt. Peter F. Walker, had sent out a detail to find the brigade ordnance train, but the men were long overdue and presumed killed or captured. The Illinoisans emptied the cartridge boxes of their prisoners, which yielded an additional round or two per man, hardly the windfall they had hoped for.[43]

Sergeant Widney saw Mitchell's reaction to the news that the 34th's ammunition was almost exhausted. Until then, Widney recollected, Mitchell had appeared "alert and cheerful," but now the general "looked at his watch with such an expression as Wellington may have worn when he exclaimed, 'Oh! that Blücher or night were here.' Then, instead of replacing his timepiece in his pocket, he thrust it into his boot preliminary to being shot or captured." Not to be undone by Mitchell's gesture, "the boys asked the General for the time of day," recalled Lt. R. J. Heath of the 34th.[44]

An anxious General Davis sat on his horse a short distance to the rear, utterly powerless to assist Morgan. His view obscured by smoke and thick pine woods, Davis could only listen to the incessant roar of musketry that rolled up from Morgan's position. To Davis' adjutant, Lieutenant Colonel McClurg, "It seemed more than men could bear." Turning to McClurg, Davis said, "If Morgan's troops can stand this, all is right; if not, the day is lost. There is no reserve —not a regiment to move—they must fight it out." Davis had even sent his personal escort and headquarters guard into the fray. He dispatched an aide to Slocum with a plea for one brigade to plug the gap between Mitchell and Fearing. When the firing in Morgan's sector finally slackened, Davis ordered McClurg to ride forward and reconnoiter.[45]

McClurg had gone no more than a few yards when he glimpsed a column of soldiers marching off to his right, straight across his path and in rear of Morgan's position. "They looked like rebels," McClurg noted, "and my sharp-sighted orderly, Batterson, said they were 'rebs'; but the view was obscured by smoke, and the idea that the enemy could be in that position was preposterous." McClurg and his orderly pressed on. After riding for about a hundred yards through a dense wood, the two Federals entered a clearing occupied by a column of Confederate troops. McClurg was greeted with cheers and shouts of "Come down off that horse, Yank!" Spurring his mount, McClurg galloped out of the clearing, only to collide with his orderly. Their two frightened horses plunged headlong into a swamp just as a shower of Rebel minie balls clipped the twigs and branches above their heads. McClurg and his orderly remounted and sped southward until they were able to steal around the Confederates' right flank. McClurg found General Morgan behind Vandever's works and apprised him of his "perilous situation." Given the circumstances, McClurg was surprised to find the morale of Morgan's men so high, but as one of their officers explained, they "had often attacked works, but [until now] they had rarely had the pleasure of fighting behind them."[46]

The 14th Michigan and the 60th Illinois had begun their counterattack against Hoke around the time of McClurg's arrival. Soon afterward, the men of the 16th and 78th Illinois glanced over their shoulders and saw a column of troops advancing through the woods toward Fearing's abandoned works. Many of the soldiers in the column were dressed in blue. The Illinoisans hesitated to fire on them, but bearing in mind McClurg's warning, the 16th Illinois leaped to the front side of the first line of Vandever's works, while the 78th Illinois sprinted back to the second line just as the advancing column poured a withering fire into their ranks.[47]

Across the way, along the front of Baker's Brigade, the color bearer of the 54th Alabama, Sgt. James Flinn, left the safety of Fearing's works, advanced halfway into the no man's land—or "bull pen"—separating Vandever's works from Fearing's, and planted the 54th's colors in plain view of both sides. As Flinn turned to wave his comrades forward, a Yankee minie ball pierced his heart, killing him instantly. With Flinn's death, the Alabamians' assault on Morgan's line collapsed before it had properly begun. Private Hadaway and a member of the 54th's color guard both raced forward to rescue the colors. The color guardsman reached Flinn's corpse first and seized the flag. Hadaway gathered up Flinn's personal effects, including some "very nice Confederate gray cloth" which Flinn had bought for his new color bearer's uniform. Hadaway recalled that it took him several minutes to collect Flinn's possessions, "and strange to say[,] there was not a gun fired during the time, nor was there a Federal in sight."[48]

On the Confederate right flank, in the swamp before the "bull pen," General Palmer was on horseback directing the fire of his Tennesseans and Virginians when he received a report "that there was a considerable Federal force not more than 100 yards to my right, and moving upon my rear." Hearing the crack of musketry behind him, Sgt. Tom Corn of the 32nd Tennessee turned around and saw the Stars and Stripes, and a line of Federals advancing beneath it. An uneasy Corn told comrades George Winford and Sid Bryant, "The enemy is going to rout us."

"I've run for the last time," Winford replied.

"If they want to get me," Corn declared, "they'll have to *shoot me* first."[49]

The force confronting Palmer's command was Brig. Gen. William Cogswell's brigade of Ward's division, XX Corps. Cogswell's men were running on straight adrenaline at this time, for they had had little else to sustain them since breaking camp at dawn on March 18. For the past two days they had been doing double duty as rear guard and escort for the XX Corps wagon train. Owing to the slow progress of the column, Cogswell's brigade had made just 10 miles on the 18th, and did not stumble into camp until 5:00 a.m. on the 19th. By 9:00 a.m. Cogswell's exhausted troops were back on the march. But the men soon forgot their fatigue, for in the words of one soldier, they were "enjoying the balmy air of spring [and] snuffing in the delicious fragrance of the apple and peach blossoms." About 1:00 p.m. Cogswell's brigade was ordered to leave the wagons behind and hurry to the front with the rest of Ward's division. They reached Morris' farm two hours later after a fast march covering seven miles, "without dinner or a halt," wrote General Cogswell. The brigade halted in an open field on Morris' farm, in rear of the line held by Jackson's division and north of the Goldsboro Road. From this position General Ward intended to "hurl" Cogswell's brigade wherever it was most needed. As it transpired, Ward would "hurl" it nowhere.[50]

About 4:00 p.m. Lt. Col. Charles W. Asmussen of General Williams' staff informed Cogswell that Williams was ordering him to move his brigade to the right and report to General Davis of the XIV Corps. Asmussen assured Cogswell that he would notify Ward of the order. As Cogswell's brigade was crossing the Goldsboro Road, Slocum rode up and told Cogswell that he had brought along a XIV Corps staff officer who would lead him to Davis. On the way, the staff officer told Cogswell that Davis intended to use his brigade to plug a gap in the XIV Corps' line. Cogswell met Davis just

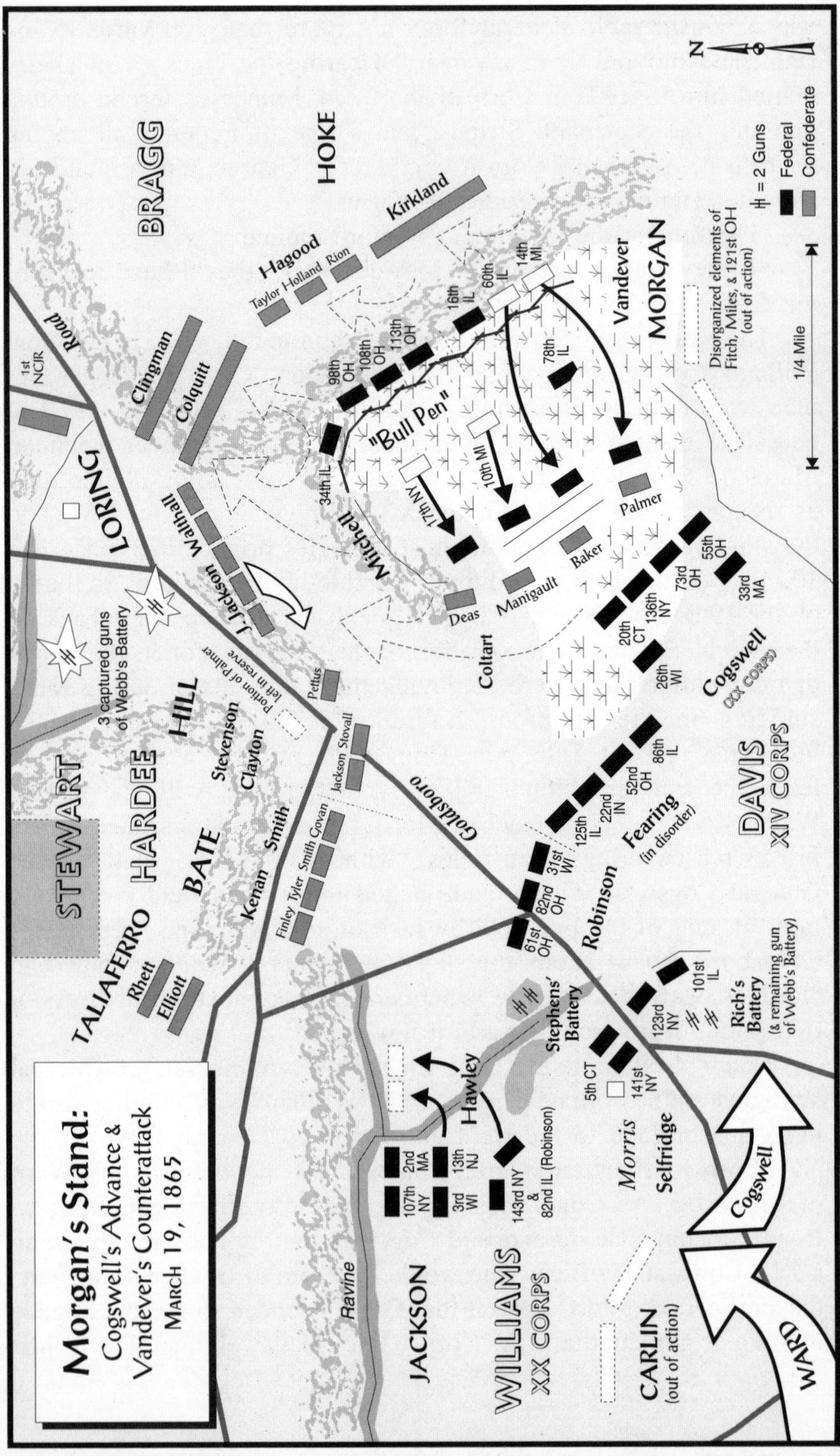
Morgan's Stand:
Cogswell's Advance &
Vandever's Counterattack
March 19, 1865
BRAGG
HOKE
Kirkland
Hagood
Taylor Holland Rion
Clingman
Colquitt
1st NCJR
Road
LORING
Walthall
J. Jackson
3 captured guns of Webb's Battery
STEWART
HARDEE
HILL
Stevenson
Clayton
Pettus
Portion of Palmer left in reserve
BATE
Kenan
Smith
Finley Tyler Smith Govan
Jackson Stovall
TALIAFERRO
Rhett
Elliott
Mitchell
34th IL
98th OH
108th OH
113th OH
16th IL
60th IL
14th MI
"Bull Pen"
17th NY
10th MI
78th IL
Vandever
MORGAN
Deas
Manigault
Baker
Palmer
Coltart
20th CT
136th NY
73rd OH
55th OH
33rd MA
26th WI
Cogswell
(XX CORPS)
125th IL
22nd IN
52nd OH
86th IL
Fearing
(in disorder)
DAVIS
XIV CORPS
31st WI
82nd OH
61st OH
Robinson
Goldsboro
Stephens' Battery
123rd NY
101st IL
Rich's Battery
(& remaining gun of Webb's Battery)
5th CT
141st NY
Morris
Selfridge
Hawley
107th NY
2nd MA
3rd WI
13th NJ
143rd NY & 82nd IL (Robinson)
Ravine
JACKSON
WILLIAMS
XX CORPS
CARLIN
(out of action)
Cogswell
WARD
Disorganized elements of Fitch, Miles, & 121st OH (out of action)
= 2 Guns
Federal
Confederate
1/4 Mile
N
Mark A. Moore

beyond the right of Robinson's brigade's new position on the Morris farm and astride the Goldsboro Road.[51]

Private A. A. Velie of the 136th New York recalled that Davis rode up to Cogswell and asked him how many regiments he had.

"Six," Cogswell replied.

"Hold three of your regiments here in line and charge with the other three," Davis ordered.[52]

If Velie's recollection of Davis's order is correct, then Cogswell modified it, placing instead four regiments on the front line and two in the rear. From left to right, the front line regiments were the 20th Connecticut, 136th New York, 73rd Ohio and 55th Ohio. The 26th Wisconsin and 33rd Massachusetts anchored the left and right flanks of the rear line, respectively. This veteran brigade had originally belonged to the XI Corps, Army of the Potomac, and most of the regiments had served together as a unit since the Chancellorsville and Gettysburg campaigns. But their commander, William Cogswell, was new to the brigade, having led it for barely two months. "[O]n the 16th of January I came to this brigade a stranger," he reported, "and commenced the campaign with them the next morning." Cogswell was pleased with his new command, finding the men "brave in action, willing and obedient on the march, quiet and soldierly in camp."[53]

Cogswell's line of battle swung around the right flank of Fearing's brigade, which held the Union line on Robinson's right. According to Private Velie, Davis ordered Cogswell to "have the men give a yell" when they charged. Velie's regiment, the 136th New York, "was near the center of the line, and when Gen. Davis gave the order he was not over 40 feet from where I stood," Velie recalled. "I shall never forget it, and I thought he did wrong in giving the order as he did. . . .I thought it would have been much better to go through the swamp with as little noise as possible, and when we got in sight of [the enemy] to give a yell and give them the benefit of our Springfields."[54]

Cogswell's line advanced about 150 yards through a gloomy pine forest, then wheeled to the left while slogging through a knee-deep swamp. Their yells notwithstanding, the Federals elicited nothing more severe than some scattered fire from the Confederate skirmishers. Once the brigade emerged from the swamp, Company B of the 55th Ohio and two companies of the 33rd Massachusetts deployed as skirmishers on Cogswell's right. The Ohioans found it difficult to dart from tree to tree, because most of the pines they came to were in flames. To the surprise of Pvt. J. W. Rumple, a skirmisher in the 55th, "numbers of rebel soldiers began to pour into our lines and give themselves up."[55]

Then, without warning, the 55th Ohio collided with the right flank of Palmer's Confederate brigade. The officers and men of each side were so stunned by the others' sudden appearance that, for several interminable moments, not a shot was fired. The Federals held fast, but the Confederates who could do so fell back toward the Goldsboro Road. The rest found themselves trapped behind the enemy's line of battle, and either hid out in the swamp or surrendered to the Yankees. Captain Blasland and his two skirmish companies of the 33rd Massachusetts mopped up behind the 55th Ohio, capturing most of the troops belonging to the 26th and 45th Tennessee regiments, plus the regimental colors of the 26th.[56]

Seeing their chance, Lieutenant Colonels Grummond and Evans ordered a bayonet charge to the rear. The men of the 14th Michigan and 60th Illinois bounded over their works with a shout and assaulted the Confederates from Palmer's Brigade occupying Fearing's works. The Federals routed the stunned Southerners, capturing more than 100 prisoners and the flag of the 54th Virginia. Captain Dunphy of the 10th Michigan and Captain Marshall of the 17th New York also chose this moment to order their troops forward into the bloody "bull pen." Together, they attacked Baker's Brigade and Hill's Division, driving them off after a brief struggle. In addition to capturing a large number of Confederates, the Federals rescued several dozen of their comrades who had been captured earlier in the day.[57]

If the timing of these various Federal assaults was fortuitous, their effect on Confederate morale was nothing short of devastating. Only minutes earlier, the soldiers of Hoke's Division and Lee's Corps had had Morgan's division all but surrounded; now it was a portion of Lee's Corps that was virtually entrapped.

Private R. A. Lambert of the 42nd Alabama was near the right flank of Baker's line when it gave way. "I saw that our entire line was doomed to go, so I debated in a hurry whether or not to remain and be captured, or to take my chance of being shot in the back by fleeing from an enemy so very close," he later wrote. Lambert chose to skedaddle with the rest of his command:

> Having a horror of being taken prisoner, I took my chances as all others seemed to be doing. In hurrying back as fast as my feet and legs would take me, I finally saw through the big pine timber in front of me a line of Yanks—the woods looked blue with them—but they were standing still and not firing a gun, which they could not do without endangering the line we had just left in front of us, hence we found ourselves. . .in a hollow square, the enemy on four sides of us in heavy timber, and each line close by at that!. . .Our men who got out were either those who hid themselves in the thick gallberry bushes until after dark[,] or those fleet of foot. I was in the latter class, and I am not ashamed to own up to such on that particular occasion.[58]

Private Hadaway of the 54th Alabama had heard no order to retreat, yet nearly all his comrades had fled toward the Goldsboro Road. It appeared to Hadaway that only he and Lt. Joe Abney remained at Fearing's works:

> we stood there dumb with astonishment and expectancy. Finally without a word to me Joe started off. . . .I called to him and asked him if he was going to leave me. He replied there was no use in staying there. His answer was not satisfactory [to me] or in line with my conception of duty.

Once Lieutenant Abney was out of sight, Hadaway decided that perhaps discretion *was* the better part of valor. "There being no one else present nor [sic] in sight I assumed command of myself," he later recalled, "as I had a right to do both military and civil." Like Private Lambert before him, Hadaway joined the "fleet of feet" who were fleeing toward the Goldsboro Road:

> I started at a lively clip, but had not gone far before firing in my immediate rear and commands of "halt" were heard. I looked back and the Federals had risen up from behind that "bull pen" as thick as black birds on a horse-lot fence. . . .I simply pulled the throttle wide open and shut my mouth to prevent the unnecessary escape of steam, and went. . . .I had often said that the Federals had never made a bullet to kill me, nor organized an army big enough to capture me, but the situation seemed to place my boasts in the doubtful

> column this time. . . .The bullets were whistling all around me so thick that only the protecting hand of the good Lord enabled me to escape.

Hadaway was covered with mud by the time he emerged from the bushes bordering the Goldsboro Road, where he found himself standing before Lt. Gen. A. P. Stewart, who towered above him on his great horse. General Stewart found "my bedraggled and drenched appearance. . .very amusing and very ludicrous," Hadaway recalled. "I asked the general if he could tell me where Baker's brigade was."

"Bless you[,] my boy," "Old Straight" said with a chuckle, "I do not know where anybody is."[59]

Much like the men in the ranks, General Palmer also realized that retreat was his best alternative. Estimating the Union force at "more than double my number," Palmer ordered his Tennesseans and Virginians to fall back "on or near the Goldsboro Road. . .as rapidly as possible." As he was leading his men north in an attempt to escape the converging lines of Federals, his horse was shot from under him. Supposing that the animal's wound was mortal, Palmer left it for dead, only to reach the Goldsboro Road and discover that the poor beast had followed him out of the wilderness.[60]

At about the same time that Palmer realized his men were almost trapped, Sergeant Corn looked to his left and saw that his regiment, the 32nd Tennessee of Palmer's Brigade, was in full retreat. Corn tried to overtake his comrades, but the advancing Federals—"cursing me and firing at me at the same time," he recalled—cut off his northerly escape route. He hid behind a tree and waited until the firing had died away before he left his cover. Returning to his regiment's former position, he learned from a comrade who had hidden there the fate of his two comrades, Sid Bryant and George Winford. Bryant was wounded and Winford was captured, having kept his word that he had run for the last time. As he absorbed the sad news, Corn heard someone call out his name. He turned and saw Col. Anderson Searcy of the 45th Tennessee step out from behind a tree. "I never in my life was so glad to see anyone," Corn remembered. Searcy asked Corn what he thought of the situation, and the sergeant replied that he believed the enemy had surrounded them.[61]

Soon other soldiers from Palmer's Brigade left their hiding places and stepped forward. There were 70 men in all, including a handful of Alabamians from Baker's Brigade that had wandered south into Searcy's sector. Searcy—who was joined by three other field officers: Col. E. S. Gully of the 40th Alabama, Lt. Col. Alexander Hall of the 45th Tennessee, and Maj. William H. Joyner of the 18th Tennessee—called his men together and laid the facts before them. "The Colonel told us the only thing we could do would be to throw away our guns and cartridge boxes to keep the Yankees from getting them," remembered one Tennessean. "[T]hat we were a mile or more inside of their lines, and they were liable to come upon us at any moment." Realizing that they were all standing in an ankle-deep swamp, Searcy saw no reason why their wait should be an uncomfortable one. "Boys," he said, "let's get back here a little bit on dry land." Searcy's band moved back a short distance and halted beside an old log. "To our surprise," wrote Corn, "a Yank crawled out from underneath [the log] and said that he would surrender." Other Federals appeared and gave themselves up, including a captain who handed over his sword to Searcy. One Union captive even remarked: "Well, Johnnies, you seem to have the earth to-day, and we might as well surrender."[62]

Searcy counted heads and found that he had a dozen Union prisoners. The colonel allowed his men to divide the Federals' rations, then led them southward into the swamp bordering Vandever's right flank, where they waited for nightfall. Searcy warned his prisoners to "keep quiet and make no attempts to escape or betray us." That night Searcy and his motley command stole around Vandever's right flank and marched until dawn, establishing a pattern of marching by night and resting by day. They maintained this pattern for the first several days of their perilous odyssey behind Union lines. Although Searcy and his men had several close calls eluding the enemy, their constant preoccupation was with finding enough food to sustain 80 hungry men. "I followed the Confederate flag from the beginning to the end of the war," Sergeant Corn wrote 40 years later, "but in all that time [I] never suffered as much from hunger as I did those eight days we were trying to get through the Yankee lines." Of one rare and memorable meal Pvt. W. H. Ogilvie of the 45th Tennessee rhapsodized:

> Were I a poet I would sing its praises. But alas for me; I can only say it was a *corn bread dinner*. It was a *3 days['] rations dinner*. . . .It was a *soul-cheering dinner*. . . .It was a *never-to-be-forgotten dinner*. . . .Thirty years ago! [I]t lingers in our memories and makes us wish we could enjoy it again.

"Smack your mouths[,] boys," Ogilvie chaffed his former comrades, "you'll never enjoy another such."[63]

Colonel Searcy and his men resurfaced at Raleigh on the morning of March 28. They tramped proudly down to the provost marshal's office and turned over their prisoners, who by now "were loath to leave us," recalled one Tennessean. "[W]e gave them letters to send to our wives & sweethearts when they should be exchanged." The Federals later sent the letters as promised. That afternoon, Searcy and his command boarded the cars for Mitchener's Station, where they received a hero's welcome. Private Ogilvie recalled that Palmer's Brigade "turned out to greet us." In a speech to his troops, Palmer declared the march of Searcy's little band "to be the most wonderful feat of the war." Ogilvie recalled that, "Gen. John C. Brown, our former brigade commander. . .came over to see us, and made a speech, in which he pronounced it the greatest campaign of any war, comparing it to Napoleon crossing the Alps." Ogilvie found the generals' praise a bit extravagant, realizing all the same that they were carried away by the enthusiasm of the moment.[64]

But the celebrations were yet to come. For now, Searcy and his men would lay low in the swamp, keeping a sharp eye on their prisoners and waiting for night to fall.

* * *

Vandever's Federal troops were rounding up prisoners when a squad of Michigan soldiers happened upon a lone Rebel huddled behind Fearing's first line of works. The Confederate's name was Hiram Smith Williams, a private in Company C, 40th Alabama, Baker's Brigade. Williams had previously served in the Confederate Pioneer Corps, building bridges and corduroying roads for the Army of Tennessee. The 32-year-old was an atypical Confederate soldier. A native of West Bloomfield, New Jersey, he had been a journalist, a painter, and an actor before the war.[65]

Private Williams had remained behind at Fearing's works because he had no intention of being shot in the back while trying to make his escape. Williams recorded that his captors were generous victors: "They gave us credit for fighting them as hard as they were ever fought and some told me it was the first time their line was ever broken. Some thought we had whiskey to incite us on. Quite a compliment."[66]

As the sun dipped low in the pines, Vandever mounted his brigade's bullet-riddled works and bid his men gather 'round. Then, according to Peter Meagher of the 17th New York, the former Iowa congressman "drank a toast to the men, in which he complimented them upon their 'cool courage and discipline displayed in the victory just won.'"[67]

The next day Lieutenant Colonel Fitch returned to the area of Mitchell's refused line. "I thought the Confederate dead on the battle-fields of Perryville and Stone [sic] River were numerous," he recalled, "but they were not equal in number to those in front of this position." Regarding the fighting along the angle of Morgan's line, Capt. Will Robinson of the 34th Illinois told his father that "all agree in saying it was the hottest place we were ever in. The rebels had us completely surrounded and nothing but the most obstinate resistance saved the entire division from capture." Another veteran of the 34th, Lt. R. J. Heath, later wrote:

> I was there [at Bentonville] with a regiment that had faced Beauregard at Shiloh and Bragg at Stone's [sic] River; that had participated in nearly every battle of the Army of the Cumberland. We had taken a hand in the terrible assaults at Kenesaw Mountain and Jonesboro; but for desperate valor on the part of the rebels, and for a desperate resistance and a determination to whip them on the part of our own men, we saw nothing in four years of army life to compare with that 19th of March at Bentonville.[68]

While the battle continued to rage on the Morris farm behind them, Morgan's exhausted troops knelt down once more behind their works and peered into the darkening thickets, no doubt hoping that they had seen the Confederates for the last time on this bloody Sunday.

~ *twelve* ~

"Like One Continuous Peal of Heavy Thunder"

—Capt. G. B. Gardner of Hardee's Escort

The Confederates now faced a serious crisis. Daniel Harvey Hill needed troops to fill the gap left by the rout of Baker's and Palmer's brigades and Hill's (Coltart's) Division, and he had no time to lose. The fiery Tarheel galloped off to where he had last seen Pettus' and Smith's brigades, and nearly collided with Cogswell's skirmish line, unaware that the two brigades he was searching for had moved since the repulse of Fearing's spoiling attack. Hill galloped back to the Goldsboro Road and continued his search for Pettus.[1]

As Hill searched for reinforcements, General Palmer managed to rally his Confederate brigade just above the Goldsboro Road, where he found his two North Carolina regiments, the 58th and the 60th, waiting in reserve. The two Tarheel regiments had remained north of the road when the rest of Palmer's Brigade had vanished into the wilderness. Nevertheless, Palmer's Tennesseans and Virginians were spent, and D. H. Hill had no intention of deploying these exhausted troops on the front line. As for Baker's Brigade, Hill later reported that "General Baker retired entirely across the Goldsboro Road, and was no more engaged that day. I did not know his location until [it was] too late to put him again in position." Like Baker's Brigade, Hill's former division had lost all cohesion and was stampeding to the rear.[2]

Fortunately for Hill, Stewart's Corps arrived to plug the gap in Hill's line. Since crossing the Goldsboro Road about an hour beforehand, Stewart's Corps had alternately advanced and sidled to the right, with the apparent intention of joining on the right of Colquitt's Brigade. But when Hoke's assault lost its momentum, either Stewart or General Loring ordered the 900-man corps to move several hundred yards further to the right to reinforce Lee's (D. H. Hill's) Corps. Edward Walthall reported that as soon as his division came up, he received a message that the enemy was approaching his left flank. Walthall passed the message on to Loring, who in turn instructed Walthall to stay where he was. While Walthall was deploying his command, some panic-stricken troops, probably from Hill's Division, began to rush through his line. Colonel Harry Toulmin, the commander of Deas' Brigade, reported to Walthall at this time with 50 men—all that remained of his shattered unit. Walthall directed Toulmin to form on the left of his division, and to refuse his line "so as to protect my flank." Loring's Division (under Colonel Jackson) deployed on Walthall's right.[3]

On the right of Jackson's position, Pettus' Brigade was advancing in line of battle along the Goldsboro Road toward Morris' farm when D. H. Hill rode up and ordered him to halt his command. Hill explained "that the enemy were advancing in force, and probably with fresh troops." Pettus ordered his men to move by the left flank and deploy on the right of Loring's Division, and "to lie down in their places." The right of Pettus' line was thrown back until it touched the Goldsboro Road, in an effort to connect with Bate's command beyond that flank. "It was then about sunset," Pettus wrote, "and from the smoke of the guns and the burning woods it was difficult to see objects at a distance."[4]

Hill ordered Palmer to form his shattered brigade in rear of Pettus. Major George W. F. Harper, whose 58th North Carolina held the left of Palmer's line, found his reserve position a warm place nonetheless. The Tarheels received a steady small arms fire from both their front and right flank. In addition, the XIV Corps' Battery I, 2nd Illinois, Lt. Judson Rich commanding, had unlimbered south of the Goldsboro Road and about three-fourths of a mile to the southwest, from which point it was hurling shot and shell in Palmer's and Pettus' direction. Major Harper described the fire of Rich's battery as "most aggravating." Harper added that the Federal battery's fire would have made his position "extremely uncomfortable if the gunners had slightly depressed their pieces. . . .As it was,. . .their shells. . .flew almost harmlessly through the

GEN. JOSEPH E. JOHNSTON.
On February 22, 1865, Johnston assumed command of the scattered forces opposing Sherman in the Carolinas. One month later, on March 19, "Old Joe" routed a portion of Sherman's army near Bentonville—a phenomenal turnabout. This assault proved to be the last Confederate open field offensive of the war. Only once before, at Seven Pines, did Johnston display such aggressiveness, and only because his back was to Richmond. Bentonville may have been the most shining moment in Johnston's uneven Civil War career, for it was there that he displayed an audacity that until then had been seemingly absent in his character.

ɴ. BRAXTON BRAGG.
gg had led the hard-luck Army of nessee longer than any other gen-, from Corinth to the rout on Misıary Ridge. By then it was obvious n to the dour North Carolinian that officers and men no longer believed im. He therefore resigned his comd and went on to serve as President is' military advisor, only to find self serving alongside some of his enemies from the Army of Tennes- in March 1865. Although Bragg nmitted several blunders at tonville, his performance there was as egregious as some of his detrac- later insisted.

LT. GEN. WILLIAM J. HARDEE.
"Old Reliable" proved to be Johnst strong right hand at Bentonville. W the Confederate grand assault on M 19 threatened to sputter out on the n ern fringes of the Cole field, the co geous Hardee rode into the field waved his troops forward. Altho Hardee ultimately failed to do all he could to ensure Confederate suc on the 19th, he redressed this laps organizing and personally leading Southern counterattack that turned Mower's charge on the afternoon o 21st. Yet Hardee's moment of triu was marred by tragedy.

LT. GEN. WADE HAMPTON.
The ablest of Johnston's lieutenants, Hampton had secured a transfer from his post as commander of the Army of Northern Virginia's cavalry corps in order to defend his home state of South Carolina against Sherman's invading forces. Yet Hampton and his cavalry had to bide their time until their surprise attack on Kilpatrick's camp at Monroe's Crossroads in North Carolina. Although this engagement showed Hampton at less than his best, the South Carolinian turned in one of his finest performances of the war at Bentonville just one week later.

. GEN. JOSEPH WHEELER.
ɜeler served as Hampton's second ›mmand during the North Carolina ıpaign—a situation he heartily de- ·d, since he had been the ranking ɜral in the Confederate cavalry ser- until Hampton's promotion in Feb- y 1865. During this time, "Little ' also came under fire for failing to › his hard-riding command under ı a semblance of discipline. Wheeler ›red some luster to his tarnished ıtation by leading a portion of his mand in the counterattack that ed Mower's charge at Bentonville ⁄Iarch 21, 1865.

LT. GEN. ALEXANDER P. STEWART.
Though a graduate of West Point, Stewart was a college professor for most of his adult life. The professor proved to be an apt student of war, and rose steadily through the ranks of the Army of Tennessee, reaching the level of corps command during the Atlanta Campaign. In March 1865, Johnston rewarded Stewart's competence and perseverance by placing him at the head of the Army of Tennessee contingent. Stewart's performance at Bentonville is shrouded in mystery, for he left no after-action report.

Maj. Gen. Daniel Harvey Hill.
Unlike so many other of his peers at Bentonville outspoken Hill left a detailed account of his do during the three-day battle. In one of the w supreme ironies, Hill found himself in March 1 serving alongside his old nemesis, Gen. Bra Bragg. "I beg you to forget the past for this er gency," Johnston had pleaded. Hill relented, subsequently used his Bentonville report as a p form from which to hurl several accusations aga the hated Bragg. As further irony, the ubiquitous briefly commanded troops in Bragg's sector du the second day of the battle.

Maj. Gen. William B. Bate.
At Bentonville, "Old Grits" commanded the remnant of Cheatham's Corps, which consisted of his former division and Cleburne's Division. Hobbled by numerous wounds, Bate rode into battle on March 19 with a pair of crutches strapped to his saddle. Acutely jealous of the reputation of his old division, Bate served notice to the men of Cleburne's Division that he would not tolerate their insults any longer. Bate's command fought bravely at Bentonville, losing a quarter of its 900 officers and men.

Maj. Gen. Robert F. Hoke.
In late 1864, Gen. Robert E. Lee detached Ho veteran division from the Army of Northern ginia and sent it south to defend Fort Fisher. S then, Hoke and his men had suffered one set after another under the dispirited Bragg Bentonville on March 19, Hoke's Division fo fiercely and earned the unqualified admiratio their enemy, many of whom called the battle most desperate fight of the war. The part that H played in this and subsequent fighting at Benton is a matter for conjecture, since neither he o brigade commanders filed reports on the battl

MAJ. GEN. WILLIAM T. SHERMAN. Perhaps the war's most "modern" general, Sherman fully utilized the North's superior logistics and technology to win the crucial Atlanta Campaign, and thus ensure President Abraham Lincoln's re-election. And though Sherman cannot properly be called the creator of "total war," he certainly emerged as its most eloquent and ardent exponent. If the 1865 Carolinas Campaign reveals Sherman's strategic mastery, the final day's fighting at Bentonville demonstrates that at the operational—or grand tactical—level, Sherman lacked the decisiveness of Thomas or Sheridan. Fortunately for Sherman, Lee's surrender to Grant at Appomattox Court House persuaded Johnston to surrender his army at Bennett Place on April 26.

J. GEN. HENRY W. SLOCUM. eteran of the Army of the Potomac, cum had taken part in two of the 's bloodiest and most decisive tles—Antietam and Gettysburg. ing the Carolinas Campaign he comnded the Army of Georgia, or rman's Left Wing. As the ranking eral commander at Bentonville on rch 19, Slocum was slow to realize extent of the Confederate threat, but e he did, he reacted swiftly, choosgood defensive ground and offera stout resistance.

MAJ. GEN. OLIVER O. HOWARD.
Howard commanded the Army of the Tennesse
Sherman's Right Wing. Like Slocum, Howard
a veteran of the war's Eastern theater, where
luckless XI Corps was routed at Chancellorsv
then driven back during the first day's fightin
Gettysburg. Howard believed that Slocum
dragged his feet on his approach march to Gettysb
and later remarked that at Bentonville the ta
were turned. Known variously within the arm
the "Christian Soldier" and "Old Prayer Bo
Howard was respected for his bravery, though
staff officers often resented the danger to whi
subjected them. At Bentonville Howard was e
to support Mower's breakthrough on March 21
he was overridden by the ever-cautious Sherm

BVT. MAJ. GEN. JUDSON KILPATRICK.
After an uneven career in the Eastern theater that ended with the disastrous Kilpatrick–Dahlgren Raid, General Kilpatrick was transferred to the West, where he served as Sherman's cavalry commander on the March to the Sea and during the Carolinas Campaign. At first Kilpatrick flourished in his new role, but his rashness nearly led to a catastrophe at Monroe's Crossroads. Moreover, Kilpatrick's poor reconnaissance led Sherman and Slocum to believe that the Confederates had conceded Goldsboro to them without a fight, and nearly resulted in disaster at Bentonville. It is therefore no surprise that by mid-March Sherman was eager to have Sheridan and his cavalry on hand in the Carolinas.

MAJ. GEN. JOSEPH A. MOWER.
A favorite of Sherman, "Fighting Joe" Mower
the most aggressive general in the Federal arm
Bentonville. Mower was hot-tempered, but was
ways quick with an apology for those whom
wronged in his anger. Mower's so-called "rec
naissance" of the Confederate left flank on Marc
was actually a full-scale assault intended to cut
the Southerners' sole line of retreat at Bentonv
Mower's charge might have succeeded had Sher
allowed Howard to support it. Instead, Sher
recalled Mower, not realizing at the time the ex
of "Fighting Joe's" breakthrough.

. MAJ. GEN. JEFFERSON C. DAVIS.
ortunately named—for a general dressed in on blue—the irascible Davis had a facility for ing enemies within the Federal army. In 1862 he murdered his superior officer, Maj. Gen. Will- Nelson, and later feuded with several of his own rdinates, including Brig. Gen. William P. Carlin. n so, Sherman valued Davis as a proven field mander. At Bentonville two of Davis' divisions the brunt of the Confederate assault on March His decision to order Fearing's brigade's spoil- attack was a calculated risk, but it proved to be right thing, done at the right time."

BRIG. GEN. WILLIAM P. CARLIN.
Carlin commanded the First Division in Davis' XIV Corps. The Illinoisan chafed under the inimical Davis, fearful that even one slip might lead to his downfall. That slip came at Bentonville, where Carlin's division was routed on the afternoon of March 19. Following the battle, Carlin resigned his command, no doubt dreading Davis' retaliation. Although the rout was not Carlin's fault, he could never live it down, and subsequently wrote several articles absolving himself of the blame while shifting it to others.

. GEN. JAMES D. MORGAN.
gan commanded the Second Division, XIV os. Though lacking in dash, Morgan more than pensated for this shortcoming with his bulldog city. The valiant stand of Morgan's division h of the Goldsboro Road turned the tide of the ch 19 battle by blunting the Confederates' mo- tum and by buying time for the deployment of Federal XX Corps on Morris' farm. In one of the s unfortunate ironies, Morgan received a pro- on to major general by brevet for services ered at Bentonville, as did Carlin.

Union Maj. Gen. Jefferson C. Davis (left) photographed in his tent attending to paperwork with his chief of staff, Lt. Col. Alexander C. McClurg. McClurg's postwar Atlantic Monthly article, "The Last Chance of the Confederacy," proved to be one of the best eyewitness accounts of the Battle of Bentonville.

timber some ten feet or more overhead, and most of them burst in rear [of my position]."[5]

While Harper observed the Illinois battery's fearsome pyrotechnic display, General Palmer rode up and asked, "Where is the right of your regiment?" A strange question, the Tarheel major thought, from such a source at such a time. But Harper's surprise turned to amazement when his reply was followed by, "Major, countermarch your regiment."

Although "it seemed just a little unnecessary" to do so, Harper reminded the general "that the regiment was already facing the enemy, who was close at hand, and being heard to that effect in a most convincing. . .way."

"Yes, I know," Palmer said, "but I want you to look after these fellows over here." The general pointed over his shoulder to the right and rear of the 58th's present position—that is, in the direction of Bate's line.[6]

"The regiment was accordingly countermarched," Harper wrote, "halted on the spot and fronted—this time facing north, or opposite to the direction we had just before faced." The 58th was probably dispatched at Bate's request to guard his open right flank. As Bate's line was now facing almost due west, this would appear to be the most plausible explanation for the 58th's new alignment. Harper prudently ordered his men to lie down, but Palmer remained "quietly seated on his horse," the Tarheel major recalled, "apparently unconscious that anything unusual was going on, though musket balls were flying pretty thick, and some of the enemy's shells must have passed near his head." Once the 58th had filed into position, Palmer "leisurely rode off to some other part of the brigade," Harper wrote, "where the business in hand was not so dull and uninteresting."[7]

The shells that passed above Palmer and Harper were bursting over the Cole field, where McLaws' Division had halted in reserve after its march from Hoke's left. According to McLaws, Generals Johnston, Bragg and Stewart were also in the field, presumably within range of the enemy's shells. McLaws noted that the Federal artillery fire "became so troublesome" that he was forced to march his troops down the slope on the western half of the Cole field and into position on the reverse side of the abandoned log works constructed earlier by Robinson's Federal brigade. Perhaps it was their unfinished state that led McLaws to believe these Union works may have been "our own[,] as they looked the other way, towards the enemy." Aside from the "troublesome" shell bursts, all seemed quiet to McLaws, who concluded that the day's fighting was over. The general permitted his men to scavenge the Cole field for arms and ammunition, but then "the musketry recommenced with great fury." Soon afterward, Lieutenant Colonel Roy, Hardee's adjutant, galloped up and ordered McLaws to send two brigades toward the firing.[8]

McLaws dispatched his two best brigades. Conner's (under Brig. Gen. John D. Kennedy) advanced westward on the left and Col. George P. Harrison's Brigade moved out on the right. These units were followed by Col. Washington Hardy's Brigade in reserve. "We moved in a hurry," recalled one of Kennedy's men, W. A. Johnson of the 2nd South Carolina, "and passing along the [Goldsboro] road we saw Gen. Johnston sitting on a log by the side of the road. We cheered him, and he saluted us."[9]

Kennedy ordered his brigade to march left oblique, while Harrison's Brigade continued its advance toward Bate's position further to the southwest. "This oblique movement was performed very handsomely by the brigade under a terrific shelling," Kennedy reported. He halted his brigade in rear of Stewart's Corps, the left of his line extending across the Goldsboro Road, and the center almost on it. By this stage of the war, Conner's (Kennedy's) Brigade outnumbered Stewart's entire corps by 300 effectives. Lieutenant Colonel William Wallace's 2nd South Carolina held the left of Kennedy's line, which meant that the 2nd had to stand in the road and dodge the enemy's shells until it was ordered forward. But according to W. A. Johnson, the shells were the least of the Carolinians' worries. "[T]he musketry fire in our front was the heaviest I had heard during the war," wrote Johnson, a veteran of Antietam and Gettysburg. "Our division commander, Gen. McLaws, made the same observation. I wondered how enough men could survive under it to keep it up, but somehow they did. I guessed we would find out when we got into it."[10]

* * *

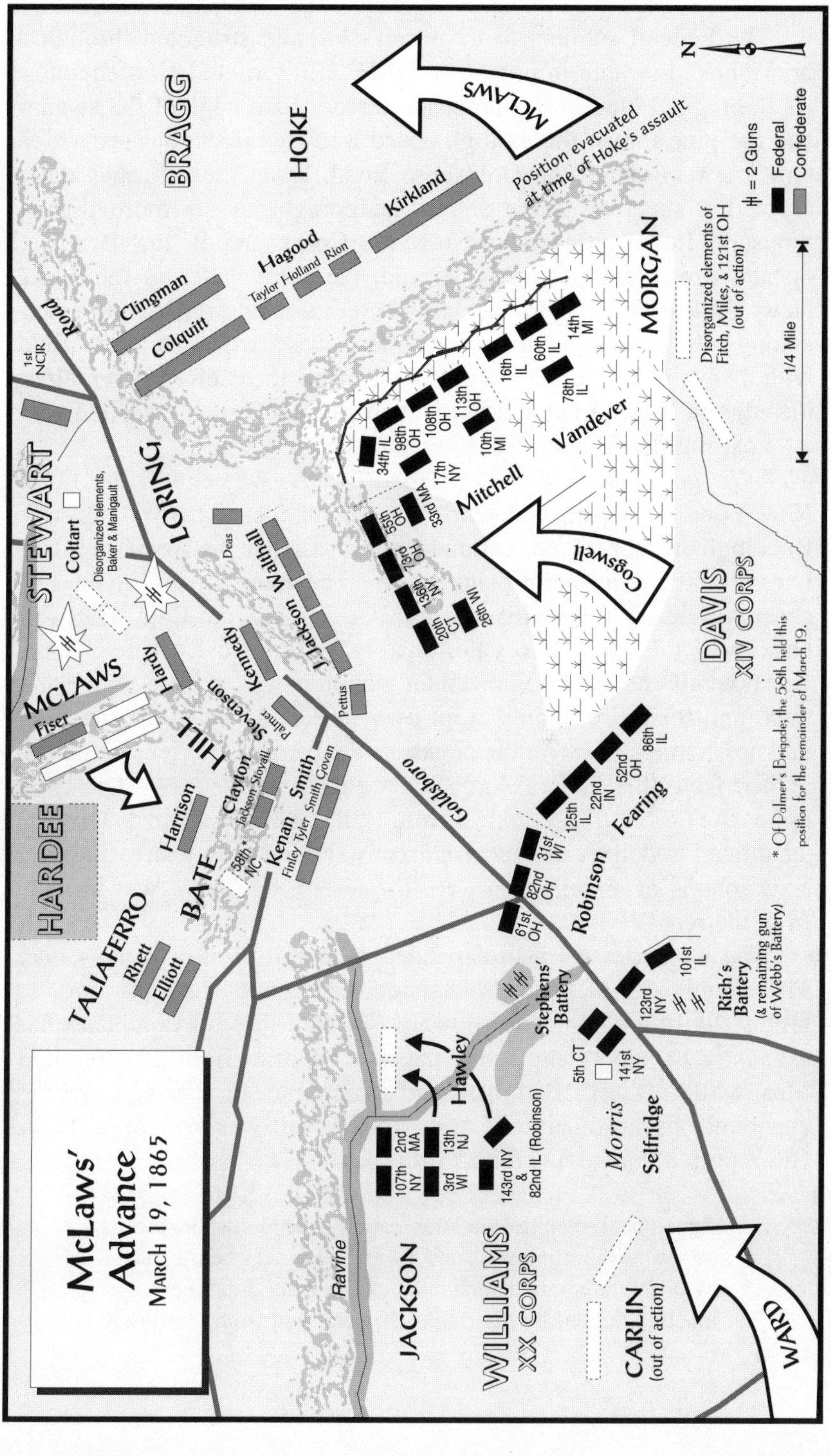
McLaws' Advance
March 19, 1865
BRAGG
HOKE
McLAWS
Position evacuated at time of Hoke's assault
Kirkland
Hagood
Taylor Holland Rion
Clingman
Colquitt
Road
1st NCJR
STEWART
Coltart
Disorganized elements, Baker & Manigault
LORING
Deas
Walthall
J. Jackson
Kennedy
MCLAWS
Fiser
Hardy
Stevenson
Palmer
HILL
Clayton
Jackson Stovall
Smith
Smith Govan
Pettus
HARDEE
Harrison
BATE
58th NC *
Kenan
Finley Tyler
TALIAFERRO
Rhett
Elliott
Goldsboro
34th IL
98th OH
108th OH
113th OH
17th NY
33rd MA
55th OH
73rd OH
136th NY
20th CT
26th WI
10th MI
16th IL
60th IL
14th MI
78th IL
Mitchell
Vandever
MORGAN
Cogswell
Disorganized elements of Fitch, Miles, & 121st OH (out of action)
1/4 Mile
= 2 Guns
Federal
Confederate
N
DAVIS
XIV CORPS
* Of Palmer's Brigade; the 58th held this position for the remainder of March 19.
125th IL
22nd IN
52nd OH
86th IL
Fearing
31st WI
82nd OH
61st OH
Robinson
101st IL
123rd NY
Rich's Battery
(& remaining gun of Webb's Battery)
Stephens' Battery
5th CT
141st NY
Morris
Selfridge
Hawley
2nd MA
13th NJ
107th NY
3rd WI
143rd NY & 82nd IL (Robinson)
Ravine
JACKSON
WILLIAMS
XX CORPS
CARLIN
(out of action)
WARD

Mark A. Moore

The Federal soldiers of Cogswell's brigade struggled through a briar-choked swamp in pursuit of D. H. Hill's routed Confederates. As the ragged blue line approached the northern edge of the swamp and the pine forest, the men glimpsed a row of thick bushes which they knew bordered the Goldsboro Road. From those bushes there erupted a sheet of flame and a deafening roar, as more than a thousand Rebel rifles from Stewart's Corps and Pettus' Brigade, opened fire. Major Henry L. Arnold, the commander of the 136th New York—which held the left center of Cogswell's line—was among the Union casualties. As Arnold was carried from the field with a severe wound, Cogswell's men threw themselves down along the edge of the swamp, and in the words of one Federal, replied with a "most murderous fire."[11]

"We got close to them," recalled Pvt. A. A. Velie of the 136th New York. The 20th Connecticut's commander, Lt. Col. Philo B. Buckingham, concurred, estimating the distance between the two lines at 200 feet, or point-blank range. "The enemy. . .endeavored by sheer weight of fire to drive [back] our line," wrote Capt. Hartwell Osborn of the 55th Ohio. "Fortunately," observed Lt. Col. Samuel H. Hurst of the 73rd Ohio, "their position was a little above our own, and their fire mainly went over us." Because of approaching darkness, combined with the clouds of smoke and the dense thickets in their front, the Federals' aim proved to be no better. "Thus lying upon the ground," Hurst wrote, "the Seventy-Third Ohio. . .continued to deliver and receive a constant and telling fire, until our sixty rounds of ammunition were exhausted, and more was brought from the rear."[12]

The Confederates also expended ammunition at a furious rate. The commander of Loring's Division, Col. James Jackson, notified fellow division commander Edward Walthall that his command had exhausted its supply and would have to withdraw from the front line. Meanwhile, D. H. Hill assumed command in Loring's sector, apparently because neither Loring nor Stewart was present to do so. Hill reported that he had found:

> a good deal of confusion after reaching the Goldsboro Road, owing to the mixture of troops and to orders being issued by different commanders, but. . .when natural darkness was much increased by the smoke of battle and from thousands

> of smouldering pine stumps and logs, it was greater than I ever witnessed before.

General McLaws noted that a "fog also came on, which, added to the smoke[,] made it impossible to see [beyond] a very short distance." It was under these chaotic conditions that Hill attempted to bolster the Confederate line opposing Cogswell's brigade.[13]

Unaware that Loring's Division had run out of ammunition, Hill directed Kennedy to deploy his brigade on Walthall's left instead of relieving Loring's Division. General Johnston rode up alongside McLaws while Kennedy was dressing his ranks. "Old Joe" halted in the road, indifferent to the shells which screamed overhead, but very much interested in the result of Kennedy's advance. Johnston regarded Cogswell's counterattack as a last-minute attempt by the Yankees to seize the initiative, and he wanted it stopped at once. As Kennedy ordered his brigade forward, Johnston raised his hat to the South Carolinians.[14]

One of Hill's staff officers led Kennedy's Brigade into position. Only one or two regiments—Kennedy was unsure of the exact number—had deployed on Walthall's left when the rest of the brigade was directed to relieve Loring's Division on Walthall's right, D. H. Hill having learned that Colonel Jackson's troops had exhausted their ammunition. W. A. Johnson of the 2nd South Carolina recalled that his regiment advanced into the timber, where it "came upon a line of Alabama troops lying down and firing as fast as they could load their guns. I could not see the Federals on account of the woods and brush," Johnson wrote, "but they were surely imitating the Alabama troops in shooting. It looked like both sides were trying to see which side could make the most noise without exterminating each other. . . .The roar of the guns was terrific." Colonel Henry Bunn, the acting commander of Reynolds' Brigade, Walthall's Division, reported: "At this point the contest was more obstinate and the musketry more terrific than at any other time of the engagement." Oddly enough, Kennedy characterized the enemy's fire as "not very severe," but few other Confederate commanders on that part of the field shared his opinion. By nightfall Yankee minie balls had wounded Colonel Bunn and General Pettus, and had killed Pettus' nephew and aide-de-camp, Lieutenant Pettus. Though Bunn's wound compelled him to turn over his command to Lt. Col. Morton G. Galloway, Pettus received a flesh wound in the left leg and was able to remain on the field.[15]

Though Kennedy may have remembered the firing as "not very severe," the Federals in Cogswell's brigade found it overwhelming. Lieutenant Colonel Hurst of the 73rd Ohio recalled that, "Just at sunset, the enemy was reinforced with a fresh line of battle [Kennedy's Brigade]; from their double line now came such a storm of bullets as we had never before witnessed. So terrible and withering was this fire of small arms, that, had our battalions stood up, they must have been utterly annihilated." Hurst described the air around him as being "thick with hissing bullets."[16]

"I think I was never under such a terrible storm of bullets in my life," echoed Lieutenant Colonel Buckingham of the 20th Connecticut, "and I have been in a good many very hot places I will assure you." Buckingham directed his men to take shelter behind "trees & logs otherwise I should have had my regiment annihilated." At one point Buckingham was struck in the thigh by a spent ball, but his rubber poncho absorbed most of the blow, leaving him with only a mild bruise. He noted that it "stung quite sharply. . .as it was." When the fighting was over, Buckingham counted 34 bullet holes in the tree that he had used for cover.[17]

Since his Company B of the 55th Ohio anchored the right flank of Cogswell's line, Capt. Hartwell Osborn, with only the 55th's adjutant accompanying him, set out to find Morgan's left flank, which he supposed was on his immediate right. To his chagrin, Osborn discovered that the gap between Morgan and Cogswell was still not closed. As Osborn and Adjutant Chase traversed the ground at twilight under a canopy of smoke, they found this no man's land littered with Rebel dead. The two Union officers went among the corpses and collected a dozen rifle-muskets and cartridge boxes each, which they somehow carried back to the 55th Ohio. As a precaution in case the Rebels attempted to advance through the gap, Osborn directed his company to refuse its right flank until a junction with Morgan's division could be made.[18]

It was dark when Kennedy's South Carolina regiments began their advance against Cogswell's Federals. As the South Carolinians passed over the prone Alabamians of Scott's Brigade, Loring's Division, the Federals opened fire on the advancing Rebels, killing and wounding several. The 2nd South Carolina's W. A. Johnson cast a rueful glance over his shoulder when the Alabamians—their ammunition supply exhausted—jumped up and headed for the rear. Now that Kennedy was in position on his right, Walthall shifted his small division "a little to the left. . .to resist an attack which had been threatened by the enemy," reported Brig. Gen. George D. Johnston of Quarles' Brigade.[19]

Kennedy attempted one assault against Cogswell's line, but the, piecemeal attack, delivered with only a few hundred men, was doomed to failure. As the brigade moved into the open and advanced southeast against the center of Cogswell's line, the 2nd South Carolina's color bearer was sent sprawling when a bullet struck him in the chest. Fortunately, the ball imbedded itself in a small Bible the soldier kept in the breast pocket of his jacket: "The book saved his life," W. A. Johnson wrote, "but the blow knocked him out." A member of the 2nd's color guard seized the flag as it fell and was killed a moment later. The honorable but perilous duty now devolved upon W. A. Johnson, who had never coveted the color bearer's post. For three years Johnson had seen numberless comrades fall while carrying the regiment's colors. As a result of his observations, he concluded:

> [N]o firing line should have a. . .single flag bearer. The idea of a man carrying a flag and being a target for every gun of the enemy is, to my mind, radically wrong. . . .War is a business, [and] to be successful [one must wage it] on business principles: that is, every man must be armed to fight.

Johnson believed that an emblem worn on each soldier's shirt or jacket would serve as an effective substitute for the regimental colors. His objections notwithstanding, he bore the flag through the rest of the battle. One ball grazed his cheek and another cut the bridge of his nose, but Johnson emerged from the fight without serious injury, though he noted that his clothing was "pretty badly shot up."[20]

The 2nd South Carolina advanced in the darkness by the light of the burning pitch pines, which occasionally flared up like huge Roman candles. The smoke from these fires burned the eyes and throats of the men. Suddenly, the Carolinians received a volley from their left-rear, and Lieutenant Colonel Wallace immediately ordered the 2nd to halt, cease fire and hit the ground. "We obeyed," a laconic W. A. Johnson recalled. Wallace's men waited until the firing from both their front and rear had ceased before rising to resume the advance. Soon after regaining their feet, they were again fired upon from front and rear, and were again ordered to lie down. The Carolinians repeated this scenario several more times, with the same result. Lieutenant Colonel Wallace sent several couriers to the rear "to notify these people that we were not the enemy," Johnson wrote, "but it seems they never got the word."[21]

The smoke of the burning pines grew so thick that the 2nd South Carolina was able to escape under its cover. To prevent any further firing from the rear, Wallace instructed his men to hold their fire even if fired upon by the enemy. The Carolinians withdrew by the right flank and returned to the main line, where they rejoined the rest of Conner's brigade. Johnson and his comrades of the 2nd learned that they had been fired on from the rear by Walthall's troops, who had mistaken them for a line of Union skirmishers.[22]

By 8:30 p.m. the musketry along Cogswell's front had faded into scattered picket firing. McLaws ordered Kennedy to withdraw Conner's brigade to its starting point west of the Cole field. Walthall reported that Kennedy's withdrawal left a gap several hundred yards wide between his right and Pettus' left, which he covered by deploying his 200-man division in skirmish formation.[23]

Cogswell's brigade had accomplished its objective. It had slammed the door shut on the Confederates' attempt to envelope Morgan's salient and now provided a link, however tenuous, between Morgan and the rest of Slocum's line. But while the fighting raged along Cogswell's front, Generals Bate and Taliaferro were launching their own assaults on the Federal position at Morris' farm.

* * *

Earlier in the day, at about 3:15 p.m. on the far left of Slocum's battle line, Maj. Frederick H. Harris' 13th New Jersey was helping the 2nd Massachusetts fortify its position when his men heard "heavy and continuous firing" erupt in the woods along their right flank. The noise intensified and seemed to draw nearer, indicating to William Hawley's brigade that at least a portion of the XIV Corps was being driven back toward Morris' farm. Minutes later, Major

Harris received an order from Colonel Hawley to move the 13th New Jersey from behind the New Englanders and across the wooded ravine on his right, there to form a line extending beyond the right flank of the 2nd Massachusetts. The 13th crossed the ravine and entered a large open field. In their front was a stand of trees and another ravine, well-suited for a defensive line. The veterans of the 13th liked their new position. The swampy, briar-strewn ravines bordering their front and left flank made excellent natural obstacles to an enemy advance, and the strip of trees provided good cover, yet afforded the men a commanding view of the field that stretched before them.[24]

The 13th New Jersey had a rail breastwork underway when, according to one soldier, "the firing became furious" and the fugitives from Buell's and Briant's commands burst into view. "[T]he vast field was soon covered with men, horses, artillery, caissons, &c., which brought vividly to our minds a similar scene at the Battle of Chancellorsville," recalled the 13th's historian, Samuel Toombs. Hawley, meanwhile, sent the 82nd Illinois, one of the two regiments on loan from General Robinson, to the 13th's support. As his Illinoisans hustled into position, Lt. Col. Edward S. Salomon saw "a great many [of Carlin's] men and officers coming out of the woods in the greatest confusion and disorder. It looked to me like a stampede," he reported. From his vantage point across the ravine, a soldier in the 3rd Wisconsin saw men "throwing away guns, knapsacks, & every thing & all running like a flock of sheep." A New Yorker from Hawley's brigade also described the rout:

> At once I understood the situation. I had never seen a panic, but I knew this was one, and hence it was possible for it to be a serious affair. . . .No matter how well some may keep their heads, the very fact that the great body of the troops have lost the bonds of discipline and the power to reason, and have in fact become insane for the time being, puts every one in danger.[25]

Here and there a few of Carlin's soldiers attempted to halt the rout. A color sergeant from Buell's brigade drew up alongside the 13th New Jersey and planted his regiment's colors before him. Brandishing his sword, the color bearer exhorted his comrades to "rally around. . .and not give up the field," but they swept past him without breaking stride. Flag in hand, the color bearer sheathed his sword and ran after them. Major Harris attempted to rally enough of Carlin's men to fill the 400-yard gap between the 13th New Jersey and Robinson's brigade to the south. Even with the help of his enlisted men, Harris found that it was a futile effort. "Officers and men called upon the fleeing crowd to rally and join on our line but in vain," Toombs wrote. When the 82nd Illinois trotted into view, the soldiers of the 13th "cheered long and loud," mindful that the 82nd was all the support they could expect to receive. While the Illinoisans filed into position on the 13th New Jersey's right, Lieutenant Colonel Salomon and his officers managed to rally about 50 fugitives, most of them belonging to the 13th Michigan of Buell's brigade. Salomon put them in line with his regiment.[26]

Most of Carlin's troops continued running until they reached the vicinity of the Morris farmhouse, near where Slocum had established his headquarters. Since mid-morning the Morris house had served as the XIV Corps' hospital. New York *Herald* correspondent E. D. Westfall described the house as a plain log structure "situated in a fifty acre cornfield." Inside the house, XIV Corps medical director Waldo Daniels and his surgeons had been hard at work since noon tending the wounded. "Pale and bloody men lay under the blooming peach trees or against the outbuildings of the place," Westfall wrote. "In the woods opposite the wagons of the two corps had been parked. The road, the garden, and all available space around, were crowded with pack-mules, negroes and 'bummers' on their lank, lean horses."[27]

When Confederate bullets began to patter against the logs of the Morris house, Surgeon Daniels ordered his hospital moved at once to the John Harper farm a half-mile to the rear. Some of the hospital tents had to be abandoned because they now stood dangerously close to the Rebels' front line. "Wounded and fainting men made a last desperate effort, got up and straggled off in the direction Dr. Daniels pointed out," Westfall wrote. Some of the wounded were mounted on horses and mules and led to the rear. Those men too severely wounded to ride or walk were "handled rather roughly," noted one onlooker, "being pitched into the ambulances and army wagons most any way." The wounded were then bounced and jostled back to Harper's farm amid "a bedlam of oathes [sic] and snapping of whips and rattling of wheels," a Union surgeon recalled.[28]

A few rounds of solid shot that plunged into the ground near the XIV Corps wagons on the Morris farm were sufficient to panic animals and teamsters alike. "[T]here was a regular stampede," recorded hospital steward William Humphrey. "'[B]ummers,' horses and pack mules rushed against each other in a mad race for the rear and safety," wrote newspaperman Westfall. "[W]agons, hopelessly stalled in the black earth of the woods, were jerked out by the convulsions attendant upon the bursting of shells just behind them." To Westfall and many veterans of the XIV Corps, the scene unfolding before them was a disturbing "reminder of Chickamauga."[29]

Lieutenant Colonel John B. LeSage galloped up the Goldsboro Road toward Morris' farm, the men of his 101st Illinois following at a dog trot and deploying in line of battle. The 101st was arriving on the field about an hour later than the rest of its brigade, General Robinson having detailed it to guard the Smithfield-Goldsboro crossroads. A squad of dismounted cavalry passed through the 101st's ranks on its way to the rear. One of the Illinoisans asked a trooper "how it was in front."

"[H]ot as h—l," came the reply.[30]

The 101st spent several anxious minutes waiting in the rear for orders while the musketry and cannonading rose to a thunderous fortissimo. "Suddenly," recalled H. C. Robbins, the 101st's surgeon, "a staff officer rode rapidly to Col. LeSage and gave him [an] order." The lieutenant colonel turned to face the 101st, then ordered it to double-quick to the front.[31]

On reaching the 101st's assigned position, Lieutenant Colonel LeSage dismounted and led the regiment to the line just formed by Selfridge's brigade. Colonel Selfridge had earlier received orders to shift his brigade from Hawley's left to a position astride the Goldsboro Road when it appeared that the Confederate line was sweeping westward along that route. Fortunately for the Federals, Robinson's and Fearing's brigades had rallied on the Morris farm, so Selfridge directed his men to deploy on a slight rise of ground 150 yards to the rear. Selfridge's men were building a fence rail barricade when the 101st arrived. The Illinoisans rolled up their sleeves and pitched in. "We then obtained a few shovels and strengthened our breast-works with earth," reported Col. James C. Rogers of the 123rd New York, whose left flank was resting near the road bed. Surgeon Robbins marveled at the diggers' progress:

> It is surprising to see the rapidity with which men will intrench themselves under fire, a few rails piled up in a twinkling then dirt thrown upon them with numberless tools, bayonets, frying pans bits of board bare hands anything to move dirt and it is not long before a protecting mound rises sufficient to cover men lying behind it and as the digging proceeds the ditch deepens as fast as the mound rises, till in an almost incredible space of time an intrenchment has been thrown up sufficient to protect [men] from cannon shot as well as rifle balls[.][32]

In the open field behind Selfridge's line, Rich's battery hurled fused shells at the Confederates massing along the Goldsboro Road three-fourths of a mile to the northwest. The lone gun of Webb's battery not seized by the Rebels was wheeled into position on the right of Rich's flaming guns, from which point it added its mettle to the growing din of battle. Across the road, the men of Lt. Jerome Stephens' battery (Battery C, 1st Ohio) rested in Reddick Morris' peach orchard and awaited orders. Stephens' battery had gone into park around 3:00 p.m., the first of the XX Corps batteries to arrive on the field. "Soon after our arrival we heard a great uproar toward the front," recalled one of Stephens' artilleryman, "then pack-mules, baggage-wagons, and a part of a battery came back in great disorder." A wild-eyed officer dashed past Stephens' battery yelling, "Lee's whole army is after us; run for your life boys, run!" The artillerymen found the rout of Carlin's veteran troops a trifle unsettling: "The Fourteenth Corps boys were not in the habit of running away from a fight," wrote L. Hendrick of Stephens' battery, "so we knew that there must be something ahead worth running [from]."[33]

At 3:30 p.m. came the command, "Right wheel into line!" Lieutenant Stephens led his four 12-pounder Napoleons up to a small knoll between Robinson's and Hawley's brigades, north of the Goldsboro Road. Stephens' battery held an excellent position: before it stretched the Morris field, 250 yards wide, and sloping eastward for 500 yards down to the wooded swampland bordering the Cole plantation. Whether firing canister or spherical case, the Ohioans could rapidly transform that field into a slaughter pen—provided Hawley and Robinson could hold their positions. The ground in rear of the battery dipped into a narrow wooded ravine, which widened and became marshy as it wound northward toward Hawley's position. Lieutenant Stephens kept his draft animals and caissons on the opposite side of this natural barrier to protect them from enemy fire. Hendrick recalled that by 3:45 p.m., Stephens' battery was "in good shape for callers."[34]

* * *

At noon the head of General Ward's column halted on the Goldsboro Road for lunch, having marched to within seven miles of Morris' farm. The 22nd Wisconsin of Dustin's brigade had the advance. Since breaking camp at 8:00 a.m., it had assisted a battalion of the 1st Michigan Engineers in corduroying the road. For several hours the men in the 22nd had heard the distant thunder of cannon fire, but they trusted the XIV Corps to brush aside whatever opposition it might encounter.[35]

The Wisconsinites had just sat down to eat when a staff officer, his horse covered with foam, came galloping up the road. Drawing rein before a company of the 22nd, the officer inquired for General Ward. In reply the men pointed to an ambulance parked under a nearby tree. The general was sleeping off another bender.[36]

The staff officer dismounted and approached the wagon. "Wake up[,] General," he shouted "for God's sake[,] wake up!"

Ward awoke, and in his gruff way, asked, "What's the matter now[?]"

The staff officer explained that a division of the XIV Corps had been overrun by a superior force of the enemy, and that the boys at the front were "getting tired out" and needed support.

"Huh," Ward replied, "I'll bet I'm tireder nor they are now, 'n I don't believe thars many rebs no how, [sic] I could put 'em all in my pocket."[37]

Just then Ward's adjutant, Capt. John Speed, walked up. Seeing that Ward "was in no condition to do business," the staff officer took Captain Speed aside and explained the situation to him.

"[N]ow Adjutant," the staff officer said, "get the men under arms as quick as you can, and double quick them to the front."

While Speed conferred with Ward, Sgt. John Dickinson of the 22nd Wisconsin offered the staff officer a cup of coffee and some hardtack. One of Dickinson's men asked the officer "how the affair commenced."

"Them dam [sic] bummers of ours," the staff officer snapped:

> started out this morning before daylight, as they always do, to get ahead of the soldiers; and before breakfast we knew they'd run against a snag, for we could hear the firing; and before we got through eating, back come one of them hellaty scoot, his horse just laying down to it when he rode into camp; and he says[,]["][H]urry up boys, and give us some help, for the rebs don't drive worth a dam to day.["]

With that, the staff officer mounted his horse and galloped back to the front.[38]

The staff officer was only the first of several sent by Slocum to hurry Ward's division to the front. By the time Capt. William Moseley appeared on the scene, Ward was on horseback leading his troops forward. Before Moseley could speak, "Ward laughingly motioned him away," recalled one eyewitness, "as if he already knew the message by heart." Then "Old Shaky" urged his horse into a trot, compelling the men of the 22nd Wisconsin to break into a run to keep up.[39]

Colonel Henry Case's brigade brought up the rear of Ward's division. A mounted courier dashed past urging the men to quicken their pace. "We knew what the next word would be, of course," wrote Robert Hale Strong of the 105th Illinois, "and every man tightened his belt for a run. The courier had hardly passed us when our brigade bugle sounded: 'Attention. Forward March, Double Quick!'" In the words of a veteran of Dustin's brigade, the orders were to "push forward and let the wagon train go to hell." The men of Ward's division were soon trotting along in single file on either side of the slow-moving wagons. Some of the soldiers fell out and jogged alongside the main column in the adjoining fields. Sergeant Dickinson noted that whenever the din of battle increased, the men would quicken their pace in response, "as though afraid the turning point in the battle would be reached before we came on the field." Ward's troops feared that they might arrive too late to prevent the Confederates from breaking through the Federal line. "In that case," Private Strong wrote, "it meant for us either a fight at a disadvantage or a retreat. We never had been driven from the field, but we knew that if the Union line in front of us was broken and the Rebs charged us while we were in marching column instead of line of battle, we would be at a great disadvantage."

After advancing several miles at the double quick, men began to drop out of the column from exhaustion. Ward's troops had managed to steal no more than a few hours' sleep since dawn the day before, and had been carrying their rifles, canteens, cartridge boxes, knapsacks and haversacks at the double-quick for some time. Their shoes, if they still had any, were hardly suitable for long-distance running. Yet most of the soldiers remained with their regiments throughout this grueling four-to-eight-mile jog. [40]

At length Ward's head of column reached the gradual upward slope that stretched for a half-mile from the Harper farm to the Morris farm. An occasional stray bullet zipped by to remind the men, if they needed reminding, that they were nearing the front. Ward's troops could now hear the all too familiar "demoniac yell" of the Rebels, as well as the reassuring tones of the Yankees' "huzzah's!" A South Carolinian from Hardee's Corps described the two sides' war cries:

> In the assaults of the Federals the cries were regular, like "Hurrah! Hurrah! Hurrah!" simply cheers, lacking stirring life. But the Confederate cries were yells of an intensely nervous description, every man for himself yelling "Yai, Yai, Yi, Yai, Yi!" They were simply fierce shrieks made from each man's throat individually. . . .I do not know any reason for this marked difference unless it was in the more pronounced individuality of the average Confederate soldier.[41]

The 22nd Wisconsin was the first regiment in Ward's division to crest the gentle rise, and the Wisconsinites were presented with a commanding view of the spectacle unfolding in the Morris field. "And a wilder battle scene we never saw during the war," Sergeant Dickinson wrote in his diary:

> Riderless horses were galloping over the plain. Artillery was scattered over the hillside, some busily engaged throwing shells into the swamp, others acted as tho trying to leave the field, their horses on the run towards the rear; they might have been simply changing for a better position; who could tell in such confusion[?] Down in the rear of the battle line were scores of wounded soldiers limping and dragging themselves to a place of safety; it might have been an orderly confusion, but to a newcomer [on the scene] it looked like a stampede, a perfect rout.[42]

On the eastern slope of the Morris farm, just beyond the protective confines of the Federal lines, stood the XIV Corps hospital tents. Several ambulances and wagons were parked nearby. Only a handful of surgeons and stewards remained behind to care for the wounded not yet transported to the rear. One of these was 17-year-old Cyrus Fox of the 86th Illinois, who had witnessed the advance of Carlin's division that morning, only to see it come tumbling back eight hours later.[43]

While young Fox and his fellow stewards did what they could to protect their charges, several hundred yards to the south the men of Fearing's brigade, now under the command of Lt. Col. James Langley, piled up fence rails in a desperate effort to protect themselves. Joining the 125th Illinois and the left wing of the 22nd Indiana on this new line were the battered remnants of the 52nd Ohio and the 86th Illinois. Even with the addition of these troops, Langley estimated that no more than half his brigade was present. Langley was therefore delighted when Robinson's brigade formed on his left and began building rail works in continuation of his own. Langley's next concern was to refill the empty cartridge boxes of his men. He delegated the task to Adjutant Charles Swift who, though unable to locate the division's ammunition wagons, obtained a plentiful supply from the XX Corps. "My works were scarcely strong enough to protect men lying down," Langley reported, "when the enemy's skirmishers advanced to within shooting distance and commenced a lively fire."[44]

One of those skirmishers was Sgt. Walter Clark of the 1st Georgia Volunteers of Bate's command. When the call for skirmishers was made Clark held back, but the first man to volunteer turned to him and said, "Come on, Walter." Clark recalled that he was "not advertising for that sort of a job, but the call is a personal one and not caring to let the boys know how badly scared I am, I step[ped] out of the ranks." Private Will Dabney of the 1st Georgia also stepped forward, though laboring under a presentiment that he was to be killed that day. But it was another of Clark's comrades, John Miller, who would receive his death wound while skirmishing with Langley's Federals. As the line of battle moved up to join the skirmishers, Miller clutched his belly and cried out to the Volunteers' color bearer, Frank Stone, "Frank, I'm killed."

"I hope not, John," replied Stone.

As the line of battle passed by him, Miller lay down under a pine tree to die. Moments later, Stone himself was wounded by a bullet in the side. He handed his flag to a comrade and hobbled to the rear. Sergeant Clark noted that of the 19 officers and men of his company who went into battle, one had been killed and three wounded, and 13 others could point to at least one bullet hole in their clothing or accouterments.[45]

While Bate's skirmishers traded shots with the Federals, a staff officer sent by General Hardee rode up and directed Bate to "halt and await further orders before moving." Bate brought up his main line alongside his skirmish line and ordered his command to lie down. Then he refused his flanks, having lost connection with Pettus on his left and not yet having established it with Taliaferro on his right. Convinced that his small force "was too weak, from casualties and exhaustion," to break the Federal line on Morris' farm, Bate informed Hardee of his predicament and requested reinforcements.[46]

At about this time, Taliaferro's undersized, two-brigade division approached and formed on Bate's right. Stephen Elliott's Brigade still had the advance and was ordered to halt at the tree line bordering the Morris field. The Confederates looked on as Carlin's men dashed across the open field and vanished into the woods 500 yards away. While they dressed ranks along the woods' edge, Elliott's men had ample time to contemplate their fate. Across the field, the woods along their left front looked blue with Union soldiers. In their immediate front a battery of Federal artillery (Stephens' guns) dominated the gentle slope they were about to ascend. Off to their right stood the Yankees' abandoned hospital tents.[47]

"There was now a lull in the action," wrote the 13th New Jersey's Samuel Toombs, who witnessed the action from the right flank of Hawley's brigade. "It was that great stillness we had often before noticed which precedes the breaking out of a storm." As they gazed out across the open field, Major Harris and Lieutenant Colonel Salomon, commanders of the 13th New Jersey and 82nd Illinois, respectively, both realized that their position could easily be flanked by Taliaferro's Rebels. Accordingly, the regimental commanders wisely swung back their line until it was at right angles to the rest of the brigade. Their new position was well-concealed, lying on the edge of the wooded ravine they had crossed just minutes before. While the men of the 13th New Jersey and the 82nd Illinois were hauling rails from their old position to fortify their new line, they heard the sharp "Ky-yi!" of the enemy.[48]

At the command "Forward!," Elliott's Brigade, followed by Rhett's Brigade in close support, left the cover of the woods raising the Rebel yell. Surgeon H. C. Robbins of the 101st Illinois found the yells "blood curdling." Another noncombatant, Chaplain Earle of the 21st Michigan, wrote: "such fiendish yells never saluted my ears before. Why, it seemed to me as though the doors of perdition had been thrown wide open, and that all the devils were out!" Elliott's troops advanced at the double quick and in good order and were met almost immediately by a "leaden hailstorm" of shrapnel, noted one Confederate eyewitness.[49]

Stephens' Ohio battery, which stood in the path of the Rebel assault, "had redoubts started three rails high in front of our pieces," wrote artilleryman L. Hendrick, "when the rebels came out of the woods in the front and on the left of us, about 500 yards away." The crews of Stephens' battery primed and loaded their guns, and in the words of Hendrick, "we sent them a volley of case shot [with fuses] cut just right to burst among them. We kept this up as fast as we could load and fire."[50]

With each salvo hundreds of iron and lead balls tore into the ranks of Elliott's Brigade or plunged into the sandy soil at the Southerners' feet, creating a blinding sandstorm. "My eyes were in a moment filled with sand dashed up by the [shrapnel] which struck around," wrote Cpl. A. P. Ford of Elliott's Brigade. "I wiped them with my hand, and keeping them closed as much as I could, kept on at a run." Elliott's line of battle rushed past the XIV Corps hospital

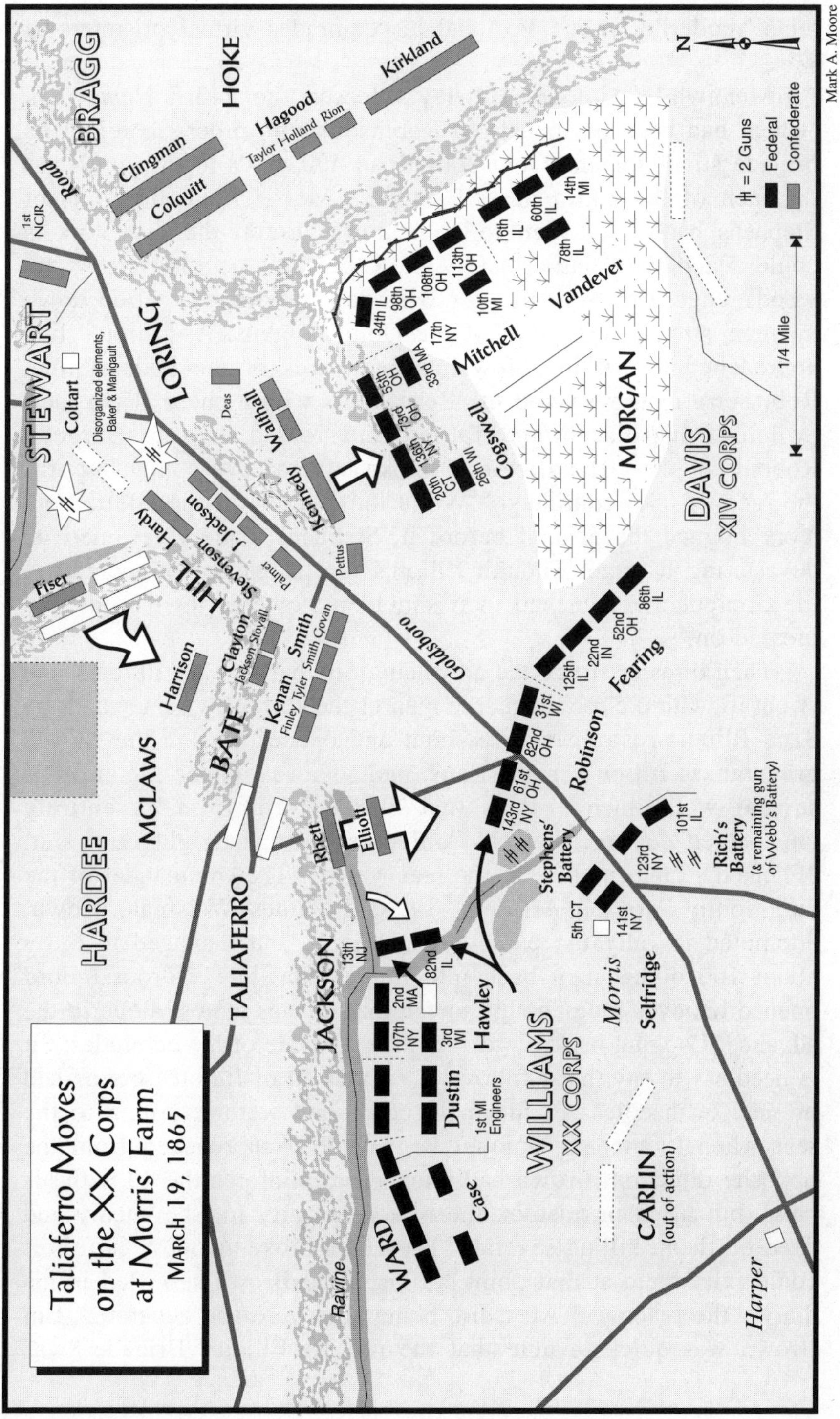
Taliaferro Moves
on the XX Corps
at Morris' Farm
March 19, 1865
HARDEE
MCLAWS
TALIAFERRO
JACKSON
Rhett
Elliott
Harrison
BATE
Kenan
Finley Tyler
Smith
Smith Govan
Clayton
Jackson Stovall
Stevenson
J. Jackson
Palmer
Pettus
HILL
Hardy
Fiser
STEWART
Coltart
Disorganized elements,
Baker & Manigault
LORING
Deas
Walthall
Kennedy
1st NCJR
Road
Goldsboro
BRAGG
HOKE
Clingman
Colquitt
Hagood
Taylor Holland Rion
Kirkland
Ravine
WARD
Case
Dustin
1st MI Engineers
107th NY
2nd MA
13th NJ
82nd IL
3rd WI
Hawley
WILLIAMS
XX CORPS
Morris
Selfridge
5th CT
141st NY
Stephens' Battery
143rd NY
61st OH
82nd OH
31st WI
Robinson
123rd NY
101st IL
Rich's Battery
(& remaining gun of Webb's Battery)
125th IL
22nd IN
52nd OH
86th IL
Fearing
CARLIN
(out of action)
Harper
DAVIS
XIV CORPS
MORGAN
Cogswell
20th CT
26th WI
136th NY
73rd OH
55th OH
33rd MA
17th NY
Mitchell
34th IL
98th OH
108th OH
113th OH
10th MI
16th IL
60th IL
78th IL
14th MI
Vandever
1/4 Mile
= 2 Guns
Federal
Confederate
N
Mark A. Moore

tents, rendering young Fox and his comrades virtual prisoners of war.[51]

Meanwhile, Colonel Hawley released the 143rd New York (which had been on loan from Robinson) with orders to rejoin its brigade straddling the Goldsboro Road 400 yards to the south. As the men of the 143rd dashed into the Morris field, the guns of Stephens' battery fell silent to let them pass. Before the New Yorkers could reach the relative safety of Robinson's position along the woods' edge, fire from Elliott's Brigade caused them to flop down on their stomachs in front of the Ohioans' guns. As Elliott's line approached to within a few hundred yards of the Federal line, Robinson's men answered the Rebel yells with a cheer. Then their "whole front blazed and rattled and roared," wrote Surgeon Robbins of the 101st Illinois, "smoke covered everything but still the racquet [sic] continued." While the soldiers of the 143rd New York hugged the ground before it, Stephens' battery resumed its devastating barrage. Though Elliott's line staggered momentarily, the Confederates hunched their shoulders, lowered their heads and pressed on.[52]

Then disaster struck the advancing Southerners. As Elliott's line swept by within close range, the men of the 13th New Jersey and the 82nd Illinois rose up with a shout and opened fire on the serried gray ranks. Elliott's right flank melted away under the heat of several well-aimed volleys that blazed forth from an entirely unexpected quarter. Several Confederates on the right cried out, "Flanked!," and the race to the rear was on. The commander of the 2nd South Carolina Artillery, Lt. Col. James Welsman Brown, attempted to rally the panic-stricken mob, and managed to bully about 100 of his men back into line. Meanwhile, Corporal Ford opened his eyes long enough to see that he was almost alone in the advance. Looking back, Ford saw the stampede of his comrades: "It is needless to say that I followed." About 40 of Elliott's troops had pressed on heedless of the main body, and were returning to the rear when Lieutenant Colonel Brown's 100 approached from the opposite direction. Brown had intended to reinforce the 40 with his band, but his men mistook the returning party for the enemy and fired on them, killing several. "They then broke again, & no effort could rally them at that point," a disgusted Brown scrawled in his diary, "the [enemy's] Arty. fire being so severe and accurate." But Brown was quick to note that the rout of Elliott's Brigade "was mainly owing to the want of discipline in some of the Companies and the [mis]conduct of certain officers."[53]

Sam Ravenel, a 16-year-old courier on Taliaferro's staff, was looking for the general when he rode into the Morris field, "where it seemed that the land was being plowed up with cannon balls," he recalled. "Suddenly I saw men coming pell-mell into the field from the opposite side. For a moment I. . .was panic-stricken, but I then recognized [them as] our troops." Young Ravenel, who admitted to looking "more like twelve than sixteen years old," took it upon himself to rally his frightened comrades as they dashed past the V-shaped rail barricades erected by Dibrell's troopers early that morning. "I made for that place," Ravenel wrote, "and began riding up and down between the men, begging them to stop." Soon the youth was joined by several other couriers. Just then Maj. John Warley, whom Ravenel described as "red in uniform, red in temper, and red in face," ran up waving his sword over his head. In a loud voice Warley commanded the fleeing men to halt. Not one man stopped. Pointing to the row of barricades, Warley turned to an old veteran and said, "Shoot the first damned man who crosses that line!"

"It had its effect," Ravenel observed. "The boys stopped." As Major Warley was rallying about 100 men, Lieutenant Colonel Brown returned to the rear and rallied an additional 300 soldiers. Yet according to Corporal Ford, some of Elliott's men "never rallied, but went straight on home from the field, and were never heard of again." Although Ford called the panic of his comrades "inexcusable," he pointed out that most of them were sick, exhausted, undisciplined and utterly demoralized.[54]

Rhett's Brigade had been following Elliott's Brigade at a distance of 100 yards when the rout began. Although Elliott's frightened troops jostled Rhett's men on their way to the rear, most of Rhett's line held together. Captain Charles Inglesby of the 1st South Carolina Artillery attributed the steadfastness of his brigade to its "splendid discipline." Once the field in front was clear, Col. William Butler ordered Rhett's Brigade to advance. Guiding on Rhett's line of battle was the Gist Guard Artillery—the only unit from Elliott's Brigade to do so.[55]

The South Carolinians brushed aside a squad from Buell's Federal brigade that had rashly made a stand in the open field near the 13th New Jersey's position. The Confederates fired one volley at the fleeing Northerners, and among those wounded was Lt. Marcus Bates of the 21st Michigan. Unable to walk, Bates tried to crawl toward the rear, but he became nauseous and had to stop. Fortunately for Bates, a pair of Federal soldiers carried him to a fence corner behind Stephens' battery, where he fainted from exhaustion and loss of blood.[56]

Rhett's Brigade obliqued to the left, aiming for the gap in the Federal line partially occupied by Stephens' battery. The South Carolinians approached to within 30 yards of Robinson's left flank before faltering in the face of the combined firepower of the Union infantry and Stephens' artillery. Yet the South Carolinians "managed to obtain a cross-fire upon my four right regiments, which were at that time almost destitute of breastworks," reported General Robinson. "For a time," the 143rd New York's Willard Elmore recollected, "destruction seemed almost inevitable." The 143rd appeared to be in a tight spot, pinned down in Morris' open field with nothing more than a fence rail or two to hide behind. It was a regiment on the right of the 143rd, however, that panicked and broke for the rear. The 143rd's alert commander, Lt. Col. Hezekiah Watkins, galloped over from his position and halted the routed regiment's color bearer, who thereupon planted his flag staff in the ground. Brandishing his sword in one hand and his pistol in the other, Watkins rose up in his stirrups and shouted to the fleeing troops, "Halt! Who is in command?" One of the soldiers named the regiment's commander. "I outrank him," Watkins shot back. "About face and hold your line." A soldier on Selfridge's reserve line who witnessed the scene wrote, "Every one of the retreating regiment rallied to the colors, took their places, and were marched back on the double-quick to their position on the line. . . .It was handsomely done."[57]

General Slocum's anxiety manifested itself in his handling of Dustin's brigade (Ward's division), which was drawn up in reserve at the onset of Taliaferro's assault. Before the attack Slocum was the picture of self-possession as he sat on his horse by the roadside and scanned the distant tree line with his field glass. But as the Confederates advanced ever nearer to the Federal position, Slocum became agitated. Pointing to Robinson's line, Slocum told Dustin, "Col.[,] take your command down to the right of the road, and strengthen that line." Dustin's lead regiment, the 22nd Wisconsin, had advanced a few steps when the firing appeared to shift toward the guns of Stephens' battery. "And there the fight seemed to rage with redoubled fierceness," the 22nd's Sergeant Dickinson wrote. A soldier down the line from Dickinson exclaimed, "[A]in't that a perfect hell!"

"Col.," Slocum barked, "move your men to the left of the road." Dustin's brigade countermarched to a position in rear of the Ohio battery, whose busy crew members offered "warm words of welcome" to the infantrymen, noted the 22nd's William McIntosh. Yet Slocum was not satisfied with this disposition, either, and ordered Dustin to march his brigade to the extreme left of the line and deploy there. "[A]nd away we go on the run for the left," Dickinson recorded.[58]

The roar of battle abruptly ceased. The curtain of smoke lifted to reveal that the Confederate line of battle had retreated, leaving a trail of dead and wounded soldiers in its wake. "My men now collected rails and built themselves a breast-work," Robinson reported. Hospital steward Cyrus Fox took advantage of the lull to escape with his ambulance train to the Harper farm. Fox later sang the praises of Stephens' battery:

> I wish to state that the work of that battery was the most grand of any it was my lot to witness during my three years of war. . . .I shall always feel very grateful toward that battery for making it so hot for the rebs that I had the chance, and took our ambulance train out of the rebs' grasp, and to the rear.

Lieutenant Stephens noted that his battery opened fire on the enemy "with case, checking their advance and giving the infantry time to form." But artilleryman Hendrick stated what Stephens merely implied: "Battery C [1st Ohio] had the honor of saving the day by repulsing the first charge. Not that we did better than would any of the other [XX Corps] batteries, but we were there and they were not." Hendrick emphasized that Stephens' battery repulsed the first Confederate assault by firing only spherical case, "showing that to be a powerful weapon when properly used." By day's end the enemy dead would lay six-deep in places across Stephens' front, bearing silent witness to the truth of Hendrick's statement. After the battle a Union burial detail marked the Confederate mass grave on that part of the field with a crudely lettered headboard. It read: "These men were killed by Battery C, 1st O.V.A."[59]

Sergeant Thomas Goundrey of the 141st New York, Selfridge's brigade, saw firsthand the effect of the Ohio battery's barrage. That morning Goundrey and two of his comrades had been captured by the Confederates while on foraging detail. Goundrey noted that he and his fellow prisoners were in such close proximity to the front line that when Stephens' battery opened on the Rebels, "case-shot came tearing through their ranks and plowing up the ground around us. . . .The Johnnies. . .came to the rear in all shapes—hatless, bleeding, and also carried in blankets . . . .I must say that never in my experience did I see wounded men come back in such numbers. . . .We prisoners were moved out of range, as we thought not any too soon, as the ground was being torn up all about us."[60]

Colonel Butler and General Elliott had a difficult time reforming their brigades amid the screaming and bursting projectiles that tore through the treetops. The racket unnerved Elliott's troops, still shaky from their earlier rout. Even the redoubtable Lieutenant Colonel Brown found the fusillade "terrible. . . .But they stood this time as men should," Brown noted. "Besides some threats of the use of the pistol might have assisted." During the barrage Elliott received a shrapnel wound in the leg. Painful though his leg wound was, the general remained at the front to steady his men.[61]

While the Confederates were forming for their second assault, Daniel Dustin's brigade of Ward's division deployed on Hawley's left flank, facing north behind the wooded ravine in that sector. The 22nd Wisconsin's William McIntosh recalled:

> The instant our line halted, knapsacks were flung off and the rear rank, supplied with axes and spades[,] used them with marvelous energy and effect. Small trees were quickly felled, cut into logs and carried to the line, where a ditch was begun and the dirt thrown over the logs to form a parapet. In forty minutes from the halt a line of earthworks had been built from which it would have been a costly effort to dispossess their defenders.

Dustin's men also hacked away the underbrush in front of their works to give themselves a clear field of fire and deprive the enemy of a defilade.[62]

Joining on Dustin's left was a battalion of the 1st Michigan Engineers and Mechanics. The Michigan Engineers were unaccustomed to front-line duty, but XX Corps commander Alpheus Williams deemed the situation dire enough to deploy them there anyway. As they went into position, the Michiganders were greeted by the sight of some pack animals, no doubt refugees from Carlin's rout, who were roaming unattended through the woods in their front. After lining up his command alongside Dustin's brigade, Col. John B. Yates told his men, “We will whip the rebels.” Then he ordered his engineers to start digging. “They worked lively,” one engineer recalled, and before long the Michiganders had erected an entrenchment that rivaled Dustin's.[63]

Colonel Henry Case's brigade fell into line on the Michigan Engineers' left, further extending the line to the west. No sooner had Case's men stacked arms than they, too, started entrenching. Kilpatrick's cavalry division, which had screened the left of the XX Corps column and had arrived on the field around 3:00 p.m., filed into position on the extreme left of Slocum's line. From right to left, Lt. Col. William Way's dismounted brigade deployed on Case's left, followed by Col. Thomas J. Jordan's brigade, with Bvt. Brig. Gen. Smith D. Atkins' brigade and Col. George E. Spencer's brigade extending the line west and southwest as it angled back toward the Goldsboro Road. Kilpatrick's troopers erected log and rail barricades to protect their front.[64]

All this preparation, as urgent as it must have seemed at the time, proved unnecessary. The Confederates lacked the troops to outflank Slocum's left, but of course neither Slocum nor his subordinate generals could have known this.

Meanwhile, a second XX Corps battery, Lt. Edward P. Newkirk's (Battery M, 1st New York), rolled into position on Lieutenant Stephens' left, unlimbering just west of the ravine bisecting Morris' farm. The Confederates now faced eight 12-pounder Napoleons and a line of Federal infantry that was better prepared than it had been for the first assault.[65]

When Rhett's long gray line emerged from the woods a second time, the Union cannoneers and infantrymen dropped their shovels and rails and scrambled to their places. “Suddenly [we heard] the deafening cries of thousands, sounding as though all the demons of Hell had been let loose," wrote William Grunert, an Illinoisan in Case's brigade, "followed by the terrible rattle of musketry, for the time overpowering the cries." When the Federal artillery thundered forth, the noise was "so loud that we had to yell to make our nearest neighbors understand us," Grunert noted, "while the ground trembled under our feet."[66]

While advancing alongside his company, Capt. Edward Mitchell Whaley of the 1st South Carolina Regulars had 19-year-old Lt. George Stoney by the buttonhole and was shouting into his ear when an artillery projectile nearly cut Stoney in two. "I caught his upper half in my arms and called to some of the men to take him to one side and lay him down," Whaley recollected. The captain was shocked to find that not only was Stoney still alive, he was also fully conscious. The youth refused the morphine Whaley offered him, nor would he drink from Whaley's flask. Stoney only wanted to dictate a letter to his mother and have someone read from the Bible to him. Stoney lingered until dawn of the next day. His friends and relatives in Stuart's Battery learned of his death that morning: "They found an old log house. . .with an earth floor," one of Stoney's comrades recounted. "Here they dug a grave and his cousin. . .read the Episcopal service above him with the roar of battle still going on in front."[67]

For the second time Rhett's Brigade approached to within point-blank range of Robinson's line, then fell back under a blistering artillery and small arms fire, "although we peppered the Yanks severely," wrote Lt. Bill Colcock of the 1st South Carolina Artillery. While the South Carolinians dressed their thinning ranks for a third attack, the four 3-inch ordnance rifles of Scovel's battery dropped trail on the right of Stephens' battery. During the rout of Carlin's division, Lieutenant Scovel had managed to extricate his battery, but had sustained eight casualties while in position on the Cole farm. The Federals now had 12 guns trained on Morris' open field.[68] As the Confederate casualties mounted with each attack, the Union position was being strengthened to receive them.

Colonel William Butler led Rhett's Brigade into the field a third time. Braving the volleys of the 13th New Jersey and the 82nd Illinois on their right, the South Carolinians once more confronted the massed batteries on the right of the Goldsboro Road and the line of Union infantry on the left—with the same devastating result. The battered gray line withdrew and rallied once more.

According to Captain Inglesby of the 1st South Carolina Artillery, Rhett's Brigade made three charges on the Federal position at Morris' farm. Most Union eyewitnesses, however, stated that the Confederates made between five and seven assaults on that position. Perhaps the Federals exaggerated the number of charges to make their repulse of them appear that much more impressive, or perhaps the discrepancy was caused by the smoke-shrouded chaos of the battlefield, where the delineation between separate charges must have been easily blurred.[69]

However many distinct charges were made, artilleryman Hendrick recalled that at 5:30 p.m., following the repulse of at least the third Rebel assault, Winegar's battery (Battery I, 1st New York) unlimbered on the left of Newkirk's battery west of the ravine. Until now the Federal batteries on Morris' farm had been firing only spherical case and solid shot, but the crews of Winegar's battery loaded their field pieces with double-shotted canister and topped off the rounds with bullets they had begged off Hawley's infantrymen. In effect, the New Yorkers were converting their four 3-inch ordnance rifles into mammoth shotguns. Veteran gunners preferred smoothbore cannon such as the 12-pounder Napoleon for this job, because its larger bore could spray a canister load over a wider area than the 3-inch rifles, whose greater range and accuracy availed it nothing when discharging canister rounds at 200 or 300 yards. Furthermore, because a smoothbore used fixed ammunition—meaning that the charge and the round were attached—it could be loaded more rapidly than a rifled gun, which had to be loaded in two stages. When firing canister at short range, this difference often proved critical. Nevertheless, it was a brave infantryman indeed who would advance unflinching into the muzzles of *any* artillery battery. Yet this was what the men of Rhett's Brigade had done for more than an hour, and what they were about to do yet again, this time against *sixteen* Union guns.[70]

If nothing else, the assaults on the Federal position on Morris' farm demonstrated the raw courage of Rhett's Brigade, while casting doubt on General Taliaferro's competence. At some point during the assaults Taliaferro should have brought up his artillery to soften the Union position, and applied to Hardee for reinforcements (both A. Burnet Rhett's artillery battalion and McLaws' Division were waiting in reserve nearby). Taliaferro's failure to support Rhett's assaults ensured their repulse.

The New York *Herald's* E. D. Westfall described the Confederates' last assault on the XX Corps' position for his readers back home:

> The rebels, massed for final effort, emerged from the woods just as the sun went down. They came into Mr. Morris' open fields silently, without that yell, universally accounted part of a rebel charge, and marched steadily on towards Robinson and the. . .batteries. They were received with the heaviest musketry Robinson and Selfridge could give them, at which many of the gray mass put up their hands deprecatingly, as I have seen "bummers" do while fighting bees. The exertions of their officers, who were really active and truly brave, brought them on in some kind of order past a point where [the 13th New Jersey and the 82nd Illinois] could get a flank fire on them. This added to their misery; yet they stood it bravely and came on.

It was a tense moment for Union generals Slocum, Williams, Davis and Kilpatrick, who were standing in a group behind the batteries. "General Slocum stood motionless and speechless," Westfall continued, "intently watching Robinson's thin line." "Pap" Williams had earlier sent a courier to Robinson, asking the Ohio brigadier whether he could hold his position. Robinson's reply—"We've come back far enough; we'll stay here and fight till Hell freezes over"—though smacking of insubordination, must have been extremely gratifying to Williams.[71]

About 600 yards to the northeast, General Taliaferro and his staff sat on their horses and anxiously watched the advance of Rhett's Brigade. Earlier, in response to the Federal artillery fire, Taliaferro had ordered the regiments of Elliott's Brigade to lower their colors, the men to lie down, and the officers to kneel. It was a sensible order. There could have been no question of advancing Elliott's badly shaken troops into the field again, nor could anything have been gained by offering up these men as sacrifices by leaving them standing along the tree line.[72]

As Rhett's Brigade approached to within canister range, Winegar's battery opened fire. "They were terribly punished," General Williams wrote, "especially when the canister swept them

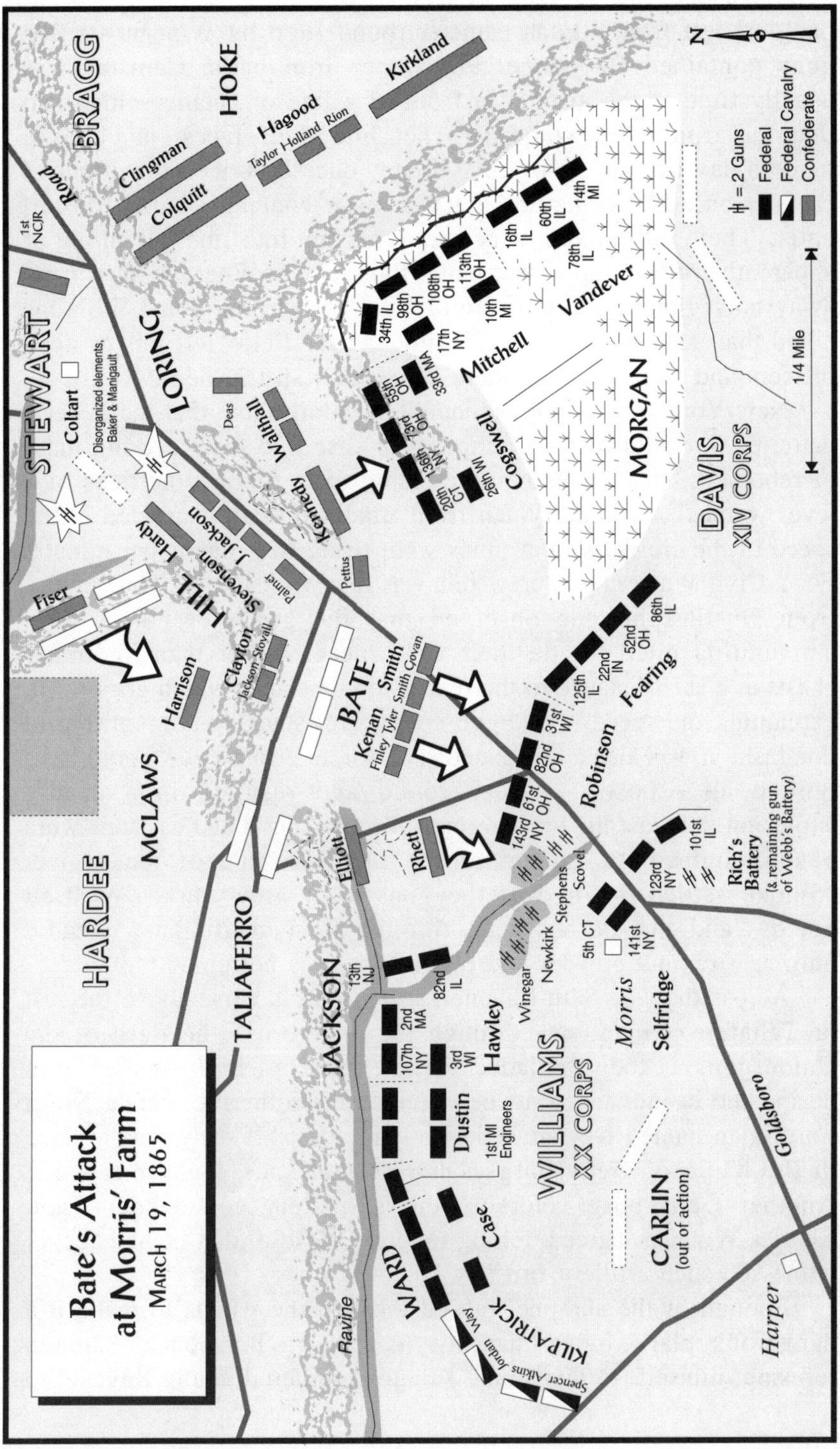
Bate's Attack
at Morris' Farm
March 19, 1865
HARDEE
MCLAWS
TALIAFERRO
JACKSON
STEWART
LORING
BRAGG
HOKE
HILL
BATE
Clingman
Colquitt
Hagood
Taylor
Holland
Rion
Kirkland
Road
1st NCJR
Coltart
Disorganized elements, Baker & Manigault
Deas
Walthall
Kennedy
Pettus
Hardy
J. Jackson
Stevenson
Palmer
Fiser
Harrison
Clayton
Jackson
Stovall
Smith
Govan
Kenan
Finley
Tyler
Elliott
Rhett
Ravine
13th NJ
82nd IL
2nd MA
107th NY
3rd WI
Hawley
Dustin
1st MI Engineers
Case
WARD
KILPATRICK
Way
Jordan
Atkins
Spencer
WILLIAMS
XX CORPS
Winegar
Newkirk
Stephens
Scovel
5th CT
141st NY
Morris
Selfridge
CARLIN
(out of action)
Goldsboro
Harper
143rd NY
61st OH
82nd OH
31st WI
Robinson
123rd NY
101st IL
Rich's Battery
(& remaining gun of Webb's Battery)
125th IL
22nd IN
52nd OH
86th IL
Fearing
20th CT
136th NY
73rd OH
55th OH
26th WI
33rd MA
17th NY
34th IL
98th OH
108th OH
113th OH
10th MI
16th IL
60th IL
78th IL
14th MI
Cogswell
Mitchell
Vandever
MORGAN
DAVIS
XIV CORPS
1/4 Mile
= 2 Guns
Federal
Federal Cavalry
Confederate
N

Mark A. Moore

on [our] left front." Each canister round fired by Winegar's rifled guns contained forty-nine .96 caliber iron balls. Canister was usually fired at the ground in front of a line of enemy soldiers so that the iron balls would ricochet into their faces, much as a modern-day riot gun is fired. Williams once described the effect of canister on a line of battle: "Each canister contains several [dozen] balls. They fell in the very front of the line and all along it apparently, stirring up a dust like a thick cloud. When the dust blew away no regiment and not a living man was to be seen." Williams noted that the Confederates crossing Morris' field "left lots of dead officers and men" behind wherever canister struck them.[73]

New York *Herald* correspondent Westfall wrote that the Federal batteries threw "canister and spherical case into the wavering mass of rebels, the discharges being as rapid for a time as the ticks of a lever watch." An infantryman from Buell's brigade marveled at the speed of the crews, who at times were firing two rounds per minute. For a Civil War-era gun crew this was fast work indeed. One soldier from Dustin's brigade observed that the gun crews kept their ammunition piled beside their field pieces rather than in limber chests at a safe distance to the rear, a circumstance which goes far in explaining the speed of the gun crews. But stacking ammunition in this fashion was also a calculated risk, for an errant spark could have ignited an exposed artillery round and resulted in a deadly explosion. At least the draft animals, limber chests and caissons were beyond immediate danger on the opposite side of the ravine. "Smoke settled down over the guns as it grew dark," Westfall noted, "and the flashes seen through it seemed like a steady, burning fire, and powder and peach blossoms perfumed the air."[74]

Across the way Sam Ravenel, seated on his horse above the rest of Taliaferro's men, saw through the underbrush the flash of the Union guns as they enfiladed Rhett's shattered line. At one point during the cannonade, Ravenel overheard another courier, a North Carolinian named Devant, tell two comrades: "If there was a place in the battle of Gettysburg as hot as that spot, I never saw it." Another Gettysburg veteran, Federal battery commander Capt. Charles Winegar, agreed, telling reporter Westfall that he had "never witnessed such artillery fire."[75]

Enough of the shrapnel rattled through the woods to make it a dangerous place for a man, or a boy, on horseback. Though refusing, himself, to dismount, Taliaferro ordered young Ravenel to do so, saying, "It is foolish to sit there." No sooner had the youth jumped off his horse and sat down behind a tree than some shrapnel dashed across the seat of his saddle and buried itself in the ground at his feet. Later, when Elliott asked him how he had felt facing those batteries, Ravenel said, "Why, General, I just felt that if I was going to be killed, all the trees could not save me; and if I was not, there was no need of one."

Elliott laughed. "My boy," he said, tapping Ravenel on the shoulder, "as long as you are a soldier, that is the best belief in the world."[76]

Although darkness now engulfed the woods, shrapnel continued to zip and hiss overhead, showering Elliott's prone troops with evergreen branches and twigs. About this time, General Hardee galloped up, followed by his staff and escort. One of Hardee's engineer officers noted that a "heavy fire of grapeshot was raking the bushes like gusts of wind." To Capt. G. B. Gardner of Hardee's escort company, "the din of battle roared like one continuous peal of heavy thunder." Hardee asked Taliaferro why Elliott's line was not advancing. Regardless of whether it was the plunging shrapnel or Taliaferro's reply that convinced him, Hardee saw the futility of ordering Elliott's Brigade forward.[77]

While Rhett's men were making their futile charges, William Bate's two divisions had been resting just to the left, or southeast, of Taliaferro's Division. At dusk, Bate ordered his command back on its feet. Though his line advanced only a short distance beyond the tree line bordering Morris' field, it fell under a withering small arms and artillery fire nonetheless. The commander of the remnant of Bate's old division, Col. Daniel L. Kenan, was severely wounded in the right leg while "in the thickest of the fight," General Bate later reported. Kenan's shattered leg was subsequently amputated. One of Kenan's two brigade commanders, Maj. W. H. Wilkinson of Tyler's Brigade, was killed while at the head of his troops. The striking down of these two officers while in full view of their men stalled the advance of Kenan's command.[78]

The assault of Cleburne's Division, which advanced on Kenan's left, was equally unsuccessful. Sergeant Walter Clark remembered advancing a short distance to the edge of "a pond or lagoon," where Cleburne's line was halted. "A Federal battery open[s] on us," Clark wrote, "and the color bearer of Olmstead's 1st Ga. regiment is knocked six or eight feet and disembow[e]lled by a solid shot as it plows through the ranks." Spotting a "friendly log" nearby, Clark decided that it would be a good idea to lie down behind it.[79]

Bate had lost a quarter of his 900-man command by this time, and had only the 58th North Carolina to show for his repeated pleas for reinforcements. Yet help was on the way in the form of Col. George P. Harrison's Brigade of McLaws' Division. Arriving just after sundown, Colonel Harrison's Georgians stepped over Bate's prone troops and advanced into the swamp a few paces, where they encountered a whirlwind of bullets, shrapnel and bursting shells, and were immediately ordered to hug the ground. "Had these fresh troops been thrown in an hour earlier," Bate contended, "our victory would have been more complete and more fruitful of advantage." But Bate was basing his contention on a misapprehension. In his report Bate stated that his command was relieved by McLaws' entire division, which was clearly not the case. At least two of McLaws' brigades, Conner's and Hardy's, were elsewhere on the field. Bate was right in one sense, however: Harrison's eleventh hour arrival was too late to affect the outcome of the battle.[80]

Another of McLaws' brigades, Col. John C. Fiser's, lay in reserve some distance behind Bate's line, but near enough to the front to undergo the same nerve-wracking experience described by Major Harper of the 58th North Carolina. "A storm of shell streamed five to twenty feet above us all, bursting far in our rear," wrote Lt. John Porter Fort of the 1st Georgia Regulars. "If any one of us had stood upright I think he would have been torn to pieces, but the artillerists could not depress their pieces sufficiently to strike us." Lieutenant Fort noted that for once even the Regulars' commander, Col. Richard A. Wayne, "lay down as we did, close upon our mother earth. . . .It would have been a very trying ordeal had we been ordered to rise and charge the enemy in our front."[81]

At nightfall Joe Johnston decided that his army had had enough, and he ordered Hardee to break off the assault. Hardee relayed the order to Taliaferro, who in turn notified the commander of Rhett's Brigade, Colonel Butler. The battered South Carolinians must have rejoiced when the order to fall back was given, yet their ordeal was far from over. As the Confederates fell back beyond canister range, the Federal batteries opened on them with spherical case, and they continued to suffer under the unrelenting fire of the

Union infantry, which the South Carolinians had to endure throughout their withdrawal. It was therefore hardly surprising that, in the words of correspondent Westfall, Rhett's Brigade "retired hastily and in confusion."[82]

Generals Kilpatrick and Slocum witnessed the Confederates' retreat from behind Robinson's line. The two generals must have presented a striking contrast: Slocum, ever-cool and undemonstrative—a few moments of agitation earlier in the day notwithstanding—alongside Kilpatrick, who was flashing a toothy grin and excitedly slapping his thighs to see the enemy on the run. A soldier in the 31st Wisconsin overheard Kilpatrick begging Slocum to let him run down the fleeing Rebels with his cavalry. Slocum wisely said no.[83]

Seldom one to credit the enemy with anything more noteworthy than his swiftness in retreat, Kilpatrick wrote Sherman: "I never witnessed more determined attacks than were made by the enemy to-day upon our center." Rhett's Brigade suffered for its tenacity. During the battles of March 16 and March 19-21, Rhett's Brigade sustained 567 casualties, more than half its effective force.[84]

The men of Rhett's Brigade finally reached the cover of the woods along the eastern edge of the Morris field. While reforming their line, the South Carolinians were subjected to a vicious cross fire from their front and right flank. The flank fire was the work of Hawley's and Dustin's skirmishers, eager no doubt to contribute their share in the enemy's repulse. Following the withdrawal of Rhett's Brigade from the woods' edge, the musketry gradually diminished until only the occasional report of a cannon could be heard.[85]

The Federal line on Morris' farm had held.

~ *thirteen* ~

"May God in His Mercy Spare Us All to Meet Again"

—Cpl. Abner C. Smith, 20th Connecticut

It was dark when Col. Washington Hardy's Brigade of McLaws' Division began its advance against the left flank of Mitchell's brigade, having veered left after following Conner's Brigade for a short distance. Colonel Hardy doubtless saw this nighttime assault as an excellent means of surprising the enemy. As it later developed, it was Hardy who was surprised.

Hardy's Brigade consisted of three North Carolina units: the 50th Regiment, the 77th Regiment (or 7th Reserves), and the 10th Battalion (or 2nd Battalion Heavy Artillery). Of these three units the 77th North Carolina was the most remarkable. Composed of men between the ages of 45 and 55, the 77th was raised in June 1864, as a home guard unit charged with rounding up deserters. But as General Sherman swept eastward across Georgia on his March to the Sea, the 77th and several other North Carolina regiments were ordered south from Wilmington to reinforce Hardee's garrison at Savannah. The North Carolina Legislature had passed a law forbidding the removal of any Reserves regiment beyond state borders, but that law was ignored in view of the Confederacy's acute manpower shortage. With the evacuation of Savannah, most of the North Carolina units returned to Wilmington. Not so the 77th. It remained with Hardee and was brigaded with two other orphaned Tarheel units—the 50th Regiment and the 10th Battalion. Hardy's Brigade numbered 329 effectives.[1]

Several hundred yards to the south, Maj. Aaron Robinson of the 121st Ohio was enjoying a few moments of comparative quiet in his front when his pickets ran in announcing that the enemy was close behind. Earlier in the day, following the rout of the 121st, Robinson had managed to rally about half of his regiment, as well as some troops from various other commands (the remainder of the 121st, under the temporary command of Capt. Jacob Banning, followed Miles' brigade of Carlin's division to the Morris farm). By the time Robinson had his makeshift command well in hand, the fighting in Morgan's sector had all but ceased. Robinson took up a position on the left of the 34th Illinois, facing slightly east of north, occupying the works abandoned by the 21st Wisconsin of Hobart's brigade, Carlin's division.[2]

Although his pickets stated that the enemy was advancing on his position, Major Robinson hesitated to open fire on an unidentified force. "Fearing that some of our troops might have become bewildered and were coming in," Robinson reported, "I ordered the men not to fire, but to lay close to their works." He challenged the unknown force to identify itself. "They were plainly to be seen not thirty paces from us," the Ohio major noted, "picking their way through a swamp, and apparently forming line in our front, unconscious of our position."[3]

Hardy's Brigade advanced "through a sparse growth of old field pines on through some thick huckleberry bushes and ponds of water," recalled Lt. Charles Stevens Powell of the 10th North Carolina Battalion. Lieutenant Powell was carrying a spade, which he held in front of his "cracker box"—that is, his stomach—as a crude shield. Fortunately for Powell, he never had a chance to discover its effectiveness. The Tarheel lieutenant and his comrades blundered up in the darkness to within point-blank range of the 121st Ohio's position.[4]

Major Robinson reported that "after some parleying" with the enemy, he persuaded a Rebel lieutenant to enter his lines. The lieutenant surrendered his sword to Robinson and stated that the 10th North Carolina Battalion was in position to attack him. This convinced Robinson that the enemy was upon him in force. He warned the 34th Illinois on his right and sent his prisoner to General Mitchell. "I then ordered the enemy to come in at once," Robinson stated, "telling them that if they did not we should fire upon them." Few if any of the Tarheels heard Major Robinson's warning.

"After a moment's pause I ordered the men to fire," the Ohio major wrote.[5]

"The sheet of fire was blinding," Tarheel lieutenant Powell recalled. "We received a terrible volley," wrote Lt. John Albright of the 77th North Carolina, and "we took shelter the best we could behind the pine trees, except some of us who were in a pond about sixty or seventy yards wide." Colonel Hardy was at the front of his brigade when it was first fired upon. Seeing that his men were falling all around him, Hardy rushed forward with his hat in one hand and his sword in the other, to a point midway between the Union and Confederate lines. "You are shooting your own men!" Hardy shouted to the Federals, hoping that in the darkness he would pass for a Union officer. As the bullets whizzed by, Hardy strode from one end of the line to the other, imploring the Yankees to cease fire while their own officers ordered them to fire at will. "Still the firing went on," Lieutenant Albright noted. The 121st Ohio's Major Robinson estimated that the fusillade lasted about 15 minutes. Albright recalled that once the firing had ceased, his company commander, Capt. W. S. Bradshaw, sent out Lt. John Blalock to determine whether the force in his front was really the enemy. When Blalock crept up to within 20 feet of the Ohioans' breastworks, two Federals leaped out of the darkness, grabbed the Tarheel lieutenant by the arms, and shoved him over the works. The Confederates retaliated by opening fire on the Federals and driving them back from their parapet—or so Albright remembered it.[6]

Lieutenant J. C. Ellington of the 50th North Carolina offered another and more plausible denouement to Hardy's catastrophic night assault. Ellington wrote that as soon as the firing ceased, "all of our men who were able. . .crawled out of the swamp and made their escape, and Colonel Hardy deliberately walked off without a scratch." The next morning the men of the 121st Ohio collected 42 rifles and one sword which Hardy's men had thrown away in their flight to the rear.[7]

According to one of Hardy's couriers, a Tennessee cavalryman named William E. Sloan, Col. George Wortham was the only member of Hardy's Brigade "to show the 'white feather.'" Wortham had been advancing in rear of his regiment, the 50th North Carolina, when it was hit by the Federals' first devastating volley. At the first opportunity Wortham bolted for the rear and safety. Sloan was delivering a dispatch sent by Colonel Hardy when

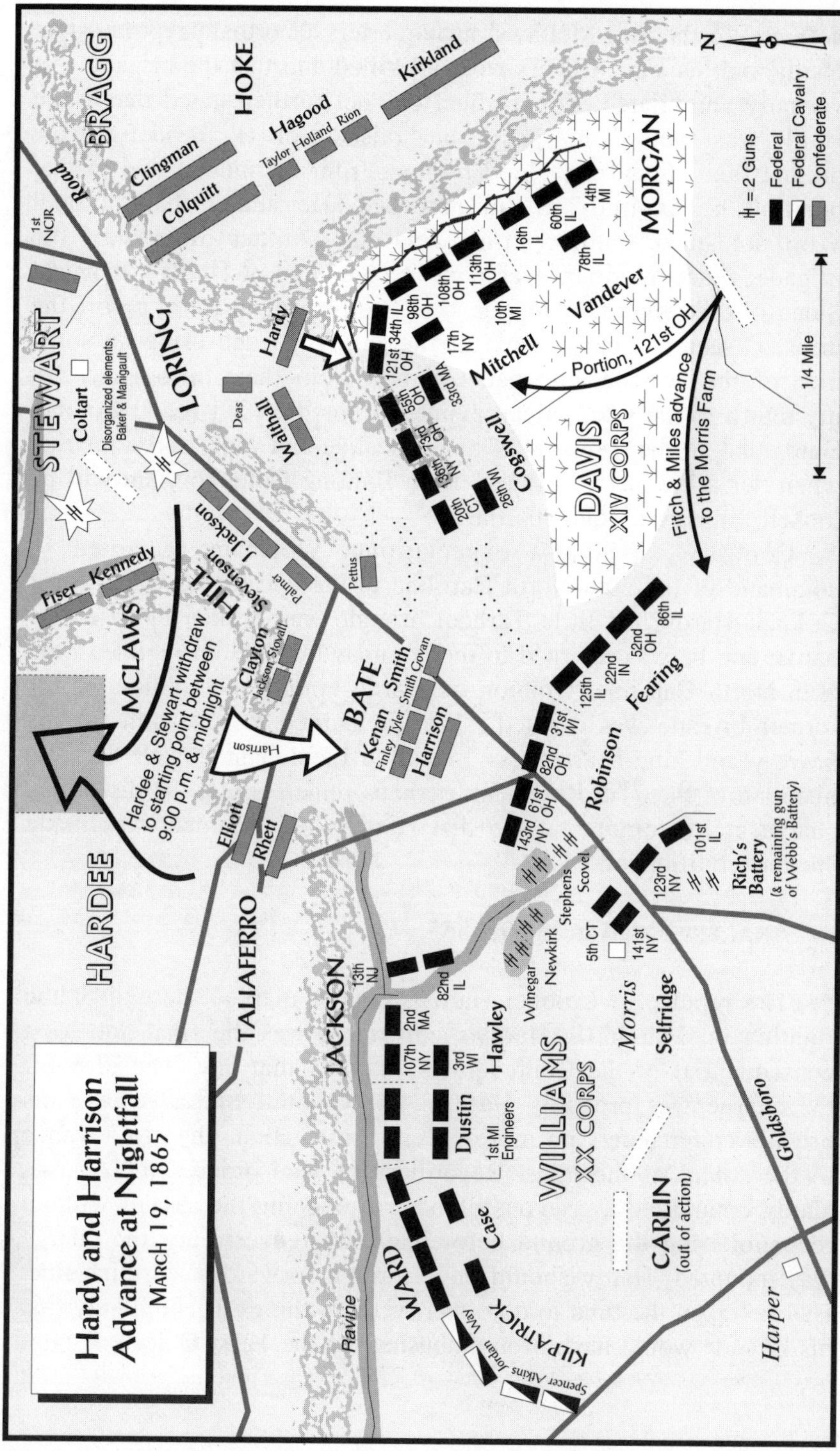

Hardy and Harrison
Advance at Nightfall
March 19, 1865
HARDEE
STEWART
LORING
BRAGG
HOKE
MCLAWS
HILL
BATE
TALIAFERRO
JACKSON
WILLIAMS
XX CORPS
DAVIS
XIV CORPS
MORGAN
CARLIN
(out of action)
KILPATRICK
WARD
Clingman
Colquitt
Hagood
Taylor Holland Rion
Kirkland
Road
1st NCJR
Coltart
Disorganized elements, Baker & Manigault
Deas
Hardy
Walthall
Pettus
Fiser
Kennedy
J. Jackson
Stevenson
Palmer
Clayton
Jackson Stovall
Kenan
Finley Tyler
Smith
Smith Govan
Harrison
Elliott
Rhett
Hardee & Stewart withdraw to starting point between 9:00 p.m. & midnight
34th IL
121st OH
98th OH
108th OH
113th OH
16th IL
60th IL
14th MI
78th IL
10th MI
17th NY
55th OH
33rd MA
73rd OH
136th NY
26th WI
20th CT
Mitchell
Vandever
Cogswell
Portion, 121st OH
Fitch & Miles advance to the Morris Farm
125th IL
22nd IN
52nd OH
86th IL
Fearing
31st WI
82nd OH
61st OH
143rd NY
Robinson
101st IL
123rd NY
Rich's Battery
(& remaining gun of Webb's Battery)
Scovel
Stephens
Newkirk
Winegar
5th CT
141st NY
Morris
Selfridge
13th NJ
82nd IL
2nd MA
107th NY
3rd WI
Hawley
Dustin
1st MI Engineers
Case
Ravine
Way
Jordan
Spencer Atkins
Goldsboro
Harper
N
= 2 Guns
Federal
Federal Cavalry
Confederate
1/4 Mile

Mark A. Moore

he met Wortham at McLaws' headquarters. Wortham reported that Hardy and his staff officers were all killed and that the brigade was virtually annihilated, The Tarheel colonel further stated that when Hardy was shot off his horse, he "raised Col. H's head from the ground [and] found the blood running from his mouth, and in that position he expired," Sloan recorded. He added that Colonel Wortham spun "similar yarns" relating to other officers of the brigade. Since Wortham was next in command of Hardy's Brigade, Sloan obeyed his order to ride back to the wagon train, report the disaster, secure some rations for the survivors, and bring up some men of the brigade who had returned from their furloughs. "On my return to the line," Sloan penned in his diary, "I found Colonel Hardy and all the members of his staff alive and well. I presume that when our army has a little rest from fighting Col. Wortham will be looked after by a court-martial."[8]

Contrary to Sloan's expectations, Wortham remained in command of the 50th North Carolina to the end of the war. As for Colonel Hardy, his little Tarheel brigade was broken up after the battle, and he was returned to the command of his old regiment, the 60th North Carolina. Opinion on Hardy among the soldiers of his former brigade was divided. "We all learned to love him for his bravery and kind-heartedness," recalled Lieutenant Powell. But the historian of the 77th Regiment, perhaps remembering the disastrous charge at Bentonville, wrote that Hardy's reassignment was made "to the gratification of all."[9]

Analysis of March 19, 1865

The repulse of Colonel Hardy's charge marked the end of the fighting on March 19. Hardy's movement was the final and least consequential of the Confederates' assaults that day. The idea for the charge was probably Hardy's, for General McLaws gave his brigade commanders no more specific instructions than to advance to the sound of the guns. Regardless of who ordered the charge, Hardy committed a grievous blunder in opening the assault without reconnoitering the ground beforehand. Moreover, once the charge was mounted, Hardy should have thrown forward a skirmish line. Had he taken the time to do either of these things, it is unlikely that his brigade would have been ambushed by the 121st Ohio.[10]

Lafayette McLaws' hands-off approach in regard to his division reflects the attitude of most of the Confederate high command at Bentonville, starting with General Johnston. "Old Joe" relegated himself to a secondary, though by no means unimportant, role—that of motivator. Numerous eyewitness accounts place Johnston nearly everywhere on the field praising and exhorting the men, who—particularly the veterans of the Army of Tennessee—responded with enthusiasm. For all his disappointment in the battle's outcome, Johnston saw Bentonville as a moral victory for his army. "One important object was gained," he wrote, "that of restoring the confidence of our troops. . . .All were greatly elated by the event." Though Johnston did much to motivate his troops, he left the work of maneuvering them to his subordinates, which, given their uneven combat record, was an unwise course.[11]

The foremost of these, at least in terms of rank, was Gen. Braxton Bragg. Johnston had retained Bragg against his better judgment: "It was a great weakness on my part, not to send him to Raleigh on the 18th [of March]," Johnston told Robert Hoke five years after the battle. Yet when Bragg pleaded (needlessly, as it turned out) for reinforcements, Johnston sent him McLaws' Division. And when Bragg failed to advance his wing—that is, Hoke's and McLaws' divisions—at the appointed hour, Johnston allowed Bragg to follow his own timetable. Bragg has been criticized on both accounts, but as Wade Hampton observed in the former case, responsibility for the decision to reinforce Bragg rested squarely on Johnston's shoulders. As for the latter case, if Bragg repeatedly failed to obey Johnston's orders to attack, as Johnston later claimed, then he should have removed Bragg from command and launched the attack himself. Such a move would have had no effect on Hoke's or McLaws' divisions, both of which were commanded by seasoned veterans. Yet like his fellow Virginian Robert E. Lee, Johnston was too much of a gentleman to have subjected even a disobedient subordinate to such humiliation.[12]

Bragg also received criticism from generals D. H. Hill and Johnson Hagood for failing to exploit Hoke's breakthrough on General Morgan's left flank. The two generals were no doubt referring to the collapse of General Mitchell's refused line that had been manned by some troops of Carlin's division and by the 121st Ohio of Mitchell's brigade. According to Hagood, when Bragg learned of Hoke's breakthrough, he directed Hoke to recall his troops and make a frontal assault instead. In his after-action report, D. H. Hill told much the same story, adding that he had heard it from General Hoke himself. Hill also stated that when the Federals saw that the right wing of Colquitt's Brigade of Hoke's Division had stolen around their flank, they threw down their weapons in surrender. But when Colquitt withdrew as ordered by Bragg, the Northerners snatched up their rifles and resumed the fight. Both Hagood and Hill implied that if Bragg had let Hoke exploit Colquitt's breakthrough, the day would have belonged to the Confederacy.[13]

Both Hill and Hagood were mistaken: the so-called "breakthrough" of Colquitt's Brigade was not the crippling blow they had supposed it to be. The 10th Michigan and the 17th New York of Vandever's brigade had been waiting in reserve when Carlin's fugitives and the 121st Ohio on the front line were routed, and were able to repulse Colquitt's assault. If Bragg ordered Colquitt's withdrawal, he did so *after* Colquitt's repulse. Furthermore, Hill had a double stake in making Bragg the scapegoat: to avenge his ill-treatment at Bragg's hands and to divert attention from the poor showing of his own command south of the Goldsboro Road.

Bragg's most serious blunder at Bentonville was in failing to utilize McLaws' Division while he had it. Had Bragg struck swiftly with Hoke's and McLaws' combined strength, Mitchell's and Vandever's isolated brigades probably would have been overwhelmed.

Johnston's other wing commander at Bentonville, Lt. Gen. William J. Hardee, has been criticized for delaying the Confederate grand assault by his late arrival on the field. This criticism is unfair. The head of Hardee's column arrived at Bentonville about 9:00 a.m., just as the Army of Tennessee began filing into position. If anyone is to blame for this delay, it is the Army of Tennessee's commander, Lt. Gen. A. P. Stewart, who should have ordered a reconnaissance of the area to uncover other routes to the battlefield.[14]

Hardee handled his wing, which consisted of Taliaferro's Division and the Army of Tennessee contingent, expertly during the early stages of the assault. Though Hardee delayed the attack a precious half-hour to deploy Taliaferro's troops, once he gave the signal his wing advanced rapidly and in good order. When the assault threatened to sputter out on the northern fringes of the Cole field, Hardee himself galloped into the field and led the way. Yet Hardee, Stewart and D. H. Hill must share responsibility for the inaction of the troops from Lee's Corps (under D. H. Hill's command) once they had settled into Fearing's abandoned works in rear of Morgan's line. The Confederates on this part of the field were all too eager to play the Federals' waiting game when they should have been assaulting Morgan's position. As wing commander, Hardee should have pressed the attack of Lee's Corps south of the Goldsboro Road. He did not do so, and in this he is culpable.

Like Bragg, Hardee also failed to utilize McLaws' Division when it was given to him, leaving McLaws to twiddle his thumbs until sundown. By then it was too late. Had McLaws reinforced Hoke or D. H. Hill or Bate about 4:00 p.m., the outcome might have been different. Instead, Hardee parceled out McLaws' brigades to all three commanders a full two hours later, with negligible results. An officer of Hardee's experience should have known better.[15]

Moreover, Hardee and Bragg failed to coordinate their attacks on Morgan's position. As historian Jay Luvaas noted: "On the whole Confederate staff work was faulty and the coordination between the individual commanders left much to be desired. This was doubtless due to the fact that Johnston's army was only recently organized and had never fought before as a unit."[16]

Lieutenant General Wade Hampton, Johnston's cavalry chief, deserves credit for delaying the Federal advance on the 18th, for selecting the battleground of the 19th and formulating the Confederates' excellent battle plan, and for screening the Confederate infantry's deployment on the 19th. Hampton was also correct in advising Johnston to deny Bragg's inopportune request for reinforcements and to open the assault without delay. Nevertheless, Hampton's cavalry missed out on the grand assault altogether. Hampton had intended to deploy his horsemen on the infantry's right flank, but with the exception of Dibrell's Division, which was exhausted from almost continual skirmishing over the past two days, he had no cavalry to deploy. Butler's Division was opposing the Federal Right Wing's advance twelve miles to the southeast, and the balance of Wheeler's Cavalry Corps was stranded on the north bank of Stone Creek about four miles north of Bentonville. Wheeler reported that Stone Creek could be forded at only one point. As for Mill Creek, which ran just above Bentonville, Wheeler found it unfordable. So much for Hampton's cavalry.[17]

As for Hampton's Federal counterpart, Maj. Gen. Judson Kilpatrick, the less said, the better. Kilpatrick's poor reconnaissance and rosy prognostications on March 18 caused Generals Sherman and Slocum to ignore the warnings of the foragers, who reported that the Confederates were massing along the Left Wing's front and left flank.

Of the Confederate generals, Maj. Gen. D. H. Hill seems to have been the most active, although this perception may spring from the fact that his after-action report is the most detailed one to come down to us. It is also one of only a handful that exist. Hill certainly never strayed far from the thick of it, judging from the four wounded staff officers he left in his wake. As if that weren't enough, Hill had loaned a fifth staff officer his horse, Magnus, who panicked and threw the unfortunate officer, bruising him badly. Yet fighting always suited Daniel Harvey Hill, who was able to write home: "I was sick. . .but the battle made me well."[18]

One of the most puzzling aspects of the March 19 battle was the absence of artillery support for Taliaferro's and Bate's commands prior to, or during, their assaults on the Federal position at Morris' farm. More surprising still, Maj. A. Burnet Rhett's artillery battalion, which was attached to Taliaferro's Division, remained in park some distance in rear of the battlefield and was never brought up. "This is the 4th fight which I have sat by & listened to, without being engaged, since I have been in artillery service," one of Rhett's cannoneers wrote his sister. "It is certainly a pretty safe arm."[19]

Several Union accounts mention that Confederate shot and shell fell on Morris' farm during the rout of Carlin's division, but there is not one reference to an enemy artillery projectile striking near the Union position on Morris' farm at any time during Bate's or Taliaferro's assaults. In short, the Federals were able to mass five batteries (for a total of 21 guns) in Reddick Morris' fields without fear of enemy counter-battery fire, and with the loss of only one artilleryman. Hardee and Taliaferro must bear the blame for failing to utilize Rhett's artillery battalion. The muddy terrain at Bentonville might have made a convenient excuse, except that the mud did not prevent the Federals from deploying their artillery.

The rising ground on the Morris farm provided the Federals with a natural rallying point, not only for Fearing's and Robinson's brigades, but for Carlin's division as well. Though Generals Buell and Hobart had rallied a portion of their respective brigades in a field several hundred yards in rear of the XX Corps line, stragglers continued to wander in throughout the night and into the next day. The units of Carlin's division that had initially deployed south of the Goldsboro Road, namely Fitch's wing of Hobart's brigade and Miles' brigade, rejoined the division later that evening. But what had become of the division's commander, General Carlin?[20]

Carlin became separated from his command the moment Buell's line fell back, and made his escape through the ravine in rear of Buell's works. The remainder of Carlin's tale borders on the ludicrous. Happening upon a squad of eight soldiers from the 31st Wisconsin of Robinson's brigade, Carlin suggested that they adopt "the Chinese system of noise" to delay the Confederate advance. "In accordance with this idea," Carlin wrote, "I commanded this squad of men to form into line, and proceeded to give commands in my loudest voice, as if maneuvering a battalion, but the system did not work well on the enemy. They continued to advance regardless of my commands and of the firing of my little squad." So Carlin dismissed his band and resumed his retreat, heading in the direction of the Goldsboro Road.[21]

On the way, Carlin nearly collided with a Confederate line of battle. A mounted officer in gray spotted Carlin and rode toward him, "muttering strange words which I did not understand," the Federal brigadier recalled. Carlin nevertheless understood that the officer meant business, for "he carried a huge horse pistol, which was leveled directly at me." Carlin backed into the woods, and to his immense relief, the Rebel officer lowered his pistol and rode back to his command.

Stepping into the road, Carlin noticed a pair of battery horses tied to an oak tree. He smiled as he imagined himself, dressed in his best uniform, riding a fully harnessed horse without saddle into friendly lines. But he found the thought of rotting away in a Rebel prison even less appealing, and "resolved to brave the laughter." Carlin tried to untie the horses, but it "proved to be a very difficult operation." After tugging away at the harnesses for a few minutes, Carlin glanced down the Goldsboro Road and saw the enemy's line of battle advancing toward him. The hapless brigadier abandoned the idea of riding, but by now was so exhausted that his pace was reduced to a walk. Fortunately for him, General Robinson's line loomed just ahead. An overjoyed Carlin met Col. Francis West of the 31st Wisconsin by the roadside and warned him that the enemy was approaching. When Carlin reached his division, he found all his staff and his horse Rosy safe and sound. Carlin asked Buell to explain why he had withdrawn his brigade on his own responsibility. Buell replied that he had done so because the enemy had overlapped his left flank and would soon have enveloped it entirely if he had remained. Buell's answer appeared to satisfy Carlin, who let the matter rest—that is, until 17 years later.[22]

In response to Alexander McClurg's *Atlantic Monthly* article entitled, "The Last Chance of the Confederacy," Carlin penned his own account of the Battle of Bentonville, which appeared in the Cincinnati *Daily Gazette* on September 11, 1882. In this letter and in subsequent writings, Carlin sought to make General Buell the scapegoat for the rout of his division at Bentonville. Carlin accused Buell of retreating "without awaiting to receive the charge, solely on account of [Taliaferro's] flanking force." Carlin also faulted Buell for withdrawing his brigade on his own responsibility. In making his case against Buell, Carlin ignored two important facts. First, Briant's wing of Hobart's brigade actually gave way *before* Buell's brigade, and second, by the time Buell gave the order to withdraw, Taliaferro's Division had nearly cut off his line of retreat. Furthermore, in his after-action report, Carlin credited Buell's brigade with holding its position until both of its flanks were turned and it was forced to retreat. In a letter written to a former subordinate several months after the battle, Carlin stated: "Had my troops on the left [that is, north] of the [Goldsboro] road held their position longer than they did, they would have been crushed by superior numbers."[23]

Nor can Carlin be blamed for the rout of his division. Having received conflicting orders from Davis and Slocum on the afternoon of the 19th, it is hardly surprising that Carlin chose a third course—that of holding his position and strengthening it. Had Carlin withdrawn behind the ravine as Slocum's engineering officer, Lieutenant Ludlow, had suggested, he would have exposed his right flank to the fire of Hoke's Division, which was what had driven Briant's wing across the ravine in the first place.

Who, then, was responsible for the rout of Carlin's division? In his study *The March to the Sea,* Jacob Cox pointed an accusing finger at Slocum. Cox wondered whether it was wise to deploy the two XIV Corps divisions "upon the line of the advanced [that is, Hobart's] brigade when it came in contact with an entrenched infantry line, and when the best information showed all of Johnston's army present." Slocum later admitted that he was slow to grasp the true situation. By the time he did, it was too late for him to implement Cox's corollary suggestion: "It would seem to be better to have placed Morgan's division and two of Carlin's brigades upon the line near the Morris house. . .and to have withdrawn Hobart's brigade to the same point." Had Slocum done this, Cox reasoned, Johnston would have been forced to pursue him through more than a mile of swamps and thickets, only to confront the Federals' strong fortifications with his own badly disjointed line. As it was, Slocum believed that a defense in depth was the best course open to him. He left Davis' two divisions at the front to absorb the shock of the Rebel assault while the XX Corps established its line on the Morris farm. Slocum's plan worked, although it resulted in the sacrifice of Carlin's division.[24]

Although Slocum was slow to shift to the defensive, once he did so, the deployment of the XX Corps line on the Morris farm was swift and effective. Slocum deserves credit for selecting a strong defensive position, and General Williams for speeding his two XX Corps divisions and three artillery batteries to the front. Fearing's spoiling attack bought valuable time for the XX Corps' deployment by stalling the Confederates' westward advance along the Goldsboro Road. Davis' decision to uncover the rear of Morgan's position by ordering Fearing's attack could have spelled disaster for Mitchell and Vandever, but it was a calculated risk that succeeded. Davis made the best decision possible under the circumstances. Even if Mitchell and Vandever had been crushed, the XX Corps line would have been strong enough to hold off Johnston's army until the arrival of the Federal Right Wing.

In the end, Morgan's line held while Carlin's crumbled. General Carlin found the dichotomy unfathomable. Captain Theo Wiseman, Morgan's adjutant, recalled a conversation that he had with Carlin on the morning of March 20. Wiseman found Carlin "sitting under a tree beside the road. . .looking sad at the mishap of his gallant division the day previous." After wondering aloud why his division had been routed, Carlin asked, "How was it that Morgan's Division stayed in there?"[25]

Morgan's troops, that is, Vandever's and Mitchell's brigades, "stayed in there" for at least five reasons. First, they had sufficient time to build strong log works. Carlin later remarked, with ample justification, that these works "proved of immense value to Sherman's army, and probably to Sherman's reputation." Second, Morgan and his two brigade commanders, Generals Vandever and Mitchell, made excellent preparations for the Confederate assault on Mitchell's vulnerable left flank, first in refusing and fortifying it, then, in shifting the 10th Michigan and 17th New York to within supporting distance of it. Third, Morgan's subordinates—General Mitchell, Lieutenant Colonel Grummond of the 14th Michigan and Captain Dunphy of the 10th Michigan, foremost among them—provided strong leadership on a front in which their troops could see no further than several yards in any direction. "We believe we owe our light loss greatly to the skill and care of our officers," a soldier in the 10th Michigan wrote to his hometown paper. Fourth, Morgan's troops were self-reliant veterans who continued to fight even when they appeared to be surrounded, the enemy's bullets zipping past them from all sides. Fifth, as stated earlier, the Confederates of Lee's Corps who stole into the rear of Morgan's position accommodated the Federals by not attacking when the opportunity presented itself. Though Fearing's spoiling attack blunted the Southerners' momentum, Fearing's subsequent retreat left the back door open for D. H. Hill's command.[26]

Both Carlin and Morgan were promoted to major general by brevet following the battle, and ironically, both promotions bear the date of March 19, 1865. The date of these two promotions is significant, for it indicates that Carlin and Morgan were both being rewarded for services rendered in the Battle of Bentonville. Carlin's promotion, though well-deserved, should have fallen on any other day than March 19, for its timing mocks Morgan's brave stand south of the Goldsboro Road. Carlin received his promotion while at home on sick leave, having fallen ill just after the battle. The promotion was little more than a symbolic gesture, for Carlin was without a post, having resigned his command of the First Division, XIV Corps. Carlin soon regretted his decision, and appealed to Sherman for another command. In a letter to Sherman, Carlin confessed that he had resigned because he feared that Davis was waiting for a chance to ruin his reputation, thereby conceding that the rout of his division at Bentonville would have given Davis such an opportunity. It is unknown whether Carlin ever received a reply from Sherman. In any case, Carlin soon received orders to report for duty in western Virginia.[27]

The Battle of Bentonville haunted Carlin for the rest of his life. In his writings on the battle, he sought to absolve himself of all blame for the rout, and rightly so. Yet in the process he struck a false note or two, particularly in his contention that he had tried to warn Davis and Sherman of the impending battle. Several eyewitness accounts portray a different Carlin, one who was confident that he could "drive the rebels out with a skirmish line." In later years Carlin never could come to grips with the fact that he had simply been unlucky at Bentonville. In the opinion of Captain Wiseman, "There was not a division of veteran troops in Sherman's army but would have given way same as Carlin's men did under the same circumstances."[28]

The rout of Carlin's division led the men of the XX Corps to refer to the fight as the "Battle of Acorn Run," in mock tribute to the XIV Corps' official insignia. "[F]or some time after[,] all that was necessary to make a member of that corps fighting mad was to mention Acorn Run," recalled one XX Corps veteran.[29]

In the end, the Confederate grand assault, which had begun so promisingly, came to grief because Johnston hadn't enough men to exploit his initial success. Had Johnston struck earlier, say at 11:00 a.m., while Morgan was deploying and before Carlin was ready to attack, he might have driven in the XIV Corps upon the XX Corps as it was advancing up the Goldsboro Road. But as Jay Luvaas observed, even if Johnston *had* crushed Slocum's wing, he still would have had to contend with Howard's wing and the forces under Terry and Schofield—without the advantage of surprise.[30]

The March 19 battle ended in a draw. Slocum's decision to shift to the defensive ensured that outcome. Although the Federals later insisted that they were heavily outnumbered, by late afternoon they had about 20,000 men on the battlefield, compared to the Confederates' 16,000. Casualty figures for the March 19 battle are sketchy, yet the losses on both sides can be estimated with a fair degree of accuracy. It is safe to fix Slocum's losses at about 1,100, given that most of his 1,144 total casualties occurred during the first day's fighting. Confederate casualties numbered about 2,000. The disparity in losses is to be expected, since the Confederate army was the predominant aggressor and failed to overwhelm the Federals, most of whom enjoyed strong defensive positions and excellent artillery support.[31]

* * *

With the day's fighting at an end, it remained for the two armies to care for their wounded and bury their dead. "This is the first time I have seen a regular fight; it looked fine but the result looks bad," Union stretcher bearer William Humphrey noted in his diary. "All over the woods could be seen officers & men with pine torches in their hands seeking after some fallen comrade or friend to take him to the hospital if alive & bury him if dead, a sad & weary task!" wrote Lt. Col. Philo Buckingham of the 20th Connecticut, Cogswell's brigade. "First our own & then the rebel wounded & dead were cared for. . . .You could have walked without stepping on the ground on the dead bodies that marked where [the Rebel] line was."[32]

Of Cogswell's 137 casualties, 13 were killed, 115 were wounded, and nine were missing. None of those casualties was more anxiously watched over that night than Cpl. Abner C. Smith of the 20th Connecticut. Corporal Smith had been wounded at the close of the fight, and his friend and tent-mate of three years, Cpl. Horatio Chapman, was therefore permitted to leave the ranks and help carry Smith to the XX Corps field hospital. Chapman described his friend's wound: "A minie ball had entered his right leg near the thigh and passed down and came out on the opposite side just above the knee. . .shattering the bone all to pieces. His leg was immediately amputated and he was laid in a tent on some straw." Chapman stayed with his friend "until the effects of the ether passed off," he recorded, and then returned to his regiment "feeling very sad at the loss of my tent-mate and brave comrade."[33]

On March 23 Corporal Smith wrote home to his family, telling his children: "I am thankful to God that I am so well as I am. I would have you be good children till I see you again of which I hope won't be long. May God in his mercy spare us all to meet again once more in the flesh." Five days later Smith was dead.[34]

By midnight Cogswell's troops had completed the task of burying the dead and carrying off the wounded. Thereafter, General Cogswell ordered his brigade to withdraw behind the swamp and entrench. Within an hour the men finished their works, and those not on picket duty fell into an exhausted sleep.[35]

The work of treating the XIV Corps wounded at the Harper house continued throughout the night of the 19th and the morning of the 20th. Fourteenth Corps medical director Waldo Daniels estimated that "about 500 men were brought in and operated on or dressed during that night and the next morning." Lieutenant Colonel William Douglas Hamilton of the 9th Ohio Cavalry visited the makeshift hospital, which he thought "resembled a slaughter house. A dozen surgeons and attendants in their shirt sleeves stood at rude benches cutting off arms and legs and throwing them out of the windows, where they lay scattered on the grass."[36]

Lieutenant Colonel Hamilton entered a room of the house that was "filled with the severely wounded whose moans and cries were heart-rending. . . .I noticed one poor boy covered with blood which was flowing from a cruel wound in his breast. . . .Amidst the confusion of sounds I heard him calling plaintively for his mother and Jesus in turns. . . .When I returned his eyes were closed and all was still."[37]

During the battle John Harper, 62, his wife Amy, 45, and six of their nine children occupied the upper story of their home. The Harper children ranged in age from 9 to 26. Two of the three eldest Harper sons, Martin and Henry, were away in the Confederate army. The third, John James, lived in Bentonville and was the preacher at nearby Mill Creek Christian Church. For the Harpers and many other families living in and around Bentonville, the battle was only the beginning of their long ordeal.[38]

Lieutenant Marcus Bates, the young officer of the 21st Michigan who had been wounded during the rout of Carlin's division, awoke on the morning of March 20 to find himself lying in a tent filled with wounded men. Bates noticed that the man on his left was dead. Division surgeon Dr. Goodale greeted Bates with a cheery, "Good morning," and asked the lieutenant how he felt. "I don't know what answer I made him," Bates wrote. "I was conscious that I was in a critical condition, and thought of my dear ones at home, thankful that I still had a fighting chance for life." Yet the comments of his friends and doctors were less than encouraging. After examining Bates' wound, Chief Surgeon Waldo Daniels remarked, "Nothing more can be done for him." Following a visit from several of his comrades, Bates overheard one of them say outside his tent that it was a shame they would have to leave him behind. "I knew my chances were slim," Bates wrote. "I remember recording a vow that I would not fill a North Carolina grave then, and I think that resolution saved me."[39]

At Bentonville Confederate surgeons worked all night amputating the shattered limbs of wounded soldiers, and were still hard at work the next morning. "The poor [boys] who were wounded are now while I am writing laying all around me on the ground suffering and bleeding," hospital steward Albert Quincy Porter noted in his diary. "Oh how I do feel for them."[40]

The highest-ranking Confederate casualty was Brig. Gen. Daniel H. Reynolds, whose mangled leg was amputated just above the knee by Dr. John T. Darby, medical director of the Army of Tennessee. At 8:00 a.m. on the 20th, Reynolds was placed on a litter, lifted into an ambulance, and jolted for 15 miles over a series of terribly cut-up roads. For Reynolds and his fellow passengers, the pain must have been excruciating. The general's ambulance arrived at Mitchener's Station just after dark, where he was put on a train bound for Raleigh. Reynolds arrived in Raleigh at 11:30 p.m., but it was 1:30 a.m. on the 21st before he was finally taken from his litter and placed in a bed at the officers' hospital. "[I]t was a day of great suffering to me," Reynolds noted. Yet the general was among the more fortunate of the Confederate wounded, many of whom died before they could be properly cared for.[41]

Sergeant John Curry of the 40th Alabama, Baker's Brigade, had been suffering from a chill since March 18, and was therefore permitted to fall out of ranks and march at his own pace. When Curry reached the battlefield on the morning of the 19th, he was unable to find his regiment, and so fell in with the nearest unit at hand—the 54th Virginia of Palmer's Brigade. Once the battle was over, Curry obtained permission to rejoin his command. Somehow he found a section of ground over which the 40th Alabama had fought. Beneath his feet, and partially concealed behind a log, lay the body of the 40th's adjutant, E. H. Ellerby. Curry heard the groans of the wounded on every side. After much searching, he located two of his comrades, David Morrow and Wiley Horton. Morrow had been shot in the body, and Horton in the leg. Curry noted that the two men must have waded a swamp, for they were soaked to the skin. "It was a sad spectacle," Curry wrote. "Morrow's sufferings were intense and his groans made the more so, because his being harelipped, were very touching indeed." Curry dragged Horton up beside Morrow and built a fire to warm his two shivering comrades. Early the next morning stretcher bearers arrived to carry Morrow and Horton to a waiting ambulance. Although Curry was now suffering from a raging fever, he refused the stretcher bearers' offer of assistance. Curry recovered and later learned that both had died, Morrow on the way to the field hospital, and Horton following the amputation of his leg.[42]

Color bearer W. A. Johnson of the 2nd South Carolina, Conner's Brigade, was examining the various bullet holes in his clothing when he heard a familiar voice call his name. He turned around and faced his brother, whom he had not seen in more than two years. Johnson's brother, a member of Stovall's Brigade, was bivouacked no more than 15 paces from him, and had recognized him in the firelight. "So I was reconciled to the left oblique business at last," Johnson wrote, referring to the 2nd South Carolina's misadventures below the Goldsboro Road. "[B]ut for this I would never have camped where I did, and of course would not have had the joyous meeting which I did."[43]

On the eastern edge of the Morris farm, Taliaferro's troops endured a steady shelling from the Federal artillery for several hours after the battle. "Here could have been seen what civilians consider a phenomenon—men sleeping on a battle-field [while] under fire," recalled Cpl. A. P. Ford of Elliott's Brigade. "Old soldiers understand this, and know that it is very common. Some of the men, worn [out] by fatigue, while lying down in line actually went to sleep, philosophically indifferent to the shells that were tearing through the trees, bursting over their heads, and occasionally causing casualties." Far more disturbing were the cries and groans of the wounded who had fallen in the assaults across the Morris field. "Some of these men were brought off," Ford wrote, "but others could not be reached, and died where they fell." Mingling with the cries of the wounded men were the screams of the wounded horses, which Ford found "particularly distressing."[44]

Between 9:00 p.m. and midnight, the Confederates withdrew to their jumping-off point, having borne off their wounded and buried most of their dead. The hapless soldiers of Elliott's Brigade became lost and did not reach their position on Bate's right until 2:30 a.m.[45]

After the battle, Slocum ordered his tent fly pitched near the Morris house. He had sent four couriers to Sherman during the day, and now he could only hold his position and wait for a reply. Of Slocum's three written messages to Sherman, the first two are almost casual in tone: "I hope you will come up on their left rear in strong force," Slocum wrote at 1:30 p.m. "I think a portion of the Right Wing should be brought forward at once," he requested a half-hour later. But the urgency of Slocum's final appeal is unmistakable: "I deem it of the greatest importance that the Right Wing come up during the night to my assistance." A far cry indeed from Slocum's first message to Sherman, in which he assured his chief that there was nothing more in his front than some stubborn Rebel cavalry.[46]

Major James Taylor Holmes spent a sleepless night on the front line with his regiment, the 52nd Ohio of Fearing's brigade. After yielding the advance to Carlin's division on the morning of the 19th, Major Holmes and his detachment of foragers were ordered to form on the extreme left of the Union line. As the firing along the front intensified, Holmes repeatedly asked permission to report to the 52nd Ohio. Each time Holmes' request was denied. At nightfall Holmes was finally permitted to rejoin his regiment. He was thoroughly disgusted. Thirty-six years later, Holmes still smarted from Carlin's snub:

> [T]he general who waded in with his division, with his nose in the air, saying to me, "get your men out of my way[,]" and whose division "got it in the neck". . . .wrote and published a glowing account of his generalship and achievements that morning. If I am spared to write it, I propose to tell the truth in a sketch of what I know of Bentonville, and to skin that general's published lies and distortions so that their father, if living, will not know them.[47]

Holmes never found the time to write his sketch, and no doubt went to his grave believing that "if some generals," meaning Morgan and Fearing, "had not been overwise and had listened to the facts and opinion which I promptly and carefully delivered to them on the evening of the 18th, Bentonville would have had a different history and many a good soldier would now be living whose bones are dust."[48]

~ *fourteen* ~

"The Army Is Coming to You as Fast as Possible"

—William T. Sherman

At 10:00 a.m. on March 19, General Howard and his staff heard the unmistakable sound of cannon fire coming from somewhere to their left and rear. The booming of the guns reminded Lt. Col. William E. Strong of the "rumbling of thunder low down in the sky." They continued to ride eastward down the new Goldsboro Road, away from the firing. Their route lay about five miles south of Slocum's.

"Hampton is pitching into Kilpatrick again," joked one staff officer. "He ought to be generous this time and leave him his boots and shirt." Howard and nearly everyone on his staff agreed that the cannon fire indicated "nothing more than a spirited cavalry engagement," Strong noted.

Twenty minutes later they reached the fork at Falling Creek Church, where the new Goldsboro Road entered the Wilmington Road. The general and his staff drew rein while Lieutenant Colonel Strong rode up to the signboard and read aloud: "12 miles to Goldsboro via State Bridge and 13 miles via Cox's Bridge." (The State Bridge and Cox's Bridge were the two crossings of the Neuse River below Goldsboro.) Strong added that the head of Slocum's column was due to arrive at Cox's Bridge by day's end. The officers again heard the distant rumbling, but this time it was louder and more distinct. Strong took out his watch: it was 10:20 a.m. "From that moment till long after sunset," he later recorded, "the sounds of distant battle never ceased."[1]

Howard decided to halt at Falling Creek Church to enable his column to catch up. For an hour or more the rumbling of artillery fire rose in a steady crescendo. At 11:30 a.m. the van of the XV Corps' column, consisting of Col. Clark R. Wever's brigade of Maj. Gen. John E. Smith's division, reached Falling Creek Church. Howard rode back a few miles to see how the rest of Smith's division was faring, and found Brig. Gen. William T. Clark's brigade snarled at the ford across Falling Creek. The ford was badly cut up by the crossing of Wever's brigade, and Clark's troops were hard at work corduroying the creek bottom when Howard rode up.[2]

The distant cannonade grew still louder. Howard and his staff now feared that Slocum was involved in a pitched battle. It was noon when Howard decided to act. He sent Maj. Thomas Osborn to the rear of the column to direct Maj. Gen. William B. Hazen's division to Slocum's support, and to inform Slocum that he "should call on the XV Corps for all the troops he might wish." Howard then ordered Lieutenant Colonel Strong to take his cavalry escort and secure Cox's Crossroads, where the Wilmington Road and the "old" Goldsboro Road intersected. Howard also sent Captain Duncan's scouts and the 7th Illinois Mounted Infantry to the State Bridge to determine whether the enemy held it in force.[3]

Major Osborn had ridden back about two miles when he met General Sherman, who told Osborn that he had just heard from Slocum. Sherman said that Slocum had run into Dibrell's cavalry, which he was driving back easily, and that there would be no need for Osborn to divert any XV Corps troops to Slocum's assistance. Sherman also said that he was on his way to meet Howard and that Osborn might as well join him. Osborn declined, replying that he had better "go on and see how the column was getting over the road." Major Osborn soon overtook Maj. Eugene Guindon, who was returning to Slocum after having delivered his message to Sherman. Guindon told Osborn that the Left Wing was driving the enemy toward Cox's Bridge, and suggested that the Right Wing seize the crossroads one mile south of the bridge and thereby cut off the Rebels' retreat. Guindon's message indicates that Slocum was still unaware of the Confederates' approach route to Bentonville. Osborn decided to heed Guindon's suggestion: "As General Howard had made my movement discretionary," he recorded, "I thought the best thing to be done was to hurry up the whole [XV] Corps to the front, as the head of column was only three or four miles from Cox's Bridge."[4]

Meanwhile, Lieutenant Colonel Strong and his mounted force narrowly averted disaster at Cox's Crossroads, the same crossroads that Major Guindon had suggested seizing. Strong ran into the enemy's videttes less than a mile from Falling Creek Church and drove them back on the main body of Confederate cavalry, about 250 troopers from Butler's Brigade of South Carolinians. The Rebels swooped down on Strong's small force and by the Yankee lieutenant colonel's own admission, the Federals barely escaped capture. Not to be undone by this setback, Strong galloped back to Falling Creek Church and asked Howard for an infantry regiment. Strong returned to the crossroads at the head of the 10th Iowa of Wever's brigade, the regiment numbering 350 effectives. When he came to within three-fourths of a mile of the crossroads, Strong threw out two companies as skirmishers and deployed the rest of the 10th in line of battle. The Iowans advanced under a heavy fire on the South Carolinians, who were lined up behind a fence-rail barricade. When the Federal skirmishers dashed up to within 150 yards of the barricade, the Confederate troopers broke for the rear. According to Lieutenant Colonel Strong's watch, the 10th Iowa secured the crossroads at precisely 4:00 p.m.[5]

* * *

As Sherman and his staff rode past the stalled column of Clark's brigade, the 4th Minnesota's brass band struck up "Hail to the Chief." The general doffed his hat as he rode by, reaching Howard's camp at Falling Creek Church about 2:00 p.m., and reporting that the XV Corps' column stretched back to Blackman Lee's store, a distance of 15 miles. Sherman also allayed Howard's fears concerning the noise coming from Slocum's direction, but said nothing about his having countermanded Howard's orders to Major Osborn (Sherman's failure to do so would later cause Osborn a few moments of embarrassment). Captain Duncan returned later that afternoon and reported that after a brief skirmish the enemy retreated, burning both the State Bridge and the adjacent railroad bridge. Lieutenant Colonel Strong informed Howard that he had

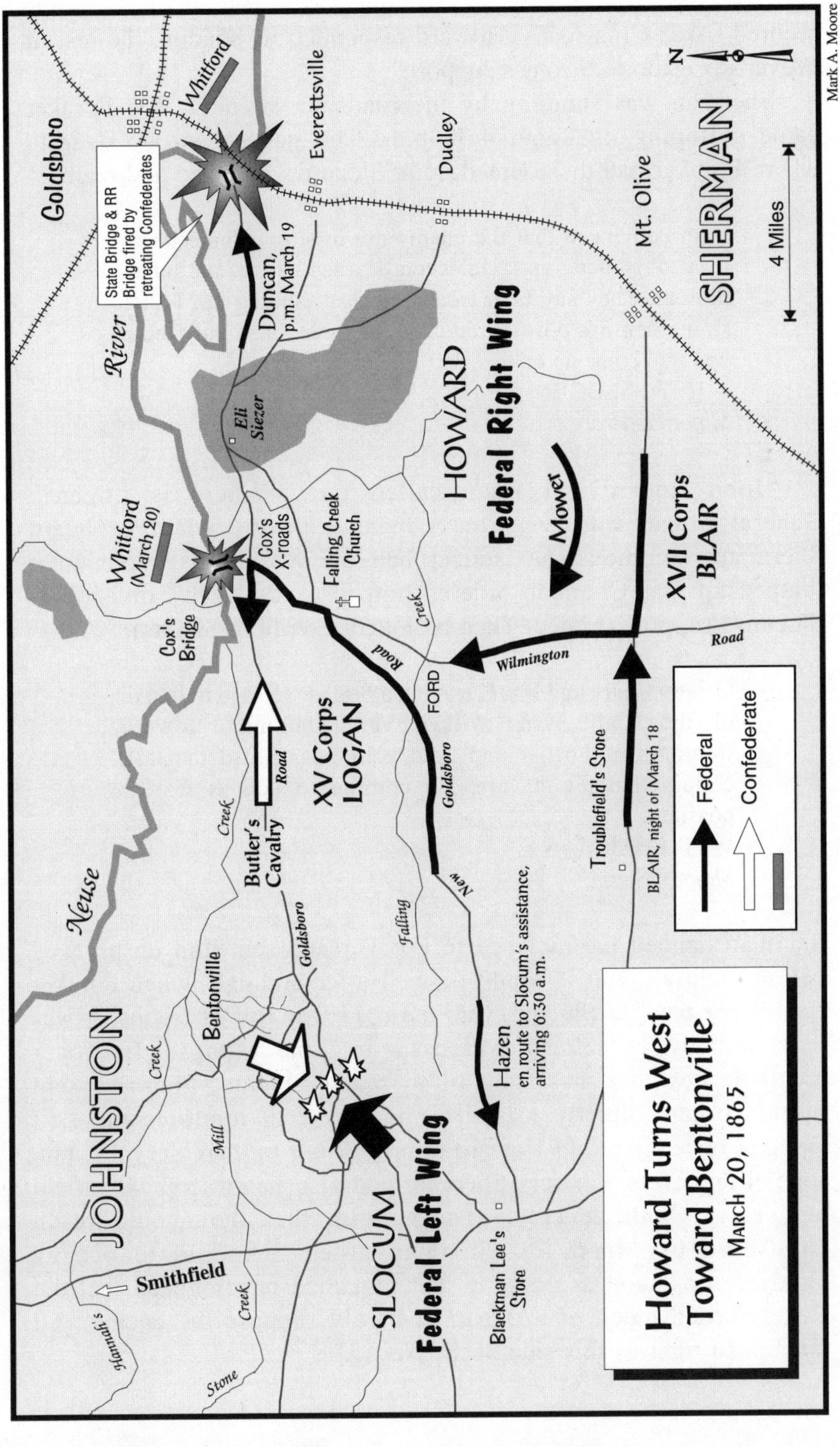
Howard Turns West
Toward Bentonville
March 20, 1865
Goldsboro
Whitford
State Bridge & RR Bridge fired by retreating Confederates
Everettsville
Dudley
Mt. Olive
SHERMAN
4 Miles
N
River
Duncan, p.m. March 19
Eli Siezer
HOWARD
Federal Right Wing
Mowet
XVII Corps
BLAIR
Whitford (March 20)
Cox's X-roads
Falling Creek Church
Cox's Bridge
Creek
Road
Wilmington
Road
FORD
Goldsboro
New
XV Corps
LOGAN
Butler's Cavalry
Road
Troublefield's Store
BLAIR, night of March 18
Federal
Confederate
Neuse
Creek
Goldsboro
Falling
Bentonville
JOHNSTON
Creek
Mill
Hazen
en route to Slocum's assistance, arriving 6:30 a.m.
SLOCUM
Federal Left Wing
Blackman Lee's Store
Smithfield
Hannah's
Creek
Stone

Mark A. Moore

secured Cox's Crossroads. Howard responded by sending the rest of Wever's brigade to Strong's support.[6]

Sherman was standing by the roadside when Lt. Joe Foraker came galloping up about 4:30 p.m. The general strode over to where Foraker had dismounted, took Slocum's message and read:

> I am convinced that the enemy are in strong force in my front. Prisoners report Johnston, Hardee, Hoke, and others present. They say their troops are just coming up. I shall strengthen my position and feel of their lines, but I hope you will come up on their left rear in strong force.
> —H. W. SLOCUM
> *Major-General*[7]

"John Logan!" Sherman called out. "Where is Logan?" General Logan was lying on a blanket nearby when he heard Sherman's summons. No sooner had the XV Corps commander jumped up than Sherman ordered him to send Hazen's division to Slocum's support at once. Then he jotted a reply to Slocum:

> Call up Geary and Baird, leaving a brigade to each train. All of the Right Wing will move at moonrise toward Bentonville. Fortify and hold your position to the last, certain that all the army is coming to you as fast as possible.
> W. T. SHERMAN
> *Major-General*

Sherman handed the message to Foraker and sent him on his way before nightfall. But it would be well after midnight when Foraker finally got back to Slocum, for "the road was full of troops, it was dark and my 'horseflesh' was used up!" the young staff officer recalled. Lest his message fail to reach Slocum, Sherman sent written orders directly to Baird and Geary to reinforce the Left Wing at once, then told Howard to order Blair to march at 3:00 a.m. for Falling Creek Church. Sherman had also heard from Schofield and Terry, both generals assuring him that they could reach Goldsboro by March 21. Sherman urged Schofield to occupy Goldsboro as soon as possible, but remained unconvinced that the Rebels posed much of a threat: "I hardly suppose the enemy will attempt to fight us this side of the Neuse."[8]

When Major Osborn reached camp that evening, he found General Howard waiting for him. Howard "was a good deal disappointed" when Osborn told him that he had neither sent Hazen's division to the Left Wing's assistance nor gone to see Slocum. Realizing that Sherman must not have told Howard about countermanding his order, Osborn explained the situation, to which Sherman interjected, "Yes, I told him so." Howard thereupon let the matter drop, and Osborn felt much relieved to be off the hook.[9]

Because of the poor condition of the roads, Sherman's headquarters wagons had not yet arrived, so Howard invited him to share his mess and tent. At 9:30 p.m. a staff officer galloped into Howard's camp. Leaping off his horse, he asked the nearest soldier to show him the way to Sherman. The officer said that he was Major Guindon from Slocum's headquarters. This time Guindon had a different tale to tell Sherman than the one he had told earlier in the day. Howard's staff officers gathered around Guindon as he recounted the events of the battle just fought near Bentonville.

Hearing the hubbub, Sherman emerged from Howard's tent. Lieutenant Colonel Strong described his appearance:

> The Commander-in-Chief would have made a good subject for "Punch" or "Vanity Fair." Every officer present was nearly bursting with laughter at [Sherman's] ludicrous appearance. . . .[B]eing of course anxious to hear the news of the fight [he] rushed out to the camp fire without stopping to put on his clothes. He stood in a bed of ashes up to his ankles, chewing impatiently the stump of a cigar, with his hands clasped behind him and with nothing on but a red flannel undershirt and a pair of drawers.[10]

Major Guindon reported that Johnston's army had routed Carlin's division of the XIV Corps, but that Morgan's division was holding its own, though hard pressed. The Rebels had made four assaults on the XX Corps' line, Guindon added. Each time they had been handsomely repulsed, but they were making another charge when he left the battlefield about 5:00 p.m. Guindon informed Sherman that Slocum estimated he was facing at least 45,000 enemy troops, and that he could not hold them without reinforcements from the Right Wing.

It was about 2:00 a.m. when Lt. Col. Charles Asmussen dashed into camp with the message Sherman and everyone else had been waiting for: *Slocum's line had held.* General Logan's troops briefly celebrated the good news, then returned to their bedrolls, mindful that they were scheduled to move out before sunrise.[11]

That night, Capt. John Alexander of the 97th Indiana commanded a XV Corps picket post. "[W]e knew we were close to the enemy," Alexander wrote, "for by putting our ears to the ground we could hear the tramping of the[ir] horses and the rattling of their sabers." A squad of the 6th Iowa had gone on picket duty "with the enemy in full view at rifle range," recalled Lt. Henry H. Wright. "Picket firing was kept up until a late hour, with several shells from the enemy's guns passing over [our] camps."[12]

Promptly at 5:00 a.m. Colonel Wever's brigade, with a section of Lt. Edward B. Wright's battery (Battery B, 1st Michigan) in tow, advanced on Cox's Bridge, which was held by Col. John N. Whitford's North Carolina Brigade and a battery from Starr's Battalion of artillery. Whitford's orders were to delay the Federal advance for as long as possible, then burn the bridge to prevent the enemy from crossing and thereby threatening both Goldsboro and Johnston's line of retreat at Bentonville. Wever's orders were to seize the bridge or, failing that, to force the enemy to burn it. Either way, Wever would deny the Rebels their only remaining crossing in rear of the Right Wing's column. Seldom during the war had Federal and Confederate objectives been so much in accord.[13]

Colonel Wever's task was far from routine. For nearly a mile the road to the bridge was flanked on either side by a deep swamp and was swept by Colonel Whitford's artillery. Furthermore, Whitford had deployed his thousand-man force wisely, posting his skirmishers in the swamp and two stronger lines at the bridge, one on the north bank and the other on the south. Worse yet for the Federals, the swamp prevented Lieutenant Wright's two 3-inch ordnance rifles from being maneuvered into effective firing range.[14]

After skirmishing with Whitford's North Carolinians for about an hour, Wever's plucky Westerners drove them across Cox's Bridge, which the Tarheels set afire to prevent its falling into Yankee hands. The troops on both sides watched it burn, each side thoroughly satisfied that it had accomplished its mission. By 7:45 a.m. the bridge was little more than a pile of cinders. The Confederates withdrew, the Federals took possession, and in the words of division commander John Smith, his men "completed the work of destruction."[15]

While Wever's brigade was thus occupied, the advance of Woods' division was rounding the corner at Cox's Crossroads a mile to the south, and heading west on the Goldsboro Road. General Woods' troops had risen early that morning to clean their rifles and refill their cartridge boxes, for as one soldier explained, it was "a certainty that the First Division as the advance of the corps column would be in the storm-center."[16]

Their commander, Bvt. Maj. Gen. Charles R. Woods, was a graduate of West Point (class of 1852), and had served as an infantry officer in Texas and Washington. The heavily bearded Woods was once described as "a tall and not altogether graceful man, with a quiet, blunt manner," rendering his nickname—"Susan"—an incongruous one, to say the least. Woods had commanded the troops on board the *Star of the West* during its ill-fated attempt to relieve Fort Sumter. Starting as colonel of the 76th Ohio, Woods had risen steadily in Sherman's old XV Corps, receiving his major general's brevet on November 22, 1864. Charles Woods' elder brother, Brig. Gen. William B. Woods, was a lawyer and Republican politician who had begun the war as lieutenant colonel of the 76th Ohio and had since filled each vacancy created by Charles' promotions. William Woods now commanded a brigade in his brother's division. The highlight of his post-war legal and political career would come in 1880, when he would be appointed to the U. S. Supreme Court.[17]

About one mile west of Cox's Crossroads, while screening Gen. Charles Woods' advance, the 7th Illinois Mounted Infantry struck a squad of Rebel cavalry from Young's Brigade of Butler's Division. The Illinoisans maintained a heavy fire with their seven-shot Spencer rifles and drove back the Confederate troopers for several miles. The Rebels' resistance stiffened as they fell back on reinforcements and as the Illinoisans reduced their rate of fire to conserve a rapidly dwindling ammunition supply. The 97th Indiana of Col. Robert F. Catterson's brigade trotted past the horsemen of the 7th Illinois and took up the chase.[18]

Catterson's brigade possessed more raw firepower than any other brigade in Sherman's army. Of Catterson's seven regiments, five brandished the Spencer rifle, and at least a portion of a sixth

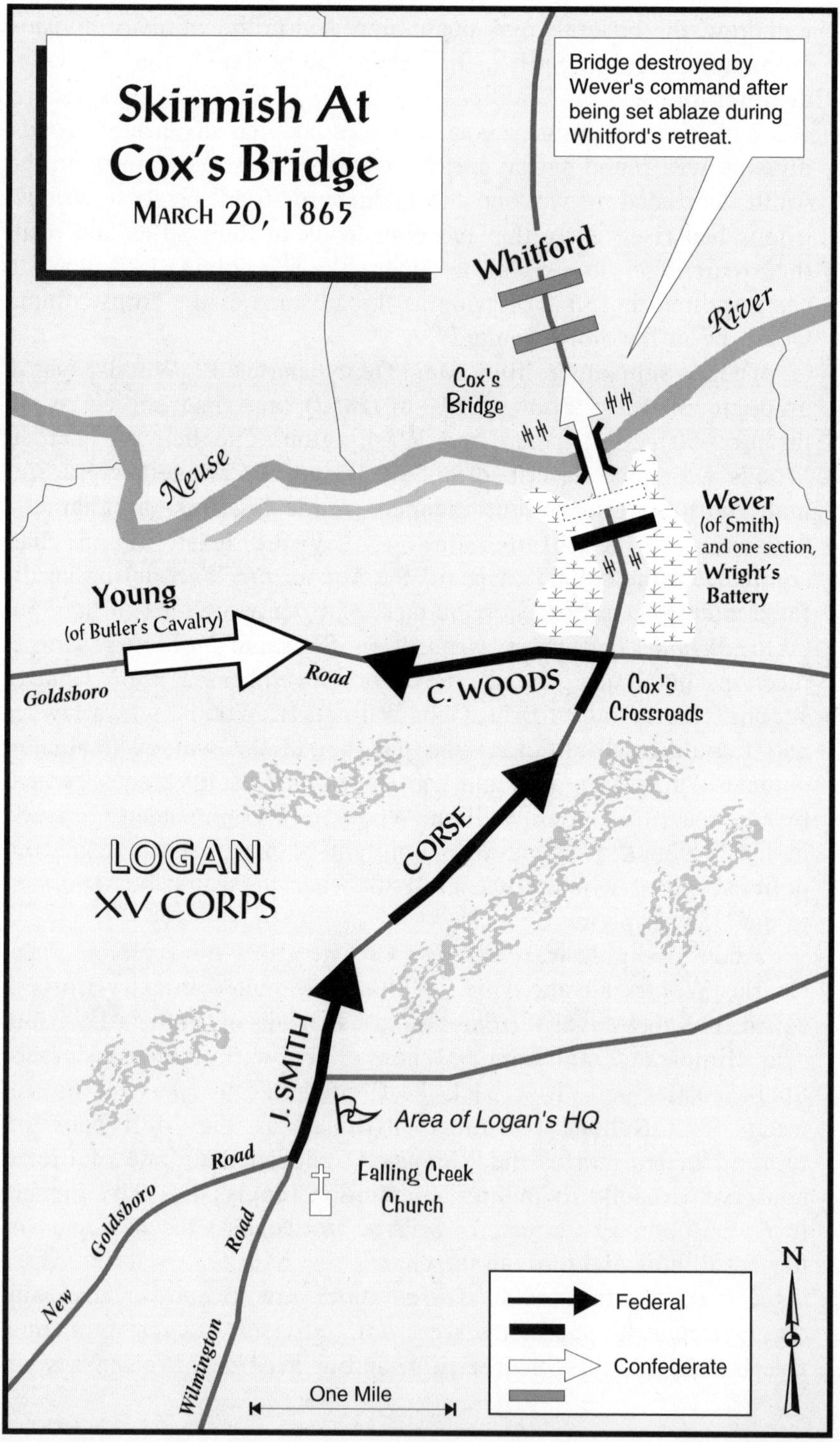

Skirmish At Cox's Bridge
March 20, 1865
Bridge destroyed by Wever's command after being set ablaze during Whitford's retreat.
Whitford
River
Cox's Bridge
Neuse
Wever
(of Smith)
and one section,
Wright's Battery
Young
(of Butler's Cavalry)
Goldsboro
Road
C. WOODS
Cox's Crossroads
CORSE
LOGAN
XV CORPS
J. SMITH
Area of Logan's HQ
Road
Falling Creek Church
New Goldsboro
Road
Wilmington
One Mile
Federal
Confederate
N

Mark A. Moore

was armed with the 16-shot Henry rifle. The purchase of these repeating rifles was both voluntary and a considerable out-of-pocket expense. Each Spencer rifle cost 35 dollars, an investment of almost four months' pay for the average enlisted man. The Spencer cartridge contained fewer than fifty grains of powder, making the rifle a relatively short-range weapon; yet its resulting low muzzle velocity gave the bullet tremendous stopping power. The Spencer rifle's only flaw was its loading mechanism—a long spring which had to be slid out of the stock when reloading. Nevertheless, in the hands of an expert, the Spencer rifle could fire 21 rounds per minute. Given its combination of reliability and firepower, the Spencer proved to be one of the finest small arms weapons of the Civil War. "I think the Johnnys are getting rattled," wrote a Hoosier in Catterson's brigade who toted a Henry rifle. "[T]hey are afraid of our repeating rifles. They say we are not fair, that we have guns that we load up on Sunday and shoot all the rest of the week. This I know, I feel a good deal more confidence in myself with a 16 shooter in my hands than I used to with a single shot rifle."[19]

Blazing away with their Spencers, the 97th Indiana kept up a running fight with the Mississippians and Georgians of Young's Brigade for about three miles. Three companies of the Hoosier regiment deployed as skirmishers on the right of the road and three more on the left, the remaining companies of the 97th following in reserve. "We followed [the Rebels] up one hill and down another," recalled Capt. John Alexander, the commander of the 97th's three right companies. "They would wait till we got to the top of a hill, give us a volley and run until they got over the next hill."[20]

Four companies of the 100th Indiana under Maj. John Headington moved up on the left of the 97th Indiana's skirmish companies. The 97th advanced across open fields, the 100th through pine woods. It soon became apparent to Capt. Eli Sherlock of the 100th that this was a mixed blessing, for the Confederates were massing in his front to exploit the cover of the timber. Meanwhile, the 97th Indiana exhausted its ammunition and was relieved by the 6th Iowa. As the Iowans double-quicked to the front, Lt. Henry Wright overheard Sherman instructing Colonel Catterson to "drive the enemy as fast as the men could travel." But Sherman also instructed Howard to "proceed with due caution, using skirmishers alone" until he formed a junction with Slocum's wing.[21]

Young's Confederate brigade was reinforced by several brigades of Wheeler's cavalry, who were fighting dismounted from behind a series of barricades that blocked the Goldsboro Road. Wheeler's orders were to delay the Federal advance long enough to enable Hoke's Division to swing back into position behind him. The 6th Iowa's Lieutenant Wright recalled:

> We charged them and flanked them from all [six of] their barricades until we came onto their main line of infantry. We heard [the Rebels] beat the "long roll" in their camps and heard the bugle sound the attention and could hear the officers giving commands to the men.[22]

The Iowans soon emptied their cartridge boxes and made way for the 46th Ohio—Colonel Catterson believing that it was more prudent to waste good ammunition than good soldiers. Yet Captain Sherlock might have questioned this statement, for the men of the 100th Indiana's four skirmish companies were sorely in need of a breather, having had to keep pace with two fresh regiments. The Hoosier skirmishers emerged into an open field with their objective, the Bentonville crossroads near the Green Flowers house, in full view just a few hundred yards away. A rail barricade held by some skirmishers from Hagood's Brigade of Hoke's Division straddled the crossroads.[23]

Suddenly, a large body of Rebel cavalry burst out of the woods opposite the 100th's skirmish line. With a loud yell the Confederates galloped around the Hoosiers' left flank. Captain Sherlock turned around and saw that the Southern troopers were dashing straight for Generals Howard, Logan and Woods, who had ridden up perilously close to the skirmish line. The sudden tumult frightened the 100th's pack mules, who bolted for the rear, "and the air for a while [sic] seemed to be as full of frying pans, coffee pots, tin plates and cups, as bullets," wrote an onlooker from the 97th Indiana. The balance of the 100th was concealed in the timber within easy supporting distance, and with a well-aimed volley the Hoosiers brought the Rebel cavalry to an abrupt halt. This was good news for the Federal generals and the 100th's pack mules, but not for the 100th's skirmishers, who were now trapped between the Confederate barricade in their front and the enemy horsemen in their rear. Several officers advised Major Headington to order the men to cut

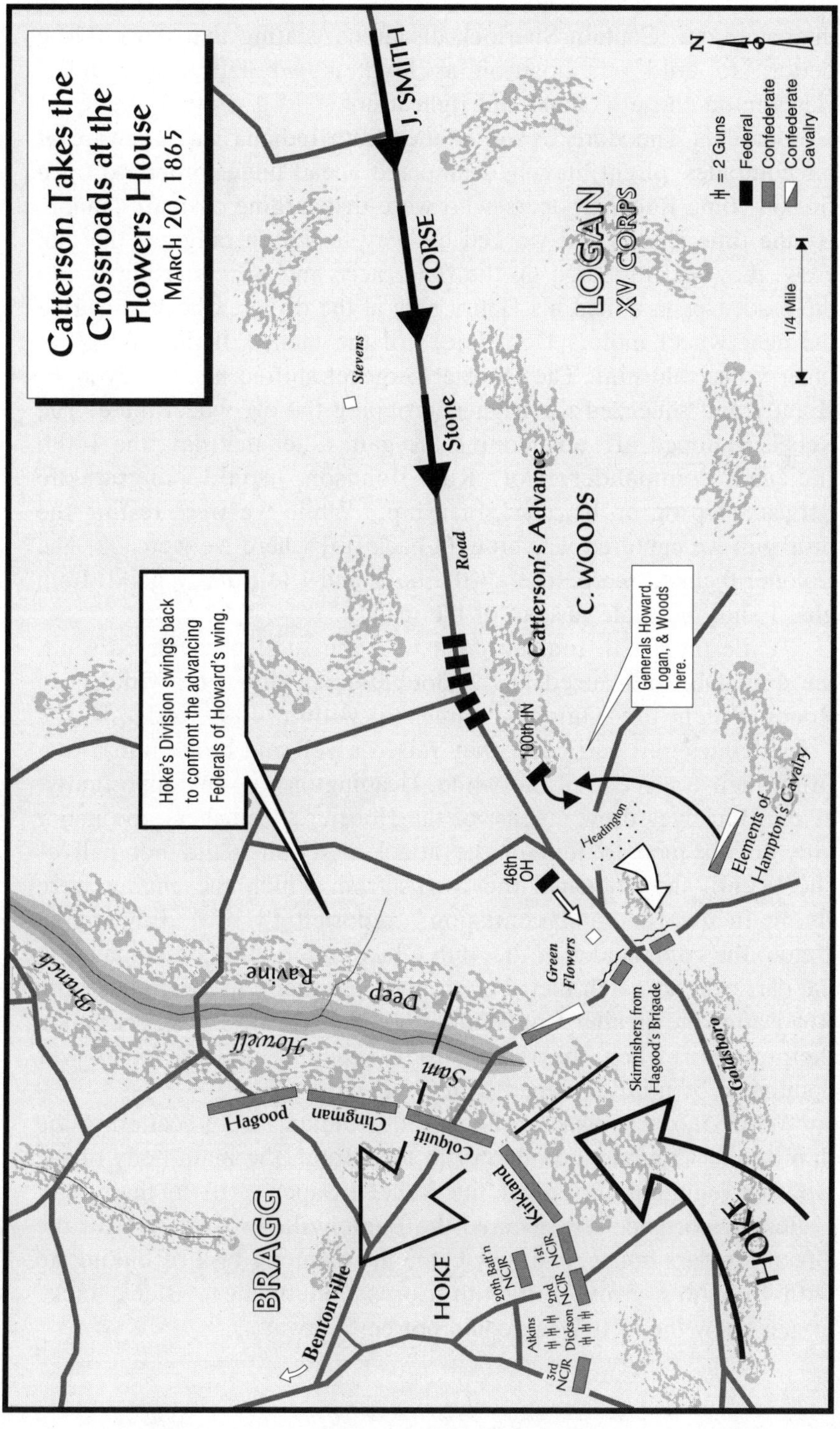
Catterson Takes the Crossroads at the Flowers House
March 20, 1865
J. SMITH
CORSE
Stone
Road
Stevens
LOGAN
XV CORPS
Catterson's Advance
C. WOODS
Generals Howard, Logan, & Woods here.
100th IN
46th OH
Headington
Elements of Hampton's Cavalry
Hoke's Division swings back to confront the advancing Federals of Howard's wing.
Green Flowers
Skirmishers from Hagood's Brigade
Goldsboro
Deep Ravine
Howell Branch
Sam
Hagood
Clingman
Colquitt
Kirkland
BRAGG
HOKE
HOKE
Bentonville
20th Batt'n NCJR
1st NCJR
2nd NCJR
Atkins
Dickson
3rd NCJR
= 2 Guns
Federal
Confederate
Confederate Cavalry
1/4 Mile
N

Mark A. Moore

their way out. Captain Sherlock disagreed, stating that it would be better "to hold our position as long as we had a man left." Headington chose to stand and fight it out.[24]

Sergeant Theodore Upson of the 100th Indiana was unaware of his comrades' plight, having scampered ahead under orders to open fire on some Rebel troopers who were discharging a small cannon. By the time Upson had worked his way to within range of the gun crew, they had limbered up the field piece and were starting it into the road. Upson aimed his Henry rifle at the driver, who was astride the near wheel mule: "Dont [sic] kill the man; kill the mule," an inner voice told him. The Hoosier sergeant shifted his aim ever-so-slightly and squeezed the trigger, dropping the off wheel mule. The Rebels galloped off, abandoning the gun. Later that day, the 100th Indiana's commander, Col. Ruel Johnson, would congratulate Sergeant Upson on his marksmanship: "While we were resting the little gun we captured was brought back [to] where we were. . . .The Colonel thanked me before all the boys and I felt pretty good. I am glad I shot the mule instead of the man."[25]

While the 100th Indiana dealt with the sudden cavalry assault, the 46th Ohio advanced at the double-quick down the Goldsboro Road. When the Ohioans came to within 400 yards of the Confederates' rail barricade, they raised a yell and broke into a run, firing their Spencers all the while. Headington saw his opportunity: as the Buckeyes drew abreast of the Hoosier skirmishers, the major ordered his men to join in the attack. "My men did not halt or check until they reached the works from which the enemy were flying in disorder and confusion," reported Lt. Col. Edward N. Upton, the commander of the 46th Ohio. Upton let his men pause at the barricade to catch their breath, then led them up the Bentonville Road after the fleeing Confederate horsemen. The Buckeyes halted their pursuit when they came to a swampy ravine, for it was dominated by a hill crowned with Rebel works.[26]

While the skirmishers of the 100th Indiana were scattering the thin line of Confederate infantry in their front, the main body of the Hoosier regiment drove off the Rebel troopers still in their rear. Catterson's brigade had secured the Bentonville crossroads near the Green Flowers house, and now came the daunting task of linking up with Slocum's army. Fifteenth Corps commander "Black Jack" Logan knew the Left Wing could not be far away:

"We could distinctly hear the musketry in General Slocum's front," he reported. It was 12 noon.[27]

* * *

Brigadier General Evander M. Law's first day as commander of Butler's Division of cavalry promised to be an eventful one. At dawn on March 20, Wade Hampton had notified Law that General Butler had fallen ill and that command of the division now devolved upon him. A few hours later, Law's videttes reported that the Federal Right Wing had turned left at Cox's Crossroads and was marching west on the Goldsboro Road. Butler's cavalry was all that now stood between the Right Wing and the rear of Johnston's army. Yet Law knew the most Butler's cavalry could do was annoy the Yankee juggernaut.[28]

As an infantry officer Law had assumed division-level command in critical situations before, first at Gettysburg and later that summer at Chickamauga, substituting both times for a severely wounded Maj. Gen. John Bell Hood. Law had been twice severely wounded himself, at Manassas and Cold Harbor. A native South Carolinian and an 1856 graduate of the Citadel, Law joined Hampton's cavalry in January 1865, to defend his homeland. He accepted command of a brigade in Maj. Gen. M. C. Butler's Division, which had been transferred from Virginia to the Palmetto State to oppose Sherman. Law had been promised command of an infantry division in Johnston's army, but soon realized that it was *infantrymen*, not infantry commanders, that Johnston needed, and so never pressed "Old Joe" for the promotion.[29]

For the moment Law was concerned only with delaying the Federal Right Wing. "The enemy's infantry and artillery is advancing rapidly from the direction of Cox's Bridge." Law wrote Johnston at 9:50 a.m. Given the circumstances, such a lapse in subject-verb agreement should be excusable, except that Law had been an instructor of *belles lettres* at the Citadel, and in the half-century following the war would make his living as a journalist. "A few regiments of infantry would check his advance, I think, very materially. Our cavalry is too weak to accomplish much," Law conceded.[30]

General Johnston received Law's message at 10:15 a.m., and immediately instructed Bragg to swing back Hoke's Division so that its line would face south and east, and run roughly parallel to the Goldsboro Road. Johnston also ordered Wheeler to deploy a part of his cavalry just east of Hoke's new position and construct a series of barricades astride the Goldsboro Road.[31]

The men of Hoke's Division had been up since dawn strengthening their line of works confronting Morgan's division. About 9:00 a.m. Lt. Col. George W. Grummond sent out four companies of his 14th Michigan (Vandever's brigade) to investigate the chopping noises that echoed across his front. Captain J. Walter Myers led the 14th's skirmish line under orders from Grummond to prevent the Confederates from improving or extending their fortifications. Captain Myers advanced his skirmishers to within close range of the works held by Kirkland's Brigade and ordered his men to open fire. The Tarheels dropped their axes, hatchets and shovels, and scrambled for cover.[32]

After trading shots with the Rebels for about a half-hour, Captain Myers noticed that their fire had slackened considerably and that they were moving rapidly to their right. Myers notified Grummond, who in turn obtained authorization from General Vandever to lead the 14th Michigan and the 16th Illinois in a charge on the enemy's works. The 16th's commander, Capt. Herman Lund, was less than enthusiastic, noting that he and his men had spent a miserable night lying "behind our breast-works on the wet ground, without fire, and the most of us with nothing to eat." The knowledge that nearly everyone else in Vandever's brigade had had to endure the same miserable conditions did little to brighten Captain Lund's outlook.[33]

Captain Myers reported that his skirmishers reached Kirkland's works "in time to see a few straggling rebels disappear in the woods and swamps." Myers led his men forward about 300 yards before halting to await further orders. Grummond directed Myers to swing his line around to the left and advance rapidly toward the Goldsboro Road, keeping his left flank within sight of the enemy's abandoned works. Myers also took the precaution of refusing his right flank.

Grummond followed at the head of the main body—six companies of the 14th Michigan on the right and the 16th Illinois on the left—pausing only long enough at the enemy's works to make sure they were deserted. "Without throwing out any skirmishers or stopping to reform our lines," the 16th's Captain Lund wrote, unaware that Myers' skirmish line was in the woods up ahead, "we were ordered to forward again at double-quick" through a swamp snarled "with a dense growth of underbrush and vines, fallen logs, &c." Grummond maintained this brisk pace for about a half-mile, at some point wheeling his main line to the left in conformity with his skirmish line, which had reached the Goldsboro Road and was sparring with the Confederates.[34]

Enter the ubiquitous D. H. Hill. Hill was observing a Federal skirmish line's advance on the Cole house when he learned that Hoke's Division was changing front. Hill dispatched Stevenson's Division to cover Hoke's withdrawal, but General Stewart met General Stevenson en route and countermanded Hill's order. Hill thereupon rode over to Hoke's new position and found the Junior Reserves and two batteries of Starr's Battalion swinging back on a line several hundred yards in rear of their old position and facing the Goldsboro Road. The boys flung up a log entrenchment "filled in with earth dug up with bayonets and tin pans and a few spades and shovels," recalled one Reservist. Seeing that Hoke's rear guard needed some help, Hill trained one six-gun battery on the Federals dashing across the Goldsboro Road.[35]

The first salvo struck the left flank of Myers' skirmish line and halted his advance. Meanwhile, Kirkland's Brigade deployed to oppose the Federal skirmishers, and in tandem with the Junior Reserves on their right, laid down a severe cross fire along the Yankees' front. Captain Myers ran back to Grummond for further orders, and was told to charge the Rebel line and seize the battery.

Grummond's main line followed the skirmishers into a storm of bullets, shrapnel and canister. "When we received this fire," reported the 16th Illinois' Captain Lund, "the men were completely exhausted by marching at double-quick so long. [O]ur line was confused, broken, and disorganized. . .and yet we were not permitted to stop for a moment, but were rushed ahead on double-quick."[36]

Kirkland's Brigade withdrew to a gap in Hoke's line left for it between Colquitt and the Junior Reserves. "Into line, faced to the rear!" Kirkland commanded. The well-disciplined Tarheels calmly turned their backs on the approaching enemy and filed into position. Most of the troops were permitted to pile up a few logs

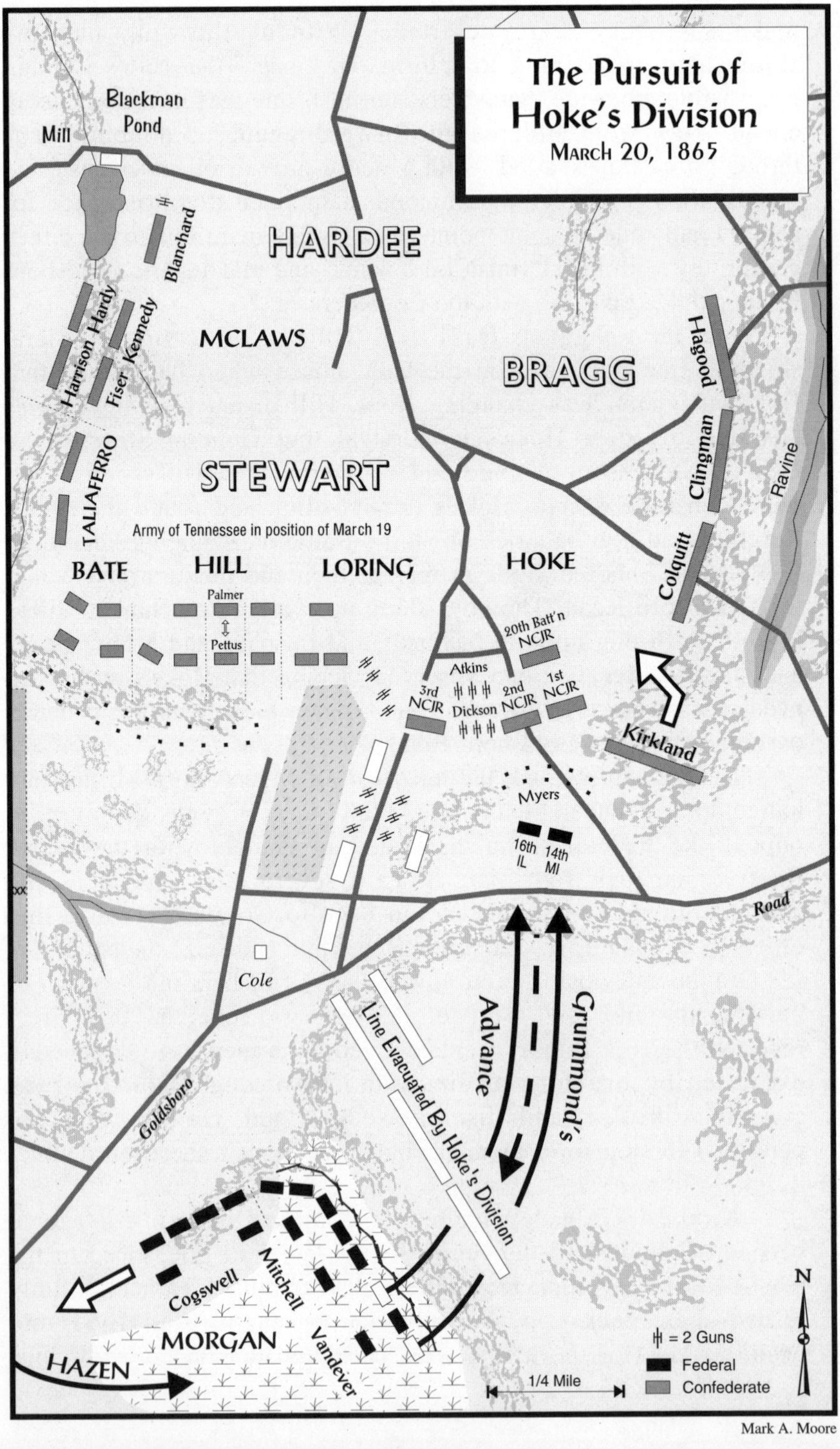
The Pursuit of
Hoke's Division
March 20, 1865
Blackman
Mill
Pond
Blanchard
HARDEE
Harrison
Hardy
Kennedy
Fiser
MCLAWS
BRAGG
Hagood
Clingman
Ravine
STEWART
TALIAFERRO
Army of Tennessee in position of March 19
BATE
HILL
LORING
HOKE
Colquitt
Palmer
Pettus
20th Batt'n
NCJR
Atkins
3rd
NCJR
Dickson
2nd
NCJR
1st
NCJR
Kirkland
Myers
16th
IL
14th
MI
Road
Cole
Line Evacuated By Hoke's Division
Advance
Grummond's
Goldsboro
Cogswell
Mitchell
MORGAN
Vandever
HAZEN
= 2 Guns
Federal
Confederate
1/4 Mile
N

Mark A. Moore

and fence rails for protection, but not Company A of the 17th North Carolina, which remained deployed in two ranks.[37]

The Tarheels held their fire until the Federals advanced to within 30 yards of their line: "[T]he order was given to fire," wrote George Rose of the 66th North Carolina. "[T]he men immediately raised upon their knees and fired a volley full in front of the advancing foe. Their ranks were mowed down like wheat before the scythe." Above the roar of musketry Capt. William Biggs of the 17th's Company A shouted, "Rear rank, ready, aim, fire! Load!," followed by the same commands for the front rank. "The volleys were very distinct amid the rattle of *firing by file* all along the line," recalled Kirkland's adjutant, Capt. Charles Elliott. "This *fire by rank* was very effective, as piles of dead were left in front of this company." Kirkland's fire struck the right flank of the 14th Michigan, and sent the survivors reeling back.[38]

Captain Lund reported that the Junior Reserves and Starr's six-gun battery poured "a most destructive fire" into the 16th Illinois' front and left flank. Every man in the 16th's color guard was wounded in the charge except Cpl. George Wheeler, who brought off the regimental colors under a murderous fire of musketry and artillery. A four-year veteran of the 16th would later write: "This was the last battle of the war the Sixteenth was engaged in, but it was the most terrible of them all."[39]

Captain Myers reported that some of his Michiganders leaped over the Junior Reserves' half-finished works and, seizing the draft horses, demanded the battery's surrender. The Reserves, undaunted by the Federals in their midst, rushed fresh troops into the breach and drove back Myers' men. "[W]e were compelled to retire somewhat in confusion," Myers admitted.[40]

Lieutenant Colonel Grummond withdrew his bloodied command to the safety of Hoke's abandoned works. Grummond had a dozen Rebel prisoners to show for his rashness, but his command had suffered at least 50 casualties. In repulsing Grummond's charge the men of Kirkland's Brigade gained some measure of revenge for their drubbing of the previous day.[41]

With the possible exception of Joe Mower, George Washington Grummond was the most aggressive fighter in Sherman's army, which was no mean feat. Two years later Grummond would achieve lasting notoriety by being killed in the frontier battle which became known as the Fetterman Massacre.[42]

While Grummond's command was licking its wounds, Col. Theodore Jones' brigade of Hazen's division, XV Corps, advanced into position on the right of Morgan's division. Moreover, two brigades of Baird's division of the XIV Corps moved up to occupy a field in rear of Carlin's division, which earlier had relieved Cogswell's brigade at the front.[43]

On the evening of the 19th, Hazen's, Geary's and Baird's divisions had been at the rear of the XV Corps column when they were ordered to join the Left Wing near Bentonville. At the time, Geary's troops were guarding the XX Corps train and Baird's men the XIV Corps train. In obedience to Slocum's orders, Geary and Baird each left behind one brigade to guard the wagons. Geary reached the John Harper farm first, at 4:30 a.m. After a grueling 20-mile march, much of it at night and over muddy roads, Hazen's division arrived at 6:30 a.m., followed by Baird's division at 8:00 a.m.[44] Charles Milton Hopper of the 70th Ohio, Oliver's brigade, described the night march of Hazen's division:

> On Guard with the Regimental Wagons 10 P.M. & no moon. We are laying around a fire wishing for the train to move. A large swamp just ahead (They) say we have to cross it yet tonight. If so we are good for the night. This is the beauty of a soldiers life. . . .we was out until 12 in the worst night I ever saw. . . .Trains just move forward until midnight, when we get orders to go back and take another road. Heavy fighting force march. Going all night. Come back to the forks of the road and took the road out to the 20th Corps.[45]

That morning, Ohioan John W. Reid of Geary's division visited the battlefield on Morris' farm, where details were burying the dead while stretcher bearers were still carrying off the wounded. "The field was strewn with dead & dying," Reid noted. "In some places the union & rebel soldiers lay together where they had fell fighting a hand to hand conflict." Or so it appeared to Reid. A more likely explanation is that the Union dead had fallen during the retreat prior to the Confederate assaults, and that some of the Confederate dead were dressed in Federal uniforms. This was as close as Geary's troops would come to the fighting at Bentonville. They would remain safely encamped on the Harper farm for the next two days before resuming the march to Goldsboro. Not so Baird's or Hazen's troops.[46]

About 1:00 p.m. Maj. Gen. Absalom Baird received orders from General Davis to push forward his two brigades and Capt. Joseph McKnight's artillery (5th Wisconsin Battery) and reconnoiter the enemy's position. Baird's line advanced at 2:00 p.m. and halted at the unfinished log works briefly held by Robinson's brigade on the 19th. Baird directed his First Brigade commander, Col. Morton Hunter, to send out a strong skirmish line across the wooded ravine bordering their left flank. Colonel Hunter assigned Maj. John H. Jolly the task of leading the skirmish line, placing the 23rd Missouri, plus one company each of the 31st, 89th and 92nd Ohio regiments, under Jolly's command.[47]

Major Jolly led his skirmish line into the swamp at the base of the ravine. This was the same ravine that had figured so prominently in Carlin's rout. One of Baird's soldiers remarked: "[T]o see how the bullets had raked the undergrowth[,] mowing it down as with a scythe and scaling the bark as they did from the trees, one can hardly realize how it could be possible for any to escape."[48]

The Missourians and Ohioans scampered up the northern slope under a sharp fire, driving the Confederate skirmishers before them. Generals Davis and Baird and their staffs followed just a few yards behind the Federal skirmish line. "While we were driving in the [Rebel] skirmishers," wrote Maj. James Connolly, one of Baird's staff officers, "I received a gentle reminder that 'a body ought to be careful' for a rebel bullet struck the limb of a pine tree some five feet above my head, and glancing downward struck the plate of my sword belt and plunged into the leaves at my feet. It didn't hurt any and I was very glad of it."[49]

The Federals halted at the Confederate rifle pits and gazed out across the field and open woods in their front. Every veteran soldier from Davis down could see that the Rebels had dug a formidable line of works. Every man knew that assaulting these entrenchments would be bloody work. On Baird's left, the skirmishers from the XX Corps also found the enemy well-entrenched.[50]

Meanwhile, the soldiers manning Baird's main line improved and extended Robinson's old works. Some of the men of Hunter's brigade were detailed to carry off the wounded from the March 19 battle who were still floundering in the swamps bordering the Cole plantation. "We [worked] under [a] heavy fire," wrote stretcher

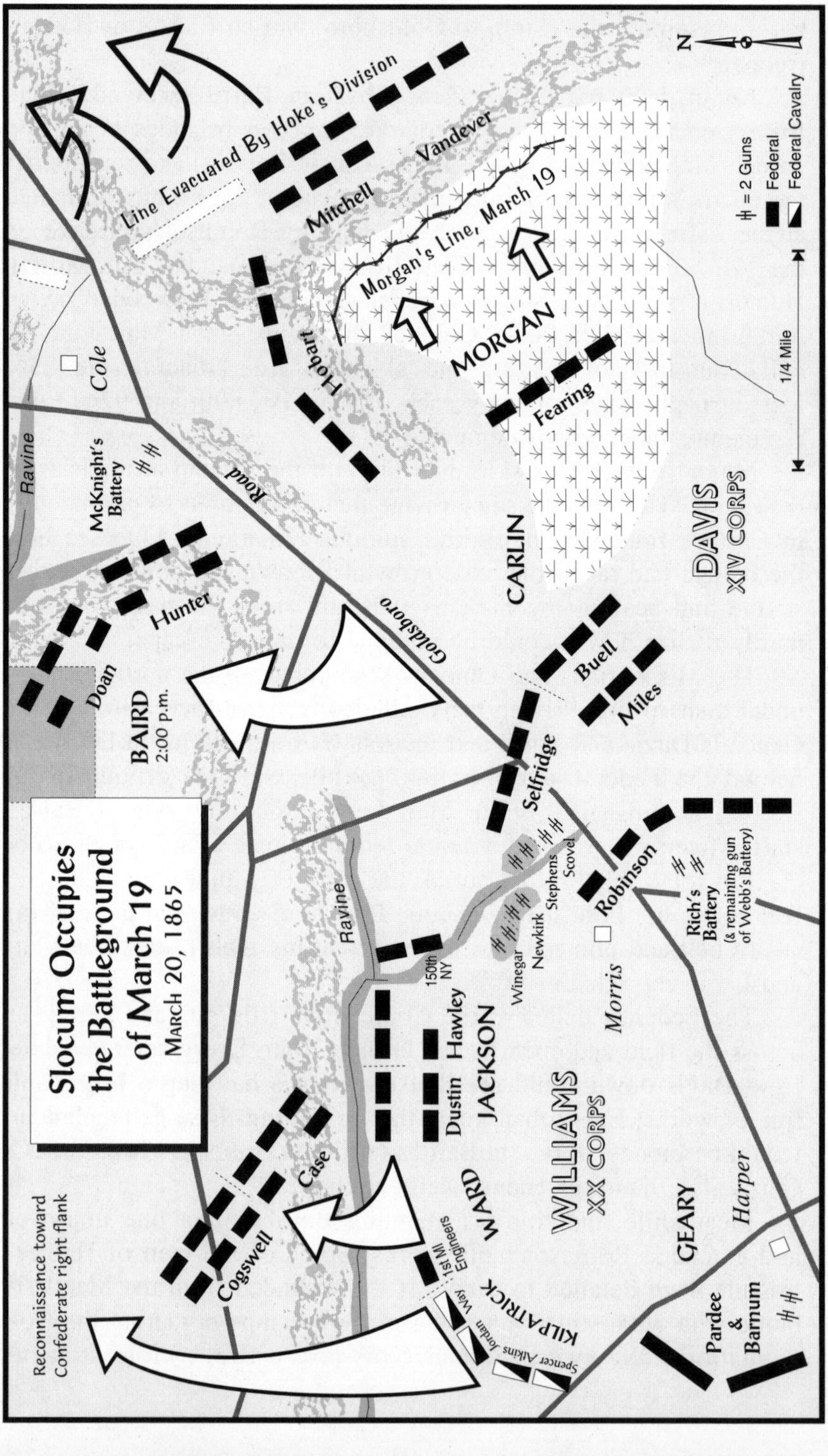
Slocum Occupies the Battleground of March 19
March 20, 1865
Line Evacuated By Hoke's Division
Mitchell
Vandever
Morgan's Line, March 19
Hobart
MORGAN
Fearing
Cole
Ravine
McKnight's Battery
Goldsboro Road
Hunter
Doan
BAIRD
2:00 p.m.
CARLIN
DAVIS
XIV CORPS
Buell
Miles
Selfridge
Stephens
Scovel
Newkirk
Winegar
Robinson
Rich's Battery
(& remaining gun of Webb's Battery)
Morris
Ravine
150th NY
Hawley
Dustin
JACKSON
WILLIAMS
XX CORPS
Case
Cogswell
WARD
1st MI Engineers
Way
Jordan
Atkins
Spencer
KILPATRICK
GEARY
Harper
Pardee & Barnum
Reconnaissance toward Confederate right flank
= 2 Guns
Federal
Federal Cavalry
1/4 Mile
N

Mark A. Moore

bearer William C. Johnson of the 89th Ohio, "shells almost continually bursting all around us."[51]

McKnight's battery unlimbered just north of the Goldsboro Road, on the spot occupied by Scovel's and Webb's batteries the day before. The Federal battery spent a routine day on the front line (if such a thing were possible), firing 20 rounds of solid shot and sustaining no casualties. Nearby, a Union work party managed to haul off the fourth gun of Webb's battery, which the Confederates had left behind because all of its draft horses had been killed. Manhandling the gun was a ticklish operation, for in the words of one laborer, the carriage "wheels was literally shot to pieces by musket balls."[52]

For the men of Baird's Second Brigade, Lt. Col. Thomas Doan commanding, the day was anything but routine. The men were subjected to a barrage of enemy artillery fire more annoying than destructive, though one shell burst wounded two men of the 2nd Minnesota. In the words of the 2nd's H. H. Hills, "We were too close and too quiet to remain inactive long, and it looked threatening."[53]

A staff officer galloped up to Lieutenant Colonel Doan, and in a voice loud enough for Hills and several other Minnesotans to hear, ordered Doan to ready his brigade for a charge on the enemy's works. "I shall never forget the uncomfortable feeling I experienced on hearing this," Hills wrote. "I imagined I was already singled out for a target. . .I did not feel as though I was of the stuff that martyrs were made." While Hills was thus contemplating his fate, another staff officer rode up and ordered Doan to cancel the attack. "I always considered this the most critical moment of my life," Hills recalled, "and that I escaped destruction by a very narrow margin."[54]

Whatever thought Generals Davis or Baird gave to an assault on the Army of Tennessee's works was now abandoned. Perhaps Davis had had to be reminded that Slocum's orders were to "move forward your skirmish line. . .but without bringing on a general engagement." At nightfall Davis ordered Baird to withdraw his division to the field it had occupied earlier in the day. The men found it a poor place to bivouac. "I learned that they call this battle ground 'Bentonville,'" wrote Sgt. William B. Miller of the 75th Indiana, Doan's brigade. "I have not seen any town or even a good place. . .[for] it seems to be all swamp here." Though they could not have realized it then, Sergeant Miller and his comrades had ample reason to celebrate, for their participation in this seemingly misnamed battle was over.[55]

At 1:00 p.m. the 6th Missouri and 30th Ohio of Col. Theodore Jones' brigade, Hazen's division, were ordered forward on the skirmish line. "We had no dinner [or] supper yesterday & no breakfast this morning," complained Edward Schweitzer of the 30th Ohio. Nor would there be time for dinner today. The Ohioans and Missourians unslung their knapsacks and deployed in skirmish formation, the 6th Missouri on the right and the 30th Ohio on the left. They moved out beyond Morgan's division's works, then passed Hoke's abandoned line, now held by Lieutenant Colonel Grummond's command. The 6th Missouri and the 30th Ohio were groping for the left flank of Howard's wing, which had been pushing toward Bentonville from the east. They advanced for more than a mile, wading swamps and hacking their way through briar thickets, until they stumbled upon the Goldsboro Road and some Confederate skirmishers from Kirkland's Brigade.[56]

While elements of Hazen's division were seeking Howard, portions of Howard's Wing were probing for Slocum. At 3:00 p.m. Gen. Charles Woods ordered Col. George A. Stone to proceed westward on the Goldsboro Road with three regiments of his Iowa brigade and make contact with Slocum's right flank. Colonel Stone deployed the 25th Iowa as skirmishers and directed the 30th and the 31st Iowa to follow in reserve. The 25th's color bearer led the way, marching down the middle of the road. This bold display soon attracted Kirkland's skirmishers, who opened fire on the Federals. Stone ordered his Iowans to oblique to the right in order to exploit the cover of the pine woods. While they were executing this maneuver, Stone's left flank collided with Kirkland's Tarheels, resulting in some severe skirmishing.[57]

At that moment the 6th Missouri and the 30th Ohio appeared on Stone's left flank. Colonel Stone and the 6th Missouri's commander, Lt. Col. Delos von Deusen, agreed to combine forces and "charge at a given signal," Stone later reported. The 6th Missouri drew up alongside the 25th Iowa. The two regiments executed a right half wheel and faced north, then advanced at a run. "[W]e had pretty warm work," wrote Sgt. Hiram Thornley, one of Colonel Stone's Hawkeyes. "The ground was well wooded and a perfect swamp. . . .Sometimes we were up to our knees in water, but

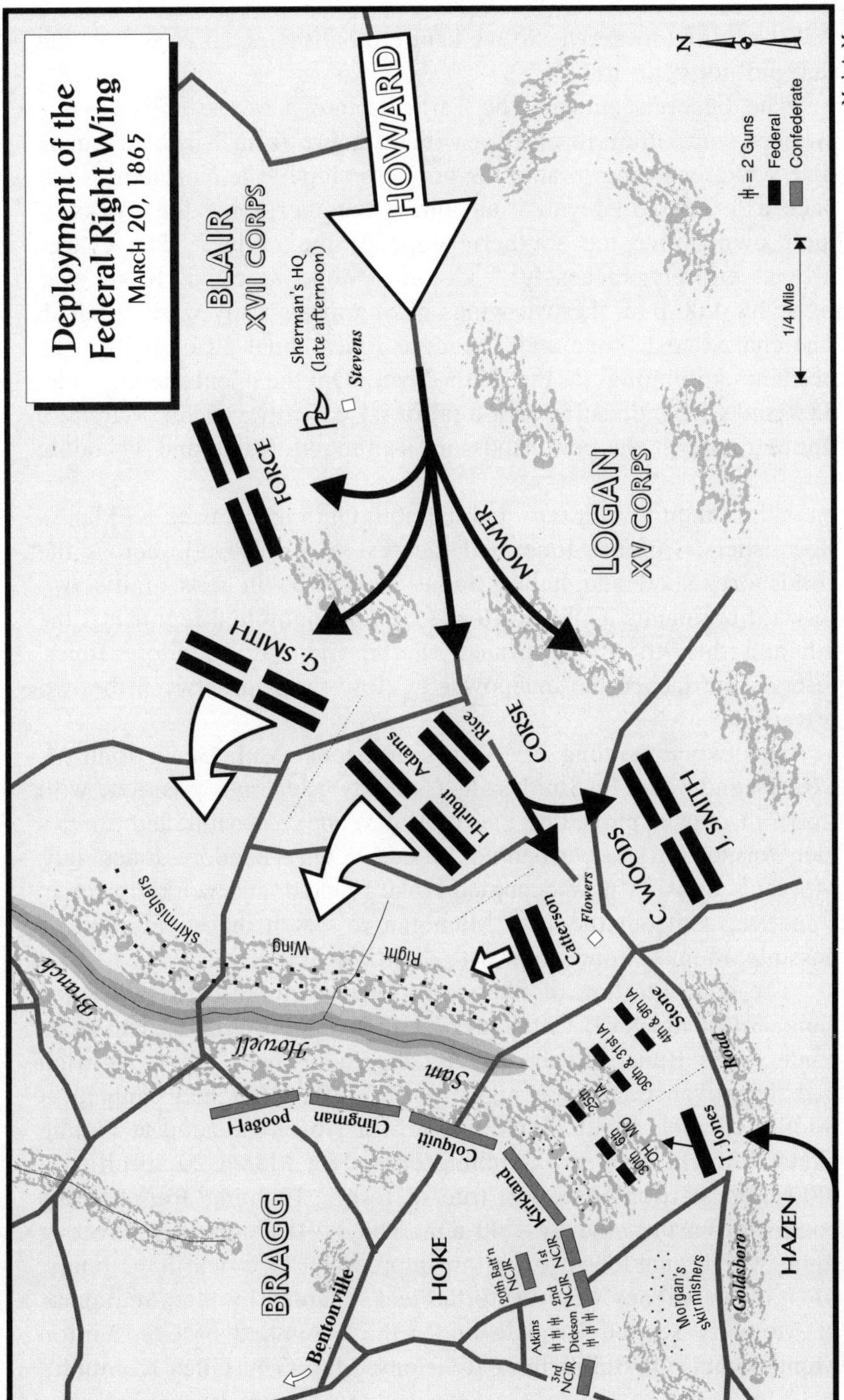
Deployment of the Federal Right Wing
March 20, 1865
HOWARD
BLAIR
XVII CORPS
Sherman's HQ (late afternoon)
Stevens
FORCE
G. SMITH
MOWER
LOGAN
XV CORPS
CORSE
Rice
Adams
Hurlbut
C. WOODS
J. SMITH
Flowers
Catterson
skirmishers
Right Wing
Branch
Howell
Sam
Stone
Road
4th & 9th IA
30th & 31st IA
25th IA
6th MO
30th OH
T. Jones
Hagood
Clingman
Colquitt
Kirkland
BRAGG
HOKE
Bentonville
90th Batt'n NCJR
1st NCJR
2nd NCJR
3rd NCJR
Atkins
Dickson
Morgan's skirmishers
Goldsboro
HAZEN
1/4 Mile
= 2 Guns
Federal
Confederate
N

Mark A. Moore

it was no time to growl. So we kept on, balls flew all around us but that did not deter us."[58]

The Federals pursued the Tarheels into a ravine and across a swamp, where they received a withering fire from Kirkland's main line, which was dug in atop the northern slope. The Northerners fell back a few hundred yards and threw together some log works of their own above the southern slope of the ravine. "The charge proved entirely successful," Colonel Stone asserted. Stone was right: by 4:00 p.m. the two wings of Sherman's army were reunited. The charge cost Stone and Theodore Jones about 50 casualties, 24 of them belonging to the 25th Iowa. On the Confederate side, Kirkland's Brigade suffered a total of 44 casualties in the March 20 fighting against the commands of Grummond, Stone and Theodore Jones.[59]

While the 6th Missouri and the 30th Ohio drove back Kirkland's skirmishers, Colonel Jones led the rest of his brigade across the Goldsboro Road and halted about 300 yards in rear of his two forward regiments. Colonel Stone's two uncommitted regiments, the 4th and the 9th Iowa, formed on the right of Theodore Jones' reserve, but lacked the manpower to close the gap between the two brigades.[60]

The two remaining XV Corps divisions, Maj. Gens. John M. Corse's and John E. Smith's, had already filed into position, with Corse's troops deployed on the right of Woods' division, and Smith's men formed in reserve behind Woods.[61] On Theodore Jones' left, Morgan's division now occupied Hoke's abandoned works in force. Vandever sent out the 10th Michigan to watch the enemy and, if possible, to make connection with the Right Wing.[62]

The concentration of Sherman's forces was effected when the vanguard of the XVII Corps arrived about mid-afternoon, led by its chief, Frank Blair, and the redoubtable Joe Mower, whose division had the advance. On the night of the 19th, Blair had camped at Smith's Chapel, about 10 miles south of Howard's camp at Falling Creek Church. Mower's marching orders for March 20 specified a 3:00 a.m. starting time but, true to form, "Fighting Joe" had his command on the road by 1:00 a.m. The XVII Corps was traveling light, which enabled it to log an impressive 25 miles in 12 hours. Most of its wagons were far to the rear, guarded by three regiments of Mower's Second Brigade under the command of Col. Milton Montgomery. Of Blair's three divisions, Maj. Gen. Giles A. Smith's joined on the right of Corse's line, Brig. Gen. Manning F. Force's formed in reserve behind Smith, and Mower deployed his men in line of battle south of the Goldsboro Road, facing west. One of Mower's men chanced to see "Billy Sherman. . .walking round, looking better pleased & dirtier than we have ever seen him before."[63]

Mower's orders were to drive off any Confederates still lurking in the woods and swamps south of the road, and to find the right flank of the XIV Corps (Morgan's division had yet to form a junction with Theodore Jones' brigade because Colonel Jones' line was already stretched too thin from trying to join on Colonel Stone's left). Mower's westward advance passed without incident, and about 4:00 p.m. his skirmishers met those of Morgan's division—that is, the 10th Michigan of Vandever's brigade.[64]

At dusk the 6th Missouri and the 30th Ohio withdrew to the main line, enabling Theodore Jones' brigade to connect with Morgan's skirmishers. Mower's division then returned to the Right Wing's sector. According to a lieutenant in Col. John Tillson's brigade, Mower's troops were so exhausted that on the return march "the men [were] sleep walking along." Those who were able to do so made camp on the left of Force's division. The rest went to sleep where they collapsed.[65]

Meanwhile, on Morgan's front, the 10th Michigan deployed four companies as skirmishers and advanced to the edge of a swamp. At sundown the 10th charged across the swamp and drove in a section of Kirkland's skirmish line, but soon finding themselves heavily outnumbered, the Michiganders fell back to their former position and entrenched.[66]

Once the junction of the two Federal armies was made, Sherman and Howard wasted no time in sending messengers to Slocum. One of the first to arrive at Slocum's headquarters was Maj. Thomas Osborn, Howard's chief of artillery. Since Gettysburg Major Osborn had harbored a grudge against Slocum. Both Osborn and Howard believed that Slocum had dragged his feet on his approach march to Gettysburg despite Howard's repeated appeals to hurry to his support. His nickname around Howard's headquarters was "Slow come." "His peculiarities are unpleasant," Osborn wrote of Slocum, "and one is not apt to reform his prejudices in favor of an unpleasant man." But then the major added, "He did well here [at Bentonville] and I am glad of it."[67]

The irony of the Right Wing's march to Slocum's support was not lost on Howard, for he remarked on it thirty years later. In 1894 Howard recalled:

> I had been a little impatient with Slocum the first day at Gettysburg. He thought that General Meade did not want an affair brought on at Gettysburg, but desired the battle at Pipe Clay Creek, so but slowly answered my call. At Bentonville I thought I would get even with him. I received word that Slocum was in trouble, so I immediately turned Hazen's division, whose rear was pretty near, to the right-about, and hastened it to his support. And he gives us credit for it in his report. So, as we say in the game of draughts, I had my revenge.[68]

"I asked Slocum how he thought the battle stood, when they ceased fighting," Osborn recorded, "as both parties held the line confronting each other."

Slocum replied, "We whipped them."[69]

* * *

Joe Johnston spent most of March 20 at his headquarters on the John Benton farm just east of Bentonville. In a dispatch to Gen. Robert E. Lee, Johnston wrote:[70]

> I concentrated our troops here yesterday morning and attacked the enemy about 3 p.m.; routed him, capturing three guns; but a mile in rear he rallied upon fresh troops. We were able to press all back slowly until 6, when receiving fresh troops, apparently, he attempted the offensive, which we resisted without difficulty until dark. This morning he is intrenched. Our loss was small. The troops behaved extremely well. Dense thickets prevented rapid operations.[71]

Sunday, March 19, had been a day of both triumph and disappointment for Joseph E. Johnston and the Army of the South. With one wing of Sherman's army confronting him already and another gathering in his front, however, it was time for Johnston to forget the missed opportunities and focus on the situation at hand. As Johnston himself admitted, "The Enemies intrenched position [and] greatly superior number. . .makes [sic] further offensive impracticable." Now was the time for Johnston to execute one of his masterful retreats, as he had done so often in similar situations during the Atlanta Campaign.[72]

Instead, Johnston chose to stay and fight.

What prompted him to do so? "We are remaining here to cover the removal of our wounded to the Rail Road at Smithfield," Johnston wrote Beauregard in Raleigh. Johnston later echoed this refrain in his postwar writings on the battle. Historian Jay Luvaas acknowledged that Johnston's avowed purpose for remaining at Bentonville was a humane one, "but scarcely defensible from a strictly military point of view," because it involved the possible sacrifice of one of the few Confederate armies left in the field for the sake of a few hundred wounded.[73]

Johnston offered Robert E. Lee a second reason for staying: "We held our ground in the hope that [the enemy's] greatly superior numbers might encourage him to attack." Johnston saw the handwriting on the wall. He could expect no reinforcements substantial enough to offset Sherman's overwhelming numerical superiority, nor could he expect another opportunity as favorable as the one presented him the day before. Clearly Johnston had reached a crisis. He was well aware that once Sherman combined with Schofield and Terry, the outcome would be reduced to a simple matter of mathematics, if it were not already.[74]

Bentonville represented Johnston's last hope, however desperate, of dealing Sherman a crippling blow. Yet Johnston knew the outcome lay in Sherman's hands. He was risking everything on the possibility that an overconfident Sherman might launch a frontal assault on the Confederates' fortified line. Of course there was the possibility that such an assault might succeed, but conversely, it was Johnston's only hope of success.

* * *

On the morning of March 20, Generals Hardee and McLaws reconnoitered the Confederate right flank to determine where best to deploy McLaws' troops. Earlier, Hardee had withdrawn Taliaferro's Division from its position of the day before and had placed it in rear of Bate's right flank, the Army of Tennessee's line remaining the same as on the morning of the 19th. From there Hardee had directed Taliaferro to deploy his troops on the eastern side of a creek that ran north a half-mile to a mill pond. Thus, Taliaferro's line formed a right angle to the Army of Tennessee's line and faced west.[75]

Hardee directed McLaws to deploy his division on the right of Taliaferro's position. McLaws replied that he would do so, but would not order his men to entrench because he believed they would soon be needed on the left flank. Hardee could not have been pleased with McLaws' reply, but apparently let the matter rest.[76]

The two generals rode on until they came to the mill, where a road running east and west crossed the mill pond. Hardee considered the road a likely approach route for the Federals, and so ordered McLaws to post a strong force on each side of it. With great reluctance McLaws placed Brig. Gen. Albert G. Blanchard's Brigade and a section of artillery there. Blanchard's Brigade consisted of about 300 junior and senior reservists from South Carolina. McLaws had little faith in the fighting ability of this brigade of old men and boys, and whenever a battle appeared imminent, sent them to the rear. Yet McLaws now placed Blanchard's Brigade on the front line because he knew he hadn't a man (or boy) to spare.[77]

McLaws apparently changed his mind about entrenching and instructed General Blanchard to fortify his position. He then rode back to supervise the deployment of his other brigades. Soon after his return, McLaws received the order he had been awaiting: he was to traverse the army's rear yet again, moving his division from the extreme right of the army to the extreme left, leaving Blanchard's Brigade at the mill pond. As he led Conner's and Fiser's Brigades into the road by the mill, McLaws noted with dismay that "Blanchard [was] fortifying along the mill race and mill pond, neglecting the high ground immediately in his rear." Sending his column ahead, McLaws remained behind to show Blanchard where to fortify his line, then hurried off to rejoin his command.[78]

While McLaws was galloping toward the left flank, he met General Hampton, who ordered him to halt two of his brigades, "as the enemy were reported moving directly upon Bentonville." McLaws relayed Hampton's order to Hardee, who rode to Johnston's headquarters for confirmation. A few minutes later, Hardee received word that the Federals had been driven off. "The reported advance on this place proves to have consisted of a small foraging party," Hampton wrote. Hampton also promised to send a squadron of cavalry to relieve Blanchard's Brigade at the mill. Meanwhile, Taliaferro's Division stretched its line to the right to compensate for McLaws' departure.[79]

When McLaws finally reached the left flank, he found Conner's Brigade (under John Kennedy) deployed in echelon on Hoke's left, about 100 yards to the rear. McLaws disliked this arrangement, and ordered Harrison's Brigade to form directly on Hoke's left. McLaws next placed Fiser's and Hardy's brigades on Kennedy's left to form a reserve line. From left to right, the Confederate main line opposing the Federal Right Wing now consisted of Harrison's Brigade of McLaws' Division, and Hagood's, Clingman's, Colquitt's, Kirkland's and Nethercutt's (Junior Reserves) brigades of Hoke's Division. The two sides confronted each other across a swampy ravine, the Confederates occupying the west bank and the Federals the east. A small stream known as the Sam Howell Branch ran through the center of this ravine and fed into Mill Creek. The outnumbered Confederates had chosen a strong defensive position.[80]

While McLaws' Division was deploying on the Confederate left, two skeleton brigades fresh from Smithfield reported for duty at Bentonville. The first was Cumming's Georgia Brigade, commanded by Col. Robert J. Henderson; the second was Granbury's Texas Brigade, led by Lt. Col. William A. Ryan. Both units were detached from their respective commands in the Army of Tennessee (the Georgians belonged to Stevenson's Division, and the Texans to Cleburne's Division). Johnston deemed them more urgently needed elsewhere, placing Cumming's Brigade in reserve behind Hoke's Division, and shuttling Granbury's Brigade from one weak point on the line to another. The two so-called brigades totaled barely 500 men. They constituted the bulk of Johnston's infantry reinforcements for March 20.[81]

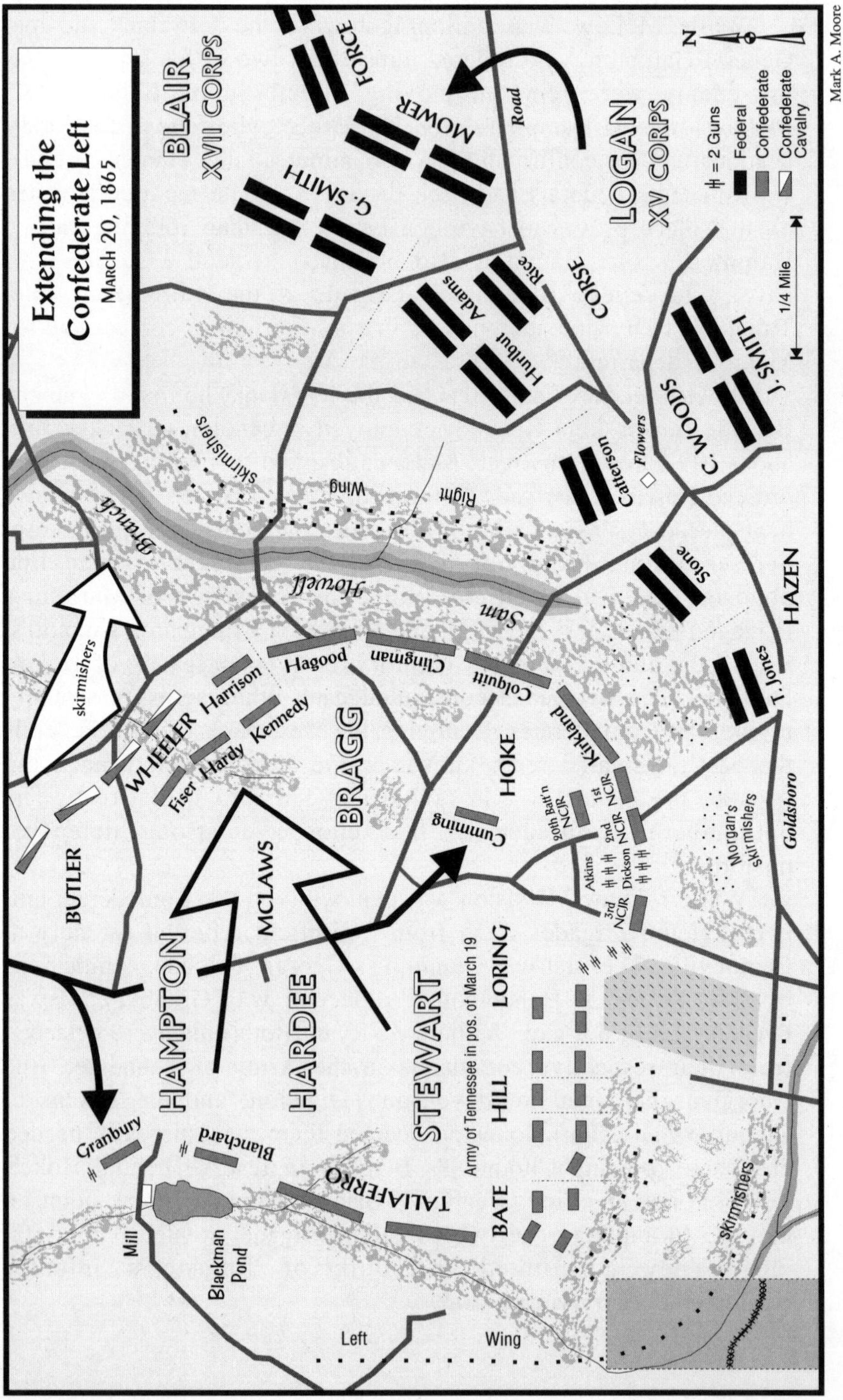

Extending the Confederate Left
March 20, 1865
BLAIR
XVII CORPS
FORCE
MOWER
G. SMITH
Road
LOGAN
XV CORPS
Rice
Adams
Hurlbut
CORSE
Catterson
Flowers
C. WOODS
J. SMITH
Stone
HAZEN
T. Jones
skirmishers
Wing
Right
Branch
Howell
Sam
skirmishers
Harrison
Hagood
Clingman
Colquitt
Kirkland
WHEELER
Fiser
Hardy
Kennedy
BRAGG
HOKE
20th Batt'n NCJR
1st NCJR
2nd NCJR
Cumming
Atkins
Dickson
3rd NCJR
Morgan's skirmishers
Goldsboro
BUTLER
MCLAWS
HAMPTON
HARDEE
STEWART
Army of Tennessee in pos. of March 19
LORING
HILL
BATE
Granbury
Blanchard
TALIAFERRO
Mill
Blackman Pond
Left
Wing
skirmishers
N
= 2 Guns
Federal
Confederate
Confederate Cavalry
1/4 Mile
Mark A. Moore

Wheeler's cavalry, meanwhile, filed into position on the left of Harrison's Brigade, and on Wheeler's left, General Law deployed Butler's Division. Wheeler had earlier ordered Law "to scout all the roads running eastwardly" from Bentonville. "I have found the right of the enemy's line," Law informed Hampton. "It is simply an extension of the line in front of our infantry by skirmishers who are stationary." Law reported that the Union line extended only a short distance north of the Goldsboro Road.[82]

Butler's Division held the extreme left of the Confederate line, which was now U-shaped and more than four miles long. In effect, the Confederate position was an enlarged bridgehead guarding the Mill Creek Bridge above Bentonville—the Confederates' sole avenue of retreat. It was a dangerous disposition.[83]

Law posted videttes on all the roads running westward from the Union line toward Bentonville while the balance of Butler's Division drew ammunition and rested. Butler's men were veterans of the Army of Northern Virginia—"Jeb" Stuart's cavalry—and many of these troopers rated themselves a cut above their counterparts from the Army of Tennessee. That afternoon Edward Laight Wells, a South Carolinian serving in General Butler's escort, wrote his aunt in New York: "Sherman will find us different customers from the Western Army & rather harder to run." Before the fighting at Bentonville was finished, Wells and his comrades would have ample opportunity to prove their superiority to Wheeler's cavalrymen.[84] The addition of Wade Hampton's 4,000 troopers gave Johnston roughly 20,000 men of all arms with which to oppose Sherman's army of 55,000.[85]

Skirmishing continued past nightfall along the line occupied by the Federal Right Wing. The incessant musketry "reminded us of the old times before Atlanta," wrote Brig. Gen. William W. Belknap, a brigade commander in Giles Smith's division of the XVII Corps. Confederate prisoners reported that Longstreet's Corps had arrived (shades of Chickamauga), and that Gen. Robert E. Lee himself was present to direct operations.[86]

For Sgt. John Risedorph of the 4th Minnesota, Clark's brigade, John Smith's division, XV Corps, March 20 had been a day of misery. Two days before, Risedorph had drawn a pair of shoes so ill-fitting that they raised a dozen blisters on his feet before he had marched five miles. Risedorph gave away the shoes and marched barefoot. "I have had to march barefoot again today and my feet keep getting worse," he penciled in his diary. "If I do not get in camp soon I will have to give up."

At 9:00 p.m. Risedorph noted that the musketry in his front was still "very heavy. . . .One year ago today I was in my own state putting on style and enjoying myself hugely," he scribbled. "but how different today, and what change times bring[.] today we may be all health and jollity[,] tomorrow we may be nothing more than a bunch of clay."[87]

* * *

General Sherman established his headquarters on the Stevens farm, about 600 yards southeast of Giles Smith's (Fourth Division, XVII Corps) position on the Union right flank. "Our camp," Sherman aide Henry Hitchcock wrote, "is a pleasant one, in a large open field, and a few rods from us is Blair's HdQrs, while Gen. Howard's is also very near."[88]

That evening Sherman assured General Schofield that he could "march into Goldsboro without opposition," and ordered General Terry "to go to Cox's, to which point I will send a pontoon train if I conclude to lay a bridge there." Sherman also instructed the two generals to be ready to march to his support if necessary. "We are now ready for battle if Johnston desires it to-morrow," Sherman wrote Terry, "but as he has failed to overcome one wing he will hardly invite battle with both. I don't want to fight now or here, and therefore won't object to his drawing off to-night toward Smithfield, as he should."[89]

Sherman directed Slocum to send all his empty wagons to Kinston for supplies in case Johnston chose to stay and fight. "I cannot see why he remains," Sherman added, "and still think he will avail himself of night to get back to Smithfield. I would rather avoid a general battle if possible, but if he insists on it, we must accommodate him."[90]

Thus, Sherman was as reluctant to open a battle at Bentonville as Johnston was eager to invite one. And yet, as so often happens in warfare, the next day's fight would assume a far different aspect from what either commander could have hoped for or anticipated.

~ *fifteen* ~

"As Exciting and Lively a P.M. As I Ever Saw"

—Maj. Charles W. Wills, 103rd Illinois

Vett Noble's duties as General Sherman's chief clerk began early on the morning of Tuesday, March 21. Sherman's adjutant, Maj. Lewis M. Dayton, "came and called me at 2 A.M.," Noble wrote. "the Genl had got a fit on and made out a Special Field Order three letter pages long, two copies to be made instanter [sic] and nine more right after. I concluded I wouldn't go to bed again although I got no good sleep the night before."[1]

Noble was referring to Sherman's "Special Field Orders No. 33," a 313-word document in six parts. In Parts I-III Sherman directed Generals Howard, Slocum and Kilpatrick to establish temporary depots near the Wilmington & Weldon Railroad where they were to deposit all unnecessary baggage. Sherman also enjoined Howard to send his empty wagons to Kinston for provisions, and Slocum to transport his wounded to a temporary hospital on the railroad just below Goldsboro. In Parts IV-VI Sherman ordered Slocum to send his pontoon train to Cox's Bridge—or rather, what was left of it—where General Terry would cross the Neuse River and establish a bridgehead. Howard, likewise, was to "send his bridge train to some good crossing" between his depot and Goldsboro. The order also directed Schofield to occupy Goldsboro, and concluded by urging Col. W. W. Wright to "use extraordinary exertions" to complete the rail link between Kinston and Goldsboro.[2]

A few miles northwest of Sherman's headquarters, General Law was also awakened at 2:00 a.m. "My scouts have just returned from the right of the enemy's lines," Law informed General Hampton. "They report no retrograde movement of the enemy; on the contrary, the indications are that he will fight to-day."[3]

The Confederates utilized the early morning hours of March 21 to bolster their vulnerable left flank. The Georgians of Fiser's Brigade, McLaws' Division, stumbled in the darkness across the swamp on their left and relieved a portion of Wheeler's cavalry, whose line accordingly shifted to the left. Wheeler ordered his troopers to entrench, and by sunup they had dug a line of works extending 1,200 yards northward from McLaws' left flank. The cavalrymen of Butler's Division erected a line of log and rail barricades in continuation of Wheeler's works, and Law's dismounted skirmishers dug some rifle pits along the swamp in their front.[4]

At dawn Colonel Fiser reported that his left flank did not connect with Wheeler's right, so McLaws dispatched Hardy's Brigade to plug the gap. Hardy's unit did not possess enough men to cover the opening, however, so Colonel Hardy immediately sent word to McLaws that his left flank was exposed and that Federal skirmishers were trying to turn it. McLaws then ordered General Kennedy to send two regiments of Conner's Brigade to join on Hardy's left and form a junction with Wheeler's cavalrymen. While Kennedy's two regiments were deploying, the Federal skirmishers attacked them. Alarmed by the rattle of musketry that suddenly erupted on his left flank, McLaws ordered Kennedy to send two more regiments to the left, then rode over to investigate.[5]

Wheeler's situation was equally uncertain. While McLaws shifted his reserves to the left in an effort to form a solid line of defense, Hampton's adjutant informed Wheeler that the Federals had been seen crossing the swamp on his left, and that that same flank did not connect with Law's right. The time was 6:45 a.m., and already the Confederates' vulnerable left flank was being pressed.[6]

* * *

On Slocum's line, some XX Corps soldiers spent a sleepless night pondering a rumored assault they were to make the next morning. "In such a case the soldiers dislike to be in suspense," wrote a veteran of the 102nd Illinois, a regiment in Case's brigade of Ward's division. The men had gone to bed early, "silent and thoughtful," and were up at 5:30 a.m. on the 21st, "ready to move on the enemy's works." The Illinoisan continued:

> I cannot describe the feelings then experienced, nor the thoughts that passed through my mind, as I sat by the fire, waiting for the time when the work should commence. I almost longed for the time to come that the work might be finished and off my mind. This thinking of a battle so long before it is to take place and knowing it must be fought, almost makes a coward of the thinker.[7]

The Illinoisan and his comrades need not have worried, because Sherman had other plans for the XX Corps. Sherman sent his chief engineer, Col. Orlando M. Poe, to Slocum with orders to avoid "a general engagement unless the enemy attacked." Furthermore, Colonel Poe outlined Sherman's plan for resuming the march to Goldsboro. On the following day, March 22, Slocum was to withdraw the XX Corps from its present position and march it down the new Goldsboro Road to a point in rear of Howard's wing. On March 23 Slocum would repeat this withdrawal with the XIV Corps. To prevent Johnston from pouncing on the rear of Slocum's column, "let the cavalry relieve by a thin skirmish line the skirmishers" of the infantry's rear guard, Sherman advised Slocum in a dispatch. Poe noted that while he was explaining these various movements, "the Enemy attacked General Slocum's command." But the supposed assault soon proved to be nothing more than some skirmishing at the Cole plantation.[8]

What did Sherman hope to accomplish by withdrawing Slocum's wing? "The left wing is now extricated," Sherman told General Force on the morning of the 21st. "I will resume the march to Goldsboro. I will not attack Johnson [sic]—fighting him would amount to nothing. I will close around him and let him attack me, if he choose[s]. But to-morrow, I will resume the march, whether he attack[s] or not." It is clear from this statement that Sherman regarded Johnston's army as little more than a nuisance, and one that he was prepared to sidestep if it refused to do the sensible thing and retreat. But was Sherman prepared to withdraw *both* wings of his army and concede the field—and the mantle of victory—to Johnston?[9]

Probably not. Sherman understood the importance his men attached to a victory at Bentonville. These veterans knew as well as their commander that this battle might very well be the culminating event of the Carolinas Campaign, and more importantly, they knew that many of their comrades had already fought and died on this field. Major Osborn stated the matter thus: "These operations appear to me to have settled down to a question of who can stay the longest, and so claim the record of a victory. . . .The point is *morale,* and who shall have it. If we back first to go for supplies, Johnston gets the *morale,* and if we make Johnston leave first, we keep our record good.[10]

Sherman's only objective at Bentonville was to allow Johnston's army to withdraw so that his own army could resume its march on Goldsboro. Sherman regarded a tactical victory at Bentonville as of secondary importance. As he told Schofield: "[Johnston's] position is in the swamps, difficult of approach, and I don't like to assail his parapets."[11]

There was yet another reason against a general assault: the weather was turning ugly. Throughout the morning the storm clouds gathered and the sky darkened, "Threatening rain," Sherman scrawled in his diary.[12]

Meanwhile, Sherman aide Maj. Henry Hitchcock was inside his tent writing a letter to his wife Mary: "It is about 8:30 A.M., and breakfast is over two hours ago. The pickets on both sides, and the skirmishers, are amusing themselves popping away as usual." The day before, Hitchcock had ventured forth for the first time "beyond the line of battle, into the woods, where they were skirmishing; learned what was going on, found out that thick woods are not favorable to landscape views, though very good to stop bullets, and went back better satisfied." Yet Hitchcock conceded:

> if one should go into danger without orders & pick up a bullet, it seems the verdict would be 'served him right'—and this most of all from the Gen'l himself. . . .I do not find that those who have faced danger oftenest are any more

> disposed to go into it needlessly; on the contrary, it seems to be regarded as simple folly.

Regarding the morning's skirmishing, Hitchcock told his wife that for all the noise "there is no prospect of an assault—indeed I know it is intended to reconnoitre the ground today for other purposes."[13]

* * *

At 10:25 a.m. Lt. Gen. A. P. Stewart sent an urgent message to General Johnston: "It has just been reported to me that the enemy's infantry are advancing on Taliaferro's extreme right, threatening to turn his flank."[14]

Fortunately for the Confederates, Stewart's warning proved to be a false alarm: Taliaferro's men had mistaken the intentions of a Union skirmish line that had appeared in their front. The Federal skirmishers, numbering several hundred men from Ward's division of the XX Corps, fired a few shots before vanishing into the woods, just as they had done on a similar reconnaissance the day before. Ward's skirmishers returned to the main line and reported what they had seen. Because of the skirmishers' indifferent reconnaissance work, General Ward—and more importantly, XX Corps commander Alpheus Williams—now believed that a strong line of Confederate works extended to Mill Creek. This misconception was of inestimable value to Johnston, for the gap beyond his right flank—a mile-long stretch from Mill Creek to the end of the infantry's entrenched line—was defended by only a thin line of cavalry videttes. At noon Johnston ordered Stewart and Taliaferro to throw out skirmishers and make their own reconnaissance. The skirmishers reported that "the enemy had drawn back his left and intrenched it, as if to cover a march toward Goldsborough."[15]

The Confederate skirmishers were correct as to the Federals' intentions, but aside from *advancing* a few hundred yards on the extreme left, Slocum's line actually had changed little since the night of March 19. The only changes of consequence involving Slocum's line on March 21 occurred along General Morgan's front. First, Vandever's and Mitchell's brigades advanced a short distance beyond Hoke's old works and changed front to the left. Their line now faced the Goldsboro Road and re-established connection with General Hazen's skirmishers. Once again, the 14th Michigan and the 16th Illinois (under the irrepressible Lieutenant Colonel Grummond) moved out to find the enemy. For several hours Grummond's command engaged in desultory skirmishing with the North Carolina Junior Reserves while the rest of Vandever's brigade constructed earthworks a few hundred yards to the rear.[16]

Grummond's Confederate counterpart was 18-year-old Maj. Walter Clark, the future chief justice of the North Carolina Supreme Court. Clark had commanded the Junior Reserves' skirmish line since the morning of the 20th. Between the "almost continuous firing" and the Yankee "scamps trying to creep up on us in the dark," Clark had been unable to sleep the night before. The youthful major called the scrap with Grummond's command "a regular Indian fight of it behind trees." Grummond merely reported that "the enemy's skirmishers kept up a brisk fire, doing but little damage. I lost one man wounded."[17]

The second change of position involved Fearing's brigade, which had returned to its old works in rear of Vandever's and Mitchell's line on the morning of the 20th. That evening, when Baird's division withdrew from Robinson's brigade's old works near the western edge of the Cole field, Morgan directed Lieutenant Colonel Langley to place two regiments of Fearing's brigade behind those works. Morgan thus sought to prevent the Confederates from gaining a foothold in the Cole field or enfilading his lines from the second-story windows of the Cole house.[18]

On the morning of the 21st Langley placed the other two available regiments of his brigade to the right of Robinson's works and astride the Goldsboro Road. "This formation put the brigade in single line, with the left much advanced," Langley reported. The 52nd Ohio held the left of the line. Major James Taylor Holmes of the 52nd thought the "left flank of the regiment stuck [out] at the enemy like a sore thumb." Moreover, the entire brigade lay several hundred yards in front of its nearest support—Carlin's division of the XIV Corps.[19]

When Carlin's skirmishers formed on Langley's flanks, Fearing's brigade inspector James Burkhalter sneered:

> The gap is now filled by the somewhat demoralized skirmishers of the 1st Division [14th] Army Corps, who have but partially recovered from the infantile stampede they staged on the 19th. In their present fearful state, without any very heavy blows against them by the rebs, these men would quickly repeat their shameful conduct.[20]

Conditions appeared ripe for a reprise of the March 19 rout. Langley's men made the best of their exposed position by improving Robinson's works on the left of the line, and by digging new works on the right. Langley reported his situation to Morgan, then awaited his chief's reply.[21]

By 10:00 a.m. Langley's position was the focal point of Slocum's line. Generals Morgan, Davis and Carlin all reconnoitered the ground, and were soon joined by Slocum, who assured Langley that he would place some troops on his left flank. But Slocum stipulated that these troops would remain in position for only one hour, long enough for a part of Langley's command to entrench along a more retired line south of the Goldsboro Road. About noon, two XX Corps brigades—Selfridge's and Robinson's—advanced into position on Langley's left, where according to division commander Nathaniel Jackson, "they took position very near that occupied by General Robinson on the 19th." (We can only speculate as to the advice the fiery Robinson might have offered Lieutenant Colonel Langley.) The XX Corps troops immediately set to work building breastworks, but after about a half-hour (according to Langley's estimate) they packed up and withdrew to their former positions. Langley in turn fell back to his new line of works just south of, and facing, the Goldsboro Road.[22]

Meanwhile, the weather worsened. A light drizzle had fallen since mid-morning, and at noon increased to a downpour, sometimes falling "in fierce torrents," according to Sherman aide Maj. George W. Nichols. This steady rainfall would continue into the following morning.[23]

To secure his new line, Langley left a picket post of 60 men under Major Holmes at his old position, advanced a skirmish line across the Cole field, and placed a detachment of sharpshooters from the 22nd Indiana in the Cole house and farm buildings. The Federal skirmish line—consisting of Company I of the 86th Illinois led by Lt. Col. Allen Fahnestock—drove back the Rebel skirmishers

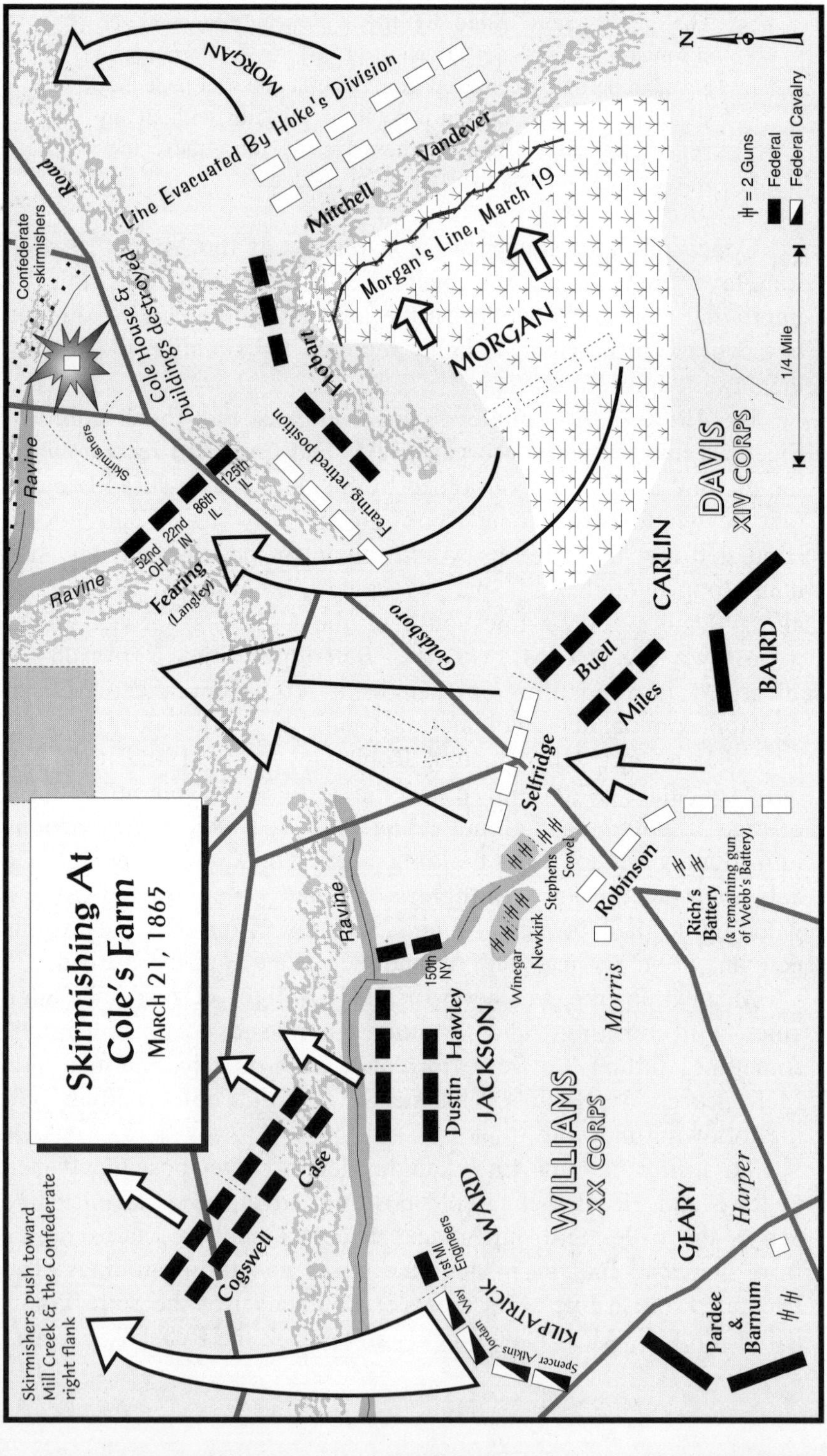
Skirmishing At Cole's Farm
March 21, 1865
MORGAN
Line Evacuated By Hoke's Division
Road
Confederate skirmishers
Cole House & buildings destroyed
Mitchell
Vandever
Morgan's Line, March 19
Hobart
MORGAN
Fearing, retired position
Ravine
Skirmishers
125th IL
86th IL
22nd IN
52nd OH
Ravine
Fearing (Langley)
Goldsboro
Buell
Miles
CARLIN
DAVIS
XIV CORPS
BAIRD
Selfridge
Robinson
Scovel
Stephens
Newkirk
Winegar
Rich's Battery (& remaining gun of Webb's Battery)
Morris
Ravine
150th NY
Hawley
Dustin
JACKSON
WILLIAMS
XX CORPS
WARD
Case
Cogswell
GEARY
Harper
Pardee & Barnum
1st MI Engineers
KILPATRICK
Way
Jordan
Atkins
Spencer
Skirmishers push toward Mill Creek & the Confederate right flank
N
= 2 Guns
Federal
Federal Cavalry
1/4 Mile

Mark A. Moore

easily, but as several other Union skirmish lines had already discovered, holding this field would prove to be a difficult matter.[24]

In his official report Lieutenant Colonel Fahnestock mentioned that his skirmishers occupied a line of rifle pits, but he failed to specify the location of these pits. They probably lined the northern slope of the ravine north of the Cole field.[25]

The Confederates reacted swiftly to the Federal advance, opening a fierce artillery and small arms fire on the Union skirmishers. Minutes later, a long gray and butternut line, comprising the skirmishers of the three Army of Tennessee corps, advanced on the swampy ravine occupied by Fahnestock's skirmishers. Once again, this ravine bore witness to an overwhelming Confederate charge and a precipitate Federal retreat. As the Illinoisans and Hoosiers raced across the Cole field, the Confederate skirmishers put the Cole house and buildings to the torch, burning them to the ground "to prevent their further use by the Yankee sharpshooters," D. H. Hill reported. The three-day battle for the Cole house had ended in a draw. Aside from some scattered picket firing, this action marked the end of the fighting on Slocum's and A. P. Stewart's side of the battlefield.[26]

That afternoon XIV Corps staff officer Captain Burkhalter questioned some Confederate prisoners and deserters and learned that "Hardee's Corps was massed on our front and ready to make a charge, and was only delayed by the heavy uproar made on our right, by our General Howard." In retrospect, the intention of these so-called Rebel prisoners and deserters is obvious. In modern parlance they would be classified as "operatives" and their work as "counterintelligence." That Captain Burkhalter and his superiors credited the Rebel prisoners' statements reveals two important facts: the Federals' uncertainty regarding the Confederates' actual strength and the Confederates' adroitness at exploiting that uncertainty.[27]

Before the day ended, Johnston would have to gamble on the Federals' misapprehension to save his Army of the South from destruction.

* * *

The Federal skirmishers along Howard's front advanced at first light. Sherman reported that his "general instructions were to press steadily with skirmishers alone, to use artillery pretty freely in the wooded space held by the enemy, and to feel pretty strongly the flanks of his position." Both Logan's and Blair's skirmishers developed a strong and continuous line of Confederate earthworks crowning the opposite side of the ravine. At 10:00 a.m., Howard's main line advanced several hundred yards to the eastern edge of this ravine and entrenched.[28]

The system used by the 50th Illinois was no doubt typical of most XV Corps regiments:

> The sergeant major was. . .ordered to take twenty men and go to the division train as quickly as possible and get what axes and spades he could. . . .Going at a double quick they soon returned with thirty-six spades and ten new axes. During this time the line was located, and the tools being given to one company at a time, they were allowed ten minutes' use of them until they had been used along the line. Others of the boys were busy with their hatchets and heavy knives in hacking down the underbrush in front and bringing it into the pile of rubbish, which was soon covered with dirt, forming a fair line of works.[29]

Across the ravine from the Federals, Hoke's and McLaws' men were similarly occupied, though considerably more hard pressed for axes and shovels. The Confederates' first line of defense was a string of rifle pits near the base of the ravine and about 100 yards in front of the main line. These pits lay from 40 to 50 feet apart and varied in size, sheltering anywhere from two to four men. The Rebels had also cleared away the interval between the rifle pits and the main line to improve their downhill field of fire. About 50 yards from their works they drove a staggered line of sharpened stakes (abatis) into the ground to break the momentum of a Yankee assault. Here and there the Confederate earthworks were surmounted by headlogs which served to protect the heads of the defenders, who aimed and fired their rifles through a narrow slit between the log and the earthwork. If a shell or a solid shot knocked the headlog loose, it would roll harmlessly down a row of logs leaning up against the entrenchment instead of toppling over on the defenders. At least this was how the headlog system worked in theory, but as will be seen, this was not always the case in battlefield conditions. The Union and Confederate field fortifications at Bentonville varied little, for experience had taught the soldiers on both sides the same harsh lessons.[30]

On the XV Corps' front, Gen. William Woods' brigade, having just reached the front after being on train guard duty, deployed along the center of younger brother Charles' divisional line. Hazen's Second and Third Brigades, commanded respectively by Col. Wells Jones and Brig. Gen. John Oliver, formed on the left of First Brigade commander Theodore Jones' line. Wells Jones' and Oliver's troops had just finished corduroying a muddy farm road that led up to their position so that the four 20-pounder Parrott guns of Capt. Francis DeGress' battery (Battery H, 1st Illinois) could be hauled into range. By then Hazen decided that he did not need DeGress' battery at the front, so it never went into action at Bentonville.[31]

Hazen's line was deployed just north of the Goldsboro Road a few hundred yards in advance of Morgan's line. A large gap separated the two divisions, meaning that Howard's and Slocum's wings had failed to form a proper junction. Thus far Hazen's skirmishers had managed to cover the gap without difficulty, and Hazen had taken the precaution of holding Oliver's brigade in reserve on his left. His division enjoyed greater success in shoring up its right flank, when about noon Theodore Jones' brigade obliqued to the right and joined on the left flank of Stone's Iowa brigade of Woods' division.[32]

By 1:00 p.m. most of Howard's new line was well-entrenched. The Union and Confederate main lines on this front were now separated by 300 yards of swampy thickets and man-made obstructions. The skirmish firing was heavy all along the ravine, but neither side appeared eager to test the other's defenses.

The stalemate proved short-lived. About 1:30 p.m. Howard received word from XVII Corps commander Blair that General Joe Mower's division had driven into the rear of the Rebels' position near Bentonville and threatened their sole line of retreat. Howard ordered Blair to support Mower's breakthrough with his other two divisions, then sent word to XV Corps commander Logan "to push forward his skirmish line and the moment he detected the enemy giving way to take advantage of it."[33]

Logan sent forward a strong skirmish line with orders to seize the enemy's rifle pits, while holding his main line in readiness for a general assault. Generals Charles Woods and Corse ordered up their batteries, and XV Corps chief of artillery Lt. Col. William H. Ross directed a section of Lt. Edward B. Wright's battery (Battery B, 1st Michigan) to report for duty on the main line. (Battery B was attached to John Smith's division, which remained in reserve throughout the day.) The six brass Napoleons of Battery H, 1st Missouri, Capt. Charles M. Callahan commanding, unlimbered on the right of Corse's position, while the four Napoleons of the 12th Wisconsin Battery under Capt. William Zickerick dropped trail on the right of Charles Woods' line. The two 3-inch ordnance rifles of Wright's battery wheeled into position on the right of Captain Zickerick's guns.[34]

General William Woods described the fighting in his front as a "hot skirmish, almost amounting to a battle." One hundred Federal skirmishers under Capt. William Burch of the 31st/32nd Missouri Consolidated drove off the left flank skirmishers of Colquitt's Georgia Brigade, and immediately began piling up earth on the reverse side of the enemy's rifle pits. The Georgians launched a desperate counterattack from their main line and retook the pits. The Federals rallied and again drove off the Confederates, only to be driven back again themselves. Woods now sent in a reinforcement of 40 fresh troops, which enabled the Northerners to seize the Georgians' pits a third time and hold them. Woods reported that during the fighting for the pits Captain Burch "received a severe and dangerous wound."[35]

On Woods' left, Colonel Stone deployed a strong skirmish line consisting of three regiments—from left to right, the 9th, 30th and 4th Iowa regiments. The Iowans captured the Georgians' pits in their front "with but slight loss," Stone reported, "but the enemy evinced so much determination to regain them that the fighting became very sharp." Colonel Stone ventured up to the skirmish line a few times and estimated that the rifle pits lay within 100 yards of the Confederates' main line.[36]

The Federal skirmishers cautiously worked their way up to the abandoned pits while the soldiers of Colquitt's Brigade fired heavy volleys down on them. Private Levi Nelson Green of the 9th Iowa wrote that after each volley, he rose up with a yell and fired away at the Rebels with his Spencer rifle, in the midst of a rain "pouring down in torrents," Green noted. According to Colonel Stone, the Georgians followed up their volleys three times by assaulting his

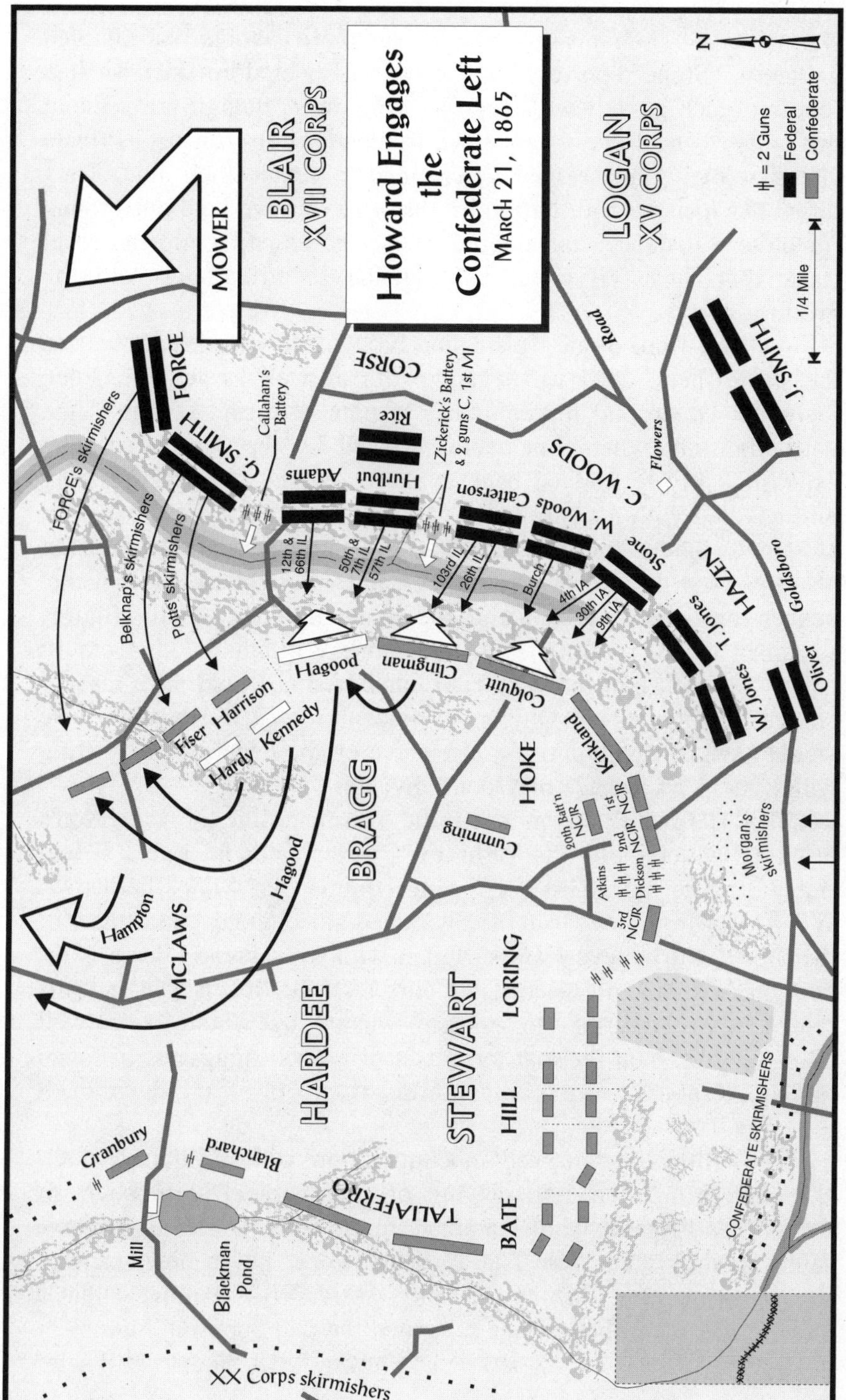
Howard Engages the Confederate Left
March 21, 1865
BLAIR
XVII CORPS
LOGAN
XV CORPS
MOWER
FORCE
G. SMITH
CORSE
Rice
Adams
Hurlbut
C. WOODS
W. Woods
Catterson
Stone
HAZEN
T. Jones
W. Jones
Oliver
J. SMITH
Callahan's Battery
Zickerick's Battery & 2 guns C, 1st MI
12th & 66th IL
50th & 7th IL
57th IL
103rd IL
26th IL
Burch
4th IA
30th IA
9th IA
FORCE's skirmishers
Belknap's skirmishers
Potts' skirmishers
Road
Flowers
Goldsboro
Hagood
Clingman
Colquitt
Kirkland
HOKE
BRAGG
Fiser
Harrison
Hardy
Kennedy
Cumming
20th Batt'n NCJR
1st NCJR
2nd NCJR
3rd NCJR
Atkins
Dickson
Morgan's skirmishers
Hampton
MCLAWS
HARDEE
STEWART
LORING
HILL
BATE
Granbury
Blanchard
TALIAFERRO
Mill
Blackman Pond
XX Corps skirmishers
CONFEDERATE SKIRMISHERS
= 2 Guns
Federal
Confederate
1/4 Mile
N

Mark A. Moore

skirmishers. "Their men swarmed over the[ir] works and charged gallantly," Stone reported, but the Iowans' beefed-up skirmish line repulsed each assault with superior firepower, though not without difficulty. "The Rebels kept up a tremendous fire on us," Private Green wrote, "and seemed determined to retake their line. They drove our men on both left and right of us, but we held our ground for quite a distance, and poured such a galling fire into the rebel flank that they fell back, and our boys rallied and held the ground."[37]

A detail from Stone's main line brought down some shovels to the skirmishers, "and we began to dig as well as shoot," Green recorded. Green and his comrades remained on the skirmish line until nightfall, when they were relieved by the 31st Iowa. The exhausted private trudged back to the main line, "a sweet looking bird covered with mud from top to toe."[38]

On Colonel Stone's left, the skirmishers of Hazen's division never pressed the skirmishers of Kirkland's North Carolina Brigade; hence, they both were spared the much higher casualty figures sustained by their comrades on the Stone-William Woods-Colquitt front. "If it had not rained so hard our Division would have made a charge," explained an Ohioan in Hazen's outfit. Such an excuse would have met with derision elsewhere on the Federal line, starting with Catterson's brigade of Woods' division.[39]

The 103rd Illinois manned the skirmish line of Catterson's brigade, which held the right of Charles Woods' line. "I feel finely," wrote the 103rd's left wing commander, Maj. Charles W. Wills, "wet from head to foot, has rained since noon[,] hard most of the time. . . .I believe I am surfeited with oven bread ('death balls' our cook calls them), biscuit, and pork." Of the Rebels, Major Wills remarked: "I would like to see them whaled, but would like to wait until we refit. You see that too much of a good thing gets *old*, and one don't enjoy even campaigning after 50 or 60 days of it together."[40]

The Illinoisans charged in conjunction with William Woods' skirmishers on their left, driving off the Tarheel skirmishers of Clingman's Brigade, who scrambled up the slope to the comparative safety of their main line. The Tarheels' works lay in plain view of the Illinoisans down at the rifle pits; Major Wills estimated that a mere 75 yards of open woods separated the two opposing lines.[41]

While the 103rd traded shots with the Tarheels, the crews of Zickerick's battery, ignoring the whizzing bullets and the knee-deep swamp at the base of the ravine, hauled their guns into position behind the Illinoisans. The four 12-pounder Napoleons now stood within 100 yards of the Confederates' main line.[42]

No sooner had Zickerick's battery unlimbered than Clingman's Brigade counterattacked simultaneously with Colquitt's. The combined brigades succeeded in dislodging the left wing of the 103rd Illinois from the rifle pits. The 500 North Carolinians were spread dangerously thin, however, having earlier been called upon to fill a gap on their left created when Hagood's Brigade hurried off to oppose Mower's division near Bentonville. The Federals soon rallied and retook the pits, but the Tarheel skirmishers mounted another counterattack.[43]

Fortunately for the 103rd and the crews of Zickerick's battery, the 26th Illinois came up on their left flank and went for the Carolinians "with a first-class yell," Major Wills wrote. "You should have seen the Rebels run. It did me a power of good." As soon as William Woods' skirmishers retook the pits on the Illinoisans' left, the 26th relieved the 103rd on the skirmish line, and Zickerick's battery roared into action. "I think this has been as exciting and lively a p.m. as I ever saw," Major Wills noted in his diary.[44]

The Federals on General Corse's skirmish line may have found their fight with the Confederates a bit *too* exciting. Company C of the 50th Illinois in Lt. Col. Frederick J. Hurlbut's brigade, held the left of that line, along the front that had just been vacated by Hagood's Brigade. The left wing of Clingman's Brigade now manned Hagood's entrenchments. Company C received orders to charge alongside the skirmish line of Col. Robert N. Adams' brigade on their right, which consisted of several companies from the 12th and 66th Illinois regiments. In this charge Company C sustained several casualties and one near-miss: Sgt. Frank McCarty received a flesh wound in his arm; Matthew Leech was shot in the upper shin of his left leg, necessitating amputation above the knee; Private Deer was grazed by a bullet along the right side of his head; and George Carter received a severe scare when a minie ball tore through his tin bucket and haversack before finally coming to rest in the tenth ply of his bedroll.[45]

Although the Illinoisans seized the enemy's rifle pits in their front, the North Carolinians launched a fierce counterattack from their main works and outflanked Colonel Adams' skirmish line, compelling it to fall back. According to Lieutenant Colonel Hurlbut, Company C of the 50th Illinois had made the charge with empty cartridge boxes and, receiving no support on either flank, was ordered to fall back by Capt. Benjamin S. Barbour of Corse's staff. By the time reinforcements arrived, the Confederates had already reoccupied their rifle pits. The 50th Illinois' historian recalled the incident differently, however, stating that Captain Barbour encountered Company C as it was returning to the main line after being relieved by Companies A, H and K of the 50th. Barbour was furious. He called the men of Company C cowards and ordered them back onto the skirmish line in the mistaken belief that he was dealing with skulkers. Company C promptly obeyed and assisted the three other companies in retaking the pits.[46]

The charge of the 50th Illinois skirmishers was brief but bloody. In Company A, Anderson Font was killed by a bullet in the chest; L. C. Hasting received a flesh wound in the left arm; J. W. McDonald was struck by a spent ball. In Company H, Jerry Clark was hit by a bullet that fractured his elbow; B. H. Lambert was wounded in the left thigh; G. W. Friday suffered a flesh wound in the calf of his right leg; W. McConnel was slightly wounded in the left shin. In Company K, Clinging Smith was grazed by a ball on his left shoulder, while N. Hoffman was nicked in the head by a bullet.[47]

The 50th Illinois' skirmishers retook the pits, but their success was temporary, for they were soon driven across the swamp by the Tarheels' augmented skirmish line. The four companies of the 50th were relieved by the 70 men of the 7th Illinois under Maj. Edward Johnson, most of whom were brandishing Henry rifles. Soon afterward, two companies of the 57th Illinois advanced to the support of the 7th. A soldier of the 57th observed that his rapid-firing comrades were "as usual having lots of fun with their sixteen-shooters."[48]

The Illinoisans on the skirmish line dug rifle pits in anticipation of a Confederate assault, which came just after the 39th Iowa had deployed alongside the main body of the 57th Illinois. The Federals repulsed the assault easily. Private Will Johnson of the 39th saw General Logan, hatless and sword in hand, calmly riding his great black horse along the main line. "Keep cool, they are coming again," "Black Jack" told his men. "Wait until you can count the buttons on their coats and see the whites of their eyes before you shoot." Logan's advice must have sounded quaint to the Henry-toting men of the 7th, who had even less trouble repulsing the second assault than the first.[49]

Like Logan, General Howard spent most of the afternoon at the front, having galloped up to Charles Woods' line the moment he had received word of Mower's breakthrough. "I have been riding with Gen. Howard for five hours, backwards and forwards along our skirmish line, exposed to a deadly fire," Lt. Col. William E. Strong wrote in his journal. "I thought both of us would be killed. I never hesitated yet to go where my duty called me. . .but I do object most seriously to being made a target for the enemy to practice on." Strong was reminded of an observation Capt. Charles Henry Howard once made about his brother the general: "[R]iding in battle with a man who is always prepared to die, is not as pleasant as one might think."

"I agree with Captain Howard," Strong wrote.[50]

At least Strong did not have to worry about being hit by a Confederate cannon ball. While riding up and down the Right Wing's skirmish line, Howard noticed that the Rebels were not using any artillery in his front and concluded that they had withdrawn it in preparation for a retreat that night.[51] Given the nature of the terrain, Howard was fortunate to have 12 of his own field pieces in position. Major Osborn characterized the ground at Bentonville as "a quicksand flat" which supported infantry well enough, but swallowed gun carriage wheels and draft animals' hooves. Of course this did not prevent Zickerick's and Callahan's batteries from assuming forward positions on the XV Corps line, but the three XVII Corps batteries would remain in park throughout the day.[52]

The Confederates suffered no less than the Federals in the see-saw fighting for the rifle pits. Among the 18 casualties suffered by Clingman's Brigade on March 21 was its commander, Col. William S. Devane, and the commander of the 61st North Carolina, Lt. Col. Edward Beatty Mallett. Devane was severely wounded and Mallett was killed during the afternoon's fighting. Mallett's last words were, "My wife! my poor wife!"[53]

News of Mallett's death soon reached his widow, who was refugeeing in Chapel Hill, North Carolina, with their five children.

The Malletts had lived there since March 1862, having fled the family estate in New Berne rather than live under Yankee occupation. Soon after the death of her husband, Mrs. Mallett's health began to fail. "The wife made an effort to live for [her] children," wrote Cornelia Phillips Spencer, one of her Chapel Hill neighbors. "But the brown hair turned gray rapidly, the easy-chair was relinquished for the bed, and before winter came the five children were left alone in the world."[54]

With the exception of one incident, the skirmishing along the front occupied by Giles Smith's and Force's divisions of the XVII Corps lacked the ferocity of the fighting in Corse's and Charles Woods' sectors. About 2:00 p.m. Giles Smith's skirmish line splashed across a swamp and seized the rifle pits held by Harrison's and Fiser's Brigades of McLaws' Division. The skirmishers of Brig. Gen. William W. Belknap's brigade paused for a breather at the pits, then advanced on the Confederates' main line, led by the 32nd Illinois on the right flank. One of the Illinoisans, a draftee or conscript, lagged behind the skirmish line and knelt down as if to avoid the Rebels' bullets.

"You d—d 'connie,' come on and fight!" yelled an officer of the 32nd, displaying the volunteer soldier's contempt for the drafted man.

"Wait till I tie my shoe, and you'll see how a 'connie' will fight!" the draftee replied, and then dashed off after his comrades.[55]

On the Confederate line, McLaws ordered the rifle pits retaken at all hazards. While the 1st Georgia Regulars of Fiser's Brigade were organizing their skirmish detail amid a barrage of enemy shell bursts, the Union skirmishers raced up the smoke-covered, thickly wooded slope, realizing too late that they had blundered to within point-blank range of the Rebels' main earthworks. For a moment the Illinoisans stood dumbfounded in the clearing, then turned and ran. The Regulars opened fire and shot them all in the back, or so they thought. When the smoke cleared, the conscript's body was found lying face down on the Confederate parapet. "They should have thrown down their arms when they saw the situation," wrote Lt. John Fort of the Regulars.[56]

Just a few yards away, a handful of Yankees raised their hands in surrender. "I saw some of the Fifth Georgia regiment jump over their works, collar the boys in blue and pull them in while the rest retreated," recalled Sgt. Williams H. Andrews of the Regulars. The Georgians hauled in a total of seven prisoners from the 32nd Illinois. One of the Illinoisans who had been shot down near the Rebel works and presumed dead by his comrades returned to the regiment a few days later. "He was scarcely recognizable," wrote the 32nd's adjutant, Fenwick Hedley, "for his uniform was horribly dilapidated, and he wore a large patch near his nose, and a bandage around his head, a rifle ball having passed through his cheek, making its exit behind the opposite ear. . . .[He] was looked upon as a modern Lazarus."[57]

As soon as the Federal assault had been repulsed, the Confederates of McLaws' Division resumed preparations for the counterattack. "Where is Fort?" echoed down the line. When the young lieutenant heard Col. Richard A. Wayne call his name, he knew his "time had come." Colonel Wayne informed Fort that he was to lead the charge to retake the rifle pits, and that his force would consist of four men from each company of Fiser's Brigade, about 100 men in all. "I handed my overcoat and blanket to Sergeant Duke," Fort remembered, "and standing upon our intrenchments[,] sword in hand, I commanded. . .'Forward!'"[58]

Fort's men rose up from behind their parapets and charged "with alacrity," but the Georgians' own abatis so disordered their line that the lieutenant ordered his detail to halt and dress ranks. The Georgians then raised "a spirited yell" and resumed the attack. The Illinoisans and Iowans of Belknap's brigade fired a single ragged volley at the charging Rebels before fleeing into the swamp. Fort estimated that his line was within 20 paces of the Federals when they opened fire, but because of the cover provided by the smoke and the dense pine woods, his detail lost only three or four killed, while inflicting about the same number of fatalities on the enemy.[59]

On Belknap's left, the skirmishers of Brig. Gen. Benjamin Potts' brigade fell back before Colonel Harrison's advancing skirmish line. Although the Confederates now controlled all of their rifle pits from Corse's left to Giles Smith's right, it proved to be a double-edged sword. With the Federal batteries now up behind the front lines, they were able to direct their fire anywhere on McLaws' line without risk of harming their own men. Two sections of Callahan's battery moved up in support of both Corse's and Giles Smith's skirmishers, adding their firepower to that of Zickerick's battery on Charles Woods' right.[60]

The Federal artillery fire surprised the Confederates, most of whom had not expected to face Yankee cannon in such heavily wooded swampland. When Callahan's battery opened fire on McLaws' line with solid shot, the first round grazed one of the 1st Georgia Regulars' headlogs. "Then the line of men rose up like one man and our logs were tumbled over our works," Sergeant Andrews recalled, "for a cannon ball bursting one of the logs would have caused more damage than a dozen shells." One of McLaws' men recorded that his position was so pelted with "canister shot. . .[that] a man is not safe for one moment out of the intrenchments."[61]

Callahan's battery also directed its fire on McLaws' rifle pits, "but we refused to abandon them," Lieutenant Fort wrote. During the barrage a shell exploded near the pit occupied by Fort and several of his men, showering them with a column of sand, but leaving them without so much as a scratch.[62]

General Force reported that his Federal skirmishers crossed the swamp in their front and advanced to within 100 paces of the Confederates' main line, where they dug in and fired away at their Rebel counterparts. On the left Force's division was opposed by Hardy's and Conner's brigades of McLaws' Division, and on the right by Ashby's Brigade of Humes' Division and Anderson's Brigade of Allen's Division, Wheeler's Cavalry Corps.[63]

Earlier in the day, when McLaws learned that Conner's left flank did not connect with Wheeler's right, he ordered General Kennedy to deploy a strong skirmish line to cover the gap separating the two commands. Kennedy assigned Capt. D. Augustus Dickert, 3rd South Carolina, the task of commanding this skirmish line. By mid-afternoon, Captain Dickert's command was so hard pressed that McLaws sent him the only reinforcements he could scrape up: two companies of teenage boys from Fiser's Brigade and a regiment of Tarheel senior reserves, probably the 77th North Carolina from Hardy's Brigade.

Dickert recalled that "as these old men were coming up on line the enemy were giving us a rattling fire." The captain could neither threaten nor cajole the senior reserves onto the skirmish line because their colonel, "a venerable old gray-beard," had taken cover behind a large tree "as soon as the bullets began to pelt the pines in his front." Dickert likewise failed to coax the colonel from his hiding place: "[A]ll he would do was. . .grasp me by the hand, and try to jerk me down beside him."

"Lie down, young man," the colonel pleaded, "or by God you'll be shot to pieces! Lie down!"

Dickert broke free of the colonel's grasp and walked down to the skirmish line, where he found the youths from Fiser's Brigade "fighting with a glee and abandon I never saw equalled. I am sorry to record that several of these promising young men. . .were killed and many wounded."[64]

On Captain Dickert's left, Ashby's Brigade of Tennesseans, commanded by Lt. Col. James H. Lewis, and Brig. Gen. Robert H. Anderson's Brigade of Georgians, fought dismounted, trading shots with Force's Union skirmishers from behind a strong line of works. "About 2 PM heard heavy firing to the rear of our left flank," noted Capt. William W. Gordon of Anderson's Brigade. The Confederate troopers shot nervous glances in the direction of Bentonville, fearing that the Mill Creek Bridge was under attack.[65]

Under normal circumstances, Mill Creek was a shallow and sluggish stream bordered by steep, muddy banks, yet offering several good fords above Bentonville. But this was 1865—the year of "Sherman's freshet," as the local citizens called it—and Mill Creek had flooded its banks, transforming the pine woods on the north side into a vast swamp. Moreover, the creek threatened to wash out both the foot bridge and the wagon bridge above Bentonville. On March 19 Wheeler's troopers had discovered just how formidable a barrier Mill Creek was, having traced its course for several miles in either direction without finding one ford. An army forced to retreat across Mill Creek would have to abandon its artillery, supply and baggage wagons, ambulances, horses and mules. In short, it would cease to be an army.[66]

Wheeler's cavalrymen knew that if the bridge across Mill Creek was threatened, Johnston's army was fighting for its very survival.

~ *sixteen* ~

"We Would Have Charged Old Nick Himself"

—M. J. Davis of Cumming's Brigade

> It is [Monday,] March 21, 1864. . . ."Crazy Joe" is on the rampage, and there is no rest for the Live Eagle Brigade. It is a wet, drizzling morning; the ground is soaked, and the deep dust of the alluvial soil of this region is now changed to soft and sticky mud. The conditions for marching could not be more forbidding.[1]

So begins S. C. Miles' account of Joe Mower's daring raid on Henderson's Hill, Louisiana, at the opening of Maj. Gen. Nathaniel P. Banks' Red River campaign. On that auspicious day, Mower led his command on a grueling 30-mile march, calculating that the Confederates would least expect such a movement in rainy weather. The fortuitous capture of a Confederate courier had enabled Mower to learn the enemy's countersign, as well as their strength and position. The raid was a stunning success: without firing a shot, "Mower's Guerrillas" captured 250 enemy horsemen, 200 horses, and a four-gun battery. On this raid "Fighting Joe" outdid even himself. According to Miles, Mower strode into one enemy camp wearing the uniform of a captured Confederate officer and announced to the unsuspecting Southern troopers that they were all prisoners of the U. S. Army, whereupon "Mower's Guerrillas" sprang up from their hiding places surrounding the camp.[2]

Exactly one year later, on the morning of Tuesday, March 21, 1865, Joe Mower received notification from XVII Corps commander Frank Blair to have his division in readiness to move out on the right flank. "At the sound of the bugel [sic] we fell in," one of Mower's soldiers noted in his diary. As the men filed into line, it began to drizzle. Mower's command at Bentonville consisted of his First and Third Brigades and the 25th Wisconsin of the Second Brigade, which Mower retained as a guard for his ambulance train, and Lt. William W. Hyser's battery (Battery C, 1st Michigan).[3]

The First Brigade under Brig. Gen. John W. Fuller had the advance, followed by the Third Brigade under Col. John Tillson. Mower's troops had enjoyed a good night's sleep—"best rest last night that we have had in ten days," recorded an officer in Tillson's brigade—and a leisurely breakfast before breaking camp at 10:00 a.m.[4] By 11:00 a.m. Mower's division was on the march, heading almost due north. When the head of the column reached General Blair's headquarters, Mower gave the order to halt and rode over to confer with Blair, who was on horseback and awaiting him by the roadside. The two generals discussed the position that Mower was to occupy. At some point during the discussion Blair sent ahead his inspector general, Lt. Col. Andrew Hickenlooper, with Capt. Albert Koehne of Mower's staff to show him where to deploy.[5]

Because his regiment had the advance, Col. Charles Sheldon of the 18th Missouri was in an excellent position to overhear the generals' conversation. According to Sheldon, Mower's parting words to Blair were: "I suppose, General, after I get into position, there will be no objection to my making a little reconnoisance [sic]."

"None at all," Blair replied.[6]

Mower's column resumed the march, winding past Generals Giles Smith's and Force's earthworks, and finally Force's picket line. As the men passed the videttes of the 9th Illinois Mounted Infantry, they knew that the column had reached the end of the Federal line, the extreme right flank of Sherman's army. A few of Mower's soldiers observed with some uneasiness that a half-mile gap separated them from Force's position. Mower's left flank would remain unsupported throughout the afternoon's operations, an oversight that would prove costly.[7]

Captain Koehne showed Mower where Blair wanted his division to entrench—on the brow of a hill overlooking the Sam Howell Branch, as had the rest of Howard's line. But Mower was far more interested in a nearby road that Koehne said led to the Confederate left flank. This road ran due north for about a half-mile before curving westward toward the Rebel lines. The northward section ran parallel to the Sam Howell Branch to the east and a second stream to the west, which crossed the road at a ford along the curve before feeding into Mill Creek.[8]

With Koehne and Mower leading the way, Fuller's and Tillson's brigades marched up the road and halted when the 18th Missouri came to the ford. Mower decided that it would be unwise to proceed any further with his two brigades in column, so he directed General Fuller to post a strong guard at the ford in case the Confederates attempted such a maneuver themselves. Fuller ordered Colonel Sheldon to deploy five companies of the 18th Missouri along the ford, and to hold it at all hazards.[9]

John Fuller was Joe Mower's most experienced subordinate. He had led the division during the Atlanta Campaign, where his finest hour came during the desperate battle of July 22. There he had rallied his faltering troops by waving the colors of his old regiment, the 27th Ohio. When Mower assumed command in October 1864, the English-born Fuller reverted to his former brigade command.[10]

Mower ordered his two brigades to face about and countermarch a few hundred yards before directing them to halt and face right. His line now faced almost due west, and before it stretched a wide swamp. Fuller's brigade manned the right of the line and Tillson's brigade the left. From left to right, Tillson's brigade consisted of the 10th Illinois, 25th Indiana and 32nd Wisconsin. Joining on Tillson's right were Fuller's three regiments, the 39th Ohio, 27th Ohio and the remaining four companies of the 18th Missouri. The main line numbered about 1,800 men. While Colonel Tillson sent forward just two companies of the 10th Illinois as his skirmish line, Fuller deployed the entire 64th Illinois, about 350-strong, many of them brandishing the deadly Henry repeating rifle.[11]

Some of the men in the 64th had been waiting since November 1864, to receive their Henry rifles. A few days before the March to the Sea began, the 64th's commander, Lt. Col. Michael W. Manning, returned to Illinois to oversee the shipment of a supply of the rifles that the Henry-less men had paid for several months previously. After a series of delays, Manning and the rifles finally arrived at Hilton Head, South Carolina, on February 1, 1865, but by then the

64th was marching deep into enemy territory on the mainland. Manning also bore commissions for several of his men, including one for the regiment's senior captain, 27-year-old Joseph S. Reynolds. According to his commission, Reynolds had been a major since November 1, 1864, but without that document the army still considered him a captain. For obvious reasons, Manning's presence was in great demand among the officers and men of the 64th, to say nothing of Generals Mower and Fuller.[12]

Captain Reynolds had commanded the 64th Illinois in Manning's absence. Like Manning, Reynolds was in hot water with his superiors, facing charges of absence without leave. By mid-1864, Reynolds had been wounded in battle three times, but it was a bout with chronic diarrhea that had led him to obtain 20 days' medical leave in July of that year. Upon the expiration of his leave, Reynolds had not recovered from his illness, and was granted an extension by medical officers in Illinois. To make matters worse, the ailing Reynolds was also diagnosed as tubercular. Nevertheless, the 64th's regimental books listed Reynolds as AWOL from August 21-October 12, 1864.[13]

The regiment that Reynolds commanded possessed more firepower than any other in Fuller's brigade, and for that reason was usually found on the skirmish line. On its bloodiest day—the July 22 Battle of Atlanta—the 64th Illinois had suffered 89 casualties while spearheading a Federal counterattack, recovering in the process the body of Maj. Gen. James B. McPherson.[14]

Once the 64th was in formation, Captain Reynolds "stepped in front of the regiment and made a little speech," remembered one veteran. Pointing over his shoulder, Reynolds told the men that the enemy was just beyond the swamp and that they were going to attack him. He concluded by saying that he expected every man to do his duty.[15]

Mower deployed his command in single line of battle, meaning that the line was two ranks deep. The order reverberated down the line: "Forward!" An officer in Tillson's brigade complained that Mower, in his eagerness to push ahead, scarcely had allowed them time enough "to form the line and to allow the skirmishers to deploy." Still, the two brigades lurched forward, the line of battle following closely behind the skirmishers. The rain was falling steadily now. By noon, Joe Mower's "little reconnaissance" was underway.[16]

* * *

An anxious General Law galloped up to General Hampton and reported that his pickets had spotted a column of Federals marching into position across the swamp in his front. Law reminded Hampton that his line was too weak to repulse anything more substantial than an enemy skirmish line. Hampton told Law to ask Wheeler to extend his line to the left, and added that he would notify Johnston of Law's predicament. When Law found Wheeler, he repeated Hampton's suggestion to him. Wheeler refused to comply with Law's request, explaining that his own line was already overextended. Just then, Law heard his artillery open fire, and galloped off to rejoin his command.[17]

While Law was pleading his case with Wheeler, McLaws reconnoitered the ground on his division's left flank, which was defended only by Captain Dickert's skirmish line. McLaws ordered one of his aides, Capt. G. B. Lamar, to locate Wheeler's right flank. Captain Lamar rode northward a short distance and found a portion of Wheeler's skirmish line defending a road that branched off the Bentonville Road and headed straight for the Federal lines. This road ran northeast for about a mile, then curved southeast for another mile before intersecting with the Goldsboro Road. Wheeler was on the skirmish line when Lamar rode up, and may have told the young staff officer that the road would make an excellent approach route for a Union assault. Lamar galloped back to McLaws and informed the general of what he had learned, then the two rode off to reconnoiter the area in question.[18]

When McLaws arrived at the road, he saw "at a glance" the importance of the position. McLaws immediately sped off to General Johnston's headquarters, where he reported Wheeler's vulnerable position to both Johnston and Hardee. Hampton arrived soon afterward and reported that the Federals were advancing in strength along Law's front. Hampton warned General Johnston "that there was no force present able to resist an attack, and that if the enemy broke through at that point, which was near the [Mill Creek] bridge. . .our only line of retreat would be cut off."

Johnston directed Hampton to ride back to Law's position "to ascertain the exact condition of affairs."[19]

Joe Johnston realized that it was time to gamble. Emboldened by A. P. Stewart's report that Slocum's wing was swung back as if to cover a withdrawal, he ordered Stewart to send him Palmer's and Baker's brigades of Lee's Corps, and instructed Hardee to shift Taliaferro's Division and Granbury's Brigade from the army's right flank to the left. In response to McLaws' warning, Johnston also directed Hardee to send Cumming's Brigade to Wheeler's support. Then "Old Joe" placed "Old Reliable" in command of these multifarious reserves.[20]

While Johnston was making these dispositions, Maj. Gen. Frank Cheatham reported to him at the head of his thousand-man contingent—Brown's Division and Lowrey's Brigade of Cleburne's Division. Cheatham's troops had arrived at Mitchener's Station about 5:00 p.m. the day before, after a nightmarish rail journey that had included an engine breakdown outside of Raleigh. Mindful of the numerous delays caused by the railroad, Frank Cheatham set a grueling pace on the march to Bentonville the next morning. The men struggled to keep up and many of them dropped out from exhaustion, doubtless the result of two weeks' inactivity caused by the haphazard nature of travel on the North Carolina Railroad.[21]

The first troops to arrive were the Tennesseans of Vaughan's Brigade, who forgot their exhaustion at the sight of General Johnston and raised a "loud, hearty cheer," remembered one veteran. After all, was it not "Old Joe" who, just the year before, had reunited Cheatham's Tennessee brigades that Bragg had so callously dispersed? The commander of Vaughan's Brigade, Col. William P. Bishop, informed Johnston that his men were ready for duty, but then confessed that they were exhausted from the day's march. Johnston told Colonel Bishop to have his men fall out and rest in the yard at his headquarters. As the other brigades of Cheatham's contingent arrived on the field they, too, collapsed as soon as they heard the order to fall out. "The music of battle seemed to lull them to sleep," recalled one Tennessean."[22]

While Johnston waited for Hardee to concentrate his scattered forces, Hampton sent him alarming news: the Federals were across the swamp and driving Law's skirmishers before them. Johnston no doubt wondered whether there was enough time to shore up his weak left flank.[23]

* * *

The 64th Illinois plunged into the swamp, led by Captain Reynolds and the regiment's color sergeant, Jerome Evans. "It was a terrible job getting over the swamp, sinking in to the knees and sometimes to the hips," recalled Pvt. Abel Stilwell of the 64th. Sergeant Francis M. Karber of the 39th Ohio remembered having to hack his way through dense patches of vines and sweetbriars while the Rebel minies zipped past him. "In our front," wrote Colonel Sheldon of the 18th Missouri, "the marsh was so deep, and such a tangle of vines, that all the mounted officers were speedily on foot," and some of the men who had been issued entrenching tools threw them away to lighten their burden.[24]

Captain Jacob DeGress of Mower's staff appeared in front of Fuller's line and ordered all barefoot men to the rear. The order applied to many of Fuller's rank and file, for in the 39th Ohio alone there were 130 barefoot men. Yet no more than a handful of officers and men heard the order, and only a few of those affected actually heeded it. The misunderstanding engendered by the "barefoot order" resulted in at least one court-martial trial for cowardice.[25]

Tillson's brigade advanced about 400 yards across a field and through a belt of woods before receiving an order from Mower to halt while Fuller's line struggled through the swamp. Tillson used the 45-minute delay to reinforce his skirmish line with two additional companies of the 10th Illinois, which he deployed on his open left flank. To pass the time, both the 64th Illinois and the skirmish companies of the 10th Illinois traded shots with the Confederate skirmishers while Earle's South Carolina Battery, which had rejoined Butler's Division on March 20, subjected the Federals to a steady shelling. Once Fuller's line finally drew abreast, Tillson's brigade resumed the advance, entering a swamp no less formidable than the one Fuller's troops were wading. While crossing this swamp, Tillson received word that his skirmish line did not connect with Fuller's. "I had only time to report the fact to the general commanding," Tillson wrote, "and urge watchfulness in that quarter,"[26]

Private Stilwell of the 64th Illinois was one of the first Federals to reach dry land. He remembered being numb with fatigue, and

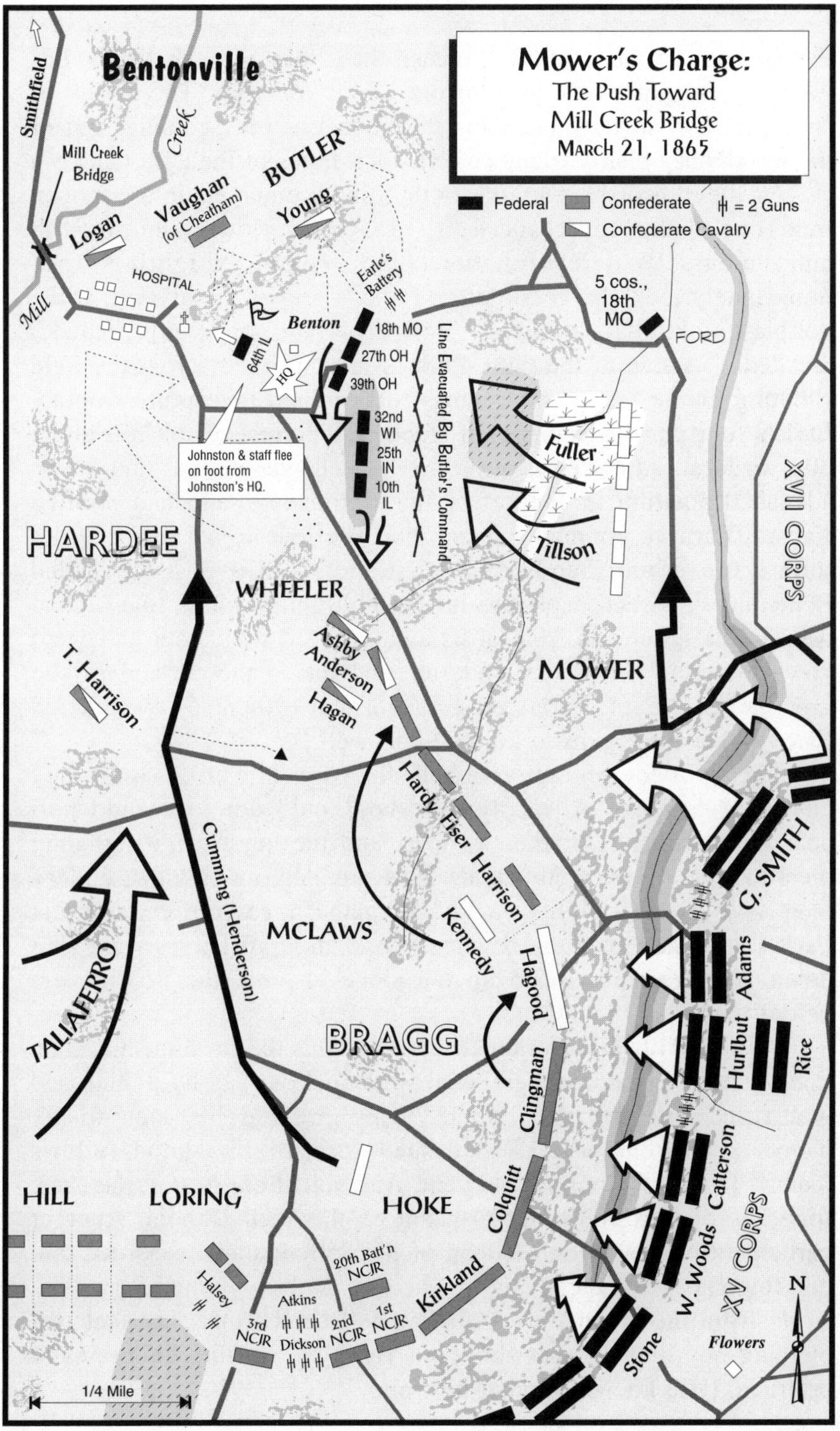

Mower's Charge:
The Push Toward
Mill Creek Bridge
March 21, 1865
Federal
Confederate
= 2 Guns
Confederate Cavalry
Bentonville
Smithfield
Mill Creek Bridge
Creek
Mill
BUTLER
Logan
Vaughan (of Cheatham)
Young
HOSPITAL
Earle's Battery
Benton
HQ
64th IL
18th MO
27th OH
39th OH
32nd WI
25th IN
10th IL
Line Evacuated By Butler's Command
Johnston & staff flee on foot from Johnston's HQ.
5 cos., 18th MO
FORD
Fuller
Tillson
XVII CORPS
HARDEE
WHEELER
Ashby
Anderson
Hagan
T. Harrison
MOWER
Hardy
Fiser
Harrison
G. SMITH
Cumming (Henderson)
MCLAWS
Kennedy
Hagood
Adams
TALIAFERRO
BRAGG
Hurlbut
Rice
Clingman
Catterson
HILL
LORING
HOKE
Colquitt
W. Woods
XV CORPS
20th Batt'n NCJR
Halsey
Atkins
Kirkland
3rd NCJR
Dickson
2nd NCJR
1st NCJR
Stone
Flowers
N
1/4 Mile

Mark A. Moore

that a blast of the enemy's canister that "tore through the woods with a great noise" shook him out of his lethargy. The shriek of shot and shell so frightened some deer that as they bounded out of the woods they nearly trampled Pvt. John Bates of the 27th Ohio.[27]

As the skirmishers of the 64th Illinois emerged into an open field, one of the men chanced to see General Mower and asked in amazement, "Where did he come from?" "Fighting Joe" immediately took charge, ordering Fuller's brigade to advance at the double-quick. "He shouted, 'Forward!' and on [we] rushed," recalled a veteran of the 64th. Fuller's men sprinted across the field shouting at the top of their lungs, determined to capture Captain Earle's four-gun battery, which stood at the crest of the hill about 300 yards ahead. General Law had placed one of the guns in an advanced position in support of the skirmishers, and had ordered Captain Earle to command it himself. The lone Rebel gun belched forth a few errant rounds. "The first shot went over us," recalled Benjamin F. Sweet, a private in the 39th Ohio, while "the second went in the ground in front of us and the third was about half[way] down the gun," when Law rode up, and seeing the onrushing blue line, barked, "Capt. Earle, get your gun out of here!" Law ordered Earle's other three guns to limber up as well.[28]

As the Federals approached the opposite tree line they continued to cheer so loudly that they could not (or would not) hear the commands of their officers and the bugle calls signaling them to halt. As the Confederate guns rumbled out of view, Fuller's men now set their sights on smaller game: a reserve caisson that Earle's crew had abandoned when two of its draft horses were shot down. The Yankees raced up the slope, driving the Southerners before them.[29]

Colonel Tillson reported that on leaving the swamp, his main line overtook his skirmishers, who were "held at bay by a thick and well-filled line of rifle pits." Tillson ordered his men to fix bayonets and charge. "[W]e dashed forward like good fellows lodeing [sic] and firing as we went. And yelled our best at the same time," wrote Lt. John H. Ferguson of the 10th Illinois. Another participant, Captain John Nilson of the 25th Indiana, recorded that his company "advanced under Shelling & heavy muskettry [sic] firing from the enemy. . . .Cap Ren fell dead from a musket ball piercing his forehead just above his right eye causing his brains to protrude. [H]e knew not what hurt him."[30]

Bearing the brunt of Mower's charge were the South Carolinians of Butler's former brigade, now led by a 24-year-old brigadier named Thomas Muldrop Logan—otherwise known to his friends as "Mully." For the past few weeks Law had commanded Butler's Brigade, relegating Mully Logan to supernumerary status. But upon Law's elevation to division-level command, Logan resumed his place at the head of Butler's Brigade. Though penniless at the war's close, Logan would eventually become one of the country's wealthiest and most powerful railroad barons.[31]

Hopelessly outnumbered and poorly entrenched, Logan's troopers fired off a few rounds at the massive blue line before fleeing. While their dismounted comrades streamed to the rear, the men of Logan's mounted reserve spurred their horses and galloped off toward the Mill Creek Bridge. One of Wheeler's troopers happened to be near the bridge when a body of Logan's horsemen thundered across:

> Soon the causeway was filled by a disorderly mob of Confederate cavalry making good time in finding the rear. From them it was learned that they, a brigade of Butler's Division of cavalry of the Army of Northern Virginia, had been stationed on the opposite side of the creek to defend the approach to the bridge. That at least a corps of the enemy's infantry had attacked and driven them back; and that while they were telling the tale they were sure the enemy had gained the high bank on the opposite end of the creek and had cut off the only line of retreat for [Johnston's] army.[32]

Fortunately for Law, only one of his two brigades stampeded to the rear. The other—Young's Brigade, commanded by Col. Gilbert J. "Gib" Wright—held the left of Law's position. While Wright's line actually extended beyond Mower's right flank, the collapse of Mully Logan's line forced "Gib" Wright to swing back his own line until it stood parallel to Mill Creek.[33]

General Fuller's troops finally halted at the line of abandoned rail and log barricades, but Mower galloped to the front of Fuller's brigade and ordered it forward once more. The men scampered over the Confederate works and up the slope. "After gaining the crest of the hill I ordered a halt," Mower later wrote. While Fuller's main line dressed ranks, "Fighting Joe" sent the 64th Illinois toward Bentonville and the Mill Creek Bridge. It was 1:30 p.m. and pouring rain.[34]

At this moment Mower must have sensed that victory was within his grasp. He had moved his command deep into the left rear of Johnston's army, and had met but little opposition. He sent word of his situation to Blair and called upon him for support.[35]

At this point Mower received Colonel Tillson's message that his skirmish line did not connect with Fuller's. This news should have come as no surprise to Mower—after all, he had just directed the 64th Illinois to press ahead unsupported—yet he inferred from Tillson's message that his entire command had obliqued to the right while crossing the swamp. Mower's next move was uncharacteristically tentative. Instead of driving on toward Bentonville, he directed Fuller and Tillson to move by the left flank and close up on the main XVII Corps line. He then galloped off toward Tillson's position to see to the execution of the order. Fuller and Tillson dutifully obliqued to the left and rear for nearly the length of a brigade front—that is, a few hundred yards—before they received orders to halt, face about, and prepare to advance.[36]

As Fuller and Tillson shifted their commands, the 64th Illinois overran Johnston's headquarters on the John Benton farm. The regiment's attack was so swift and unexpected that it succeeded in driving off "Old Joe" and his staff and cavalry escort—all of them on foot, no less—together with the sleepy-eyed Tennesseans of Vaughan's Brigade. It appeared to Private Stilwell "as tho Johnston's whole army was retreating" before the 64th. Stilwell recalled that at the time he and his comrades "did not know [we] were making history." Yet they were, for it was a rare occurrence on a Civil War battlefield when an army captured the enemy commander's headquarters.[37]

For a few precious moments the Illinoisans had free run of Benton's farm. In later years two veterans of Fuller's brigade made competitive claims as to who had plundered what belonging to whom. Brigade historian Charles Smith stated that "Captain W. H. H. Mintern of the Thirty-ninth Ohio, gallantly rushing forward, captured Johnston's sash, sword, belt, his horse saddled and bridled, and his private correspondence." The 64th's adjutant, Robert Mann Woods, reminded Captain Smith that it was the Illinoisans who had captured "Genl Jo Johnstons headquarters and the horses of his staff officers." But Captain Woods believed the real coup was the horse that Captain Reynolds had galloped off with—"a fine bay stallion" belonging to Hardee.[38]

Regardless of the truth of these claims, the charge of the 64th Illinois was much more than a gigantic souvenir hunt. The Illinoisans had swept forward into Bentonville—just a few hundred yards shy of the Mill Creek Bridge—and were now poised to cut off the Rebels' sole line of retreat. Albert Quincy Porter, a Confederate hospital steward who witnessed the Illinoisans' advance, believed "there was no chance for us [sic] only to be captured."[39]

* * *

About 2:00 p.m., while he and his men waited in reserve behind Hoke's line, Col. Robert J. Henderson received a dispatch from Johnston's adjutant, Col. Archer Anderson, stating that Cumming's Brigade "was subject to the orders of Gen. Hardee, & to proceed with it down the Bentonville Road." The bearer of the dispatch was Hardee's adjutant, Lt. Col. Thomas B. Roy, whose job it was "to designate the position the Brigade was to occupy," Henderson reported. Colonel Henderson ordered his men onto their feet and soon had them double-quicking northward.

Henderson and Roy rode ahead to reconnoiter. About a half-mile south of Bentonville, they turned right onto a farm road, leaving a courier behind at the intersection to direct the troops. As they rode on, Roy informed Henderson that his brigade was to reinforce Wheeler's cavalry. Moments later, the courier came dashing after them, shouting that Cumming's Brigade had not turned off behind them and instead had continued up the main road. Fearing the worst, the two officers galloped off for Bentonville.[40]

* * *

The troopers of Harrison's Brigade of Confederate cavalry were resting in a field about a half-mile south of Bentonville when their daily ration arrived: two quarts of corn apiece, to be shared by man and horse alike. Although these cavalrymen may have grumbled at their scant fare, they didn't stint their mounts. "The fact is," wrote inspection officer Alfred Roman, "the men seem to take better care of the horses than they do of themselves."[41]

Harrison's Brigade consisted of the 3rd Arkansas, 4th Tennessee, 8th Texas, and 11th Texas Cavalry regiments, and was led by Col. Baxter Smith. Their appearance was distinctly unmilitary: discipline was lax, no two of the men dressed alike, and in the words of Colonel Roman, "There seems to be an independent, careless way, about most of the officers and men, which plainly indicates how little they value the details of Army regulations."[42]

When it came to fighting, however, the men of Harrison's Brigade were in deadly earnest. When scrapping at close range, they had no use for sabers, wielding instead a pair of Colt Army or Navy revolvers. The brigade ordnance reports list more than twice as many rifles as carbines and shotguns, which indicates that these troopers were as adept at fighting on foot as on horseback. Moreover, the brigade had more than 80 men armed with Spencer rifles, and though ammunition was often scarce, they must have welcomed the increased firepower nonetheless. Harrison's Brigade was known throughout the army as the "Texas brigade." Within Wheeler's Corps it was also called the "charging brigade."[43]

The men of the 8th Texas Cavalry—the renowned Terry's Texas Rangers—were parching and eating their corn when the regiment's newest, and perhaps youngest, recruit reported for duty. Sixteen-year-old Willie Hardee was thereupon led to the Rangers' commander, Capt. Doc Matthews. Young Hardee may have been surprised to discover that Captain Matthews was himself a "smooth-faced boy." Matthews was a newcomer to his post, having assumed command after all three of the Rangers' field officers had fallen severely wounded during the recent fighting. According to a veteran of the Rangers, Doc Matthews "presented an ungainly and unmilitary aspect. . .although able, brave, and well-qualified to handle the veterans" under his command. And as for Private Hardee, Captain Matthews doubtless saw that the boy was brimming over with enthusiasm.[44]

Willie Hardee must have felt keenly the responsibility of being the only son of Lt. Gen. William J. Hardee. Since that early spring day in 1864 when he ran away from school to join the Rangers, Willie had sought to emerge from the general's shadow. But the

Rangers sent the boy to his father, who made him an aide on his staff—the better to keep an eye on him. Young Willie "won his spurs at Resaca, where he had a horse killed under him," Hardee's adjutant, Lieutenant Colonel Roy wrote, "and did a soldier's duty throughout the [Atlanta] campaign." In another effort to strike out on his own, Willie joined Capt. H. M. Stuart's Battery in February 1865, but soon learned that artillery service could be as safe—and as dull—as school life back in Georgia.[45]

While on the march to Bentonville, Willie again met the Rangers, "and the boy's first love revived," Roy noted. Private Hardee begged his father to let him join. As a last-minute counter-proposal—and most likely at Hardee's urging—General Johnston offered Willie an appointment as his aide. But the youth declined, saying "he would not have rank until he won it." General Hardee gave his reluctant consent. "Swear him into service in your company," the general told the Rangers' Capt. Kyle, "as nothing else will satisfy."[46]

Willie Hardee was regaling the Rangers with the latest news from headquarters "when a sharp rattle and then a roar was heard [coming from] the bridge," recalled A. P. Harcourt. "There was no mistaking what it meant." A staff officer galloped up from the direction of Bentonville and informed Colonel Smith that his command was needed at once to defend the bridge, adding "that such were the orders of General Hardee."[47]

A few minutes earlier, in response to an order from Wheeler, Colonel Smith had sent forward the 3rd Arkansas and 11th Texas, leaving only the 8th Texas and 4th Tennessee in reserve. The colonel ordered his two remaining regiments to mount up, and in their haste, the Texans and Tennesseans rode off without regard to formation. "Companies continued intermixed," Harcourt wrote, "but into [column of] 'fours' was effected on the ride under spur."[48]

* * *

When Colonel Henderson and Lieutenant Colonel Roy finally overtook Cumming's brigade, it was advancing in line of battle astride the Bentonville Road. They could see the Federal skirmishers just ahead in the village itself, darting between the houses and other buildings. The Army of Tennessee's field hospital stood in the Federals' path, and the wounded who could move were escaping as fast as their injuries would allow. But their peril was short-lived. Thanks to Cumming's Brigade, the Union advance had reached its high-water mark. As the Northerners withdrew from the village, Colonel Henderson ordered his Georgians to change front while advancing, the left flank pivoting on the right until the entire line faced east. Cumming's Brigade drove the 64th Illinois with ease through the open woods east of Bentonville. "They fled. . .leaving a line of ditching tools and knapsacks as far as we could see," remembered one Georgian. "We had passed this line some thirty or forty yards when they began to pepper us at a lively rate. We halted some eighty yards away [from them], and all that could got behind trees. We were giving them the best that we had in our shop, when we heard a yell to our right."[49]

The yell on the Georgians' right proved to be from Col. Baxter Smith's two cavalry regiments, the 4th Tennessee and 8th Texas. "We found General Hardee standing in the road about half a mile or more from where we started," wrote Capt. George Guild, the 4th Tennessee Cavalry's historian. "He at once ordered the regiments into line along the road and to charge through the woods." Guild recalled that "the Eighth Texas deployed in line of battle to the right and the Fourth Tennessee to the left."[50]

"Forward, Rangers!" Doc Matthews hollered. "Front into line!" One of the Texans noticed that as Private Hardee took his place in the front rank, the general and his son "tipped their caps to each other." For a moment there was a terrible stillness: "Everything was so plain and clear," recalled one Ranger, "you could see the [Yankees] handling their guns and hear their shouts of command." Drawing his sword, General Hardee gave the order and led the charge on a borrowed horse. "With a wild shout we rushed through the woods," Captain Guild remembered. As the Rebel horsemen thundered past Cumming's Brigade, they fired their rifles and carbines at the approaching line of blue, then tossed them aside and grabbed their revolvers. The Yankee skirmishers "were taken by surprise at the suddenness of the attack," Guild continued, "and as we rode in among them using our 'navies,' we scattered them and forced them back to their main line" several hundred yards to the rear.[51]

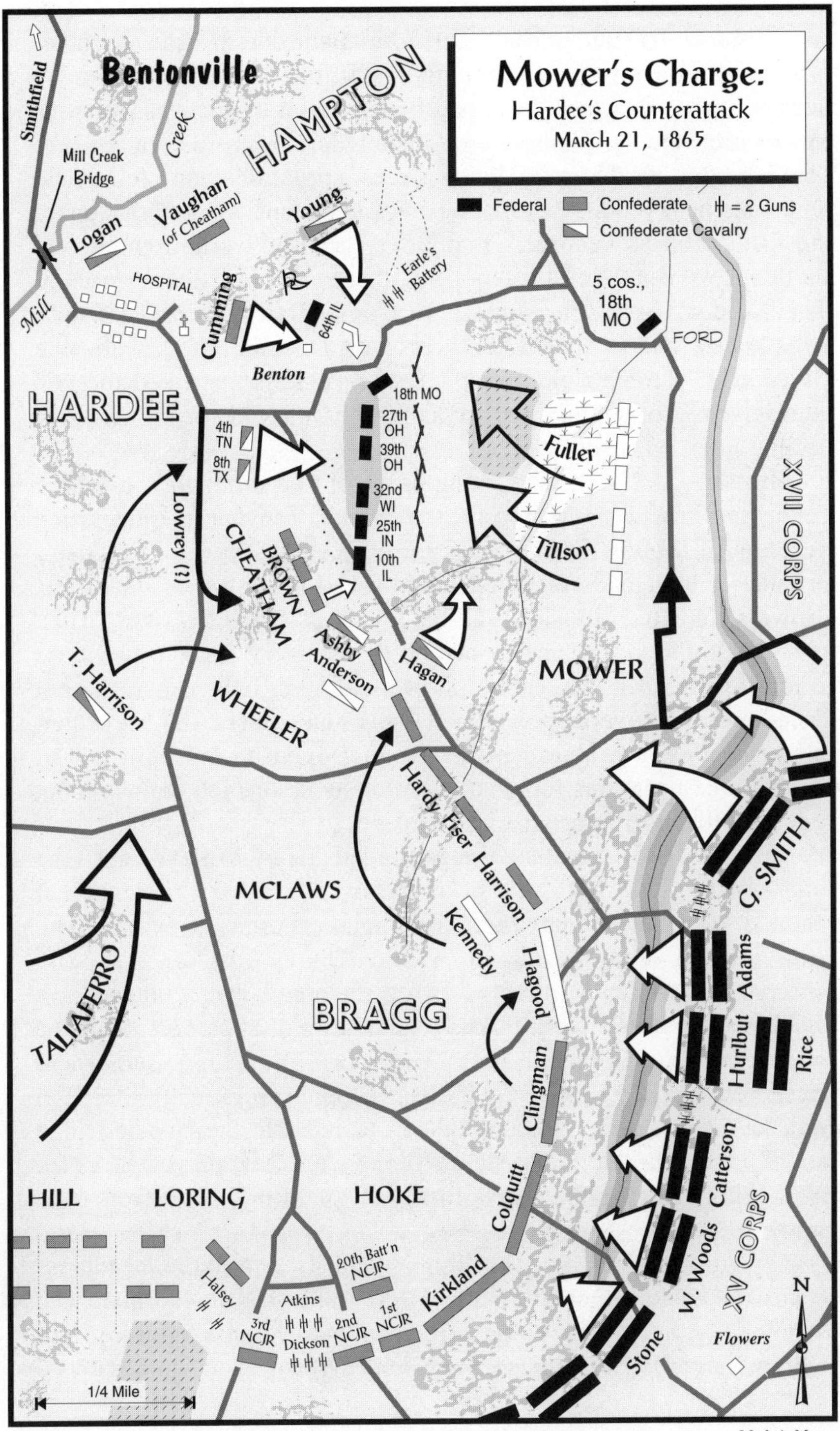
Mower's Charge:
Hardee's Counterattack
March 21, 1865
Federal
Confederate
Confederate Cavalry
= 2 Guns
Bentonville
Smithfield
Mill Creek Bridge
Mill
Creek
HAMPTON
Logan
Vaughan (of Cheatham)
Young
Earle's Battery
HOSPITAL
Cumming
64th IL
Benton
5 cos., 18th MO
FORD
HARDEE
18th MO
27th OH
39th OH
32nd WI
25th IN
10th IL
4th TN
8th TX
Fuller
Tillson
XVII CORPS
Lowrey (?)
BROWN
CHEATHAM
Ashby
Anderson
Hagan
T. Harrison
WHEELER
MOWER
Hardy
Fiser
Harrison
G. SMITH
MCLAWS
Kennedy
Hagood
Adams
TALIAFERRO
BRAGG
Hurlbut
Rice
Clingman
Catterson
HILL
LORING
HOKE
Colquitt
W. Woods
XV CORPS
20th Batt'n NCJR
Kirkland
Halsey
Atkins
3rd NCJR
Dickson
2nd NCJR
1st NCJR
Stone
Flowers
N
1/4 Mile

Mark A. Moore

Colonel Tillson had just gotten his main line in hand when the officers commanding the two right skirmish companies came to him, reporting that their lines had been broken by a cavalry charge. Meanwhile, the skirmishers on Tillson's left "were driven in," the colonel later wrote, "and being urged forward again, fell back, reporting heavy odds before them." Lieutenant John Ferguson of the 10th Illinois recorded that after "running[,] hollowing and shooting, we run against a rebel line that would not flee from us as the[y] did at first." In addition to Confederate cavalry, Tillson's brigade now had to contend with Brown's Division, or "Cheatham's Division of Hardee's old corps," as the Tennesseans liked to style themselves. And rightly so, for it was Frank Cheatham who was leading them on this day.[52]

Brown's Division was composed of the remnants of three Tennessee brigades—Maney's, Strahl's and Vaughan's—plus Gist's Brigade of South Carolinians and Georgians. Less Vaughan's Brigade, which had remained behind at Johnston's headquarters, Brown's depleted division numbered about 600 effectives. They advanced through the pine woods on the Rangers' right in two lines of battle roughly 50 yards apart. Colonel Tillson wrote that Cheatham's line overlapped his left flank and extended to his center, "with a very heavy skirmish line running opposite my right front." Mower rode up at this time, and as soon as he learned the situation, ordered Tillson to refuse his left flank.[53]

Tillson's and Cheatham's men traded a few volleys, but "the rebels finding we would not be drove by a fair stand up and fight made a charge on our line," Lieutenant Ferguson wrote. The Confederates approached to within 100 yards of the 32nd Wisconsin. "Our well directed firing did good work," the 32nd's Ole Leigram jotted in his diary, "and after a short but hot time drove them to flight in great disorder." But the Southerners succeeded in pressing back Tillson's center regiment, the 25th Indiana. At one point Colonel Tillson feared that the Hoosiers' line would break, but the 25th's Maj. William Crenshaw prevented a rout by seizing the regimental colors and planting them front and center.[54]

On Tillson's left, the 10th Illinois held its own until Cheatham's troops discovered that the Federal left flank was in the air. "The enemy. . .came down in our front in heavy mass hooping and yelling," recorded Lieutenant Ferguson. "We ingaged them with all

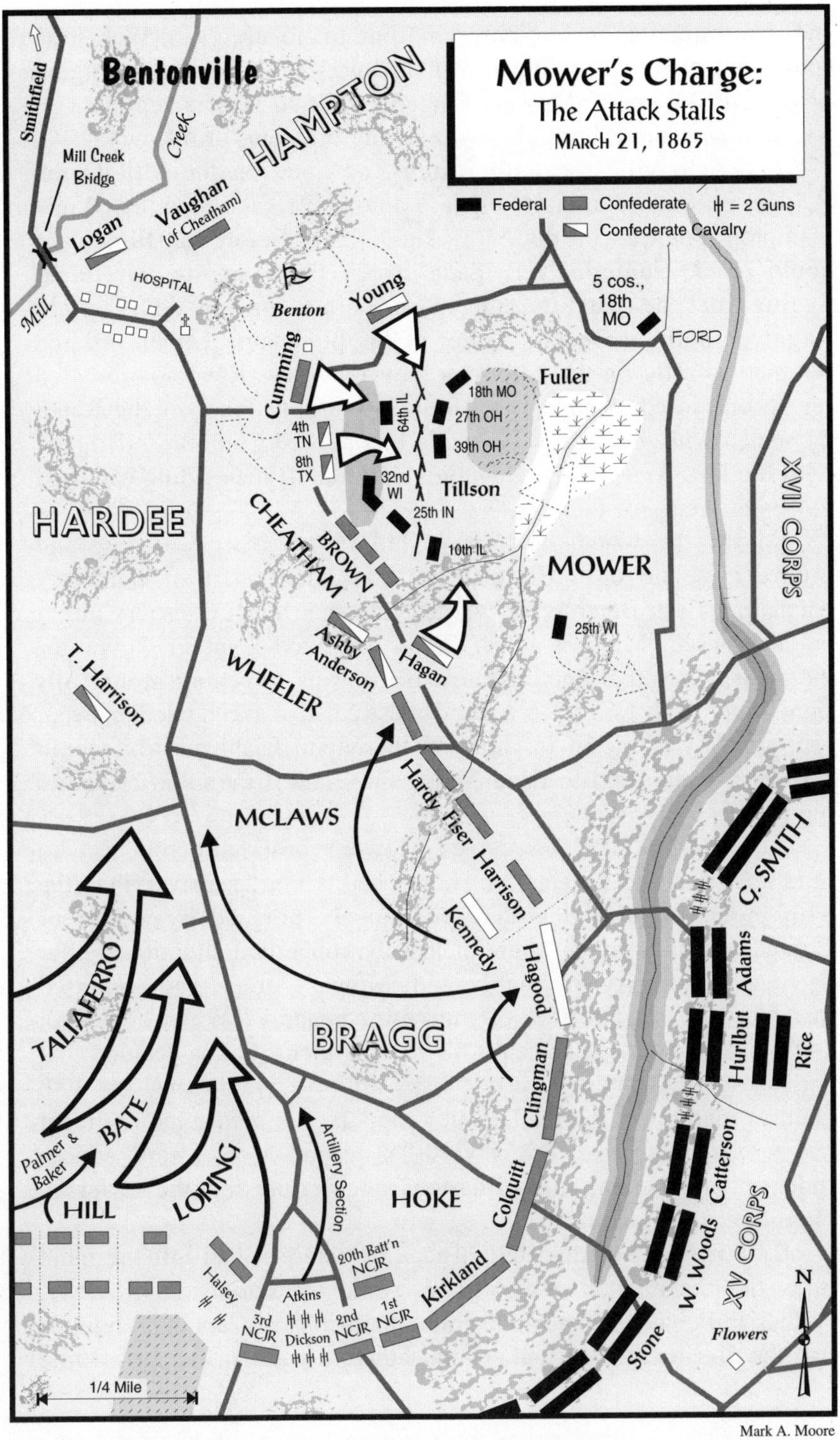

Mower's Charge:
The Attack Stalls
March 21, 1865
Federal
Confederate
= 2 Guns
Confederate Cavalry
Bentonville
Smithfield
Mill Creek Bridge
Creek
Mill
HAMPTON
Logan
Vaughan (of Cheatham)
HOSPITAL
Benton
Young
Cumming
5 cos., 18th MO
FORD
Fuller
18th MO
27th OH
39th OH
64th IL
4th TN
8th TX
32nd WI
Tillson
25th IN
10th IL
HARDEE
CHEATHAM
BROWN
MOWER
XVII CORPS
25th WI
Ashby
Anderson
Hagan
WHEELER
T. Harrison
MCLAWS
Hardy
Fiser
Harrison
Kennedy
G. SMITH
Hagood
Adams
Hurlbut
Rice
TALIAFERRO
BRAGG
BATE
Palmer & Baker
LORING
Artillery Section
Clingman
Catterson
HOKE
Colquitt
HILL
20th Batt'n NCJR
Kirkland
W. Woods
XV CORPS
Halsey
Atkins
3rd NCJR
2nd NCJR
1st NCJR
Dickson
Stone
Flowers
N
1/4 Mile

Mark A. Moore

the determination in our power. . .but to no use. . . .[We] soon found the enemy comeing down on our left flank, and swinging around in our rear." Mower ordered Fuller to send a regiment to Tillson's assistance, but Fuller was having problems of his own.[55]

At Bentonville the 64th Illinois' advance on the Mill Creek Bridge ground to a halt when Young's Brigade, led by Wade Hampton, pounced on the 64th's right flank. Before the Illinoisans could react, Cumming's Brigade struck them on the left flank. Seeing that he was in danger of being surrounded, Captain Reynolds notified General Fuller of his predicament, then ordered his men to rally on the colors as they fell back. Reynolds directed his second-in-command, Capt. John J. Long, to fend off the Rebel horsemen with the right wing while he opposed Cumming's Brigade with the left. And finally, Reynolds ordered all men riding captured horses to break for the rear.[56]

So far the woods had prevented Fuller from watching the progress of the 64th Illinois, but a sudden burst of musketry emanating from Bentonville warned him that his skirmishers might be in trouble. Minutes later, Fuller received Captain Reynolds' message that some Confederate cavalry was sweeping around his right flank, followed by a second message that the horsemen were supported by a line of infantry. "I thereupon faced the Eighteenth Missouri to the right to better cover that flank," the Ohio brigadier reported.[57]

At this point Fuller received Mower's order directing him to send a regiment to Tillson. No sooner had the order arrived than the 64th burst into the Benton field, closely pursued by a line of Confederate infantry. In view of his own uncertain situation, Fuller deemed it too risky to comply with Mower's order, and "reported that fact to a staff officer of the major general." When a second, and more strident, order came for the regiment, Fuller decided that perhaps the movement wasn't so risky after all. He directed the 39th Ohio to march to Colonel Tillson's support, but before the regiment had moved more than a few yards, a second Mower staff officer rode up and, seeing the situation, countermanded the order in "Fighting Joe's" name.[58]

By now the 64th had fallen back to where it had left the main line—but the main line was gone. Amid the confusion of battle, neither Fuller nor Mower had thought to inform Captain Reynolds that the division had shifted several hundred yards to the left. While

Reynolds' Illinoisans back-pedaled to Fuller's new position, the companies on the right under Captain Long dueled with "Gib" Wright's Georgia and Mississippi horsemen. Colonel Sheldon of the 18th Missouri recalled that he and his troops looked on from a safe distance: "We certainly could not avoid laughing at the peculiar antics of some of the skirmishers as they jabbed the horses. . .in the flanks. . .with the[ir] bayonets, while the confederate riders were slashing at them around the great pine trees." Fuller was not amused, however. Seeing that Young's Brigade was galloping around his right flank, he ordered "the right of the line to swing back, so as to present a strong front" to the Southern cavalrymen.[59]

Once again, Cumming's Brigade struck when the enemy was off-balance, this time while the right half of Fuller's line was executing its change of front. The Georgians drove Fuller's brigade from the crest, but according to Fuller, the Federals "speedily rallied," some on the slope and the rest at the Rebels' works near the base of the ridge. While the 64th Illinois dressed ranks along the slope, Young's Brigade mounted a charge. "The timber being scattering and [there being] no underbrush, it was almost as good as open field for them," wrote Sgt. Robert Russell of the 64th. But a volley from Fuller's main line stopped the Confederate horsemen in their tracks: "such a falling out of saddles I never saw," Russell remembered.[60]

Meanwhile, the troopers of the 8th Texas and 4th Tennessee cavalry regiments wreaked havoc along Tillson's right and center. They rode down dozens of the 10th Illinois skirmishers, killing or capturing most of them. But at least one Ranger, William Andrew Fletcher, got more than he bargained for when he overtook a squad of Union skirmishers with some fight left in them. Private Fletcher recalled the incident:

> I was about fifty yards to their front demanding, 'Surrender!,' thinking they were cowed, but two shots from the bunch made me think they were not a surrendering lot, so I got out of the scrape, scared but not hurt. After their two shots, I was satisfied they were onto their job. . .and were reserving their fire or they would, no doubt, have emptied my saddle. I have often thought, of all the simple acts of my life, this one headed the list. . . .After this bullets seemed to make a greater noise than usual.[61]

Some of the Texans and Tennesseans slipped through a gap between the 39th Ohio and 32nd Wisconsin—the left flank of Fuller's brigade and the right flank of Tillson's brigade, respectively—and in the course of their mad dash to the rear of Tillson's brigade's line nearly defeated Tillson's efforts to rally the shaken 25th Indiana. By the time Tillson realized what had happened, the 8th Texas and 4th Tennessee had vanished into the pine woods.[62]

Observing that the cavalry on both of his flanks had retired, and that the Federal line advancing up the slope stretched far beyond his right, Colonel Henderson ordered his brigade to withdraw beyond range of the Federals' rifles. M. J. Davis of Cumming's Brigade recalled:

> We fell back to the edge of a field, where we met General Johnston. . . .It was the first time we had seen "Old Joe" since he was relieved of his command at Atlanta. We gave him three cheers. He raised his hat and spoke some words that I failed to catch, but some that were nearer him said he told Col. Henderson to compliment the brigade for him; that they had saved the army. That set us on fire again, and we would have charged Old Nick himself if Joe Johnston had ordered us to.[63]

While the 64th Illinois reoccupied the crest of the hill in its front, the 10th Illinois faced imminent disaster. Cheatham's troops pushed up to within 20 yards of the Illinoisans' crumbling line and called on them to surrender. "[W]e about faced and made for the rear as fast as we could," recorded Lieutenant Ferguson, but the 10th soon discovered that the Rebels were as numerous there as they had been at the front.[64]

Augmenting Cheatham's flanking force were the dismounted troopers of Ashby's Brigade and Hagan's Alabama Brigade of Allen's Division. The Alabamians were commanded by Col. D. G. White, a former staff officer under Hardee. Hagan's Brigade was drawn up in reserve behind Anderson's Brigade when General Wheeler galloped up and ordered them to follow him into the rear of the Federal position. On Anderson's left, some of Ashby's Tennesseans jumped over their works and joined in the charge.[65]

Seeing that the Southern troopers had cut off their line of retreat, the Illinoisans broke to their left and formed a new line at the rifle pits near the bottom of the slope. Fortunately for the 10th, the Confederates did not press the attack, though they did maintain a steady small arms fire. When Colonel Tillson reached the 10th's front, he ordered the men to strengthen their works and sent out a skirmish line to develop the enemy's position. Colonel Tillson's line now resembled a ram's horn: on the right, the 32nd Wisconsin's position remained unchanged, though its left was thrown back about 30 degrees; in the center, the 25th Indiana continued on the same line as the 32nd, but at a more retired angle; and on the left, the 10th Illinois formed the inward curve to guard against another flank attack. The Illinoisans peered into the dense clouds of smoke that obscured their front, and awaited the next onslaught. Colonel Tillson noted that the Confederates' "musketry had nearly ceased, but a brisk artillery fire was kept up on us."[66]

Now that his two brigades were disengaged, Mower ordered Fuller to move by the left flank across the swamp in rear of Tillson and form on his left. The maneuver was executed without incident, though Fuller's men were surprised to find that they had been preceded by four companies of the 25th Wisconsin from Mower's Second Brigade. Ordered forward by Mower at 1:00 p.m., the Wisconsinites had held their advanced position since Mower's breakthrough, but had been unable to connect on Tillson's left. With Fuller's arrival, the detachment withdrew and rejoined the rest of the 25th on train guard duty.[67]

Mower was now satisfied that he had shifted to within supporting distance of the main XVII Corps line. He formed his division in line of battle, ordered up a fresh supply of ammunition, and prepared to advance a second time.[68]

When Sherman received word of Mower's charge from Blair, he was furious. "I don't like it at all," he fumed. "It might bring on a general engagement." Despite the obvious—and remarkable—opportunity Mower's "reconnaissance" provided Sherman, he added that the army had nothing to gain from a pitched battle. Sherman sent Blair and Mower orders to break off the assault at once. Fearing that Johnston might "let go his parapets to overwhelm Mower," Sherman ordered a general attack by the skirmish line along Howard's entire front. "The skirmishers are keeping up a continual roar of musketry and two or three batteries are playing," wrote Sherman clerk Vett Noble. "The result is yet to be seen." It was an anxious time for Sherman, who had issued his orders and now had to await news of the outcome.[69]

A young soldier named Melvin Grigsby chose this moment to seek out Sherman, "so as to see how a great commander would act while a battle was in progress." Grigsby found Sherman standing in the yard of the Stevens farm, surrounded by his orderlies and staff officers. When not receiving messages and sending orders, Sherman nervously paced back and forth under some large shade trees, an unlit cigar clenched between his teeth. At one point he asked the officer nearest him for a light. The officer handed Sherman his cigar, which the general used to light his own smoke. Turning away to listen to the distant noise of battle, Sherman absently dropped the officer's cigar on the ground. The officer glared at Sherman for a moment, then laughed as he picked up the cigar and continued his smoke.[70]

* * *

When Howard received the news of Mower's charge, he was also furious—at Sherman, no less. Howard was misinformed that the commanding general had personally ordered Mower forward without first notifying him. Howard immediately ordered Blair to advance his remaining two divisions to Mower's support, and directed Logan to throw out a strong skirmish line and seize the enemy's rifle pits in his front. But when Howard reached the XVII Corps' position, he found the main line retiring instead of advancing, and began to scold Blair for disobeying his orders.

"The withdrawal is by Sherman's order!" Blair shot back.[71]

Once more Howard was furious at Sherman, this time for *calling off* Mower's attack. Howard believed that he could "not only whip Joseph E. Johnston, but capture him." Twenty-five years later, Sherman's decision would prompt Howard to write:

> I do not think that in the conduction of a battle, with its details and changes, [Sherman's] judgment was as good as that of Sheridan, Thomas or Grant. My memory reverts. . .to the last operations at Bentonville, where, I think, Sheridan

> might have been more effective and successful in immediate results.[72]

When Mower received Sherman's order, there was nothing left for him to do but obey. A thoroughly disappointed "Fighting Joe" ordered Tillson to pass around Fuller's rear, form on his left, and make connection with Force's division. Mower's division now overlooked the Sam Howell Branch, where it dug in and awaited further orders. Thus ended the affair known as "Mower's Charge."[73]

The charge had promised much and delivered little—a few dozen prisoners and captured horses and one artillery caisson full of ammunition. In return, it had cost Mower 166 casualties. A soldier in the 32nd Wisconsin called the charge "the hardest fight that we have ever had," while a veteran in the 39th Ohio groused, "We accomplished simply nothing." The charge had failed because Mower had flinched at the critical moment. Instead of pressing on to Bentonville when he had the chance, Mower chose to shift his division closer to the main XVII Corps line, thus surrendering the initiative to Hardee. Had Mower advanced in force on the Mill Creek Bridge, he doubtless would have risked being surrounded and overwhelmed, but he also would have compelled Sherman to rush to his assistance. This seems to have been Mower's original intention.[74]

Mower's offhand remark to Blair about "making a little reconnaissance" looks ahead to Gen. George S. Patton's own free use of the term, "reconnaissance-in-force"—also known as the "rock soup method." Patton himself best describes the means by which an impetuous subordinate can overcome the objections of a reluctant commander:

> A tramp once went to a house and asked for some boiling water to make rock soup. The lady was interested and gave him the water, in which he placed two polished white stones. He then asked if he might have some potatoes and carrots to put in the soup to flavor it a little, and finally ended up with some meat. In other words, in order to attack, we had first to pretend to reconnoiter, then reinforce the reconnaissance, and finally put on an attack.[75]

The rock soup method describes perfectly Mower's *modus operandi* at Bentonville. "Fighting Joe" knew that he lacked the force to deal Johnston a crippling blow, but by attacking he hoped to manipulate Sherman into reinforcing his so-called "reconnaissance." It is unclear whether Mower's plan had Blair's approval, tacit or otherwise, but Blair at least knew that he was tempting fate when he placed Mower on the extreme right of the Federal line, and then approved his "reconnaissance."

Sherman later regretted his decision to recall Mower: "I think I made a mistake there, and should rapidly have followed Mower's lead with the whole of the right wing, which would have brought on a general battle, and it could not have resulted other than successfully to us, by reason of our vastly superior numbers." Then Sherman cited his reason for *not* supporting Mower's attack: the desire to link up with reinforcements before undertaking a decisive battle against an enemy whose numbers were "utterly unknown" at the time. His McClellan-esque excuse notwithstanding, Sherman's failure to exploit Mower's breakthrough (combined with Carlin's rout on March 19) might not have been so readily overlooked had it occurred a few months earlier. But both time and circumstances now favored Sherman: Northern victory was just around the corner and it would overshadow all of his errors save one.[76]

The Confederates were slow to react to Mower's charge, requiring almost two hours to mount a counterattack. But when they struck, they did so with their old spirit and dash, hitting Mower on all sides and driving back most of his line in confusion. Hardee deserves much of the credit for organizing and leading the counterattack, though ably assisted by Generals Hampton, Wheeler and Cheatham and Colonel Henderson. Contrary to the statements of Johnston, Hampton, Hardee and other Confederate commanders, the Rebels opposed Mower with comparable numbers—roughly 2,000 infantry and cavalry.[77]

If Mower was disappointed at the outcome of his charge, his Confederate counterpart, General Hardee, was thoroughly delighted. As "Old Reliable" trotted to the rear—"his face bright with the light of battle,"—he turned to Hampton and said, "That was Nip and Tuck, and for a time I thought Tuck had it." But Hardee's triumph abruptly turned to tragedy when he saw his son Willie slumped over in his saddle, held up by a Ranger who rode behind him. Willie Hardee had received a mortal chest wound. As his father looked on, the boy was placed on a stretcher and carried to a waiting ambulance. Wade Hampton doubtless empathized with Hardee, for his own son Preston had been killed in battle less than five months earlier.[78]

Hardee gave instructions for his son to be transported to Hillsborough, where his wife and daughter were staying with his niece, Susannah Hardee Kirkland, the wife of Brig. Gen. William W. Kirkland. Willie lingered a few days before dying on March 24. He was given a military funeral which his father attended, as did many of his former comrades from Hardee's artillery reserve. Willie Hardee was buried in the cemetery of St. Matthew's Episcopal Church in Hillsborough.[79]

During the 1850's, Willie's father had befriended a young lieutenant who later rose to the rank of major general in the Union army. That officer was O. O. Howard—the same Howard who so desperately wanted to thrash Hardee at Bentonville. Howard and Hardee had been close friends at West Point, despite considerable differences in age, rank and temperament. Hardee, the commandant of cadets, had even entrusted Howard, a lowly assistant professor of mathematics, with tutoring his son Willie. Howard later received the news of Willie's death from a former West Point classmate, Confederate general Stephen D. Lee.[80]

The grief-stricken Hardee had to shift his thoughts from his dying son to the job at hand. His reinforcements were arriving and had to be deployed: Baker's Brigade from the Army of Tennessee had even reached the Confederate left in time to assist in Mower's repulse, and Taliaferro's Division had arrived just after the last shots had been fired. As an added precaution, Johnston called upon Bragg for Hagood's Brigade and A. P. Stewart for Stewart's Corps and a portion of Bate's contingent from Cheatham's Corps.[81]

From left to right—that is, running southward from Mill Creek to Wheeler's left flank—Hardee deployed Taliaferro's Division, Cumming's Brigade of Stevenson's Division, Stewart's Corps, Baker's Brigade of Clayton's Division, and Brown's Division. Hardee also had at least eight field pieces at his disposal, including Earle's Battery and a section each from A. Burnet Rhett's and Starr's battalions. The remaining reinforcements—Hagood's, Palmer's and Granbury's brigades, plus Bate's troops—were held in reserve, as was Law's cavalry. This arrangement gave Johnston a strong left flank, but left Stewart with fewer than 2,000 men to defend his position on the right, which stretched for two miles.[82]

Generals Bate and D. H. Hill spread their lines ever thinner in a vain attempt to cover the vacated ground on the Confederate right. "I am from three to five feet apart in single rank," Bate informed Stewart at 5:00 p.m. "The enemy is confronting us. . .in what force I do not know. I have kept Taliaferro's pickets on post; will retain them. There is no cavalry on my right that I can find, and I made search. The enemy can come in there with impunity."[83]

Federal cavalry demonstrated the aptness of Bate's last statement. Two companies each from the 8th Indiana and the 9th Pennsylvania cavalry regiments swept around the Rebel right flank, which was defended by a few batteries from Maj. A. Burnet Rhett's artillery battalion. The Union horsemen made off with some forage, but lacked the numbers to further exploit their opportunity.[84]

By now it was obvious to Johnston that he must retreat from his position at Bentonville. So far he had been able to rely on Sherman's passivity and caution, but Mower's breakthrough had revealed the vulnerability of the Confederate position. Moreover, all of the wounded who could be moved had been sent off to Smithfield, and it was obvious that Sherman had no intention of attempting a desperate frontal assault as he had at Kennesaw Mountain. In short, retreat was Johnston's only viable option.

* * *

Although the repulse of Mower's charge marked the end of large-scale fighting at Bentonville, the skirmishers along the Sam Howell Branch maintained a constant and deadly fire. Chaplain E. P. Burton of the 7th Illinois crept down to the XV Corps' main line, where he noted that the bullets zipped past with alarming frequency, "& two or three came so near as to produce a peculiar nervous wineing." Just down the line from Chaplain Burton, Pvt. Thomas Larue of the 2nd Iowa found the passing minies terrifying. "I hate those damed little whizing sonabiches," Larue wrote his brother, "they clip damed cloce sometimes." To the misfortune of some, those whizzing bullets occasionally found their mark. Not far from Private Larue's sector, Sgt. J. B. Hawkes of the 50th Illinois was

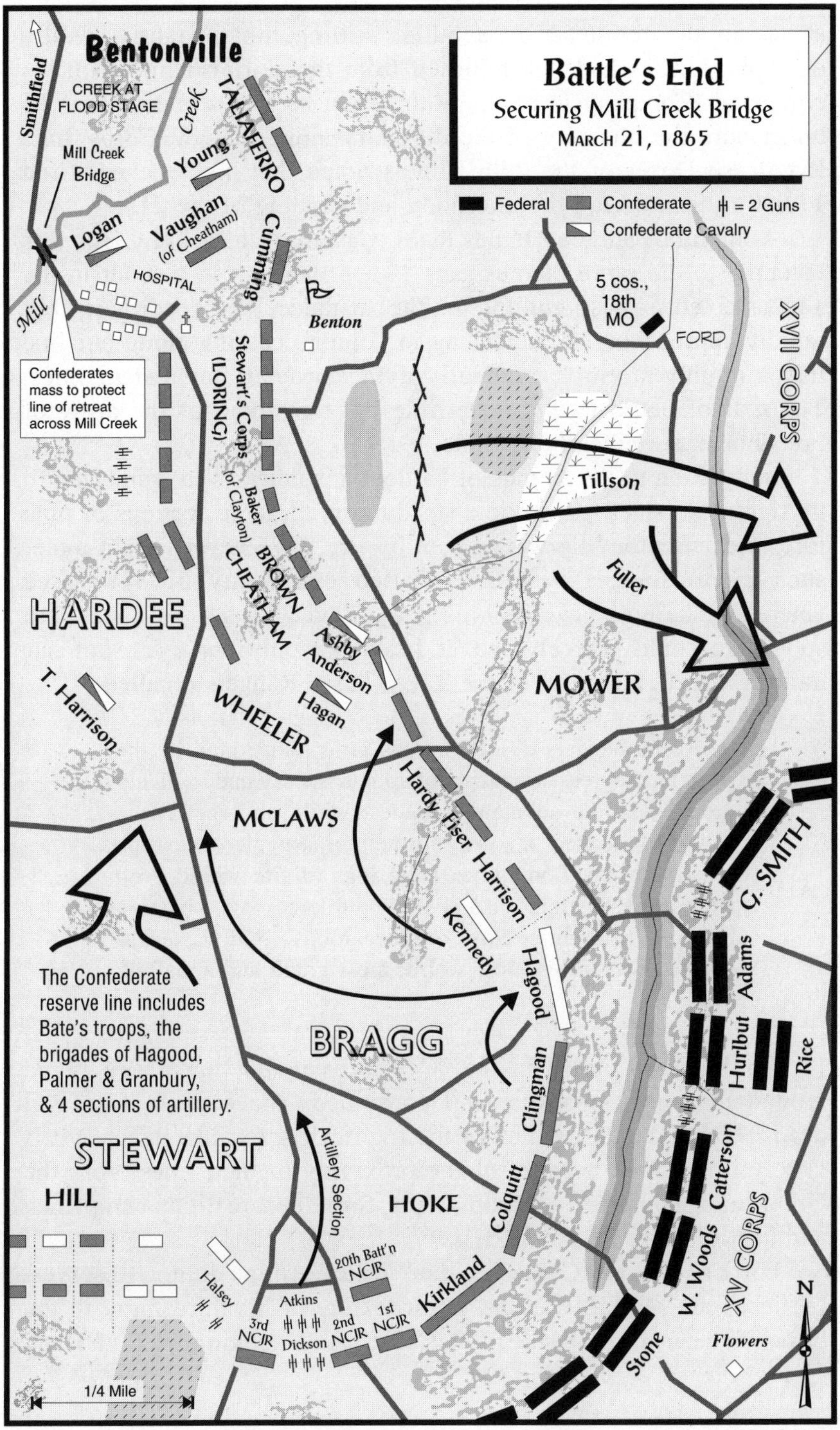
Battle's End
Securing Mill Creek Bridge
March 21, 1865
Federal
Confederate
Confederate Cavalry
= 2 Guns
Bentonville
Smithfield
CREEK AT FLOOD STAGE
Creek
Mill Creek Bridge
Mill
HOSPITAL
Confederates mass to protect line of retreat across Mill Creek
TALIAFERRO
Young
Logan
Vaughan (of Cheatham)
Cumming
Benton
Stewart's Corps (LORING)
Baker (of Clayton)
BROWN
CHEATHAM
Ashby
Anderson
Hagan
WHEELER
HARDEE
T. Harrison
5 cos., 18th MO
FORD
XVII CORPS
Tillson
Fuller
MOWER
MCLAWS
Hardy
Fiser
Harrison
Kennedy
Hagood
G. SMITH
Adams
Hurlbut
Rice
The Confederate reserve line includes Bate's troops, the brigades of Hagood, Palmer & Granbury, & 4 sections of artillery.
BRAGG
Clingman
Colquitt
STEWART
HILL
HOKE
Artillery Section
Catterson
W. Woods
XV CORPS
Kirkland
20th Batt'n NCJR
1st NCJR
2nd NCJR
3rd NCJR
Atkins
Dickson
Halsey
Stone
Flowers
N
1/4 Mile

Mark A. Moore

struck in the forehead by a bullet, killing him instantly. Oddly enough, Hawkes had just returned from the skirmish line with his command, Company H of the 50th, when he was struck down. To underscore the intensity of the musketry along the XV Corps' line, Pvt. Jesse Dozer of the 26th Illinois noted that his regiment fired 17,000 rounds during the afternoon and evening of the 21st.[85]

At nightfall Surgeon James R. M. Gaskill of the XVII Corps was listening to the rattle of musketry "when there arose a shout in the 14 & 15 corps just audible in the distance," he recorded, "but rapidly approaching & increasing in volume, passing along our line like a mighty storm & gradually dying away in our distant lines. The roar of battle had been terrible but this shout of the army of Freedom was eminently sublime."[86]

In addition to the sounds of battle, the soldiers were subjected to its sights and smells. Despite a steady rainfall, large sections of pine forest near Bentonville were swept by fire. "We never fought under such circumstances before," recalled one Army of Tennessee veteran. "The entire woods was [sic] filled with smoke, black and sooty, we could scarcely see. It filled not only our eyes, but our mouths." A. P. Harcourt of the Terry Texas Rangers recalled:

> the scene beggars description, as lurid flames, fed by the rosin on the trees, would shoot up into the sky and suddenly drop back like so many tongues, while underneath the wounded moaned piteously for help or struggled to escape roasting alive. Sometimes huge logs of fire would drop from a great height, or a shell would knock off a blazing tree top upon a litter corps or other troops. . . .It was grim-visaged war in his most weird, most grand and appalling aspect.

An Indiana soldier in the XV Corps noted that a fire raged around his unit's position, and consumed "the bodies of several dead. . .Confederates, which in the fog made a terrible stench." It is grimly ironic that, because of the proximity of their lines, both the Union and Confederate troops were forbidden to light campfires, and had to shiver in the darkness.[87]

For Lt. William Calder of the North Carolina Junior Reserves, the incessant rainfall was the worst feature of his third night in the trenches near Bentonville. "My feet were soaking wet and my overcoat saturated," he scrawled in his diary. "I laid on the cold wet ground with nothing over me and got a few moments of hurried sleep. I passed a miserable night." On the Federal side of the Sam Howell Branch, a veteran of the 7th Illinois, his poetic impulse undampened by the rain, noted: "The chilling winds make mournful music through the branches of the tall pines."[88]

As midnight approached, the soldiers on both sides huddled in their muddy trenches and waited for dawn, uncertain as to what the next day would bring.

~ *seventeen* ~

"An Emblem of Coming Peace"

—William McIntosh of the 22nd Wisconsin

The Confederate army began the evacuation of its position near Bentonville at 10:00 p.m. on March 21. The artillery withdrew first, followed by the infantry in the early morning hours of the 22nd. A South Carolina private noted that he and his comrades had to march "through fearful & interminable depths of mud," caused by the incessant rain. Nevertheless, the rainfall muffled the tread of thousands of marching feet and the creaking of wagon and gun carriage wheels. Despite the inclement weather and the early morning hour, the Confederate retreat was not entirely unopposed. Lieutenant John Fort of the 1st Georgia Regulars recalled that a Union battery maintained a steady fire on the Mill Creek Bridge, hurling shot and shell throughout the night, but doing little damage. By dawn, Johnston's Army of the South was across and on the march for Smithfield. The Confederate rear guard, consisting of Wheeler's cavalry, set fire to the bridge in an effort to delay the Federals' expected pursuit. Sherman had allowed Johnston's all-but-trapped army to escape unmolested.[1]

On the XV Corps' front, Federal pickets reported that the Confederate skirmish firing began to diminish about 2:00 a.m., then ceased an hour later. General Logan instructed Col. Robert F. Catterson, the commander of the Second Brigade of Woods' division, to determine whether the Rebels had abandoned their earthworks. Catterson led his brigade forward at first light, with the 26th Illinois in the advance. His men were delighted that the rain had stopped and that the day dawned clear and pleasant. The 26th's skirmishers found the Confederate works in their front abandoned and raised a loud cheer. Catterson's brigade double-quicked to Bentonville and discovered that the Southerners had completed their evacuation only minutes before. Just north of town, the men of the 26th Illinois found the Mill Creek Bridge in flames, but they doused the fire in time to save the bridge.[2]

While the Illinoisans were smothering the flames and dumping burning barrels of rosin off the bridge, General Mower galloped up. "Fighting Joe" was furious, swearing at Catterson's men for allowing the Confederate rear guard to set fire to the bridge and make its escape. But a more likely reason for Mower's anger was his discovery that Catterson's brigade had beaten his own troops to the bridge. As the Federal command nearest to the Mill Creek Bridge, Mower's division should have been the first Union troops on the scene, and no one was more aware of this than Mower.[3]

Having saved the bridge, Catterson's brigade resumed its pursuit of the Confederate rear guard. A running fight ensued between the 26th Illinois and a detachment of dismounted troopers from Wheeler's cavalry. The skirmishing intensified as the 26th approached the bridge across Hannah's Creek two miles north of Bentonville. Led by their color bearer, Sgt. James Smith, the Illinoisans rushed the bridge, which the Rebels had torched as soon as Wheeler's cavalrymen were across. As Sergeant Smith and the 26th's color company charged across the burning bridge, a Confederate battery on the opposite bank opened fire with canister, killing Smith and wounding several of his comrades. When Smith fell, the colors of the 26th Illinois plunged into Hannah's Creek. Braving a severe small arms and artillery fire, Lt. Arthur Webster and his command, Company E of the 26th, rushed forward and rescued the colors, then saved the bridge. The heroism of the 26th was for naught, however, for soon afterward Catterson received orders to immediately withdraw to the Mill Creek Bridge. Catterson's brigade had been sent forward to hasten the Confederate retreat—nothing more.[4]

By the time Catterson's brigade returned to Mill Creek, the area was teeming with soldiers from the XV and XVII corps. Many of these Federal troops combed the woods and fields near Bentonville for dead and wounded comrades. During their search they happened upon the charred remains of soldiers who had been burned in the fires of the previous day. They also found several abandoned Confederate hospitals littered with amputated limbs and unburied corpses. But the most grisly sights awaited them along the banks of Mill Creek. William David Evans, an Ohio private in the XVII Corps, described what he saw:

> Near the creek we found the body of one of our men who had been hanged by the rebels, & chopped with an axe. One leg was broken, one foot cut in two, & his head split in two or three places. During the morning we found 3 more of our men, mutilated in a similar manner. They had all been evidently taken prisoners & butchered, their [sic] being no gunshot wounds to be found on [any] of them. Three men belonging to the 10th Illinois were also found hanging on trees, & were taken down and buried.

Private Evans noted that several Union generals saw these mutilated corpses, but he neglected to mention the generals' names. A large crowd of Federal soldiers gathered around the corpses, and some of the men swore before the generals that they would take no more prisoners. In response to these threats, the Union provost guards were strengthened to prevent the men from murdering captured Confederates.[5]

According to Pvt. George W. Girton of the 47th Ohio, a slave led him and some of his comrades to a ditch where yet another mutilated corpse had been dumped and then covered with leaves. Saying that he was an eyewitness to the prisoner's torture and death, the slave explained that the man had been tortured for information concerning the Union army's strength and position. His inquisitors had begun by cutting off some of his toes, then they amputated his legs below the knees. When that failed to make the prisoner talk, they hung him by the neck, then cut him down and beat him to death with clubs. Girton added that Howard soon learned of the atrocity and arrested a local citizen who had been found with the dead soldier's papers in his possession.[6]

In truth, the Federals arrested every adult white male residing in Bentonville for the murder of the mutilated soldiers. Among those arrested were the town's two most prominent citizens, John James Harper and John C. Hood. As was mentioned earlier, Harper was a minister and the son of John Harper, whose house served as the XIV Corps hospital. Hood was a mechanic, and as the owner of a local carriage shop, was the community's largest employer. After his arrest, the younger Harper asked to be taken before the Federal wounded left behind by the Confederates in Bentonville. Harper had nursed the wounded of both sides throughout the battle, and when he was presented to the Union soldiers, they acclaimed him as their friend. Apparently Hood and the other local men were freed due to lack of evidence.[7]

Strangely enough, neither Howard nor his subordinates mentioned this macabre episode in their reports or postwar memoirs. Only the common soldiers and a few local citizens left a record of the incident. It is not known who committed the atrocities.

Upset by the lack of successful prosecutions, some of the Union soldiers took justice into their own hands. They burned Hood's carriage shop, storehouse and turpentine distillery, young Harper's house (including his sizable library), and the Bentonville Methodist Church. We can only surmise that these burnings were a reprisal for the murder of Federal prisoners, since some of Sherman's men required no pretext whatsoever for destroying civilian property. Most of the homes and buildings left standing housed the 63 Confederates who were too severely wounded to be transported to Smithfield. A soldier in General Terry's command who passed through Bentonville three weeks later noted that the village "consists of scarcely a dozen small unpainted weather-beaten dwellings. Two or three of these primitive tenements were still occupied by several severely wounded rebel soldiers. They were destitute of hospital conveniences, were indifferently attended and appeared to be subsisting on the plainest quality of food." In fairness to the citizens of Bentonville, they were no doubt left destitute by the passing of the Union and Confederate armies, and cared for the wounded soldiers as well as their limited means would allow.[8]

The John Harper family was no exception. During the battle, their house had served as a Union hospital; afterward, it served as a hospital for 45 critically wounded Southern soldiers. Throughout the spring and summer of 1865, John and Amy Harper and their children nursed these wounded men. Despite the Harpers' care, many of the wounded died and were buried in a field adjacent to the Harper family cemetery. The Harpers' ordeal did not end with the burial of the last dead Confederate. Their farm had been so devastated by the Union army that John Harper and most of his sons were forced to work as sharecroppers on a neighboring farm.[9]

The Willis Cole family was even more unfortunate than the Harpers. They lost nearly all their worldly goods when their house and plantation buildings were burned by the Confederates, forcing them to start anew.

But those who suffered most grievously were the soldiers themselves. The official Confederate casualty list for the Battle of Bentonville indicates 239 killed, 1,694 wounded and 673 missing, for a total of 2,606 casualties. There are, however, a few discrepancies. Brown's Division lists no casualties and is noted as not having been engaged in the battle, contrary to contemporary accounts from both Union and Confederate sources. Moreover, the monument to the Confederate dead at Bentonville states that there are *360* Southern soldiers buried on the battlefield, a 50 per cent increase over the official tally of 239 killed. The true death count is probably somewhere between the two figures. Even so, it would be a mistake to assume from the discrepancy between the death tally on the monument and that of the official total that the Confederates willfully misrepresented their casualty figures.[10]

On the Federal side, the official count is 194 killed, 1,112 wounded and 221 missing, for a total of 1,527 casualties. Like the Confederate casualty figure, this number is probably low. In his *Memoirs*, Sherman reports the Federal loss as 1,604. Nevertheless, the Battle of Bentonville resulted in more than 4,100 casualties, making it one of the bloodiest conflicts of the war in 1865.[11]

Although both the Union and Confederate armies had opportunities to score an overwhelming victory at Bentonville, the battle proved to be indecisive. On the first day, the Confederates failed to capitalize on their initial success, and their primary assault ended in a series of bloody repulses. When the Union Right Wing reached the battlefield on the second day, the momentum shifted to the Federals. On the third day, Mower led his division in an unauthorized assault on the Confederate left flank and nearly succeeded in cutting off the Southern army's sole line of retreat. Only a desperate counterattack saved the Rebel army from possible destruction—with some help from Sherman, who allowed Johnston to escape from Bentonville with his army intact.

Sherman's role in the Battle of Bentonville was a negative one. The March 19 battle was Slocum's fight, and on March 20 and 21,

Sherman restrained his army, choosing to skirmish with Johnston rather than bring him to battle. Even when Mower's breakthrough exposed the vulnerability of the Confederates' flanks, Sherman held back, squandering a golden opportunity to crush one of the Confederacy's few remaining field armies. It is tempting to credit Sherman with prescience for checking his army, but the truth is that on the afternoon of March 21, 1865, he believed that the war was far from over. At Bentonville, Sherman was more concerned with meeting his timetable for occupying Goldsboro than with the larger objective of ending the war in his theater of operations as soon as possible.

Given Sherman's lackluster performance at Bentonville, it is hardly surprising that he devoted less than four pages to the battle in his *Memoirs*. Typical of his attitude is this comment: "After the first attack on Carlin's division [on the 19th], I doubt if the fighting was as desperate as described by him [that is, by Johnston in his *Narrative*]. I was close up with the Fifteenth Corps, on the 20th and 21st, considered the fighting as mere skirmishing, and know that my orders were to avoid a general battle, till we could be sure of Goldsboro', and of opening up a new base of supply." Of course Sherman fails to mention that he was miles from the battlefield during the fiercest fighting on the 19th. "Many an old soldier who was in that leaden rain and iron hail," wrote one Union veteran of Bentonville, Lt. Col. Alexander McClurg, "and who perhaps carries with him a memento of it in a shattered limb or the recollection of a dead comrade, has smiled grimly as he has read Sherman's scanty reference to it." Unfortunately, Civil War historians seem to have taken Sherman at his word, which explains in part why Bentonville has received so little attention over the thirteen decades following the battle.[12]

Although in his *Memoirs* Sherman downplayed the battle's significance, in contemporary dispatches he acclaimed Bentonville as a great victory for his army. "We whipped Joe Johnston's army yesterday," Sherman informed Schofield on March 22, "and he retreated in disorder in the night. We are in possession of the field and our skirmishers are after his rear guard two miles north of Mill Creek." And, in Special Field Orders No. 35, Sherman declared: "The general commanding announces to his army that yesterday it beat on its chosen ground the concentrated armies of the enemy, who has fled in disorder, leaving his dead, wounded, and prisoners in our hands and burning his bridges on his retreat." But Howard's astute chief of artillery, Maj. Thomas Osborn, cast a dubious eye upon Sherman's claim. "In General Sherman's congratulatory address he says: 'We beat the enemy yesterday,'" Osborn recorded in his diary. "I was really unaware that any one was beat or whipped *yesterday*." Although Johnston retreated and left Sherman in possession of the field, the Federal victory was anything but decisive. Johnston's army was still intact and still dangerous if taken lightly, as the Federals had been wont to do of late.[13]

If Sherman's tactical judgment was poor, Johnston's was scarcely better, as his performance during the March 19 battle indicates. Nevertheless, Johnston should be credited for forging an army in less than one month's time, for his aggressiveness on March 19, and for his impressive show of strength on the 20th and the 21st. Still, Johnston took an extraordinary gamble by remaining at Bentonville on the 20th and 21st, and it nearly cost him his army. Perhaps he did so because he could see the handwriting on the wall, and knew that this was his last opportunity to strike Sherman's army with any prospect of success.

Johnston perceived Bentonville as a moral victory for his army, particularly for the soldiers of the Army of Tennessee, who retrieved their sinking reputation and—more importantly—their faith in themselves. "Troops of Tennessee army have fully disproved slanders that have been published against them," Johnston wrote Gen. Robert E. Lee from Smithfield on March 23. "The moral effect of these operations has been very beneficial. The spirit of the army is greatly improved and is now excellent."[14]

Regardless of the morale of Johnston's army, the weight of the enemy's numbers was now overwhelming. On March 21, Schofield's command occupied Goldsboro; meanwhile, Terry's Provisional Corps reached the site of Cox's Bridge, and by the 22nd had two pontoon bridges across the Neuse River and a bridgehead established on the north bank. The addition of Schofield's and Terry's commands swelled Sherman's ranks to roughly 88,000 officers and men. Johnston, on the other hand, could expect to receive only enough reinforcements to offset his losses at Bentonville. "Sherman's force cannot be hindered by the small force I have," Johnston informed Lee. "I can do no more than annoy him. I respectfully suggest that it is no longer a question whether you leave present position; you have only to decide where to meet Sherman. I will be near him." [15]

* * *

On the morning of March 22, Major Osborn and several other members of Howard's staff visited the scenes of the fighting on March 19. "We. . .visited the field of General Slocum's fight which has the characteristic of a battle field where a desperate battle has been fought," Osborn wrote. "The graves of the enemy's dead, the dead horses, broken material, the line of earth works, trees cut down with artillery, and the whole forest scarred and cut with musketry &c. &c." When Terry's corps passed through the battlefield several weeks later, Chaplain Henry McNeal Turner of the 1st U. S. Colored Troops noted that "the trees were in many places riddled with balls. I was amused at one tree, through which seven cannon balls had passed, yet it continued to stand. That tree must have been a rebel."[16]

While Osborn and his fellow staff officers examined the battlefield, the Federal Left Wing resumed its march to Goldsboro. The day was windy and the road muddy, but the men did not complain, mindful that rest, mail from home, and new clothes and shoes awaited them in Goldsboro. During the march—at midday, no less—the soldiers glimpsed "a star which shone bright, high in the heavens, an emblem of coming peace," noted William McIntosh of the 22nd Wisconsin. "Thousands gazing upward observed the phenomenal star, and not a few connect its singular apparition with the waning chances of the Confederacy and held it an omen of a restored Union."[17]

The Right Wing resumed its march to Goldsboro on March 23, the day after the Left Wing's departure. While some of Sherman's men meditated on the prospect of peace, others such as Howard's inspector general, Lt. Col. William E. Strong, reflected on "those brave and gallant companions in arms who will come back to us no more. Peace to the gallant dead, sleeping, some of them in far away and unmarked graves." Strong ticked off the far-flung places to which the war had carried him and his comrades: Belmont, Corinth, Memphis, Vicksburg, Missionary Ridge, Chattanooga, Atlanta,

Savannah, and now on to Goldsboro. After Goldsboro, Strong wondered, "Where next?"[18]

* * *

Where next, indeed. After resting and refitting in Goldsboro, Sherman's next destination was Petersburg, Virginia, to form a junction with Grant and close out the war by defeating the combined armies of Lee and Johnston. But events unfolded swiftly—more swiftly than either Sherman or Johnston anticipated. Contrary to the expectations of the two commanders, Bentonville proved to be their last pitched battle of the war. Lee's surrender to Grant at Appomattox Court House on April 9 convinced Johnston that further resistance was futile. Instead of meeting in battle one last time, "Cump" and "Old Joe" next met over a bottle of whiskey in James Bennett's farmhouse near Durham, North Carolina to discuss surrender terms. Lee's surrender at Appomattox, combined with President Lincoln's assassination on April 14 and Johnston's surrender at Bennett Place on April 26, swept Bentonville from the pages of the newspapers and from the consciousness of Americans both North and South. Since then, Civil War historians have consigned the battle to obscurity. There are several reasons for this.

Although it is the largest battle fought on North Carolina soil and the culminating event of Sherman's Carolinas Campaign, the Battle of Bentonville neither shortened the war nor significantly altered its outcome. This, combined with the cursory treatment accorded it in both Sherman's and Johnston's memoirs—neither general performed well at Bentonville, and neither general dwelled upon the subject in his reminiscences—accounts for its consignment to obscurity in Civil War annals. Yet Bentonville—particularly the March 19 battle—was a desperate struggle that proved to an overconfident Federal high command that the Confederates were far from beaten. "We have injured Sherman a good deal," Wade Hampton wrote his sister on March 22, "so that he cannot boast of getting through free." Lieutenant Colonel Alexander McClurg agreed with Hampton. Referring to those of his Federal comrades who fought in the March 19 battle, McClurg wrote: "He may have looked back to Chickamauga, and to twenty pitched battles besides, and may still have thought that in none of them had he a hand in such stubborn work as that at Bentonville."[19]

Above all else, the Battle of Bentonville should be remembered in honor of the soldiers in blue and gray who fought there for their beliefs—just as they did at hundreds of other Civil War battlefields across the nation—and in the process, helped to reshape the United States of America.

~ Afterword ~

The Carolinas Campaign of 1865 had more than its share of notable—and in some cases, notorious—generals. Not surprisingly, the first name to come to mind is Maj. Gen. William T. Sherman, since this undertaking was his brainchild. The Carolinas Campaign was well-conceived and skillfully executed. Sherman's only significant blunder was in failing to destroy Johnston's army at Bentonville when he had the opportunity. Yet history was kind to "Uncle Billy," for barely one month after the battle he accepted Johnston's surrender at the Bennett Place.

Sherman's Confederate counterpart, Gen. Joseph E. Johnston, wrought a minor miracle in forging an army less than one month after assuming command in the Carolinas. In March 1865, he displayed a decisiveness conspicuously lacking earlier in his Civil War career. Johnston's aggressiveness at Bentonville may have been the result of desperation, but it nonetheless indicated that he would take chances when he perceived that the potential benefits outweighed the risks involved. Although Johnston's decision to remain at Bentonville on March 20-21 appears reckless, it was based on his belief that it offered him his last opportunity of defeating Sherman.

Of course Johnston had not calculated the effect Sherman's boldest general, Joseph A. Mower, would have on the fighting at Bentonville. Acting on his own initiative, Mower came within a whisker of cutting off Johnston's only route of retreat. Mower conducted operations at Bentonville as if he were living on borrowed time—and in a sense he was. During the spring of 1865 he was suffering from a pulmonary ailment contracted in the icy swamps of South Carolina, an illness that would claim his life five years later.

The most unfortunate of Sherman's generals at Bentonville was Brig. Gen. William P. Carlin. Given the circumstances, the rout of Carlin's division was inevitable, yet Carlin could never come to terms with that sad fact. In his post-war reminiscences, he claimed to have warned his superiors that a battle was imminent, and placed the blame for the collapse of his command on one of his brigade commanders. Not unexpectedly, Carlin's version of events elicited an angry response from many Union veterans of Bentonville, most notably Maj. James Taylor Holmes—the commander of a detachment of foragers in Morgan's division. Holmes planned to write a sketch that would "skin" Carlin's "published lies," but died before he was able to do so. As a result, Carlin's account remained unchallenged for more than a century.

The man responsible for the rout of Carlin's division was Maj. Gen. Henry W. Slocum, the commander of the Federal Left Wing. Slocum deployed Carlin's and Morgan's divisions of the XIV Corps carelessly, in the mistaken belief that he faced only a large force of cavalry. When Slocum learned that Johnston's entire army was before him, he left the two XIV Corps divisions at the front to absorb the shock of the Confederate assault. Although this move resulted in the rout of Carlin's men, it blunted the Confederate attack and bought precious time for the XX Corps to establish its line on the Morris farm. Slocum's decision to shift to the defensive, and his judicious deployment of the XX Corps infantry and artillery, ensured that the March 19 battle would end in a draw.

Slocum received invaluable assistance from Brig. Gen. James D. Morgan and his fine division, which held its position even after finding itself virtually surrounded. Brevet Brigadier General William Cogswell's brigade deserves credit for its timely assistance in driving off the Confederates attacking Morgan from the rear. Morgan's successful stand south of the Goldsboro Road marked a crucial shift in momentum favoring Slocum's wing. Had Morgan's salient given way, the Federal line on the Morris farm would have been hard pressed to hold against the victorious Confederates.

Sherman's cavalry chief, Bvt. Maj. Gen. Judson Kilpatrick, deserves much of the blame for the Federals' lack of preparedness in the early stages of the battle. Kilpatrick's reports stating that Johnston's army was falling back on Raleigh encouraged Sherman and Slocum to believe that their advance on Goldsboro was opposed by nothing more than a large cavalry force. Incidents such as this and Kilpatrick's near-disaster at Monroe's Crossroads prompted Sherman to request the transfer of Maj. Gen. Philip H. Sheridan and his cavalry force from Virginia to North Carolina. Fortunately for Kilpatrick, General Grant considered Sheridan too valuable to spare.

The performance of Johnston's cavalry chief, Lt. Gen. Wade Hampton, presents a striking contrast to that of Kilpatrick. Hampton chose the battlefield and devised the Confederates' plan of battle. To buy time for the Confederate deployment, he delayed the Federal advance on the afternoon of March 18 and on the morning of the 19th. Moreover, the South Carolinian aided in the repulse of Mower's charge on the afternoon of the 21st. Given his lack of resources, it is all the more remarkable that Hampton's effort at Bentonville was one of his best of the war.

Johnston's trusted subordinate, Lt. Gen. William J. Hardee, provided inspiring leadership during the main Confederate assault on March 19. When the advance threatened to sputter out on the northern fringes of the Cole field, Hardee rode into the field and waved his men forward, thus re-igniting the attack. Yet Hardee failed to exploit the breakthrough of Lee's Corps into the rear of Morgan's position, nor did he provide Taliaferro's or Bate's troops with the artillery support they so desperately needed when undertaking their assault on the Federal position on the Morris farm. "Old Reliable" redeemed himself, however, by organizing and leading the counterattacking force that repulsed Mower's charge on the afternoon of March 21. Hardee's triumph was marred by tragedy, for his only son, Willie—a youth of 16—was mortally wounded during the charge that halted Mower's advance.

General Braxton Bragg's final effort as a field commander was tragic in its own right. A virtual pariah within his own command, Bragg wielded authority over soldiers who had long since ceased to believe in him. During the March 19 battle, Bragg committed two serious tactical blunders that Johnston had only himself to blame for not correcting. Several Confederate generals blamed Bragg's poor generalship for the failure of Hoke's Division to carry General Morgan's position, but such blame overlooks the determined resistance of Morgan's veteran troops.

If there is little that can be said with certainty about Bragg's performance at Bentonville, there is even less to say about that of his subordinate, Maj. Gen. Robert F. Hoke. It is a telling commentary on the paucity of Confederate after-action reports for Bentonville that Hoke's name is mentioned as often in the reports of the Federals as in those of the Confederates. The historian can only guess as to Hoke's role in the battle, for at no time does he emerge from Bragg's shadow. This omission is as much Hoke's fault as Bragg's, for neither general submitted a report on the battle. This silence persisted into the post-war years, and included most of Hoke's brigade commanders and enlisted men. Hoke himself set the precedent: Johnston twice asked the North Carolinian to provide him with an account of his division's part in the battle, but Hoke failed to respond to both requests.

Seldom one to remain silent on any topic, D. H. Hill was the antithesis of his fellow Tarheel. Hill provided a detailed account of his actions during the Battle of Bentonville. Depending on one's point of view, Hill was either the most industrious Confederate general at Bentonville, or the most meddlesome. On two occasions Hill assumed command of troops not properly under his authority, and on one of those occasions, the troops happened to be commanded by his nemesis, Braxton Bragg. During the March 19 battle, Hill was present everywhere except where he was needed most—with his troops south of the Goldsboro Road. His failure to assault Morgan's position from the rear in tandem with Bragg's attacks on Morgan's front and left flank gave the Federals in that sector the breathing room they needed to repulse the Confederates' assaults.

Most of the officers and enlisted men on both sides fought creditably, and in many cases, heroically. Happily for Johnston, his Army of Tennessee veterans proved that they could still fight with their old grit, and the boys of the North Carolina Junior Reserves Brigade proved their worth through three days of continuous fighting. Sherman's veteran troops further solidified their fine reputation, Carlin's rout notwithstanding.

Bentonville Today

The Bentonville battleground is a fitting memorial to those Northern and Southern soldiers who fought there. If those long-dead veterans could walk the battlefield again, they would find much of it unchanged, though a good deal quieter. Thanks to 130 years of neglect, the battlefield largely remains in an excellent state of preservation, but we can no longer rely on that happy accident. Developments (yes, the pun is intended) occurring during the next 10 years will probably decide the battlefield's fate. In 1993, the Congressionally-established Civil War Sites Advisory Commission, numbering such luminaries as James M. McPherson and Edwin C. Bearss, ranked the Bentonville battleground sixth on its list of 384 battlefield sites. This ranking placed Bentonville in the top class of nationally significant battlefields requiring immediate preservation action.

In 1986, the Bentonville Battleground Historical Association (BBHA) was formed for the purpose of preserving the battlefield and interpreting the events that occurred there on March 19-21, 1865. Only two percent of the 6,000-acre battlefield is contained within the Bentonville Battleground State Historic Site. The BBHA is a non-profit organization relying on donations to purchase battlefield land and to educate the public on the importance of preserving that land. The Bentonville Battleground Historical Association can be reached at BBHA, P. O. Box 432, Newton Grove, NC 28366.

M. L. B.

APPENDIX A:

The Opposing Forces in the Skirmish at Cheraw, South Carolina

★ Union Forces Engaged ★

ARMY OF THE TENNESSEE
Maj. Gen. Oliver O. Howard

SEVENTEENTH ARMY CORPS
Maj. Gen. Frank P. Blair, Jr.

First Division
Maj. Gen. Joseph A. Mower

First Brigade[1]
Brig. Gen. John W. Fuller
27th Ohio
1st Michigan, Battery C (Hyser's)

★ Confederate Forces Engaged ★

HARDEE'S CORPS
Lt. Gen. William J. Hardee

McLAWS' DIVISION
Maj. Gen. Lafayette McLaws

[1] As Mower's Division advanced on Cheraw, Fuller's Brigade had the lead, with the 27th Ohio out in front. The remainder of the brigade (consisting of the 64th IL, 18th MO, and 39th OH) followed in close support.

Fiser's Brigade
Col. John C. Fiser
1st Georgia Regulars[2]

Elements of Butler's Cavalry[3]
Maj. Gen. M. C. Butler

[2] As a veteran regiment of Fiser's Brigade, it appears the Regulars were chosen to serve as rear guard on the retreat from Cheraw.

[3] Butler's Division consisted of Butler's and Young's Brigades. It is not clear which units from these commands participated in the skirmish with Brig. Gen. John Fuller's Federal brigade. For the organization of Butler's Division see the troop roster for Monroe's Crossroads elsewhere in this appendix.

APPENDIX B:

The Opposing Forces in the Battle of Monroe's Crossroads, North Carolina

★ ORGANIZATION OF UNION FORCES ★

CAVALRY

Third Division
Bvt. Maj. Gen. Judson Kilpatrick

Kilpatrick's Scout Company
Capt. Theo Northrop

Third Brigade
Col. George E. Spencer
1st Alabama   5th Kentucky
5th Ohio

Fourth Brigade (provisional)[1]
Lt. Col. William B. Way
1st Regiment   2nd Regiment
3rd Regiment

ARTILLERY

One Section 10th Wisconsin Battery (Beebe's)
Lt. Ebenezer W. Stetson

---

[1] The Fourth Brigade was composed of dismounted men from the Third Division, with regimental numbers coinciding with the parent brigade numbers.

★ ORGANIZATION OF CONFEDERATE FORCES ★

CAVALRY

Lt. Gen. Wade Hampton

WHEELER'S CORPS

Maj. Gen. Joseph Wheeler
(Army of Tennessee)

HUMES' DIVISION

Brig. Gen. W. Y. C. Humes (W)

Harrison's Brigade

Col. Thomas Harrison (W)

3rd Arkansas Cav. 4th Tennessee Cav.
8th Texas Cav. 11th Texas Cav.

Ashby's Brigade

Col. Henry M. Ashby

1st Tennessee Cav. 2nd Tennessee Cav.
5th Tennessee Cav. 9th Tennessee Battalion

ALLEN'S DIVISION

Brig. Gen. William W. Allen

Hagan's Brigade

Col. James Hagan (W)

1st Alabama Cav. 3rd Alabama Cav.
9th Alabama Cav. 12th Alabama Cav.
51st Alabama Cav. 53rd Alabama Cav.
24th Alabama Battalion

Anderson's Brigade

Brig. Gen. Robert H. Anderson

3rd Confederate Cav. 8th Confederate Cav.
10th Confederate Cav. 5th Georgia Cav.

DIBRELL'S DIVISION[2]
Col. George G. Dibrell

Dibrell's Brigade
Col. William S. McLemore
4th Tennessee (McLemore's) Cav.
13th Tennessee Cav.
Shaw's Tennessee Battalion

Breckinridge's Brigade (Lewis')
Col. W. C. P. Breckinridge
1st Kentucky Cav. 2nd Kentucky Cav.
9th Kentucky Cav. 2nd Kentucky Mounted Infantry
4th Kentucky Mounted Infantry
5th Kentucky Mounted Infantry
6th Kentucky Mounted Infantry
9th Kentucky Mounted Infantry

Butler's Division
(From the Army of Northern Virginia)
Maj. Gen. M. C. Butler

Young's Brigade
Col. Gilbert J. Wright
10th Georgia Cav. Cobb's Georgia Legion[3]
Jeff Davis Legion Phillips' Georgia Legion

Butler's Brigade
Brig. Gen. Evander M. Law
4th South Carolina Cav. 5th South Carolina Cav.
6th South Carolina Cav.

---

[2] Dibrell's Division remained in reserve during the attack on Kilpatrick's camp, but served as rear guard for the Confederate retreat.

[3] Commander Lt. Col. Barrington S. King killed.

APPENDIX C:

The Opposing Forces in the Battle of Averasboro, North Carolina

★ ORGANIZATION OF UNION FORCES ★

LEFT WING
ARMY OF GEORGIA (Late ARMY OF THE CUMBERLAND)
Maj. Gen. Henry W. Slocum

TWENTIETH ARMY CORPS
Bvt. Maj. Gen. Alpheus S. Williams

First Division
Brig. Gen. Nathaniel J. Jackson

First Brigade
Col. James L. Selfridge
5th Connecticut 46th Pennsylvania
123rd New York 141st New York

Second Brigade
Col. William Hawley
2nd Massachusetts 3rd Wisconsin
13th New Jersey 107th New York
150th New York

Third Brigade
Brig. Gen. James S. Robinson
82nd Illinois 61st Ohio
82nd Ohio 31st Wisconsin
143rd New York 101st Illinois

Third Division
Bvt. Maj. Gen. William T. Ward

First Brigade
Col. Henry Case
70th Indiana 79th Ohio
102nd Illinois 105th Illinois
129th Illinois

Second Brigade
Col. Daniel Dustin
33rd Indiana 85th Indiana
19th Michigan 22nd Wisconsin

Third Brigade
Bvt. Brig. Gen. William Cogswell
20th Connecticut 33rd Massachusetts
55th Ohio 73rd Ohio
26th Wisconsin 136th New York

Artillery
Maj. John A. Reynolds

1st New York Light, Battery I (Winegar's)
1st New York Light, Battery M (Newkirk's)
1st Ohio Light, Battery C (Stephens')
Pennsylvania Light, Battery E (Sloan's)[1]

FOURTEENTH ARMY CORPS
Bvt. Maj. Gen. Jefferson C. Davis

First Division
Brig. Gen. William P. Carlin

First Brigade
Bvt. Brig. Gen. Harrison C. Hobart
42nd Indiana 88th Indiana
33rd Ohio 94th Ohio
21st Wisconsin 104th Illinois

Second Brigade
Bvt. Brig. Gen. George P. Buell
13th Michigan 21st Michigan
69th Ohio

Third Brigade
Lt. Col. David Miles
38th Indiana 21st Ohio
79th Pennsylvania 74th Ohio

Second Division
Brig. Gen. James D. Morgan

[1] Not engaged. The battery accompanied Geary's division, which escorted the XX Corps' trains in rear of the Right Wing.

Provost Guard
110th Illinois (Company B; Company A, 24th Illinois attached)

First Brigade
Brig. Gen. William Vandever
16th Illinois 14th Michigan
10th Michigan 60th Illinois
17th New York

Second Brigade
Brig. Gen. John G. Mitchell
34th Illinois 98th Ohio
78th Illinois 108th Ohio
113th Ohio 121st Ohio

Third Brigade
Bvt. Brig. Gen. Benjamin D. Fearing
86th Illinois 22nd Indiana
52nd Ohio 125th Illinois
37th Indiana (one company)
85th Illinois

CAVALRY

Third Division
Bvt. Maj. Gen. Judson Kilpatrick

First Brigade
Col. Thomas J. Jordan
3rd Indiana (battalion) 8th Indiana
2nd Kentucky 3rd Kentucky
9th Pennsylvania

Second Brigade
Bvt. Brig. Gen. Smith D. Atkins
92nd Illinois (mounted) 10th Ohio
9th Ohio 9th Michigan
McLaughlin's Squadron (Ohio)

Third Brigade
Col. George E. Spencer
1st Alabama 5th Kentucky
5th Ohio

Fourth Brigade (provisional)[2]
Lt. Col. William B. Way
1st Regiment 2nd Regiment
3rd Regiment

★ ORGANIZATION OF CONFEDERATE FORCES ★

DEPARTMENT OF SOUTH CAROLINA, GEORGIA, AND FLORIDA

HARDEE'S CORPS
Lt. Gen. William J. Hardee

Taliaferro's Division
Brig. Gen. William B. Taliaferro

Elliott's Brigade
Brig. Gen. Stephen Elliott, Jr.
22nd Georgia Battalion 28th Georgia Battalion (Bonaud's)
2nd South Carolina Heavy Artillery Hanleiter's Battalion
Gist Guard Artillery

Rhett's Brigade
Col. Alfred M. Rhett (C)
Col. William Butler
1st South Carolina Infantry (Regulars)
1st South Carolina Heavy Artillery
Lucas' South Carolina Battalion

MCLAWS' DIVISION
Maj. Gen. Lafayette McLaws

Conner's Brigade
Brig. Gen. John D. Kennedy
2nd South Carolina 3rd South Carolina
7th South Carolina 8th South Carolina
15th South Carolina 20th South Carolina
3rd South Carolina Battalion

[2] The Fourth Brigade was composed of dismounted men from the Third Division, with regimental numbers coinciding with the parent brigade numbers.

Fiser's Brigade
Col. John C. Fiser
1st Georgia Regulars 2nd Georgia Battalion Reserves
5th Georgia Reserves 6th Georgia Reserves
27th Georgia Battalion

Harrison's Brigade
Col. George P. Harrison
5th Georgia 32nd Georgia
47th Georgia

Hardy's Brigade
Col. Washington Hardy
50th North Carolina
77th North Carolina (7th Senior Reserves)
10th North Carolina Battalion

Blanchard's Brigade
Brig. Gen. Albert G. Blanchard
1st Battalion South Carolina Reserves
2nd Battalion South Carolina Reserves
6th Battalion South Carolina Reserves
7th Battalion South Carolina Reserves
Kay's Company, South Carolina Reserves

Battalion Artillery
Maj. A. Burnet Rhett
Le Gardeur's Battery
H. M. Stuart's Battery (Beaufort Light Artillery)

CAVALRY
Lt. Gen. Wade Hampton

WHEELER'S CORPS
Maj. Gen. Joseph Wheeler
(Army of Tennessee)

HUMES' DIVISION
Col. Henry M. Ashby

Harrison's Brigade
Col. Baxter Smith
3rd Arkansas Cav. 4th Tennessee Cav.
8th Texas Cav. 11th Texas Cav.

Ashby's Brigade
Lt. Col. James H. Lewis
1st Tennessee Cav. 2nd Tennessee Cav.
5th Tennessee Cav. 9th Tennessee Battalion

ALLEN'S DIVISION
Brig. Gen. William W. Allen

Hagan's Brigade
Col. D. G. White
1st Alabama Cav. 3rd Alabama Cav.
9th Alabama Cav. 12th Alabama Cav.
51st Alabama Cav. 53rd Alabama Cav.
24th Alabama Battalion

Anderson's Brigade
Brig. Gen. Robert H. Anderson
3rd Confederate Cav. 8th Confederate Cav.
10th Confederate Cav. 5th Georgia Cav.

APPENDIX D:

The Opposing Forces in the Battle of Bentonville, North Carolina

★ ORGANIZATION OF UNION FORCES[1] ★

Maj. Gen. William T. Sherman, Commanding

Headquarters Guard
7th Company, Ohio Sharpshooters

Engineers and Mechanics
1st Michigan
1st Missouri (five companies)

RIGHT WING:
ARMY OF THE TENNESSEE
Maj. Gen. Oliver O. Howard

Escort
15th Illinois Cavalry
4th Company Ohio Cavalry
Pontoon Train Guard
14th Wisconsin (Company E)

FIFTEENTH ARMY CORPS
Maj. Gen. John A. Logan

First Division
Bvt. Maj. Gen. Charles R. Woods

1. This order of battle is based on *OR* 47, pt. 1, pp. 46-55, with corrections based on additional sources.

First Brigade
Bvt. Brig. Gen. William B. Woods
12th Indiana 26th Iowa
27th Missouri
31st/32nd Missouri (six companies)
76th Ohio

Second Brigade
Col. Robert F. Catterson
26th Illinois 40th Illinois
103rd Illinois 97th Indiana
100th Indiana 6th Iowa
46th Ohio

Third Brigade
Col. George A. Stone
4th Iowa 9th Iowa
25th Iowa 30th Iowa
31st Iowa

Second Division
Maj. Gen. William B. Hazen

First Brigade
Col. Theodore Jones
55th Illinois 116th Illinois
127th Illinois
6th Missouri (Cos. A and B, 8th Missouri attached)
30th Ohio 57th Ohio

Second Brigade
Col. Wells S. Jones
111th Illinois 83rd Indiana
37th Ohio 47th Ohio
53rd Ohio 54th Ohio

Third Brigade
Brig. Gen. John M. Oliver
48th Illinois 90th Illinois
99th Indiana 15th Michigan
70th Ohio

Third Division
Bvt. Maj. Gen. John E. Smith

First Brigade
Brig. Gen. William T. Clark
63rd Illinois
93rd Illinois (with detachment non-veterans of 18th Wisconsin)
48th Indiana 59th Indiana
4th Minnesota

Second Brigade
Col. Clark R. Wever
56th Illinois 10th Iowa
17th Iowa (one company)
26th Missouri (two companies, and detachment 10th Missouri)
80th Ohio

Fourth Division
Bvt. Maj. Gen. John M. Corse

First Brigade
Brig. Gen. Elliott W. Rice
52nd Illinois 66th Indiana
2nd Iowa 7th Iowa

Second Brigade
Col. Robert N. Adams
12th Illinois 66th Illinois
81st Ohio

Third Brigade
Col. Frederick J. Hurlbut
7th Illinois 50th Illinois
57th Illinois 39th Iowa

Unassigned

110th United States Colored Troops

ARTILLERY

Lt. Col. William H. Ross

1st Illinois Light, Battery H (DeGress')

1st Michigan Light, Battery B (Wright's)

1st Missouri Light, Battery H (Callahan's)

12th Wisconsin Battery (Zickerick's)

SEVENTEENTH ARMY CORPS

Maj. Gen. Frank P. Blair, Jr.

Escort

11th Illinois Cavalry (Company G)

First Division

Maj. Gen. Joseph A. Mower

First Brigade

Brig. Gen. John W. Fuller

64th Illinois 18th Missouri

27th Ohio 39th Ohio

Second Brigade[2]

Col. Milton Montgomery

35th New Jersey 43rd Ohio

63rd Ohio 25th Wisconsin

Third Brigade

Col. John Tillson

10th Illinois 25th Indiana

32nd Wisconsin

2. The 25th Wisconsin was the only regiment of Montgomery's Brigade to reach the battlefield. The remainder served as train guard.

Third Division
Brig. Gen. Manning F. Force

Provost Guard
20th Illinois
First Brigade
Col. Cassius Fairchild
30th Illinois 31st Illinois
45th Illinois 12th Wisconsin
16th Wisconsin

Second Brigade
Col. Greenberry F. Wiles
20th Ohio 68th Ohio
78th Ohio 17th Wisconsin

Fourth Division
Bvt. Maj. Gen. Giles A. Smith

First Brigade
Brig. Gen. Benjamin F. Potts
14th/15th Illinois (battalion)
53rd Illinois 23rd Indiana
53rd Indiana 32nd Ohio

Third Brigade
Brig. Gen. William W. Belknap
32nd Illinois
11th Iowa 13th Iowa
15th Iowa 16th Iowa

ARTILLERY
Maj. Allen C. Waterhouse
1st Michigan Light, Battery C
1st Minnesota Battery 15th Ohio Battery

Unassigned
9th Illinois (mounted)

LEFT WING:
ARMY OF GEORGIA
(Late ARMY OF THE CUMBERLAND)
Maj. Gen. Henry W. Slocum

Pontoniers
58th Indiana

FOURTEENTH ARMY CORPS
Bvt. Maj. Gen. Jefferson C. Davis

First Division
Brig. Gen. William P. Carlin

First Brigade
Bvt. Brig. Gen. Harrison C. Hobart
104th Illinois 88th Indiana
33rd Ohio 94th Ohio
21st Wisconsin 42nd Indiana

Second Brigade
Bvt. Brig. Gen. George P. Buell
13th Michigan[3] 21st Michigan
69th Ohio

Third Brigade
Lt. Col. David Miles (W)
Lt. Col. Arnold McMahan
38th Indiana[4] 21st Ohio
74th Ohio[5] 79th Pennsylvania

Second Division
Brig. Gen. James D. Morgan

3. Commander Maj. Willard G. Eaton killed.
4. Commander Capt. James H. Low killed.
5. The 74th Ohio remained in the rear as train guard. Owens, *Greene County Soldiers*, p. 102.

Provost Guard

110th Illinois (Company B; Company A, 24th Illinois attached)

First Brigade

Brig. Gen. William Vandever

16th Illinois   60th Illinois

10th Michigan   14th Michigan

17th New York

Second Brigade

Brig. Gen. John G. Mitchell

34th Illinois   78th Illinois

98th Ohio   108th Ohio

113th Ohio   121st Ohio

Third Brigade

Bvt. Brig. Gen. Benjamin D. Fearing (W)

Lt. Col. James W. Langley

86th Illinois   125th Illinois

22nd Indiana   37th Indiana (one company)

52nd Ohio   85th Illinois[6]

Third Division[7]

Bvt. Maj. Gen. Absalom Baird

First Brigade

Col. Morton C. Hunter

82nd Indiana

23rd Missouri (four companies)

17th Ohio   31st Ohio

89th Ohio

92nd Ohio (11th Ohio attached)

6. The 85th Illinois remained in the rear as train guard. *OR* 47, pt. 1, p. 534.

7. The Third Division remained with the trains March 19, and arrived on the battlefield March 20. The Third Brigade remained in the rear on train guard duty.

Second Brigade
Lt. Col. Thomas Doan
75th Indiana 87th Indiana
101st Indiana 2nd Minnesota
105th Ohio

Third Brigade
Col. George P. Este
74th Indiana 18th Kentucky
14th Ohio 38th Ohio

ARTILLERY

Maj. Charles Houghtaling
1st Illinois Light, Battery C (Scovel's)
2nd Illinois Light, Battery I (Rich's)
19th Indiana Battery (Webb's)[8]
5th Wisconsin Battery (McKnight's)

TWENTIETH ARMY CORPS
Bvt. Maj. Gen. Alpheus S. Williams

First Division
Brig. Gen. Nathaniel J. Jackson

First Brigade
Col. James L. Selfridge
5th Connecticut 123rd New York
141st New York 46th Pennsylvania

Second Brigade
Col. William Hawley
2nd Massachusetts 13th New Jersey
107th New York 150th New York
3rd Wisconsin

8. Commander Lt. Samuel D. Webb killed.

Third Brigade

Brig. Gen. James S. Robinson

82nd Illinois 101st Illinois

143rd New York 82nd Ohio

61st Ohio 31st Wisconsin

Second Division[9]

Bvt. Maj. Gen. John W. Geary

First Brigade

Bvt. Brig. Gen. Ario Pardee, Jr.

5th Ohio 29th Ohio

66th Ohio 28th Pennsylvania

147th Pennsylvania

Second Brigade

Col. George W. Mindil

33rd New Jersey 73rd Pennsylvania

109th Pennsylvania 119th New York

134th New York 154th New York

Third Brigade

Bvt. Brig. Gen. Henry A. Barnum

60th New York 29th Pennsylvania

102nd New York 137th New York

149th New York 111th Pennsylvania

Third Division

Bvt. Maj. Gen. William T. Ward

First Brigade

Col. Henry Case

70th Indiana 79th Ohio

102nd Illinois 105th Illinois

129th Illinois

9. Remained in the rear as train guard March 19. The First and Third Brigades reached the battlefield March 20.

Second Brigade
Col. Daniel Dustin
33rd Indiana 85th Indiana
19th Michigan 22nd Wisconsin

Third Brigade
Bvt. Brig. Gen. William Cogswell
20th Connecticut 33rd Massachusetts
55th Ohio 73rd Ohio
26th Wisconsin 136th New York

ARTILLERY

Maj. John A. Reynolds
1st New York Light, Battery I (Winegar's)
1st New York Light, Battery M (Newkirk's)
1st Ohio Light, Battery C (Stephens')
Pennsylvania Light, Battery E (Sloan's)[10]

CAVALRY

Third Division[11]
Bvt. Maj. Gen. Judson Kilpatrick

First Brigade
Col. Thomas J. Jordan
3rd Indiana (battalion) 8th Indiana
2nd Kentucky 3rd Kentucky
9th Pennsylvania

Second Brigade
Bvt. Brig. Gen. Smith D. Atkins
92nd Illinois (mounted) 10th Ohio
9th Ohio 9th Michigan
McLaughlin's Squadron (Ohio)

10. Not engaged. The battery arrived with Geary on March 20.
11. Not actively engaged.

Third Brigade
Col. George E. Spencer
1st Alabama 5th Kentucky
5th Ohio

Fourth Brigade (provisional) [12]
Lt. Col. William B. Way
1st Regiment 2nd Regiment
3rd Regiment

ARTILLERY

10th Wisconsin Battery (Beebe's)

12. Composed of dismounted men from the Third Division, with regimental numbers coinciding with the parent brigade numbers.

★ ORGANIZATION OF CONFEDERATE FORCES[13] ★

Gen. Joseph E. Johnston, Commanding

ARMY OF TENNESSEE
Lt. Gen. Alexander P. Stewart

LEE'S CORPS
Maj. Gen. D. H. Hill

Stevenson's Division
Maj. Gen. Carter L. Stevenson

Palmer's Brigade
Brig. Gen. Joseph B. Palmer
3rd Tennessee 18th Tennessee
26th Tennessee 32nd Tennessee
45th Tennessee 46th Tennessee[14]
58th North Carolina 60th North Carolina
54th Virginia 63rd Virginia
23rd Tennessee Battalion

Pettus' Brigade
Brig. Gen. Edmund W. Pettus (W)
20th Alabama 23rd Alabama
30th Alabama 31st Alabama
46th Alabama

13. Regiments, battalions, and batteries are listed individually to credit all units represented on the field of battle. By March 1865 many of these depleted, campaign-weary entities were consolidated, with some brigades having two or more units combined under a single commander. Thus Bentonville-specific command structures at the regimental level cannot be determined in every case. The army was partly reorganized at the end of March, and again more radically on April 9, 1865. See *OR* 47, pt. 1, pp. 1061-1066, and *OR* 47, pt. 3, pp. 732-736.

14. The Confederate troop roster for March 31, 1865 lists the 46th Tennessee simultaneously in Palmer's and Quarles' Brigades. *OR* 47, pt. 3, pp. 733, 735.

Cumming's Brigade (Arrived on the battlefield March 20)
Col. Robert J. Henderson
34th Georgia 36th Georgia
39th Georgia 56th Georgia

Clayton's Division
Maj. Gen. Henry D. Clayton

Stovall's Brigade
Col. Henry C. Kellogg
40th Georgia 41st Georgia
42nd Georgia 43rd Georgia
52nd Georgia

Jackson's Brigade
Lt. Col. Osceola Kyle
25th Georgia 29th Georgia
30th Georgia 66th Georgia
1st Confederate
1st Battalion Georgia Sharpshooters

Baker's Brigade
Brig. Gen. Alpheus Baker
37th Alabama 40th Alabama
42nd Alabama 54th Alabama

Hill's Division
Col. John G. Coltart

Deas' Brigade
Col. Harry T. Toulmin
19th Alabama 22nd Alabama
25th Alabama 39th Alabama
50th Alabama

Manigault's Brigade
Lt. Col. John C. Carter
24th Alabama 34th Alabama
10th South Carolina 19th South Carolina

STEWART'S CORPS
Maj. Gen. William W. Loring

Loring's Division
Col. James Jackson

Adams' Brigade
Lt. Col. Robert J. Lawrence
6th Mississippi 14th Mississippi
15th Mississippi[15] 20th Mississippi
23rd Mississippi 43rd Mississippi

Scott's Brigade
Capt. John A. Dixon
27th Alabama 35th Alabama
49th Alabama 55th Alabama
57th Alabama 12th Louisiana

Featherston's Brigade
Maj. Martin A. Oatis
1st Mississippi Battalion 1st Mississippi
3rd Mississippi 22nd Mississippi
31st Mississippi 33rd Mississippi
40th Mississippi

Walthall's Division
Maj. Gen. Edward C. Walthall

Reynolds' Brigade
Brig. Gen. Daniel H. Reynolds (W)
Col. Henry C. Bunn (W)
Lt. Col. Morton G. Galloway
4th Arkansas 9th Arkansas
25th Arkansas
1st Arkansas Mounted Rifles (dismounted)
2nd Arkansas Mounted Rifles (dismounted)

15. The Confederate troop roster for March 31, 1865 lists the 15th MS simultaneously in Adams' and Lowrey's Brigades. *OR* 47, pt. 3, pp. 734, 736.

Quarles' Brigade
Brig. Gen. George D. Johnston
1st Alabama 17th Alabama
29th Alabama 42nd Tennessee
48th Tennessee 49th Tennessee
53rd Tennessee 55th Tennessee

CHEATHAM'S CORPS
Maj. Gen. William B. Bate

Cleburne's Division
Brig. Gen. James A. Smith

Govan's Brigade
Col. Peter V. Green
1st Arkansas 2nd Arkansas
5th Arkansas 6th Arkansas
7th Arkansas 8th Arkansas
13th Arkansas 15th Arkansas
19th Arkansas 24th Arkansas
3rd Confederate

Smith's Brigade
Capt. J. R. Bonner
1st Georgia (Volunteers) 54th Georgia
57th Georgia 63rd Georgia

Granbury's Brigade
(Arrived on the battlefield March 20)
Maj. William A. Ryan
35th Tennessee 6th Texas
7th Texas 10th Texas
15th Texas 17th Texas
18th Texas 24th Texas
25th Texas 5th Confederate

Lowrey's Brigade
(Arrived on the battlefield March 21)[16]
Lt. Col. John F. Smith
3rd Mississippi 8th Mississippi
16th Alabama 32nd Mississippi

Bate's Division
Col. D. L. Kenan (W)

Tyler's Brigade
Maj. W. H. Wilkinson (K)
2nd Tennessee 10th Tennessee
15th Tennessee 20th Tennessee
30th Tennessee 37th Tennessee
37th Georgia
4th Georgia Battalion Sharpshooters

Finley's Brigade
Lt. Col. Eli Washburn
1st Florida 3rd Florida
4th Florida 6th Florida
7th Florida 1st Florida Cavalry (dismounted)

Brown's Division [17]
(Arrived on the battlefield March 21)
Brig. Gen. Roswell S. Ripley

Gist's Brigade
Col. Hume R. Feild
16th South Carolina 24th South Carolina
46th Georgia 65th Georgia
3rd Georgia Battalion
2nd Battalion Georgia Sharpshooters

Maney's Brigade
Lt. Col. Christopher C. McKinney

---

16. Lowrey appears as Lowry on the Confederate troop roster for March 31, 1865. *OR* 47, pt. 3, p. 736.
17. Corps commander Frank Cheatham led Brown's Division into the fight.

1st Tennessee 8th Tennessee
16th Tennessee 27th Tennessee
28th Tennessee

Strahl's Brigade
Col. James D. Tillman
4th Tennessee 5th Tennessee
19th Tennessee 24th Tennessee
31st Tennessee 33rd Tennessee
38th Tennessee 41st Tennessee

Vaughan's Brigade
Col. William P. Bishop
11th Tennessee 12th Tennessee
13th Tennessee 29th Tennessee
47th Tennessee 51st Tennessee
52nd Tennessee 154th Tennessee

DEPARTMENT OF NORTH CAROLINA
Gen. Braxton Bragg

Hoke's Division[18]
(From the Army of Northern Virginia)
Maj. Gen. Robert F. Hoke

Clingman's Brigade
Col. William S. Devane (W)
8th North Carolina 31st North Carolina
51st North Carolina 61st North Carolina[19]

18. Though Hoke's Division belonged to the Army of Northern Virginia, it was operating at Bentonville with several local detachments. These included three companies of the 13th Battalion North Carolina Light Artillery, three regiments and one battalion of North Carolina Junior Reserves, and two regiments and one battalion from the Fort Fisher garrison (brigaded with Johnson Hagood's South Carolinians).

19. Commander Lt. Col. Edward G. Mallett killed.

Kirkland's Brigade
Brig. Gen. William W. Kirkland
17th North Carolina 42nd North Carolina
66th North Carolina

Hagood's Brigade
Brig. Gen. Johnson Hagood
Contingent of Lt. Col. James H. Rion:
11th South Carolina 21st South Carolina
25th South Carolina 27th South Carolina
7th South Carolina Battalion
Contingent of Lt. Col. John D. Taylor (W):
1st North Carolina Battalion Heavy Artillery
(9th North Carolina Battalion)
36th North Carolina
Adams' Battery (Company D, 13th Battalion
North Carolina Light Artillery)
Contingent of Maj. William A. Holland:
40th North Carolina

Colquitt's Brigade
Col. Charles T. Zachry
6th Georgia 19th Georgia
23rd Georgia 27th Georgia
28th Georgia

North Carolina Junior Reserves Brigade
Col. John H. Nethercutt
70th North Carolina (1st North Carolina JR)
71st North Carolina (2nd North Carolina JR)
72nd North Carolina (3rd North Carolina JR)
20th Battalion North Carolina JR

ARTILLERY[20]

13th Battalion North Carolina Light Artillery[21]

Lt. Col. Joseph B. Starr

Atkins' Battery (Company B) Dickson's Battery (Company E)

DEPARTMENT OF SOUTH CAROLINA, GEORGIA, AND FLORIDA

HARDEE'S CORPS

Lt. Gen. William J. Hardee

Taliaferro's Division

Brig. Gen. William B. Taliaferro

Elliott's Brigade

Brig. Gen. Stephen Elliott, Jr. (W)

22nd Georgia Battalion 28th Georgia Battalion (Bonaud's)

2nd South Carolina Heavy Artillery Hanleiter's Battalion

Gist Guard Artillery

Rhett's Brigade

Col. William Butler

1st South Carolina Infantry (Regulars)

1st South Carolina Heavy Artillery

Lucas' South Carolina Battalion

---

20. The following artillery batteries may have been present with Hoke's Division: 3rd North Carolina Battalion: Co. A, Capt. Andrew J. Ellis; Co. B, Capt. William Badham, Jr.; and detachments, Co. C, Lt. Alfred M. Darden. 10th North Carolina (detachment): Co. I, Capt. Thomas J. Southerland; Sampson Artillery, Capt. Abner M. Moseley; and the Staunton Hill (Virginia) Battery, Capt. Andrew B. Paris. If these units were present, no accounts have surfaced to state specifically where on the field, or with what brigade, they served. It is also unclear whether they served as infantry or artillery. See *OR* 47, pt. 3, p. 1155.

21. The six companies of this battalion were widely scattered in March 1865. Company F was attached to Longstreet's Corps of the Army of Northern Virginia; Company A was operating out of Weldon, North Carolina; and one section of Company C, known as Cumming's Battery, was stationed at Kinston, North Carolina. It may have been this section of Cumming's Battery that, with Col. John Whitford's brigade, opposed the Federal Right Wing at Cox's Bridge near Goldsboro. Of the three companies present at Bentonville Company D (Adams' Battery) probably fought as infantry with Hagood's Brigade, while Companies B and E (Atkins' and Dickson's Batteries) fought as artillery under the direct command of Colonel Starr. Manarin, *North Carolina Troops* 1, pp. 551, 558, 568, 576, 585, 594.

McLaws' Division
Maj. Gen. Lafayette McLaws

Conner's Brigade
Brig. Gen. John D. Kennedy
2nd South Carolina 3rd South Carolina
7th South Carolina 8th South Carolina
15th South Carolina 20th South Carolina
3rd South Carolina Battalion

Fiser's Brigade
Col. John C. Fiser
1st Georgia Regulars 2nd Georgia Battalion Reserves
5th Georgia Reserves 6th Georgia Reserves
27th Georgia Battalion

Harrison's Brigade
Col. George P. Harrison
5th Georgia 32nd Georgia
47th Georgia

Hardy's Brigade
Col. Washington Hardy
50th North Carolina
77th North Carolina (7th Senior Reserves)
10th North Carolina Battalion

Blanchard's Brigade
Brig. Gen. Albert G. Blanchard
1st Battalion South Carolina Reserves
2nd Battalion South Carolina Reserves
6th Battalion South Carolina Reserves
7th Battalion South Carolina Reserves
Kay's Company, South Carolina Reserves

Battalion Artillery
Maj. A. Burnet Rhett
LeGardeur's Battery
H. M. Stuart's Battery (Beaufort Light Artillery)

CAVALRY COMMAND
Lt. Gen. Wade Hampton

WHEELER'S CORPS
Maj. Gen. Joseph Wheeler
(Army of Tennessee)

Humes' Division
Col. Henry M. Ashby

T. Harrison's Brigade
Col. Baxter Smith
3rd Arkansas Cav. 4th Tennessee Cav.
8th Texas Cav. 11th Texas Cav.

Ashby's Brigade
Lt. Col. James H. Lewis
1st Tennessee Cav. 2nd Tennessee Cav.
5th Tennessee Cav. 9th Tennessee Battalion

Allen's Division
Brig. Gen. William W. Allen

Hagan's Brigade
Col. D. G. White
1st Alabama Cav. 3rd Alabama Cav.
9th Alabama Cav. 12th Alabama Cav.
51st Alabama Cav. 53rd Alabama Cav.
24th Alabama Battalion

Anderson's Brigade
Brig. Gen. Robert H. Anderson
3rd Confederate Cav. 8th Confederate Cav.
10th Confederate Cav. 5th Georgia Cav.

Dibrell's Division
Col. George G. Dibrell

Dibrell's Brigade
Col. William S. McLemore

4th Tennessee (McLemore's) Cav.
13th Tennessee Cav.
Shaw's Tennessee Battalion

Breckinridge's Brigade (formerly Lewis')
Col. W. C. P. Breckinridge
1st Kentucky Cav. 2nd Kentucky Cav.
9th Kentucky Cav. 2nd Kentucky Mounted Infantry
4th Kentucky Mounted Infantry
5th Kentucky Mounted Infantry
6th Kentucky Mounted Infantry
9th Kentucky Mounted Infantry

Butler's Division
(From the Army of Northern Virginia)
Maj. Gen. M. C. Butler
Brig. Gen. Evander M. Law

Young's Brigade
Col. Gilbert J. Wright
10th Georgia Cav. Cobb's Georgia Legion
Jeff Davis Legion Phillips' Georgia Legion

Butler's Brigade
Brig. Gen. Evander M. Law
Brig. Gen. Thomas M. Logan
4th South Carolina Cav. 5th South Carolina Cav.
6th South Carolina Cav.

HORSE ARTILLERY

Earle's South Carolina Battery
Hart's (Halsey's) South Carolina Battery

APPENDIX E:

VIEWS OF THE BATTLEFIELD

The elevation map on the facing page, titled "Bentonville and Vicinity," is keyed to provide a directional reference for the 13 photographs that follow. The numbered arrows on the map represent views of the battlefield from the perspective of the combatants, as well as views of extant earthworks and the Harper House. The numbers correspond to like-numbered photographs, and individual captions beneath each image relate the shot to a particular scene in the battle. The arrows provide an approximate angle of view (based on many battlefield walks) but are not positioned on the exact spots where the photos were taken. Cross-referencing the tactical maps will be helpful in understanding these modern views as they relate to troop positions during the battle. For this reason the key map shows the area's historic road configuration.

Mark A. Moore

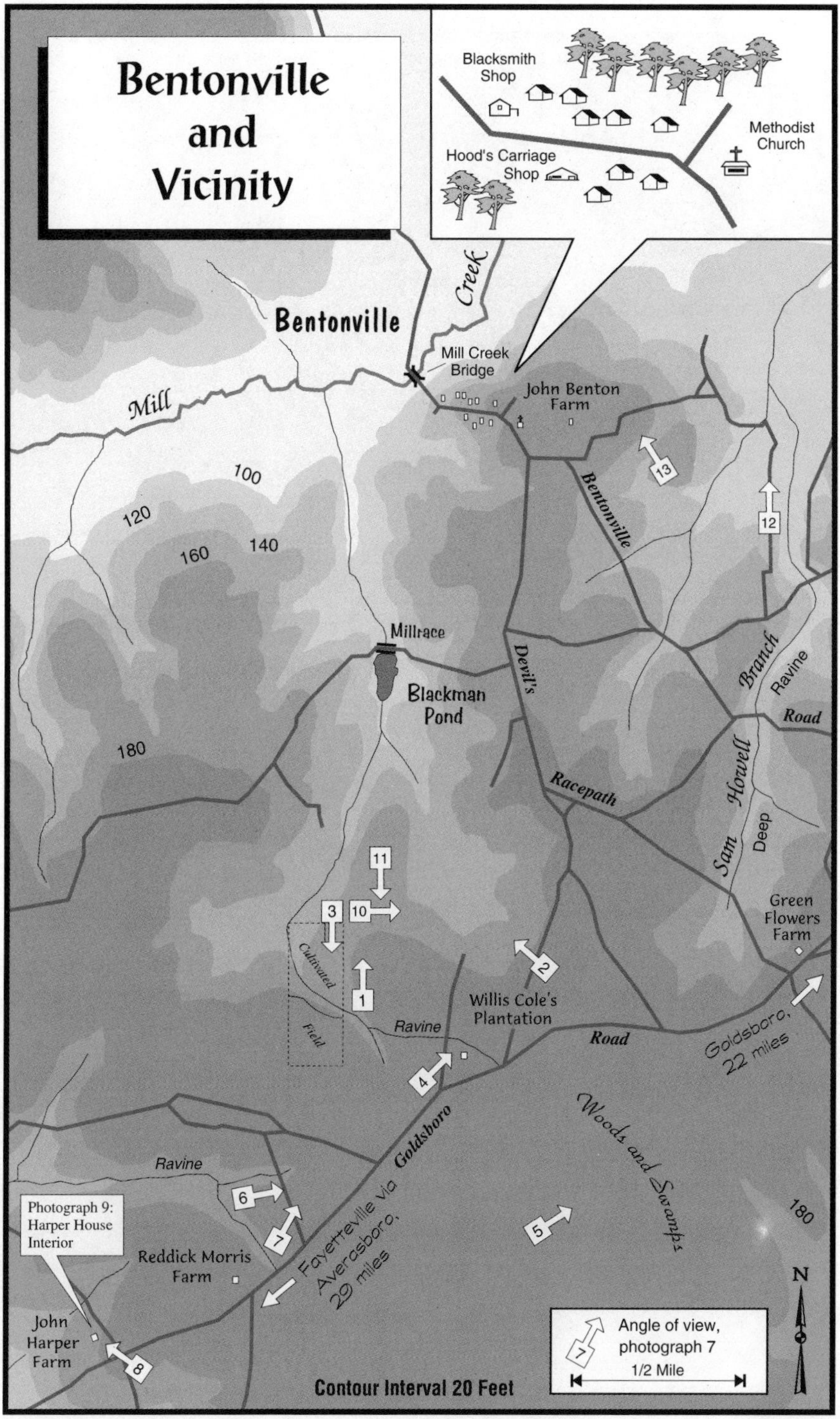
Bentonville and Vicinity
Blacksmith Shop
Methodist Church
Hood's Carriage Shop
Creek
Bentonville
Mill Creek Bridge
Mill
John Benton Farm
100
120
160
140
13
Bentonville
12
Millrace
Blackman Pond
Devil's
Branch
Ravine
Road
180
Racepath
Howell
Sam
Deep
11
3
10
Cultivated
Field
1
2
Green Flowers Farm
Willis Cole's Plantation
Ravine
Road
Goldsboro, 22 miles
4
Woods and Swamps
Goldsboro
Ravine
6
7
Fayetteville via Averasboro, 29 miles
5
180
Photograph 9: Harper House Interior
Reddick Morris Farm
John Harper Farm
8
N
Angle of view, photograph 7
1/2 Mile
Contour Interval 20 Feet
Mark A. Moore

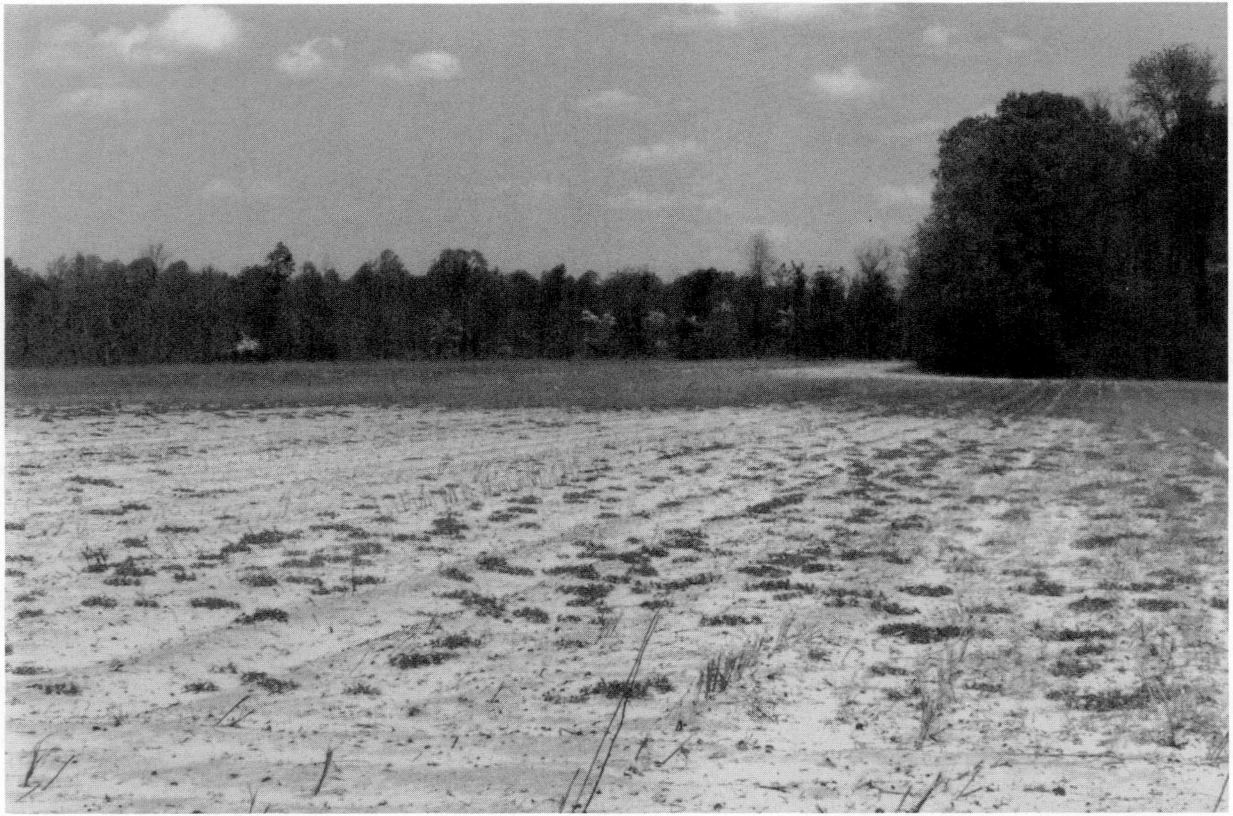

1. *Scene of Buell's noontime assault, facing north toward Bate's position.* The Federals of Buell's brigade advanced across this field toward the treeline in the background. "[The Rebels] opened fire and gave us an awful volley," wrote a lieutenant in Buell's brigade. "I tell you it was a tight place. . . .I was awfully scart [scared], but I'll be hanged if I was going to show it." (Refer to map on p. 185) Photo by Nancy Bradley.

2. *Scene of Walthall's advance during the Confederate grand assault, facing northwest.* At Bentonville, Maj. Gen. Edward C. Walthall's veteran division numbered a scant 240 officers and men. Yet their advance across this field (from the right background to the left middle-ground) presented a stirring sight to the boys of the North Carolina Junior Reserves, many of whom watched from this vantage point. Colonel Charles Broadfoot of the 1st Reserves described the memorable scene: "Several officers led the charge on horseback across an open field in full view, with colors flying and line of battle in such perfect order as to be able to distinguish the several field officers in proper place. . . .It was gallantly done, but it was painful to see how close their battle flags were together, regiments being scarcely larger than companies and [the] division not much larger than a regiment should be."
(Refer to map on p. 207) Photo by Nancy Bradley.

3. *Bate's view of the Confederate grand assault, facing south.* "In our front and gently sloping upwards for three hundred yards was an old field dotted with second growth pines," wrote a Georgian in Bate's command. "[A]s we advanced, we passed over the bodies of the enemy [Buell's brigade] who had been killed in the assault and whose faces, from exposure to the sun, had turned almost black." (Refer to map on p. 207) Photo by Nancy Bradley.

4. *View of the Cole field, facing northeast.* The Willis Cole house stood in front of the grove of trees standing in the right center of the photograph. During the Confederate grand assault, the Army of Tennessee troops emerged from the treeline and advanced toward the foreground. A Union staff officer described their approach: "I saw the rebel regiments in front in full view, stretching through the fields as far as the eye could reach, advancing rapidly and firing as they came. . . .The onward sweep of the rebel lines was like the waves of the ocean, resistless." (Refer to map on p. 207) Photo by Nancy Bradley.

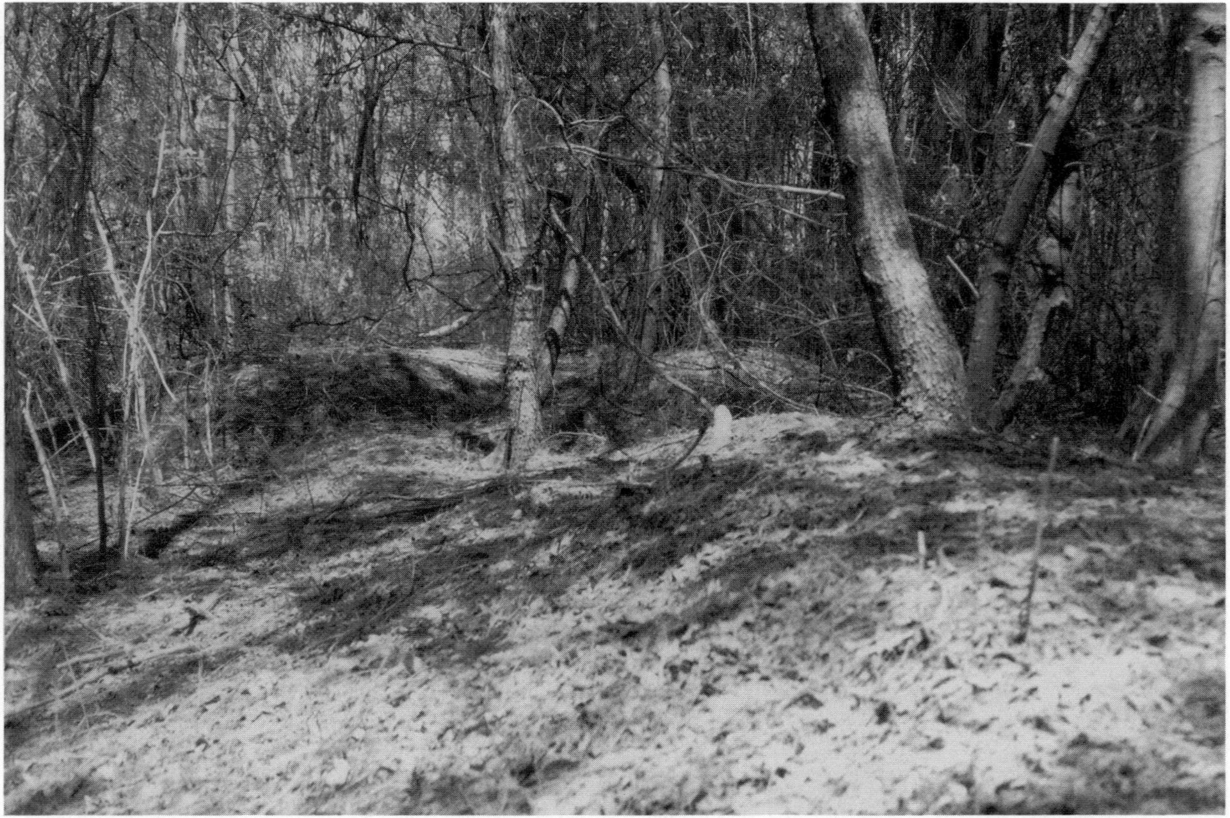

5. *View of Morgan's log works, facing northeast toward Hoke's position.* The works are in the middle-ground and run from left to right. "The surging masses of our assailants recoiled from our barricades like spray from the sides of a well-built ship," one of Morgan's veterans recalled. (Refer to map on p. 236) Photo by Nancy Bradley.

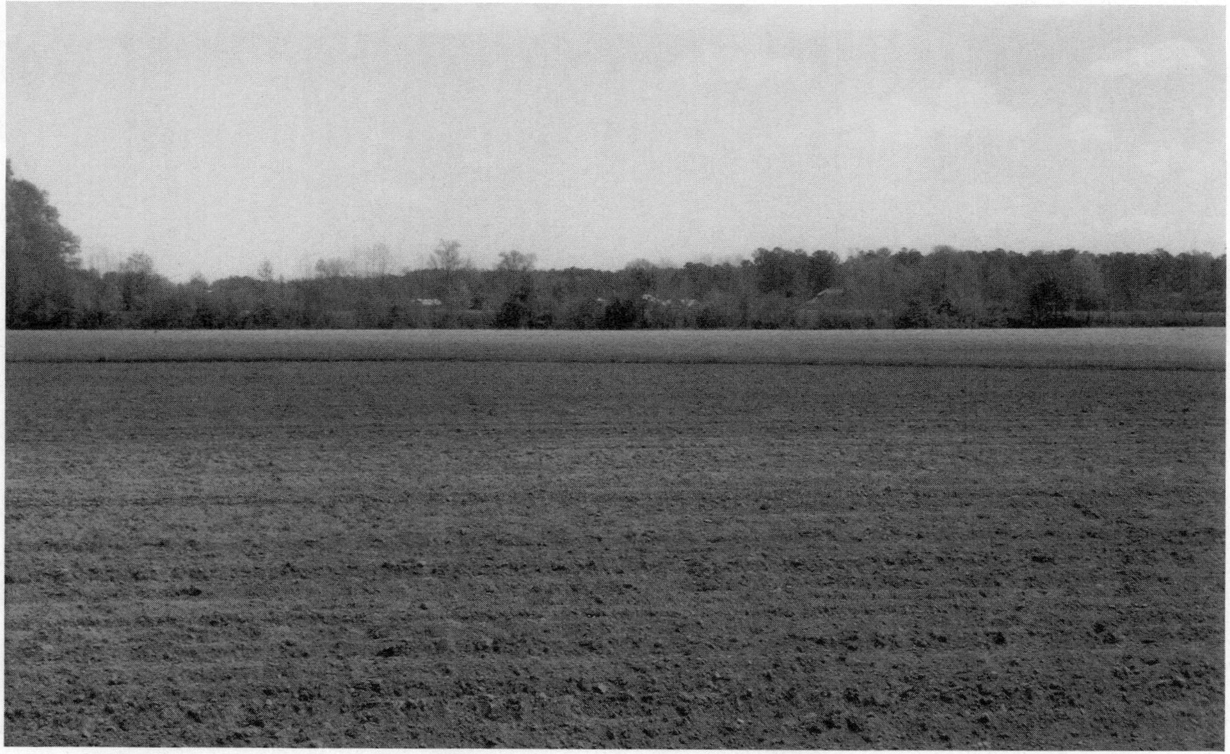

6. *The 13th New Jersey's view of Carlin's rout across Morris' field, facing east.* In 1865, there was no secondary growth vegetation lining this field to obstruct the view of the soldiers of the 13th New Jersey. During the rout, Carlin's fugitives raced from the left of this view to the right. "The vast field was soon covered with men, horses, artillery, caissons, &c., which brought vividly to our minds a similar scene at the Battle of Chancellorsville," wrote the 13th New Jersey's historian, Samuel Toombs. (Refer to map on p. 281) Photo by Nancy Bradley.

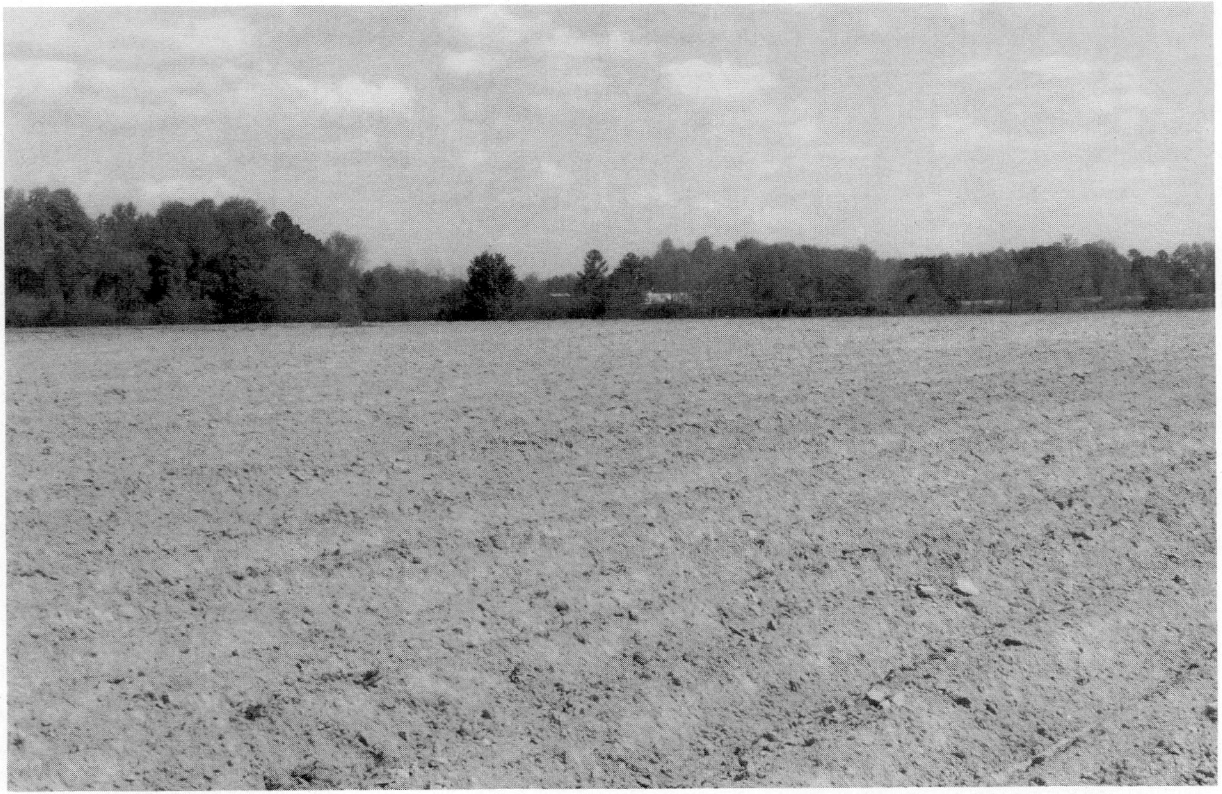

7. *View of Morris' field, as seen by the men of Battery C, 1st Ohio (Stephens' battery), facing northeast.* Stephens' battery was the only artillery in position when the Confederates made their first assault on the Union line on Morris' farm. Taliaferro's Division approached from the center, and Bate's command from the right, of the photograph. When the Confederates emerged from the woods in the background, the crews of Stephens' battery "sent them a volley of caseshot [with fuses] cut just right to burst among them," recalled one Ohio gunner. "We kept this up as fast as we could load and shoot." (Refer to map on p. 281) Photo by Nancy Bradley.

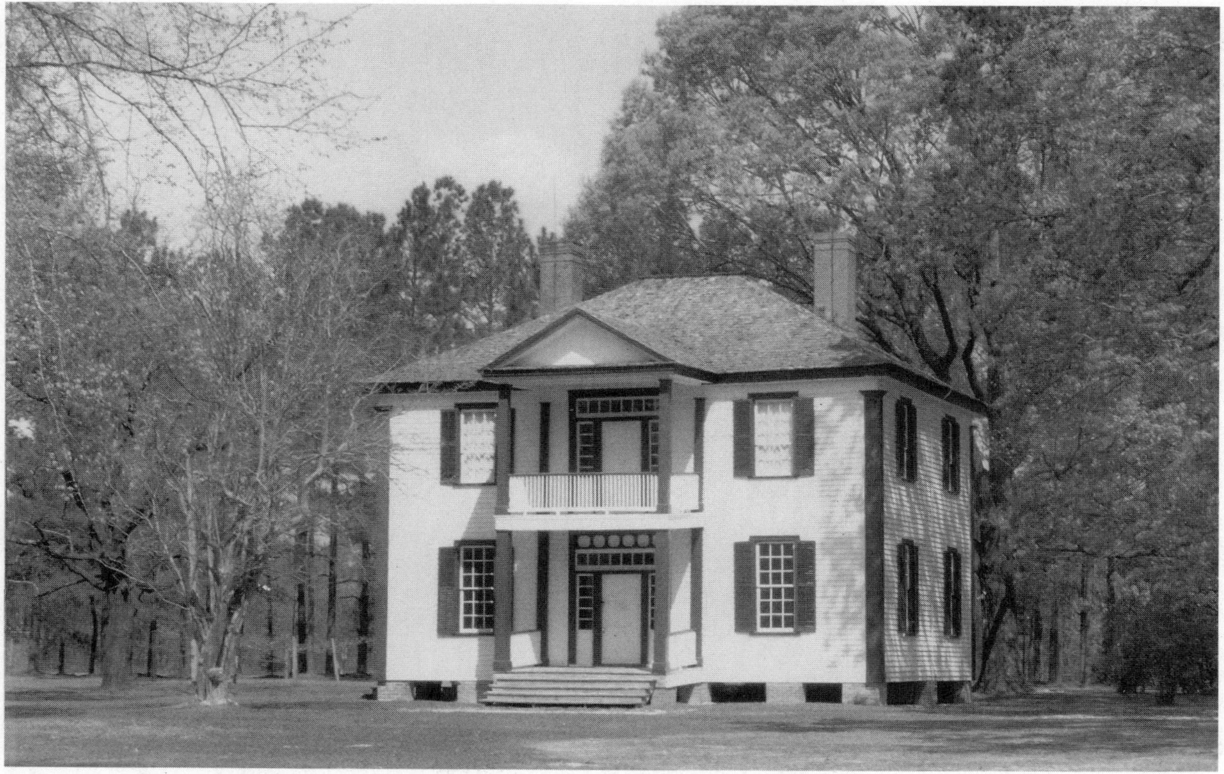

8. *View of the John Harper house, facing northwest.* The Harper house served as the Union XIV Corps' hospital during the battle. The XIV Corps' chief surgeon estimated that 500 Federals were treated here. Afterward, the house served as a hospital for 45 Confederates who were too grievously wounded to be transported with the army to Smithfield. (Refer to map on p. 291) Photo by Nancy Bradley.

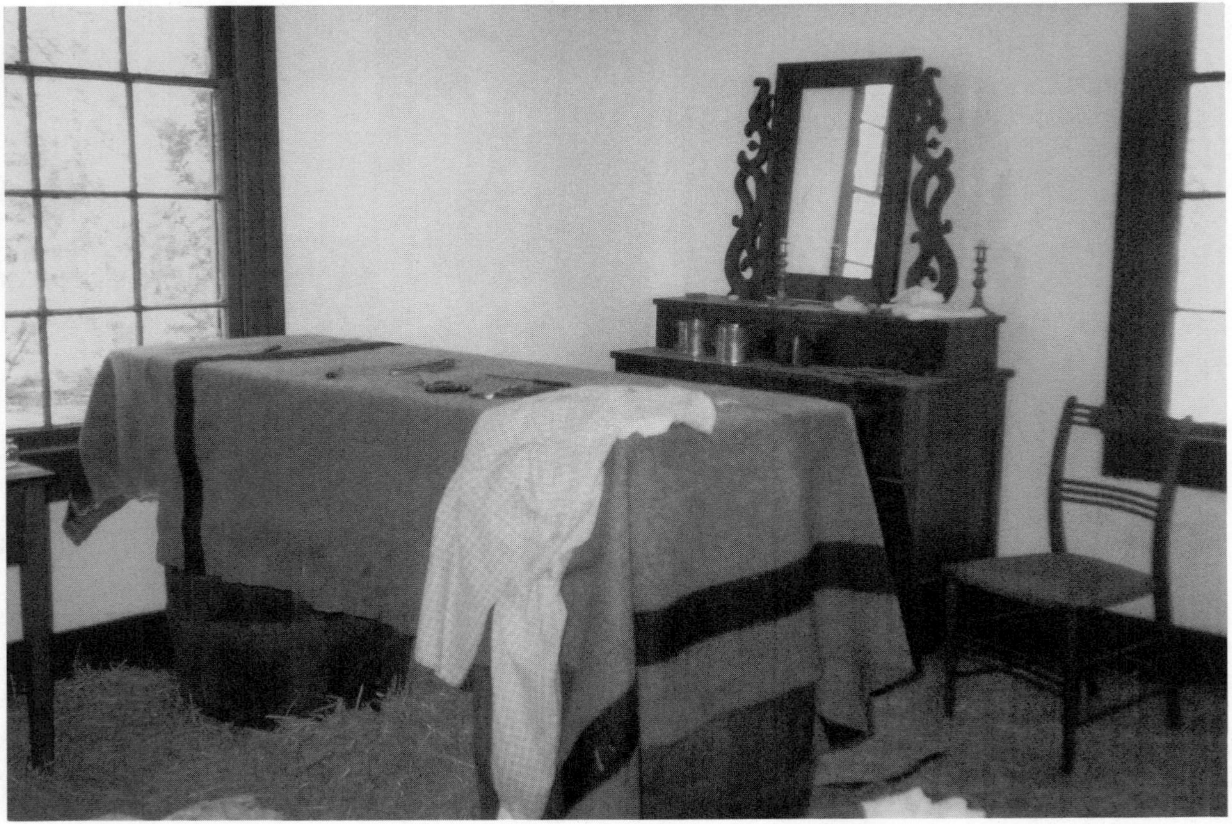

9. During the battle, the *Harper house interior* "resembled a slaughter house," wrote one eyewitness. "A dozen surgeons and attendants in shirt sleeves stood at rude benches cutting off arms and legs and throwing them out of the windows, where they lay scattered on the grass."
(Refer to map on p. 291) Photo by Nancy Bradley.

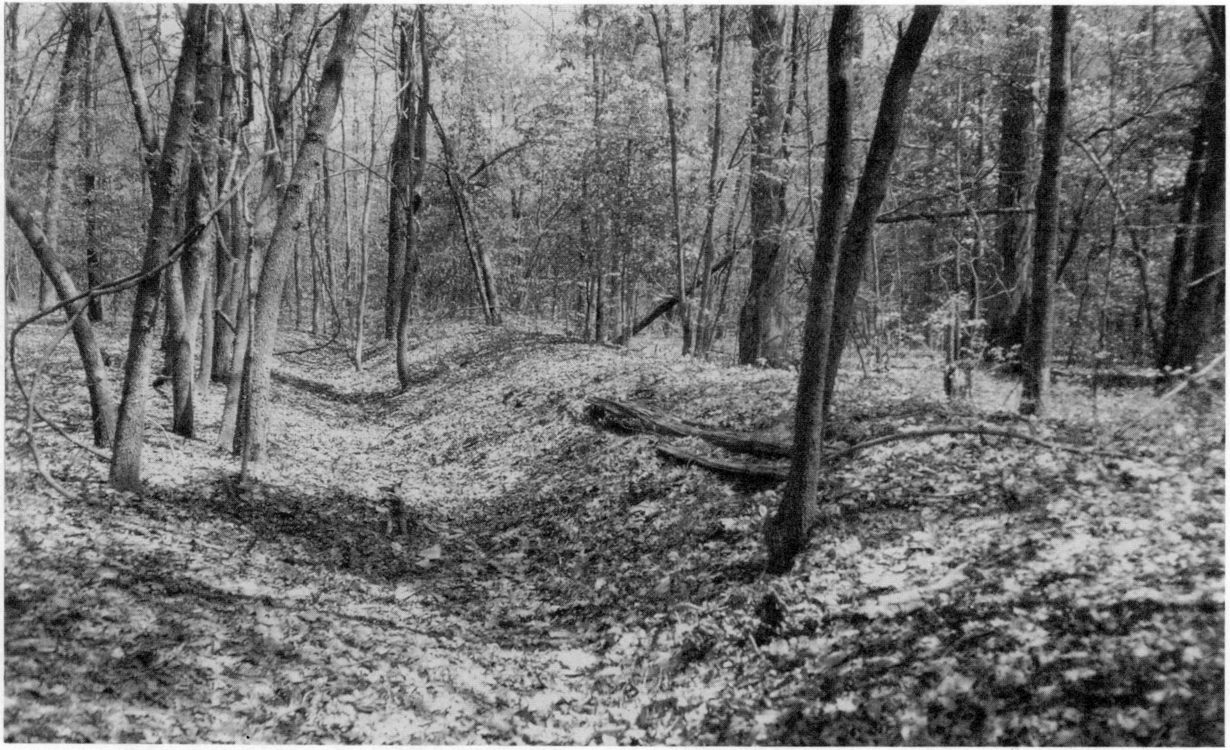

10. *Section of the Army of Tennessee's entrenchments, facing east.* Both the Union and Confederate armies at Bentonville had mastered the art of field fortification. In a dispatch to General Schofield, General Sherman explained his reluctance to assault Johnston's smaller army: "[H]is position is in the swamps, difficult of approach, and I don't like to assail his parapets." These well-preserved entrenchments bear eloquent witness to the wisdom of Sherman's statement. (Refer to map on p. 346) Photo by Nancy Bradley.

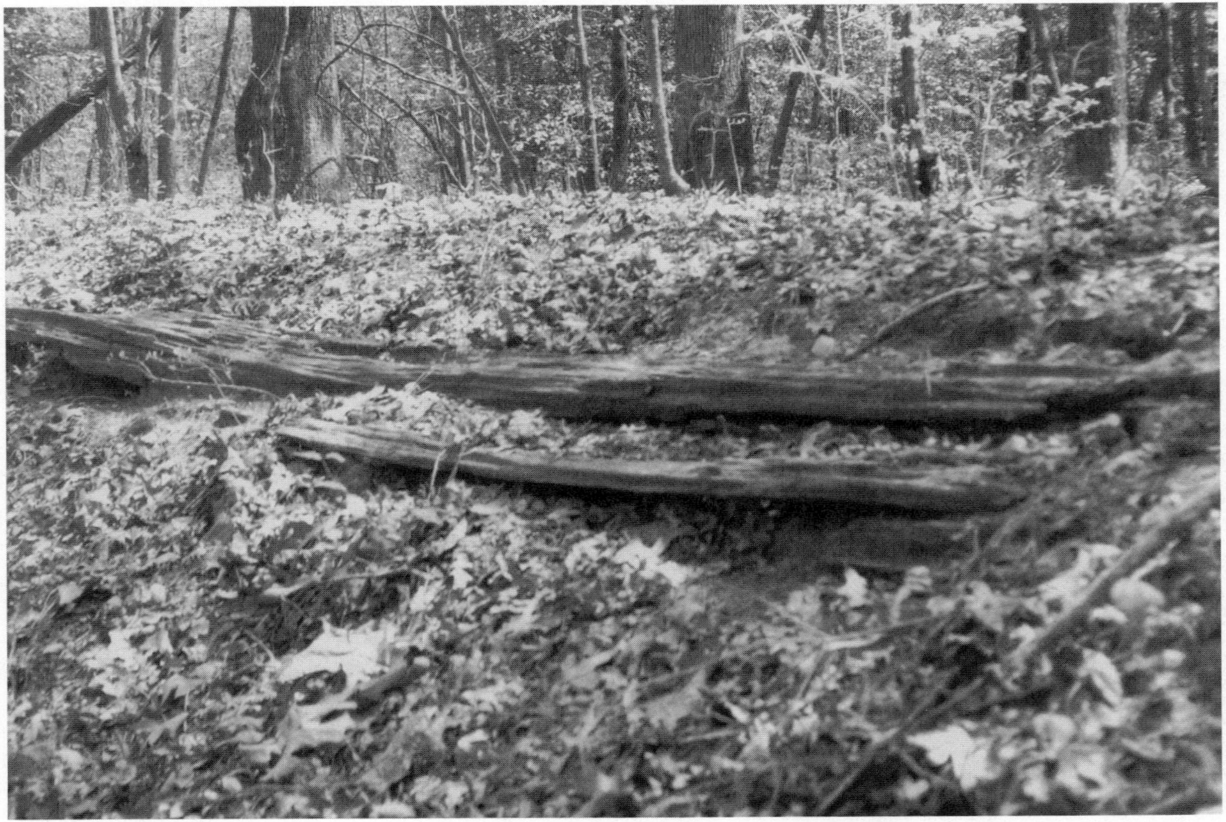

11. *Close-up of Army of Tennessee entrenchments, showing log revetment.* (Refer to map on p. 346) Photo by Nancy Bradley.

12. *Mower's approach route, facing north.* General Mower's two brigades formed line of battle along this road, facing to the left (or west). In his eagerness to push ahead, Mower scarcely gave his brigades time enough "to form the line and to allow the skirmishers to deploy," complained one officer. (Refer to map on p. 377) Photo by Nancy Bradley.

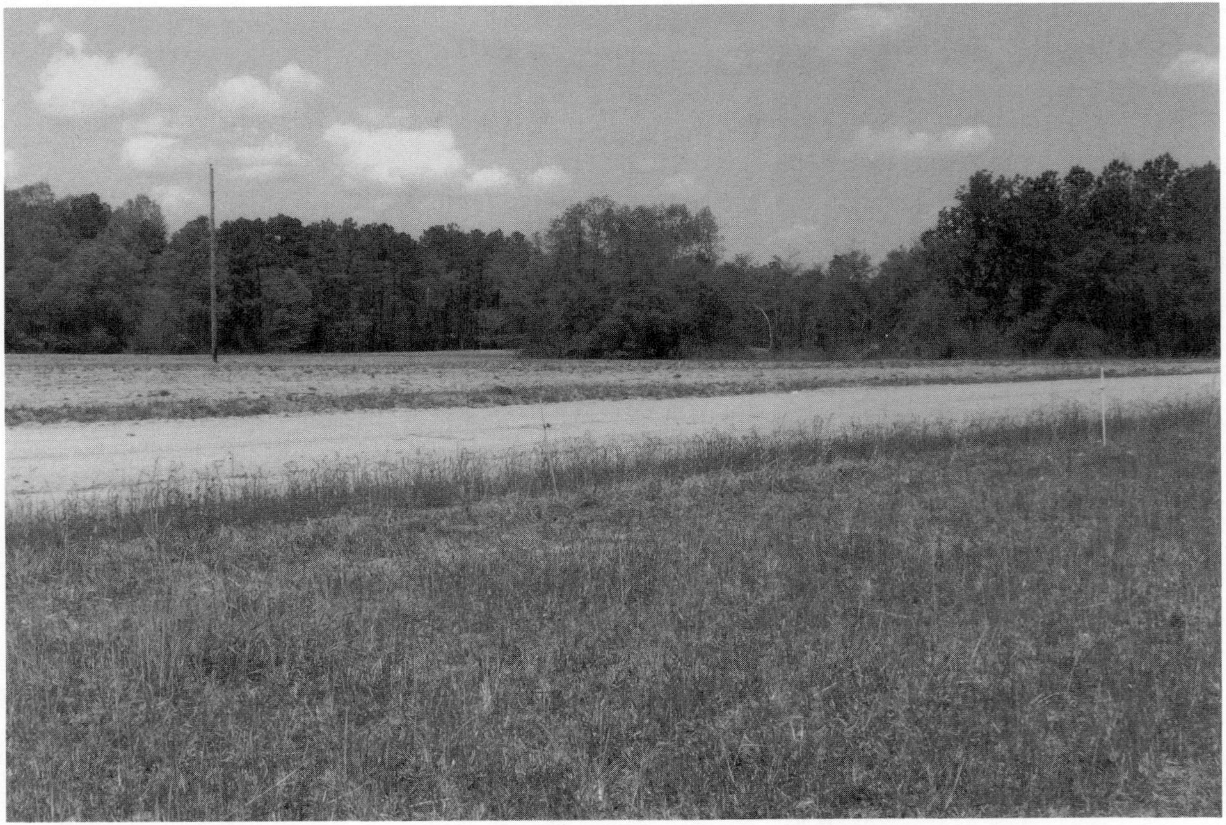

13. *Location of Earle's Battery during Mower's charge, facing northwest.* Earle's Battery stood between the utility pole on the left and the treeline on the right. Prior to the rout of Butler's Brigade, the four cannon faced to the right (or east) toward the advancing Federals of Mower's division. After driving off the Confederate cavalry and artillery defending this portion of the line, Fuller's brigade halted on the crest of this hill, marked by the road in the foreground. (Refer to map on p. 385) Photo by Nancy Bradley.

A contemporary view of Mower's charge showing the Confederates' abandoned artillery caisson in the center foreground. Earle's Battery is pictured on the left, heading for the rear. (Refer to map on p. 385) *Frank Leslie's Illustrated Newspaper.*

~ NOTES ~

ABBREVIATIONS OF MANUSCRIPT REPOSITORIES

ALDAH	Alabama Department of Archives and History
AAS	American Antiquarian Society
UAK-F	University of Arkansas at Fayetteville
AHS	Atlanta Historical Society
CAH-UTX	Center for American History, University of Texas
CHS	Chicago Historical Society
CTSL	Connecticut State Library
DU	Perkins Library, Duke University
EU	Woodruff Library, Emory University
GADAH	Georgia Department of Archives and History
GAHS	Georgia Historical Society
UGA	University of Georgia
HEHL	Henry E. Huntington Library
ILSHL	Illinois State Historical Library
INHS	Indiana Historical Society
INSL	Indiana State Library
KMNP	Kennesaw Mountain National Park
LC	Library of Congress
BL-UMI	Bentley Historical Library, University of Michigan
MNHS	Minnesota Historical Society
WHMC-UMO	Western Historical Manuscript Collection, University of Missouri Library
NA	National Archives
NCDAH	North Carolina Division of Archives and History

NCC-UNC	North Carolina Collection, Wilson Library, University of North Carolina
SHC-UNC	Southern Historical Collection, Wilson Library, University of North Carolina
UND	University of Notre Dame
OHS	Ohio Historical Society
HSPA	Historical Society of Pennsylvania
SCHS	South Carolina Historical Society
USC	South Caroliniana Library, University of South Carolina
SHSW	State Historical Society of Wisconsin
TNSLA	Tennessee State Library and Archives
USAMHI	United States Army Military History Institute, Archives Branch
UWA	University of Washington
UWI-Parkside	University of Wisconsin-Parkside
WRHS	Western Reserve Historical Society

DISPATCHES PRECEEDING CHAPTER ONE

1. Sherman, *Memoirs*, 2, p. 231.
2. A. Lincoln to W. T. Sherman, December 26, 1865, W. T. Sherman Papers, OHS.

Chapter One: *This Is a Great Game That Is Being Played. . .*

1. Sherman, *Memoirs*, 2, p. 221.
2. Ibid., pp. 206, 213.
3. Ibid., pp. 224-225.
4. Ibid., pp. 225, 237.
5. Ibid., pp. 23-238; *OR*, pt. 1, p. 17.
6. Grant, *Personal Memoirs*, p. 518; Sherman, *Memoirs*, 2, pp. 257-259.
7. For biographical information on General Logan, I consulted Castel, "Black Jack Logan," pp. 4-10, 41-45; Dawson, *Gen. John A. Logan*; and Warner, *Generals in Blue*, pp. 281-283.
8. Morris, 31st Illinois, p. 9; Grant, *Personal Memoirs,* pp. 300, 487; Sherman, Memoirs, 2, pp. 81, 85-86. Grant believed that Logan was the general best qualified to succeed McPherson.
9. Ibid., pp. 85-86.
10. Grant, *Personal Memoirs*, p. 505; Sherman, *Memoirs*, 2, p. 232.

11 Trimble, *Ninety-Third Illinois*, p. 180.

12. Warner, *Generals in Blue*, pp. 35-36; Battle, *History of UNC*, 1, p. 474.
13. Grant, *Personal Memoirs*, 300.
14. Davis, "With Sherman," p. 202; Hemstreet, "Little Things," pp. 159.
15. Ibid., pp. 159-160.
16. Warner, *Generals in Blue*, p. 237; McFeely, *Yankee Stepfather*, pp. 29-38.
17. For an excellent account of Howard's role in the first day's battle, see Pfanz, *Gettysburg: Cemetery Hill*, pp. 31-58.
18. Warner, *Generals in Blue*, p. 238; Glatthaar, *March to the Sea*, p. 23; Henry Hitchcock Diary, January 31, 1865, Henry Hitchcock Papers, LC.
19. Harwell, *Fiery Trail*, p. 100.
20. Hickenlooper Reminiscences, pp. 107-108, *CWTI* Coll., USAMHI.
21. William B. Miller Journal, February 28, 1865, INHS; Stormont, *Fifty-Eighth Indiana*, pp. 426, 490; W. P. Carlin to W. T. Sherman, April 21, 1865, W. T. Sherman Papers, LC. See Jones, "Jefferson Davis in Blue," for the most thorough account of the general's Civil War career.
22. Warner, *Generals in Blue*, p.115; Jones, "General Jeff C. Davis," p. 231; Weems, *To Conquer a Peace*, pp. 307-308; Boatner, *Civil War Dictionary*, p. 226.
23. Warner, *Generals in Blue*, pp. 116, 344, 646; Greene, "Killing of Nelson"; Wright, "Notes of a Staff-Officer," pp. 60-61; Buell, "East Tennessee," pp. 42-44.
24. Ibid., pp. 43-44; Greene, "Killing of Nelson"; Wright, "Notes of a Staff-Officer," p. 61.
25. Sherman, *Memoirs*, 2, pp. 244-245.
26. Committee, *Ninety-Second Illinois*, p. 197; T. H. Pendergast Journal, December 9, 1864, W. W. Pendergast Family Papers, MNHS; Angle, *Three Years*, pp. 354-355; Glatthaar, *March to the Sea*, p. 64; Jones, "General Jeff C. Davis," pp. 242-245.
27. Quaife, *From the Cannon's Mouth*, pp. 8, 349.
28. Ibid., pp. 3-7 *passim*; Warner, *Generals in Blue*, pp. 559-560.
29. Ibid., p. 560.
30. Quaife, *From the Cannon's Mouth*, pp. 375-376.
31. Warner, *Generals in Blue*, p. 451; Slocum, *Henry Warner Slocum*, pp. 6-12.
32. Ibid., pp. 13-15, 31, 53-54, 88-93, 127-131; Warner, *Generals in Blue*, p. 452.
33. Ibid. General Sherman had designated Slocum's wing the Army of Georgia prior to the March to the Sea, but did not inform the War Department of this change until his arrival at Goldsboro in March 1865. See Slocum, *Henry Warner Slocum*, p. 296; *OR* 47, pt. 3, p. 43.
34. Nichols, *Story*, p. 271; Harwell, *Fiery Trail*, p. 199; Glatthaar, *March to the Sea*, pp. 22-24 *passim*.
35. Wilson, *Under the Old Flag* 2, p. 13.
36. Warner, *Generals in Blue*, p. 266; Longacre, "Judson Kilpatrick," pp. 25-26. This crimson banner subsequently became known as the "Blood Red Flag." Kilpatrick carried it with him to the end of the war. See W. W. Prichard Journal, p. 24, Civil War Misc. Coll., USAMHI.
37. Longacre, "Judson Kilpatrick," pp. 26-28.
38. Ibid., pp. 28-29.
39. Freeman, *Lee's Lieutenants*, 3, pp. 261-262; Longacre, "Judson Kilpatrick," pp. 29-30; Warner, *Generals in Blue*, p. 266.
40. Ibid; Longacre, "Judson Kilpatrick," p. 30.
41. Ibid., pp. 30-32 *passim*.
42. Ibid., pp. 25, 32-33.

43. *OR* 47, pt. 1, p. 48; Sherman, *Memoirs*, 2, pp. 172, 269, 387; Glatthaar, *March to the Sea*, pp. 19-21.

44. Sherman, *Memoirs*, 2, pp. 175, 176-178 *passim*, 183, 269; Nichols, *Story*, p. 130.

45. Ibid., pp. 183, 192, 388; Glatthaar, *March to the Sea*, p. 123.

46.*OR* 47, pt. 2, pp. 1084-1085.

47. Ibid., pt. 1, p. 19; ibid., pt. 2, pp. 1079, 1084-1085.

48. "Mem[orandum] of conversations with Jefferson Davis held on Thursday Jany 12 & Jany 14 1865 by Francis P. Blair. . .," Blair Family Papers, LC; Davis, *Rise and Fall*, 2, pp. 610-617; Basler, *Collected Works of Lincoln*, 8, pp. 275-276.

49. For the accounts of the five principals involved, see: [Lincoln] Ibid., pp. 284-285; [Seward] *OR* 4, ser. 3, pp. 1163-1165; Campbell, *Reminiscences*, pp. 3-19; Hunter, "Peace Commission of 1865," pp. 168-176; Stephens, *Constitutional View*, 2, pp. 589-624.

50. James to "Sister Sarah," February 3, 1865, James Royal Ladd Papers, in the possession of Mabel Prescott, Mooresville, Indiana.

51. J. E. Johnston to William [Mackall], January 26, 1865, Mackall Papers, SHC-UNC; Symonds, *Joseph E. Johnston*, p. 341. On February 17, Beauregard stated that he had only about 3,000 infantry and cavalry with which to defend Columbia. *OR* 47, pt. 2, p. 1208.

52. For the definitive account, see Lucas, *Sherman and the Burning of Columbia*. On the same night much of Charleston also burned, the result of the firing of supply and munitions warehouses by the retreating Confederates.

53. *OR* 47, pt. 2, pp. 1217-1218, 1222-1223 *passim*; Thomas B. Roy Diary, February 19-21, 1865, photocopy in the possession of Nat. C. Hughes, Chattanooga, TN.

54. Dowdey, *Wartime Papers*, p. 906.

55. *OR* 47, pt. 2, p. 1238.

56. Ibid., p. 1237; Dowdey, *Wartime Papers*, pp. 904, 909. Davis became so alarmed over Beauregard's inability to slow Sherman's advance that on February 19 he suggested to Lee that he travel to Beauregard's headquarters for a conference. When Lee dodged the suggestion, Davis sent the Confederate army's chief engineer, Maj. Gen. J. F. Gilmer, instead. *OR* 47, pt. 2, pp. 1222, 1229; Dowdey, *Wartime Papers*, p. 905; Rowland, *Jefferson Davis*, 8, pp. 448-451, 516-518.

57. Dowdey, *Wartime Papers*, p. 906; *OR* 47, pt. 2, p. 1247.

Chapter Two: . . *And Great Men Are Playing It*

1. *OR* 47, pt. 2, p. 1247; Johnston, *Narrative*, p. 371; Woodward, *Mary Chesnut's Civil War*, pp. 729, 731. In his *Narrative*, Johnston states that he received Lee's order on February 23, but his reply is dated February 22.

2. *OR* 47, pt. 2, pp. 1257, 1274; Johnston, *Narrative*, pp. 371-372; George to Father, February 24, 1865, Confederate Soldiers' Letters: M. J. Blackwell, ALDAH. Although Johnston did not issue the order announcing his return to command until February 25, he was already in Charlotte on February 23 organizing and reviewing his forces.

3. *OR* 47, pt. 2, p. 1271; Hampton, "Battle of Bentonville," p. 701.

4. Roman, *Military Operations*, 2, pp. 331-332; McMurry, *John Bell Hood*, p. 182; Connelly, *Autumn of Glory*, pp. 513-514; Horn, *Army of Tennessee*, p. 422.

5. Black, *Railroads,* pp. 272, 275; *OR* 47, pt. 2, pp. 1047, 1052.

6. Hill, "Palmer's Brigade," p. 332; *OR* 47, pt. 2, pp. 1088, 1100, 1168, 1185, 1197, 1232; Francis H. Nash Diary, February 20-23, 1865, UGA; A. Q. Porter Diary, January 27-February 10, 1865, A. Q. Porter Coll., LC.

7. According to the journal of Maj. Henry Hampton, the adjutant for Cheatham's Corps, the train that he and General Cheatham were riding on derailed twice within the first three days of their journey. *OR* 47, pt. 1, pp. 1080-1082; Black, *Railroads,* pp. 272-274 *passim*; Horn, *Army of Tennessee,* p. 423.

8. William E. Stanton to Cousin, March 30, 1865, William E. Stanton Letters, CAH-UTX; Jno. M. G[oodman] to Sister, March 1, 1865, W. T. Sherman Papers, LC. See also Curry, "A History of Company B,," p. 218; McNeill, "The Stress of War," Phd. diss., Rice University; Glatthaar, Unpublished essay on Confederate soldier morale.

9. *OR* 47, pt. 2, pp. 1281-1282, 1288; Thomas B. Roy Diary, February 25, 1865; Ford, *Life*, p. 42; Ford, "A March." General Hardee at first believed that the Federals were advancing on Florence or Darlington; it wasn't until February 28 that he decided that their next objective was Cheraw. *OR* 47, pt. 2, pp. 1290-1291.

10. Thomas B. Roy Diary, February 18-20, 1865; Andrews, *Diary*, p. 14.

11. Thomas B. Roy Diary, February 20, 1865; Ford, *Life*, pp. 43-44.

12. Thomas B. Roy Diary, February 17 and 22, 1865; *OR* 47, pt. 2, pp. 1205, 1274.

13. Warner, *Generals in Gray*, pp. 204-205; Freeman, *Lee's Lieutenants*, 3, pp. 300-301.

14. The evacuation of the Pocotaligo line occurred on the night of January 14, 1865. For letters attesting to McLaws' sobriety on the night in question, see J. C. Farley to L. P. Yandell, January 19, 1865, and nine others to Yandell on the same date, McLaws Papers, SHC-UNC.

15. Warner, *Generals in Gray*, pp. 297-298; Freeman, *Lee's Lieutenants*, 1, p. 327; ibid., 2, pp. 45, 109, 341, 505.

16. Thomas B. Roy Diary, February 22, 1865; Freeman, Lee's *Lieutenants*, 3, pp. 545, 547; *OR* 47, pt. 2, p. 1274.

17. For biographical information on Hardee, I consulted Hughes, *Old Reliable*; Warner, *Generals in Gray*, pp. 124-125; and Woodworth, *Davis and His Generals*, pp. 162, 164-166.

18. McMurry, *John Bell Hood*, p. 16.

19. Hughes, *Old Reliable,* p. 183.

20. Ibid., pp. 223-224, 231-232, 241-242, 303.

21. Ibid., p. 270.

22. Thomas B. Roy Diary, February 17 and 21, 1865; *OR* 47, pt. 2, pp. 1231, 1242. It is unknown exactly when Hardee re-established telegraphic communication with Beauregard. The earliest date mentioned is February 24. See ibid., p. 1320.

23. Andrews, *Diary*, p. 14; McLaws Order Book, February 24, 1865, McLaws Papers, SHC-UNC; Johnson," Closing Days," May 22, 1902; *OR* 47, pt. 2, pp. 1281-1282, 1288, 1290-1291.

24. Ibid., pt. 1, pp. 22, 421, 427, 431, 550-551; ibid., pt. 2, pp. 573, 589; Hight, *Fifty-Eighth Indiana*, pp. 490-493; Sherman, *Memoirs*, 2, pp. 288-289; Harwell, *Fiery Trail,* p. 153; Allee, "Civil War History," p. 167, MNHS.

25. Beight, "Night We Crossed the Catawba."

26. *OR* 47, pt. 1, pp. 339, 343, 349; ibid., pt. 2, p. 586; John N. Ferguson Diary, February 26, 1865, LC.

27. Blume," Crossing Lynch's Creek."

28. Ibid; *OR* 47, pt. 1, p. 349; ibid., pt. 2, p. 586.
29. Ibid., pt. 1, p. 380.
30. Ibid., pt. 1, pp. 380-381; ibid., pt. 2, pp. 598-599, 611-612.
31. Ibid., pt. 2, pp. 612, 628, 631; Sherman, *Memoirs*, 2, pp. 292, 299. In his *Memoirs*, Sherman states that he learned of Johnston's restoration to command while at Cheraw, but the above-cited dispatches indicate that he received this news several days beforehand.
32. *OR* 47, pt. 2, p. 1297. On March 1 Beauregard reversed himself and stated that he believed Sherman was headed on a more eastward course. See ibid., p. 1298.
33. Ibid., pp. 1297-1298.
34. J. E. Johnston to B. T. Johnson, August 2, 1887, B. T. Johnson Papers, DU; J. E. Johnston to L. T. Wigfall, March 14, 1865, Wigfall Papers, LC. For biographical information on Johnston, I consulted Symonds, *Joseph E. Johnston*; Govan, *A Different Valor*; and Warner, *Generals in Gray*, pp. 161-162.
35. For recent appraisals of the Davis-Johnston feud, see Glatthaar, *Partners in Command*, pp. 95-133; Davis, *Jefferson Davis*; Symonds, *Joseph E. Johnston*; Woodworth, *Davis and His Generals*, pp. 173-185, 196-221; Lash, *Destroyer of the Iron Horse*; McMurry, "'Enemy at Richmond,'" pp. 5-31. See also James, "Joseph E. Johnston, Storm Center," pp. 342-359.
36. "Sketch of the Career of General Joseph E. Johnston, 'The Very God of War'" from *Richmond Times-Dispatch,* Feb. 19, 1911, *SHSP*, vol. 38 (1910), p. 344.
37. For an incisive analysis of Joseph Johnston's command tenure during the Atlanta Campaign, see Richard McMurry, "A Policy So Disastrous: Joseph E. Johnston's Atlanta Campaign," pp. 223-248, in Theodore P. Savas and David Woodbury, editors, *The Campaign for Atlanta & Sherman's March to the Sea, Essays on the American Civil War* (Campbell, CA., 1994), pp. 223-248.
38. For recent appraisals of Johnston's conduct of the Atlanta Campaign, see Symonds, *Joseph E. Johnston,* pp. 269-335; McMurry, "A Policy so Disastrous," pp. 223-250; Castel, *Decision in the West*; Woodworth, *Davis and His Generals,* pp. 258-286 *passim*. See also Hay, "Davis-Hood-Johnston Controversy," pp. 54-84.
39. Connelly, *Autumn of Glory,* pp. 517-518.
40. A. H. Stephens et al. to R. E. Lee, February 4, 1865, and R. E. Lee to A. H. Stephens et. al., February 13, 1865, Wigfall Papers, LC.
41. *OR* 47, pt. 2, pp. 1304-1311.
42. Ibid., pp. 1303,1311.
43. J. E. Johnston to L. T. Wigfall, December 15, 1862 and March 14, 1865, Wigfall Papers, LC; Woodward, *Mary Chesnut's Civil War,* p. 725; Symonds, *Joseph E. Johnston,* pp. 192, 199, 343.
44. Johnston, *Narrative,* p. 372; J. E. Johnston to L. T. Wigfall, March 14, 1865, Wigfall Papers, LC; W. T. Sherman to Jno. W. Draper, August 17, [1868], Draper Papers, LC; Harwell, *Fiery Trail,* p.84.
45. Among the best Sherman biographies and special studies I consulted were: Marszalek, *Sherman*; Marszalek, *Sherman's Other War*; Royster, *Destructive War*; Lewis, *Sherman, Fighting Prophet*; Williams, *McClellan, Sherman and Grant*; Barrett, *Sherman's March*. For a thumbnail sketch, see Warner, *Generals in Blue,* pp. 441-444.
46. Sherman, *Memoirs,* 1, pp. 201-202.
47. Simon, *Papers of U. S. Grant,* 5, p. 215.

48. Sherman, *Memoirs,* 1, p. 400. Two excellent studies of the Grant-Sherman partnership are Williams, *McClellan, Sherman and Grant*, pp. 57-61; and Glatthaar, *Partners in Command*, pp. 135-161.

49. W. T. Sherman to Ellen [Sherman], March 10, 1864, W. T. Sherman Papers, UND.

50. In his three-volume study, *The Campaign for Vicksburg* (Dayton, 1985-1986), vol. 2, pp. 480-481, Edwin C. Bearss makes the point that the idea of Grant cutting himself off from his supply base at Grand Gulf was "one of the Civil War's major misconceptions," since Grand Gulf was transformed into a fortified camp out of which heavily guarded wagon trains ventured forth daily to supply the army.

51. Sherman, *Memoirs,* 1, p. 400; W. T. Sherman to Ellen [Sherman], July 5, 1863, W. T. Sherman Papers, UND.

52. Sherman, "Grand Strategy," p. 247; Sherman, *Memoirs,* 2, pp. 25-26.

53. Sherman, *Memoirs,* 1, p. 400.

54. Ibid., 2, p. 399. For a detailed look into Sherman's logistical preparations for the Atlanta Campaign, see Castel, *Decision in the West,* pp. 91-93, 117-118. Cooke, "Feeding Sherman's Army," pp. 97-116; and Bogle," The Western & Atlantic Railroad," pp. 325-339.

55. *OR* 38, pt. 3, p. 162; Sherman, *Memoirs,* 2, p. 154; A. Lincoln to W. T. Sherman, December 26, 1864, W. T. Sherman Papers, OHS.

56. Byers, *Fire and Sword,* p. 179; Young [J. Powell] to "Friend Ellen," March 27, 1865, Ellen Aumack Papers, DU; Hemstreet, "Little Things," pp. 160-161.

57. Davis, "With Sherman," pp. 204-205; Harwell, *Fiery Trail,* p. 98.

58. For an example from Sherman's own pen of one such exchange, see Sherman, *Memoirs,* 2, p. 290. Davis, "With Sherman," p. 197.

59. Vett to Sister, March 14, 1865, Sylvester C. Noble Papers, Ypsilanti Hist. Soc.

60. M. F. Force to Capt. [Cornelius Cadle], March 1, 1865, Force Papers, UWA.

61. *OR* 47, pt. 2, pp. 533, 537, 544, 546, 554-555, 596-597.

62. Ibid., pt. 1, pp. 859-861 *passim*; ibid., pt. 2, p. 615; William M. Heath Diary, February 27, 1865, OHS; Reynolds, "Diary of James W. Chapin," p. 51.

63. *OR* 47, pt. 2, pp. 649-650; Rood, *Twelfth Wisconsin,* p. 416; M. J. Hough to D. H. Hill, November 26, 1865, D. H. Hill Papers, NCDAH.

64. Lawson Daily Memorandum, March 2, 1865, Lawson Correspondence, AHS.

65. Ibid.; Rood, *Twelfth Wisconsin,* p. 416; McDonald, *Thirtieth Illinois,* pp. 99-100; Dihel, "Death to Foragers."

66. Lawson Daily Memorandum, March 2, 1865, Lawson Correspondence, AHS; McDonald, *Thirtieth Illinois*, p. 100; Dihel, "Death to Foragers."

67. Rood, *Twelfth Wisconsin,* p. 417; Lawson Daily Memorandum, March 2, 1865, Lawson Correspondence, AHS; Dihel, "Death to Foragers"; McDonald, *Thirtieth Illinois,* pp. 99-100; Andersen, *Diary of Allen Morgan Geer,* p. 200; Force Letterbook-Journal, March 1 [2?], 1865, Force Papers, UWA.

68. M. J. Hough to D. H. Hill, November 26, 1865, D. H. Hill Papers, NCDAH.

69. *OR* 47, pt. 2, p. 649.

Chapter Three: *You Could Have Played Cards on Der Coat-tails*

1. Butler, "Curtain Falls," p. 472.

2. Ibid., pp. 472-473; McLaws Order Book, March 2, 1865, McLaws Papers, SHC-UNC; *OR* 47, pt. 2, pp. 1316-1317. The order that Butler refers to was not

published in the *Official Records*. If a copy of it still exists, I have been unable to locate it.

3. Ibid; McLaws Order Book, March 2-3, 1865, McLaws Papers, SHC- UNC.

4. Evans Diary, March 3, 1865, Evans Papers, WRHS; Jamison, *Recollections,* p. 314; Nilson Diary, March 3, 1865, Nilson Papers, INHS; Ferguson Diary, March 3, 1865, MacMurray College.

5. Evans Diary, March 3, 1865, Evans Papers, WRHS; Smith, *Fuller's Brigade,* p. 269; Strickling, "Reminiscences, p. 37, OHS.

6. Harwell, *Fiery Trail,* pp. 148, 162; *Report of Society of the Army of the Tennessee,* 36, pp. 241-242.

7. Warner, *Generals in Blue,* p. 339; *OR* 39, pt. 2, p. 233.

8. Ibid., pp. 338-339; *Report of Society of the Army of the Tennessee,* 36, pp. 238, 244-50; Hemstreet, "Little Things," p, 160.

9. Warner, *Generals in Blue,* p. 339; *Report of Society of the Army of the Tennessee,* 36, pp. 247-249; Sherman, *Memoirs,* 2, p. 159.

10. *OR* 47, pt. 1, p. 387; *Report of Society of the Army of the Tennessee,* 36, pp. 241, 243; Glatthaar, *March to the Sea,* pp. 24-25; Pittenger Diary, March 31, 1865, OHS.

11. *Report of Society of the Army of the Tennessee,* 36, p. 243.

12. Ibid., p. 242; *OR* 47, pt. 1, p. 387.

13. Strickling, "Reminiscences," p. 37, OHS.

14. Andrews, *Footprints,* p.166; Andrews, "At the Pee Dee Bridge," L. P. Thomas Scrapbooks, 1, p. 24, L. P. Thomas Papers, AHS.

15. Ibid; Andrews, *Footprints,* p. 166-167; Harwell, *Fiery Trail,* p. 163.

16. Strickling Reminiscences, p. 37, OHS; Benjamin F. Sweet War Record, p. 26, WHMC-UMO; Andrews, *Footprints,* p. 167; Andrews, "At the Pee Dee Bridge," L. P. Thomas Scrapbooks, 1, p. 24, L. P. Thomas Papers, AHS; Harwell, *Fiery Trail,* p. 163.

17. Susan to Sister, March 16, 1865, Susan B. Lining Letter, SCHS.

18. Butler, "Curtain Falls," pp. 473-474; Evans Diary, March 3, 1865, Evans Papers, WRHS; Jamison, *Recollections*, p. 314; Smith, *Fuller's Brigade*, p. 269.

19. Andrews, *Footprints*, pp. 167-168; Andrews, *Diary*, p. 15; Andrews, "At the Pee Dee Bridge," L. P. Thomas Scrapbooks, 1, p. 24, L. P. Thomas Papers, AHS; Smith, *A Charlestonian's Recollections*, p. 99; Alfred Chisolm to [?], March 16, 1865, Chisolm Family Papers, SHC-UNC; Hardee, "Memoranda," JO 483, March 3, 1865, J. E. Johnston Papers, HEHL.

20. Evans Diary, March 3, 1865, Evans Papers, WRHS; Nilson Diary, March 3, 1865, Nilson Papers, INHS.

21. Ibid; Evans Diary, March 3, 1865, Evans Papers, WRHS; Lybarger, *Leaves*, March 3, 1865 [n.p.]; Sargeant, *Personal Recollections*, [n.p.].

22. Kittelson [Leigram] Diary, March 3, 1865, Kittelson [Leigram] Papers, SHSW; R. Mead Jr. to "Folks at Home," March 30, 1865, Mead Papers, LC; Richmond *Examiner*, March 24, 1865; Susan to Sister, March 16, 1865, Susan B. Lining Letter, SCHS.

23. Sherman, *Memoirs*, 2, pp. 291-292; Slocum, "Sherman's March," p. 687; Potter, *Reminiscences*, p. 125; Jamison, *Recollections*, p. 315.

24. *OR*, pt. 1, p, 182-183, 381; Robertson, "Cheraw and Fayetteville"; Neal, *Missouri Engineer*, p. 171; Butt, "Cheraw"; O. M. Poe to R. Delafield, April 1, 1865, O. M. Poe Papers, LC; Twombly, "Explosion at Cheraw."

25. *OR* 47, pt. 1, pp. 180, 182; Roseberry, "Gun at Cheraw"; Lamb, *My March*, March 5, 1865 [n.p.]; Smith, *Fuller's Brigade*, pp. 269, 271; Jamison,

Recollections, pp. 314-315; Elliott, "Through the Carolinas"; Gee, "Capture of the Gun"; Hedley, *Marching Through Georgia*, p. 398.

26. Sherman, *Memoirs*, 2, p. 290.

27. Ibid., pp. 290-291; Byers, *Fire and Sword*, p. 183; *OR* 47, pt. 1, pp. 202, 230-231, 381-382; Smith, *Fuller's Brigade*, p. 271.

28. Evans Diary, March 4, 1865, Evans Papers, WRHS; Ferguson Diary, March 4, 1865, MacMurray College; Kittelson [Leigram] Diary, March 4, 1865, Kittelson [Leigram] Papers, SHSW; Smith, *Fuller's Brigade*," p. 271; Jamison, *Recollections*, p. 315.

29. *OR* 47, pt. 1, p. 202; ibid., pt. 2, p. 701; Howard, *Autobiography*, 2, pp. 135-136; Harwell, *Fiery Trail*, pp. 168-169; Neal, *Missouri Engineer*, p. 171; Butt, "Cheraw"; Twombly, "Explosion at Cheraw"; Johnson, "Cheraw Explosion."

30. Winther, *With Sherman to the Sea*, pp. 155-156.

31. Ibid., p. 156; *OR* 47, pt. 1, p. 202; Byers, *Fire and Sword*, p. 183; Arbuckle, *Civil War Experiences*, p. 136; Neal, *Missouri Engineer*, p. 171; Johnson, "Cheraw Explosion"; Susan to Sister, March 16, 1865, Susan B. Lining Letter, SCHS.

32. Ibid.

33. James E. Graham Diary, March 6, 1865, OHS.

34. Howard, *Autobiography*, 2, p. 136; Harwell, *Fiery Trail*, p. 169; Arbuckle, *Civil War Experiences*, p. 138.

35. *OR* 47, pt. 1, pp. 422, 427, 432, 492, 861; ibid., pt. 2, pp. 691-692, 704; Stormont, *Fifty-Eighth Indiana*, pp. 495-496; Shiman, "Engineering Sherman's March," Phd. dissertation, Duke University, p. 645.

36. Sherman, *Memoirs*, 2, p. 292; Lybarger, *Leaves*, March 5, 1865 [n.p.]; W. T. Sherman to John W. Draper, March 15, 1870, Draper Papers, LC; Marszalek, *Sherman*, p. 327; Marszalek, *Sherman's Other War*, p. 176.

37. McLaws Order Book, March 3-4, 1865, McLaws Papers, SHC-UNC; Thomas B. Roy Diary, March 3-4, 1865; *OR* 47, pt. 2, p. 1320.

38. Ibid.

39. Ibid., pp. 1321, 1329-1333 *passim*, 1335-1337 *passim*.

40 Ibid., pp. 1333, 1337.

41. E. B. Middleton Diary, March 7, 1865, Cheves-Middleton Papers, SCHS; Ford, *Life*, pp. 44-45.

42. Lankford, *An Irishman in Dixie*, p. 33.

43. *OR* 47, pt. 2, pp. 1321, 1337; Johnston, *Narrative*, p. 378.

44. Johnston, *Narrative*, p. 378; *OR* 47, pt. 2, pp. 1257, 1320, 1328.

45. Woodward, *Mary Chesnut's Civil War*, p. 793.

46. *OR* 47, pt. 2, pp. 1334, 1338-1339 *passim*.

47. Ibid., pt. 1, p. 1088; ibid., pt. 2, pp. 1334, 1338-1339 *passim*; Johnston, *Narrative*, pp. 378-379; Freeman, *Lee's Lieutenants*, 3, pp. 335-336. General Hill had only 1,300 effectives from the Army of Tennessee on March 8, but with the arrival of several hundred men from Stewart's Corps on the 10th, he had approximately the above-cited figure.

48. I use Cox's statement of losses; Bragg's tally is three guns and 1,500 prisoners. *OR* 47, pt. 1, pp. 62, 932-933, 976-979, 1078-1079; 1086-1088; ibid., pt. 2, p. 1354; Johnston, *Narrative*, pp. 379-380.

49. In *Autumn of Glory,* Connelly argues that Johnston's decision to reinforce Bragg at Kinston was "foolhardy" because, "If disaster befell Bragg, Johnston's small command would probably be cut in two." Connelly also calls the Battle of Wise's Forks "fruitless and wasteful," because even with the Army of Tennessee contingent, Bragg hadn't enough men to "have hoped for any lasting success." In

making his argument, Connelly ignores the fact that Johnston had to be just as concerned about Schofield's advance as Sherman's. Furthermore, it was anything but wasteful of Johnston to use the manpower at his disposal, even with limited prospects of success. At that point in the war, Johnston *had* to take long chances—something he should have tried earlier in the war. See Connelly, *Autumn of Glory*, p. 524.

50. *OR* 47, pt. 2, pp. 1349, 1351, 1353, 1355-1356, 1363-1364; Lash, *Destroyer*, pp. 158, 164-165.

51. Ibid., p. 168; *OR* 47, pt. 1, p. 1082; ibid., pt. 2, pp. 1374, 1388.

52. Worsham, *Old Nineteenth Tennessee*, p. 172.

53. *OR* 47, pt. 2, pp. 1406-1407.

54. Johnston, *Narrative*, pp. 374-375; *OR* 47, pt. 2, pp. 1313, 1320, 1324-1325, 1330, 1332.

55. Ibid., pp. 1290, 1296-1297, 1373-1374; Johnston, *Narrative*, pp. 374-376.

56. *OR* 47, pt. 2, p. 1373.

57. Hamilton, *Recollections*, pp. 195-196; Widney, "From the Sea, " August 20, 1903; Benton, *As Seen*, p. 265.

58. *OR* 47, pt. 2, p. 735; Sherman, *Memoirs*, 2, p. 293.

59. Byers, *Fire and Sword*, pp. 181-182; *OR* 47, pt. 2, p. 739.

60. Sherman, *Memoirs*, 2, p. 293; W. T. Sherman Diary, March 9, 1865, W. T. Sherman Papers, UND; Byers, *Fire and Sword*, p. 181.

61. *OR* 47, pt. 2, pp. 756-757; Brown, *Fourth Minnesota*, pp. 386-387.

62. Trimble, *Ninety-Third Illinois*, pp. 179-180; Brown, *Fourth Minnesota*, p. 387; Risedorph Diary, March 10, 1865, Risedorph Papers, MNHS; Stauffer, *Civil War Diary*, [n.p.] March 9, 1865.

63. *OR* 47, pt. 2, pp. 754, 763-764; Harwell, *Fiery Trail*, pp. 171, 173.

Chapter Four: *An Infernal Surprise*

1. For biographical information on Hampton, I consulted Wellman, *Giant in Gray*; Cauthen, *Family Letters*; Freeman, *Lee's Lieutenants*, 3 vols.; and Warner, *Generals in Gray*, pp. 122-123.

2. Wade Hampton to L. T. Wigfall, January 20, 1865, Wigfall Papers, LC.

3. Freeman, *Lee's Lieutenants*, 3, p. 195.

4. Ibid., 3, p. 639; Freeman, *Lee's Dispatches*, p. 317.

5. Wellman, *Giant in Gray*, p. 168; Cauthen, *Family Letters*, pp. 113-114; Wade Hampton to L. T. Wigfall, January 20, 1865, Wigfall Papers, LC.

6. *OR* 47, pt. 2, p. 1207; Wade Hampton to L. T. Wigfall, January 20, 1865, Wigfall Papers, LC; Warner, *Generals in Gray*, pp. 332-333.

7. For biographical information on Wheeler, I consulted Dyer, *"Fightin' Joe" Wheeler* and Warner, *Generals in Gray*, pp. 332-333. For Wheeler's nicknames, see Castel, *Decision in the West*, p. 111; Holman, "Participant," p. 544.

8. Roman, "Inspection Report of Wheeler's Cavalry Corps," 1, pp. 12, 15-17, 20-22, Roman Papers, LC.

9. Dubose, *General Joseph Wheeler*, p. 430; Dodson, *Campaigns of Wheeler*, pp. 331-345; Wade Hampton to E. L. Wells, April 4, 1900, Wells Correspondence, SCHS; Scott, "Monroe's Crossroads," p. 26.

10. Butler, "Curtain Falls," pp. 468-475 *passim*; J. F. Waring Diary, March 8, 1865, SHC-UNC; *OR* 47, pt. 1, pp. 867, 873-878 *passim*, 880, 882, 885, 894,

901, 904, 906-907, 1130; ibid., pt. 2, pp. 682, 1317, 1337-1338; Committee, *Ninety-Second Illinois*, pp. 221-223 *passim*; Cavalryman, "Campaign," April 28, 1892.

11. *OR* 47, pt. 1, pp. 867, 875; Cavalryman, "Campaign," April 28, 1892; Committee, *Ninety-Second Illinois*, p. 223.

12. *OR* 47, pt. 1, pp. 861, 867, 894; ibid., pt. 2, p. 786; Committee, *Ninety-Second Illinois*, p. 223.

13. *OR* 47, pt. 1, p. 863; ibid., pt. 2, pp. 721, 786-787. Sherman states that he never received Kilpatrick's message. *OR* 47, pt. 2, p. 788. Kilpatrick's vague description of the roads on which Hampton was traveling, as well as his omission of their proper names, indicates that he had a poor reference map of the area's transportation network. For an accurate historic roads map of the area, see Loftfield, "Cultural Resource Reconnaissance," fig. 2 (following p. 17).

14. *OR* 47, pt. 1, p. 43. The estimate for Hampton's effective strength is based on his earliest troop return, which is dated March 27, 1865. See ibid., pt. 3, p. 707.

15. [Brooks], "Charge on Kilpatrick's Camp," p. 424.

16. Butler, " Kilpatrick's Narrow Escape," p. 443; M. C. Butler to Edward L. Wells, March 27, 1900, Wells Correspondence, SCHS. Two eyewitnesses recalled that the escort belonged to the 5th Ohio Cavalry. See [Brooks], "Charge on Kilpatrick's Camp," p. 425; Bunch, "Surprise of Kilpatrick's Camp," *Confederate Veteran* Papers, Box 1, DU.

17. Ibid; Butler, "Kilpatrick's Narrow Escape," pp. 443; [Brooks], "Charge on Kilpatrick's Camp," p. 425.

18. Butler, "Kilpatrick's Narrow Escape," p. 443; M. C. Butler to Edward L. Wells, March 27, 1900, Wells Correspondence, SCHS; *OR* 47, pt. 1, p. 861; ibid., pt. 2, p. 786. Kilpatrick reported that his escort of one officer and 15 men was captured, but Butler remembered capturing "twenty-eight or thirty men."

19. Warner, *Generals in Gray*, pp. 40-41; Wells, "A Morning Call," p. 127.

20. Butler, "Curtain Falls," p. 443; M. C. Butler to Edward L. Wells, March 27, 1900, and Wade Hampton to E. L. Wells, April 8, 1900, Wells Correspondence, SCHS.

21. *OR* 47, pt. 1, pp. 894, 899, 904; Bunch, "Surprise of Kilpatrick's Camp," *Confederate Veteran* Papers, Box 1, DU.

22. *OR* 47, pt. 1, 861, 867; ibid., pt. 2, p. 786; Committee, *Ninety-Second Illinois* p. 223.

23. Loftfield, "Cultural Resource Reconnaissance," fig. 4 (following p. 30); Scott, "Monroe's Crossroads," p. 98, various maps accompanying study; McLaws Order Book, March 8, 1865, McLaws Papers, SHC- UNC; William M. Heath Diary, February 19, 1865, OHS. The identity of these two women is unknown. Historians have long supposed that Kilpatrick's female companions were Amelia Feaster and her daughter, Marie Boozer. (The daughter retained the name of her natural father, who was said to have been Mrs. Feaster's fourth husband.) Lamentably, popular legend must give way to dry fact: Mrs. Feaster and Miss Boozer were the guests of Maj. Gen. Oliver O. Howard throughout the march from Columbia to Fayetteville. Howard marveled at the way they had "completely mastered all the discomforts of military life. . . .I have mentioned them," Howard wrote his wife, "because we have seen so much of them for the last three weeks and I have learned that ladies can campaign." The general added that the two women had lost everything in the fire at Columbia, and were returning to Mrs. Feaster's hometown of Philadelphia. O. O. Howard to Wife, [March 12,] 1865, O. O. Howard Papers, BC.

24. *OR* 47, pt. 1, pp. 904; Northrop, "Other Side," p. 423; Scott, "Monroe's Crossroads," pp. 97-98, fig. 43; Nye, "Monroe's Cross-roads," pp. 6-7.

25. Northrop, "Other Side," p. 423.

26. Nye, "Monroe's Cross-roads," p.7; *OR* 47, pt. 1, p. 894; Reneau, "Montrose [sic] Crossroads."

27. *OR* 47, pt. 1, pp. 867, 883, 886, 889; Cavalryman, "Campaign," May 5, 1892; Committee, Ninety-Second Illinois, pp. 223-225.

28. *OR* 47, pt. 1, p. 1130; Wade Hampton to E. L. Wells, April 8, 1900, Wells Correspondence, SCHS; Lomax, "At Monroe's Crossroads."

29. A. F. Hardie quoted in Dubose, "Fayetteville Road Fight," p. 85; H. C. Reynolds to Thomas M. Owen, September 17, 1913, H. C. Reynolds Papers, ALDAH; Sparkman Diary, March 9, 1865, Box 3, Diaries, Memoirs, Etc., TNSLA; Howard, *Sketch of Cobb Legion*, p. 13. However, Butler and two others recall that there was no picket on Way's brigade's side of the camp. See Butler, "Kilpatrick's Narrow Escape," p. 445; Wells, "A Morning Call," p. 126; Bunch, Surprise of Kilpatrick's Camp, *Confederate Veteran* Papers, Box 1, DU.

30. Butler, "Curtain Falls," 443-444; Wells, "A Morning Call," p. 12; Bunch, "Surprise of Kilpatrick's Camp," *Confederate Veteran* Papers, Box 1, DU.

31. Butler, "Kilpatrick's Narrow Escape," p. 444; M. C. Butler to Edward L. Wells, March 27, 1900, and Wade Hampton to E. L. Wells, April 8, 1900, Wells Correspondence, SCHS; A. F. Hardie quoted in Dubose, "Fayetteville Road Fight," p. 85; Dodson, *Campaigns of Wheeler*, p. 344.

32. M. C. Butler to Edward L. Wells, March 27, 1865, Wells Correspondence, SCHS.

33. Mims, *War History*, p. 14; Watkins, "Another Account," p. 84; Allen, "About Fight," p. 433; Hamilton, "Effort to Capture Kilpatrick," p. 329; Holman, "Participant," p. 544; Lindsley, *Military Annals*, p. 675; W. W. Gordon Diary, March 10, 1865, Gordon Family Papers, SHC-UNC; Scott, "Monroe's Crossroads," pp. 98-99, fig. 43.

34. Wells, "A Morning Call," p. 126; Wells, *Hampton and Reconstruction*, p. 63; Swan, "Kilpatrick's Cavalry."

35. Jones, "Report," p. 434; A. F. Hardie quoted in Dubose, "Fayetteville Road Fight," p. 85. H. C. Reynolds of Shannon's scouts had escaped from Kilpatrick's camp several days before, and reported to Wheeler that "Kil" had told him, "that he & 'Joe' were classmates at W[est] P[oin]t and boasted to me how many times he had beaten him &c &c." See H. C. Reynolds to Thomas M. Owen, September 17, 1913, H. C. Reynolds Papers, ALDAH.

36. Wade Hampton to E. L. Wells, March 25, 1900, and April 8, 1900; Wells Correspondence, SCHS. Although Wheeler reported that he assumed command of both his and Butler's cavalry, Hampton denied ever turning over authority to Wheeler. *OR* 47, pt. 1, p. 1130; Dodson, *Campaigns of Wheeler*, p. 344.

37. Wells, *Hampton and His Cavalry*, p. 404; Swan, "Kilpatrick's Cavalry"; Butler, "Kilpatrick's Narrow Escape," p. 445; M. C. Butler to Edward L. Wells, March 27, 1900, Wells Correspondence, SCHS; *OR* 47, pt. 1, pp. 899, 904; Wells, *Hampton and His Cavalry*, pp. 405-406.

38. Dubose, *Joseph Wheeler*, pp. 448-449; A. F. Hardie quoted in Dubose, "Fayetteville Road Fight," p. 85; Butler, "Kilpatrick's Narrow Escape," p. 446; M. C. Butler to Edward L. Wells, March 27, 1900, Wells Correspondence, SCHS.

39. *OR* 47, pt. 1, p. 861; Butler, "Kilpatrick's Narrow Escape," pp. 446-447; M. C. Butler to Edward L. Wells, March 27, 1900, Wells Correspondence, SCHS; Northrop, "Other Side," p. 423; Jenkins, "Kilpatrick's Capture."

40. M. C. Butler to Edward L. Wells, March 27, 1900, Wells Correspondence, SCHS; John Ash Memoranda, John Ash Papers, EU; Mims, *War History*, p. 14; Gordon, "War Stories," pp. 2-3, J. F. Waring Papers, GAHS; Hamilton, "Effort to Capture Kilpatrick," p. 329; Calhoun, "Credit to Wheeler," p. 83; Guild, *Fourth Tennessee Cavalry*, p. 124.

41. Wells, "A Morning Call," pp. 127-128; Dubose, *General Joseph Wheeler*, p. 449.

42. [Brooks], "Charge on Kilpatrick's Camp," pp. 426-428; Butler, "Kilpatrick's Narrow Escape," p. 446; W. W. Gordon Diary, March 10, 1865, Gordon Family Papers, SHC-UNC; John Ash Memoranda, John Ash Papers, EU; A. F. Hardie quoted in Dubose, "Fayetteville Road Fight," p. 85. Scales was probably one of Captain Shannon's scouts. See Witcher, "Shannon's Scouts," p. 512.

43. Allen, "About Fight at Fayetteville," p. 433; Guild, *Fourth Tennessee Cavalry*, pp. 123-124; Lindsley, *Military Annals*, p. 695.

44. For a history of the 1st Alabama Cavalry (U. S.), see, Hoole, *Alabama Tories*.

45. Gardner, "Alabama's Sons Fought"; Scott, "Monroe's Crossroads," pp. 92, 99.

46. Butler, "Kilpatrick's Narrow Escape," p. 445; M. C. Butler to Edward L. Wells, March 27, 1900, Wells Correspondence, SCHS.

47. *OR* 47, pt. 1, 894, 899; Butler, "Kilpatrick's Narrow Escape," p. 445; M. C. Butler to Edward L. Wells, March 27, 1900, Wells Correspondence, SCHS.

48. Ibid; Butler, "Kilpatrick's Narrow Escape," pp. 445-446; [Brooks], "Heroic Deeds," pp. 433-434; Zimmerman Davis to Edward L. Wells, June 10, 1898, Wells Correspondence, SCHS; Howard, *Sketch of Cobb Legion*, p. 14.

49. Mims, *War History*, pp. 14-15; H. C. Reynolds to Thomas M. Owen, September 17, 1913, H. C. Reynolds Papers, ALDAH; Gardner, "Alabama's Sons Fought"; Reneau, "Montrose [sic] Crossroads"; Northrop, "Other Side," p. 423; *OR* 47, pt. 1, pp. 904-905.

50. *OR* 47, pt. 1, 1130; Dodson, *Campaigns of Wheeler*, p. 345; Lindsley, *Military Annals*, pp. 675-676; Scott, "Monroe's Crossroads," p. 100, fig. 47. In his *OR* report, Wheeler states that Brig. Gen. Moses W. Hannon was among the wounded at Monroe's Crossroads, a curious statement, since Hannon's Brigade was broken up on January 2, 1865. *OR* 47, pt. 2, p. 1073.

51. *OR* 47, pt. 1, pp. 524, 862, 894; ibid., pt. 2, pp. 764-765, 787; Payne, *Thirty-Fourth Illinois*, pp. 196-197; Widney, "From the Sea," August 20, 1903; Carlin, "Military Memoirs," July 30, 1885; Atkins' brigade finally extricated itself from the swamp and rejoined Kilpatrick at noon. *OR* 47, pt. 1, pp. 886, 889.

52. *OR* 47, pt. 1, pp. 862, 894-895, 1130; ibid., pt. 2, p. 787.

53. Ibid., pt. 1, p. 862; ibid., pt. 2, p. 787.

54. J. F. Waring Diary, March 10, 1865, SHC-UNC; *OR* 47, pt. 1, pp. 867-868; Kyle, "Incidents of Hospital Life," p. 42; Nye, "Monroe's Cross-roads," pp. 12, 14-15.

55. J. F. Waring Diary, March 10, 1865, SHC-UNC.

56. Butler, "Kilpatrick's Narrow Escape," p. 445; Dodson, *Campaigns of Wheeler*, pp. 345-346; Wade Hampton to E. L. Wells, March 25, 1900, and April 8, 1900, Wells Correspondence, SCHS.

57. *OR* 47, pt. 1, p. 862.

Chapter Five: *Remember Us Very Kindly To Mr. Sherman*

1. *OR* 47, pt. 2, pp. 1356-1357; Thomas B. Roy Diary, March 9, 1865; Sarah Ann Tillinghast to Mary [n.d.], p. 7, Tillinghast Family Papers, DU.

2. *OR* 47, pt. 2, pp. 1357, 1362-1363; Thomas B. Roy Diary, March 10-11, 1865; John Johnson Diary, March 10, 1865, DU; Andrews, *Footprints*, p. 170; Johnson, "Closing Days," May 22, 1900; E. B. Middleton Diary, March 10, 1865, Cheves-Middleton Papers, SCHS; C. W. Hutson to Sister, March 10, 1865, C. W. Hutson Papers, SHC-UNC; Worth, "Sherman's Raid," p. 46.

3. Sarah Ann Tillinghast to Mary, [n.d.], p. 8, Tillinghast Family Papers, DU; E. B. Middleton Diary, March 10, 1865, Cheves-Middleton Papers, SCHS; Johnson, "Marching, Camping, Fighting, 2, p. 141, L. P. Thomas Scrapbooks, L. P. Thomas Papers, AHS; Hawthorne, "Memories," p. 60, NCDAH; Worth, "Sherman's Raid," pp. 46-48 *passim*.

4. *OR* 47, pt. 1, p. 1130; Bryan, "Sherman's Army," p. 1.

5. Hawthorne, "Memories," p. 61, NCDAH.

6. Wade Hampton to Edward L. Wells, December 20, 1897, and Edward L. Wells to Wade Hampton, February 8, 1899, Wells Correspondence, SCHS; Scott, "Story of a Scout," pp. 112-113; Cauthen, *Family Letters*, pp. 161-162; Wells, "Hampton at Fayetteville," *SHSP*, pp. 145-146. Hampton may have had additional help from other Confederates. See Williams, "Veteran Williams's Story." Charleston *Sunday News*, December 5, 1897.

7. *OR* 47, pt. 1, pp. 46, 203; Duncan, "With the Army," pp. 518-519; Collins, "First to Enter Fayetteville"; Harwell, *Fiery Trail*, p. 174.

8. Scott, "Story of a Scout," pp. 112-113; Wade Hampton to Edward L. Wells, December 20, 1897, Wells Correspondence, SCHS; Wells, "Hampton at Fayetteville," *SHSP*, p. 146; Wells, "Hampton at Fayetteville," Charleston *Sunday News*, December 12, 1897; Smith, *Mason Smith Family Letters*, p. 172.

9. A Federal scout named David Day was captured in the melee wearing a Confederate uniform. Hampton informed Day that he intended to hang him at the earliest opportunity, but Day escaped before the South Carolinian could carry out his threat. Duncan, "With the Army," pp. 519-521; Wade Hampton to Edward L. Wells, December 20, 1897, Wells Correspondence, SCHS; Cauthen, *Family Letters*, pp. 161-162.

10. *OR* 47, pt. 1, pp. 204, 413; Charles Brush Diary, March 11, 1865, Brush Family Papers, ILSHL; Jefferson J. Hibbets to Addison Ware, Jr., March 12, 1865, in Hibbets, "Fayetteville, N. C."

11. Ibid., *OR* 47, pt. 1, p. 413.

12. *OR* 47, pt. 1, pp. 562-563; William B. Miller Journal, March 11, 1865, INHS; Harwell, *Fiery Trail*, pp. 174-175.

13. In his Special Field Orders No. 28, Sherman did not list the newspaper offices among the property to be destroyed at Fayetteville, but Baird's mention of them in his report implies that he received approval from a superior authority—most likely Sherman. *OR* 47, pt. 1, p. 551; ibid., pt. 2, p. 779; Sherman, *General and Special Field Orders*, pp. 195-196; Raleigh *Daily Confederate*, April 11, 1865; Raleigh *Daily Conservative*, April 5, 1865; Fayetteville *Daily Telegraph*, March 10, 1865, quoted in (Raleigh) *North Carolina Standard*, March 15, 1865.

14. W. T. Sherman Diary, March 11, 1865, W. T. Sherman Papers, UND; O. M. Poe Diary, March 11, 1865, O. M. Poe Papers, LC; Henry to Mary, March 12, 1865, Henry Hitchcock Papers, LC; Harwell, *Fiery Trail*, p. 175; Byers, *Fire and Sword*, pp. 184-186; Broadfoot, "Interesting Story," Fayetteville *Observer*, May 15, 1928. In his article on the 6th North Carolina Battalion, M. P. Taylor writes that Sgt. Thomas Stevens (or Stephens) "was an old United States Sergeant, and

joined the Southern Army at great peril." See Taylor, "Sixth Battalion," in Clark, *Histories*, 4, pp. 296, 298. Taylor had been a major in the 6th Battalion. Some 60 years after the fact, Broadfoot recalled that the name of Sherman's former comrade was Edward Monaghan. See op. cit.

15. Sherman, *Memoirs*, 2, p. 295; *OR* 47, pt. 2, p. 795; ibid., Ser. 3, Vol. 5, pp. 479-481; Henry to Wife, March 12, 1865, Henry Hitchcock Papers, LC; Morse, *Letters*, p. 212. The commander at Wilmington, General Terry, sent the *Davidson* to Fayetteville in response to Sherman's message of March 8. But Sherman's messenger, Cpl. James Pike, arrived at Terry's headquarters in Wilmington several hours after General Howard's two scouts, Sgt. Myron J. Amick and Pvt. George W. Quimby, reached Terry with the same message. See Pike, *Scout and Ranger*, p. 387; Howard, *Autobiography*, 2, p. 139; Harwell, *Fiery Trail*, p. 180. One of General Terry's scouts reached Sherman with a message before Captain Ainsworth did. *OR* 47, pt. 2, pp. 725-726, 791.

16. *OR* 47, pt. 2, pp. 793-794; W. T. Sherman to Ellen [Sherman], March 12, 1865, W. T. Sherman Papers, UND; W. T. Sherman to Thomas Ewing, March 12, 1865, Thomas Ewing Family Papers, LC.

17. *OR* 47, pt. 2, pp. 799-800, 803. During the halt at Fayetteville, Sherman also made plans to supply his army upon its arrival at Goldsboro. See ibid., p. 795.

18. O. M. Poe Diary, March 12, 1865, and O. M. Poe to Richard Delafield, April 1, 1865, O. M. Poe Papers, LC; *OR* 47, pt. 1, pp. 171-172; ibid., pt. 2, p. 779, 794; Sherman, *General and Special Field Orders*, p. 196. Sherman's chief ordnance officer, Lt. Col. Thomas G. Baylor, oversaw the destruction of the arsenal's powder and small arms stores.

19. O. M. Poe to John B. Yates, March 11, 1865, and O. M. Poe to Wife, March 12, 1865, O. M. Poe Papers, LC; Hackett, "Fayetteville Arsenal"; Robertson, "Cheraw and Fayetteville"; W. W. Prichard Journal, March 13, 1865, Civil War Misc. Coll., USAMHI; Mellon, "Letters of James Greenalch," p. 236; Anderson, "What Sherman Did," p. 139. On March 11, the commander of the arsenal, Lt. Col. Frederick L. Childs, had removed such machinery as he could by railroad to the Egypt Coal Mines northwest of Fayetteville, which proved to be outside of Sherman's line of march. See Samuel A. Ashe to Mary Childs, January 3, 1901, quoted in Mary Childs to Yates Snowden, ca. 1901, Frederick L. Childs Collection, USC; Anderson, "Confederate Arsenal," p. 223.

20. *OR* 47, pt. 1, p. 172; O. M. Poe to Richard Delafield, April 1, 1865, O. M. Poe Papers, LC.

21. Byers, "Some Recollections"; Vett to Sister, March 14, 1865, Sylvester C. Noble Papers, Ypsilanti Hist. Soc.

22. Howard's destination initially was Faison's Depot, about 20 miles south of Goldsboro, but it was soon changed to Goldsboro. *OR* 47, pt. 1, p. 24; ibid., pt. 2, pp. 822-823, 829. Although Sherman states that there were only four unencumbered divisions in the Right Wing, there were in fact five—four from the XV Corps and one from the XVII Corps. See Harwell, *Fiery Trail*, pp. 183-184.

23. *OR* 47, pt. 1, pp. 204, 320, 340; ibid., pt. 2, pp. 803, 807, 823, 828, 847; O. O. Howard to Wife, March 15, 1865, O. O. Howard Papers, BC; Harwell, *Fiery Trail*, pp. 183-184, 186. Major Osborn estimated that the refugee column numbered 7,000 men, women and children.

24. Ibid., p. 183; Campbell, "Return," p. 32; Sarah Ann Tillinghast to Mary, [n.d.], p. 52, Tillinghast Family Papers, DU; Harwell, *Fiery Trail*, p. 183.

25. Terry also sent Sherman some pants, but only enough for a fraction of his army. *OR* 47, pt. 1, p. 204; ibid., pt. 2, pp. 803, 840-841, 861, 971; Harwell, *Fiery Trail*, p. 183.

26. *OR* 47, pt. 2, p. 803.

Chapter Six: *We Heard the Bullets Whistling Their Death Song*

1. George Wortham to Father, March 13, 1865, Pittman Coll., NCDAH; McLaws Order Book, March 12, 1865, McLaws Papers, SHC-UNC; Andrews, *Footprints*, p. 170.

2. Hardee, "Memoranda," March 16, 1865, JO 483, J. E. Johnston Papers, HEHL.

3. Ibid. On March 11, Hardee told one of his staff officers that he wanted "to remain in front of the Enemy as long as possible." See H. D. Bulkley to W. M. Tunno, March 11, 1865 [second dispatch], Confederate Miscellany, EU.

4. On February 3, Beauregard stated that Hardee had 13,000 troops at Charleston. Ibid; *OR* 47, pt. 2, pp. 1084, 1361, 1386, 1397. One source states that the loss of Goodwyn and the Citadel Cadets was partially offset by the addition of the 6th North Carolina Battalion, a 200-man outfit that had garrisoned the Fayetteville Arsenal. See Daves, "Battle of Averasboro," pp. 125-126. A second source, however, states that the 6th Battalion escorted the Arsenal machinery to the Egypt Coal Mines, where it remained until the end of the war. See Taylor, "Sixth Battalion," Clark, *Histories*, 4, p. 299.

5. E. B. Middleton Diary, March 15, 1865, Cheves-Middleton Papers, SCHS; Henry to [Mary], April 7, 1865, Henry Hitchcock Papers, LC.

6. *OR* 47, pt. 1, p. 1084; E. B. Middleton Diary, map accompanying March 16, 1865 entry, Cheves-Middleton Papers, SCHS; McLaws Order Book, March 14-15, 1865, McLaws Papers, SHC-UNC.

7. *OR* 47, pt. 1, p. 1084; Hardee, "Memoranda," March 16, 1865, JO 483, J. E. Johnston Papers, HEHL.

8. *OR* 47, pt. 1, pp. 880, 886, 1084.

9. Northrop, "Gen. [sic] Rhett's Capture"; Northrop, "Capture of Gen. [sic] Rhett"; Northrop, "Capture of Col. Rhett."

10. Ibid; Northrop, "Gen. [sic] Rhett's Capture." One source states that the men on both sides were wearing waterproof overcoats, thus concealing their identities from each other. See "Colonel Alfred Rhett," p. 5, MSS Rhett, Museum of the Confederacy.

11. Northrop, "Capture of Col. Rhett"; Camburn, "Capture of Col. Rhett"; Hamilton, *Recollections*, p. 191.

12. Sherman, *Memoirs*, 2, pp. 300-301; Slocum, "Sherman's March," p. 691; A. S. Williams Diary, March 15, 1865, A. S. Williams Papers, Detroit Pub. Lib.; Henry to [Mary], April 7, 1865, Henry Hitchcock Papers, LC; "Colonel Alfred Rhett," p. 1, MSS Rhett, Museum of the Confederacy.

13. Henry to [Mary], April 7, 1865, Henry Hitchcock Papers, LC.

14. "Colonel Alfred Rhett," p. 1, MSS Rhett, Museum of the Confederacy; "Trial of Major Alfred Rhett," #11-324, Mitchell-Pringle Collection, SCHS; R. B. Rhett, Jr. to William Porcher Miles, December 28, 1862, R. B. Rhett Papers, SHC-UNC; P[aul] H[amilton] Hayne to Alfred Rhett, September 7, 1862, A. M. Rhett Papers, USC; Cincinnati *Daily Commercial*, April 13, 1865.

15. "Colonel Alfred Rhett," p. 5, MSS Rhett, Museum of the Confederacy; Henry to [Mary], April 7, 1865, Henry Hitchcock Papers, LC.

16. Slocum, "Sherman's March," p. 691; William Thomas quoted in Rowell, *Yankee Cavalrymen*, p. 241; Northrop, "Capture of Gen. [sic] Rhett"; Sherman, *Memoirs*, 2, pp. 301-303 *passim*.

17. *OR* 47, pt. 1, 422, 448, 585; A. S. Williams Diary, March 15, 1865; Toombs, *Reminiscences*, p. 209.

18. Ibid; Meffert Diary, March 15, 1865, SHSW; Bryant, *Third Wisconsin*, pp. 315-316; Cook, *Dutchess County Regiment*, p. 156.

19. Oakey, "Marching Through Georgia," p. 678; *OR* 47, pt. 1, pp. 637, 644, 880; Meffert Diary, March 15, 1865, SHSW; Bryant, *Third Wisconsin*, p. 316.

20. *OR* 47, pt. 2, pp. 835, 861, 867; Nichols, *Story,* p. 256.

21. E. B. Middleton Diary, March 15, 1865, Cheves-Middleton Papers, SCHS.

22. McIntosh, "Annals," p. 205, McIntosh Papers, SHSW; Fallis, "Kilpatrick at Averasboro"; Williamson D. Ward Journal, March 16, 1865, INHS; E. B. Middleton Diary, March 16, 1865, Cheves-Middleton Papers, SCHS; *OR* 47, pt. 1, pp. 664, 868, 871, 1085; Northrop, "Capture of Col. Rhett"; Inglesby, *First South Carolina Artillery*, p. 16.

23. Ibid; "Life of Andrew Woodley," p. 55, D. M. Tedder Book, SHC-UNC; *OR* 47, pt. 1, pp. 868, 871, 873, 875, 880, 883, 886; Tom to Jane, March 25, 1865, T. J. Jordan Papers, HSPA.

24. *OR* 47, pt. 1, pp. 637, 644, 895, 897, 900, 901; Peter Funk Diary, March 16, 1865, New York Infantry: 150th Regiment, Civil War Misc. Coll., USAMHI; W. F. Colcock to Father, March 25, 1865, letter in the possession of George Slaton, Wilmington, NC; Meffert Diary, March 16, 1865, SHSW.

25. Toombs, *Reminiscences*, pp. 212-213; *OR* 47, pt. 1, pp. 895.

26. *OR* 47, pt. 1, pp. 585, 600, 611, 617, 623, 633, 637, 644, 664, 783, 789, 807, 824; Morhous, *Reminiscences*, p. 169; Bauer, *Soldiering*, pp. 226-227.

27. *OR* 47, pt. 1, pp. 585-586, 600, 783-784, 807-808, 816, 901; McIntosh, "Annals," pp. 205-206, McIntosh Papers, SHSW; C. H. Dickinson Diary, March 16, 1865, C. H. Dickinson Papers, SHSW; Brant, *Eighty-Fifth Indiana*, p. 104; McBride, *Thirty-third Indiana*, pp. 171-172; G. S. B., "19th Michigan Infantry," Detroit *Advertiser and Tribune*, April 10, 1865.

28. *OR* 47, pt. 1, pp. 807, 846-847, 849-850, 851-852, 854, 1085; McBride, *Thirty-third Indiana*, p. 172; C. H. Dickinson Diary, March 16, 1865, C. H. Dickinson Papers, SHSW; W. F. Colcock to Father, March 25, 1865; Castle, "Averysboro [sic]"; Castle, "In North Carolina."

29. *OR* 47, pt. 1, p. 1084-1085; ibid., pt. 2, 1386.

30. Ibid., pt. 1, pp. 24, 422, 586, 784, 789; Sherman, *Memoirs*, 2, p. 301; Slocum, "Sherman's March," p. 691; A. S. Williams Diary, March 16, 1865; James A. Congleton Journal, March 16, 1865, LC; Thomas Y. Finley Diary, March 16, 1865, Civil War Misc. Coll., USAMHI. General Ward reported that he ordered Colonel Case to make the flanking maneuver, but Case stated that he received the order from General Williams.

31. *OR* 47, pt. 1, pp. 808, 817; C. H. Dickinson Diary, March 16, 1865, C. H. Dickinson Papers, SHSW; McIntosh, "Annals," p. 207, McIntosh Papers, SHSW; David A. Fateley Diary, March 16, 1865, INHS; Conner, "Guns at Averasboro"; G. S. B., "19th Michigan Infantry," Detroit *Advertiser and Tribune*, April 10, 1865; Brant, *Eighty-fifth Indiana*, p. 105; W. F. Colcock to Father, March 25, 1865; E. B. Middleton Diary, March 16, 1865, Cheves-Middleton Papers, SCHS; Sam to Maggie, March 26, 1865, Harryman Papers, INSL; Thomas Y. Finley Diary, March 16, 1865, Civil War Misc. Coll. USAMHI; DeRosier, *Through the South*, pp. 168-

169; [T. E. Smith] to Brother, March 23, 1865, T. E. Smith and Family Coll., Cincinnati Hist. Soc.; Grunert, *One-hundred and Twenty-ninth Illinois*, p. 215.

32. Halsey, *A Yankee Private's Civil War*, p. 186; Castle, "Averysboro [sic]"; Castle, "In North Carolina"; Thomas Y. Finley Diary, March 16, 1865, Civil War Misc. Coll., USAMHI; C. H. Dickinson Diary, March 16, 1865, C. H. Dickinson Papers, SHSW; McIntosh, " Annals," pp. 207-208, McIntosh Papers, SHSW.

33. *OR* 47, pt. 1, pp. 847, 852, 1085.

34. C. H. Dickinson Diary, March 16, 1865, C. H. Dickinson Papers, SHSW; Ezra Button Diary, March 16, 1865, John B. Tripp Papers, SHSW; C. G. Michael Diary, March 16, 1865, INHS; [T. E. Smith] to Brother, March 23, 1865, T. E. Smith and Family Coll., Cincinnati Hist. Soc.; E. B. Middleton Diary, March 16, 1865, Cheves-Middleton Papers, SCHS.

35. *OR* 47, pt. 1, pp. 586, 600, 611, 623, 644-645, 664-665, 784, 790, 799, 808, 824-825, 889, 1085.

36. McLaws Order Book, March 16, 1865, McLaws Papers, SHC-UNC; Andrews, *Footprints*, p. 171; Andrews, "At Averysboro [sic] and Bentonville," L. P. Thomas Scrapbooks, 1, p. 44, L. P. Thomas Papers, AHS; *OR* 47, pt. 1, pp. 889-890.

37. Ibid; Andrew, *Footprints*, p. 171; Andrew, "At Averysboro [sic] and Bentonville," L. P. Thomas Scrapbooks, 1, p. 44, L. P. Thomas Papers, AHS.

38. McLaws Order Book, March 16, 1865, McLaws Papers, SHC-UNC; Johnson, "Marching, Camping, Fighting," L. P. Thomas Scrapbooks, 2, p. 141, L. P. Thomas Papers, AHS; Johnson, "Closing Days," May 29, 1902; *OR* 47, pt. 1, p. 1085.

39. McLaws Order Book, March 16, 1865, McLaws Papers, SHC-UNC; *OR* 47, pt. 1, pp. 1085-1086, 1126, 1130; ibid., pt. 2, p. 1402.

40. *OR* 47, pt. 1, pp. 484, 493, 514, 516, 521-522, 525, 533, 541, 547-548.

41. Ibid., pp. 433, 484, 495-496, 503-504, 507, 533; W. F., "10th Michigan Cavalry [sic]," Detroit *Advertiser and Tribune,* April 10, 1865; Westervelt, *Lights and Shadows*, p. 98.

42. *OR* 47, pt. 1, pp. 495-496, 502, 504, 507; Shaw, "At Averasboro, N. C."; Westervelt, *Lights and Shadows*, p. 98. Another of Vandever's regimental commanders, Capt. Eben White of the 16th Illinois, was mortally wounded.

43. *OR* 47, pt. 1, p. 484.

44. Castle, "In North Carolina"; Castle, "Averysboro [sic]"; Daniels, "Averysboro [sic] Fight"; Grunert, *One-hundred and Twenty-ninth Illinois*, p. 216.

45. A. S. Williams Diary, March 16, 1865; *OR* 47, pt. 1, 586.

46. McLaws Order Book, March 16, 1865, McLaws Papers, SHC-UNC.

47. *OR* 47, pt. 1, pp. 63-66, 448, 452, 586, 645; A. S. Williams Diary, March 16, 1865; Sanders, "Battle of Averasboro," p. 216; Cook, *Dutchess County Regiment*, pp. 156-157; Grunert, *One-hundred and Twenty-ninth Illinois*, p. 216.

48. McLaws Order Book, March 16, 1865, McLaws Papers, SHC-UNC; Sanders, "Battle of Averasboro," p. 216.

49. Thomas B. Roy Diary, March 16, 1865; W. F. Colcock to Father, March 25, 1865.

50. *OR* 47, pt. 2, p. 871; Sherman, *Memoirs*, 2, p. 302.

51. *OR* 47, pt. 2, pp. 869-870; Nichols, *Story*, pp. 258-259.

Chapter Seven: *Old Hampton Is Playing a Bluff Game*

1. *OR* 47, pt. 1, pp. 25, 784, 808, 826; ibid., pt. 2, pp. 870-871 *passim*.

2. Sherman, *Memoirs*, 2, p. 302; C. G. Michael Diary, March 17, 1865, INHS; [T. E. Smith] to Brother, March 23, 1865, T. E. Smith and Family Coll., Cincinnati Hist. Soc.

3. Sherman, *Memoirs*, 2, p. 302.

4. Janie Smith to Janie [Robeson], April 12, 1865, Mrs. Thomas Webb Coll., NCDAH; Raleigh *News and Observer*, May 10, 1953; "Lebanon," National Register of Historic Places Study.

5. Baxter Smith Reminiscences, p. 29, Civil War Misc. Coll., USAMHI; McIntosh, "Annals," p. 210, McIntosh Papers, SHSW; *OR* 47, pt. 1, p. 784.

6. *OR* 47, pt. 1, pp. 448, 484, 493.

7. Ibid., pp. 205, 484-485, 493, 934; ibid., pt. 2, pp. 622, 818, 855, 871, 880; Sladen, "Official Diary," March 17, 1865, Sladen Family Papers, USAMHI; Harwell, *Fiery Trail*, p. 189.

8. *OR* 47, pt. 2, pp. 1363, 1372, 1375, 1387-1388, 1392; Johnston, *Narrative*, p. 382.

9. L. T. Wigfall to J. E. Johnston, February 27, 1865, and March 3, 1865, JO 304 and JO 305, J. E. Johnston Papers, HEHL; Symonds, *Joseph E. Johnston*, pp. 343-344.

10. J. E. Johnston to L. T. Wigfall, March 14, 1865, Wigfall Papers, LC.

11. A. Q. Porter Diary, March 15, 1865, A. Q. Porter Coll., LC; Ridley, *Battles and Sketches*, p. 452.

12. Ibid; *OR* 47, pt. 2, p. 1399.

13. Wingfield, *General A. P. Stewart*, pp. 22-40; Warner, *Generals in Gray*, p. 293; Woodworth, *Davis and His Generals*, p. 264.

14. Polk's Corps was still officially called the Army of Mississippi at the time of Stewart's promotion. Wingfield, *General A. P. Stewart*, pp. 42-104 *passim*; Woodworth, *Davis and His Generals*, pp. 264-265; Boatner, *Civil War Dictionary*, p. 798; Castel, *Decision in the West*, pp. 336, 338, 381-383, 433.

15. *OR* 47, pt. 1, p. 1088; ibid., pt. 2, p. 1408; Ridley, *Battles and Sketches*, p. 452. The above-cited troop strength figure for the Army of Tennessee is for March 19 prior to the Battle of Bentonville.

16. Busbee, "Junior Reserves Brigade," in Clark, *Histories*, 4, pp. 585, 588-589.

17. *OR* 47, pt. 1, p. 1087; Broadfoot, "Seventieth Regiment," in Clark *Histories*, 4, pp. 19-20.

18. *OR* 47, pt. 1, pp. 1073-1074; ibid., pt. 2, pp. 1400-1401, 1409.

19. J. W. Brown Diary, March 16-17, 1865, Private Papers, Mf Drawer 187, Reel 13, GADAH; Ford, *Life*, pp. 52-53; *OR* 47, pt. 2, 1409, 1411; Inglesby, *First South Carolina Artillery*, p. 17.

20. Andrews, "Averysboro [sic] and Bentonville," L. P. Thomas Scrapbooks, 1, p. 44, L. P. Thomas Papers, AHS; Andrews, *Footprints*, p. 173.

21. *OR* 47, pt. 2, pp. 1410-1411, 1417.

22. Ibid., pt. 2, pp. 1410, 1414-1416 *passim*, 1418.

23. Ibid., pp. 1414-1415, 1418.

24. Ibid., pp. 1411, 1413, 1422.

25. Ibid., p. 1415.

26. If Hampton's reply to Johnston was a written message, it has not come down to us. In his *Century* article on the Battle of Bentonville, Hampton recalled that he gave Johnston a detailed description of the location of the four Federal corps, yet in a dispatch written on the afternoon of March 18, Hampton stated that he was uncertain as to which of the four Union corps was in his front. See Hampton,

"Battle of Bentonville," p. 701; Johnston, *Narrative*, p. 384; *OR* 47, pt. 2, p. 1430.

27. Ibid., p. 1429.

28. Ibid., pp. 1428-1429 *passim*, 1435; Johnston, *Narrative*, pp. 384-385.

29. Holmes, A. G. *Diary of Henry McCall Holmes*, p. 32; G. W. F. Harper Diary, March 18, 1865, G. W. F. Harper Papers, SHC-UNC; *OR* 47, pt. 1, p. 1056; ibid., pt. 2, p. 1427; Johnston, *Narrative*, p. 385. According to a local legend, the Devil's Race Path received its name when a dark stranger appeared on a magnificent black stallion, and without so much as a word, joined in a horse race between some of the neighborhood's young men. In the words of folklorist C. S. Powell, the mysterious horseman "followed in the wake of the first go, passed all on the half way, his horse's nostrils blowing smoke like a tar-kiln, going on and on, never looking back and never returning." The road was "ever afterward called the 'Devil's race path.'" See newspaper clipping entitled, "On Road to Bentonsville [sic]," in Lowry Shuford Coll., NCDAH.

30. *OR* 47, pt. 2, p. 1427; McLaws Order Book, March 18, 1865, McLaws Papers, SHC-UNC; Johnson, "Closing Days," May 29, 1902; J. W. Brown Diary, March 18, 1865, Private Papers, Mf Drawer 187, Reel 13. On the march, McLaws' Division had the advance, and was followed by Taliaferro's Division.

31. *OR* 47, pt. 1, pp. 484-485, 493; ibid., pt. 2, p. 1433.

32. Ibid., pt. 1, pp. 434, 484-485, 493, 514, 525; W. F., "10th Michigan Cavalry [sic], Detroit *Advertiser and Tribune*, April 5, 1865; Branum, "Letters," June 21, 1900.

33. *OR* 47, pt. 1, p. 493; Carlin, "Battle of Bentonville," MOLLUS-OH, 3, p. 233; Carlin, "Battle of Bentonsville [sic]," Cincinnati *Daily Gazette*, September 11, 1882; Carlin, "Military Memoirs," July 30, 1885.

34. Ibid; Carlin, "Battle of Bentonville," MOLLUS-OH, 3, p. 234; Carlin, "Battle of Bentonsville [sic]," Cincinnati *Daily Gazette*, September 11, 1882.

35. Ibid; Carlin, "Military Memoirs," July 30, 1885.

36. *OR* 47, pt. 1, p. 172; ibid., pt. 2, pp. 885-886, 890, 892; Sherman, *Memoirs*, 2, p. 303; Nichols, *Story of the Great March*, p. 262; *OR* 47, pt. 1, p. 172; ibid., pt. 2, p. 890; *Outline Tenth Regiment Michigan Infantry*, pp. 25-26; Shiman, "Engineering Sherman's March," pp. 594-595. The state maps of North Carolina conspired to mislead both Sherman and Johnston. Sherman's chief engineer, Col. Orlando M. Poe, described the maps of North Carolina as "almost worthless. I have seen two State maps of North Carolina," Poe reported, "one dated 1833, & the other 1857. They vie with each other in inaccuracy." See O. M. Poe to Richard Delafield, April 1, 1865, O. M. Poe Papers, LC.

37. *OR* 47, pt. 1, pp. 205, 485, 493; ibid., pt. 2, p. 886; Howard, *Autobiography*, 2, p. 142; Sladen, "Official Diary," March 18, 1865; Harwell, *Fiery Trail*, p. 191. Although Howard stated that the head of his column was six miles south of Slocum's, he neglected to mention that his encampments at Lee's store were just two miles south of Slocum's nearest bivouac.

38. Hampton, "Battle of Bentonville," pp. 701-702.

39. Ibid., p. 703; *OR* 47, pt. 2, p. 992, 1415; Halsey, "Last Duel," p. 8.

40. Ibid., pp. 8, 31.

41. Holmes, *52d O. V. I.*, p. 25; J. T. Holmes to [J. B.] Work, September 20, 1901, Box 3, Vol. 3: "Correspondence File, Vol. 6, September-June, 1901-1902," J. T. Holmes Papers, OHS; Hampton, "Battle of Bentonville," p. 702.

42. Holmes, *52d O. V. I.*, p. 25; J. T. Holmes to [J. B.] Work, September 20, 1901, Box 3, Vol. 3: "Correspondence File, Vol. 6, September-June, 1901-1902," J. T. Holmes Papers, OHS.

43. D. H. Reynolds Diary, March 18, 1865, D. H. Reynolds Papers, UAK-F; Corn, "In Enemy's Lines," p. 507; "Thomas Jefferson Corn," *TCWVQ*, 2, p. 563; Calder Diary, March 18, 1865, Calder Papers, DU; Ridley, *Battles and Sketches*, p. 452.

44. *OR* 47, pt. 2, pp. 1427-1428; McLaws Order Book, March 18, 1865, McLaws Papers, SHC-UNC; J. W. Brown Diary, March 18, 1865, Private Papers, Mf Drawer 187, Reel 13, GADAH; John Johnson Diary, March 18, 1865, DU.

45. Hampton, "Battle of Bentonville," p. 702; Johnston, *Narrative* p. 385.

46. Ibid., pp. 385-386; *OR* 47, pt. 1, p. 1056; Hampton, "Battle of Bentonville," pp. 702-703. One of Johnston's biographers refers to the Confederate plan of attack at Bentonville as Johnston's, and notes that it is virtually identical to the plan he intended to implement at Cassville during the Atlanta Campaign of 1864. Yet Johnston himself concedes that the Bentonville plan was Hampton's. Furthermore, Gen. Robert E. Lee employed a similar plan at Second Manassas on August 30, 1862. Hampton might have gotten the idea for his plan from that battle, but it is more likely that his plan was dictated by the nature of the terrain on the Cole plantation. See Symonds, *Joseph E. Johnston*, p. 348.

47. Halsey, "Last Duel," pp. 8, 31.

Chapter Eight: *The Rebels Don't Drive Worth a Damn*

1. Belknap, "Bentonville," pp. 6, 8.

2. Ibid., p. 6; Belknap, "Recollections," p. 345.

3. J. T. Holmes to [J. B.] Work, September 20, 1901, Box 3, Vol. 3: "Correspondence File, Vol. 6, September-June, 1901-1902," J. T. Holmes Papers, OHS.

4. Allee, "Civil War History," 2, p. 179, MNHS.

5. Belknap, "Bentonville," pp. 6-7; Overley, "What Marching Through Georgia Means," p. 446.

6. Belknap, "Bentonville," pp. 7-10.

7. Holmes, *52d O. V. I.*, p. 25; J. T. Holmes to [J. B.] Work, September 20, 1901, Box 3, Vol. 3: "Correspondence File, Vol. 6 September-June, 1901-1902," J. T. Holmes Papers, OHS.

8. Halsey, "Last Duel," p. 31.

9. Ibid.

10. Schaum Diary, March 19, 1865, DU; Earle, "Sherman's March," [n.p.], Civil War Misc. Coll., USAMHI; Branum, "Letters," June 21, 1900; *OR* 47, pt. 1, p. 448; Payne, *Thirty-Fourth Illinois*, pp. 199-200.

11. Nichols, *Story*, p. 261; Dougall, "Bentonville," p. 214; McClurg, "Last Chance," p. 389, 391; Allee, "Civil War History," 2, pp. 167, 178, 186, MNHS.

12. *OR* 47, pt. 1, p. 25; Sherman, *Memoirs*, 2, p. 303; Slocum, "Sherman's March," p. 692; McClurg, "Last Chance," p. 391; Foraker, *Notes*, 1, p. 59.

13. *OR* 47, pt. 1, p. 448; Payne, *Thirty-Fourth Illinois*, p. 199; Widney, "From the Sea," August 27, 1903; Fox, "Bentonville," May 7, 1896; J. T. Reeve Memorandum, March 19, 1865, J. T. Reeve Diary, SHSW; Carlin, "Battle of Bentonville," MOLLUS-OH, 3, pp. 235-236; Carlin, "Battle of Bentonsville [sic], Cincinnati *Daily Gazette*, September 11, 1882; Carlin, "Military Memoirs," July 30, 1885; W. P. Carlin to Marcus Bates in, Bates, "Battle of Bentonville," p. 142; Bill Brown, lecture on Battle of Bentonville to Harnett County Historical Society, Erwin, NC, March 11, 1995.

14. W. C. Johnson Journal, March 19, 1865, LC; Payne, *Thirty-Fourth Illinois*, p. 199.

15. *OR* 47, pt. 1, p. 448; M. H. Fitch Diary, March 19, 1865, SHSW; Carlin, "Battle of Bentonsville [sic]," Cincinnati *Daily Gazette*, September 11, 1882; W. P. Carlin to W. T. Sherman, April 21, 1865, W. T. Sherman Papers, LC.

16. Warner, *Generals in Blue*, pp. 69-70; "Gen. Wm. P. Carlin."

17. *OR* 20, pt. 1, pp. 261-266, 279-283; ibid., 30, pt. 1, pp. 515-519; W. P. Carlin to T. W. Morrison, January 19, 1863, J. C. Davis Papers, INHS; W. P. Carlin to W. T. Sherman, April 21, 1865, W. T. Sherman Papers.

18. Ibid.

19. Dougall, "Bentonville," p. 215; Otto, "War Memories," p. 103, Otto Papers, SHSW.

20. J. T. Holmes to [J. B.] Work, September 20, 1901, Box 3, Vol. 3: "Correspondence File, Vol. 6, September-June, 1901-1902," J. T. Holmes Papers, OHS; Dougall, "Bentonville," p. 215; Westfall, "Battle of Bentonville."

21. J. T. Holmes to [J. B.] Work, September 20, 1901, Box 3, Vol. 3: "Correspondence File, Vol. 6, September-June, 1901-1902," J. T. Holmes Papers, OHS; Statement of Thomas Thatcher, Henry Hysman, Albert Felheisen and Henry Allee, quoted in Allee, "Civil War History," 2, p. 179, MNHS; Fox, "Bentonville," July 1, 1886, and "Bentonville," May 7, 1896.

22. Ibid.

23. *OR* 47, pt. 1, pp. 452- 453.

24. Ibid.; Hinson, "Bentonville"; *Record of the Ninety-Fourth Ohio*, p. 88.

25. Earle, "Sherman's March," [n.p.], Civil War Misc. Coll., USAMHI; Foraker, *Notes*, 1, p. 59.

26. Ibid; Hinson, "Bentonville."

27. Foraker, *Notes*, 1, pp. 59-60; *OR* 47, pt. 1, p. 452; Hinson, "Bentonville."

28. John Herr to Sister, March 26, 1865, Herr Papers, DU; Hinson, "Bentonville."

29. Foraker, *Notes*, 1, p. 60; J. B. Foraker to H. W. Slocum, in Slocum, "Sherman's March," p. 691.

30. *OR* 47, pt. 1, p. 463.

31. Ibid., p. 434; Charlie to Mother & Etta, April 18, 1865, C. S. Brown Papers, DU; Westfall, "Battle of Bentonville."

32. *OR* 47, pt. 1, pp. 423, 434, 449, 467; ibid., pt. 2, 908; Bowman Diary, March 19, 1865, Bowman Family Papers, USAMHI; Carlin, "Battle of Bentonville," MOLLUS-OH, 3, p. 237; Carlin, "Military Memoirs," July 30, 1885.

33. Johnston, *Narrative*, pp. 385-386; *OR* 47, pt. 2, p. 1424.

34. For the definitive account of the Fort Fisher-Wilmington Campaign, see Chris E. Fonvielle, Jr., "'The Last Rays of Departing Hope': The Battles of Fort Fisher, the Fall of Wilmington, North Carolina, and the End of the Confederacy." Ph.D. diss., University of South Carolina, 1994.

35. Ibid., p. 223; Barrett, *Civil War in North Carolina*, pp. 279-280, 287-288; Gragg, *Confederate Goliath*, pp. 187-189.

36. Warner, *Generals in Gray*, p. 140; Barrett, *Civil War in North Carolina*, pp. 213-220; Fonvielle, "Last Rays," pp. 222-223; Freeman, *Lee's Lieutenants*, 3, p. 593; Sommers, *Richmond Redeemed*, pp. 116-117.

37. Hagood, *Memoirs*, pp. 358, 362; *OR* 47, pt. 2, pp. 1259, 1280; Ramsay, "Sixty-First Regiment," 3, p. 503, Rose, "Sixty-Sixth Regiment," 3, p. 698; Hinsdale, "Seventy-Second Regiment," 4, pp. 56-57, and Myrover, "Thirteenth Battalion," 4, p. 351, in Clark, *Histories*.

38. For a general description of the Cole plantation, see Joseph Hoffhines to Wife, March 27, 1865, Hoffhines Papers, OHS; *OR* 47, pt. 1, p. 666; Payne, *Thirty-Fourth Illinois*, p. 204; Myrover, "Thirteenth Battalion," 4, p. 351, in Clark, *Histories*.

39. J. B. Foraker to H. W. Slocum, in Slocum, "Sherman's March," p. 693.

40. *OR* 47, pt. 1, pp. 448-449, 453, 456-457, 463, Calkins, *One Hundred and Fourth Illinois*, pp. 300-301. Paradoxically, Hobart's "left wing" was on the right side of the road, and his "right wing" was on the left side.

41. *OR* 47, pt. 1, pp. 453, 460; Joseph Hoffhines to Wife, March 27, 1865, Hoffhines Papers, OHS; Hinson, "Bentonville."

42. Hinsdale, "Seventy-Second Regiment," 4, p. 57, and Myrover, "Thirteenth Battalion," 4, p. 351, in Clark, *Histories*; Joseph Hoffhines to Wife, March 27, 1865, Hoffhines Papers, OHS. At Bentonville, Atkins' Battery consisted of one section of 12-pounder Napoleons and two sections of 10-pounder Parrotts. See Myrover, op. cit., and Halcott Pride Jones Journal, March 19, 1865, NCDAH.

43. Hinson, "Bentonville"; Joseph Hoffhines to Wife, March 27, 1865, Hoffhines Papers, OHS; Hinsdale, "Seventy-Second Regiment," 4, p. 56, in Clark, *Histories*; *OR* 47, pt. 1, p. 453.

44. *OR* 47, pt. 1, pp. 457, 463; Calkins, *One Hundred and Fourth Illinois*, p. 301; Carlin, "Battle of Bentonville," MOLLUS-OH, 3, p. 237; Fitch, *Echoes*, p. 265.

45. *OR* 47, pt. 1, pp. 457, 463; Calkins, *One Hundred and Fourth Illinois*, pp. 301-302, 308; M. H. Fitch Diary, March 19, 1865, SHSW; Fitch, *Echoes*, p. 256.

46. Calkins, *One Hundred and Fourth Illinois*, p 308.

47. Ibid., pp. 307-309, *passim*.

48. M. H. Fitch Diary, March 19, 1865 (see map at the end of the March 19 entry), SHSW; Cornelius Courtright Diary, March 19, 1865, CHS.

49. *OR* 47, pt. 1, pp. 449, 463, 577; Otto, "War Memories," p. 104, Otto Papers, SHSW. *OR* 38, pt. 1, p. 825, for status report on Scovel's battery's guns.

50. *OR* 47, pt. 1, pp. 1056, 1101; ibid., pt. 2, p. 1408; ibid., pt. 3, p. 698; Sword, *Embrace an Angry Wind*, pp. 216-219. In a March 26 letter to President Davis, General Bragg wrote: "I passed that noble soldier Walthall a few days since on the field, and inquired for his command. He pointed me to a small squad and said, 'My Division consists of two brigadiers and 63 men for duty.'" Walthall may have understated his numbers for dramatic effect, although his actual troop strength was hardly less appalling. See Braxton Bragg to "Mr. President," March 26, 1865, Box 3, Folder 18, Bragg Papers in the William P. Palmer Coll., WRHS.

51. Hampton, "Battle of Bentonville," p. 703; Halsey, "Last Duel," p. 31; Bunn, "Battle of Bentonville," Stephen B. Weeks Scrapbook, 4, p. 44, NCC-UNC; *OR* 47, pt. 3, p. 698.

52. Ibid., pt. 1, pp. 1056, 1101; Bunn, "Battle of Bentonville," Stephen B. Weeks Scrapbook, 4, p. 44, NCC-UNC; D. H. Hill to Daughter, March 23, 1865, D. H. Hill Papers, USAMHI; Corn, "In Enemy's Lines," p. 507.

53. Bunn, "Battle of Bentonville," Stephen B. Weeks Scrapbook, 4, p. 44, NCC-UNC; *OR* 47, pt. 1, pp. 1101, 1103, 1104-1105.

54. D. H. Reynolds Diary, March 19, 1865, D. H. Reynolds Papers, UAK-F; Dacus, *Reminiscences of Company H*, [n.p.]. D. H. Hill witnessed Reynolds' wounding, and wrote that the shell killed two other horses besides Old Bob. See D. H. Hill to Daughter, March 26, 1865, D. H. Hill Papers, USAMHI.

55. Halsey, "Last Duel," p. 31.

56. Ibid.

57. Casualty list for Halsey's Battery, March 19, 1865, Edwin L. Halsey Papers, SHC-UNC; Ford, *Life*, p. 60.
58. Otto, "War Memories," p. 104, Otto Papers, SHSW; Fitch, *Echoes*, p. 256.
59. *OR* 47, pt. 1, p. 1099; ibid., pt. 2, pp. 1362, 1412; Hattaway, *Stephen D. Lee*, pp. 146, 153.
60. Bridges, *Lee's Maverick General*, pp. 25, 148-149, 153-154; Royster, *Destructive War*, pp. 49-50, 268.
61. Warner, *Generals in Gray*, pp. 136-137; Bridges, *Lee's Maverick General*, pp. 2, 149-151, 190.
62. Hill's promotion was officially dated July 11, 1863. Warner, *Generals in Gray*, p. 137; Bridges, *Lee's Maverick General*, pp. 193-194.
63. See Peter Cozzens, *This Terrible Sound: The Battle of Chickamauga*, for the definitive study of this battle.
64. Bridges, *Lee's Maverick General*, pp. 226-227, 234-236; Horn, *Army of Tennessee*, p. 286. According to *OR* 30, pt. 2, pp. 65-66, the petition was supposed to have been written by Maj. Gen. Simon Bolivar Buckner, a corps commander in the Army of Tennessee. Buckner was an outspoken advocate of Bragg's removal from command.
65. Bridges, *Lee's Maverick General*, pp. 236-240.
66. Ibid., pp. 238-239, 246; Connelly, *Autumn of Glory*, pp. 247-250.
67. Bridges, *Lee's Maverick General*, pp. 246, 254-259, 264-265, 268-269, 271; Williams, *Papers of William A. Graham*, 6, pp. 102-104, 109, 132-134. For Vance's letter and Lee's endorsement, see *OR* 42, pt. 3, pp. 1163-1170. For Davis' tardy reply, see *OR* 46, pt. 2, p. 1016.
68. Bridges, *Lee's Maverick General*, pp. 270-272; Williams, *Papers of William A. Graham*, 6, pp. 199-201, 209-211; *OR* 47, pt. 2, pp. 991, 1000-1003, 1006, 1023, 1038, 1317.
69. *OR* 47, pt. 2, p. 1338; D. H. Hill to "Genl" [J. E. Johnston], March 16, 1865, J. E. Johnston Papers, William & Mary College.
70. *OR* 47, pt. 1, pp. 1089-1090. The other two brigades of Hill's Division, Sharp's and Brantly's, were marching northward with Stephen D. Lee.
71. Ibid., pp. 1093, 1098.
72. Ibid., p. 1090; H. D. Clayton to J. W. Ratchford, March 30, 1865, H. D. Clayton Papers, UAL; Thomas, "Their Last Battle," p. 216.
73. *OR* 47, pt. 1, pp. 1089, 1106; sketch map accompanying George P. Buell's MS report, Union Battle Reports, Box 109, #729, RG 94, NA; Bates, "Battle of Bentonville," p. 143.
74. *OR* 47, pt. 1, pp. 467-468; Charlie to Mother & Etta, April 18, 1865, C. S. Brown Papers, DU; sketch map accompanying George P. Buell's MS report, Union Battle Reports, Box 109, #729, RG 94, NA; Bates, "Battle of Bentonville," pp. 143-144. By the time Carlin recalled Buell, his brigade was heading straight for Lieutenant Colonel Briant's position anyway. See Carlin, "Battle of Bentonville," MOLLUS-OH, 3, p. 237; William J. Carroll to Brother & Sister, March 30, 1865, W. J. Carroll Papers, BL-UMI.
75. *OR* 47, pt. 1, pp. 453, 460; Hinson, "Bentonville."
76. *OR* 47, pt. 1, p. 468; map accompanying George P. Buell's MS report, Union Battle Reports, Box 109, #729, RG 94, NA; Carlin, "Military Memoirs," July 30, 1885; Carlin, "Battle of Bentonville," MOLLUS-OH, 3, p. 237; Bates, "Battle of Bentonville," p. 143; Bowman Diary, March 19, 1865, Bowman Family Papers, USAMHI. Carlin later stated that a 400-yard gap separated Buell's and Hobart's brigades, but he was probably referring to the open space between Briant's and Fitch's wings.

77. *OR* 47, pt. 1, pp. 447, 457, 463, 473, 476, 480; Calkins, *One Hundred and Fourth Illinois*, pp. 302-303; John Eicker Memoir, Harrisburg CWRT Coll., USAMHI. Miles' fourth regiment, the 74th Ohio, remained in the rear on wagon guard duty and did not take part in the battle. See Owens, *Green County Soldiers*, p. 102.

78. *OR* 47, pt. 1, p. 485.

79. Warner, *Generals in Blue*, p. 334; Collins, "James D. Morgan," p. 274.

80. Warner, *Generals in Blue*, pp. 334-335; Collins, "James D. Morgan," pp. 275-276.

81. Warner, *Generals in Blue*, pp. 334-335; Collins, "James D. Morgan," pp. 275-276.

82. Warner, *Generals in Blue*, p. 335; Schenck, "In the Carolinas"; Nichols, *Story*, p. 272; Collins, "James D. Morgan," pp. 276-281.

83. Pepper, *Personal Recollections*, p. 379.

84. *OR* 47, pt. 1, pp. 485, 510-511, 516, 525, 534; Schenck, "In the Carolinas"; Litvin, "Captain Burkhalter's Georgia War," *Voices*, 2, pp. 537-538; McAdams, *Every-Day Soldier Life*, p. 144.

85. Widney Diary-Reminiscences, chap. 45, p. 2, KMNP; *OR* 47, pt. 1, pp. 511, 514, 522, 534; McAdams, *Every-Day Soldier Life*, p. 144. Morgan reported that he ordered Fearing to deploy one company of the 125th Illinois, but Fearing wrote that he deployed the entire regiment. *OR* 47, pt. 1, pp. 485, 534.

86. *OR* 47, pt. 1, pp. 485, 516; Hagood, *Memoirs*, pp. 358-359.

87. Slocum, "Sherman's March," p. 692; *OR* 47, pt. 1, pp. 423-424, 434, 449; Carlin, "Battle of Bentonville," MOLLUS-OH, 3, pp. 238-239; Carlin, "Military Memoirs," July 30, 1885.

88. *OR* 47, pt. 1, pp. 1089, 1099.

89. Ibid., pp. 1060, 1106-1108; ibid., pt. 3, p. 698. Bate commanded roughly half of Cheatham's Corps at Bentonville. Cleburne's Division fought at Bentonville on March 19 (without Mark Lowrey's and Hiram Granbury's brigades). Granbury's Brigade arrived at Bentonville either late on the night of March 19 or early on the morning of March 20. Lowrey's Brigade arrived on March 21 with Brown's Division, the third and last of the three divisions of Cheatham's Corps. See Worsham, *Old Nineteenth Tennessee*, p. 172; Darst, "Robert Hodges, Jr.," p. 39; Lindsley, *Military Annals*, p. 438.

90. Clark, *Stars and Bars*, p. 167.

91. Marshall, *William B. Bate*, pp. 160, 168, 171; Warner, *Generals in Gray*, pp. 19-20; Clark, *Stars and Bars*, p. 197.

92. *OR* 47, pt. 1, pp. 449, 473, 476, 480; Carlin, "Battle of Bentonville," MOLLUS-OH, 3, p. 238; Carlin, "Military Memoirs," July 30, 1885. Fitch's wing of Hobart's brigade took no part in Miles' assault, although the 104th Illinois was under instructions to advance to Miles' support if he achieved a breakthrough.

93. *OR* 47, pt. 1, p. 476.

94. Ibid., p. 473; Hagood, *Memoirs*, p. 358.

95. Johnston, *Narrative* pp. 386-387; Hampton, "Battle of Bentonville," pp. 703-704; *OR* 47, pt. 1, p. 1056; J. E. Johnston to R. F. Hoke, January 27, 1871, R. F. Hoke Papers, NCDAH.

96. McLaws Order Book, March 19, 1865, McLaws Papers, SHC-UNC; Williams, *War Diary*, p. 16; Johnson, "Closing Days," May 29, 1902; Johnson, "Marching, Camping, Fighting," L. P. Thomas Scrapbooks, 2, p. 148, L. P. Thomas Papers, AHS; Thomas B. Roy Diary, March 19, 1865.

97. McLaws Order Book, March 19, 1865, McLaws Papers, SHC-UNC; Andrews, "Averysboro [sic] and Bentonville," L. P. Thomas Scrapbooks, 1, p. 44, L. P. Thomas Papers, AHS; Andrews, *Footprints*, p. 173.

98. McLaws Order Book, March 19, 1865, McLaws Papers, SHC-UNC; Johnston, *Narrative*, pp. 386-387; Hampton, "Battle of Bentonville," pp. 703-704; Dickert, *Kershaw's Brigade*, p. 523.

Chapter Nine: *Old Joe Will Give Billy Sherman Hell To-day*

1. *OR* 47, pt. 1, pp. 449, 453, 460, 468; Carlin, "Battle of Bentonville," MOLLUS-OH, 3, pp. 238-239.
2. *OR* 47, pt. 1, pp. 468, 471; Bates, "Battle of Bentonville," p. 144.
3. Ibid; sketch map accompanying George P. Buell's MS report.
4. Bates, "Battle of Bentonville," p. 145.
5. Ibid; John Wesley Daniels Diary, March 19, 1865, BL-UMI; William J. Carroll to Brother & Sister, March 30, 1865, and William J. Carroll Diary, March 19, 1865, W. J. Carroll Papers, BL-UMI; John Hickman Diary, March 19, 1865, Squier Family Papers, BL-UMI; H. D. Clayton to J. W. Ratchford, March 30, 1865, H. D. Clayton Papers, UAL; *OR* 47, pt. 1, p. 1099. Beginning with the William J. Carroll Diary, all of the above-cited Union and Confederate sources state that Buell's and Briant's joint assault began about noon.
6. H. D. Clayton to J. W. Ratchford, March 30, 1865, H. D. Clayton Papers, UAL; Thomas, "Their Last Battle," pp. 216-217.
7. Ibid; p. 217; *OR* 47, pt. 1, pp. 453, 1093, 1099; Hinson, "Bentonville."
8. *OR* 47, pt. 1, pp. 1089-1090, 1093-1094; Hinson, "Bentonville."
9. Thomas, "Their Last Battle," p. 217; Corn, "In Enemy's Lines," p. 507.
10. Thomas, "Their Last Battle," pp. 217-218; "Thomas Jefferson Corn," *TCWVQ*, 2, p. 563; Corn, "In Enemy's Lines," p. 507.
11. *OR* 47, pt. 1, pp. 453, 460; Dougall, "Bentonville," p. 216; Boltz Diary, March 19, 1865, Boltz Papers, DU; Hinson, "Bentonville"; Joseph Hoffhines to Wife, March 27, 1865, Hoffhines Papers, OHS.
12. *OR* 47, pt. 1, p. 468; Bates, "Battle of Bentonville," pp. 145-146.
13. Charlie to Father, December 16, 1864, and January 5, 1864[5], Chas. S. Brown to "Folks. . .or anyone else," [n.d., March 1865?], Chas. S. Brown to Etta, April 26, 1865, C. S. Brown Papers, DU; Glatthaar, *March to the Sea*, p. 35.
14. Charlie to Mother & Etta, April 18, 1865, and Chas. S. Brown to Etta, April 26, 1865, C. S. Brown Papers, DU; John Wesley Daniels Diary, March 19, 1865, BL-UMI; William J. Carroll to Brother & Sister, March 30, 1865, and William J. Carroll Diary, March 19, 1865, W. J. Carroll Papers, BL-UMI; *OR* 47, pt. 1, pp. 468, 1106, 1108; Bates, "Battle of Bentonville," p. 146; Clark, *Stars and Bars*, p. 167; H. D. Clayton to J. W. Ratchford, March 30, 1865, H. D. Clayton Papers, UAL.
15. William J. Carroll to Brother & Sister, March 30, 1865, W. J. Carroll Papers, BL-UMI.
16. *OR* 47, pt. 1, pp. 468, 472, 1106; Chas. S. Brown to "Folks. . .or anyone else," [n.d., March 1865?], and Chas. S. Brown to Etta, April 26, 1865, C. S. Brown Papers, DU; Bates, "Battle of Bentonville," p. 146; H. D. Clayton to J. W. Ratchford, March 30, 1865, H. D. Clayton Papers, UAL.
17. Bates, "Battle of Bentonville," p. 146; Bowman Diary, March 19, 1865, Bowman Family Papers, USAMHI.

18. Thomas, "Their Last Battle," p. 218; Bates, "Battle of Bentonville," pp. 144, 146; Chas. S. Brown to "Folks. . .or anyone else," [n.d., March 1865?], C. S. Brown Papers, DU; Bowman Diary, March 19, 1865, Bowman Family Papers, USAMHI.

19. *OR* 47, pt. 1, p. 423; ibid., pt. 2, p. 906; Slocum, "Sherman's March," p. 692.

20. Carlin, "Battle of Bentonville," MOLLUS-OH, 3, pp. 239-240; W. P. Carlin to Marcus Bates, in Bates, "Battle of Bentonville," p. 147; Carlin, "Military Memoirs," July 30, 1885; *OR* 47, pt. 1, pp. 434, 449; ibid., pt. 2, p. 906; Slocum, "Sherman's March," p. 692.

21. Carlin, "Battle of Bentonville," MOLLUS-OH, 3, pp. 240, 250; Carlin, "Military Memoirs," July 30, 1885; *OR* 47, pt. 1, pp. 423, 434; Slocum, "Sherman's March," p. 692; McClurg, "Last Chance," p. 392.

22. Slocum, "Sherman's March," pp. 693, 695; McClurg, "Last Chance," p. 392.

23. *OR* 47, pt. 1, pp. 423-424; J. B. Foraker to H. W. Slocum, in Slocum, "Sherman's March," p. 693; Foraker, *Notes*, 1, pp. 62-63;

24. J. B. Foraker to H. W. Slocum, in Slocum, "Sherman's March," p. 693; Foraker, *Notes*, 1, pp. 62-63; *OR* 47, pt. 2, p. 904.

25. Ibid., pt. 1, pp. 496, 502, 504; Westervelt, *Lights and Shadows*, p. 94.

26. *OR* 47, pt. 1, pp. 496, 499, 502, 504, 534; Schenck, "In the Carolinas."

27. Inglesby, *First South Carolina Artillery*, p. 17; Ford, "Last Battles," p. 141; C. Woodward Hutson to Em, March 19[, 1865], C. W. Hutson Papers, SHC-UNC; J. W. Brown Diary, March 19, 1865, Private Papers, Mf Drawer 187, Reel 13, GADAH.

28. Inglesby, *First South Carolina Artillery*, pp. 17-18.

29. *OR* 47, pt. 1, p. 1106; Inglesby, *First South Carolina Artillery*, p. 18; Sanders, "Battle of Bentonville," p. 299.

30. Ford, "Last Battles," pp. 141-142; Ford, *Life*, pp. 55-56; J. W. Brown Diary, March 19, 1865, Private Papers, Mf Drawer 187, Reel 13, GADAH.

31. *OR* 47, pt. 1, p. 1113 (also published in *OR* 47, pt. 2, pp. 1437-1438.)

32. *OR* 47, pt. 1, p. 1094; Thomas B. Roy Diary, March 19, 1865; J. E. Johnston to R. F. Hoke, January 27, 1871, R. F. Hoke Papers, NCDAH; Ridley, *Battles and Sketches*, pp. 452-453.

33. *OR* 47, pt. 1, pp. 575, 577, 579-580.

34. McClurg, "Last Chance," p. 393; *OR* 47, pt. 1, pp. 587, 645, 658.

35. *OR* 47, pt. 1, pp. 423-424, 587, 600, 611, 645, 653, 665, 671; Elmore, "Bentonville and Averysboro [sic]." General Jackson reported that his division left camp at 7:00 a.m., but most of his subordinates recorded an earlier departure time.

36. *OR* 47, pt. 1, pp. 665-666, 671, 674, 679; J. S. R[obinson] to "Friend Hunt," April 20, 1865, J. S. Robinson Papers, OHS; Packer, "Warfield Forgot"; Bartley, "Fighting at Bentonville"; "Overwhelmed by Sherman's Kindness," Beyer, *Deeds of Valor*, 1, p. 493.

37. Warner, *Generals in Blue*, pp. 406-407.

38. *OR* 47, pt. 1, pp. 468, 665-666; J. S. R[obinson] to "Friend Hunt," April 20, 1865, J. S. Robinson Papers, OHS.

39. Hinson, "Bentonville."

40. *OR* 47, pt. 1, pp. 1094, 1106.

41. Ibid., p. 1094.

42. Inglesby, *First South Carolina Artillery*, p. 18; Ford, *Life*, p. 56.

43. *OR* 47, pt. 1, p. 468; sketch map accompanying George P. Buell's MS report; [Landstrom], "Civil War Experiences," p. 319.
44. Ibid., pp. 314-319.
45. *OR* 47, pt. 1, pp. 434-435, 449-450.
46. McClurg, "Last Chance," p. 392.
47. *OR* 47, pt. 1, pp. 587, 600-601; A. S. Williams Diary, March 19, 1865.
48. *OR* 47, pt. 1, pp. 600-601, 637, 645; Toombs, *Reminiscences*, pp. 213-214. The other regiments in Hawley's brigade were the 107th New York, 150th New York and 3rd Wisconsin. The 150th New York remained in the rear on guard duty and took no part in the March 19 battle. *OR* 47, pt. 1, p. 653.
49. Ibid., pp. 612, 624.
50. Ibid., pp. 577, 579-580.
51. Ibid., p. 666.
52. Hinson, "Bentonville."

Chapter Ten: *We Run Like the Duce*

1. *OR* 47, pt. 1, pp. 1098-1099; G. B. Gardner to Wife [n.d.], Mf Drawer 283, Reel 25, Civil War Misc.—Personal Papers, GADAH; Ogilvie, "Brown's Brigade at Bentonville," Box 14, Folder 8, Confederate Coll., TNSLA.
2. *OR* 47, pt. 1, pp. 1101-1102, 1105; Bunn, "Battle of Bentonville," Stephen B. Weeks Scrapbook, 4, pp. 45-46, NCC-UNC.
3. *OR* 47, pt. 1, p. 1103; Bunn, "Battle of Bentonville," Stephen B. Weeks Scrapbook, 4, pp. 45-46, NCC-UNC; A. P. Stewart quoted in, "Gen. E. C. Walthall," p. 306; Halcott Pride Jones Journal, March 19, 1865, NCDAH.
4. Broadfoot, "Seventieth Regiment," 4, p. 21, in Clark, *Histories*.
5. *OR* 47, pt. 1, p. 1105; Bunn, "Battle of Bentonville," Stephen B. Weeks Scrapbook, 4, p. 45, NCC-UNC.
6. *OR* 47, pt. 1, pp. 666-667, 1102-1103, 1105; Packer, "Warfield Forgot"; Bartley, "Fighting at Bentonville."
7. *OR* 47, pt. 1, p. 1099; Johnston , *Narrative*, p. 387; Hinson, "Bentonville"; "R. S. Cowles," *TCWVQ*, 2, p. 577; Harper, "Fifty-Eighth Regiment," 3, p. 440, in Clark, *Histories*. Concerning the Federal works along Lieutenant Colonel Briant's front, D. H. Hill wrote: "The Yankees had some rifle-pits for skirmishers, but no connected line except in front of Palmer's Brigade of this corps." The "connected line" that Hill refers to was doubtless the line of works dug by the 33rd Ohio. The 33rd had an hour's head start on the other Union regiments defending that line. As for Buell's works, General Bate described them as "continuous and well constructed." *OR* 47, pt. 1, pp. 453, 1090, 1106.
8. Hinson, "Bentonville."
9. Ibid; Joseph Hoffhines to Wife, March 27, 1865, Hoffhines Papers, OHS.
10. Ibid; Hinson, "Bentonville."
11. Ibid; *OR* 47, pt. 1, p. 461.
12. H. D. Clayton to J. W. Ratchford, March 30, 1865, H. D. Clayton Papers, UAL; *OR* 47, pt. 1, pp. 453, 460; Dougall, "Bentonville," p. 217; Boltz Diary, March 19, 1865, Boltz Papers, DU.
13. *OR* 47, pt. 1, pp. 1106, 1108; Ridley, *Battles and Sketches*, p. 454.
14. Clark, *Stars and Bars*, p. 192; Buck, *Cleburne and His Command*, p. 130.
15. Clark, *Stars and Bars*, pp. 158, 192.
16. Ibid., pp. 192-193.

17. Bates, "Battle of Bentonville," p. 148; *OR* 47, pt. 1, p. 449.

18. Carlin, "Military Memoirs," July 30, 1885; Carlin, "Battle of Bentonville," MOLLUS-OH, 3, p. 240; Chas. S. Brown to "Folks. . .or anyone else," [n.d., March 1865?], Chas. S. Brown to Etta, April 26, 1865, C. S. Brown Papers, DU.

19. *OR* 47, pt. 1, p. 468.

20. Ibid., pp. 449, 468; Chas. S. Brown to Etta, April 26, 1865, C. S. Brown Papers, DU.

21. Carlin, "Military Memoirs," July 30, 1885; Carlin, "Battle of Bentonville," MOLLUS-OH, 3, pp. 241-242; Chas. S. Brown to "Folks. . .or anyone else," [n.d., March 1865], C. S. Brown Papers, DU.

22. Carlin, "Military Memoirs," July 30, 1885; Carlin, "Battle of Bentonville," MOLLUS-OH, 3, p. 242.

23. Sanders, "Battle of Bentonville," p. 299.

24. Warner, *Generals in Gray*, p. 82; Inglesby, *First South Carolina Artillery*, p. 18.

25. Sanders, "Battle of Bentonville," p. 299; J. W. Brown Diary, March 19, 1865, Mf Drawer 187, Reel 13, Private Papers, GADAH; Ford, *Life*, pp. 56-57.

26. Clark, *Stars and Bars*, p. 193. General Bate reported: "not a man [of my command] stopped to plunder the knapsacks of the enemy." *OR* 47, pt. 1, p. 1107.

27. Bates, "Battle of Bentonville," p. 148; Chas. S. Brown to "Folks. . .or anyone else," [n.d., March 1865?], C. S. Brown Papers, DU; *OR* 47, pt. 1, p. 577; Townsend, "With the Ambulance Train."

28. Lyman Widney Diary-Reminiscences, chap. 45, p. 2, KMNP; A. M. Ayers to Wife, March 25, 1865, A. M. Ayers Papers, EU.

29. Lyman Widney Diary-Reminiscences, chap. 45, p. 3, KMNP.

30. *OR* 47, pt. 1, p. 1106; Charlie to Mother & Etta, April 18, 1865, C. S. Brown Papers, DU.

31.G. B. Gardner to Wife, [n.d.], Mf Drawer 283, Reel 25, Civil War Misc.—Personal Papers, GADAH.

32. [Roy], "Sketch of W. J. Hardee," p. 48, W. J. Hardee Papers, ALDAH. Although many of the troops in Lee's Corps witnessed the carnage at Franklin, few of them took part in the charge.

33. Hughes, *Old Reliable*, p. 288; [Roy], "Sketch of W. J. Hardee," p. 48, W. J. Hardee Papers, ALDAH. An abridged version of Roy's biographical sketch can be found in Pollard, *Lee and His Lieutenants*, pp. 808-829.

34. *OR*, pt. 1, pp. 666, 679.

35. *OR* 47, pt. 1, pp. 580, 1094, 1099, 1102, 1103; Harper, "Fifty-Eighth Regiment," 3, p. 440, in Clark, *Histories*; Harper, "Palmer's Brigade," NCC Clipping File #1081, NCC-UNC; Lambert, "Battle of Bentonville," p. 221; H. D. Clayton to J. W. Ratchford, March 30, 1865, H. D Clayton Papers, UAL. *OR* 38, pt. 1, p. 825, for a description of the 19th Indiana Battery's ordnance.

36. The March 20 morning report for Webb's battery indicates that it lost eight horses killed, 12 horses captured and two mules killed. RG 94: Regimental Records. Muster Rolls, Descriptive Rools, Morning Reports, and Letter Books, 19th Indiana Battery; "Overwhelmed by Sherman's Kindness," in Beyer, *Deeds,* 1, pp. 493-494.

37. Ibid.; *OR* 47, pt. 1, pp. 679, 1043; *Medal of Honor Recipients,* p. 20.

38. Lyman Widney Diary-Reminiscences, chap. 45, p. 3, KMNP; McClurg, "Last Chance," p. 393. McClurg appears to be describing Robinson's orderly retreat along the Goldsboro Road.

39. Ibid.

40. L. W. Earle, "Sherman's March," [n.p.], Civil War Misc. Coll., USAMHI.

41. Fitch, *Echoes,* p. 257.

42. Ibid., pp. 257-258, 260; Otto, "War Memories," p. 106, Otto Papers, SHSW; *OR* 47, pt. 1, p. 463. Fitch must have known more about Carlin's troop dispositions than he was willing to admit. One of Fitch's subordinates, Maj. John Widmer of the 104th Illinois, reported that he was instructed to advance to the support of Miles' brigade during Carlin's noontime assault if it proved successful. In his memoirs, Fitch stated that he was unaware of Miles' position on the field. Yet in his after-action report, Fitch stated that he was with Widmer's regiment at the time of Miles' assault, and most likely was the one who ordered Widmer to advance to Miles' support if there was a breakthrough.

43. Fitch, *Echoes,* pp. 258, 265; M. H. Fitch Diary, March 19, 1865, M. H. Fitch Papers, SHSW; Otto, "War Memories," pp. 106-107, Otto Papers, SHSW; *OR* 47, pt. 1, pp. 457, 459, 463-464.

44. *OR* 47, pt. 1, p. 473; J. L. Keller quoted in Canfield, *21st Ohio*, p. 182; Povenmire, "Diary of Jacob Adams," p. 701.

45. John Eicker Memoir, p. 26, Harrisburg CWRT Coll., USAMHI.

46. *OR* 47, pt. 1, p. 511; Will C. Robinson quoted in Payne, *Thirty-Fourth Illinois*, pp. 200-201.

47. *OR* 47, pt. 1, pp. 511, 526.

48. Ibid., pt. 1, pp. 485, 502; W. F., "10th Michigan Cavalry [sic]," *Detroit Adveriser and Tribune*, April 5, 1865.

49. [Roy], "Sketch of W. J. Hardee," p. 48, W. J. Hardee Papers, ALDAH; Harper, "Fifty-Eighth Regiment," 3, p. 440, in Clark, *Histories*; Hughes, *Old Reliable,* pp. 288-289.

50. J. E. Johnston to R. F. Hoke, January 27, 1871, R. F. Hoke Papers, NCDAH; McLaws Order Book, March 19, 1865, McLaws Papers, SHC-UNC; Dickert, *Kershaw's Brigade,* p. 523.

51. McLaws Order Book, March 19, 1865, McLaws Papers, SHC-UNC; J. E. Johnston to R. F. Hoke, January 27, 1871, R. F. Hoke Papers, NCDAH; France, *Battle of Bentonville,* p. 12; *OR* 47, pt. 1, p. 1056.

52. Hagood, *Memoirs,* p. 360; *OR* 47, pt. 1, pp. 1090, 1104-1105, 1108.

53. *OR* 47, pt. 1, pp. 1094, 1099-1100; H. D. Clayton to J. W. Ratchford, March 30, 1865, H. D. Clayton Papers, UAL; B. F. Watson to Editor, *Confederate Veteran,* January 14, 1929, Box 7, *Confederate Veteran* Papers, DU (also published with a few changes as Watson, "Battle of Bentonville," p. 95).

54. *OR* 47, pt. 1, pp. 485, 494; McClurg, "Last Chance," pp. 393-394; [Dawes], *Memorial of Benjamin D. Fearing,* p. 16; Levi A. Ross Diary, March 19, 1865, ILSHL.

55. A. L. Fahnestock Diary, March 19, 1865, Peoria Public Library; A. L. Fahnestock to Charles Swift, March 24, 1865, J. W. Langley Papers, KMNP; *OR* 47, pt. 1, pp. 485-486, 534, 1106, 1108.

56. *OR* 47, pt. 1, pp. 534, 541, 548.

57. Ibid., pp. 1090, 1094, 1098.

58. Ibid., pp. 1090, 1100; H. D. Clayton to J. W. Ratchford, March 30, 1865, H. D. Clayton Papers, UAL.

59. A. L. Fahnestock to Charles Swift, March 24, 1865, J. W. Langley Papers, KMNP; A. L. Fahnestock Diary, March 19, 1865, Peoria Public Library; Kinnear, *Eighty-Sixth Illinois,* p. 106; Lambert, "Battle of Bentonville," p. 221.

60. *OR* 47, pt. 1, pp. 534-535, 541.

61. A. L. Fahnestock Diary, March 19, 1865, Peoria Public Library; A. L. Fahnestock to Charles Swift, March 24, 1865, J. W. Langley Papers, KMNP; *OR* 47, pt. 1, p. 535.

62. A. L. Fahnestock Diary, March 19, 1865, Peoria Public Library; A. L. Fahnestock to Charles Swift, March 24, 1865, J. W. Langley Papers, KMNP; T. J. Cochran quoted in [Dawes], *Memorial of Benjamin Dana Fearing,* p. 25; *OR* 47, pt. 1, p. 535. At this point in the fight, Fearing believed that Mitchell's brigade was moving up to his support, but he was soon disabused of that notion.

63. *OR* 47, pt. 1, pp. 535, 548; A. L. Fahnestock to Charles Swift, March 24, 1865, J. W. Langley Papers, KMNP.

64. *OR* 47, pt. 1, p. 541; Allee, "Civil War History," 2, pp. 180, 182, MNHS.

65. *OR* 47, pt. 1, pp. 537, 541.

66. Ibid., p. 541; Hardee, *Tactics*, 2, pp. 169-170.

67. *OR* 47, pt. 1, pp. 541-542.

68. Ibid., pp. 537, 542-544 *passim*; Litvin, "Captain Burkhalter's Georgia War," *Voices*, 2, p. 538. Besides Fearing and Langley, the other brigade commanders were Dan McCook, Oscar Harmon and Caleb Dilworth. During the June 27, 1864, assault on Kennesaw Mountain, McCook was mortally wounded and Harmon was killed minutes after replacing him.

Chapter Eleven: *It Seemed More Than Men Could Bear*

1. *OR* 47, pt. 1, pp. 511, 514; Payne, *Thirty-Fourth Illinois*, p. 201; Heath, "Bentonville."

2. Clingman's Brigade played a minor role in Hoke's assault, suffering only 20 casualties compared to Colquitt's 214. *OR* 47, pt. 1, pp. 511, 1080; Widney, "From the Sea," August 27, 1903; Lyman Widney Diary-Reminiscences, chap. 45, p. 4, KMNP; Payne, *Thirty-Fourth Illinois*, p. 202; Hagood, *Memoirs*, p. 202. Hagood's account of the battle is the only one written by a brigade-level commander in Hoke's Division. Worse yet, neither Bragg nor Hoke wrote an account of the battle. On two occasions in 1871, Joseph E. Johnston asked Hoke to furnish a summary of his division's actions at Bentonville, but Hoke ignored Johnston's requests. See J. E. Johnston to R. F. Hoke, January 27, 1871, and September 27, 1871, R. F. Hoke Papers, NCDAH.

3. John W. Carson to Alexander Branum, March 26, 1865, in J. M. Branum, "Letters," June 21, 1900.

4. Seaman, "Battle of Bentonville."

5. Warfield, "Benton's Crossroads."

6. *OR* 47, pt. 1, p. 526; Warfield, "Benton's Crossroads," and "Fighting at Bentonville."

7. *OR* 47, pt. 1, p. 526.

8. Ibid., pp. 473-474; J. L. Keller quoted in Canfield, *21st Ohio*, pp. 182-183.

9. *OR* 30, pt. 1, pp. 387-395; Cozzens, *This Terrible Sound*, p. 505.

10. *OR* 47, pt. 1, pp. 457, 459, 464; Fitch, *Echoes*, pp. 258-259; G. R. Kellams to Lt. Gentry, March 27, 1865, Gibson County Civil War Papers, INHS.

11. *OR* 47, pt. 1, pp. 457, 459, 464; Fitch, *Echoes*, p. 259; J. L. Keller quoted in Canfield, *21st Ohio*, p. 183.

12. *OR* 47, pt. 1, pp. 526-527.

13. Ibid.

14. McNeill, "Ninth Battalion," 4, p. 311, William Lamb, "Thirty-Sixth Regiment," 2, p. 650, and Davis, "Fortieth Regiment," 2, pp. 761-763 in Clark, *Histories*; Taylor, "Personal Recollections," p. 4, J. D. Taylor Papers, NCDAH; Hagood, *Memoirs*, pp. 351, 360.

15. Hagood, *Memoirs* p. 360; McNeill, "Ninth Battalion," 4, p. 304, in Clark, *Histories*; Taylor, "Personal Recollections, pp. 2-3, J. D. Taylor Papers, NCDAH.

16. McAdams, *Every-Day Soldier Life*, p. 145.

17. Davis, "Fortieth Regiment," 2, pp. 763-764, in Clark, *Histories*.

18. Taylor, "Personal Recollections," pp. 6-7, J. D. Taylor Papers, NCDAH; McNeill, "Ninth Battalion," 4, p. 312, and William Lamb, "Thirty-Sixth Regiment," 2, pp. 650-651, in Clark, *Histories*; Hagood, *Memoirs*, pp. 360-361; *OR* 47, pt. 1, p. 499. Major Frederick Beck, the commander of the 108th Ohio, reported: "the enemy came on in full force and charged our works. A terrible battle ensued, which lasted for some two hours, when the enemy retired, leaving many dead and wounded on the field in our front." The charge of the "Red Infantry" would have lasted just a fraction of two hours.

McNeill wrote that only *one* officer in Taylor's command escaped unharmed, but both Taylor and Lamb state that the figure was in fact *two* officers—Lieutenants Allen and Gilchrist of the 9th North Carolina Battalion. The casualty figures for Taylor's contingent are those supplied by Taylor and Lamb.

19. Taylor, "Personal Recollections," pp. 7-8, J. D. Taylor Papers, NCDAH. The three mortally wounded officers were Captains McDougal, Rankin and Taylor (no relation to the lieutenant colonel) of the 9th North Carolina Battalion. See William Lamb, "Thirty-Sixth Regiment," 2, p. 651, in Clark, *Histories*.

20. *OR* 47, pt. 1, pp. 504, 516-517.

21. Ferguson, "Battle of Averysboro & Bentonville N Carlina [sic]," p. 2, Ferguson Reminiscences, *CWTI* Coll., USAMHI; *OR* 47, pt. 1, pp. 496, 499, 504, 517.

22. *OR* 47, pt. 1, pp. 496, 499, 504, 517.

23. McAdams, *Every-Day Soldier Life*, p. 145.

24. Schenck, "In the Carolinas."

25. *OR* 47, pt. 1, pp. 496, 499, 504; Beyer, *Deeds of Valor*, 1, p. 491.

26. Ibid., pp. 491-492; Compiled Service Record of George W. Clute, Company I, 14 Regt. Michigan Infantry, NA; *A Study in Valor*, pp. 34-35; Robertson, *Michigan in the War*, p. 350; *Medal of Honor Recipients*, p. 190.

27. Beyer, *Deeds of Valor*, 1, p. 492; *A Study in Valor*, pp. 9-10, 34-35; *Medal of Honor Recipients*, p. 190.

28. Henry Plant received his medal on April 27, 1896, and George Clute received his on August 26, 1898. Ibid., pp. 58, 190.

29. McClurg, "Last Chance," p. 396; *OR* 47, pt. 1, pp. 497, 504; Robertson, *Michigan in the War*, pp. 350-351. In his report, Lieutenant Colonel Grummond wrote: "One general officer [possibly Hoke] was taken, but I think escaped from the guard in the swamp [while] going to the rear."

The casualties for Hoke's Division on March 19 are: 45 killed, 370 wounded and 178 missing. *OR* 47, pt. 1, p. 1059.

30. Ibid., pp. 499, 504, 517; Robertson, *Michigan in the War*, pp. 350-351. Grummond reported that the Confederates held the works first occupied by the 10th Michigan, but Lieutenant Colonel Vernon of the 78th Illinois stated that his regiment held those works.

31. Lambert, "Battle of Bentonville," pp. 221-222; Shingleton, "With Loyalty and Honor," p. 258.

32. Ibid; B. F. Watson to Editor, *Confederate Veteran*, January 14, 1929, *Confederate Veteran* Papers, Box 7, DU (published with a few changes as Watson, "In the Battle of Bentonville," p. 95); Lambert, "Battle of Bentonville," pp. 221-222.

33. Shingleton, "'With Loyalty and Honor,'" pp. 258-259.

34. *OR* 47, pt. 1, p. 1100.

35. Lambert, "Battle of Bentonville," p. 221.

36. *OR* 47, pt. 1, pp. 480, 494, 496-497, 502, 508.

37. Otto, "War Memories," p. 107, Otto Papers, SHSW; Meagher, "17th New York"; Stewart, *52nd O. V. I.,* p. 164. The 35th New Jersey enjoyed a similar distinction: it was the only Eastern regiment in the XVII Corps, and the 35th's members wore a Zouave uniform. See *National Tribune Scrapbook*, 1, pp. 159-160.

38. *OR* 47, pt. 1, pp. 502, 508.

39. Hill's Division held the left, Baker's Brigade the center, and Palmer's Brigade the right of the Confederate line confronting the rear of Morgan's position. Ibid; Westervelt, *Lights and Shadows*, p. 94; Lyman Widney Diary-Reminiscences, chap. 45, p. 6, KMNP; W. F., "10th Michigan Cavalry [sic]," Detroit *Advertiser and Tribune*, April 5, 1865.

40. Ibid; *OR* 47, pt. 1, p. 502.

41. Ibid., pp. 502, 1090; W. F., "10th Michigan Cavalry [sic]," Detroit *Advertiser and Tribune*, April 5, 1865. In his report, General Vandever cited Captain Dunphy for his "distinguished gallantry." *OR* 47, pt. 1, pp. 497-498.

42. Ibid., p. 508.

43. Payne, *Thirty-Fourth Illinois*, p. 202; *OR* 47, pt. 1, p. 514. Captain Walker reported that at this point in the battle "the enemy did not make any regular and persistent attack on our front; they sometimes advanced in considerable force, but were easily driven back." Walker noted that "there was a scattering fire in our rear, so that it was at one time necessary to jump to the opposite side of the works for protection."

44. Lyman Widney Diary-Reminiscences, chap. 45, p. 6, KMNP; Widney, "From the Sea," August 27, 1903; Heath, "Bentonville."

45. McClurg, "Last Chance," pp. 394-395; A. C. McClurg to Benson J. Lossing, February 18, 1868, in Lossing, *Pictorial History*, 3, p. 501.

46. McClurg, "Last Chance," pp. 395-396. McClurg wrote that General Morgan was unaware of the Confederates in rear of his position until he warned him of their presence. Since McClurg noted that "Mitchell's brigade had already discovered the intruders in their rear," it is probable that Morgan was with Vandever's brigade at the time of McClurg's arrival.

47. *OR* 47, pt. 1, pp. 499, 517; Batchelor Diary, March 19, 1865, ILSHL.

48. Shingleton, "With Loyalty and Honor," p. 259; Lambert, "Battle of Bentonville," p. 222.

49. *OR* 47, pt. 1, p. 1100; Corn, "In Enemy's Lines," p. 507; "Thomas Jefferson Corn," *TCWVQ*, 2, p. 563.

50. *OR* 47, pt. 1, pp. 784, 826, 828, 834, 838; Cogswell, "Bentonville, N. C."; William K. Winkler, *Letters of Frederick C. Winkler*, p. 203; Storrs, *Twentieth Connecticut*, p. 164; Underwood, *Thirty-Third Massachusetts*, p. 282.

51. *OR* 47, pt. 1, pp. 424, 435, 587, 826.

52. Velie, "Charged in a Swamp."

53. *OR* 47, pt. 1, pp. 826-827 *passim*, 834, 838, 842- 843; Velie, "Charged in a Swamp"; Osborn, "A Few Words about Bentonville"; Storrs, *Twentieth Connecticut*, p. 164.

54. Velie, "Charged in a Swamp."

55. *OR* 47, pt. 1, pp. 538, 834, 838; Storrs, *Twentieth Connecticut*, p. 164; Rumple, "Coggswell's [sic] Brigade at Bentonville"; Osborn, "Sherman's Carolinas Campaign," p. 113.

56. *OR* 47, pt. 1, p. 826; Osborn, *Trials and Triumphs*, p. 201; Underwood, *Thirty-Third Massachusetts*, pp. 283-284; Hurst, *Seventy-Third Ohio*, p. 175; Rumple, "Coggswell's [sic] Brigade at Bentonville."

57. *OR* 47, pt. 1, pp. 486, 497, 499, 502-503, 504, 508; W. F., "10th Michigan Cavalry [sic]," Detroit *Advertiser and Tribune*, April 5, 1865; Robertson, *Michigan in the War*, p. 351; Stewart, *52nd O.V.I.*, p. 162.

58. Lambert, "Battle of Bentonville," p. 222.

59. Shingleton, "With Loyalty and Honor," pp. 259-260.

60. *OR* 47, pt. 1, p. 1100; Ogilvie, "Brown's Brigade at Bentonville," p. 1, Box 14, Folder 8, Confederate Coll., TNSLA; Ogilvie, "Days and Nights," p. 361.

61. Corn, "In Enemy's Lines," p. 507; "Thomas Jefferson Corn," *TCWVQ*, 2, pp. 563-564.

62. In addition to the Tennesseans and Alabamians, General Stevenson reported that several soldiers from the 54th Virginia were in Colonel Searcy's squad. *OR* 47, pt. 1, pp. 1090, 1095, 1100; O'Neal, "From the Western Border," p. 125; Corn, "In Enemy's Lines," p. 507; "Thomas Jefferson Corn," *TCWVQ*, 2, p. 564; "R. S. Cowles," *TCWVQ*, 2, p. 577; Ogilvie, "Brown's Brigade at Bentonville," p. 5.

63. Corn, "In Enemy's Lines," p. 507; Ogilvie, "Brown's Brigade at Bentonville," pp. 1-5 *passim*; O'Neal, "From the Western Border," p. 125. Captain Wood, the adjutant for Manigault's Brigade of Hill's Division, led a party of 10 men and eight prisoners around the Union right, and reached the Confederate lines on March 20. *OR* 47, pt. 1, pp. 1090-1091; Yeary, *Reminiscences*, p. 365.

64. Ogilvie, "Brown's Brigade at Bentonville," p. 5. The reception accorded Searcy's Alabama contingent was no less emotional. According to Private O'Neal, the 17-year-old color bearer of the 40th Alabama, division commander Henry D. Clayton "took me in his arms as a child," when the general was told that the youth had carried out his regiment's flag. See O'Neal, "From the Western Border," p. 125.

65. Wynne, *This War*, pp. 1-14 *passim*, p. 129.

66. Ibid., pp. 127-129.

67. Meagher, "17th New York."

68. Fitch, *Echoes*, p. 259; Will to Father, March 24, 1865, W. C. Robinson Papers, ILSHL; Heath, "Bentonville."

Chapter Twelve: *Like One Continuous Peal of Heavy Thunder*

1. *OR* 47, pt. 1, p. 1090.

2. Ibid., pp. 1091, 1095, 1100.

3. Ibid., pp. 1091, 1102, 1104.

4. Ibid., pp. 1090-1091, 1094-1095, 1098. General Stevenson reported that Loring's Division formed on Pettus' left, but Hill's and Pettus' reports indicate that Loring may have reached the front line ahead of Pettus.

5. Ibid., pp. 435, 485, 575; Harper, "Fifty-Eighth Regiment," 3, p. 441, in Clark, *Histories*.

6. Ibid.

7. *OR* 47, pt. 1, p. 1107; Harper, *Fifty-Eighth Regiment*, 3, pp. 441-442, in Clark, *Histories*.

8. McLaws Order Book, March 19, 1865, McLaws Papers, SHC-UNC; *OR* 47, pt. 1, p. 1109; Hughes, *Old Reliable*, p. 290.

9. McLaws Order Book, March 19, 1865, McLaws Papers, SHC-UNC; Johnson, "Marching, Camping, Fighting," L. P. Thomas Scrapbooks, 2, p. 148, L. P. Thomas Papers, AHS; Johnson, "Closing Days," May 29, 1902.

10. *OR* 47, pt. 1, p. 1109; ibid., pt. 2, pp. 1397, 1408; Johnson, "Closing Days," May 29, 1902.

11. *OR* 47, pt. 1, pp. 826, 834, 840, 842-843, 1098-1099; Velie, "Charged in a Swamp"; Hurst, *Seventy-Third Ohio*, p. 176; Osborn, *Trials and Triumphs*, pp. 201-202.

12. Velie, "Charged in a Swamp"; *OR* 47, pt. 1, pp. 834, 842-843, 1110; Hurst, *Seventy-Third Ohio*, p. 176; Osborn, *Trials and Triumphs*, p. 202.

13. *OR* 47, pt. 1, pp. 1091, 1102, 1109; McLaws Order Book, March 19, 1865, McLaws Papers, SHC-UNC.

14. *OR* 47, pt. 1, p. 1056; Johnston, *Narrative*, p. 388; Johnson, "Closing Days," May 29, 1902.

15. *OR* 47, pt. 1, pp. 1091, 1096, 1099, 1102, 1105, 1109; Johnson, "Closing Days," May 29, 1902; Johnson, "Marching, Camping, Fighting," L. P. Thomas Scrapbooks, 2, p. 148, L. P. Thomas Papers, AHS; Raleigh *Conservative*, March 27, 1865.

16. Hurst, *Seventy-Third Ohio*, p. 176; *OR* 47, pt. 1, p. 843.

17. P. B. Buckingham to Wife, March 26, 1865, P. B. Buckingham Papers, AAS.

18. Osborn, *Trials and Triumphs*, p. 202; Osborn, "A Few Words."

19. Johnson, "Closing Days," May 29, 1902; Johnson, "Marching, Camping, Fighting," L. P. Thomas Scrapbooks, 2, p. 148, L. P. Thomas Papers, AHS; *OR* 47, pt. 1, 1104.

20. *OR* 47, pt. 1, p. 1110; Johnson, "Closing Days," May 29, 1902; Johnson, "Marching, Camping, Fighting," L. P. Thomas Scrapbooks, 2, p. 148, L. P. Thomas Papers, AHS.

21. Ibid., Johnson, "Closing Days," May 29, 1902.

22. Ibid., Johnson, "Marching, Camping, Fighting," L. P. Thomas Scrapbooks, 2, p. 148, L. P. Thomas Papers, AHS; Rumple, "Coggswell's [sic] Brigade at Bentonville."

23. *OR* 47, pt. 1, pp. 1102-1104 *passim*, 1110.

24. Ibid., p. 645; Toombs, *Reminiscences*, p. 214.

25. Ibid., pp. 214-215; *OR* 47, pt. 1, pp. 645, 671; Meffert Diary, March 19, 1865, SHSW; Benton, *As Seen from the Ranks*, pp. 269-270.

26. Toombs, *Reminiscences*, p. 215; *OR* 47, pt. 1, pp. 645, 671.

27. Westfall, "Battle of Bentonsville [sic]."

28. Ibid.; *OR* 47, pt. 1, p. 441; Robbins, "Autobiography," p. 13, H. C. Robbins Papers, SHSW; Morhous, *Reminiscences*, p. 171.

29. Westfall, "Battle of Bentonsville [sic]"; *OR* 47, pt. 1, pp. 629, 653; Kinnear, *Eighty-Sixth Illinois*, p. 105.

30. Robbins, "Autobiography," pp. 13-14, H. C. Robbins Papers, SHSW; *OR* 47, pt. 1, pp. 665, 674.

31. Robbins, "Autobiography," p. 14, H. C. Robbins Papers, SHSW.

32. Ibid., pp. 15, 18-19; *OR* 47, pt. 1, 601, 612, 624.

33. *OR* 47, pt. 1, pp. 575, 847, 854; Hendrick, "Bentonville." For a map showing the position of Rich's battery (Battery I, 2nd Illinois), see Payne, *Thirty-Fourth Illinois*, map following p. 208.

34. *OR* 47, pt. 1, pp. 847, 854; Hendrick, "Bentonville"; McIntosh, "Annals," p. 212, McIntosh Papers, SHSW.

35. Ezra Button Diary, March 19, 1865, John B. Tripp Papers, SHSW; McIntosh, "Annals," p. 211, McIntosh Papers, SHSW; C. H. Dickinson Diary, March 19, 1865, C. H. Dickinson Papers, SHSW; Robertson, *Michigan in the War*, p. 506; *OR* 47, pt. 1, p. 809.

36. C. H. Dickinson Diary, March 19, 1865, C. H. Dickinson Papers, SHSW. A few days prior to Johnston's surrender, Bvt. Maj. Gen. John W. Geary wrote his wife: "Ward & [Alpheus] Williams both drink too much, and neither could be trusted." J. W. G. to Mary [Geary], April 23, 1865, J. W. Geary Papers, HSPA.

37. C. H. Dickinson Diary, March 19, 1865, C. H. Dickinson Papers, SHSW. Sergeant Charles Dickinson accurately transcribed General Ward's rustic mode of speech. During the Battle of Averasboro, New York *Herald* journalist E. D. Westfall overheard a conversation between Generals Williams and Ward, whom Westfall referred to as the "rough b'ar of Kentucky." When Williams told Ward not to press the Confederates too hard, Ward replied that he "would not hit anybody without they struck first." See Westfall, "Battle of Bentonville [sic]."

38. C. H. Dickinson Diary, March 19, 1865, C. H. Dickinson Papers, SHSW.

39. Westfall, "Battle of Bentonsville [sic]"; C. H. Dickinson Diary, March 19, 1865, C. H. Dickinson Papers, SHSW.

40. Halsey, *A Yankee Private's Civil War*, pp. 189-190; Ezra W. Button Diary, March 19, 1865, John B. Tripp Papers, SHSW; C. H. Dickinson Diary, March 19, 1865, C. H. Dickinson Papers, SHSW; McIntosh, "Annals," pp. 211-212, McIntosh Papers, SHSW; McBride, *Thirty-Third Indiana*, p. 173; Brant, *Eighty-Fifth Indiana*, p. 106; *OR* 47, pt. 1, pp. 809, 816, 818. The mileage estimates vary greatly among Ward's troops. Their relative positions in the column would account for some of the difference—the estimates of the men who were understandably prone to exaggerate would probably account for the rest.

41. Halsey, *A Yankee Private's Civil War*, p. 190; Ford, *Life*, p. 58.

42. C. H. Dickinson Diary, March 19, 1865, C. H. Dickinson Papers, SHSW.

43. Ibid; Halsey, *A Yankee Private's Civil War*, p. 190; Fox, "Bentonville," July 1, 1886, and "Bentonville," May 7, 1896; Bradley, *Star Corps*, p. 273.

44. *OR* 47, pt. 1, p. 537.

45. Clark, *Stars and Bars*, pp. 193-195 *passim*,

46. *OR* 47, pt. 1, pp. 1107, 1109.

47. Ford, *Life*, pp. 57-58; Ford, "A March"; Ford, "Last Battles," p. 142; *OR* 47, pt. 1, pp. 666-667; Luvaas, "Johnston's Last Stand," p. 347.

48. Toombs, *Reminiscences*, p. 215; *OR* 47, pt. 1, pp. 645, 671.

49. Ford, *Life*, p. 58; Ford, "Last Battles," p. 142; Ford, "A March"; Sanders, "Battle of Bentonville," p. 299; Ravenel, "Ask the Survivors," p. 124; Robbins, "Autobiography," p. 16, H. C. Robbins Papers, SHSW; Earle, "Sherman's March," [n.p.], Civil War Misc. Coll., USAMHI.

50. Hendrick, "Bentonville."

51. Ford, *Life*, pp. 58-59; Fox, "Bentonville," July 1, 1886, and "Bentonville," May 7, 1896.

52. *OR* 47, pt. 1, p. 666; Elmore, "A Comrade"; Robbins, "Autobiography," p. 16, H. C. Robbins Papers, SHSW.

53. Toombs, *Reminiscences*, pp. 215-216; Devor, "Twentieth Corps at Bentonville"; *OR* 47, pt. 1, pp. 645, 671-672; J. W. Brown Diary, March 19, 1865, Private Papers, Mf Drawer 187, Reel 13, GADAH; Ford, *Life*, p. 59; Ford, "Last Battles," p. 142; Ford, "A March"; Ravenel, "Boy Brigade," p. 418; Sanders, "Battle of Bentonville," p. 299; Sanders, "More About," p. 460; W. F. Colcock to Father, March 25, 1865, in the possession of George Slaton, Wilmington, NC.

54. Ravenel, "Boy Brigade," p. 418; J. W. Brown Diary, March 19, 1865, Private Papers, Mf Drawer 187, Reel 13, GADAH; Ford, *Life*, p. 59; Ford, "A March."

55. Inglesby, *First South Carolina Artillery*, pp. 18-19; W. F. Colcock to Father, March 25, 1865. The Gist Guard Artillery was also called Manigault's Battalion, and was commanded by Capt. Theodore Boag. According to Inglesby, "Boag was recommended for promotion to a Majority" on the basis of his excellent showing at Bentonville, but the war ended before the recommendation could be acted upon.

56. Bates, "Battle of Bentonville," pp. 148-149.

57. *OR* 47, pt. 1, pp. 666-667; Elmore, "A Comrade"; W. F. Colcock to Father, March 25, 1865; Committee, *143rd New York*, pp. 45-46; Morhous, *123rd New York*, pp. 170-171.

58. C. H. Dickinson Diary, March 19, 1865, C. H. Dickinson Paper, SHSW; McIntosh, "Annals," McIntosh Papers, SHSW. Just before the assault, New York *Herald* reporter E. D. Westfall saw the "decidedly cool" Slocum sitting under a tree on the Morris farm. See Westfall, "Battle of Bentonsville [sic]."

In addition to directing Dustin's movements, General Slocum also sent a staff officer to Lieutenant Colonel Langley with orders that Fearing's brigade line be "thrown back about seventy-five yards," Langley reported. "This direction I could not obey, even if the point selected by him had been more advisable, for the main line of the enemy at this moment vigorously assaulted my works." *OR* 47, pt. 1, pp. 537-538.

59. Robbins, "Autobiography," pp. 16-17, H. C. Robbins Papers, SHSW; *OR* 47, pt. 1, pp. 667, 854; Fox, "Bentonville," May 7, 1896; Hendrick, "Bentonville"; King, "Fighting at Bentonville"; C. H. Dickinson Diary, March 19, 1865, C. H. Dickinson Papers, SHSW.

60. Goundrey, "Battle of Bentonville."

61. J. W. Brown Diary, Private Papers, Mf Drawer 187, Reel 13, GADAH; Hendrick, "Bentonville"; [C. W. Hutson] to Em, March 21, 1865, C. W. Hutson Papers, SHC-UNC.

62. McIntosh, "Annals," pp. 212-213, McIntosh Papers, SHSW; *OR* 47, pt. 1, p. 809.

63. Robertson, *Michigan in the War*, p. 506; *OR* 47, pt. 1, p. 595.

64. Ibid., pp. 790, 873, 880, 905; Grunert, *One-Hundred and Twenty-Ninth Illinois*, p. 219.

65. Hendrick, "Bentonville." Artilleryman Hendrick wrote that Capt. Charles Winegar's battery (Battery I, 1st New York) was the second XX Corps battery to unlimber on the Morris farm, but the corps' ordnance report indicates that on March 19, 1865, Winegar's battery fired 56 rounds, whereas Newkirk's battery fired 133. It is therefore probable that Newkirk's battery unlimbered before Winegar's.

66. Robbins, "Autobiography," p. 17, H, C. Robbins Papers, SHSW; *OR* 47, pt. 1, p. 667; Grunert, *One-Hundred and Twenty-Ninth Illinois*, p. 219.

67. Whaley, "Short Account," pp. 33-34, E. M. Whaley Papers, DU; James Stuart quoted in Barnwell, *Story*, pp. 196-197; C. Woodward Hutson to Sister [Journal-Letter], March 21, 1865, C. W. Hutson Papers, SHC-UNC.

68. W. F. Colcock to Father, March 25, 1865; Hendrick, "Bentonville"; *OR* 47, pt. 1, pp. 575, 577.

69. Inglesby, *First South Carolina Artillery*, p. 19. Lieutenant Colcock stated that there were only two charges. See W. F. Colcock to Father, March 25, 1865. For a sampling of the Federal estimates, see *OR* 47, pt. 1, pp. 587, 667; ibid., pt. 2, p. 909; Grunert, *One-Hundred and Twenty-Ninth Illinois*, p. 220; Ezra Button

Diary, March 19, 1865, John B. Tripp Papers, SHSW; C. H. Dickinson Diary, March 19, 1865, C. H. Dickinson Papers, SHSW; Halsey, *A Yankee Private's Civil War*, p. 193; Bradley, *Star Corps*, p. 273; Elmore, "A Comrade." One Federal eyewitness counted no fewer than *nine* distinct charges. See Sam to Maggie, March 26, 1865, S. K. Harryman Papers, INSL.

70. Hendrick, "Bentonville"; Bryant, *Third Wisconsin*, p. 323; Coggins, *Arms and Equipment*, p. 76.

71. Westfall, "Battle of Bentonsville [sic]." "The most violent attack was made as the sun was setting," reported Brig. Gen. Nathaniel J. Jackson, the commander of the First Division, XX Corps. *OR* 47, pt. 1, p. 601.

72. Ravenel, "Ask the Survivors," p. 124; Ravenel, "Boy Brigade," p. 417.

73. Coggins, *Arms and Equipment*, p. 76; Quaife, *From the Cannon's Mouth*, pp. 129, 386.

74. Westfall, "Battle of Bentonsville [sic]"; Charlie to Mother & Etta, April 18, 1865, C. S. Brown Papers, DU; McIntosh, "Annals," p. 212, McIntosh Papers, SHSW.

75. Ravenel, "Ask the Survivors," p. 124; Westfall, "Battle of Bentonsville [sic]."

76. Ravenel, "Ask the Survivors," p. 124; Ravenel, "Boy Brigade," p. 417.

77. James Stuart quoted in Barnwell, *Story*, p. 196; G. B. Gardner to Wife, [n.d.], Mf Drawer 283, Reel 25, Civil War Miscellany—Personal Papers, GADAH.

78. *OR* 47, pt. 1, p. 1107.

79. Clark, *Stars and Bars*, p. 195.

80. *OR* 47, pt. 1, p. 1107.

81. Fort, "First Georgia Regulars," p. 27, *CWTI* Coll., USAMHI. "I saw the fewest men running out of battle I have ever seen while [we were] lying in the rear as reinforcements," recalled Sgt. W. H. Andrews of the Regulars. "While everyone knows that the Confederacy is on its last legs, still our boys fight as desperate as ever." See Andrews, *Footprints*, p. 174.

82. Johnston, *Narrative*, pp. 388-389; Thomas B. Roy Diary, March 19, 1865; Westfall, "Battle of Bentonsville [sic]."

83. Ibid; Bartley, "Fighting at Bentonville."

84. *OR* 47, pt. 1, pp. 1059-1060; ibid., pt. 2, p. 909; *OR* 47, pt. 3, p. 716. At Bentonville, Taliaferro's Division sustained 31 killed, 166 wounded and 126 missing, for a total of 323 casualties. The final casualty list for Taliaferro's Division indicates 809 killed, wounded and missing for Rhett's Brigade and Elliott's Brigade from March 13 to March 29, 1865, but does not specify where and on what day the casualties occurred. Moreover, Livermore's assumption that all of Taliaferro's casualties at Bentonville occurred on March 19 is incorrect. A substantial number of Taliaferro's troops were captured on the morning of March 22. See Livermore, *Numbers and Losses*, p. 135, n. 3; Inglesby, *First South Carolina Artillery*, p. 19. Given the cryptic nature and incomplete status of the returns filed for Taliaferro's Division, it is impossible to be more precise regarding Confederate casualties.

85. Ibid., Halsey, *A Yankee Private's Civil War*, p. 192.

Chapter Thirteen: *May God in His Mercy Spare Us All to Meet Again*

1. McLaws Order Book, March 19, 1865, McLaws Papers, SHC-UNC; *OR* 47, pt. 2, pp. 1069, 1397; Albright, "Seventy-Seventh Regiment," 4, pp. 101-103, in Clark, *Histories*.

2. *OR* 47, pt. 1, p. 527.

3. Ibid.

4. Powell, "Additional Sketch Tenth Battalion," 4, p. 336, and Albright, "Seventy-Seventh Regiment," 4, p. 104, in Clark, *Histories*; Powell, "Last Days," pp. 7-8, NCC-UNC.

5. *OR* 47, pt. 1, p. 527. Major Robinson reported that the Rebel lieutenant belonged to the "Tenth North Carolina *Regiment*" (italics mine), but that is an understandable slip. In his article, "The Last Chance of the Confederacy," Alexander McClurg credited General Mitchell with organizing the ambush of Hardy's Brigade. McClurg confused the facts, however, by spelling Hardy's name *Hardee*, and by placing the Tarheel colonel in command of Colquitt's Georgia Brigade. It is also improbable that the "bright young fellow" sent by Hardy to deliver a message to the nearest Confederate commanding officer could have gotten past Mitchell's pickets and one of Mitchell's staff officers without first being told to identify himself. Yet that is what McClurg would have us believe. "Colonel Hardee [sic] presents his compliments to you," the Confederate staff officer began, "and asks that you will apprise your line that he is forming in your front to charge the Yankee lines on your left." A flabbergasted Mitchell thereupon commended the unwitting Rebel staff officer to his brigade provost marshal, then repulsed the advancing Confederates with a single devastating volley. McClurg knew how to tell a good story, but Major Robinson's report is more credible. McClurg's tale is so compelling that it was repeated in several Union regimental histories. See Osborn, *Trials and Triumphs*, pp. 202-203; McClurg, "Last Chance," p. 397. The historian of the 34th Illinois mentions two incidents of mistaken identity involving several officers and men from Colquitt's Brigade similar to the incident related by Major Robinson. Perhaps McClurg combined elements of these various incidents into one story. See Payne, *Thirty-Fourth Illinois*, p. 203.

6. Albright, "Seventy-Seventh Regiment," 4, pp. 104-105, Ellington, "Fiftieth Regiment," 3, p. 198, and Powell, "Additional Sketch," 4, p. 336, in Clark, *Histories*; *OR* 47, pt. 1, p. 527.

7. Ellington, "Fiftieth Regiment," 3, p. 198, in Clark, *Histories*. Major Robinson reported that his men also found three Confederate dead in their front. *OR* 47, pt. 1, pp. 527-528.

8. William E. Sloan Diary, March 19, 1865, Confederate Coll., Box 7, TNSLA. Concerning this incident, the regimental historian of the 50th North Carolina wrote: "At the first volley every man fell to the ground and Colonel Wortham and Lieutenant Lane, of the Fiftieth, and Lieutenant Powell, of the Tenth Battalion, crawled out of the thicket and reported to General McLaws for duty, stating that the entire brigade was killed or wounded." See Ellington, "Fiftieth Regiment," 3, p. 198, in Clark, *Histories*.

9. *OR* 47, pt. 1, p. 733; Powell, "Additional Sketch," 4, p. 334, and Albright, "Seventy-Seventh Regiment," 4, p. 105, in Clark, *Histories*.

10. McLaws Order Book, March 19, 1865, McLaws Papers, SHC-UNC.

11. Johnston, *Narrative*, p. 389; Hoole, *Forty-Sixth Alabama*, p. 38; Dacus, *First Arkansas Mounted Rifles*, [n.p.].

12. J. E. Johnston to R. F. Hoke, January 27, 1871, Robert F. Hoke Papers, NCDAH.

13. Hagood, *Memoirs*, pp. 360-361; *OR* 47, pt. 1, p. 1091. The lack of after-action reports from Bragg, Hoke and Hoke's brigade commanders forced me to rely

almost exclusively on the reports of their Federal counterparts to trace the events that transpired on this part of the field.

14. Hardee and Stewart also failed to file reports on the battle. After the war Hardee wrote his "Memoranda of the Operations of My Corps" in response to a request from Johnston, who at the time was writing his *Narrative*. Hardee's account, however, is a mere outline and leaves many questions unanswered. As previously stated, we know that Hardee commanded the right, and Stewart the center, of the army, but we know little else about Stewart's role in the battle. See Thomas B. Roy Diary, March 19, 1865; Hardee, "Memoranda," March 19, 1865, JO 483, J. E. Johnston Papers, HEHL; Johnston, *Narrative*, pp. 387, 583; Ridley, *Battles and Sketches*, p. 452.

15. McLaws Order Book, March 19, 1865, McLaws Papers, SHC-UNC.

16. Luvaas, "Johnston's Last Stand," p. 356.

17. *OR* 47, pt. 1, pp. 1128-1131 *passim*; Johnston, *Narrative*, p. 389.

18. *OR* 47, pt. 1, pp. 1092-1093; D. H. Hill to Daughter, March 23, 1865, D. H. Hill Papers, USAMHI.

19. C. Woodward Hutson to Sister [Letter-Journal], March 1865, "On the march from Fayetteville," C. W. Hutson Papers, SHC-UNC.

20. Westfall, "Battle of Bentonsville [sic]"; *OR* 47, pt. 1, pp. 450, 453, 468-469; Hinson, "Bentonville"; Carlin, "Military Memoirs," July 30, 1885.

21. Carlin, "Battle of Bentonsville [sic]," Cincinnati *Daily Gazette*, September 11, 1882; Carlin, "Military Memoirs," July 30, 1885; Carlin, "Battle of Bentonville," MOLLUS-OH, 3, pp. 240-243, 246. In his MOLLUS article, Carlin claimed to have discovered the effect of his delaying action upon the Confederate advance when he read the following quotation from Johnston's *Narrative* (p. 388): "Some distance in the rear there was a very thick wood of young pines, into which the Federal troops were pursued, and in which they rallied and renewed the fight." But it is doubtful that Johnston and his men would have mistaken Carlin's eight-man squad for a line of battle.

22. Carlin, "Military Memoirs" July 30, 1885; Carlin, "Battle of Bentonville," MOLLUS-OH, 3, pp. 246-247.

23. Carlin, "Battle of Bentonsville," [sic] Cincinnati *Daily Gazette*, September 11, 1882; Carlin, "Military Memoirs," July 30, 1885, and August 6, 1885; Carlin, "Battle of Bentonville," MOLLUS-OH, 3, pp. 241, 245; *OR* 47, pt. 1, p. 449; W. P. Carlin to M. H. Fitch, May 27, 1865, in Fitch, *Echoes*, p. 266. "Buell was not driven back," Carlin asserted in 1889. "He had, without order or authority, directed his brigade to fall back." Given the circumstances, Carlin drew too fine a distinction between falling back and being driven back. Carlin was in fact fortunate that Buell fell back when he did.

24. Cox, *March to the Sea*, pp. 197-198. How great was the sacrifice? Carlin's division suffered 453 casualties on the 19th. Of that number, Carlin lost one brigade commander wounded and two regimental commanders killed. Buell's brigade alone suffered 205 casualties, or nearly one-third of its 630 officers and men. *OR* 47, pt. 1, pp. 71, 76, 449-450.

25. Wiseman, "Bentonville."

26. Carlin, "Battle of Bentonville," MOLLUS-OH, 3, p. 239; W. F., "10th Michigan Cavalry [sic]," Detroit *Advertiser and Tribune*, April 5, 1865; Hatch, "From Savannah to Goldsboro," Quincy[, IL] *Daily Whig and Republican*, April 7, 1865.

27. Amann, *Personnel*, 2, pp. 7, 15. The brevets that Carlin and Morgan received from March 19, 1865, were for their service in the U. S. Volunteers. Carlin also received an equivalent promotion by brevet in the Regular Army, which

dated from March 13, 1865. *OR* 47, pt. 3, pp. 372, 476; W. P. Carlin to W. T. Sherman, April 21, 1865, W. T. Sherman Papers, LC; Carlin, "Military Memoirs," August 6, 1885.

28. Fox, "Bentonville," July 1, 1886; Wiseman, "Bentonville."

29. Hinkley, *Third Wisconsin*, p. 172; Elmore, "A Comrade."

30. Luvaas, "Johnston's Last Stand," pp. 354-355.

31. Livermore, *Numbers and Losses*, pp. 134-135; *OR* 47, pt. 1, pp. 27, 43, 71-76, 1057-1060; *OR* 47, pt. 2, p. 1408; Johnston, *Narrative*, p. 393. There are numerous discrepancies in the casualty figures, particularly on the Confederate side: Livermore's total (2,118) is too high, whereas Johnston's (1,915) is too low. Nor are the *Official Records* very helpful, since the Confederate casualty list for March 19 lacks a figure for Hardee's Corps.

The Union casualty total is less problematic, though the figure cited by Sherman (1,186) is higher than Slocum's final tally (1,144). Slocum's casualty figure was for all three days of the battle, but his losses on March 20-21 were light. Livermore's estimate (1,103) for March 19 is close to the mark.

In calculating the number of Confederate troops present at Bentonville on March 19, I consulted Johnston's field return on p. 1057 of *OR* 47, pt. 1. I added 500 troops of Bate's command who reached the army the day after the field return, and arrived at a total of 15,413 effectives. If Dibrell's Division of cavalry is added to that total, it gives the Confederates about 16,200 effectives. Historian Wilbur S. Nye estimated that Johnston had "not less than 25,000 men. . .in action on the 19th." This figure is far too high. Nye credited Johnston with having 6,000 cavalry at Bentonville, which "Old Joe" must have pulled out of thin air. See Nye, "Battle of Bentonville," NCC-UNC.

Although Kilpatrick's cavalry took no part in the fighting at Bentonville, it provided Slocum with a 4,000-man reserve.

32. William Humphrey Diary, March 19, 1865, Chicago Pub. Lib.; P. B. Buckingham to Wife, March 26, 1865, P. B. Buckingham Papers, Box 1, AAS.

33. *OR* 47, pt. 1, p. 75; Chapman, *Civil War Diary*, p. 113.

34. Abner C. Smith to Wife, March 23, 1865, and Chas. N. Lyman to Mrs. Abner C. Smith 2nd, March 29, 1865, Abner C. Smith Letters, CTSL.

35. *OR* 47, pt. 1, pp. 826, 834; P. B. Buckingham to Wife, March 26, 1865, P. B. Buckingham Papers, Box 1, AAS.

36. *OR* 47, pt. 1, p. 441; Hamilton, *Recollections*, p. 194. Hamilton's quotation ends with this statement: "The legs of the infantry could be distinguished from those of the cavalry by the size of their calves, as the march of 1,000 miles had increased the size of one and diminished the size of the other." A telling comparison, but for one fact: there were no casualties among the Union cavalry at Bentonville. *OR* 47, pt. 1, pp. 75-76.

37. Hamilton, *Recollections*, p. 194.

38. Harper Family Genealogy, Bentonville Battleground State Hist. Site; 1860 Census-Johnston County, Battle of Bentonville File, Johnston County Pub. Lib.; Jordan, *NC Troops*, 6, p. 505; Smithfield[, NC] *Herald*, September 13, 1927; Hill, *Confederate Military History: North Carolina*, 5, p. 532; "Harper House," National Register of Historic Places Study.

39. Bates, "Battle of Bentonville," pp. 150-151.

40. A. Q. Porter Diary, March 19, 1865, A. Q. Porter Coll., LC.

41. D. H. Reynolds Diary, March 19-20, 1865, D. H. Reynolds Papers, UAK-F.

42. [Curry], "A History of Company B," pp. 219-220.

43. Johnson, "Marching, Camping, Fighting," L. P. Thomas Scrapbooks, 2, p. 148, L. P. Thomas Papers, AHS; Johnson, "Closing Days," May 29, 1902.

44. Ford, *Life*, pp. 59-60; Ford, "Last Battles," p. 142; Ford, "A March."

45. *OR* 47, pt. 1, pp. 1095, 1107; J. W. Brown Diary, March 19, 1865, Private Papers, Mf Drawer 187, Reel 13, GADAH.

46. Westfall, "Battle of Bentonsville [sic]"; *OR* 47, pt. 2, pp. 903-906 *passim*. See MS map H-280, No. 9, RG 77, NA–Cartographic Branch, Alexandria, VA, for penciled-in location of Slocum's headquarters; it is marked by a "Δ" (pyramid symbol) and is labeled, "Hd Qrs Army of Ga." This correction was not made on the map that appeared in the *OR Atlas* as Plate 79, No. 4.

47. J. T. Holmes to [J. B.] Work, September 20, 1901, Box 3, Vol. 3: "Correspondence File, Vol. 6, September-June, 1901-1902," J. T. Holmes Papers, OHS; Holmes, *52d O.V.I.*, p. 25.

48. J. T. Holmes to [J. B.] Work, September 20, 1901, Box 3, Vol. 3: "Correspondence File, Vol. 6, September-June, 1901-1902," J. T. Holmes Papers, OHS. Holmes' correspondent, Julius Birney Work (himself a veteran of the 52nd Ohio), was a publisher who must have found Holmes' letter too provocative to ignore. "The Bentonville story would hardly do to publish in the broken and imperfect form given it in my hurried letter," Holmes answered Work. "That was a mere sketch on my knee, truthful but not full. . .with no thought of publication." Work was persistent, as this subsequent reply from Holmes attests: "The reasons against the publication of the Bentonville letter are still in full force. . . .*Don't do it*." See op. cit., J. T. Holmes to [J. B.] Work, October 22, 1901, and March 12, 1902.

Chapter Fourteen: *The Army is Coming to You as Fast as Possible*

1. Strong, "Battle of Bentonville," March 19, 1865 entry from "Extracts from Journal," W. E. Strong Papers, ILSHL; Harwell, *Fiery Trail*, p. 192; Sladen, "Official Diary," March 19, 1865.

2. Howard, *Autobiography*, 2, p. 143; Howard, "Marching Through Georgia," March 19, 1896; Strong, "Battle of Bentonville," March 19, 1865 entry from "Extracts from Journal," W. E. Strong Papers, ILSHL; *OR* 47, pt. 1, pp. 205.

3. Ibid; Sladen, "Official Diary," March 19, 1865; Howard, *Autobiography*, 2, p. 143; Harwell, *Fiery Trail*, p. 192; *OR* 47, pt. 1, pp. 205-206; Strong, "Battle of Bentonville," March 19, 1865 entry from "Extracts from Journal," W. E. Strong Papers, ILSHL. Howard's and Strong's accounts conflict in one crucial area: Strong wrote that Howard ordered him to seize Cox's Crossroads *before* receiving word from Sherman, whereas Howard reported that he sent Strong to the crossroads *after* Sherman had notified him that Slocum faced only a small force of enemy cavalry.

4. Harwell, *Fiery Trail*, pp. 192-193; *OR* 47, pt. 1, p. 206; Howard, *Autobiography*, 2, p. 143; Howard, "Marching Through Georgia," March 19, 1896. Like Slocum, Howard at first believed that Johnston's only avenue of retreat was via Cox's bridge.

5. Strong, "Battle of Bentonville," March 19, 1865 entry from "Extracts from Journal," W. E. Strong Papers, ILSHL; *OR* 47, pt. 1, p. 206.

6. Brown, *Fourth Minnesota*, p. 391; *OR* 47, pt. 1, pp. 25, 205-206,; ibid., pt. 2, p. 904; Strong, "Battle of Bentonville," March 19, 1865 entry from "Extracts from Journal," W. E. Strong Papers, ILSHL; Sladen, "Official Diary," March 19, 1865; Harwell, *Fiery Trail*, p. 193.

7. Foraker, *Notes*, 1, p. 63; Slocum, "Sherman's March," p. 693; *OR* 47, pt. 2, pp. 903-904.

8. Foraker, *Notes*, 1, p. 63; Slocum, "Sherman's March," p. 693; *OR* 47, pt. 1, pp. 25, 206, 383; ibid., pt. 2, pp. 899, 901-902, 905, 909-910, 912-913; Howard, *Autobiography*, 2, pp. 143-144.

9. Harwell, *Fiery Trail*, p. 193.

10. Strong, "Battle of Bentonville," March 19, 1865 entry from "Extracts from Journal," W. E. Strong Papers, ILSHL; McClurg, "Last Chance," p. 399.

11. Strong "Battle of Bentonville," March 19, 1865 entry from "Extracts from Journal," W. E. Strong Papers, ILSHL; *OR* 47, pt. 2, pp. 905-906, 918.

12. Alexander, *Ninety-Seventh Indiana*, p. 24; Wright, *Sixth Iowa*, p. 429; Harwell, *Fiery Trail*, p. 192.

13. *OR* 47, pt. 1, p. 321; ibid., pt. 2, pp. 916, 1436; Wharton, "Sixty-Seventh Regiment," 3, pp. 708-709, in Clark, *Histories*; Pepper, "Army Correspondence," [Columbus,] *Ohio State Journal*, April 8, 1865.

14. *OR* 47, pt. 1, p. 321; ibid., pt. 2, p. 916.

15. Ibid., pt. 1, p. 321; Wharton, "Sixty-Seventh Regiment," 3, p. 709, in Clark, *Histories*; Pepper, "Army Correspondence," [Columbus,] *Ohio State Journal*, April 8, 1865.

16. *OR* 47, pt. 1, pp. 235, 246; ibid., pt. 2, p. 914; Wright, *Sixth Iowa*, p. 429.

17. Warner, *Generals in Blue*, pp. 571-572; Nichols, *Story*, pp. 272-273.

18. Sladen, "Official Diary," March 20, 1865.

19. Coggins, *Arms and Equipment*, pp. 35-36; Winther, *With Sherman to the Sea*, pp. 157-158.

20. Alexander, *Ninety-Seventh Indiana*, p. 24; *OR* 47, pt. 1, p. 259.

21. Sherlock, *One Hundredth Indiana*, pp. 208-209; Wright, *Sixth Iowa*, p. 430; Harwell, *Fiery Trail*, p. 195; *OR* 47, pt. 1, pp. 26, 259; Sherman, *Memoirs*, 2, p. 304.

22. *OR* 47, pt. 1, pp. 1129, 1131; Guild, *Fourth Tennessee Cavalry*, pp. 130-131; Monnett, "Awfulest Time," p. 287.

23. *OR* 47, pt. 1, pp. 259, 262; Sherlock, *One Hundredth Indiana*, p. 209; [Rose], "Tour of the Battlefield," p. 3, Bentonville Battleground; Sketch map showing the position of the XV Corps near Bentonville, March 20, 1865, File Z12-199, RG 77, NA Cart. Branch.

24. Ibid., pp. 209-210; Winther, *With Sherman to the Sea*, pp. 158-159; Alexander, *Ninety-Seventh Indiana*, p. 24; Hubert, *Fiftieth Illinois*, p. 370.

25. Winther, *With Sherman to the Sea*, p. 159.

26. *OR* 47, pt. 1, pp. 262-263; Sherlock, *One Hundredth Indiana*, p. 210.

27. Sherlock, *One Hundredth Indiana*, pp. 210-211; *OR* 47, pt. 1, pp. 26, 235; Harwell, *Fiery Trail*, p. 195. Captain Sherlock wrote that his regiment routed Hagood's Brigade, but Hagood in fact opposed the Hoosiers with only a skirmish line. Hagood's Brigade suffered a total of eight casualties (all wounded) on March 20. *OR* 47, pt. 1, p. 1080.

28. Hampton, "Battle of Bentonville," p. 704; Johnston, *Narrative*, p. 389; E. M. Law to Stokes, March 26, 1865, Mss2 L4109 a 1, Virginia Hist. Soc.; *OR* 47, pt. 2, p. 1443.

29. Warner, *Generals in Gray*, pp. 174-175; *OR* 47, pt. 2, pp. 998, 1207, 1320; E. M. Law to Stokes, March 26, 1865, Mss2 L4109 a 1, Virginia Hist. Soc. Before assuming command of Butler's Brigade, General Law briefly commanded the remounted detachment of that brigade. See Holmes, "Dismounted Battalion," pp. 381-382.

30. *OR* 47, pt. 2, p. 1443; Warner, *Generals in Gray*, pp. 174-175.

31. Johnston, *Narrative*, p. 389; *OR* 47, pt. 1, pp. 1129, 1131.

32. *OR* 47, pt. 1, pp. 505-506.

33. Ibid., pp. 497, 499, 505-506.

34. Ibid., pp. 499, 505-506.

35. Ibid., p. 1091; Halcott Pride Jones Journal, March 20, 1865, NCDAH; Calder Diary, March 20, 1865, Calder Papers, DU; Broadfoot, "Seventieth Regiment," in Clark, *Histories*. Both Grummond and Lund counted only four Confederate cannon, perhaps because one section of the battery was concealed from their view. Captain Myers counted only *three* guns. *OR* 47, pt. 1, pp. 499, 505-507. Yet Robertson, *Michigan in the War*, p. 351, mentions a six-gun battery.

36. *OR* 47, pt. 1, pp. 499, 505-507; Elliott, "Martin-Kirkland Brigade," 4, p. 548, in Clark, *Histories*.

37. Ibid.

38. Rose, "Sixty-Sixth Regiment," 3, pp. 698-699, and Elliott, "Martin-Kirkland Brigade," 4, p. 548, in Clark, *Histories*.

39. *OR* 47, pt. 1, pp. 499-500; *Report of the Adjutant General-Illinois*, 2, p. 37.

40. *OR* 47, pt. 1, p. 507.

41. Ibid., pp. 72, 504-505. Grummond stated that his loss on March 20 was 27 casualties, but this includes the losses for the 14th Michigan only. Judging from Captain Lund's report, the 16th Illinois' loss was comparable to the 14th Michigan's. Grummond's claim of 100 prisoners is exaggerated. Even if *all* of Hoke's wounded and missing for March 20 had fallen into Grummond's hands, they would have amounted to no more than 60 prisoners. See ibid., p. 1080.

42. Nevin, *Old West: The Soldiers*, pp. 136-143; "Fetterman Massacre," pp. 131-132.

43. Ibid., pp. 288, 294, 424, 436, 450, 554; Hazen, *Narrative*, p. 366.

44. *OR* 47, pt. 1, pp. 274, 283, 551-552, 567, 694; Hazen, *Narrative*, p. 366.

45. C. M. Hopper Letter-Journal, March 19, 1865, C. M. Hopper Papers, SHC-UNC.

46. John W. Reid to Will, March 28, 1865, W. G. McCreary Papers, DU; *OR* 47, pt. 1, pp. 74, 694. Geary's division sustained no casualties at Bentonville.

47. *OR* 47, pt. 1, pp. 436, 552, 554; ibid., pt. 2, p. 920.

48. W. C. Johnson Journal, March 19, 1865, LC.

49. *OR* 47, pt. 1, pp. 552, 554; John D. Inskeep Diary, March 20, 1865, OHS; Angle, *Three Years*, p. 386.

50. *OR* 47, pt. 1, pp. 436, 554, 588, 649, 653, 785, 809, 816; Angle, *Three Years*, p. 386; John D. Inskeep Diary, March 20, 1865, OHS.

51. W. C. Johnson Journal, March 20, 1865, LC.

52. *OR* 47, pt. 1, pp. 575, 581; William B. Miller Journal, March 20, 1865, INHS.

53. *OR* 47, pt. 1, pp. 563, 567; "Brother Judson" to Sister, March 29, 1865, Box 1, J. W. Bishop Papers, MNHS; Hills, "Second Minnesota," July 27, 1899.

54. Ibid.

55. *OR* 47, pt. 1, pp. 436, 552, 554-555; ibid., pt. 2, p. 920; William B. Miller Journal, March 20, 1865, INHS.

56. *OR* 47, pt. 1, pp. 288, 294; Edward E. Schweitzer Diary, March 20, 1865, *CWTI* Coll., USAMHI.

57. *OR* 47, pt. 1, p. 267.

58. Corbin, *A Star*, pp. 457-458; *OR* 47, pt. 1, 267, 288.

59. Edward E. Schweitzer Diary, March 20, 1865, *CWTI* Coll., USAMHI; *OR* 47, pt. 1, pp. 26, 67, 235, 267, 1080.

60. Ibid., pp. 288, 294; Edward E. Schweitzer Diary, March 20, 1865, *CWTI* Coll., USAMHI.

61. *OR* 47, pt. 1, pp. 321, 341, 343, 346, 354, 356, 358, 365-366, 368, 370.

62. Ibid., pp. 494, 497, 503, 512, 514, 517, 520, 528.

63. Ibid., pp. 93, 96, 383, 399, 409, 413, 414; ibid., pt. 2, p. 903; Sladen, "Official Diary," March 20, 1865; Hickenlooper Diary, March 19-20, 1865, Hickenlooper Family Coll., Cincinnati Hist. Soc.; Hickenlooper, "Reminiscences," p. 107, *CWTI* Coll., USAMHI; Jackson, *Colonel's Diary*, p. 199; Evans Diary, March 20, 1865, Evans Papers, WRHS. Of Colonel Montgomery's four regiments, the 25th Wisconsin accompanied Mower to Bentonville, while the 35th New Jersey, 43rd Ohio and 63rd Ohio remained with the trains.

64. *OR* 47, pt. 1, pp. 487, 494; Elias Perry Diary, March 20, 1865, WHMC-UMO; Rockwood Diary, March 20, 1865, WHMC-UMO; Sargeant, *Personal Recollections*, [n.p.]; Evans Diary, March 20, 1865, Evans Papers, WRHS; Kittelson [Leigram] Diary, March 20, 1865, Kittelson [Leigram] Papers, SHSW; Ferguson Diary, March 20, 1865, MacMurray College; Nilson Diary, March 20, 1865, Nilson Papers, INHS; Anders, *Eighteenth Missouri*, p. 316.

65. *OR* 47, pt. 1, pp. 487, 494; Edward E. Schweitzer Diary, March 20, 1865, *CWTI* Coll., USAMHI; Ferguson Diary, March 20, 1865, MacMurray College.

66. *OR* 47, pt. 1, p. 503.

67. Harwell, *Fiery Trail*, pp. 196, 199; C. H. Howard to E. Whittlesday, July 9, 1863, C. H. Howard Papers, BC; Howard, *Autobiography*, 2, pp. 148-149.

68. Howard, "Campaign of the Carolinas," p. 29. It *was* Howard's intention to send Hazen's division to Slocum's support, but as was stated earlier, Sherman countermanded Howard's order to Hazen. It was Sherman himself who finally ordered Hazen to Slocum's assistance. But Howard was right in one sense: the tables were turned on Slocum at Bentonville.

69. Harwell, *Fiery Trail*, p. 196; Howard, *Autobiography*, 2, pp. 148-149.

70. [Rose], "Tour of the Battlefield," p. 4, Bentonville Battleground. The precise location of General Johnston's headquarters is unknown. Johnston's dispatches for March 20-21 are of no help, for they are simply headed, "Near Bentonville." Nor do there appear to be any maps—either Federal or Confederate—of the battleground that mark Johnston's headquarters site. I have been unable to locate *any* Confederate maps of the Bentonville battlefield.

In a January 30, 1993, phone conversation with the author, historian Jay Luvaas recalled that local historian Herschel V. Rose (1887-1959) pointed to the former John Benton field east of Bentonville and stated that it had been the site of General Johnston's headquarters. This is also the location mentioned in Rose's brief manuscript guidebook entitled, "A Tour of the Battlefield." Rose was a native of Bentonville and an authority on the battle. Many of his relatives and acquaintances were present at Bentonville during the three-day engagement. Unless more substantial evidence should one day surface, Herschel Rose's statement must stand as the only lead we have in placing Johnston's headquarters site.

71. *OR* 47, pt. 1, p. 1440.

72. J. E. Johnston to G. T. Beauregard, March 21, 1865, J. E. Johnston Papers, Museum of the Confederacy.

73. Ibid; Luvaas, "Johnston's Last Stand," pp. 356-357.

74. *OR* 47, pt. 1, p. 1056.

75. McLaws Order Book, March 20, 1865, McLaws Papers, SHC-UNC. The map that accompanied General Slocum's report of the battle (drawn by H. M. McDowell—see *OR Atlas*, Plate 79, No. 4) places Taliaferro's works on the west side of the creek facing an open field. Except for a few rifle pits, I have found no trace of these works, if any ever existed. On the east side of the stream, however, a

line of works still remains, and like most of the battlefield, it lies on private property.

76. McLaws Order Book, March 20, 1865, McLaws Papers, SHC-UNC. McLaws did not mention this incident with Hardee in any contemporary letters or journal entries; rather, it appears in a recollection he wrote for Henry W. Graber, a veteran of his escort company—Company B of the renowned Terry Rangers (8th Texas Cavalry). McLaws recalled that one of his Rangers, a scout named Tom Paysinger, had come to his tent about 3:00 a.m. on the 20th and reported that the enemy was advancing on the Confederates' rear. See L. McLaws to Graber, April 9, 1897, in Graber, *A Terry Texas Ranger*, pp. 224-225. McLaws may also have been resentful because he suspected—correctly, as it turned out—that he would soon be relieved of command. See L. McLaws to Wife, March 23, 1865, McLaws Papers, SHC-UNC.

77. McLaws Order Book, March 16, 20, 1865, McLaws Papers, SHC-UNC. At Averasboro, for example, McLaws kept Blanchard's Brigade well behind the front lines guarding the wagons. In his order book entry for March 19, McLaws did not even mention Blanchard's Brigade, most likely because it took no part in the day's fighting. Furthermore, General Blanchard had retained his command solely because a March 9, 1865, War Department directive relieving him of command had not yet reached Johnston's headquarters. See Albert Blanchard to J. C. Breckinridge, April 1, 1865, Letters Recd. by Confed. Secy. of War (Mf), NA.

78. McLaws Order Book, March 20, 1865, McLaws Papers, SHC-UNC; L. McLaws to Graber, April 9, 1897, in Graber, A *Terry Texas Ranger*, pp. 224-225. McLaws recalled that General Hardee himself rode up and gave him the order.

79. McLaws Order Book, March 20, 1865, McLaws Papers, SHC-UNC; *OR* 47, pt. 2, p. 1443. The Union foraging party that Hampton was referring to may have been a battalion of the 8th Indiana Cavalry commanded by Capt. Justice G. Crowell. See ibid., pt. 1, p. 871.

80. McLaws Order Book, March 20, 1865, McLaws Papers, SHC-UNC; Hagood, *Memoirs*, pp. 361-362; *OR* 47, pt. 1, pp. 235, 341; [Rose], "Tour of the Battlefield," p. 2, Bentonville Battleground.

81. *OR* 47, pt. 1, p. 1097; ibid., pt. 2, p. 1444; Darst, "Robert Hodges, Jr.," p. 39. Granbury's Brigade may have arrived at Bentonville late on the night of March 19. One of the brigade's probable locations on March 20 was on the Confederate right, in rear of Blanchard's Brigade. According to one Texan, General Johnston placed Granbury's Brigade "in rear of a Brigade of S. C. reserve State Cadets which he thought rather unable to trust in front."

Cumming's Brigade had become separated from Stevenson's Division while opposing Sherman's advance through South Carolina in February 1865. The brigade was temporarily attached to Hardee's Corps, which it accompanied on the march from Charleston, South Carolina, to Averasboro, North Carolina. Cumming's Brigade then escorted Hardee's reserve artillery to Smithfield, where it arrived on March 19. See Davis, "Eighth Texas Cavalry," p. 184; *OR* 47, pt. 2, p. 1397.

82. McLaws Order Book, March 20, 1865, McLaws Papers, SHC-UNC; *OR* 47, pt. 1, p. 1131; ibid., pt. 2, p. 1443; W. W. Gordon Diary, March 20, 1865, Gordon Family Papers, SHC-UNC.

83. J. F. Waring Diary, March 20, 1865, SHC-UNC; Howard, *Autobiography*, 2, p. 147; *OR* 47, pt. 1, p. 206; ibid., pt. 2, p. 1443.

84. Ibid.; Smith, *Mason Smith Family Letters*, p. 172.

85. Of the approximately 4,000 cavalrymen under Hampton's command at Bentonville, 3,000 served in Wheeler's Cavalry Corps and 1,000 in Butler's

Division. *OR* 47, pt. 3, p. 707. Hampton's effective strength as of March 27, 1865, is the nearest estimate that we have.

86. Belknap, *Fifteenth Iowa*, p. 469; Brush Diary, March 20, 1865, Brush Family Papers, ILSHL; Wills, *Army Life*, p. 365. "Those who were on the Atlanta campaign are much reminded of the way things used to be then." Henry Hitchcock to Mary, March 21, 1865, Henry Hitchcock Papers, LC.

William Worth Belknap later served in President Grant's Cabinet as secretary of war, and was eventually compelled to resign or face impeachment on charges of corruption. Belknap tendered his resignation once it appeared certain that he would be convicted by the Senate. See Warner, *Generals in Blue*, p. 29.

87. Risedorph Diary, March 18-20, 1865, Risedorph Papers, MNHS.

88. *OR Atlas*, Plate 133, No. 2; Henry Hitchcock to Mary, March 21, 1865, Henry Hitchcock Papers, LC.

89. *OR* 47, pt. 2, pp. 922, 925.

90. Ibid., p. 919.

Chapter Fifteen: *As Exciting and Lively a P.M. As I Ever Saw*

1. Vett to Mother, March 21, 1865, S. C. Noble Papers, Ypsilanti Hist. Soc.

2. Sherman, *General and Special Field Orders*, pp. 200-201; *OR* 47, pt. 2, p. 930.

3. Ibid., pt. 2, p. 1447.

4. McLaws Order Book, March 20[-21], 1865, McLaws Papers, SHC-UNC; *OR* 47, pt. 1, p. 1131; Fort, "First Georgia Regulars," pp. 28-29; *CWTI* Coll., USAMHI; W. W. Gordon Diary, March 20-21, 1865, Gordon Family Papers, SHC-UNC.

5. McLaws Order Book, March 20[-21], 1865, McLaws Papers, SHC-UNC. Although McLaws had trouble connecting with Wheeler's cavalry on his left flank, there *was* a regiment of Anderson's cavalry brigade in his front on the morning of the 21st, whose commander warned him that the Federal skirmish line extended beyond his own. *OR* 47, pt. 2, p. 1448.

6. Ibid., p. 1447.

7. Fleharty, *Our Regiment*, pp. 161-162. The rumor probably sprang from a March 20 dispatch sent by General Williams to General Ward notifying him to have his division "in readiness to move at daybreak tomorrow." *OR* 47, pt. 2, p. 922.

8. O. M. Poe Diary, March 21, 1865, O. M. Poe Papers, LC; *OR* 47, pt. 2, pp. 936-938 *passim*.

9. Force Letterbook-Journal, March 21, 1865, and M. F. Force to Mr. Kebler, March 25, 1865, Force Papers, UWA.

10. Harwell, *Fiery Trail*, p. 198.

11. *OR* 47, pt. 2, p. 942.

12. W. T. Sherman Diary, March 21, 1865, W. T. Sherman Papers, UND; Nichols, *Story,* p. 267.

13. Henry Hitchcock to Mary, March 21, 1865, and April 5, 1865, Henry Hitchcock Papers, LC.

14. *OR* 47, pt. 2, p. 1446.

15. Ibid., pt. 1, pp. 588, 785, 797, 809, 816, 826, 838, 844-845, 1057; ibid., pt. 2, p. 922; Johnston, *Narrative*, p. 390.

16. *OR* 47, pt. 1, pp. 487, 494, 497, 500, 503, 505, 515.

17. Brooks, *Papers of Walter Clark*, 1, p. 136; Broadfoot, "Seventieth Regiment," 4, p. 21, and Hinsdale, "Seventy-Second Regiment," 4, p. 57, in Clark, *Histories*; *OR* 47, pt. 1, p. 505.

18. *OR* 47, pt. 1, p. 538.

19. Ibid; Holmes, *52d O.V.I.*, p. 25; Litvin, "Captain Burkhalter's Georgia War," *Voices*, 2, p. 539.

20. Ibid.

21. *OR* 47, pt. 1, p. 538.

22. Ibid., pp. 538, 601, 612, 624, 633, 667, 672, 679. Slocum may have changed his mind regarding this maneuver, for in a March 21 dispatch to Morgan, Davis directed that Fearing's brigade immediately withdraw to its more retired position, because "General Slocum is not going to move out the Twentieth Corps." Nevertheless, Slocum kept his promise and ordered the two XX Corps brigades to advance to Langley's support. See ibid., pt. 2, p. 939.

23. Nichols, *Story,* p. 267.

24. *OR* 47, pt. 1, p. 538; A. L. Fahnestock Diary, March 21, 1865, Peoria Pub. Lib.; Allen L. Fahnestock to Charles Swift, March 24, 1865, J. W. Langley Papers, KMNP; Holmes, *52d O.V.I.*, p. 25.

25. Allen L. Fahnestock to Charles Swift, March 24, 1865, J. W. Langley Papers, KMNP.

26. A. L. Fahnestock Diary, March 21, 1865, Peoria Pub. Lib.; Holmes, *52d O.V.I.*, p. 25; Payne, *Thirty-Fourth Illinois*, pp. 204-205; *OR* 47, pt. 1, pp. 512, 538, 1091-1092.

27. Litvin, "Captain Burkhalter's Georgia War," *Voices*, 2, p. 539.

28. *OR* 47, pt. 1, pp. 26-27, 235, 247, 366, 368, 409; ibid., pt. 2, pp. 934-935.

29. Hubert, *Fiftieth Illinois*, p. 371. Not all of the XV Corps regiments were as fortunate as the 50th Illinois. Charles M. Hopper of the 70th Ohio, Hazen's division, wrote: "In mud and rain we build works only one old axe to cut all the logs with." C. M. Hopper Journal-Letter, March 21, 1865, C. M. Hopper Papers, SHC-UNC.

30. Fort, "First Georgia Regulars," p. 29, *CWTI* Coll., USAMHI; Andrews, "Averysboro [sic] and Bentonville," L. P. Thomas Scrapbooks, 1, p. 44, L. P. Thomas Papers, AHS.

31. *OR* 47, pt. 1, pp. 283-284; Hazen, *Narrative*, p. 366. General Hazen may have based his decision on the inferior quality of the Parrotts' ammunition. Fifteenth Corps chief of artillery Lt. Col. William H. Ross pronounced the powder in the shells as "insufficient and poor," and the fuses as unreliable. *OR* 47, pt. 1, p. 373.

32. Ibid., pp. 288, 298; ibid., pt. 2, p. 934; William F. Thayer Diary, March 21, 1865, NCDAH. In his March 21 journal entry, General Morgan merely noted that the "Fifteenth Corps closed to our right." *OR* 47, pt. 1, p. 494.

33. Ibid., pp. 207, 236, 383; Howard, *Autobiography*, 2, p. 149.

34. *OR* 47, pt. 1, pp. 236, 247, 341, 372-373 *passim*; ibid., pt. 2, pp. 934-935.

35. Ibid., pt. 1, pp. 253-254.

36. Ibid.

37. L. N. Green Diary, March 21, 1865, MNHS.

38. *OR* 47, pt. 1, p. 268; L. N. Green Diary, March 21, 1865, MNHS.

39. *OR* 47, pt. 1, pp. 67-68, 1080; Edward E. Schweitzer Diary, March 21, 1865, *CWTI* Coll., USAMHI.

40. *OR* 47, pt. 1, pp. 259, 261; Wills, *Army Life*, p. 365.

41. *OR* 47, pt. 1, p. 261; Wills, *Army Life*, p. 365.

42. *OR* 47, pt. 1, p. 372.

43. Wills, *Army Life*, pp. 365-366; Hagood, *Memoirs*, p. 362.

44. *OR* 47, pt. 1, pp. 259, 261; Wills, *Army Life*, p. 366.

45. *OR* 47, pt. 1, pp. 354, 366, 370; C. C. Platter Diary, March 21, 1865, UGA; Hubert, *Fiftieth Illinois*, pp. 371-372; Bigger, "From the 50th Illinois," [Quincy, IL] *Daily Whig and Republican*, April 10, 1865; Childress Diary, March 21, 1865, ILSHL. Brigadier General Elliott W. Rice's brigade of Corse's division remained in reserve on March 21.

46. *OR* 47, pt. 1, pp. 354, 356, 358, 366, 370; Hubert, *Fiftieth Illinois*, p. 372.

47. Bigger, "From the 50th Illinois," [Quincy, IL] *Daily Whig and Republican*, April 10, 1865.

48. *OR* 47, pt. 1, pp. 366, 368, 370; Hubert, *Fiftieth Illinois*, p. 372; Cluett, *57th Illinois*, p. 98; Ambrose, *Seventh Illinois*, pp. 300-301. There was also a mounted detachment of the 7th Illinois commanded by Lt. Col. Hector Perrin.

49. Johnson, *Union to the Hub*, p. 102; *OR* 47, pt. 1, p. 366.

50. *OR* 47, pt. 1, p. 207; Strong, "Battle of Bentonville," March 21, 1865, entry from "Extracts from Journal," W. E. Strong Papers, ILSHL.

51. *OR* 47, pt. 1, p. 207.

52. Harwell, *Fiery Trail*, pp. 196, 198.

53. Hagood, *Memoirs*, p. 362; Spencer, *Last Ninety Days*, pp. 74-75.

54. Ibid., pp. 73-75.

55. *OR* 47, pt. 1, pp. 414, 417; Chas. H. Brush to Mother, March 25, 1865, Brush Family Papers, ILSHL; Belknap, *15th Iowa*, pp. 469-470; Hedley, *Marching Through Georgia*, pp. 406-408.

56. Fort, "First Georgia Regulars," p. 29, *CWTI* Coll., USAMHI; Hedley, *Marching Through Georgia*, pp. 406-408.

57. Andrews, "Averysboro [sic] and Bentonville," L. P. Thomas Scrapbooks, 1, p. 44, L. P. Thomas Papers, AHS; Andrews, *Footprints*, p. 174; *OR* 47, pt. 1, p. 70; Hedley, *Marching Through Georgia*, p. 407.

58. Fort, "First Georgia Regulars," pp. 29-30, *CWTI* Coll., USAMHI.

59. Ibid., p. 30.

60. *OR* 47, pt. 1, pp. 341, 373.

61. Andrews, "Averysboro [sic] and Bentonville," L. P. Thomas Scrapbooks, 1, p. 44, L. P. Thomas Papers, AHS; Andrews, *Footprints*, p. 174; William E. Sloan Diary, March 21, 1865, Confederate Coll., Box 7, TNSLA.

62. Fort, "First Georgia Regulars," p. 30, *CWTI* Coll., USAMHI.

63. Force Letterbook-Journal, March 21, 1865, Force Papers, UWA; *OR* 47, pt. 1, p. 409; McLaws Order Book, March 20[-21], 1865, McLaws Papers, SHC-UNC; W. W. Gordon Diary, March 21, 1865, Gordon Family Papers, SHC-UNC; Lindsley, *Military Annals*, p. 895; Guild, *Fourth Tennessee Cavalry*, p. 125. Colonel Henry M. Ashby commanded Humes' Division at Bentonville.

64. Dickert, *Kershaw's Brigade*, p. 524.

65. W. W. Gordon Diary, March 21, 1865, Gordon Family Papers, SHC-UNC; "Judge G. K. Miller," p. 71.

66. *OR* 47, pt. 1, pp. 1128-1129, 1130-1131; ibid., pt. 2, pp. 1438-1439. One of Wheeler's cavalrymen recalled that a "high causeway" led northward from Mill Creek "through marshy and boggy ground. . .for some quarter of a mile. This marsh was impassable except by persons on foot." See Friend, "Rangers at Bentonville."

Chapter Sixteen: *We Would Have Charged Old Nick Himself*

1. Miles, "Live Eagle Brigade," September 28, 1893.

2. *OR* 34, pt. 1, pp. 306-307, 315-316; Miles, "Live Eagle Brigade," September 28, 1893.

3. *OR* 47, pt. 1, pp. 391, 399; Ferguson Diary, March 21, 1865, MacMurray College; Kittelson [Leigram] Diary, March 21, 1865, Kittelson [Leigram] Papers, SHSW.

4. Sargeant, *Personal Recollections*, [n.p.]; Jamison, *Recollections*, p. 321; Kittelson [Leigram] Diary, March 21, 1865, Kittelson [Leigram] Papers, SHSW; *OR* 47, pt. 1, p. 403.

5. Kittelson [Leigram] Diary, March 21, 1865, Kittelson [Leigram] Papers, SHSW; *OR* 47, pt. 1, p. 403; Sargeant, *Personal Recollections*, [n.p.]; Andrew Hickenlooper Diary, March 21, 1865, Hickenlooper Family Coll., Cincinnati Hist. Soc.

6. Sargeant, *Personal Recollections*, [n.p.].

7. Jamison, *Recollections*, p. 321; *OR* 47, pt. 1, p. 403; Chas. H. Brush to Mother, March 25, 1865, Brush Family Papers, ILSHL.

8. *OR* 47, pt. 1, p. 391; Anders, *Eighteenth Missouri*, pp. 316-317; map entitled, "Battle near Bentonville, North Carolina, March 21st, 1865," in Evans Diary, Evans Papers, WRHS.

9. *OR* 47, pt. 1, pp. 391, 395; Sargeant, *Personal Recollections* [n.p.]; Anders, *Eighteenth Missouri*, p. 317.

10. Warner, *Generals in Blue*, pp. 164-165; Sherman, *Memoirs*, 2, p. 159; Castel, *Decision in the West*, p. 397.

11. Although Fuller's line faced "nearly west," Tillson reported that his line was "facing almost to the southwest," which might explain why the two brigades later diverged on their advance. Sargeant, *Personal Recollections* [n.p.]; *OR* 47, pt. 1, pp. 391, 395, 397, 403-404.

The exact number of troops Mower took into battle on March 21 is unknown. The XVII Corps' "Weekly Report of Effective Force for March 19" lists 1,438 effectives for Fuller's brigade and 1,430 effectives for Tillson's brigade. Yet in his after-action report, General Fuller wrote that he had only 600 men on the main line, not including the skirmishers or the five-company guard at the ford. The actual number lies somewhere between the two figures, perhaps 2,500 total in Mower's two-brigade force. If we subtract 500 for the men on the skirmish line (see this note below for the 64th Illinois total) and 200 for the men guarding the ford, that would leave approximately 1,800 men on the main line. *OR* 47, pt. 1, p. 395; RG 98: 17th Army Corps—Letters Received, Reports, Orders, and Lists. Weekly Report of the Effective Force for the Week of March 19, 1865, Box 1, NA.

The February 1865 muster roll for the 64th Illinois lists seven officers and 377 enlisted men present for duty. RG 94: Descriptive Rolls, etc., for the 64th Regiment Illinois Infantry. Muster Rolls for February 1865, NA.

12. J. W. Fuller to S. A. Adams, April 5, 1865, RG 393 No. 413, 6265. Vol. 23/60. Letters Sent, February-June, 1865, 1st Brig., 1st Div., 17th AC, NA; *Report of the Adjutant General-Illinois*, 4, p. 309; RG 94: Compiled Service Records 64th Rgt. Ill. Inf. Joseph S. Reynolds, NA. Captain Reynolds' service record lists his age as 27 as of April 9, 1865.

On April 9, 1865, the men finally received their rifles and Captain Reynolds received his commission. Some of the men immediately resold their new Henry rifles because the war was drawing to a close and they saw no prospect of using them. See Jamison, *Recollections*, p. 325.

13. *Report of the Adjutant General-Illinois*, 4, p. 309; RG 153: Records of the Office of the Judge Advocate General-Army. File No. OO 605/3: Court-Martial Case File for Capt. J. S. Reynolds; medical certificate enclosed in RG 94: Compiled Service Records 64th Rgt. Ill. Inf. Joseph S. Reynolds, NA; Boatner, *Civil War Dictionary*, p. 695. On March 26, 1865, Captain Reynolds was tried and acquitted on a charge of absence without leave.

14. Castel, *Decision in the West*, p. 402; *Report of the Adjutant General-Illinois*, 4, p. 346; Robert Mann Woods to Charles H. Smith, January 15, 1910, Box 1, Charles and Louisa Smith Papers, WRHS.

15. Stilwell, "Battle of Bentonville."

16. Sargeant, *Personal Recollections* [n.p.]; *OR* 47, pt. 1, pp. 391, 403; Jamison, *Recollections*, p. 321; Ferguson Diary, March 21, 1865, MacMurray College.

17. Holmes, "Artillery at Bentonville," p. 103; Hampton, "Battle of Bentonville," p. 704.

18. McLaws Order Book, March 20[-21], 1865, McLaws Papers, SHC-UNC.

19. Ibid; Hampton, "Battle of Bentonville," p. 704.

20. *OR* 47, pt. 1, pp. 1057, 1092; Johnston, *Narrative*, pp. 390-391; Thomas B. Roy Diary, March 21, 1865; Darst, "Robert Hodges, Jr.," p. 39.

21. Lindsley, *Military Annals*, p. 439; Worsham, *Old Nineteenth Tennessee*, pp. 172-173; *OR* 47, pt. 1, pp. 1082-1083. Of the 2,005 effectives present in Cheatham's Corps on March 23, roughly half of those troops would have been with Bate's contingent and Granbury's Brigade, leaving the other half with Brown's Division and Lowrey's Brigade. Cheatham therefore had from 1,000 to 1,100 men present with him at Bentonville on March 21. Ibid., pt. 3, p. 706.

22. Lindsley, *Military Annals*, pp. 378, 438; Worsham, *Old Nineteenth Tennessee*, pp. 172-173; Losson, *Tennessee's Forgotten Warriors*, pp. 132-135 *passim*.

23. Johnston, *Narrative*, p. 391; Hampton, "Battle of Bentonville," p. 704.

24. J. W. Fuller to Captain [S. A. Adams?], March 28, 1865, RG 393 No. 413, 6265. Vol. 23/60. Letters Sent, February-June, 1865, 1st Brig., 1st Div., 17th AC, NA; Stilwell, "Battle of Bentonville"; RG 153: Records of the Office of the Judge Advocate General-Army. File No. OO 605/9: Court-Martial Case File for Private Thomas Delaney, NA; Sargeant, *Personal Recollections*, [n.p.]; *OR* 47, pt. 1, p. 395.

25. William H. Pittenger Diary, March 17, 1865, OHS. At least two men from Mower's division were charged with cowardice in connection with the March 21 engagement. One of the accused, Pvt. Thomas Delaney of the 39th Ohio, was acquitted because he was barefoot at the time of the battle and one of the witnesses testified that he had heard Captain DeGress order all barefoot men to the rear. The other accused man, Pvt. Jacob Schreader of the 10th Illinois, was also acquitted, but not because he was barefoot. Moreover, Schreader was charged with two other counts of cowardice stemming from earlier engagements, and pleaded guilty to one of them. See RG 153: Records of the Office of the Judge Advocate General-Army. File No. OO 605/9: Court-Martial Case File for Private Thomas Delaney, and File No. OO 605/11: Court-Martial Case File for Private Jacob Schreader, NA.

26. *OR* 47, pt. 1, pp. 391, 395, 403; Elias Perry Diary, March 21, 1865, WHMC-UMO; Jamison, *Recollections*, p. 321. According to a soldier in the 27th

Ohio, the 64th Illinois collided with the Confederate skirmishers about 200 yards west of their starting point on the road. See Evans Diary, March 21, 1865, Evans Papers, WRHS.

27. Stilwell, "Battle of Bentonville"; *OR* 47, pt. 1, pp. 395, 397; Benjamin F. Sweet War Record, pp. 26-27, WHMC-UMO; Holmes, "Artillery at Bentonville," p. 103.

28. Stilwell, "Battle of Bentonville"; John W. Bates Diary, March 21, 1865, Civil War Misc. Coll., USAMHI.

29. *OR* 47, pt. 1, pp. 391, 395, 397; Lane to Mother, March 28, 1865, Thurman D. Maness Collection, NCDAH; Smith, *Fuller's Brigade*, p. 273. One of Law's staff officers recalled that the caisson had to be abandoned because the driver had run it into a tree, wedging the trunk between a wheel and the limber chest. See Holmes, "Artillery at Bentonville," p. 103.

30. *OR* 47, pt. 1, p. 403; Ferguson Diary, March 21, 1865, MacMurray College; Nilson Diary, March 21, 1865, Nilson Papers, INHS.

31. Warner, *Generals in Gray*, pp. 189-190; Hutson, "My Reminiscences," p. 121, and C. Woodward Hutson to Sister [Journal-Letter], March 17, 1865, C. W. Hutson Papers, SHC-UNC; Holmes, "Dismounted Brigade," p. 382.

32. Sparkman Diary, March 21, 1865, Box 3, Diaries, Memoirs, Etc., TNSLA; J. F. Waring Diary, March 21, 1865, SHC-UNC; Friend, "Rangers at Bentonville." After the battle, some local residents told General Force that "Mower's movements made [that is, caused] a wild stampede across Mill creek." See Force Letterbook-Journal, March 22, 1865, Force Papers, UWA.

33. J. F. Waring Diary, March 21, 1865, SHC-UNC.

34. *OR* 47, pt. 1, pp. 391, 395, 397; Sargeant, *Personal Recollections*, [n.p.]; Woodruff, *Fifteen Years Ago*, p. 219. Colonel Waring of the Jeff Davis Legion, Young's Brigade, stated that Mower's breakthrough occurred about 1:30 p.m., which agrees with the time estimates of Mower's troops. Generals Johnston and Wheeler reported that the breakthrough occurred at 4:00 p.m., which is much too late. See J. F. Waring Diary, March 21, 1865, SHC-UNC; *OR* 47, pt. 1, pp. 1057, 1131.

35. Sargeant, *Personal Recollections*, [n.p.].

36. Fuller's and Tillson's skirmish lines probably became separated because Tillson's brigade had been heading "almost southwest," while Fuller's brigade was advancing west-northwest. At any rate, General Mower seems to have been unnerved by his isolation from the rest of Sherman's army. "Fighting Joe" must have decided to await reinforcements from General Blair before advancing on Bentonville. His decision to move by the left flank instead of attacking indicates that he had second thoughts about acting independently. *OR* 47, pt. 1, pp. 391, 395, 403. Colonel Sheldon of the 18th Missouri mistakenly believed that this shift to the left had been made at General Sherman's behest. Sargeant, *Personal Recollections*, [n.p.].

37. Woodruff, *Fifteen Years Ago*, p. 219; Case, "A Word About Bentonville"; *Report of the Adjutant General-Illinois*, 4, p. 347; Sargeant, *Personal Recollections*; Smith, *Fuller's Brigade*, p. 273.

38. Stilwell, "Battle of Bentonville"; Smith, *Fuller's Brigade*, p. 273; Robert Mann Woods to Charles H. Smith, January 15, 1910, Box 1, Charles and Louisa Smith Papers, WRHS. "The crowning infamy of your book," Captain Woods wrote Captain Smith, "is your account of the Battle of Bentonville in which neither the 18th Mo or 64th Ill are mentioned. . . .You steal the entire credit of it for your two Ohio Regiments. Your action is only equaled by that of Admiral Sampson at

Santiago [during the Spanish-American War] trying to take all the credit from Admiral Schley."

39. Hardee, "Memoranda," March 21, 1865, JO483, J. E. Johnston Papers, HEHL; Thomas B. Roy Diary, March 21, 1865; Holmes, A. G., *Diary of Henry McCall Holmes*, pp. 32-33; A. Q. Porter Diary, March 21, 1865, A. Q. Porter Coll., LC.

40. R. J. Henderson to John J. Reeve, March 29, 1865, J. E. Johnston Papers, HEHL (published in *OR* 47, pt. 1, p. 1097); Thomas B. Roy Diary, March 21, 1865.

41. Harcourt, "Terry's Texas Rangers," p. 96; Roman, "Inspection Report of Wheeler's Cavalry Corps," January 22, 1865, Letterbook, 1, p. 10, Alfred Roman Papers, LC.

42. Ibid., pp. 13-14 *passim*; Guild, *Fourth Tennessee Cavalry*, p. 125; Dodson, *Campaigns of Wheeler*, p. 421.

43. Roman, "Inspection Report of Wheeler's Cavalry Corps," January 22, 1865, Letterbook, 1, p. 8, Alfred Roman Papers, LC; Ordnance Report for Harrison's Brigade—"For the term ending January 9th, 1865," CSA Archives, Army Units, Wheeler's Cavalry Corps, DU. In an inspection report on Wheeler's Cavalry Corps for the months of January-February 1865, Col. Charles C. Jones wrote: "Many, if not all, of the breech-loading rifles and pistols are captured arms; for some of them, as the Spencer, there is great difficulty in procuring the requisite amount of ammunition, the supply now in the cartridge boxes of the men, and in the ordnance train, having been obtained exclusively by capture." Colonel Jones also noted that "ammunition for the Spencer rifles. . .is now being freely prepared at the Richmond arsenal." See "Report of Inspection Made by Colonel C. C. Jones, Jr. and Captain Whitehead," reprinted in Dodson, *Campaigns of Wheeler*, pp. 408-409 *passim*.

44. The Rangers' three wounded field officers were Col. Gustave Cook, Lt. Col. S. P. "Pat" Christian and Maj. W. R. Jarmon. Fitzhugh, *Terry's Texas Rangers*, p. 21; Harcourt, "Terry's Texas Rangers," p. 96; Holman, "Concerning the Battle of Bentonville," p. 425; Blackburn, "Reminiscences," p. 169; Friend, "Rangers at Bentonville."

45. Ibid; Roy, "W. J. Hardee," p. 50, W. J. Hardee Papers, ALDAH; [Roy], "Lieut.-Gen. Hardee," in Pollard, *Lee and His Lieutenants*, p. 827; Garrison, "General Hardee's Son," p. 7; Pickett, "Willie Hardee," p. 182; Pickett, *William J. Hardee*, p. 43; Blackburn, "Reminiscences," p. 170. Depending on the source, the school that Willie Hardee ran away from was in Athens, Milledgeville, or Marietta, Georgia. Even Hardee's adjutant and future son-in-law, Thomas B. Roy, confuses matters. In his two written accounts of Willie Hardee's life, Roy gives the names of two different towns—Athens and Marietta.

46. [Roy], "Lieut.-Gen. Hardee," in Pollard, *Lee and His Lieutenants*, p. 827; Harcourt, "Terry's Texas Rangers," p. 96; Blackburn, "Reminiscences," p. 170." Willie Hardee left Stuart's Battery on March 20. See Hutson, "My Reminiscences," p. 122, and [C. Woodward Hutson] to Em, March 21, 1865, C. W. Hutson Papers, SHC-UNC.

Captain Kyle commanded Company D of the Terry Rangers. Although several other Rangers besides Blackburn remembered Willie Hardee joining Company D, at least one believed otherwise. For the Terry Rangers' 1882 reunion, John Claiborne provided a roster of the Rangers which he reconstructed largely from memory, and which places Willie in Company B. Two facts mitigate against the accuracy of Claiborne's roster. First, a veteran of the Rangers named Oswald Tilghman published his own roster of Company B in the *Confederate Veteran*, and Willie's name does not appear on that roster. Second, Company B of the Rangers served as Maj. Gen. Lafayette McLaws' escort throughout the Carolinas Campaign, and was not present with the regiment at Bentonville. See "Muster Rolls of Terry's Texas Rangers. . . .Compiled by Jno. M. Claiborne," Texas St. Lib.; Tilghman, "Membership of a Famous Escort Company," p. 210; Friend, "Rangers at Bentonville"; Graber, *A Terry Texas Ranger*, pp. 226-227.

47. Harcourt, "Terry's Texas Rangers," p. 96; Guild, *Fourth Tennessee Cavalry*, p. 132.

48. Ibid; Harcourt, "Terry's Texas Rangers," p. 97.

49. R. J. Henderson to John J. Reeve, March 29, 1865, J. E. Johnston Papers, HEHL (published in *OR* 47, pt. 1, p. 1097); Thomas B. Roy Diary, March 21, 1865; Guild, *Fourth Tennessee Cavalry*, p. 132; Davis, "Eighth Texas Cavalry," p. 184; *OR* 47, pt. 1, p. 1131.

50. Guild, *Fourth Tennessee Cavalry*, pp. 132-133; Guild, "Battle of Bentonville," p. 64. About 200 troopers from the 8th Texas and 4th Tennessee were present with Colonel Smith at the time of the Confederate counterattack. See note by George Guild in Hampton, "Battle of Bentonville," p. 705.

51. Friend, "Rangers at Bentonville"; Lieutenant Briscoe quoted in Giles, *Terry's Texas Rangers*, p. 97; Guild, "Battle of Bentonville," p. 64; Guild, *Fourth Tennessee Cavalry*, p. 133; Harcourt, "Terry's Texas Rangers," p. 97.

52. *OR* 47, pt. 1, p. 403; Ferguson Diary, March 21, 1865, MacMurray College. Many of the Confederates who were taken prisoner along Mower's front told their Union captors that they belonged to Hardee's Corps—that is, the corps that General Hardee had commanded the previous year—*not* Hardee's current command. See Evans Diary, March 21, 1865, Evans Papers, WRHS; Nilson Diary, March 21, 1865, Nilson Papers, INHS. Although General Johnston stated that Cumming's Brigade was the only infantry that opposed Mower's charge, it is clear from numerous Confederate eyewitness accounts that Cheatham's command was the infantry that counterattacked Tillson's brigade. See Davis, "Eighth Texas Cavalry," p. 184; Holman. "Concerning the Battle of Bentonville," p. 425; Worsham, *Old Nineteenth Tennessee*, p. 172. A veteran of Taliaferro's Division recalled that as his unit went into line on the left flank, a soldier returning from the front told him and his comrades, "Don't be uneasy, boys; the Tennesseans are down there." See Sanders, "Battle of Bentonville," p. 300.

53. *OR* 47, pt. 1, pp. 391, 403; Kittelson [Leigram] Diary, March 21, 1865, Kittelson [Leigram] Papers, SHSW. Brown's Division was mauled in the charge at Franklin, Tennessee. Among the casualties were its commander, Maj. Gen. John C. Brown, who was severely wounded, and its four brigade commanders, three of whom—Brigadier Generals Gist, Strahl and Carter—were killed or mortally wounded. The fourth, Brigadier General Gordon, was captured. See Sword, *Embrace an Angry Wind*, pp. 269, 445-446.

Lowrey's Brigade of Cleburne's Division may have been present with Brown's Division on March 21, 1865, which would have swelled Cheatham's numbers to 800 effectives.

54. Ferguson Diary, March 21, 1865, MacMurray College; Kittelson [Leigram] Diary, March 21, 1865, Kittelson [Leigram] Papers, SHSW; Frank to Fannie, March 27, 1865, Francis M. Guernsey Letters, typed copies in the possession of John M. Coski, Richmond, VA; *OR* 47, pt. 1, pp. 403-404 *passim*.

55. Ferguson Diary, March 21, 1865, MacMurray College; *OR* 47, pt. 1, p. 391.

56. *OR* 47, pt. 1, pp. 395, 1057; Woodruff, *Fifteen Years Ago*, p. 219; Stilwell, "Battle of Bentonville"; Johnston, *Narrative*, p. 391.

57. *OR* 47, pt. 1, p. 395.

58. Ibid.

59. Sargeant, *Personal Recollections*; *OR* 47, pt. 1, p. 395.

60. Ibid., pp. 395-396; Russell, "Fighting at Bentonville."

61. Guild, *Fourth Tennessee Cavalry*, p. 133; Guild, "Battle of Bentonville," p. 64; Harcourt, "Terry's Texas Rangers," p. 97; Fletcher, *Rebel Private*, p. 144.

62. Harcourt, "Terry's Texas Rangers," p. 97; *OR* 47, pt. 1, p. 403.

63. R. J. Henderson to John J. Reeve, March 29, 1865, J. E. Johnston Papers, HEHL (published in *OR* 47, pt. 1, p. 1097); Davis, "Eighth Texas Cavalry," p. 184.

64. *OR* 47, pt. 1, pp. 391, 403-404; Ferguson Diary, March 21, 1865, MacMurray College; Jamison, *Recollections*, p. 322.

65. *OR* 47, pt. 1, pp. 1057, 1131; Johnston, *Narrative*, p. 391; Roy, "W. J. Hardee," p. 49, W. J. Hardee Papers, ALDAH; Lindsley, *Military Annals*, p. 895. Sergeant J. J. Hawthorne of the 3rd Alabama, Hagan's Brigade, wrote: "At Bentonville, on the last day of the fight, I ordered a charge on my own responsibility against the wishes of Colonel White, commanding our brigade." See Hawthorne, "Active Service," p. 336.

66. *OR* 47, pt. 1, pp. 391, 403-404; Ferguson Diary, March 21, 1865, MacMurray College; Jamison, *Recollections*, p. 322; Frank to Fannie, March 27, 1865, Francis M. Guernsey Letters, typed copies in the possession of John M. Coski, Richmond, VA; George W. Gee to Clarence Caldwell, March 29, 1865, Gee Papers, SHSW; Coski, "Bandbox Regiment," p. 340.

67. *OR* 47, pt. 1, pp. 391, 396, 399; Philip Roesch Memorandum, March 21, 1865, Federal Coll., Box F-23, Folder 9, TNSLA.

68 *OR* 47, pt. 1, p. 391.

69. Vett to Mother, March 21, 1865, S. C. Noble Papers, Ypsilanti Hist. Soc.; *OR* 47, pt. 1, p. 27.

70. Grigsby, *Smoked Yank*, pp. 237-238.

71. Harwell, *Fiery Trail*, p. 197. "I understand General Sherman ordered Mower in person to make the advance," Maj. Thomas Osborn wrote on March 21, "and neither General Blair, or [sic] General Howard knew of it, and were not responsible for failing to support him. . . .Had General Sherman given General Howard the order instead of doing the unsoldierly thing of giving a division commander orders direct, we should have gained a splendid victory, instead of a repulse." Osborn, of course, was mistaken: General Mower attacked on his own responsibility. *OR* 47, pt. 1, p. 207; Howard, *Autobiography*, 2, pp. 149-150.

72. O. O. Howard quoted in Boyd, *Life of William T. Sherman*, p. 533; Howard, "Campaign of the Carolinas," p. 29.

73. *OR* 47, pt. 1, 391, 404.

74. Frank to Fannie, March 27, 1865, Francis M. Guernsey Letters, typed copies in the possession of John M. Coski, Richmond, VA; Pittenger Diary, March 22, 1865, OHS. The casualty returns published in *OR* 47, pt. 1, indicate 150 casualties in Mower's division at Bentonville, but the "Report of Losses in 17 A. C. Mch 21 1865," and General Howard's report, list *166* casualties. *OR* 47, pt. 1, pp. 69-70, 207; RG 98: 17th Army Corps. Letters Received, etc. "Report of Killed, Wounded and Missing in 17 Army Corps on Mch 21 1865," Box 2, NA.

75. Patton, *War As I Knew It*, p. 95.

76. Sherman, *Memoirs*, 2, p. 304.

77. Nearly two hours elapsed from the time Law's pickets first spotted Mower's division marching into position about noon, until Young's Brigade struck the 64th Illinois between 1:30 and 2:00 p.m.

In calculating the number of Confederates who opposed Mower, I allowed 600 effectives for Young's Brigade, 250 for Cumming's Brigade, 200 for the 8th Texas and 4th Tennessee cavalry regiments, 600 for Cheatham's infantry, and 350 for Hagan's and Ashby's troopers under Wheeler, for a total of 2,000 infantry and cavalry. This figure is a conservative estimate. *OR* 47, pt. 1, p. 407; ibid., pt. 2, p. 1397; ibid., pt. 3, p. 706; note by George Guild in Hampton, "Battle of Bentonville," p. 705.

78. Hampton, "Battle of Bentonville," p. 705; Friend, "Rangers at Bentonville"; Hutson, "My Reminiscences," p. 122, [C. Woodward Hutson] to Em, March 21, 1865, C. W. Hutson Papers, SHC-UNC; Wellman, *Giant in Gray,* pp. 160-163; Freeman, *Lee's Lieutenants*, 3, pp. 615-616.

79. Thomas B. Roy Diary, March 24, 1865; Hillsborough (N. C.) *Recorder*, March 29, 1865. Perhaps in deference to Willie Hardee's former rank as his father's aide, the *Recorder* referred to him as "Lt. Hardee."

Susannah Hardee Kirkland was the daughter of Noble Andrew Hardee, an older brother of General Hardee. William and Susannah Kirkland had a daughter, Bessie, who became famous on the Broadway stage under the name of Odette Tyler. See Warner, *Generals in Gray*, p. 172; D. Hardee, *Eastern North Carolina Hardy-Hardee Family*, pp. 103-105 *passim*.

Willie Hardee died at Ayr Mount, the Kirkland family home, owned at the time by John Umstead Kirkland (1802-1879), the father of General Kirkland. Both Susannah Kirkland and the Hardee ladies were staying there as guests of Mr. Kirkland. See Anna D. Hardee to Gen. Howard, April 14, 1865, O. O. Howard Papers, BC; Anderson, *Kirklands of Ayr Mount*, pp. 149, 165, 187.

80. Howard, *Autobiography*, 2, pp. 151-152; Anna D. Hardee to Gen. Howard, April 14, 1865, and Otis to Wife, April 29, 1865, O. O. Howard Papers, BC; Warner, *Generals in Blue*, p. 237. In the April 29 letter to his wife, Howard mentioned having received Anna Hardee's letter that morning, and that she had "besought" him for protection for her friends the Kirklands, "recalling old times." In his *Autobiography*, Howard misquoted his letter of April 29 and erroneously stated that the John Kirkland family lived in Raleigh instead of Hillsborough. Howard, *Autobiography*, 2, p. 152.

81. Baker's Brigade suffered two killed and 12 wounded in the repulse of Mower's charge. *OR* 47, pt. 1, p. 1092; Ridley, *Battles and Sketches*, p. 453; Hagood, Memoirs, p. 362; Lambert, "Battle of Bentonville," p. 222; Shingleton, "'With Loyalty and Honor,'" p. 261; Ford, "Last Battles," p. 142; Sanders, "Battle of Bentonville," pp. 299-300 *passim*.

82. According to Cpl. A. P. Ford, Taliaferro's Division held the extreme left of the Confederate line: "Here. . .the Eighteenth Battalion of Elliott's Brigade, under the command of [Capt.] T. G. Boag, was on the left of the division and [was] stationed directly on the edge of Mill Creek." See Ford, "A March"; Ford, *Life*, p. 61. Colonel Robert J. Henderson reported that Cumming's Brigade deployed on Taliaferro's right. The location of the remaining Confederate units on the left flank is less clear. *OR* 47, pt. 1, p. 1098; Darst, "Robert Hodges, Jr.," p. 39; [C. Woodward Hutson] to Em, March 21, 1865, C. W. Hutson Papers, SHC-UNC; Myrover, "Thirteenth Battalion," 4, p. 352, in Clark, *Histories*.

83. *OR* 47, pt. 1, p. 1092; ibid., pt. 2, p. 1447.

84. Williamson D. Ward Journal, March 21, 1865, INHS; [C. Woodward Hutson] to Em, March 21, 1865, C. W. Hutson Papers, SHC-UNC.

85. Burton, *Diary of E. P. Burton*, pp. 71-72; Thomas P. Larue to Brother, April 8, 1865, Harrisburg CWRT Coll., USAMHI; Hubert, *Fiftieth Illinois*, p. 372;

Bigger, "From the 50th Illinois," (Quincy, Ill.) *Daily Whig and Republican*, April 10, 1865; Black, "Civil War Diary," p. 469.

86. James R. M. Gaskill Memoranda, March 21, 1865, CHS.

87. Worsham, *Old Nineteenth Tennessee*, p. 173; Harcourt, "Terry's Texas Rangers," p. 96; Sherlock, *One Hundredth Indiana*, p. 212; Sherlock Diary, March 21, 1865, Sherlock Papers, INHS; Calder Diary, March 21, 1865, Calder Papers, DU; Hubert, *Fiftieth Illinois*, p. 374.

88. Calder Diary, March 21, 1865, Calder Papers, DU; Ambrose, *Seventh Illinois*, p. 301.

Chapter Seventeen: *An Emblem of Coming Peace*

1. John B. Sale to J. B. Starr, March 21, 1865, J. B. Starr Papers, NCDAH; Calder Diary, March 21, 1865, Calder Papers, DU; G. W. F. Harper Diary, March 22, 1865, G. W. F. Harper Papers, SHC-UNC; Francis H. Nash Diary, March 22, 1865, UGA; Holmes, A. G., *Diary of Henry McCall Holmes*, p. 33; [C. W. Hutson] to Em, March 21, 1865, C. W. Hutson Papers, SHC-UNC; Fort, "First Georgia Regulars," pp. 30-31, *CWTI* Coll., USAMHI; *OR* 47, pt. 1, p. 1131.

2. *OR* 47, pt. 1, pp. 247, 259; ibid., pt. 2, pp. 954-955; Black, "Civil War Diary," p. 469; Ferguson Diary, March 22, 1865, MacMurray College; Ambrose, *Seventh Illinois*, p. 301.

3. Sherlock Diary, March 22, 1865, Sherlock Papers, INHS.

4. *OR* 47, pt. 1, p. 259, pp. 1131-1132; Black, "Civil War Diary," p. 469; Lindsley, *Military Annals*, pp. 895-896; *Report of the Adjutant General*—Illinois, 2, pp. 368, 388.

5. Wills, *Army Life,* p. 366; Sherlock, *One Hundredth Indiana*, p. 212; Jamison, *Recollections*, pp. 322-323; Evans Diary, March 22, 1865, Evans Papers, WRHS; Nilson Diary, March 22, 1865, Nilson Papers, INHS; Corbin, *A Star* , p. 458.

6. George W. Girton quoted in Saunier, *Forty-Seventh Ohio*, pp. 418-419; Corbin, *A Star,* p. 458.

7. Smithfield (NC) *Herald*, September 13, 1927, and June 4, 1940; Johnston County, North Carolina Census, 1860: Harper, John, and Hood, John C., Battle of Bentonville File, Johnston County Public Library.

8. Smithfield (NC) *Herald*, September 13, 1927; Methodist Church Book for Smithfield and Waynesboro Circuit, North Carolina, 1840-1886: "Proceedings of 3d Quarterly Meeting for Smithfield Circuit, 1865," Johnston County Public Library; *OR* 47, pt. 1, p. 1060; Mowris, *One Hundred and Seventeenth New York,* pp. 208-209; Sanders, "Battle of Bentonville," p. 300; Sanders, "More About," p. 461.

9. *OR* 47, pt. 1, p. 1060; ibid., pt. 3, pp. 703-705 *passim*; Hill, *Confederate Military History: North Carolina*, p. 532. A note appended to General Johnston's casualty list states that his ambulances later removed 28 wounded from Bentonville and 26 wounded from the Harper house.

10. *OR* 47, pt. 1, p. 1060.

11. Sherman also states that there are wide discrepancies between the number of prisoners reported captured by the Federals at Bentonville and the number reported by Confederates as missing. According to Sherman's figures, General Slocum reported 338 prisoners captured and General Howard 1,287, for a total of 1,625, whereas General Johnston reported only 653 (actually 673) missing at Bentonville. The reason for this discrepancy is easy to explain: Howard's figure for

prisoners captured is inclusive for the entire campaign, and not just the Battle of Bentonville. See Sherman, *Memoirs*, 2, pp. 305-306; *OR* 47, pt. 1, pp. 209, 1060.

12. Sherman, *Memoirs*, 2, pp. 303-306; McClurg, "Last Chance," p. 400.

13. *OR* 47, pt. 1, p. 44; ibid., pt. 2, p. 44; Sherman, *General and Special Field Orders*, p. 202; Harwell, *Fiery Trail*, p. 199. Three days after the Battle of Bentonville, the Unionist New Berne, *North Carolina Times* announced to its readers: "Tecumseh puts on his War Paint and Drubs them." See (New Berne) *North Carolina Times,* March 24, 1865.

14. *OR* 47, pt. 1, pp. 1055, 1057.

15. Ibid., p. 1055.

16. Harwell, *Fiery Trail*, p. 199; Philadelphia *Christian Recorder*, May 6, 1865. According to a newspaper account written at the turn of the century, "Eight cannon balls passed through the shell of a pine tree in the yard [of the Harper house, each ball] making a separate hole. This tree stood in its original place for several years, and was finally cut down and removed to the court house yard at Smithfield, where it may still be seen." See Rightsell, "Gory Battle of Bentonville," L. P. Thomas Scrapbook, 2, p. 172, L. P. Thomas Papers, AHS.

17. *OR* 47, pt. 1, p. 424; McIntosh, "Annals," p. 216, McIntosh Papers, SHSW; Kittinger Diary, March 22, 1865, Earl Hess Coll., USAMHI; Harvey Reid Diary, March 22, 1865, Harvey Reid Papers, UWI-Parkside.

18. *OR* 47, pt. 1, pp. 236, 383; Strong, "Battle of Bentonville," March 24, 1865 entry from "Extracts from Journal," W. E. Strong Papers, ILSHL.

19. Wade Hampton to Fisher, March 22, 1865, Hampton Family Papers, USC; McClurg, "Last Chance," p. 400.

Bibliographical Note

When I first began my research on the Battle of Bentonville, quite a few people warned me that I wouldn't find much material on the battle. I soon discovered that they were mistaken. On the contrary—there is a wealth of material regarding the battle from a variety of sources. My only real disappointment was in finding almost no material for Maj. Gen. Robert F. Hoke's Division, which played a crucial role in the March 19 fighting.

By far the best source is *The War of the Rebellion: A Compilation of the Official Records of the Union and Confederate Armies* (or *OR*), Volume 47, Parts 1 and 2. The reports and correspondence contained therein formed the core of my research material.

I visited dozens of manuscript repositories across the country—many of them familiar to Civil War historians, and some of them less well known. The material found by this means proved to be an excellent supplement to the *OR*, often supplying information omitted by it. I enjoyed this aspect of my research most, for it frequently assumed the character of a treasure hunt.

I utilized a large selection of published primary sources, which I have placed under one general heading. I found that dividing them by book and article was both superfluous and misleading (some are available in both formats), and that categorizing them by type was no less so. For example, many so-called unit histories are really the diaries or reminiscences of their authors, just as many so-called journals or memoirs are actually amalgams of both genres. Hence my decision to use an umbrella heading. In this category, I limited my list to only those books and articles that I have cited, as well as a few others. Had I listed all the titles that I had consulted but did not cite, I would have doubled the present list.

I found three bibliographical guides to be particularly helpful:

• Cole, Garold L., *Civil War Eyewitnesses: An Annotated Bibliography of Books and Articles, 1955-1986*. Columbia: University of South Carolina Press, 1988.

• Coulter, E. Merton, *Travels in the Confederate States: A Bibliography*. Norman: University of Oklahoma Press, 1948.

• Dornbusch, C. E., *Regimental Publications and Personal Narratives of the Civil War*. 2 vols. New York: The New York Public Library, 1961, 1967.

One crucial source that will not be found in this bibliography is one that I consulted repeatedly—the Bentonville battleground itself. I spent time at the Monroe's Crossroads and Averasboro battlefields as well, but I devoted most of my battlefield stomping time to Bentonville because of its greater significance. The Bentonville battleground is no two-dimensional chessboard: the topography played an important role in the fighting there, and the only way to understand the battle is to know the battlefield. It is a moving experience to walk the same ground once trod by those soldiers in blue and gray, while reading their descriptions of the battle. Fortunately, the battlefield retains much of its original character, including several miles of Union and Confederate entrenchments that denote both armies' positions. In a few cases, I discovered that the actual location of the earthworks differs from their placement on the official maps. In short, I found the Bentonville battleground to be just as important a primary source as any I encountered on the shelves or in the vaults of any library or archive. And, as in the case of any original manuscript, it is irreplaceable.

A Selected Bibliography

MANUSCRIPTS

Alabama Department of Archives and History, Montgomery, Alabama
Civil War Soldiers' Letters
M. J. Blackwell Letters: George —Letter
William Joseph Hardee Papers
Thomas B. Roy: "Sketch of William J. Hardee"
Henry Clay Reynolds Papers
University of Alabama, Tuscaloosa, Alabama, William Stanley Hoole Special Collections Library
Henry David Clayton Papers
American Antiquarian Society, Worcester, Massachusetts
Philo B. Buckingham Papers
University of Arkansas at Fayetteville, Special Collections Division, University Libraries
Daniel Harris Reynolds Papers
Atlanta Historical Society, Atlanta, Georgia, Library and Archives Room, McElreath Hall
George Lawson Correspondence
Lovic P. Thomas Papers
Bowdoin College, Brunswick, Maine, Special Collections, The Library
Charles Henry Howard Papers
Oliver Otis Howard Papers
Chicago Historical Society, Chicago, Illinois, Archives and Manuscripts Department
Cornelius C. Courtright Diary
James R. M. Gaskill Memoranda
Chicago Public Library, Chicago, Illinois, Special Collections
William T. Humphrey Papers
Cincinnati Historical Society Research Library, Cincinnati, Ohio
Hickenlooper Family Collection
Andrew H. Hickenlooper Papers
Thomas Edwin Smith and Family Collection
Connecticut State Library, Hartford, Connecticut
Abner C. Smith Letters
John M. Coski Collection, Richmond, Virginia
Francis M. Guernsey Letters

Detroit Public Library, Detroit, Michigan
Alpheus Starkey Williams Papers
Duke University, Durham, North Carolina, Special Manuscripts Department, William R. Perkins Library
Miss Ellen Aumack Papers
Young J. Powell Letters
Ferdinand F. Boltz Papers
Charles S. Brown Papers
William Calder Papers
Confederate States of America Archives: Army Units. Wheeler's Cavalry Corps
Ordnance Report for Harrison's Brigade
Confederate Veteran Papers
J. J. Bunch Letter
B. F. Watson Letter
John Herr Papers
John Johnson Diary
Bradley Tyler Johnson Papers
Joseph E. Johnston Letters
William G. McCreary Papers
John W. Reid Letters
William Schaum Diary
Tillinghast Family Papers
Sarah Ann Tillinghast Reminiscence
Edward Mitchell Whaley Papers
Emory University, Atlanta, Georgia, Special Collections Department, Robert W. Woodruff Library
John H. Ash Papers
Alexander Miller Ayers Papers
Confederate Miscellany I
H. D. Bulkley Dispatches
Georgia Department of Archives and History, Atlanta, Georgia
Civil War Miscellany—Personal Papers
G. B. Gardner Letter
Private Papers
James Welsman Brown Diary
Georgia Historical Society, Savannah, Georgia
Joseph Frederick Waring Papers
William Washington Gordon Reminiscences
University of Georgia Libraries, Athens, Georgia, Hargrett Rare Book and Manuscript Library
Francis H. Nash Diary
C. C. Platter Diary
Nathaniel Cheairs Hughes Collection, Chattanooga, Tennessee
Thomas Benton Roy Diary (Photocopy)
Henry E. Huntington Library, San Marino, California

Joseph Eggleston Johnston Papers
Illinois State Historical Library, Springfield, Illinois
John Batchelor Diary
Brush Family Papers
Charles H. Brush Diary and Letters
George Lemon Childress Diary
William Culbertson Robinson Papers
Levi Adolphus Ross Diary
William E. Strong Papers
Indiana Historical Society, Indianapolis, Indiana, William E. Smith Memorial Library
Jefferson Columbus Davis Papers
William P. Carlin Letter
David A. Fateley Diary
Gibson County Civil War Papers
Gideon R. Kellams Letter
Charles Gottlieb Michael Diary
William Bluffton Miller Journal
John Nilson Diary and Papers
Eli J. Sherlock Papers
Williamson D. Ward Journal
Indiana State Library, Indianapolis, Indiana, Manuscript Section, Indiana Division
Samuel K. Harryman Papers
Johnston County Public Library, Smithfield, North Carolina, Johnston County Room
Battle of Bentonville File
Methodist Church. Church Book for Smithfield and Waynesboro Circuit, North Carolina, 1840-1886.
Kennesaw Mountain National Park Library, Kennesaw Mountain National Park, Marietta, Georgia
James W. Langley Papers
Allen L. Fahnestock Report
Lyman S. Widney Papers
Library of Congress, Washington, DC, Geography and Map Division, Madison Building
Battle of Bentonville (Three Maps)
Library of Congress, Washington, DC, Manuscript Reading Room, Madison Building
Blair Family Papers
James A. Congleton Journal
John William Draper Papers
William T. Sherman Letters
Thomas Ewing Family Papers
William T. Sherman Letters
John N. Ferguson Diary
Henry Hitchcock Papers

W. C. Johnson Journal
Rufus Mead Papers
Orlando Metcalfe Poe Papers
Albert Quincy Porter Collection
Alfred Roman Papers
William Tecumseh Sherman Papers
Louis Trezevant Wigfall Family Papers
Wade Hampton Letter
Joseph E. Johnston Letters
MacMurray College, Jacksonville, Illinois, Henry Pfeiffer Library
John H. Ferguson Diary
University of Michigan, Ann Arbor, Michigan, Bentley Historical Library
William J. Carroll Papers
John Wesley Daniels Diary
Squier Family Papers
John Hickman Diary and Letters
Minnesota Historical Society, St. Paul, Minnesota
William Franklin Allee: "A Civil War History"
Judson W. Bishop Papers
Levi Nelson Green Papers
William Wirt Pendergast and Family Papers
Timothy Harrison Pendergast Journal
John E. Risedorph Papers
University of Missouri Library, Columbia, Missouri, Western Historical Manuscript Collection
Elias Perry Diary
Rhoderick R. Rockwood Diary
Benjamin F. Sweet Reminiscences
Museum of the Confederacy, Richmond, Virginia, Eleanor S. Brockenbrough Library
"Biographical Sketch of Colonel Alfred Rhett"
Joseph Eggleston Johnston Papers
National Archives, Washington, DC.
Microcopy No. 437: Letters Received by Confederate Secretary of War, 1861-1865
Record Group 94
Compiled Service Records
64th Regiment Illinois Infantry
14th Regiment Michigan Infantry
The Office of the Adjutant General
Battle Reports, Union
Papers and Books, General W. T. Sherman
Regimental Records: Muster Rolls, Descriptive Rolls, Morning Reports, and Letter Books
64th Regiment Illinois Infantry
19th Battery Indiana Light Artillery
Record Group 98

Letters Received, Reports, Orders, Lists, and Telegrams
17th Army Corps
Record Group 109
War Department Collection of Confederate Records, Department and Army of Tennessee, General J. E. Johnston
Record Group 153
Proceedings of the U. S. Army General Courts -Martial, 1809-1890
OO 605/3: Capt. Joseph S. Reynolds Case File
OO 605/9: Pvt. Thomas Delaney Case File
OO 605/11: Pvt. Jacob Schreader Case File
Record Group 393, Part II
Letters Sent February-June, 1865, 1st Brig., 1st Div., 17th Army Corps
National Archives Cartographic and Architectural Branch, Alexandria, Virginia
Record Group 77
File Z12-145: "Battlefield near Bentonsville [sic] March 20 [1865]"
File Z12-199: Map showing the position of the XV Corps near Bentonville, March 20, 1865
US 280 2.143: "Topographical Map No. 9. Positions of 14th and 20th Corps at Averasboro and Bentonville."
North Carolina Division of Archives and History, Raleigh, North Carolina
Daniel Harvey Hill Papers
Robert F. Hoke Papers
Joseph E. Johnston Letters
Sally Hawthorne Reminiscences
Halcott Pride Jones Journal
Thurman D. Maness Collection
Thomas Merritt Pittman Collection
George Wortham Letter
Lowry Shuford Collection
C. S. Powell Reminiscence
Joseph B. Starr Papers
William Frederick Thayer Diary
John Douglas Taylor Papers
Mrs. Thomas Webb Collection
Janie Smith Letter
Arthur T. Wyatt Collection
University of North Carolina at Chapel Hill, North Carolina Collection, Louis Round Wilson Library
North Carolina Clipping File
Wilbur S. Nye Notebooks
Charles Stevens Powell Reminiscences
Stephen B. Weeks Scrapbooks
University of North Carolina at Chapel Hill, Southern Historical Collection, Louis Round Wilson Library
William Calder Papers
Chisolm Family Papers

Alfred Chisolm Letter
Burke Davis Papers
Gordon Family Papers
W. W. Gordon Diary
Edwin L. Halsey Papers
George Washington Frederick Harper Papers and Books
Charles Milton Hopper Papers
Charles Woodward Hutson Papers
Lafayette McLaws Papers
William Whann Mackall Papers
Joseph E. Johnston Letters
Robert Barnwell Rhett Papers
Daniel Miles Tedder Book
Andrew Woodley Reminiscences
Joseph Frederick Waring Diary
University of Notre Dame, South Bend, Indiana, Archives
William Tecumseh Sherman Papers
Ohio Historical Society, Columbus, Ohio, Archives and Research Center
James E. Graham Diary
William McKindree Heath Diary
Joseph Hoffhines Papers
James Taylor Holmes Papers
John D. Inskeep Diary
William Henry Pittenger Diary
James Sidney Robinson Papers
William Tecumseh Sherman Papers
Joseph Mitchell Strickling Reminiscences
Historical Society of Pennsylvania, Philadelphia, Pennsylvania
John White Geary Letters
Thomas Jefferson Jordan Letters
Peoria Public Library, Peoria, Illinois
Allen L. Fahnestock Diary
Mabel Prescott Collection, Mooresville, Indiana
James Royal Ladd Papers
George Slaton Collection, Wilmington, North Carolina
William Colcock Letter
South Carolina Historical Society, Charleston, South Carolina
Cheves-Middleton Papers
Edward B. Middleton Diary
Susan Bowen Lining Letter
Mitchell-Pringle Collection
Edward Laight Wells Correspondence
M. C. Butler Letters
Zimmerman Davis Letter
Wade Hampton Letters
University of South Carolina, Columbia, South Carolina, South Caroliniana Library

Frederick L. Childs Collection
Hampton Family Papers
Alfred Moore Rhett Papers
Tennessee State Library and Archives, Nashville, Tennessee
Confederate Collection
W. H. Ogilvie Reminiscence
William Erskine Sloan Diary
Diaries, Memoirs, Etc.
Jesse Roderick Sparkman Diary
Federal Collection
Philip Roesch Memorandum
Texas State Library, Austin, Texas, Lorenzo De Zavala Library and Archives Building
John M. Claiborne: "Muster Rolls of Terry's Texas Rangers"
University of Texas, Austin, Texas, Center for American History (formerly Barker Texas History Center)
William E. Stanton Letters
United States Army Military History Institute, Carlisle Barracks, Pennsylvania, Archives Branch
Bowman Family Papers
Charles F. Bowman Diary
Civil War Miscellaneous Collection
John W. Bates Diary
L. W. Earle Reminiscences
Thomas Y. Finley Diaries
New York Infantry, 150th Regiment
Peter Funk Diary
W. W. Prichard Journal
Baxter Smith Reminiscences
Civil War Times, Illustrated Collection
Frank L. Ferguson Reminiscences
John Porter Fort: "History of the Last Campaign of the First Georgia Regulars"
Andrew H. Hickenlooper Reminiscences
Edward E. Schweitzer Diaries and Correspondence
Harrisburg Civil War Round Table Collection
John Eicker Memoir
Thomas P. Larue Letters
Earl Hess Collection
Isaac Kittinger Diary
Daniel Harvey Hill Papers
Sladen Family Papers
Joseph Sladen: "Official Diary of the Army of the Tennessee"
Virginia Historical Society, Richmond, Virginia
Evander McIvor Law Letter
University of Washington Libraries, Seattle, Washington
Manning Ferguson Force Papers

Western Reserve Historical Society, Cleveland, Ohio
William David Evans Papers
William Pendleton Palmer Collection
Braxton Bragg Papers
Regimental Papers of the Civil War. Tennessee. Dibrell's Brigade
Charles and Louisa Smith Papers
Robert Mann Woods Letter
College of William and Mary, Williamsburg, Virginia, Manuscripts and Rare Book Department, Earl Gregg Swem Library
Joseph Eggleston Johnston Papers
State Historical Society of Wisconsin, Madison, Wisconsin
Charles H. Dickinson Papers
Michael Hendrick Fitch Papers
George W. Gee Papers
Ole Kittelson [Leigram] Papers
William H. McIntosh Papers
William C. Meffert Papers
John Henry Otto Papers
James Theodore Reeve Diary
Henry Clay Robbins Papers
John B. Tripp Papers
Ezra W. Button Diary
University of Wisconsin-Parkside, Kenosha, Wisconsin, University Archives and Area Research Center, The Library/Learning Center
Harvey Reid Papers
Ypsilanti Historical Society, Ypsilanti, Michigan
Sylvester C. Noble Papers

OFFICIAL PUBLICATIONS

Medal of Honor Recipients, 1863-1978. Washington, D.C.: U. S. Government Printing Office, 1979.

United States War Department. *The War of the Rebellion: A Compilation of the Official Records of the Union and Confederate Armies,* 128 vols., Washington, D. C.: Government Printing Office, 1880-1901.

—. *Atlas to Accompany the Official Records of the Union and Confederate Armies*. Washington, D. C.: Government Printing Office, 1891-1895.

PUBLISHED PRIMARY SOURCES

NEWSPAPERS

Charleston (S. C.) *Sunday News*
Cincinnati *Daily Commercial*

Cincinnati *Daily Gazette*
(Columbus) *Daily Ohio State Journal*
Detroit *Advertiser and Tribune*
Detroit *Free Press*
Fayetteville (N. C.) *Observer*
Frank Leslie's Illustrated Newspaper
Harper's Weekly
Hillsborough (N. C.) *Recorder*
National Tribune
(New Bern) *North Carolina Times*
New York *Herald*
(Philadelphia) *Christian Recorder*
Philadelphia *Weekly Times*
(Quincy, Ill.) *Daily Whig and Republican*
Raleigh *Daily Confederate*
Raleigh *Daily Conservative*
Raleigh *News and Observer*
(Raleigh) *North Carolina Standard*
Richmond *Examiner*
Smithfield *(N. C.) Herald*

PUBLISHED PRIMARY SOURCES

(Includes Autobiographies, Diaries, Journals, Memoirs, Reminiscences and Unit Histories)

Alexander, John D. *History of the Ninety-Seventh Regiment Indiana Volunteer Infantry*. Terre Haute, Ind.: Moore & Langen, 1891.

Allen, W. G. "About Fight at Fayetteville, N. C.," *Confederate Veteran*, 19, no. 9 (September 1911), pp. 433-434.

Ambrose, Daniel Leib. *History of the Seventh Regiment Illinois Volunteer Infantry*. Springfield, Ill.: Illinois Journal Company, 1868.

Andersen, Mary Ann, ed. *The Civil War Diary of Allen Morgan Geer, Twentieth Regiment, Illinois Volunteers*. Denver: Robert C. Appleman, 1977.

Anderson, Mrs. John H. "Confederate Arsenal at Fayetteville, N. C.," *Confederate Veteran*, 36, no. 6 (June 1928), pp. 222-223, 238.

—. "What Sherman Did to Fayetteville, N. C.," *Confederate Veteran*, 32, no. 4 (April 1924), pp. 138-140.

Andrews, W. H. *Diary of W. H. Andrews, 1st Sergt. Co. M, 1st Georgia Regulars, from February, 1861, to May 2, 1865*. n.p., n.p., n.d.

—. *Footprints of a Regiment: A Recollection of the First Georgia Regulars 1861-1865*. Edited by Richard M. McMurry. Marietta, GA: Longstreet Press, 1992.

Angle, Paul M., ed. *Three Years in the Army of the Cumberland. The Letters and Diary of Major James A. Connolly*. Bloomington: Indiana University Press, 1959.

Arbuckle, John C. *Civil War Experiences of a Foot-Soldier Who Marched with Sherman*. Columbus, Ohio: n.p., 1930.

Bartley, M. "Fighting at Bentonville. Twentieth Corps Man Tells About the Tightest Place He Was Ever In," *National Tribune*, June 17, 1897.

Basler, Roy P., ed. *The Collected Works of Abraham Lincoln*. 8 vols. New Brunswick, N. J.: Rutgers University Press, 1953.

Bates, Marcus W. "The Battle of Bentonville," *Glimpses of the Nation's Struggle. Papers Read Before the Minnesota Commandery of the Military Order of the Loyal Legion of the United States, 1897-1902*, 5, pp. 136-151. 5 vols. St. Paul: Review Publishing Company, 1903.

Bauer, K. Jack, ed. *Soldiering: The Civil War Diary of Rice C. Bull*. San Rafael, Cal.: Presidio Press, 1977.

Beight, Samuel. "The Night We Crossed the Catawba," *National Tribune*, January 25, 1912.

Belknap, Charles E. "Bentonville: What a Bummer Knows About It," *War Papers Read Before the Military Order Loyal Legion of the United States, Commandery of the District of Columbia*, War Paper No. 12. Washington, D. C.: Published by the Commandery, 1893.

—. "Recollections of a Bummer," *The War of the 'Sixties*, pp. 345-355. Edited by E. R. Hutchins. New York: The Neale Publishing Company, 1912.

Belknap, William W., and Tyler, Loren S., eds. *History of the Fifteenth Regiment, Iowa Veteran Volunteer Infantry*. Keokuk, Iowa: R. B. Ogden and Son, 1887.

Benton, Charles E. *As Seen from the Ranks: A Boy in the Civil War*. New York: G. P. Putnam's Sons, 1902.

Beyer, W. F., and Keydel, O. F., eds. *Deeds of Valor from Records in the Archives of the United States Government*. Detroit: The Perrien-Keydel Company, 1907.

Black, Wilfred W., ed. "Marching with Sherman Through Georgia and the Carolinas: Civil War Diary of Jesse L. Dozer," *Georgia Historical Quarterly*, 52, Nos. 3 and 4 (September and December 1968), pp. 308-336, 451-479.

Blackburn, J. K. P. "Reminiscences of the Terry Rangers," *The Southwestern Historical Quarterly*, 22 (July and October 1918), pp. 38-77, 143-179.

Blume, John W. "Crossing Lynch's Creek," *National Tribune*, June 12, 1902.

Bradley, G. S. *The Star Corps or, Notes of an Army Chaplain During Sherman's March to the Sea*. Milwaukee: Jermain and Brightman, 1865.

Brant, J. E. *History of the Eighty-Fifth Indiana Volunteer Infantry*. Bloomington, Ind.: Cravens Brothers, 1902.

Branum, John Marshall. "Letters from the Field," *National Tribune*, May 24, June 21, 1900.

Broadfoot, Andrew. "Interesting Story of Arsenal Recollections," Fayetteville *Observer*, May 15, 1928.

Brooks, Aubrey Lee, and Lefler, Hugh Talmadge, eds. *The Papers of Walter Clark*. 2 vols. Chapel Hill: The University of North Carolina Press, 1948.

[Brooks, U. R.] "The Charge on Kilpatrick's Camp," in U. R. Brooks, ed., *Butler and His Cavalry in the War of Secession*, pp. 417-431. Columbia, S. C.: The State Company, 1909.

[—.] "Heroic Deeds," in U. R. Brooks, ed., *Butler and His Cavalry in the War of Secession*, pp. 432-440. Columbia, S. C.: The State Company, 1909.

Brown, Alonzo L. *History of the Fourth Regiment of Minnesota Infantry Volunteers*. St. Paul: The Pioneer Press Company, 1892.

Bryan, R. K. "Sherman's Army in Fayetteville," (Fayetteville, N. C.) *The People's Advocate*, July 23, 1925.

Bryant, Edwin E. *History of the Third Regiment of Wisconsin Veteran Volunteer Infantry, 1861-1865*. Cleveland: The Arthur H. Clark Company, 1891.

Buck, Irving A. *Cleburne and His Command*. New York: The Neale Publishing Company, 1908.

Buell, Don Carlos. "East Tennessee and the Campaign of Perryville," in Robert U. Johnson and Clarence C. Buel, eds., *Battles and Leaders of the Civil War*, 3, pp. 31-51. 4 vols. New York: The Century Company, 1884-1889.

Burton, E. P. *Diary of E. P. Burton*. Des Moines: The Historical Records Survey, 1939.

Butler, M. C. "The Curtain Falls—Butler Surrenders His Cavalry," in U. R. Brooks, ed., *Butler and His Cavalry in the War of Secession*, pp. 465-477. Columbia, S. C.: The State Company, 1909.

—. "General Kilpatrick's Narrow Escape," in U. R. Brooks, ed., *Butler and His Cavalry in the War of Secession*, pp. 443-447. Columbia, S. C.: The State Company, 1909.

Butt, C. M. "Cheraw. Destruction of Ordnance Stores There," *National Tribune*, August 7, 1884.

Byers, S. H. M. "Some Recollections of Grant," Philadelphia *Weekly Times*, October 27, 1877.

—. *With Fire and Sword*. New York: The Neale Publishing Company, 1911.

Calhoun, M. C. "Credit to Wheeler Claimed for Others," *Confederate Veteran*, 20, no. 2 (February 1912), pp. 82-83.

Calkins, William Wirt. *The History of the One Hundred and Fourth Regiment of Illinois Volunteer Infantry*. Chicago: Donohue and Henneberry, 1895.

Camburn, T. E. "Capture of Col. Rhett," *National Tribune*, August 23, 1906.

Campbell, Alice. "Return of the Bethel Heroes," *War Days in Fayetteville, North Carolina*, pp. 28-34. Fayetteville, N. C.: Judge Printing Company, 1910.

Campbell, John A. *Reminiscences and Documents Pertaining to the Civil War During the Year 1865*. Baltimore: John Murphy & Co., 1887.

Canfield, S. S. *History of the 21st Regiment Ohio Volunteer Infantry*. Toledo, Ohio: Anderson and Bateman, 1893.

Carlin, William P. "The Battle of Bentonville," *Sketches of War History, 1861-1865. Papers Prepared for the Ohio Commandery of the Loyal Legion of the United States*, 3, pp. 231-251. 6 vols. Cincinnati: Robert Clarke and Company, 1888-1908.

—. "The Battle of Bentonsville [sic]," Cincinnati *Daily Gazette*, September 11, 1882.

—. "Military Memoirs," *National Tribune*, July 23, 30, August 6, 1885.

Case, Charles M. "A Word about Bentonville," *National Tribune*, November 19, 1885.

Castle, Charles M. "Averysboro [sic]," *National Tribune*, March 25, 1886.

—. "In North Carolina. How Harrison's Brigade Put Rhett's Artillery to Flight," *National Tribune*, May 28, 1891.

Cauthen, Charles E., ed. *Family Letters of the Three Wade Hamptons, 1782-1901*. Columbia: University of South Carolina Press, 1953.

Cavalryman, A 10th Ohio. "Campaign Through the Carolinas," *National Tribune*, April 28, May 5, 12, 1892.

Chapman, Horatio Dana. *Civil War Diary of a Forty-Niner*. Hartford: ALLIS, 1929.

Clark, Walter, ed. *Histories of the Several Regiments and Battalions from North Carolina in the Great War 1861-'65. Written by Members of the Respective Commands*. 5 vols. Goldsboro, N. C.: Nash Brothers, 1901.

Clark, Walter A. *Under the Stars and Bars, or Memories of Four Years' Service with the Oglethorpes of Augusta, Georgia*. Augusta: Chronicle Printing Company, 1900.

Cluett, William W. *History of the 57th Regiment Illinois Volunteer Infantry*. Princeton: Lessee Republican Job Department, 1886.

Cogswell, William. "Bentonville, N. C. The Part Cogswell's Brigade Took in the Fight," *National Tribune*, September 10, 1885.

Collins, R. "The First to Enter Fayetteville," *National Tribune*, May 13, 1887.

Committee of the Regiment. *Ninety-Second Illinois Volunteers*. Freeport, Ill.: Journal Steam Publishing House and Bookbindery, 1875.

Committee of the Regiment. *A Condensed History of the 143d Regiment New York Volunteer Infantry*. n.p.: Newburgh Journal Printing House and Book Bindery, 1909.

Conner, W. H. "The Guns at Averasboro," *National Tribune*, February 22, 1912.

Conyngham, David P. *Sherman's March Through the South with Sketches and Incidents of the Campaign*. New York: Sheldon and Company, 1865.

Cook, S. G., and Benton, Charles E., eds. *The "Dutchess County Regiment" (150th Regiment of the New York State Volunteer Infantry) in the Civil War*. Danbury, Conn.: The Danbury Medical Printing Company, 1907.

Corbin, William E., ed. *A Star for Patriotism: Iowa's Outstanding Civil War College*. Monticello, Iowa: William E. Corbin, 1972.

Corn, Thomas Jefferson. "In Enemy's Lines with Prisoners," *Confederate Veteran*, 11, no. 11 (November 1903), pp. 506-507.

"Thomas Jefferson Corn," in Colleen Morse Elliott and Louise Armstrong Moxley, eds., *The Tennessee Civil War Veterans Questionnaires*, 2, pp. 561-566. 5 vols. Easley, S. C.: Southern Historical Press, 1985.

"R. S. Cowles," in Colleen Morse Elliott and Louise Armstrong Moxley, eds., *The Tennessee Civil War Veterans Questionnaires*, 2, pp. 574-578. 5 vols. Easley, S. C.: Southern Historical Press, 1985.

[Curry, J. H.] "A History of Company B, 40th Alabama Infantry, C. S. A. From the Diary of J. H. Curry of Pickens County," *Alabama Historical Quarterly*, 17, no. 3 (Fall 1955), pp. 159-222.

Dacus, Robert H. *Reminiscences of Company "H", First Arkansas Mounted Rifles*. Dayton, Ohio: The Press of Morningside Bookshop, 1992 (Reprint).

Daniels, Orange. "The Averysboro [sic] Fight," *National Tribune*, June 21, 1900.

Darst, Maury, ed. "Robert Hughes, Jr.: Confederate Soldier," *East Texas Historical Journal*, 9, no. 1 (March 1971), pp. 20-49.

Daves, Graham. "The Battle of Averasboro'," *Southern Historical Society Papers*, 7, no. 3 (March 1879), pp. 125-126.

Davis, Jefferson. *The Rise and Fall of the Confederate Government*. 2 vols. New York: D. Appleton and Company, 1881.

Davis, M. J. "Eighth Texas Cavalry at Bentonville," *Confederate Veteran*, 24, no. 4 (April 1916), p. 184.

Davis, Theo R. "With Sherman in His Army Home," *The Cosmopolitan*, 12, no. 2 (December 1891), pp. 195-205.

[Dawes, E. C., Cochran, T. J., et al.] *Memorial of Benjamin Dana Fearing*. n.p., n.p., [1882?].

Devor, Thomas R. "The Twentieth Corps at Bentonville," *National Tribune*, June 3, 1897.

DeRosier, Arthur H., Jr., ed. *Through the South with a Union Soldier*. Johnston City: Publications of the East Tennessee State University Advisory Council, 1969.

Dickert, D. Augustus. *History of Kershaw's Brigade, with Complete Roll of Companies, Biographical Sketches, Incidents, Anecdotes, Etc*. Newberry, S. C.: Elbert H. Aull Company, 1899.

Dihel, William L. "Death to Foragers—Sherman's Retaliatory Order," *National Tribune*, June 12, 1884.

Dougall, Allan H. "Bentonville," *War Papers Read Before the Indiana Commandery, Military Order of the Loyal Legion of the United States*, pp. 212-219. Indianapolis: Published by the Commandery, 1898.

Dowdey, Clifford, and Manarin, Louis H., eds. *The Wartime Papers of R. E. Lee*. New York: Bramhall House, 1961.

DuBose, John W. "The Fayetteville (N. C.) Road Fight," *Confederate Veteran*, 20, no. 2 (February 1912), pp. 84-86.

Duncan, William H. "With the Army of the Tennessee Through the Carolinas," *Glimpses of the Nation's Struggle, Fourth Series. Papers Read Before the Minnesota Commandery of the Military Order of the Loyal Legion of the United States, 1892-1897*, 4, pp. 517-529. 5 vols. St Paul: H. L. Collins Company, 1898.

Elliott, William. "Through the Carolinas," *National Tribune*, March 10, 1887.

Elmore, Willard. "A Comrade of the 147th [sic] N. Y. Tells of Averysboro [sic] and Bentonville," *National Tribune*, June 3, 1886.

Ewing, Joseph H., ed. *Sherman at War*. Dayton, Ohio: Morningside House, 1992.

Fallis, Leroy. "Kilpatrick at Averasboro," *National Tribune*, November 17, 1904.

Fitch, Michael H. *Echoes of the Civil War as I Hear Them*. New York: R. F. Fenno and Company, 1905.

Fleharty, S. F. *Our Regiment. A History of the 102d Illinois Infantry Volunteers with Sketches of the Atlanta Campaign, the Georgia Raid, and the Campaign of the Carolinas*. Chicago: Brewster and Hanscom, 1865.

Fletcher, William Andrew. *Rebel Private Front and Rear*. Austin: University of Texas Press, 1954.

Foraker, Joseph Benson. *Notes of a Busy Life*. 2 vols. Cincinnati: Stewart and Kidd Company, 1916.

Force, Manning F. "Marching Across Carolina," *Sketches of War History, 1861-1865. Papers Prepared for the Ohio Commandery of the Military Order of the Loyal Legion of the United States*, 1, pp. 1-18. 6 vols. Cincinnati: Robert Clarke and Company, 1888-1908.

Ford, Arthur P. "The Last Battles of Hardee's Corps," *The Southern Bivouac*, 1 (New Series: June 1885-May 1886), pp. 140-143.

—. "A March Across the Carolinas," Philadelphia *Weekly Times*, July 7, 1883.

—. and Ford, Marion J. *Life in the Confederate Army*. New York: Neale Publishing Company, 1905.

Fox, Cyrus A. B. "Bentonville. Chickamauga Fifer-Boy Tells His Experiences," *National Tribune*, May 7, 1896.

—. "Bentonville. How Carlin's Men Were Beaten Back," *National Tribune*, July 1, 1886.

Freeman, Douglas Southall, ed. *Lee's Dispatches. Unpublished Letters of General Robert E. Lee, C. S. A., to Jefferson Davis and the War Department of the Confederate States of America, 1862-1865*. New York: G. P. Putnam's Sons, 1957.

Friend, W. R. "Rangers at Bentonville," Philadelphia *Weekly Times*, November 12, 1887.

Gardner, J. H. "Alabama's Sons Fought. Comrade Gardner Has Something to Say About Comrade Wentz's Story," *National Tribune*, August 13, 1896.

Garrison, G. C. "General Hardee's Son," *Confederate Veteran*, 24, no. 1 (January 1916), p. 7.

Gee, F. M. "Capture of Gun at Cheraw, S. C.," *National Tribune*, October 2, 1884.

Giles, Leonidas B. *Terry's Texas Rangers*. Austin: The Pemberton Press, 1967.

Goundrey, Thomas D. "The Battle of Bentonville," *National Tribune*, July 21, 1892.

Graber, H. W. *A Terry Texas Ranger: The Life Record of H. W. Graber*. Austin: State House Press, 1987 (Reprint).

Grant, Ulysses S. *Personal Memoirs*. 2 vols. New York: Da Capo Press, 1982 (Reprint).

Greene, J. H. "The Killing of Nelson," Philadelphia *Weekly Times*, December 31, 1887.

Grigsby, Melvin. *The Smoked Yank*. Sioux Falls, S. D.: Melvin Grigsby, 1888.

Grunert, William. *History of the One-Hundred and Twenty-Ninth Regiment Illinois Volunteer Infantry*. Winchester, Ill.: R. B. Dedman, 1866.

Guild, George B. "Battle of Bentonville: Charge of the Fourth Tennessee and Eighth Texas Cavalry," *The Annals of the Army of Tennessee and Early Western History*, 1, No. 2 (May 1878), pp. 62-64.

—. *A Brief Narrative of the Fourth Tennessee Cavalry Regiment*. Nashville: n.p., 1913.

—. *Letter to the Confederate Veteran*, 3, no. 2, (February 1895), p. 87.

Hackett, Henry C. "The Fayetteville Arsenal: The Way It Was Destroyed by Union Troops," *National Tribune*, May 18, 1916.

Hagood, Johnson.. *Memoirs of the War Of Secession, from the Original Manuscripts of Johnson Hagood*. Columbia, S. C.: The State Company, 1910.

Halsey, Ashley, ed. *A Yankee Private's Civil War by Robert Hale Strong*. Chicago: Henry Regnery Company, 1961.

Hamilton, Posey. "The Effort to Capture Kilpatrick," *Confederate Veteran*, 29, no. 9 (September 1921), p. 329.

Hamilton, William Douglas. *Recollections of a Cavalryman After Fifty Years*. Columbus: F. J. Heer Printing Company, 1915.

Hampton, Wade. "The Battle of Bentonville," in Robert U. Johnson and Clarence C. Buel, eds., *Battles and Leaders of the Civil War*, 4, pp. 700-705. 4 vols. New York: The Century Company, 1884-1889.

Harcourt, A. P. "Terry's Texas Rangers," *The Southern Bivouac*, 1, no. 8 (Old Series: November 1882), pp. 89-97.

Hardee, William J. *Rifle and Light Infantry Tactics*. 2 vols. Philadelphia: Lippincott and Company, 1860.

Harwell, Richard, and Racine, Philip N., eds. *The Fiery Trail: A Union Officer's Account of Sherman's Last Campaigns*. Knoxville: The University of Tennessee Press, 1986.

Hawthorne, J. J. "Active Service with the Third Alabama Cavalry," *Confederate Veteran*, 34, no. 9 (September 1926), pp. 334-336.

Hazen, William Babcock. *A Narrative of Military Service*. Boston: Ticknor and Company, 1885

Heath, R. J. "Bentonville. A Spirited Account from One Who Was There," *National Tribune*, October 1, 1885.

Hedley, Fenwick Y. *Marching Through Georgia. Pen-Pictures of Every-Day Life in General Sherman's Army from the Beginning of the Atlanta Campaign Until the Close of the War*. Chicago: R. R. Donnelley and Sons, 1887.

Hemstreet, William. "Little Things About Big Generals," *Personal Recollections of the War of the Rebellion. Addresses Delivered Before the Commandery of the State of New York, Military Order of the Loyal Legion of the United States*, 3, pp. 148-166. New York: G. P. Putnam's Sons, 1907.

Hendrick, L. "Bentonville, N. C. The Part Taken by Battery C, 1st Ohio L. A., in One of Sherman's Last Fights," *National Tribune*, June 30, 1892.

Hibbets, Jeff J. "Fayetteville, N. C. An Account from the Officer Who Commanded the Capturing Party," *National Tribune*, June 11, 1885.

Hill, G. W. "Palmer's Brigade in the Carolinas," *Confederate Veteran*, 18, no. 7 (July 1910), p. 332.

Hills, H. H. "The Second Minnesota. Reminiscences of Four Years' Service at the Front," *National Tribune*, July 27, 1899.

Hinkley, Julian Wisner. *A Narrative of Service with the Third Wisconsin Infantry*. Madison: Wisconsin Historical Commission, 1912.

Hinson, J. "Bentonville. The Commander of the 33rd Ohio Gives a Graphic Account of the Battle," *National Tribune*, July 8, 1886.

Holman, J. A. "Concerning the Battle of Bentonville," *Confederate Veteran*, 6, no. 9 (September 1898), p. 425.

Holman, Natt. "Participant in the Battle of Fayetteville, N. C.," *Confederate Veteran*, 19, no. 11 (November 1911), p. 544.

Holmes, Alester G., Jr., ed. *Diary of Henry McCall Holmes, Army of Tennessee, Assistant Surgeon Florida Troops, with Related Letters, Documents, Etc.*. State College, Miss.: n.p., 1968.

Holmes, James G. "The Artillery of Bentonville," *Confederate Veteran*, 3, no. 4 (April 1895), p. 103.

—. "Dismounted Battalion, Butler's Cavalry Brigade," in U. R. Brooks, ed., *Butler and His Cavalry in the War of Secession*, pp. 380-382. Columbia, S. C.: The State Company, 1909.

Holmes, James Taylor. *52d O. V. I., Then and Now*. Columbus: The Berlin Printing Company, 1898.

Hoole, William Stanley, ed. *History of the Forty-Sixth Alabama Regiment Volunteer Infantry, 1862-1865, by Captain George Evans Brewer*. University, Ala.: Confederate Publishing Company, 1985 (Reprint).

Howard, Oliver Otis. *Autobiography of Oliver Otis Howard, Major General United States Army*. 2 vols. New York: Baker and Taylor Company, 1907.

—. "The Campaign of the Carolinas," *Eleventh Annual Dinner Ohio Commandery, MOLLUS. Burnet House—Cincinnati, May 2nd, 1894*, 11, pp. 18-31.

—. "Marching Through Georgia," *National Tribune*, March 12, 19, 26, 1896.

Howard, Wiley C. *Sketch of Cobb Legion Cavalry and Some Incidents and Scenes Remembered*. Atlanta: Atlanta Camp 159, U. C. V., 1901.

Hubert, Charles F. *History of the Fiftieth Regiment Illinois Volunteer Infantry in the War for the Union*. Kansas City, Mo.: Western Veteran Publishing Company, 1894.

Hunter, Robert M. T. "The Peace Commission of 1865," *Southern Historical Society Papers*, 3 (April 1877), pp. 168-176.

Hurst, Samuel H. *Journal-History of the Seventy-Third Ohio Volunteer Infantry*. Chillicothe, Ohio: n.p., 1866.

Inglesby, Charles. *Historical Sketch of the First Regiment of South Carolina Artillery. (Regulars)*. n.p.: Walker, Evans & Cogswell Co., n.d.

Jackson, Oscar L. *The Colonel's Diary. Journals Kept Before and During the Civil War by the Late Colonel Oscar L. Jackson, Sometime Commander of the Sixty-Third Regiment Ohio Volunteer Infantry*. Sharon, Penn.: Published by His Family, 1922.

Jamison, Matthew H. *Recollections of Pioneer and Army Life*. Kansas City, Mo.: Hudson Press, 1911.

Jenkins, George C. "Kilpatrick's Capture," *National Tribune*, October 15, 1885.

Johnson, Crosby. "The Cheraw Explosion," *National Tribune*, May 29, 1884.

Johnson, W. A. "Closing Days with Johnston," *National Tribune*, May 22, 29, June 5, 1902.

Johnson, William Benjamin. "*Union to the Hub and Twice Around the Tire": Reminiscences of the Civil War*. Balboa, Cal.: n.p., 1950.

Johnston, Joseph E. "The Dalton-Atlanta Operations: A Review, in Part, of General Sherman's *Memoirs*," *The Annals of the Army of Tennessee and Early Western History*, 1, no. 1 (April 1878), pp. 1-13.

—. *Narrative of Military Operations During the Civil War*. New York: Da Capo Press, 1990 (Reprint).

Jones, Joseph A. "Report by Joseph A. Jones, Birmingham, Ala., Company K, 51st Alabama, Partisan Rangers," *Confederate Veteran*, 19, no. 9 (September 1911), p. 434.

Kerr, Charles D. "From Atlanta to Raleigh," *War Papers Read Before the Commandery of the State of Michigan, Military Order of the Loyal Legion of the United States*, 1, pp. 202-223. Detroit: Winn and Hammond, 1893.

King, R. "Fighting at Bentonville. Battery C, 1st Ohio L. A., Wants Credit for Prompt Response to a Call," *National Tribune*, September 17, 1896.

Kinnear, J. R. *History of the Eighty-Sixth Regiment Illinois Volunteer Infantry, During Its Term of Service*. Chicago: Tribune Company's Book and Job Printing Office, 1866.

Kyle, Anne K. "Incidents of Hospital Life," *War Days in Fayetteville, N. C.*, pp. 35-45. Fayetteville, N. C.: Judge Printing Company, 1910.

Lamb, Alfred. *My March with Sherman to the Sea*. n.p., Paddock Publications, 1951.

Lambert, R. A. "In the Battle of Bentonville," *Confederate Veteran*, 37, no. 6 (June 1929), pp. 221-223.

[Landstrom, Russell C.] "Civil War Experiences of John McAllister," *Annals of Iowa*, 39, no. 4 (Spring 1968), pp. 314-320.

Lankford, Nelson D., ed. *An Irishman in Dixie: Thomas Conolly's Diary of the Fall of the Confederacy*. Columbia: University of South Carolina Press, 1988.

Lindsley, John Berrien, ed. *The Military Annals of Tennessee. Confederate. First Series: Embracing a Review of Military Operations, with Regimental Histories and Memorial Rolls, Compiled from Original and Official Sources*. Nashville: J. M. Lindsley and Company, 1886.

Litvin, Martin, ed. "Captain Burkhalter's Georgia War," *Voices of the Prairie Land*, 2, pp. 459-549. 2 vols. Galesburg, Ill.: Bickerdyke, 1972.

Lomax, W. M. "At Monroe's Crossroads," *National Tribune*, July 6, 1899.

Lutz, Stephen M. "Surely in Columbia," *National Tribune Scrapbook*, No. 1, pp. 159-160. Washington, D. C.: The National Tribune, n.d.

Lybarger, Edwin L. *Leaves from My Diary*. Warsaw, Ohio: Edwin L. Lybarger, n.d.

McAdams, Francis M. *Every-Day Soldier Life, or a History of the One Hundred and Thirteenth Ohio Volunteer Infantry*. Columbus: Charles M. Cott and Company, 1884.

McBride, John R. *History of the Thirty-Third Indiana Veteran Volunteer Infantry*. Indianapolis: William B. Buford, 1900.

McClurg, Alexander. "The Last Chance of the Confederacy," *The Atlantic Monthly*, 50 (September 1882), pp. 389-400.

McDonald, Granville B. *A History of the 30th Illinois Veteran Volunteer Regiment of Infantry*. Sparta, Ill.: Sparta News, 1916.

Meagher, Peter. "The 17th New York," *National Tribune*, October 28, 1886.

Mellon, Knox, Jr., ed. "Letters of James Greenalch," *Michigan History*, 44, no. 2 (June 1960), pp. 188-240.

Miller, G. K. Letter to *Confederate Veteran*, March 7, 1895, *Confederate Veteran*, 3, no. 3 (March 1895), p. 71.

Mims, Wilbur F. *War History of the Prattville Dragoons*. n.p., n.p., n.d.

Monnett, Howard Norman, ed. "'The Awfulest Time I Ever Seen': A Letter from Sherman's Army," *Civil War History*, 8, no. 3 (September 1962), pp. 283-289.

Morhous, Henry C. *Reminiscences of the 123d Regiment, N. Y. S. V., Giving a Complete History of Its Three Years Service in the War*. Greenwich, N. Y.: People's Book and Job Office, 1879.

Morris, W. S. *History 31st Regiment Illinois Volunteers Organized by John A. Logan*. Evansville, Ind.: Keller Printing and Publishing Company, 1902.

Morse, Charles Fessenden. *Letters Written During the Civil War, 1861-1865*. Boston: Privately Printed, 1898.

Mowris, J. A. *A History of the One Hundred and Seventeenth Regiment, New York Volunteers*. Hartford: Case, Lockwood and Company, 1866.

Neal, W. A. *An Illustrated History of the Missouri Engineer and the 25th Infantry Regiments*. Chicago: Donohue and Henneberry, 1889.

Nichols, George Ward. *The Story of the Great March from the Diary of a Staff Officer*. New York: Harper & Brothers, 1866.

Northrop, Theo F. "The Capture of Col. Rhett. The Captor Tells the Story of Its Occurrence," *National Tribune*, December 7, 1911.

—. "Capture of Gen. [sic] Rhett," *National Tribune*, January 18, 1906.

—. "Gen. [sic] Rhett's Capture. As Told by the One Who Took Him to Sherman," *National Tribune*, April 23, 1891.

—. "Other Side of the Fayetteville Road Fight," *Confederate Veteran*, 20, no. 9 (September 1912), p. 423.

Oakey, Daniel. "Marching Through Georgia and the Carolinas," in Robert U. Johnson and Clarence C. Buel, eds., *Battles and Leaders of the Civil War*, 4, pp. 671- 679. 4 vols. New York: The Century Company, 1884-1889.

Ogilvie, W. H. "Days and Nights Cut Off in Swamps," *Confederate Veteran*, 15, no. 8 (August 1907), pp. 361-362.

O'Neal, H. "From the Western Border of Texas," *Confederate Veteran*, 5, no. 3 (March 1897), p. 125.

Osborn, Hartwell. "A Few Words About Bentonville," *National Tribune*, October 8, 1885.

—. "Sherman's Carolinas Campaign," *Western Reserve University Bulletin*, 15 (1912), pp. 101-119.

— and Others. *Trials and Triumphs. The Record of the Fifty-Fifth Ohio Volunteer Infantry*. Chicago: A. C. McClurg and Company, 1904.

Outline of the Veteran Service of the Tenth Regiment of Michigan Veteran Volunteer Infantry. n.p., n.p., n.d.

Overley, Milford. "What 'Marching Through Georgia' Means," *Confederate Veteran*, 12, no. 9 (September 1904), pp. 444-446.

Owens, Ira S. *Greene County Soldiers in the Late War*. Dayton: Christian Publishing House, 1884.

Packer, S. J. "Warfield Forgot. There Were Some Twentieth Corps Fellows at Bentonville," *National Tribune*, October 29, 1896.

Payne, Edwin W. *History of the Thirty-Fourth Regiment of Illinois Volunteer Infantry*. Clinton, Iowa: Allen Printing Company, 1903.

Pepper, George W. *Personal Recollections of Sherman's Campaigns in Georgia and the Carolinas*. Zanesville: Hugh Dunne, 1866.

Pickett, W. D. "Willie Hardee," *Confederate Veteran*, 24, no. 4 (April, 1916), p. 182.

Pike, James. *The Scout and Ranger, Being the Personal Adventures of Corporal Pike, of the Fourth Ohio Cavalry*. Cincinnati: J. R. Hawley and Company, 1865.

Potter, John. *Reminiscences of the Civil War in the United States*. Oskaloosa, Iowa: The Globe Press, 1897.

Povenmire, H. M., ed. "Diary of Jacob Adams, Private in Company F, 21st O. V. V. I.," *Ohio Archaeological and Historical Quarterly*, 38, no. 4 (October 1929), pp. 627-721.

Quaife, Milo M., ed. *From the Cannon's Mouth: The Civil War Letters of General Alpheus S. Williams*. Detroit: Wayne State University Press and the Detroit Historical Society, 1959.

Ravenel, Samuel W. "Ask the Survivors of Bentonville," *Confederate Veteran*, 18, no. 3 (March 1910), p. 124.

—. "The Boy Brigade of South Carolina," *Confederate Veteran*, 29, nos. 11-12 (November-December 1921), pp. 417-418.

Record of the Ninety-Fourth Regiment Ohio Volunteer Infantry, in the War of the Rebellion. Cincinnati: The Ohio Valley Press, n.d.

Reneau, T. W. "Montrose [sic] Crossroads," *National Tribune*, September 6, 1900.

Reynolds, Donald E., and Kele, Max H. "A Yank in the Carolinas Campaign: The Diary of James W. Chapin, Eighth Indiana Cavalry," *North Carolina Historical Review*, 46, no. 1 (Winter 1969), pp. 42-57.

Ridley, Bromfield. *Battles and Sketches of the Army of Tennessee*. Mexico, Mo.: Missouri Printing and Publishing Company, 1906.

Robertson, John I. "Cheraw and Fayetteville. Work of Destruction Carried on by the 1st Mich. Engrs.," *National Tribune*, July 1, 1920.

Roman, Alfred. *The Military Operations of General Beauregard in the War Between the States*. 2 vols. New York: Harper & Brothers, 1884.

Rood, Hosea W. *Story of the Service of Company E, and of the Twelfth Wisconsin Regiment, Veteran Volunteer Infantry*. Milwaukee: Swain and Tate Company, 1893.

Roseberry, Jasper. "The Gun at Cheraw," *National Tribune*, July 31, 1919.

Rowland, Dunbar, ed. *Jefferson Davis, Constitutionalist: His Letters, Papers and Speeches*. 10 vols. Jackson, Miss.: Mississippi Department of Archives and History, 1923.

Rumple, J. W. "Coggswell's [sic] Brigade at Bentonville," *National Tribune*, June 17, 1886.

Russell, Robert. "Fighting at Bentonville," *National Tribune*, July 23, 1896.

Sanders, Robert W. "The Battle of Averasboro," *Confederate Veteran*, 34, no. 6 (June 1926), pp. 215-216.

—. "The Battle of Bentonville," *Confederate Veteran*, 34, no. 8 (August 1926), pp. 299-300.

—. "More About the Battle of Bentonville," *Confederate Veteran*, 37, no. 12 (December 1929), pp. 460-461.

Sargeant, Charles Sheldon. *Personal Recollections of the 18th Missouri Infantry in the War for the Union*. Unionville, Mo.: Stille and Lincoln, 1891.

Saunier, Joseph A. *A History of the Forty-Seventh Regiment Ohio Veteran Volunteer Infantry*. Hillsboro, Ohio: The Lyle Printing Company, n.d.

Schenck, John S. "In the Carolinas," *National Tribune*, March 25, 1886.

Scott, Hugh Henderson. "The Story of a Scout Told in His Own Way," in U. R. Brooks, ed., *Butler and His Cavalry in the War of Secession*, pp. 96-113. Columbia, S. C.: The State Company, 1909.

Seaman, William H. "The Battle of Bentonville, N. C.," *National Tribune*, August 20, 1885.

Shaw, Alfred J. "At Averasboro, N. C.," *National Tribune*, July 16, 1914.

Sherlock, Eli J. *Memorabilia of the Marches and Battles in Which the One Hundredth Regiment of Indiana Infantry Volunteers Took an Active Part*. Kansas City, Mo.: Gerard-Woody Printing Company, 1896.

Sherman, William T. *General and Field Orders, Campaigns of the Army of the Tennessee, Ohio and Cumberland, Maj. Gen. W. T. Sherman, Commanding, 1864-5*. St. Louis: R. F. Studley and Company, 1865.

—. *General Sherman's Official Account of the Great March Through Georgia and the Carolinas*. New York: Bunce and Huntington, 1865.

—. "The Grand Strategy of the Last Year of the War," in Robert U. Johnson and Clarence C. Buel, eds., *Battles and Leaders of the Civil War*, 4, pp. 247-259. 4 vols. New York: The Century Company, 1884-1889.

—. *Memoirs*. 2 vols. New York: Da Capo Press, 1984 (Reprint).

Shingleton, Royce, ed. "'With Loyalty and Honor as a Patriot': Recollections of a Confederate Soldier," *Alabama Historical Quarterly*, 33, nos. 3-4 (Fall-Winter 1971), pp. 240-263.

Simon, John Y, ed. *The Papers of Ulysses S. Grant*. 18 vols. Carbondale: Southern Illinois University Press, 1967–.

"Sketch of the Career of General Joseph E. Johnston, 'The Very God of War,'" from Richmond *Times-Dispatch*, February 19, 1911, reprinted in Southern Historical Society Papers, 38 (1910).

Slocum, Henry W. "Sherman's March from Savannah to Bentonville," in Robert U. Johnson and Clarence C. Buel, eds., *Battles and Leaders of the Civil War*, 4, pp. 681-695. 4 vols. New York: The Century Publishing Company, 1884-1889.

Smith, Charles H. *The History of Fuller's Ohio Brigade*. Cleveland: Press of A, J. Watt, 1909.

Smith, D. E. Huger. *A Charlestonian's Recollections, 1846-1913*. Charleston, S. C.: Carolina Art Association, 1950.

—. Smith, Alice R. Huger, and Childs, Arney R., eds. *Mason Smith Family Letters, 1860-1868*. Columbia: University of South Carolina Press, 1950.

Stauffer, Nelson. *Civil War Diary*. Northridge: California State University, 1976.

Stephens, Alexander H. *A Constitutional View of the Late War Between the States*. 2 vols. Philadelphia: National Publishing Company, 1870.

Stewart, Nixon B. *Dan McCook's Regiment, 52nd O. V. I. A History of the Regiment, Its Campaigns and Battles*. Alliance, Ohio: Published by the Author, 1900.

Stilwell, Abel. "The Battle of Bentonville," *National Tribune*, February 8, 1912.

Stormont, Gilbert R., ed. *History of the Fifty-Eighth Regiment of Indiana Volunteer Infantry. Its Organization, Campaigns and Battles from 1861 to 1865. From the Manuscript Prepared by the Late Chaplain John J. Hight,*

During His Service with the Regiment in the Field. Princeton: Press of the Clarion, 1895.

Storrs, John W. *The Twentieth Connecticut. A Regimental History*. Ansonia, Conn.: Press of the Naugatuck and Valley Sentinel, 1886.

A Study in Valor: Michigan Medal of Honor Winners in the Civil War, n.p., Michigan Civil War Centennial Observance Commission, 1966.

Swan, J. W. "Kilpatrick's Cavalry. A Boy's Experiences at the Front," *National Tribune*, April 6, 1905.

Thomas, L. P. "Their Last Battle," *Southern Historical Society Papers*, 29 (1901), pp. 215-222.

Tilghman, Oswald. "Membership of a Famous Escort Company," *Confederate Veteran*, 8, no. 5 (May 1900), p. 210.

Toombs, Samuel. *Reminiscences of the War, Comprising a Detailed Account of the Experiences of the Thirteenth Regiment New Jersey Volunteers*. Orange, N. J.: Printed at the Journal Office, 1878.

Townsend, O. C. "With the Ambulance Train from Atlanta to Bentonville," *National Tribune*, January 4, 1912.

Trimble, Harvey M. *History of the Ninety-Third Regiment Illinois Volunteer Infantry from Organization to Muster Out*. Chicago: The Blakely Printing Company, 1898.

Twombly, V. P. "Explosion at Cheraw. Staff Officer Tells of the Terrible Experience There," *National Tribune*, August 13, 1896.

Underwood, Adin B. *The Three Years' Service of the Thirty-Third Mass. Infantry Regiment 1862-1865*. Boston: A. Williams and Company, 1881.

Velie, A. A. "Charged in a Swamp," *National Tribune*, November 19, 1896.

Warfield, C. R. "Benton's Crossroads. The Personal Experience of an Ohio Boy at That Engagement," *National Tribune*, July 6, 1893.

—. "Fighting at Bentonville," *National Tribune*, October 1, 1896.

Watkins, E. W. "Another Account," *Confederate Veteran*, 20, no. 2 (February 1912), p. 84.

Watson, B. F. "In the Battle of Bentonville," *Confederate Veteran*, 37, no. 3 (March 1929), p. 95.

Wells, Edward Laight. "Hampton at Fayetteville," *Southern Historical Society Papers*, 13 (1885), pp. 144- 148.

—. "A Morning Call on Kilpatrick," *Southern Historical Society Papers*, 12 (March 1884), pp. 123-130.

Westervelt, William B. *Lights and Shadows of Army Life, as Seen by a Private Soldier*. Marlboro, N. Y.: C. H. Cochrane, 1886.

Widney, Lyman S. "From the Sea to the Grand Review," *National Tribune*, August 13, 20, 27, September 3, 1903.

Williams, Julie Carpenter, ed. *War Diary of Kinchen Jahu Carpenter, Confederate Soldier, May, 1862-May, 1865*. Rutherfordton, N. C.: Mrs. Julie Carpenter Williams, 1955.

Williams, Max R., ed. *The Papers of William Alexander Graham*. 7 vols. Raleigh: North Carolina Department of Cultural Resources, Division of Archives and History, 1976, 1984.

Wills, Charles W. *Army Life of an Illinois Soldier*. Washington, D. C.: Globe Printing Company, 1906.

Wilson, James Harrison. *Under the Old Flag. Reminiscences of Military Operations in the War for the Union, the Spanish War, the Boxer Rebellion, Etc.* 2 vols. New York: D. Appleton and Company, 1912.

Winkler, William K., ed. *Letters of Frederick C. Winkler, 1862-1865*. n.p., William K. Winkler, 1963.

Winther, Oscar Ogburn, ed. *With Sherman to the Sea. The Civil War Letters, Diaries, and Reminiscences of Theodore F. Upson*. Baton Rouge: Louisiana State University Press, 1943.

Wiseman, Theodore. "Bentonville. The Story Told by the A. A. G. of the Second Division, Fourteenth Corps," *National Tribune*, November 5, 1885.

Witcher, J. C. "Shannon's Scouts—Kilpatrick," *Confederate Veteran*, 14, no. 11 (November 1906), pp. 511-512.

Woodruff, George H. "History of the Sixty-Fourth Regiment; Or Yates Sharpshooters," *Fifteen Years Ago; Or the Patriotism of Will County*, pp. 180-223. Joliet, Ill.: Joliet Republican Book and Job Steam Printing House, 1876.

Woodward, C. Vann, ed. *Mary Chesnut's Civil War*. New Haven: Yale University Press, 1981.

Worsham, W. J. *The Old Nineteenth Tennessee Regiment*. Knoxville, Tenn.: Press of Paragon Printing Company, 1902.

Worth, Josephine Bryan. "Sherman's Raid," *War Days in Fayetteville, N. C.*, pp. 46-56. Fayetteville, N. C: Judge Printing Company, 1910.

Wright, Henry H. *A History of the Sixth Iowa Infantry*. Iowa City: State Historical Society of Iowa, 1923.

Wright, J. Montgomery. "Notes of a Staff-Officer at Perryville," in Robert U. Johnson and Clarence C. Buel, eds., *Battles and Leaders of the Civil War*, 3, pp. 60-61. 4 vols. New York: The Century Company, 1884-1889.

Wynne, Lewis N., and Taylor, Robert A., eds. *This War So Horrible: The Civil War Diary of Hiram Smith Williams*. Tuscaloosa, Ala.: The University of Alabama Press, 1993.

Yeary, Mamie, ed. *Reminiscences of the Boys in Gray*. Dallas, Tex.: Smith & Lamar, 1912.

PUBLISHED SECONDARY SOURCES

Amann, William Frayne, ed. *Personnel of the Civil War*. New York: Thomas Yoseloff, 1961 (Reprint).

Anders, Leslie. *The Eighteenth Missouri*. Indianapolis: The Bobbs-Merrill Company, 1968.

Anderson, Jean Bradley. *The Kirklands of Ayr Mount*. Chapel Hill: The University of North Carolina Press, 1991.

Barnwell, Robert W., Sr. "Bentonville—The Last Battle of Johnston and Sherman," *The Proceedings of the South Carolina Historical Association*, (1943), pp. 42-54.

Barnwell, Stephen B. *The Story of an American Family*. Marquette: n.p., 1969.

Barrett, John G. *The Civil War in North Carolina*. Chapel Hill: The University of North Carolina Press, 1963.

—. *Sherman's March Through the Carolinas*. Chapel Hill: The University of North Carolina Press, 1956.

Battle, Kemp P. *History of the University of North Carolina*. 2 vols. Raleigh: Edwards and Broughton Printing Company, 1907.

Beach, Lansing H. "The Civil War Battle of Bentonville," *The Military Engineer*, 21 (January-February 1929), pp. 24-30.

Bearss, Edwin C. *The Campaign for Vicksburg*. 3 vols. Dayton: Morningside Press, 1986.

Black, Robert C. *The Railroads of the Confederacy*. Chapel Hill: The University of North Carolina Press, 1952.

Boatner, Mark Mayo, III. *The Civil War Dictionary*. New York: David McKay Company, 1959.

Bogle, James G. "The Western & Atlantic Railroad in the Campaign for Atlanta," in Theodore P. Savas and David A. Woodbury, eds., *The Campaign for Atlanta*, pp. 313-342. Campbell, Cal.: Savas Woodbury Publishers, 1994.

Boyd, James P. *The Life of General William T. Sherman*. n.p., Publisher's Union, 1891.

Bridges, Hal. *Lee's Maverick General: Daniel Harvey Hill*. New York: McGraw-Hill Book Company, 1961.

Burne, Alfred H. *Lee, Grant and Sherman: A Study in Leadership in the 1864-65 Campaign*. New York: Charles Scribner's Sons, 1939.

Castel, Albert. "Black Jack Logan," *Civil War Times Illustrated*, 15 (November 1976), pp. 4-10, 41-45.

—. *Decision in the West: The Atlanta Campaign of 1864*. Lawrence: University Press of Kansas, 1992.

Coggins, Jack. *Arms and Equipment of the Civil War*. Wilmington, N. C.: Broadfoot Publishing Company, 1989 (Reprint).

Collins, William H. "Biographical Sketch of Maj. Gen. James D. Morgan," *Transactions of the Illinois State Historical Society*, 9 (1904), pp. 274-285.

Cooke, James J. "Feeding Sherman's Army: Union Logistics in the Campaign for Atlanta," in Theodore P. Savas and David A. Woodbury, eds., *The Campaign for Atlanta*, pp. 97-116. Campbell, Cal: Savas Woodbury Publishers, 1994.

Coski, John M. "The 'Bandbox Regiment': The 32nd Wisconsin Infantry," *Civil War Regiments*, 2, no. 4, pp. 313-342.

Cox, Jacob Dolson. *The March to the Sea—Franklin and Nashville*. New York: Charles Scribner's Sons, 1882.

Cozzens, Peter. *This Terrible Sound: The Battle of Chickamauga*. Urbana: University of Illinois Press, 1992.

Davis, Burke. *Sherman's March*. New York: Random House, 1980.

Davis, William C. *Jefferson Davis: The Man and His Hour. A Biography*. New York: HarperCollins, 1991.

Dawson, George Francis. *Life and Services of General John A. Logan as Soldier and Statesman*. Washington, D. C.: The National Tribune, 1884.

Dodson, William C. *Campaigns of Wheeler and His Cavalry, 1862-1865*. Atlanta: Hudgins Publishing Company, 1899.

Draper, John William. *History of the American Civil War*. 3 vols. New York: Harper & Brothers, 1870.

DuBose, John Witherspoon. *General Joseph Wheeler and the Army of Tennessee*. New York: Neale Publishing Company, 1912.

Dyer, Frederick H. *A Compendium of the War of the Rebellion*. Des Moines: Dyer Publishing Company, 1908.

Dyer, John P. *Fightin' Joe Wheeler*. Baton Rouge: Louisiana State University Press, 1941.

"The Fetterman Massacre," *Acts of Bravery*, pp. 131-132. Detroit: Perrien-Keydel Company, 1907.

Fitzhugh, Lester. *Terry's Texas Rangers*. Houston: Civil War Round Table, 1958.

Foote, Shelby. *The Civil War: A Narrative*. 3 vols. New York: Random House, 1958-1974.

Force, Manning F. *General Sherman*. New York: D. Appleton and Company, 1899.

Fowler, Malcolm. *The Battle of Averasboro*. Raleigh: North Carolina Confederate Centennial Commission, [1965?].

—. *They Passed This Way: A Personal Narrative of Harnett County History*. n.p., Harnett County Centennial, 1955.

Fox, William F. *Regimental Losses in the American Civil War, 1861-1865*. Albany: Albany Publishing Company, 1889.

France, Eric. *Bentonville*. n.p., n.p., n.d.

Freeman, Douglas Southall. *Lee's Lieutenants. A Study in Command*. 3 vols. New York: Charles Scribner's Sons, 1942-1944.

"Gen. Wm. P. Carlin," *National Tribune*, January 7, 1892.

Gibson, John M. *Those 163 Days: A Southern Account of Sherman's March from Atlanta to Raleigh*. New York: Van Rees Press, 1961.

Glatthaar, Joseph T. *The March to the Sea and Beyond: Sherman's Troops in the Savannah and Carolinas Campaigns*. New York: New York University Press, 1985.

—. *Partners in Command: The Relationships Between Leaders in the Civil War*. New York: The Free Press, 1994.

Govan, Gilbert E., and Livingood, James W. *A Different Valor: The Story of General Joseph E. Johnston, C. S. A.* New York: The Bobbs-Merrill Company, 1956.

Gragg, Rod. *Confederate Goliath: The Battle of Fort Fisher*. New York: HarperCollins, 1991.

Halsey, Ashley. "The Last Duel of the Confederacy," *Civil War Times Illustrated*, 1 (November 1962), pp. 7-8, 31.

Hardee, David L. *The Eastern North Carolina Hardy-Hardee Family in the South and Southwest*. n.p., Privately Printed, 1964.

Hattaway, Herman. *General Stephen D. Lee*. Jackson: University Press of Mississippi, 1976.

Hay, Thomas Robson. "The Davis-Hood-Johnston Controversy of 1864," *Mississippi Valley Historical Review*, 11 (June 1924-March 1925), pp. 54-84.

Hill, D. H., Jr. *Confederate Military History: North Carolina, Volume 5*. Edited by Clement A. Evans. Wilmington, N. C.: Broadfoot Publishing Company, 1987 (Reprint).

Hoole, William Stanley. *Alabama Tories. The First Alabama Cavalry, U. S. A., 1862-1865*. Tuscaloosa, Ala.: Confederate Publishing Company, 1960.

Horn, Stanley. *The Army of Tennessee: A Military History*. Norman: University of Oklahoma Press, 1952.

Hughes, Nathaniel Cheairs. *General William J. Hardee: Old Reliable*. Baton Rouge: Louisiana State University Press, 1965.

James, Alfred P. "General Joseph Eggleston Johnston, Storm Center of the Confederate Army," *Mississippi Valley Historical Review*, 14, no. 3 (December 1927), pp. 342-359.

Jeffries, C. C. *Terry's Texas Rangers*. New York: Vantage Press, n.d.

Johnson, Bradley T. *A Memoir of the Life and Public Service of Joseph E. Johnston*. Baltimore: R. H. Woodward and Company, 1891.

Jones, James P. "General Jeff C. Davis and Sherman's Georgia Campaign," *Georgia Historical Quarterly*, 47, no. 3 (September 1963), pp. 231-248.

Jordan, Weymouth T., Jr. *The Battle of Bentonville*. Wilmington, N. C.: Broadfoot Publishing Company, 1990.

Lash, Jeffrey N. *Destroyer of the Iron Horse: General Joseph E. Johnston and Confederate Rail Transport, 1861-1865*. Kent, Ohio: The Kent State University Press, 1991.

Lewis, Lloyd. *Sherman: Fighting Prophet*. New York: Harcourt, Brace and Company, 1932.

Liddell Hart, B. H. *Sherman: Soldier, Realist, American*. New York: Dodd, Mead and Company, 1929.

Livermore, Thomas L. *Numbers and Losses in the Civil War in America 1861-1865*. Boston: Houghton Mifflin and Company, 1900.

Long, E. B., with Long, Barbara. *The Civil War Day by Day: An Almanac 1861-1865*. Garden City, N. Y.: Doubleday and Company, 1971.

Longacre, Edward G. "Judson Kilpatrick," *Civil War Times Illustrated*, 10 (April 1971), pp. 24-33.

Lossing, Benson J. *Pictorial History of the Civil War in the United States of America*. 3 vols. Hartford, Conn.: Thomas Belknap, 1877.

Losson, Christopher. *Tennessee's Forgotten Warriors: Frank Cheatham and His Confederate Division*. Knoxville: The University of Tennessee Press, 1989.

Luvaas, Jay. "Johnston's Last Stand—Bentonville," *North Carolina Historical Review*, 33, no. 3 (July 1956), pp. 332-358.

McMurry, Richard M. "A Policy So Disastrous: Joseph E. Johnston's Atlanta Campaign," in Theodore P. Savas and David A. Woodbury, eds., *The Campaign for Atlanta*, pp. 223-250. Campbell, Cal.: Savas Woodbury Publishers, 1994.

—. "'The *Enemy* at Richmond': Joseph E. Johnston and the Confederate Government," *Civil War History*, 27, no. 1 (March 1981), pp. 5-31.

—. *John Bell Hood and the War for Southern Independence*. Lexington: University Press of Kentucky, 1982.

—. *Two Great Rebel Armies: An Essay in Confederate Military History*. Chapel Hill: The University of North Carolina Press, 1989.

McPherson, James M. *Battle Cry of Freedom: The Civil War Era*. New York: Oxford University Press, 1988.

Manarin, Louis H., and Jordan, Weymouth T., Jr., eds. *North Carolina Troops 1861-1865. A Roster*. 12 vols. Raleigh: North Carolina Division of Archives and History, 1968.

Marshall, Park. *A Life of William B. Bate: Citizen, Soldier and Statesman*. Nashville: The Cumberland Press, 1908.

Marszalek, John F. *Sherman: A Soldier's Passion for Order*. New York: The Free Press, 1993.

—. *Sherman's Other War: The General and the Civil War Press*. Memphis: Memphis State University Press, 1981.

Merrill, James M. *William Tecumseh Sherman*. Chicago: Rand McNally and Company, 1971.

Nevin, David. *The Old West: The Soldiers*. New York: Time-Life Books, 1973.

Nevins, Allan. *Ordeal of the Union, Vol. 4: The Organized War, 1863-1864; The Organized War to Victory, 1864-1865*. New York: Collier Books: 1992.

Oates, John A. *The Story of Fayetteville and the Upper Cape Fear*. Charlotte, N. C.: The Dowd Press, 1950.

Patton, George S., Jr. *War as I Knew It*. Boston: Houghton Mifflin Company, 1947.

Pfanz, Harry W. *Gettysburg: Culp's Hill and Cemetery Hill*. Chapel Hill: The University of North Carolina Press, 1993.

Pickett, W. D. *Sketch of the Military Career of William J. Hardee Lieutenant-General C. S. A.* Lexington, Ky.: James E. Hughes, n.d.

Pollard, Edward A. *Lee and His Lieutenants*. New York: E. B. Treat and Company, 1868.

Reid, Whitelaw. *Ohio in the War: Her Statesman, Her Generals and Soldiers.* 2 vols. Cincinnati: Moore, Wistach and Baldwin, 1868.

Report of the Adjutant General of the State of Illinois Containing Reports for the Years 1861-1866. Revised by Brigadier General J. N. Reece. 8 vols. Springfield: Phillips Brothers, State Printers, 1900-1902.

Report of the Proceedings of the Society of the Army of the Tennessee at the Thirty-Sixth Meeting Held at Council Bluff, Iowa, November 8-9, 1906. Cincinnati: Press of the Charles O. Ebel Printing Company, 1907.

Robertson, John H., ed. *Michigan in the War.* Lansing: W. S. George and Company, 1882.

Rowell, John W. *Yankee Cavalrymen. Through the Civil War with the Ninth Pennsylvania Cavalry.* Knoxville: The University of Tennessee Press, 1971.

Royster, Charles. *The Destructive War: William Tecumseh Sherman, Stonewall Jackson, and the Americans.* New York: Alfred A. Knopf, 1991.

Slocum, Charles Elihu. *The Life and Services of Major-General Henry Warner Slocum.* Toledo: The Slocum Publishing Company, 1913.

Sommers, Richard J., *Richmond Redeemed: The Siege of Petersburg.* Garden City: Doubleday, 1981.

Spencer, Cornelia Phillips. *The Last Ninety Days of the War in North Carolina.* New York: Watchman Publishing Company, 1866.

Sword, Wiley. *Embrace an Angry Wind. The Confederacy's Last Hurrah: Spring Hill, Franklin and Nashville.* New York: HarperCollins, 1992.

Symonds, Craig L. *Joseph E. Johnston: A Civil War Biography.* New York: W. W. Norton and Company, 1992.

Van Horne, Thomas B. *History of the Army of the Cumberland.* 2 vols. Wilmington, N. C.: Broadfoot Publishing Company, 1988 (Reprint).

Vetter, Charles Edmund. *Sherman: Merchant of Terror, Advocate of Peace.* Gretna, La.: Pelican Publishing Company, 1992.

Walters, John Bennett. *Merchant of Terror: General Sherman and Total War.* Indianapolis: The Bobbs-Merrill Company, 1973.

Warner, Ezra J. *Generals in Blue: Lives of the Union Commanders.* Baton Rouge: Louisiana State University Press, 1964.

—. *Generals in Gray: Lives of the Confederate Commanders.* Baton Rouge: Louisiana State University Press, 1959.

Weems, John Edward. *To Conquer a Peace: The War Between the United States and Mexico.* Garden City, N. Y.: Doubleday & Company, 1974.

Wellman, Manly Wade. *Giant in Gray: A Biography of Wade Hampton of South Carolina.* New York: Charles Scribner's Sons, 1949.

Wells, Edward Laight. *Hampton and His Cavalry in '64.* Richmond: B. F. Johnson, 1899.

—. *Hampton and Reconstruction.* Columbia, S. C.: The State Company, 1907.

Williams, T. Harry. *McClellan, Sherman and Grant.* Brunswick, N. J.: Rutgers University Press, 1962.

Wingfield, Marshall. *General A. P. Stewart.* Memphis: The West Tennessee Historical Society, 1954.

Woodworth, Steven E. *Jefferson Davis and His Generals: The Failure of Confederate Command in the West*. Lawrence: University Press of Kansas, 1990.

THESES AND DISSERTATIONS

Fonvielle, Chris E., Jr. "'The Last Rays of Departing Hope': The Battles of Fort Fisher, the Fall of Wilmington, North Carolina, and the End of the Confederacy." Phd. dissertation, University of South Carolina, 1994.

Herring, William B. "The Battle of Bentonville: March 19-21, 1865." Master's thesis, East Carolina University, 1981.

Jones, James P. "Jefferson Davis in Blue: The Military Career, 1846-1866, of General Jefferson C. Davis, U. S. A." Master's thesis, University of Florida, 1954.

McNeill, William James. "The Stress of War: The Confederacy and William Tecumseh Sherman During the Last Year of the War." Phd. dissertation, Rice University, 1973.

Shiman, Philip Lewis. "Engineering Sherman's March: Army Engineers and the Management of Modern War, 1862-1865." 2 vols. Phd. dissertation, Duke University, 1991.

UNPUBLISHED SPECIAL STUDIES

Glatthaar, Joseph T., Untitled paper on Confederate soldier morale in the Army of Tennessee from September 1, 1864, to April 26, 1865.

Historic Sites Section Files for Averasboro, Bentonville and Monroe's Crossroads, North Carolina Division of Archives and History, Raleigh.

Loftfield, Thomas C., "Cultural Resource Reconnaissance of Fort Bragg, Camp Mackall, and Simmons Army Airfield, North Carolina." 1979. Copy on file at the North Carolina Office of State Archaeology, North Carolina Division of Archives and History, Raleigh.

Material on File at Bentonville Battleground State Historic Site, Newton Grove, North Carolina.

National Register of Historic Places. National Park Service, Department of the Interior, Washington, D. C. Reports for "Lebanon" (the Farquhard Smith House) and the John Harper House. Copies on file at the Survey and Planning Office, North Carolina Division of Archives and History, Raleigh.

Nye, Wilbur S., "The Battle of Monroe's Cross-Roads." Copy on file at the State Library, North Carolina Division of Archives and History, Raleigh.

[Rose, Herschel V.] "A Tour of the Battlefield." Copy on file at the Bentonville Battleground State Historic Site, Newton Grove, North Carolina.

Scott, Douglas D., and Hunt, William J., Jr. "The Civil War Engagement at Monroe's Crossroads, Fort Bragg, North Carolina. An Historical Archaeological Perspective." Department of the Interior, National Park Service, Midwest Archeological Center, Lincoln, Nebraska, 1994.

INDEX